B
U
P

THEORY AND REALITY OF INTERNATIONAL TRADE

Massimo Roccas

Cover: Cristina Bernasconi, Milan
Typesetting: Laura Panigara, Cesano Boscone (MI)

EGEA S.p.A.
Via Salasco, 5 - 20136 Milano
Tel. 02/5836.5751 – Fax 02/5836.5753
egea.edizioni@unibocconi.it – www.egeaeditore.it

First edition: November 2021

ISBN Domestic Edition	978-88-99902-88-9
ISBN International Edition	978-88-31322-43-0
ISBN Digital International Edition	978-88-31322-54-6
ISBN Digital Domestic Edition	978-88-238-8380-2

Print: Logo s.r.l., Borgoricco (Padua)

Table of Contents

List of Abbreviations

BEPS	Base Erosion and Profit Shifting
EU	European Union
FDI	Foreign direct investment
GATT	General Agreement on Tariffs and Trade
GDP	Gross domestic product
GVC	Global value chain
HO	Heckscher–Ohlin
ICT	Information and communication technology
ILO	International Labour Organization
IMF	International Monetary Fund
IPR	Intellectual property rights
ISO	International Organization for Standardization
MNC	Multinational corporation
OECD	Organisation for Economic Co-operation and Development
R&D	Research and development
RHO	Ricardo–Heckscher–Ohlin
UBI	Universal basic income
VA	Value added
WTO	World Trade Organization

Introduction

Since the 1990s the international economy has been characterized by the rise of powerful new industrial producers in developing countries; the increasing internationalization of firms and consequent dislocations of traditional production chains; modest improvements in living standards and employment in advanced countries, followed by the most serious economic crisis since 1929; growing and persistent disequilibria of trade balances among the most important world economies; increasing power of the giant corporations providing digital networks; and a fundamental role of standards for all economic activities. To those who are looking for an explanation for these developments, the current theory of international trade has offered limited guidance, leading to widespread dissatisfaction with the analysis it provides of the causes and effects of international trade flows.

This is not the first time that international trade theory has had difficulties in providing satisfactory explanations of contemporary events. A much stronger wave of criticism against what was then the orthodox theory took place in the 1960s and mid-1970s. Based on the principle of comparative costs set out by Ricardo in 1817 and the notion of the relative availability of production factors elaborated by Heckscher in 1919 and Ohlin in 1933, trade theory had proved unable to explain the extraordinary growth of post-war trade in manufactures among industrial countries. The reason was that it continued to ignore basic developments of modern economic life, such as the role of technical progress in determining which goods each country can export, the importance of economies of scale in production and distribution, the increasing sophistication of consumers, which opened new opportunities for non-price competition, and the activities of large multinational firms.

New theories centred on these factors as causes of international trade were then advanced, and references to these new explanations started to make their appearance in standard textbooks. But what made it possible for the new theories to gain academic recognition (though the importance of the insights provided by some of their authors was then largely played down) was a development that took place in the 1980s, when some of them were translated and developed by the economists of the so-called New Trade Theory into specific models that respected all the formal requirements of orthodox economics and could be used to produce precise results.

From the 1990s onwards, in an attempt to provide explanations for the new developments in the international economy, listed in the first paragraph, international economists have moved in two directions. They have started to recognize the importance of problems previously ignored or underestimated, such as unemployment and trade balance disequilibria, that hinder the smooth working of the comparative costs principle. And they have investigated how the epochal changes that took place in this period – political, technological and organizational – gave rise to new phenomena, such as massive trade in industrial inputs and the formation of complex international production chains.

At the same time, changes in the structure of the world economy have led international trade theory to modify the very object of its analysis. It now seems aimed not so much – or not so exclusively – at explaining why given countries export given goods; rather, new objects of analysis have been developed, respectively at a higher and at a lower level of aggregation compared with traditional analysis of comparative advantage.

On the one hand, research has sought to explain why certain countries have managed to become poles of attraction for production and export activities in general or for wide categories of goods belonging to many different sectors. This development was influenced – apart from renewed interest in the spatial aspects of economic activity (which led to the establishment of a new 'economic geography' line of economic research) – by the extraordinary surge of exports from some developing countries, above all China, which have emerged as important competitive world producers of a large number of goods and services. It also seems to have been favoured by the growing realization that to an increasing extent absolute advantages, and not only comparative ones, determine countries' exports and imports.

On the other hand, an opposite tendency has developed towards more disaggregated analysis; this has taken place in two directions. First, realizing the growing importance of the fragmentation of goods' production cycles among different countries, international trade theory has increasingly concentrated on the characteristics, not of the final goods exported by a country, but of the specific phases or tasks (or components) of the exported goods' entire production cycle that a country carries out. Second, instead of concentrating analysis on the overall characteristics of the exporting country or sector, more attention has been devoted – thanks to the availability since the 1990s of new sets of data at firm level – to the specific characteristics of a country's exporting firms. It was found that a country's firms producing the same good are characterized by large differences in productivity, and that taking part in international trade differentiates exporting firms from those producing exclusively for the domestic market. The result of this is that the stimuli to higher efficiency and competitiveness provided by increased trade integration and firms' greater involvement in export and import activity appear to produce a reshuffling of firms' composition within sectors and subsectors, which has significant positive effects on the latter's overall levels of productivity.

* * *

This book represents an attempt to provide at an elementary level – after a brief summary of the main new theories produced in 1960–1975, which were the object of detailed analysis in Roccas (1975) – a description of some lines of research in international trade or connected fields of economics developed, at very dissimilar levels of academic refinement, in the following decades, which seem to throw light upon some crucial determinants of, and problems posed by, the new features of today's international economy that have already been mentioned.

Far from trying to provide a survey of the literature in the field, the book aims to present the reader with a number of contributions, covering a large number of different areas, that provide insights helping to explain the present configuration of international trade flows and the forces that are shaping it. The importance of some of these contributions has already been widely recognized, and they have found their place in current textbooks. They are treated here in less depth than those that have received less attention, often because they did not or could not reach the same level of formal elaboration. It has also seemed important to trace particular insights in the works of economists of the past who anticipated ideas and concepts that have been developed in more recent times.

A basic goal has been to show how non-economic forces of different kinds – technological, political, social and historical – have interacted with economic forces to determine the structure of contemporary international trade flows. Therefore, an attempt has been made to highlight new – or so far ignored or insufficiently examined – underlying factors (such as power asymmetries in relationships between economic actors, or the relevance of networks and standards for economic activity) that shape the flows of international trade and investment; flows that have often been analysed by international trade theory only in their final more technical aspects and mechanisms.

There has been a tendency in economics for non-economic factors to be excluded from analysis, together with economic factors that are not amenable to precise specification and measurement. This is unfortunate, as the objective importance of a factor in causing a phenomenon does not depend on our ability to insert it in a formal model and measure it precisely; so that exclusive concentration on measurable factors can lead to a seriously distorted representation of reality. But it is also unfortunate because by ignoring important, even if not precisely quantifiable, determinants of a phenomenon, attention is diverted from the urgent need to find ways to better specify and measure these determinants.

Finally, it is hoped that this work will show the complexity, the problems of definition and often the ambiguity and contradictions of some apparently clear and precise terms and concepts that are currently employed in the analysis of international trade; and especially the debatable and controversial nature – in some cases, the shaky foundations – of many theories and propositions, and connected policy prescriptions, that have been developed by international trade theory and economic theory in general (it is significant, in this respect, that the economists who have analysed a subject most thoroughly are usually those most aware of the complexity and limits of the concepts they use and the results they have reached, and of the difficulty of advancing conclusions and prescriptions of general validity). This will contribute to expose the largely illusory nature of the claim by many economists that, alone among social fields of research, their profession shares the 'scientific character' of natural sciences. In fact - apart from the fundamental differences between the analyses of social and natural phenomena, ideological and political motivations inevitably influence economists' work, in particular as regards the very choice of the subjects to be researched, the hypotheses on which models are built and, sometimes, the analytical tools employed.

An effort has been made to present in simple words the content of a large number of more technical contributions that it might be difficult for the non-specialist to access. References are provided in the text and the footnotes to more specific or – for the economist – more formal texts. Although this work is not directed at professional economists, the hope is that some of them and, especially, students preparing to enter the profession in the future may find an interest in some of the issues discussed or mentioned here but only sporadically analysed in the economic literature; and that they will devote their efforts to develop the additional insights and the formal tools necessary for the issues to become the object of analysis and debate among economists.

Unfortunately, limits of time available to the author, and of space within which the work is to be contained, have made it impossible to analyse and evaluate the vast empirical literature underlying the arguments advanced by the economists whose ideas are presented here; to provide adequate statistical data on the phenomena under discussion; and to extend the analysis to the economic policies proposed by international economists on the basis of their theoretical arguments and to the debates that have developed over these policies.

* * *

The structure of this book is as follows. Chapter 1, after briefly explaining the concepts of absolute and comparative advantage, describes what is here called the Ricardo–Heckscher–Ohlin (RHO) model, the basic analytical framework that international trade theory adopted until the 1970s, and that to a considerable extent continued, with some adaptations, to be referred to in international trade analysis. It can be useful to view all the new trade theories developed in the last sixty years as moving from the rejection of one or more of the assumptions on which that framework was based and which increasingly appeared to be contradicted by the reality of international economic life. Chapter 2 discusses some preliminary problems, mainly conceptual and methodological, that international trade analysis must try to overcome, or at least should take into consideration; these problems highlight the inevitable limitations of many of the conclusions reached by that analysis.

Chapters 3, 4 and 5 briefly discuss three central issues (scale economies, imperfect competition and technology) that gave rise to the most interesting new theories which in the 1960s and 1970s started to challenge the 150-year-old international trade theory orthodoxy based on Ricardo and then on Heckscher and Ohlin. Reference is made to some of the new problems that emerged, and the theoretical contributions that were produced, in the following decades on these three issues.

The RHO model's hypotheses of full employment and trade balance equilibrium are the object of Chapters 6 and 7. They seem to represent the key elements of the

RHO theoretical construction: the first provides the logical basis for the importance of the comparative costs principle itself (so that when Keynes introduced the opposite assumption of resources' unemployment, the whole rationale for international trade was upset); the second is essential for the operation of the mechanisms that allow the comparative costs principle to apply in real international transactions.

In Chapter 8, Adam Smith's theory of international trade is reconsidered in order to highlight some crucial insights he provided on many issues that are at the centre of contemporary international trade theory; his contribution to trade theory is compared with that of Ricardo. The tendency for international trade theory to attribute increasing importance to countries' absolute advantages relative to comparative ones is underlined, the latter finding an obstacle to their practical operation in the weaknesses of the re-equilibrating mechanisms required for their working.

Two elements that have a strong influence on international trade flows, but which have seldom been the object of analysis in international trade theory, are discussed in Chapters 9 and 10. The first is power, which has always conditioned the types and prices of the products exchanged between countries: the different aspects of economic power are discussed, and an attempt is made to synthetically outline the main changes in countries', firms' and individuals' power relationships that have taken place in the last forty years. The second is standards and networks, factors that became important from, respectively, the last decades of the 19th century and the 1980s, but which in recent years have increasingly contributed to determining countries' hierarchy in the international economy and the structure of international trade.

The last two chapters deal with issues that have been at the centre of international economists' recent discussions. Chapter 11 retraces the debate that took place from the early 1990s, particularly in the USA, on the phenomenon of advanced countries' offshoring to low-wage developing countries phases of manufacturing and service activities previously performed at home, and on the negative consequences of this phenomenon for the levels of employment and wages of significant sections of the workforce in the West. It stresses the importance of some contributions by economists to the study of the process of international fragmentation of economic activity, and to the analysis of the large international production chains managed by powerful multinational corporations (MNCs). The difficulty of determining the distribution of trade benefits among firms and countries taking part in these chains is specifically discussed in the chapter.

Chapter 12 analyses the phenomenon that has dominated the international economic stage since the 1990s: the exceptional growth of the Chinese economy (and that of other important developing countries), and the dislocations that the rise of this new protagonist – given its gigantic size – has produced in the economies of the advanced countries and in world trade equilibria. It also discusses the measures economists have proposed to eliminate or minimize the negative consequences of these new trade equilibria in terms of increasingly unequal domestic income distribution.

A few final remarks on world trade, international trade theory and international trade economists conclude the work.

* * *

The reader is invited to note that throughout this book the words 'good' and 'product', unless otherwise indicated, will always refer not only to physical goods but also to all services that can be – and increasingly are – the object of international trade.[1]

[1] Thanks are due to Pierluigi Ciocca and Riccardo De Bonis for continuous encouragement, assistance and comments; to Andrea Boltho, Rita Cappariello, Stefano Federico, Alberto Felettigh, Alfredo Gigliobianco and Reinhard Schumacher for comments on parts of the book or individual chapters or sections; to John Smith for the revision of the English text; and to Maria Lucia Stefani for assistance at the library of the Bank of Italy in Rome.

1 The Ricardo–Heckscher–Ohlin Model

International trade theory, despite new important developments in the last two hundred years, and especially since 1960, is still largely centred on the principle of comparative costs (or comparative advantages). Though roughly anticipated by Torrens in 1815, this principle is traditionally associated with the name of Ricardo, who refined and publicized it in his 1817 *Principles of Political Economy* to demonstrate the advantages of international specialization and free trade.

Until that time, international trade had basically been viewed as the means by which a country could obtain goods not available at home, or available at a much higher cost than abroad (measured, for example, as the labour hours necessary to produce them), in exchange for goods produced domestically. If country A produced the good X more efficiently than country B and the opposite occurred for good Y, both countries would gain by concentrating on the production of the good each of them could produce more efficiently and then exchanging the two goods. International trade was therefore largely connected to an 'absolute' advantage of each country in the production of a given good. Ricardo demonstrated that this was not a necessary condition for trade to benefit both countries: international specialization would increase the welfare of both trading countries even if country A produced both good X and good Y more efficiently than country B. The only condition was that the efficiency in producing good X relative to the efficiency in producing good Y was not the same in A and B.

Suppose, for example, that country A produced the good X twice as productively as country B and the good Y three times as productively as B. Then the total amount of goods X and Y that each country would obtain using its labour force would be increased – relative to a situation of autarchy – if A concentrated its labour resources in the production of Y (where its superiority over country B was higher), importing good X from B; and country B concentrated its activity instead on the production of good X (in which it enjoyed not an absolute advantage, but a relative or 'comparative' advantage over A), importing good Y from A.[1]

[1] The principle of the benefits of specialization according to comparative costs is a principle of universal validity. In order to understand it, the following example may be helpful. Suppose students A and B live in a students' residence where they must both prepare their own meals and clean their own rooms every day. Given the capabilities of the two students in the two activities, the times necessary for each of them to perform in isolation the two tasks are as follows:

From the comparative costs theory, a precise prescription of economic policy was derived: free trade increases the welfare of both trading countries, as it eliminates the impediment to the optimal use of available resources which is represented, in autarchy, by countries having also to produce the goods in whose production they

---

	Meals	Cleaning	Total
Student A	2 hours	1 hour	3 hours
Student B	1 hour	2 hours	3 hours

The overall working time spent by the two students is 6 hours per day. As each student shows a superiority over the other (an absolute advantage) in one of the two activities, it is clearly advantageous to both to agree that each should concentrate completely on the activity in which he is more efficient than the other: student A cleaning both rooms in 2 hours of work and B preparing the meals for both students also working 2 hours. Each student will work 1 hour less than in isolation and the overall amount of work will be reduced from 6 to 4 hours.

Ricardo's principle consists of the demonstration that even if student A were more efficient than student B in both activities (and provided the efficiency gap between the two activities is not the same for both students), as in the case here:

	Meals	Cleaning	Total
Student A	2 hours	1 hour	3 hours
Student B	2½ hours	3 hours	5½ hours

a benefit in terms of reduction of the hours worked both by each student and overall will be obtained (relative to the state of isolation, in which each student performs both tasks) if A will concentrate all his work on the activity in which his superiority over B is greater and B in the activity in which his inferiority is lower (that is, in which he has not an absolute, but a 'comparative' advantage), as here:

	Meals	Cleaning	Total
Student A		2 hours	2 hours
Student B	5 hours		5 hours

Since A's superiority is greater in cleaning (1 hour against 3 of B) than in meals (2 hours against 2½), if A cleans both rooms he will work 2 hours, and if B prepares the meals for both students he will work 5 hours. Each student will thus see his working hours diminish relative to the state of isolation, and overall the hours worked by the two students will fall from 8½ to 7.

Substituting students A and B with Portugal and Britain, and meals preparation and room cleaning with producing cloth and wine, one gets near to Ricardo's famous example on the benefits of specialization and trade between countries.

However, moving from the students' example or Ricardo's cloth and wine example, which refer to the amount of labour time incorporated in the goods exchanged, to the reality of international trade introduces additional problems that will be discussed later. They are largely caused by the fact that in market economies trade between two countries does not take place, as in the students' and in Ricardo's examples, as a result of a decision of the countries to carry out the exchange on the basis of the saving of work time (or of total resources employed) that the exchange produces; but on the basis of separate decisions to import or export a good taken by individual agents in the trading countries, who compare a good's national and foreign monetary price: the exporters offering their product on the foreign market if it can be sold there at a price covering at least all the production and transport expenses, and the importers buying the foreign product if its price is lower than the domestic price. A mechanism must therefore operate to translate comparative advantages into absolute price advantages for the individual sellers and purchasers of the goods.

are relatively inefficient. The imposition of custom duties, quotas and other artificial obstacles to exchange causes, instead, a loss of welfare.[2]

Ricardo wrote his *Principles* in the aftermath of the Napoleonic Wars. In England, this was a period of deep social unrest, rapid economic change and population growth, and popular riots against the high price of basic foodstuffs produced in wartime by the trade blockade and then by the political opposition of landowners to allowing the importation of cheap corn from abroad. Ricardo was particularly interested in showing that the elimination of tariffs and other obstacles to imports would produce large benefits by reducing the price of essential foodstuffs. Ultimately, his interest in demonstrating, with the comparative costs principle, the advantages of free trade was motivated by the crucial role he attributed to profits as the variable on which investment – and therefore economic growth – depended. As he considered the reduction of wages and landowners' rents the basic factor in increasing the profit rate, he viewed agricultural protectionism as the obstacle to a free importation of cheap corn that would make it possible to reduce workers' wages and land rents.

Ricardo believed that the labour theory of value – according to which the value of a good is given by the amount of labour time necessary to produce it – only applied inside each country. He formulated his theory of comparative costs according to which each individual country finds an international transaction beneficial if the cost of the goods exported in terms of the labour time incorporated in them is lower than the cost of the goods imported in terms of the labour time that would have been incorporated in them if they had been produced domestically. But he stated that the labour theory of value does not apply between countries since, given the lack of international mobility of capital and labour, the competitive forces that domestically lead to the establishment of a uniform rate of profit and similar levels of worker remuneration do not operate (in any case it would be hard to establish the notion of 'labour content of a good at the international level' given the differences in workers' productivity in different countries); the hypothesis has even been advanced (see Morales Meoqui (2020)) that he was led to formulate the principle of comparative costs primarily in order to demonstrate the validity of this statement.

When the majority of modern economists abandoned the labour theory of value, the need was felt to free the principle of comparative costs from that theory, but it proved impossible to find any alternative measure of the 'real' cost of a good. It was Haberler (1930) who found a solution: he reformulated the Ricardian principle meas-

[2] The preceding paragraphs were meant to represent an extremely simplified summary of the treatment of the absolute and comparative advantage principles that can be found in standard international trade textbooks. However, in recent years a different reading of Ricardo's text has been advanced, leading to an extensive debate that shows how uncertain and controversial are the exact meaning and the implications of Ricardo's statements on comparative costs: see Footnote 8 at the end of this chapter.

The contributions of Torrens and Ricardo to the development of the comparative costs principle have also been thoroughly analysed and debated: see Ruffin (2002, 2005), Aldrich (2004) and Morales Meoqui (2012). The concept of absolute advantage, in turn, had been the object of a debate in the *American Economic Review* in the late 1960s: see Brandis (1967, 1968) and Ingram (1968).

uring, for each country, the value of a good X not in terms of the labour time necessary to produce it, but in terms of 'opportunity cost', that is of the number of units of a second good Y that had to be forgone to produce it.

* * *

A basic consequence of the comparative costs theory is that it leads to conclusions regarding the working and effects of competition in international markets rather different from those that apply to competition within a country. This dichotomy is mainly due to two factors: first, the hypothesis (the most important among the many, that will be shortly specified, on which the principle of comparative advantages is based) that labour and capital move freely within a country – both from one location to another and from one employment to another – while they do not move from one country to another. And, second, the fact that international trade as a rule takes place between countries with different currencies, which has important implications (discussed in Chapter 7) for the mechanism relied on to ensure the re-equilibrium between an area's imports and exports.[3]

Of course, the principle of labour division and specialization applies at all levels, from individuals to nations; and so we will often see regions of a country specializing in the production of a limited number of goods where they display a relatively higher level of efficiency, and importing the other goods from other regions. But inside a nation, competition is based on absolute advantage: firms with lower production costs will offer their goods at lower absolute prices in terms of the national currency and will thus drive higher-costs producers out of the market. The logic here is that of a struggle where the stronger eliminates the weaker. Within a country, regions with more competitive producers will increase their activity and income relative to the regions whose producers are less competitive; the latter may be progressively eliminated from the national market and their region may as a consequence experience – unless special national compensating mechanisms are activated – a progressive narrowing of its productive capabilities, income stagnation and emigration of people (in particular the most capable and enterprising) and, especially, capital to richer regions, leading to overall economic marginalization.

Between countries, on the contrary, competition takes place according to comparative advantage. This principle – based on the hypothesis that economies are resource-constrained, so that factors of production cannot be unemployed – ensures that no country can be at a disadvantage trading with other countries, no matter how inefficient and technologically backward it is and how high its production costs are. There will always be lines of production for export in which it will be able to engage

[3] A third basic factor differentiating international trade from trade between regions of the same country is the existence in the second case, and not in the first, of a political authority responsible for the economic conditions of all national economic agents. In the case of trade disequilibria between regions or disrupting consequences of internal trade for some regions, the national government will normally adopt policies of redistribution and compensation that will help the deficit regions to cover their trade imbalances and to improve their competitive capabilities.

profitably: those where its inferiority is less marked. Stronger trading partners will not eliminate weaker ones from the international market. Low productivity of domestic factors of production in a country will mean that the standard of living of that country will be lower, often much lower, than that of more efficient trading partners. But international exchange will always be beneficial to the trading countries, as it will allow them to import from abroad some goods at a lower cost (in terms of the number of units of the good exported given in exchange) than if the imported goods were produced domestically.

Ricardo did not delve into the reasons for the divergence between countries A and B in the relative costs and prices of goods X and Y, limiting himself to a reference to the advantages obtainable 'by each country producing those commodities for which by its situation, its climate, and its other natural or artificial advantages, it is adapted, and by their exchanging them' (1951, p.132). It was the work of Heckscher (1919) and – in 1933 – Ohlin (1967) that produced the second big step in the development of international trade theory: they connected the comparative advantages of countries in different goods to a precise element, namely the different national endowments of factors of production (land, labour and capital). According to the Heckscher–Ohlin (HO) theory, the production of each good requires a given combination of productive factors, and each country will tend to have a comparative advantage in the production of those goods that incorporate a larger proportion of the productive factors that are relatively more abundant in the country. Other conditions being equal, a country's greater relative supply of a factor, for instance labour as against capital, will cause the price of labour relative to the price of capital to be lower than abroad and will give the country a competitive advantage in the production of the good that requires a larger input of labour. The HO theory did not modify the Ricardian conclusion on the advantages of free trade: the elimination of all obstacles to trade would allow each country to specialize on the basis of its comparative advantages in terms of relative factor abundance, thus maximizing the welfare of trading countries.

On the basis of the HO theory, the 'factor prices equalization theorem' was then developed, according to which, given some simplifying assumptions, trade tends to operate in the long run as a substitute for international factor movements: as in each trading country it increases the demand for the good exported, it tends to push up the price of the productive factor more intensively used in the production of that good (and to push down the price of the factor more intensively used in the production of the imported good), thus triggering a move towards the equalization of both relative and absolute factor prices across the trading countries (see Section 11.1.2).

Ricardo's theory of comparative advantages and the HO factor-proportion theory were adopted, merged and further developed by neoclassical economists, leading to the standard textbooks formulation that will be here referred to as 'the RHO model' (which until the 1980s represented de facto the only accepted theoretical framework for international trade theorizing and for many years thereafter continued to influence economists' thinking on trade issues). This model can be extended – but with some important limitations – to the case of a multiplicity of countries, goods and factors.[4] The weak point of this theory – and of the economic policy prescriptions that flow from it – is that it is valid only within the limits of its highly restrictive starting hypotheses, which may not correspond to the facts of the real world. The most important of these hypotheses are the following (many of which simply follow from the general hypothesis of perfect competition in domestic and international goods markets and in domestic factor markets):

1. Absence of transport costs, transaction costs, marketing and post-sale assistance costs and of other obstacles to trade (including barriers to entry and exit, such as initial fixed costs for production and export activities).
2. Absence of scale economies and diseconomies.
3. Immobility among countries of the factors of production (labour and capital) and perfect mobility – geographical and sectorial – of factors within countries (with no adjustment costs, time lags or distributional problems when factors move from one production to another).
4. Given and unchanging supplies of the factors of production in each country, and equal quality of factors everywhere.
5. Full employment of productive factors in each country.
6. Perfect equality among countries of the characteristics of each good; all goods can be produced by trading countries, thus excluding the introduction of new goods by only some of them.
7. Perfect equality among countries, and constancy in time, of the techniques for producing each good (that is, of the 'production functions', which connect the quantities of goods produced to the quantities of productive factors employed) and perfect availability of these techniques in each country. The possibility of 'factor reversal' is excluded (so that if the production of a good is intensive in the use of one factor in one country, it will be intensive in the use of that factor in other countries as well, whatever the relative factor prices might be).[5]
8. Equilibrium in the trade balance of each country (that is, there are no compensative items – such as loans, foreign investments and transfers – allowing for disequilibria between imports and exports).
9. Absence of trade in capital goods and intermediate inputs.
10. Equality and stability of consumers' tastes and demand patterns in each country.

[4] On the much-debated analytical problems posed by the extension of the comparative costs principle to a plurality of goods, countries and factors see Ethier (1984), Deardorff (2005) and Eaton and Kortum (2012).

[5] According to Rodrik (1999), 'we think of a 'production function as representing the technology through which a set of intermediate inputs and primary factors is transformed into final goods' (p. 129). The no-factor-intensities-reversal condition is essential for connecting the relative abundance of certain factors in certain countries to the export of certain goods from those countries (otherwise countries having different relative availabilities of factors could produce and export the same good employing technologies that allow more intensive use of the factor more widely available in each country).

11. No externalities (private costs and benefits equal social costs and benefits) and equal importance of all goods for each country (which means there are no differences between essential and superfluous goods, nor differences in the dynamic effects of the production of different goods in terms of technological progress, learning by doing and the stimulus of other sectors).
12. Absence of uncertainty and risk – as regards the evolution of the demand for goods, of factor supplies, of production techniques and so on, and specifically as regards the results of establishing new enterprises and of introducing innovations – and perfect availability of information to all economic operators.
13. Absence of the time dimension. This allows all phenomena involving choices between present and future (such as saving decisions and credit) to be ignored and makes it hard to distinguish between short-term and long-term effects of economic phenomena. It also implies reversibility of allocation decisions: since initial non-recoverable costs of engaging in export activity, uncertainty and risk, learning by doing (the increase in productivity that comes from increased experience due to a larger volume of past production) and other dynamic effects of producing given goods, are all excluded from the model, it follows that countries can at any moment and without specific costs change or reverse decisions such as entering into or withdrawing from international trade, or moving from one productive sector to another).
14. Absence of power asymmetries among countries and complete separation between economics and politics.

This list of starting hypotheses is striking for its distance from reality. This is a serious defect, as the validity of a theoretical model depends on its ability to represent, at a high level of abstraction, the fundamental elements of the real world. Not only were the hypotheses listed here far from representing a schematic picture of the international economy at the times of Ricardo and, especially, of Ohlin; but the main changes in the world economy over the last sixty years consisted of a more and more marked movement away from them. Just think of the increasing role, in determining volumes and directions of international trade, played by the foreign direct investment (FDI) of large MNCs and by differences among countries in the availability of technologies and in the ability to use and improve them.

A second more general defect of RHO theory is that – in sharp contrast with the theory of international trade developed by Adam Smith in *The Wealth of Nations* published in 1776 – it is a static theory, concerning the best allocation of a set of given resources at a given time (see hypothesis 4) in the list). On the contrary, since the end of World War II the interest of economists and economic policy authorities – conscious that factors of production are not given once and for all by nature, but are largely the result of intentional efforts to favour their development over time (just think of the availability of skilled labour) – has centred on the dynamic effects of a country's international specialization, that is its effects on the strength and the characteristics of the country's potential growth.[6] And, as Williams pointed out in 1929, the importance of these dynamic effects for countries' welfare has proved to far exceed the mere benefits of a better static international allocation of resources.

One can therefore easily understand why the majority of new theories (or refinements and extensions of RHO theory) that were developed to explain the actual configuration of trade flows moved from the abandonment of one or more of the hypotheses listed here and tried to introduce dynamic factors and structural changes into the analysis of trade. In the 1967 edition of his work, Ohlin himself, while insisting that factor proportions represent the basic cause of international trade, recognized that some other more realistic and dynamic elements can influence or determine the structure of trade flows, such as economies of scale, different demand patterns, differences in production functions, product differentiation, unused capacity, risk premiums and taxation. However, he did not develop their analysis in detail.

The new theoretical developments date roughly from the 1960s, when some basic changes in the world economy became apparent. On the one hand, as decolonization of Third World countries (a term that included all countries in the world except the advanced Western and the communist ones) gained momentum, the limitations of the static RHO model became evident, since it did not provide economic policy

[6] The static framework and the basic assumptions of the classical theory of international trade based on Ricardo's principle of comparative advantages had already been scathingly criticized much earlier by Williams (1929). His criticisms, however, were practically ignored by mainstream international trade theory for three decades. He had pointed out: '1. that the premises are inaccurate in sufficient degree to raise serious question of the soundness of the theory, or at least of the range of its useful application to the trade of the world; 2. that the relation of international trade to the development of new resources and productive forces is a more significant part of the explanation of the present state of nations, of incomes, prices, well-being, than is the cross-section value analysis of the classical economists, with its assumption of given quanta of productive factors, already existent and employed; 3. that the international movement of productive factors has significance relative to comparative prices, incomes, positions of nations, at least equal to that of the trade in goods; 4. that international trade in goods, cost of transport, and mobility of economic factors – externally and internally – continually react upon each other; and by investigating these interactions – in this actual, growing, changing world – we may hope to throw light upon the causes and effects of international economic contacts – upon market and productive organization, upon prices and price processes, upon incomes and general well-being…' (pp. 196–197). His strong objection to Ricardo's hypotheses on factor movements regarded not only that of the international immobility of factors, but also, and especially, that of the free movement of factors within countries.

A few years before, Graham (1923) had attacked the traditional conclusion that economists had derived from the principle of comparative advantage (based on the hypothesis of constant returns to scale) that free trade benefits all trading countries, stressing on the contrary the importance of increasing returns in manufacturing and the dynamic advantages of specialization in industrial goods relative to agricultural and mineral goods.

The free trade policy recipe derived from the static nature of classical trade theory had been criticized long before by the American Hamilton in 1791, by the Scottish (emigrated to North America) Rae in 1834 and especially by the German List in 1827 and 1841 (see Irwin (1996) and Gomes (1987)). But their criticisms, having been formulated outside the field and without recourse to the tools of academic trade theory, were largely ignored by international economists (though J. S. Mill and Marshall gave serious consideration to their arguments for the protection of infant industries).

guidelines to help newly independent countries to come out of their state of underdevelopment. On the contrary, it seemed to condemn them to the international specialization in raw materials that had characterized them in the colonial period. The factor of 'land' – lying at the root of the production of mineral and agricultural goods – was in fact the one the supply of which was relatively more abundant in these countries, and on which, therefore, their comparative advantage was to be based. But experience had shown that production and export of different goods, contrary to hypothesis 11 in the list, have very different effects on the stimuli to further economic development, and from this point of view raw materials represent the least favourable specialization.

On the other hand, empirical observation of international trade flows showed that their most dynamic component, covering a larger and larger percentage of the total flows, was unexpectedly represented by the two-way exchange of manufactured products belonging to the same productive sector (the so-called horizontal trade) between advanced countries.[7] That is, between countries that showed very similar relative supplies of the fundamental productive factors, in contrast to the expectations of the RHO model, according to which it is big differences in relative factor availabilities that create the maximum potential for trade growth. To explain this paradox of horizontal trade, the argument was advanced – developing remarks made by Ohlin himself in 1933 – that the model should be refined so as to give consideration to more specific supplies of productive factors (no longer labour versus land or capital, but, say, skilled labour versus unskilled labour) and more restrictive definitions of goods. The fact that two countries both import and export the same good, for example footwear, could thus be explained by the fact that the country with a larger supply of unskilled labour produces and exports to the other shoes of ordinary quality, which incorporate a lot of that kind of labour, while the country where skilled labour is relatively more abundant produces and exports high-quality shoes, which require a greater proportion of skilled labour. But this argument proved insufficient to account for the effective flows of horizontal exchanges.

The search for more satisfactory explanations of trade – some altogether rejecting the RHO model, some still referring to it, but with the introduction of important changes – centred on the realization of the basic importance in modern economic life of phenomena that contradict one or more of that model's hypotheses. Among these phenomena, those that most attracted the attention of trade economists in the first 1960–1975 wave of criticisms of the RHO model were those contradicting the hypotheses of constant returns to scale, perfect equality of each good and factor, and universal availability and constancy in time of technologies. In the following decades, both criticisms and debates have centred instead on the hypotheses of full employment, trade balance equilibrium and no trade in intermediate goods; while

[7] Empirical research of trade flows has been strongly stimulated since the mid-1950s by the discovery of the 'Leontief paradox'; that is, the surprising result of a 1953 study of US trade flows by Leontief, according to which that country appeared to be specialized in labour-intensive rather than capital-intensive goods, in contradiction with the widely accepted view derived from the HO theory.

increasing attention was also drawn to the role of countries' absolute advantages. In both periods, strong attacks have been made on the hypothesis of international factors immobility. Finally, recent years, with the extraordinary development of networks based on the products of the information and communication technology (ICT) sector, have seen increasing interest in the problems connected with the definition of international standards for products and networks, and the importance of power asymmetries in international economic relations (as in economic relations in general) has started to be recognized.[8]

---

[8] In the course of this work no specific analysis will be devoted to the second basic question of comparative costs theory: the determination of the terms of trade; that is, the ratio between the prices of imported and exported goods (which, in the case of the exchange of two goods, tells us how many units of one good are exchanged for one unit of the other). The only exception will be the discussion of the terms of trade between developing and advanced countries. However, it may be useful to explain the substance of the question, going back to the example of Footnote 1.

It was shown there that the two students would find it advantageous to specialize in the task where each of them was relatively more efficient (or less inefficient): student A exchanging 1 additional hour of room-cleaning against student B's 2.5 additional hours of meals preparation. In fact this exchange ratio (or terms of trade) of 1 to 2.5 hours between room cleaning and meals preparation is only one of the many possible ratios. For student A, specialization would be advantageous even at less favourable terms of trade, provided that to obtain the 2.5 hours of B's meals preparation work he were to give less than 2 hours of cleaning work (if he were to give 2 or more hours, he would save total time preparing his meals himself). For student B, specialization would still be advantageous if in exchange for the 1 hour of A's cleaning he were to give a number of extra hours of meals preparation higher than 2.5, provided it was lower than 3. So exchange would produce a benefit to both parties and would thus be possible only at terms of trade between the limits of 1.999 to 2.5 hours (which is equivalent to 1 to 1.251) and 1 to 2.999. At the first limit almost all the benefit of exchange would accrue to student B; at the second it would accrue to student A. Where will the terms of trade stand, between these limits? Economists charged Ricardo with being unable to provide a satisfactory answer in the analogous case of cloth-for-wine exchange. In 1844, J. S. Mill, in his *Essay on Some Unsettled Questions of Political Economy* presented what became the traditionally accepted solution to the problem: when two countries trade, the international exchange ratio between the two goods, within the two limits, will be determined by 'reciprocal demand', that is by the relative intensity of the demand of each country for the good exported by the other.

The terms of trade question is extremely important since – as shown by Bhagwati's (1958) article on the possible 'immiserizing growth' of countries basing their development strategy on the exports of a few commodities – a country's benefits from specialization according to comparative costs may be reduced (and under extreme condition even become negative, thus justifying a move towards autarchy) if changes in demand and supply conditions in the trading countries were to cause a deterioration of the terms of trade. A situation may therefore arise in which a country would find it advantageous to introduce policy measures (such as import tariffs and quotas or export subsidies) capable of improving its terms of trade, even if they were to reduce trade and specialization (in the sense of physical volume of goods exchanged). On the terms of trade argument for protection see Irwin (1996).

There are three other basic issues in trade theory that will not be discussed in this work, as they would involve exceedingly complex analysis, while they are usually examined in current textbooks; but they must be mentioned because they condition the validity of important theorems and results of trade theory. The first is the possibility that – contrary to the 'small-country assumption' of perfect competition of the RHO model – a country, being the exporter or importer of a large part of a good traded internationally, may influence the price of the good on the international market. The second is the question of whether trade between two (or more) countries leads to complete or incomplete specialization in the exported product (complete specialization implying the end of any domestic production of the imported good). The third regards the existence of 'specific' production factors; that is, the necessity for the production of some goods, of using particular factors that cannot be employed in other lines of production.

* * *

It is important to consider that the whole interpretation of Ricardo's comparative costs theory (whose exposition in the *Principles* was not systematic nor free from ambiguities, thus opening the way to misunderstandings and different readings) has been radically changed since Ruffin (2002) and Maneschi (2004) pointed out that the traditional idea of Ricardo's principle being based on constant returns to scale was due to a fundamental misinterpretation. In his famous numerical example of England and Portugal and cloth and wine, Ricardo simply referred to the fact that at a given point in time a specific transaction was taking place: a given unspecified quantity of cloth produced in England with the work of a certain number of men for one year and a given unspecified quantity of wine produced in Portugal with the work of another number of men for one year, were exchanged between the two countries. Later economists (Sraffa is an exception), following J. S. Mill's interpretation, erroneously attributed to Ricardo the idea that the labour contents he mentioned refer to one unit of each of the goods and represent unitary labour coefficients (that is, labour inputs per unit of output) fixed by technology independently of quantity produced and constant in time. A large debate has developed around the issues of Ricardo's belief in the constancy or variability of returns to scale, of his precise position on the determination of the exchange ratio between the two goods, of the real innovative nature of the comparative costs principle itself, and of the traditional, but now contested, identification of Smith's view on international exchange with the principle of absolute advantages. See on these issues the contributions of Pullen (2006), Maneschi (2008, 2015), Morales Meoqui (2011, 2020), Faccarello (2015a, b), Gehrke (2015, 2017), Bernhofen and J. C. Brown (2018) and Yoshii, Fujimoto and Shiozawa (2019).

The main points that emerged from the debate seem to be the following. First, the validity of the common assertion that Ricardo was unable to establish the exchange ratio between two goods exchanged internationally is disputed: he repeatedly declared that a country's export price of a good (expressed in a given currency) is determined by the monetary cost of production – including ordinary profit – of the good in that country (the intensity of foreign demand having no influence on the price apart from temporary effects that are eliminated through supply adjustment); so the exchange ratio is univocally established (abstracting from transport costs) by the ratio between the domestic prices, expressed in a common currency, of the exported good in each exporting country. However, if one or both goods exchanged are subject to variable returns to scale – and Ricardo considered agricultural production subject to decreasing returns because of the cultivation of progressively worse-quality land – both their physical labour content and their monetary price will depend on the total amount of their production, on which the amount of foreign demand does exert an influence. Since his example of cloth and wine involved an agricultural good, no specific constant exchange ratio could be indicated.

Second, Ricardo's comparative costs principle did not represent a radical change, but only a more explicit exposition of the previous theory of international exchange, to which Adam Smith adhered (and that will be discussed in Footnote 7 in Section 8.1), together with an indication of some of its implications. This opinion, already advanced by Viner (1937), seems to have been shared by Ricardo himself, since, although he was often critical of Smith, he did not point to any basic fault or limitation in Smith's theory of foreign trade. And although Smith did not formulate the principle of comparative advantage, he clearly indicated his awareness of the fact that trade can take place between two countries even when one of them is more efficient in the production of all goods.

2 Some Preliminary Problems of International Trade Theory

Before analysing the various trade theories that have been advanced since the RHO model's hypotheses became the object of serious criticism, it is necessary to examine a number of conceptual problems that impact on the whole construction of international trade theory, as they concern the very definition and the meaning of the concepts on which that theory has been built up. They create difficulties and ambiguities of both a theoretical and empirical nature.

2.1 Factors of production

2.1.1 The concept of factor of production

The first problem regarding factors of production is the number of factors to consider. The main attraction of the RHO model is that it explains the structure of trade by relating each good to a different mix of the basic factors of production (land, labour and capital) necessary to produce it and available in various countries in different proportions. As we have seen, Ohlin suggested introducing more detailed categories of production factors to account for real-world trade flows. In his original article, Heckscher (1919) himself had stressed that "the term 'factor of production' does not refer simply to the broad categories of land, capital and labour, but to the different qualities of each of these. The number of factors of production is thus practically unlimited." (p. 279). In fact, some factors that have become fundamental in determining comparative advantage in modern times, such as technology and skilled labour, have often been added by economists to the basic ones (land, capital and undifferentiated labour). However, saving HO theory by multiplying the number of factors risks reducing that theory to a mechanical *ex post* explanation of whatever trade structure one observes: it is not particularly illuminating, to explain Switzerland's 20th-century international specialization in watches, to say that it enjoyed comparatively higher availability of workers specialized in, or particularly predisposed to, watchmaking, or of machines for watch production. It seems more realistic, adopting a dynamic view of the process of trade specialization, to suppose that once Switzerland started, for whatever reason, to gain a slight advantage in watch production, machines for watchmaking were designed and produced, and then progressively improved, and watchmakers were formed because the watch market presented favourable opportunities for their employment; these developments leading to further consolidation of the original comparative advantage.

A second but connected problem regards the distinction between factors of production and production functions. The HO model is based on the hypotheses that for each given good all countries share the same production functions (that is, the same relationship between the quantity of the inputs – of, say, capital and labour – they use and the quantity of the good they obtain), while they differ in the relative availabilities of factors of production. But as pointed out more than sixty years ago by R. Robinson (1956a), it is not easy to distinguish between the two concepts: for instance, differences in climate between two countries may be considered as giving rise to different production functions, all involving the same three production factors, land, labour and capital. But, alternatively, a particular climate itself might be considered a fourth factor of production, available in one country and scarce or absent in the other, within the same common production function.

At the limit, no matter how different are the productive environments of two countries, they could always be considered as sharing the same production function if only a sufficient number of additional factors of production are included in it. But that, again, would reduce the HO theory to a tautology, explaining everything *ex post*, but nothing *ex ante* (Samuelson (1948) had already made that point: 'The tropics grow tropical fruits because of the relative abundance there of tropical conditions'). In any case, as indicated in Footnote 4 in Chapter 1, the increase in the number of factors taken into consideration in the HO model could seriously complicate and/or reduce the explanatory power of the model and the validity of the theorems derived from it.

A third problem is the difficulty of distinguishing between goods and factors of production. The goods in which technical progress is embodied (workers' tools, equipment, plants and computers), and even technology itself – in the form of patents and licences – are at the same time both production factors and goods that are the object of commercial exchange, so that for them a conflict may arise in a country between the maximization of exports and the maintenance of a position of leadership owing to exclusive ownership of technological know-how. The same occurs with cultural and educational goods and services (whose share of consumers' expenditure rises as income increases): merely by being bought and consumed, these goods and services increase the availability of knowledge and thus the amount of the basic factor of production that is called 'human capital'. Even more important, intermediate goods, which are increasingly traded to be used as inputs in the different stages of international production chains (and represent a large share of international trade; see Chapter 11), are at the same time traded manufactured goods and – for the importing country using them as inputs for its production processes – factors of production.

A fourth problem regards the determination of the amount of available factors. The RHO model presupposes that factors are homogeneous; but in the real world each factor appears to include highly diversified components, so the problem arises of how to aggregate them. For labour, one might think of evaluating supplies in terms of units of labour having a given productivity (units of output produced per hour), measured on the basis of technical data or on the basis of market wages (so that 10 workers with productivity double that of the average worker would be counted as 20 labour units), but the calculation has to overcome a number of difficulties, particularly for workers in the service sector, which in modern economies accounts for the overwhelming share of production (just think of how to measure the productivity of a teacher, a doctor or a waiter). More importantly, workers have different degrees of skill: skilled workers perform operations that unskilled ones cannot perform, and also within each of the two groups the possibility of transferring a worker from one sector of activity to another can be extremely different.

But there is a more fundamental problem with labour: what does the expression 'labour supply' mean exactly? Traditionally, it refers to a country's population of working age. Already here there are problems, as working age is not a fixed period of life, but depends on a number of variables – basically on social and legal norms regarding the number of years of education of young people and on average health conditions and the statutory retirement age of older people. Even if we could agree on a definition of working age, a more serious problem has to be solved: do all men and women of working age really represent the available labour supply? In most societies of the past and still nowadays in many countries, half of the working-age population, women, have faced obstacles – often insurmountable – to entering the labour market. In today's advanced societies, social, cultural and religious bans against women's work outside the home were overcome after struggles that took many decades; and only technological and organizational innovations (domestic electrical appliances and public kindergartens and schools, plus birth-control devices) have allowed them to participate in the labour market. Therefore, the availability of female labour is not a fixed demographic characteristic of a country, but a function of its cultural, social, organizational and economic level. But there is a bigger problem.

In a famous paper published in 1954, Arthur Lewis, discussing the scope for industrial growth of underdeveloped countries, coined the expression 'unlimited supplies of labour' to argue that it would be a long time before the industrialization of these countries, given the vast number of unemployed, underemployed and very-low-productivity agricultural workers, encountered problems of labour availability that would require significant increases in industrial wages to attract workers from the countryside. However, one may ask whether these unlimited supplies would in all cases be really available for industrial employment, or whether even for low-skill manufacturing and the simplest modern services activities the available labour supply is limited to literate workers with a minimum of general education (so that they can be trained) and can only be utilized if a minimum of public infrastructure exists. Today, Africa enjoys 'unlimited supplies of labour', but so far this has proved scarcely employable in low-skill labour-intensive activities for the international market. One possible interpretation of the recent economic progress of China and India is that while they had always enjoyed unlimited supplies of labour, it took some decades of great educational efforts and the availability of a minimum of modern domestic and long-distance international communication infrastructure to transform these hundreds of millions of workers into an effectively employable labour supply.

This confirms that the availability of employable factors of production is not an original, natural endowment of countries, but largely the product of earlier specific investments and technological developments. Ohlin himself, while basing his factor-proportion theory on the hypothesis of given factor availabilities, stressed this fact:

> the supply of productive factors is not given once and for all, and it is affected by price variations as well as by circumstances ... Various labour qualities, for instance, are trained only insofar as they are needed and *because* they are needed. In short, the supply of industrial agents may sometimes be described more adequately as the *result* of trade rather than as its cause. ([1933] 1967, p. 49)

For capital, the problems of factor definition, measurement and aggregation are much more complex than for labour (see Section 2.1.2). But for all factors the problem of determining their amount and productivity is further complicated by the fact that the latter, as just shown, are not independent variables, but depend to a large extent on the presence of other factors of production. While economic theory concentrated on the analysis of the scope for substituting one factor with another, what is of greater interest is the complementarity that exists between different factors. Lack of capital in a labour-abundant country, for example, may lead not to the development of labour-intensive types of production but to labour unemployment whenever a minimum of capital is necessary for production; and the availability of the 'human capital' factor of production (that is, workers with knowledge and skills) is conditioned by the availability of the monetary capital necessary for investment in workers' education and training.

2.1.2 What is capital?

Among factors of production, capital is the one that gives rise to the most problems. Whenever one speaks of the factor 'capital' what does one refer to exactly? The concept has always been vague and ambiguous in economics. Capital has some characteristics – the fact that, once an investment is made in physical capital, it cannot usually be transferred to other locations or converted to other uses, and the fact that it typically renders its services for a number of years – that do not easily fit the RHO model with its assumption of the absence of the time dimension. Ricardo in his *Principles* (1817) referred to physical capital when he said: 'Capital is that part of the wealth of a country which is employed in production, and consists of food, clothing, tools, raw materials, machinery, etc. necessary to give effect to labour' (1951, p. 95). But earlier on (p. 30), he made a distinction between fixed capital (tools, machinery and buildings) and circulating capital ('capital that is to support labour'; that is, food and clothing that has to be anticipated to workers as wages before the final goods are sold). He stressed that the dividing line between the two kinds of capital cannot be accurately drawn, but indicated that circulating capital is characterized by higher perishability and the necessity of more frequent reproduction.

Later economists have largely followed Ricardo's conception of capital, particularly in the context of international trade theory. The problem is that while fixed capital is the result of investment of monetary funds into long-lasting physical goods, so that the funds employed cannot be easily disinvested for employment in other lines of activity, circulating capital, especially if the duration of the production cycle for which it is anticipated is very short, can be practically indistinguishable from monetary capital, which can easily (today at the click of a mouse) be transferred from one line of activity to another and from one place to another. When, in a HO framework, we speak of a country's availability of different factors determining the nature of its international trade flows, for capital we have in mind plants and buildings that are, certainly in the short run but often also in the long run, a given, immobile endowment (though, of course, machines are exported and imported and most buildings can be put up in just a year). But the idea that capital consisting of a monetary sum should be viewed in the same way as an original, almost natural, domestic factor of production, is not equally acceptable, as such capital can easily be transferred to or received from foreign countries.

Schumpeter (1954) observed that all major economists saw capital as a prerequisite of production consisting in physical goods; however, he thought that a rigorous definition of capital should include the stock of money available for employment in production. He noticed that even the economists who most firmly upheld the concept of physical capital, including Ricardo and J. S. Mill, often advanced propositions that could only make sense if they referred to monetary capital; and concluded that those economists' attempt to develop the analysis of capital exclusively in physical terms was hardly acceptable.

Strangely enough, Schumpeter did not mention that, half a century before, Veblen had made a rigorous criticism of the concept of capital prevailing among economists. As pointed out by Brennan (2014), in a number of articles published in 1908 Veblen had advanced two fundamental arguments. First, he had noticed that while economists defined capital in physical terms, in business practice the term had come to refer to money and investment; in fact, the common discussion of capital movements from one location to another implied that reference was made only to movements of non-physical capital. Second, he argued that, contrary to monetary capital, physical capital cannot be aggregated, as it is heterogeneous. As for Veblen's conception of capital – which anticipated views not infrequently advanced in our day – he identified it with the socially accumulated stock of technological knowledge; ownership of material equipment simply allowed the owner to control the use to be made of this common stock of technology. Therefore, he attacked the notion of profit as the measure of capital's productivity, 'arguing instead that profit was institutionally grounded in the social power of the capitalists that enabled them to appropriate the technological achievements of the society as a whole' (Cohen and Harcourt 2003, p. 211).

Caves (1967) was one of the few mainstream modern economists to take up the subject after Schumpeter (another, more recently, was Leamer: see Footnote 2). He dwelt on Ohlin's ambiguous conception of capital and pointed out how confusion on this point continued to characterize international trade theorists. Ohlin referred to capital alternatively as a collection of physical capital goods and as an amount of monetary funds. When he considered capital as a basic factor determining a country's long-run specialization, he viewed it as a sum of monetary funds that can be invested in any activity; but he recognized that the time period during which capital is frozen in the form of specialized capital goods may be long enough to have an important influence on a country's international specialization.[1]

J. Robinson (1973) again drew attention to the ambiguity of the term 'capital' as used in mainstream economics and observed that:

> The greatest obfuscation of orthodox theory was its treatment of foreign investment. The concept of "capital" as a factor of production implied that when one country lends to another it is transferring real resources to it ... Now, it is true that "capital" in the sense of capital goods, say steel ingots or machine tools, may be put onto a ship and sent from one country to another, but this is not necessarily associated with a movement of "capital" in the sense of finance, for the goods may be paid for by visible or invisible exports going in the opposite direction. On the other hand, finance may pass from one country to another to be expended exclusively in employing labour and buying property on the spot, so that there is no movement of capital goods. A country which receives an inflow of finance is not receiving a supply of a factor of production called "capital", it is enjoying the possibility of running a surplus of imports or amassing monetary reserves. (pp. 22-23)
>
> Once we have seen through the neo-classical fallacy that "capital" is a factor of production there is a great deal of rethinking to be done. (p. 25)

A second serious problem with 'capital' (already mentioned in Section 2.1.1) is that, while the RHO model postulates that it is an original factor of production, whose availability is fixed and does not move internationally, it could alternatively be conceived as a produced good whose availability can be quickly increased or decreased through imports and exports (in modern times an important part of international trade has always consisted of tools, machines and other capital goods), with a consequent logical confusion between factors and goods in that model. A further element of confusion, connected to the dual (physical and monetary) nature of capital, is that the latter could appear in the balance of payments either as a merchandise item in the

---

[1] In his 1933 work Ohlin (1967) stated that 'For purposes of comparison, the capital available in a country is expressed as a sum of money that represents the cost of reproducing the capital goods in existence ... The price of this capital during a period of time is the rate of interest.' He also stressed that 'the expression "mobility of capital" refers to abstract capital, not capital goods. The incomplete international mobility of capital is due to the preference of capitalists for home investments and not to the difficulty of moving capital goods' (p. 55); 'Greater difficulties rise when for a certain period of time capital takes the form of special goods. In the long run it can acquire new forms, but the period that elapses before this is possible may be considerable and may influence the international division of production and international trade' (p. 60); 'capital movements imply a transfer of buying power' (p. 125).

Most empirical tests of the HO theory expressed the amount of the factor capital available in a country as the value obtained from the cumulated sum of the investments effected in a given number of past years. But the procedure is highly questionable.

current section in the form of physical goods that are exported and imported; or in the capital section as a 'compensating' item, since monetary capital (gold or a currency used internationally) is the instrument used to settle current account deficits and surpluses.

A third problem is that according to many economists capital should include 'human capital', that is the stock of special capabilities, skills and knowledge that people have acquired through education (and training). It is a capital that cannot be rapidly bought on the market, as it takes years to accumulate, and seems nowadays to represent the only largely irreplaceable factor (as persons are only partially mobile), allowing goods that incorporate it in large amounts to be highly priced on the international market. It is debatable how this factor should be valued in order to add it to physical capital and reach a measure of total capital availability. Does its value correspond to the cost of a given education? Given the time needed to reproduce it, in many instances its owner can command a much higher price for its use than that corresponding to the amortization of education expenses. Alternatively, one may think of calculating that price as the present value of the expected rental rate (the hourly wage) of its services for the entire working life of the person; but the calculation would be highly unreliable given the guesses that have to be made about most of the factors involved in it (paradoxically, the calculation of human capital would be greatly facilitated if we lived in a slave economy, where slaves with different educational levels would have a specific market price). The problem is further complicated by the fact that while physical capital is mainly demanded and produced for the sole purpose of allowing the production of other goods, human capital is demanded and created through education and culture not only to allow production of certain goods, but also for other fundamental non-economic purposes.

The difficulty of defining and measuring capital is even more complicated if in the concept – as more and more economists recommend – one includes 'social capital'; that is, the attitude of trust and cooperation that must prevail in a nation or a community so as to hold its members together, making them voluntarily respect general principles of honesty, fairness, and the observance of contracts and agreements. The existence of such bonds greatly simplifies and speeds up economic transactions.

There remains a fourth, but possibly more serious, problem. The HO model and practically all subsequent international trade theorizing until the 1960s used the conceptualization of capital as a complex of given physical objects that could be aggregated – just as was the case for the factors of land and labour – into a single homogeneous, exogenously endowed category, whose amount could be measured and compared among countries. Since, as Veblen had pointed out, very different types of capital goods cannot be aggregated in terms of any physical unit measure, the only way to measure and compare capital stocks would be to assign each capital good a monetary value and then to aggregate these values into a single monetary measure of the overall capital stock (as indicated by Ohlin; see Footnote 1).

This was found theoretically unacceptable by Sraffa (1960) and the English economists in the Cambridge Capital Controversy that exploded in the 1960s – see Cohen and Harcourt (2003) for a synthesis of the controversy – since such a monetary measure does not behave as the physical quantity of a homogeneous production factor. Specifically, the inverse relationship between the quantitative amount of capital available and the price for its use (the rate of return on that capital) does not generally hold when the amount of capital is measured as the value of a heterogeneous aggregate of capital goods. Capital itself cannot actually be defined, in general, independently of the rate of interest, and the rate of interest does not seem to depend on the so-called marginal productivity of capital. The very statement that the production of good A is more capital intensive than the production of good B appears to have only a temporary significance, as capital intensities depend on the rate of interest, whose variations may continuously reverse the ranking of products according to capital intensity.

Notwithstanding the fact that the counter-arguments advanced by their main opponent, Samuelson, were insufficient to save the possibility of effecting the aggregation of capital goods, later mainstream economists resumed the vague and ambiguous traditional concept of capital and the theoretical apparatus built on it, drawing from it specific economic policy prescriptions. They largely ignored the difficulties in defining, aggregating and thus measuring capital, important exceptions being Findlay (1977) and Leamer (1984, 2012),[2] and continued to refer alternatively to physical capital, monetary capital or both.[3]

---

[2] Leamer (1984) took up the problem of 'What is Capital?', highlighting the vagueness of the concept, and more recently returned to the subject in Leamer (2012), facing squarely up to the problem. He noticed that while all factors pose problems of aggregation, for capital these problems are particularly acute. While one may somehow arrive at a measure of total labour hours used for the production of a good and calculate some kind of average hourly wage rate to measure the rental rate of labour, for capital the only way to establish the amount of the factor used in a product is to aggregate the monetary value of the different forms of capital absorbed (calculated on the basis of the prices of the different capital goods and the estimated length of their working life), while to determine the capital rental rate one may refer to the real interest rate. Such a procedure, he pointed out, leads to a serious problem: the capital intensity of a good (in the sense of the monetary value of capital absorbed per unit of output) would continuously change through time with the changes in the relative prices of different capital inputs (e.g. if the price of computers goes down and the price of college education goes up, this decreases the capital content of goods requiring a lot of capital in the form of computers and increases the capital content of goods requiring a lot of capital in the form of workers' college education). But this is contrary to the RHO model hypothesis of given capital intensities of different goods (that is, the physical amounts of capital per unit of the good is fixed by technology and independent of the prices of capital goods).

Findlay (1977) had pointed out that 'Once we permit different time-intensities of production the difficulties rapidly mount as recent work by Metcalfe and Steedman (1973) and Samuelson (1975) demonstrates. "Reswitching" and other paradoxes and perversities discovered by modern capital theory disrupt the tidy world of the orthodox trade models' (p. 64).

[3] See Suarez (2010) on the use of different conceptualizations of the factor capital by recent authors.

Wood (1994, 2008), noticing that Samuelson was careful enough to express his HO model in terms of just labour and land, argued that capital should be eliminated altogether from the HO factors as it is basically reproducible and tradable and should thus be rather treated as an intermediate good (that is, as a good used as input in the production of final goods). What is not easily reproducible is capital in the form of infrastructure, but this is an element that explains the competitive advantage of a country in general, rather than determining its comparative advantage in specific goods. In fact once capital

2.1.3 Knowledge and technology

Economists agree on the fact that nowadays knowledge and technology, as the forces producing innovation, have become the fundamental elements determining a country's competitiveness; it has therefore been proposed to consider them as a specific factor of production. But this creates a number of conceptual and practical problems.

Knowledge and technology are largely incorporated in human capital, which means that they often cannot be separated from the specific individuals that hold them; and that their acquisition and development are part of the processes of education, training and 'learning by doing' that take considerable time. They are also embodied in organizations. They frequently consist of tacit elements that make them clustered in space and persistent.

They are difficult to define and measure. For example, technological activity has been estimated either on the input side, on the basis of research and development (R&D) expenditure or of the number of researchers employed, or on the output side, on the basis of the number and characteristics of patents registered; but, as explained in Chapter 5, both practices present serious deficiencies. Attempts have also been made to estimate it indirectly through its effect on productivity, but this effect is also the result of other factors beyond technology. Knowledge and technology are in part private property, which can be bought and sold in the market, for example in the form of patents and licences; but to a greater extent they are freely available, having become a common good, or having been produced by public institutions with the specific purpose of being diffused without restrictions; accordingly, they do not have a market price and their value is impossible to calculate. They are different from all other productive factors as their availability is not reduced by the fact of being used or by being shared with other agents (though in this case their diffusion can lead to the loss of their value to their original owner). As they are largely incorporated in individuals or in equipment and machines, it is difficult to evaluate their contribution to productivity growth separately from the contribution of the factors of labour and capital.

Since they are ambiguous and elusive concepts, knowledge and technology are difficult to include in those precise formal models that form the standard tools of

---

is considered fully mobile and its rental rate the same everywhere, it has no more place in the RHO model as its original availability is no longer a factor influencing comparative advantage. For Wood, the main factor to put in the place of capital should be human capital, given that education, training and knowledge represent a vital factor of production. Since non-human capital is still an important element of production, he proposed including it in his trade model as a determinant, together with technology, of the productivity of land and labour.

The whole debate on offshoring and fragmentation that took place among economists from the mid-1990s (see Section 11.1.2) was cast in terms of the relative availability of skilled versus unskilled labour. Capital was not given much consideration, and this made it possible to avoid the problems connected with the measurement of capital discussed so far. Still, leaving capital aside had negative consequences, as it led to avoid in discussions about offshoring and global value chains, the issue of firms' profits and profit shares, which are, as Ricardo pointed out, the basic determinants of investment, innovative efforts and growth.

modern academic economic analysis. This analysis, therefore, initially tended not to take them into consideration, and when it recognized their fundamental importance mostly inserted them into economic models in an oversimplified or distorted way.

But particularly confusing is the conceptual position of knowledge and technology in the theoretical scheme traditionally adopted by international trade theory, in which there are factors of production, goods, and technologies that determine the characteristics of the goods' production functions. The RHO model assumes that production functions for given goods are the same everywhere and only the relative quantity of factors available differs between countries, thereby determining their comparative advantages in given goods. But Ricardo's original theory of comparative advantage based on goods' labour content, and thus lacking the HO concept of relative factor availabilities, has often been interpreted as referring to differences in the relative productivity of trading countries in given goods owing to the production technologies of these goods being more efficient in some countries than in others: so here differences in production functions are the cause of comparative advantage. As indicated in Section 2.1.1, some economists propose treating technology as a separate factor of production – in addition to land, labour and capital – that enters the production function (equal everywhere) of a good, and determines an advantage for the country that has a larger availability of it. There is finally a third possibility: treating technologies as goods, as they are usually incorporated in investment goods that are the object of trade, or are directly bought and sold between countries as services.

2.2 Goods

One of the basic hypotheses of the RHO model (the 11th in the list in Chapter 1) regards the nature of the goods traded: there are no external effects from the production of different goods and the goods themselves, apart from their factor content, cost and price, have no characteristics that might lead the production of one of them being preferred to the production of another ("it's indifferent whether a country exports potato chips or electronic chips"). In the real world, which type of good a country exports and imports matters very much. In international trade theory, the question of the importance of differences between goods in terms of their consequences for overall economic performance, strongly underlined by Dosi, Pavitt and Soete (1990), has been later reproposed by Hausmann, Hwang and Rodrik (2007) and – with reference to the strong impact that a country's export mix has on the nature and quality of its institutions – by Nunn and Trefler (2014) (see Section 8.2.3).

Differences in goods' characteristics may be important from several points of view. The first of these is the urgency of the need a good satisfies and the ease of replacing it with similar goods: it is not the same thing whether a good is essential to human survival (such as food) or to the very possibility of keeping the economy running (such as energy sources, basic minerals or, in today's world, computers and ICT network services), or whether it satisfies non-basic needs (such as most luxury and fashion goods). In the first case, if domestic production of the good is impossible, the country will be compelled to import it from abroad no matter what price is demanded or what other conditions are imposed for its delivery by foreign countries (of course it is important whether just one foreign country or many can deliver the product; and it makes a fundamental difference whether or not the country has kept adequate stocks of such products for emergencies). This puts strict limits on the country's freedom of choice in many fields – a point taken up in Chapter 9, where the power aspects of international economic relations are discussed.

A second difference regards risk (we refer here to risk not amenable to precise calculation and therefore uninsurable). Two products may have equal effects in terms of employment, income and rate of profit, but may have different levels of risk. In our times, a country specializing in touristic services may see the leading sector of its economy suddenly disappear as a result of just one or two terrorist acts by a few individuals, as happened to Tunisia in 2015. Had that country specialized in, say, call centre services, the consequences for the economy of similar acts directed against them would probably have been negligible. Other things being equal, specialization in one or a small number of goods and the concentration of exports in one or a few markets exposes a country to greater risk and vulnerability.

A third difference concerns the characteristics of the demand for the good and the resulting potential growth of export volumes and values. There are large differences in goods' income and price elasticities (the price elasticity of a good measures the percentage increase in the demand for it when its price decreases by 1 per cent; income elasticity measures the percentage increase in the demand for a good when the income of the purchaser increases by 1 per cent). As in practically all countries people's income grows with time, a high income elasticity of foreign demand for a country's exported goods can make a great contribution to its export sales and thus to its growth and welfare. A price elasticity greater than one means that a decrease in the price of an export results in a more than proportional increase in the quantity sold and so in an increase in the value of the receipts from its sales. For many raw materials there are also large differences in the degree to which they can be substituted with artificial materials (and in the cost of such substitutions); when substitution is easy, the scope for large increases in export prices are strictly limited. There are also differences in the historical volatility of both the traded quantities and prices of various goods, so that future demand in terms of volumes sold and income obtained can be forecast with very different degrees of uncertainty.

But much more important is a fourth type of difference, which might be called difference in dynamic potential, a label that includes various characteristics of a good – or sector of activity – thanks to which its production enjoys high rates of productivity growth and can make a large contribution to the general economic progress of a country. These characteristics regard:

1. Increasing returns: the fact that in the production of some goods, unit costs fall as the volume of production increases (increasing returns are so important that Chapter 3 will be devoted to them).

2. Technological progress, in the sense that the potential for introducing technical improvements and innovations in the production process and for improving the good's characteristics or developing more technologically advanced goods differs considerably among different goods.
3. Learning effects: the production of different goods offers widely different opportunities for improvements in learning as a result of experience and familiarity with particular production processes.
4. Demand for specialized technical or organizational skills and capabilities: because of its specific nature, the production of some goods – but not of others – requires workers and managers with special skills, which may be difficult to acquire and therefore command a high remuneration. The very existence of a demand for these special skills, in turn, makes it easier to establish particular facilities to train people in these activities and their establishment more likely.
5. Synergies or cumulative causation processes: these originate in the positive effects of certain lines of production on the demand for and the stimuli to qualitative improvements of others, in the first place through connections with products or sectors providing inputs for a given product or using it as an input.
6. Scope for product differentiation: this makes it possible both to enlarge the market for the product and to prevent cut-throat price competition. Some goods are inevitably homogeneous (typically raw materials) and firms producing them cannot exploit – or stress through advertising – differences that customers may perceive as important. As these goods can easily be replaced by competitors' products, they offer less scope for increasing prices with only limited losses of market share, relative to goods that embody differentiated features or special technological advances.[4]

[4] Meier (1963), discussing the prospects for underdeveloped countries' exports, stressed the points 2, 3 and 4: 'the degree to which the various exports are processed is significant in determining the amount of machinery used, the spread of technical knowledge, the development of labour skills available for other types of industry, and the diffusion of organizational and administrative skills. It also increases the scope for innovations in the export sector' (pp. 179–180).

The importance of the nature of the goods a country exports was increasingly recognized in the following years. For example, summarizing the results of an important 1976 conference where Ohlin himself and almost all the leading international economists of the time had discussed the theory of international trade and the location of economic activity, Corden and Findlay (1977) concluded: 'It is ... undoubtedly true that different patterns of specialisation have different long-run consequences for economic development which should be brought into the analysis. Primary product specialisation can frequently lead to a distribution of income and wealth that is highly unequal and oriented towards luxury consumption. It may fail to generate the dynamism that is often associated with industrialization, involving learning by doing and the economies of large-scale production' (p. 549).

Note, however, that some economists deny the importance of the nature of the goods produced and exported. For example, the eminent international economist Bhagwati (2009) – after pointing out that, ironically, the manufacture of potato chips in the USA in fact turned out to employ a more sophisticated technology than that of semiconductor chips – argued that 'the exaggerated concern with what you produce as defining your economic destiny is a quasi-Marxist obsession bordering on folly' (p. 5). While he was correct in so far as there are many other factors that contribute to countries' economic destiny,

The product characteristics mentioned here, which tend to create opportunities for increases in profits and wages, are usually interconnected, reinforcing one another (as when patented technologically innovative goods or scale economies generated by high initial fixed costs permit non-competitive price-fixing practices). And once these factors have created a significant gap in wages between two countries, market forces (and the comparative advantage principle) will tend to push the more advanced country to further concentrate on advanced high-tech types of production with high economies of scale and the more backward to specialize in those that are more intensive in low-skilled labour.

Production of different goods can also have very different social effects, which in turn may strongly impact on the economic performance of a country. For example, L. T. Chang (2008) described how production of manufactures in Chinese cities in recent decades had revolutionary liberating effects on young women from the countryside, despite the miserable living conditions and the ruthless exploitation they were subjected to. They could escape from the stagnant and oppressive environment of country villages, widening their cultural and social horizons; gain personal and economic independence; and improve their economic and professional conditions through education and improved skills. Some years before, Federico (1994), retracing the history of the Italian silk industry in the 19th century, had highlighted the fundamental social and economic changes – that shaped the entire evolution of the initial phase of industrialization in Italy – produced by the specific characteristics of that product.

Historically, as Reinert (1994, 2007) illustrated, the potential for reaching rapid economic growth or catching up with more advanced countries, has been, at each point in time, activity-specific; that is, the production of certain goods or sectors has proved to be the key to economic progress because of the dynamic effects it had on the improvement of the overall national economic structure – while the production of other goods or sectors has proved unable, because of specific technical characteristics, to trigger such a process of general improvement. Reinert pointed to the contemporary example of two apparently similar goods: baseballs (a main production of Haiti) and golf balls (of which the USA is a large producer). Because of the existing state of technology, baseballs are produced using a needle and thread technique that has remained basically unchanged for the last hundred years; on the contrary, the production of golf balls offers considerable scope for progressive mechanization and requires the work of highly qualified labour.

The idea that thanks to a mixture of increasing returns, technological progress and imperfect competition, certain products – and specifically manufactures – are particularly apt to induce general economic development, has been a constant in the history of the West since the end of the 15th century (only in the last decades

---

his argument for denying the importance of 'what you produce', already advanced in Bhagwati (1993a), based on the greater importance of consumption over production in determining societies' welfare, appears unconvincing.

of the 20th century did some new service sectors develop whose dynamic potential was even greater than that of manufactures). At that time, the Tudor king Henry V, having observed the wealth-creating effects of cloth manufacturing in France, implemented in England a strategy of support for the domestic production of woollen textiles – the only activity then experiencing rapid technical change – using as raw material the wool previously exported abroad. Little more than a century later, in 1613, the Italian Serra (2011) – considered by Schumpeter the world's first economist – published a treatise in which he referred to types of production subject to increasing returns to scale, which he identified with manufactures, as the activities most favourable to a nation's progress. Especially since the onset of the Industrial Revolution, the recognition of the dynamic potential of manufacturing activity (as against agricultural activity and low-skilled services) – and of the fact that industry does not originate spontaneously from the market system – was at the basis of the economic policy measures in favour of industrialization adopted by all political leaders who tried to make their countries catch up with the welfare levels of industrially more advanced nations. At the theoretical level, among those who highlighted in their works the crucial role of manufacturing, despite their very different economic and ideological views, were Adam Smith in his *The Wealth of Nations* (1776), List in his insightful *Outlines of American Political Economy* (1827), and later in *The National System of Political Economy* (1841), Marshall in his writings of the 1890s, and Graham (1923); while in more recent times (1966-1967), Kaldor formulated a series of 'laws' on the beneficial effects of manufacturing on productivity to account for differences in growth rates between advanced countries.

But very large differences in dynamic economic and social potential may also occur within the group of agricultural and extractive products. Given that the availabilities of these products are largely inexorably fixed by nature, the term 'commodity lottery' has been used to refer to the development-enhancing or development-obstructing nature of the primary product a country happens to produce (see, for example, the fascinating book by Ortiz (1940) on the Cuban experience of the different effects of tobacco versus sugar production).

Some decades ago, it began to be recognized (for instance, by R. Brown and Julius (1993)) that traditional industrial activities – characterized by low worker skill levels, slower advances of technological innovation and no scope for price-fixing because of prevalent cut-throat competition – no longer provided advanced and middle-income countries with stimuli to general economic improvement. Instead, a strong dynamic potential (in terms of large increases in productivity and wages, scope for high profits, substantial export opportunities and strong positive externalities in favour of other sectors) nowadays seems to characterize some technologically advanced industrial types of production and especially some specialized high-skill services that have strong links to them. With the increase in people's income, a growing share of it is spent on services (such as information, communication, transport and health) where the connection between high-tech manufacturing and high-tech services is particularly strong.

However, Reinert (1994) himself argued that 'Today locating these "superior" production activities concentrated in any broad industrial category, as in the past, is difficult. Almost all activities and industries ... have some segments offering the winning combination of innovation and imperfect competition' (p. 179). Indeed, we see a considerable number of sectors, including some classifiable as 'traditional' or 'mature', where top-level technology is being developed with reference to specific aspects of production. An example is the automobile sector, where massive efforts – apparently successful – are being deployed to develop electric engines and driverless cars. Still, it appears that certain specific fields of activity (such as nanotechnology, robotics, 3D printing, subsectors of ICT, artificial intelligence and genetics), characterized by a major R&D content and concerning not specific final goods, but technologies with a large potential of application to many if not all sectors, represent the key to future progress and productivity gains. This means that in industrially advanced countries the demand for government policies to stimulate and sustain the development of activities that have overall growth-enhancing effects has long since shifted from concentration on manufacturing industry as a whole to specific sectors of industry and services that appear to be of strategic importance for the whole economy or to show particular innovative potential, but are characterized (as most radical innovations are) by features that tend to discourage private initiative: high risks for the investor, large basic-research costs and only long-term prospects of profitability. In fact, as Mazzucato (2013) reminded us, the main innovations of the last fifty years – civilian nuclear energy, jet planes, satellites, computers, laser, biotechnology – were developed as a result of government intervention, largely motivated by military considerations.

2.3 Countries, firms and individuals

The concept of comparative costs has a general validity, so that it can be applied to two individuals (as in the example of Footnote 1 in Chapter 1), two firms, two regions or two countries. An important difference must be stressed, however, between the kind of competition that takes place between firms and between countries.

The principle of comparative costs as developed by Ricardo applies to countries, and trade policy has also been necessarily implemented at the level of national sectors of activity. But in market economies, trade is carried out not by countries but by firms. Therefore, if one excludes the possibility of having, in each country, a single firm producing each good, that principle seems to imply the hypothesis that there exists in each country, within each industry, a 'representative firm', from which all domestic firms producing the same good do not differ too much in terms of technology, factors availability and production costs; while all firms are compelled by perfect competition to adopt one single national price, so that the good is either exported or imported.

In real life, competition within a country is not perfect, and factors availability and technology are not the same in all areas of a country, so there are usually significant price differences among firms in domestic markets. This – together with the cost of international transport and other trade costs – explains why, when trade opens between two countries, the specialization of each country in the product where it is relatively most efficient is seldom complete (with each country completely ceasing to produce the imported good).[5] More than that, often the most competitive producers of a good in each country can have their good demanded by consumers of the other country, with consequent flows of horizontal trade (just as within a nation it happens that in many regions the producers of a good export it to consumers located in other regions, these regions in turn exporting to them the same product). This will happen all the more frequently the higher the cost variability is among domestic producers of a given good relative to the average difference in the cost of the good between the two countries.

Once the hypotheses of perfect competition and the representative firm are abandoned, so that the possibility of particular economic agents exercising market power (in the sense of influencing the price of a good) is introduced, at international level a problem arises. While national antitrust authorities can regulate and sanction the market power of firms operating in their country, they are unable to do the same for the international activities of national, and especially foreign firms; and – apart from the case of the European Union (EU) – no supra-national institutions exist with corresponding power to act against monopolistic and oligopolistic practices at international level.

The RHO model rules out divergences between the interests of firms and those of their countries. As Gomory and Baumol (2000) pointed out, it is commonly argued that if two individuals or two countries engage in voluntary exchange, it is because each party benefits from it. Just as a child will not swap his marbles for a playmate's truck unless he prefers the truck to the marbles, and his playmate will not agree to the exchange unless he prefers the marbles to the truck, so it is concluded that neither will two countries voluntarily engage in trade unless they both expect to benefit from it. The analogy is flawed, since the exchange between the two children refers to a single act of exchange of goods already existing and previously acquired (at prices they may ignore), so that the agreed exchange ratio between the two goods depends on the intensity of reciprocal demand (just as it happens with two prisoners of war exchanging the contents of their Red Cross parcels); while trade between two countries refers to reproducible goods that are continuously produced on the basis of a price determined by supply and demand conditions. But quite apart from that, the analogy would only be acceptable if trade transactions and their characteristics were determined – as was the case with communist countries until the end of the 1980s

[5] As already mentioned in Footnote 8 in Chapter 1, the question of whether trade will lead to complete or incomplete specialization will not be discussed in this work; but it has important theoretical consequences for comparative costs theory. Consider that complete specialization, in the Ricardian example of exchange of wine for cloth, would lead both England and Portugal to become a monopolistic producer of one of the goods; and no calculation of relative costs of the two products in the two countries would be possible at any time after specialization.

– by specific decisions of countries' governments (presumably acting in the interest of their citizens). On the contrary, in the international market, exchanges are not the result of national authorities' decisions. The latter can only adopt measures and policies (for instance, industrial or exchange rate policies) to favour the international competitiveness of national firms or facilitate their export activity; and they take part in multinational trade negotiations in order to reach agreements that foster national firms' activity and employment. But trade transactions are the result of the impersonal forces of the market; that is, of the decisions of many firms (some of them multinationals with a very loose connection to their country) and individuals, who do not carry out international bilateral exchanges that must be balanced, as in the cases of the two children referred to or the two students mentioned in the example in Footnote 1 in Chapter 1, or of countries with a state monopoly of foreign trade. A firm's international transaction is not a barter: a firm (or individual) decides to carry out an export or an import transaction – at a price fixed by market forces – with the only goal of maximizing its individual monetary profit, without regard to its country's comparative advantages and gains from trade; purchasers buy a good abroad if its price, expressed in a given currency, is lower than that of the same good available from domestic producers. It is thus possible that in the real world, where the fulfilment of all the hypotheses of the RHO model must be excluded, the result of what is an optimal export and import choice on the part of national firms will not be an optimal choice – or may even produce losses – for their country.

Quite apart from the fact that the purpose of the firm is limited to the maximization of its economic results while the country may also pursue non-economic goals (such as military supremacy, political and cultural influence, and national security), in practice the economic interests of the two entities may also differ. This is not just because of the 'fallacy of composition' problem (the fact that what is beneficial for the individual economic unit may not be beneficial for the sum of all national units).[6] The problem is that, although in very general terms one can expect that successful firms will make for an economically successful country and vice versa, the economic goals of the two entities are different; and in the present-day globalized world, with multinational firms, large-scale offshoring and technology transfers, this has given rise to basic contradictions.

While the goal of firms is profit (in the long term, if they have a proper perspective), countries usually aim to improve citizens' welfare: they do this by maximiz-

[6] Thus for the individual firm maximum efficiency and profitability is achieved by buying abroad all the components and inputs that cost less than at home. For the country as a whole, serious losses may follow if this leads to large balance of payments disequilibria or to widespread closures of firms and the firing of workers not employable elsewhere. A typical case of the 'fallacy of composition' is that of an economy in recession, when for an individual faced with a higher risk of losing his job the rational strategy is to reduce his expenditure and set aside a volume of savings to ensure a minimum of consumption in the event of unemployment. If followed by all individuals, such a strategy would result in the economy as a whole almost inevitably falling into a much deeper recession because of the consequent reduction in total demand.

ing national income growth, but subject to other goals, first of these being full or near-full employment; other possible goals are an acceptable income distribution, provision of a stable money value, minimization of the loss of scarce foreign currency reserves, avoidance of an excessive public debt that would weigh heavily on future generations, maintenance of an ecologically sustainable use of resources and strengthening the country's bargaining power in international negotiations and institutions. The search for high profitability may be pursued by firms, as was typical of the last decades, by trying in all possible ways to reduce the number of workers needed to produce given quantities of goods, or by moving all or part of the production of a good abroad. This may cause, at national level, an increase in unemployment, possibly the worst economic result for a country's government, as it is the authority responsible for the well-being of national workers.

If one only considers firms' goal of maximizing their profits and countries' goal of maximizing the national product, the difference in economic goals between firms and countries can also be expressed in terms of value added (VA). VA is the difference between the sale price of a product and the cost of the inputs acquired (raw materials, intermediate products and other inputs); it typically includes wages and profits. The sum of the VA of all firms in a country corresponds to the value of the country's gross domestic product (GDP). Most firms engaged in foreign trade are not individual enterprises or cooperatives, but firms with owners or managers who produce together with employee workers. The basic goal of the firm's owner or manager is not to maximize the firm's total VA – relative to the investment made to obtain the goods produced – but merely to maximize that part of its VA that represents profits. At the limit, not only could a firm obtain gains from trade in some particular instances in which the country as a whole does not, but it might also even engage in trade that produces losses to the firm as a whole, but gains from trade for the owners of its capital, while workers are burdened with losses from trade. The goal of the country, instead, is basically to maximize the GDP that can be obtained by employing the factors of production available in the country; it does this both by increasing the productivity of each of the production factors employed, and by favouring the employment of all the factors available in its territory.

The economic competition that firms must face is also different from the economic competition that takes place among countries. To begin with, firms unable to withstand competition by other firms go bankrupt and have to exit the market; countries can go bankrupt, too, but while this will create a lot of problems for them, they do not disappear, as they are not just economic entities working for the market. And while two competing firms, say Volkswagen and Renault, do not buy products from one another, Germany and France do carry out a lot of bilateral trade, so that the economic progress of Germany as a result of superior performance in export activity will probably translate into increased imports from other countries including France.

Quite apart from that, firms compete with each other on the basis of price, quality and the technological level of their products; they may also compete in attracting scarce factors of production, or in finding profitable foreign locations for offshoring phases of production. Countries compete by creating through education and vocational training a more highly qualified labour force; by attracting FDI; by increasing R&D expenditure; by improving public services and infrastructure; by employing exchange rate and commercial policies to achieve a surplus on their trade balance so as to maximize total demand for their products; and through industrial policies they may also try to directly stimulate activity in specific sectors. Their goal is usually to shift the entire national structure of production and trade towards the goods with the greatest potential for demand growth, the strongest dynamic effects on other sectors and the highest level of technological and qualitative sophistication, which makes competition by other countries more difficult and permits significant monopolistic rents. In the case of developing countries, their most important economic goal is usually to adopt policies allowing the country to overcome the vicious circles that obstruct its escape from underdevelopment.

Divergencies of interests between firms and countries were neglected by mainstream international trade theory in the past, when firms were basically nationally owned and, apart from raw materials, produced their goods using national factors of production, so that international competition between countries largely coincided with competition between their respective national firms. Nowadays, international movements of goods, capitals, technologies and managerial skills are much larger and easier, and international trade is largely carried out by MNCs, whose national seat is often unclear, and which produce for the world market from factories located in different countries and/or with inputs and components provided by firms at any place in the world. In this environment, divergencies of interest between firms and countries have become acute, particularly as regards the workers in advanced countries – as pointed out by Ozawa (2019). One of the most serious today has come about because comparative advantage seems to be driven not so much by the traditional factors' relative availabilities as by technological capabilities; and the main vehicles for international transfers of technology, particularly to developing countries, have proved to be MNCs, offshoring and global production chains.

With time, more and more developing countries have learned the key lesson of the emerging Asian countries' – and particularly China's – development experience, namely that an effective instrument to upgrade national production and labour skills is to require foreign firms from advanced countries to make substantial transfers of technological know-how and training of local workers in skilled activities as a condition for the establishment of local branches and for entering into outsourcing contracts with local producers. While satisfying these requirements may prove advantageous for the advanced countries' companies, and for total world output and welfare, it may not be in the interest of the countries in which the technologies originate (as a result, in large part, of research funded publicly by their citizens).

Palley (2008) has stressed the basic change that has occurred:

> In the pre-globalization era domestically developed science and technology innovations were likely to be applied domestically so that the benefit accrued significantly to the innovating country. Today, with corporations organizing production on a global

> basis, there is nothing to ensure that domestically produced innovations will be applied domestically. Instead, corporations may simply transfer the innovation to a foreign production location. (p. 203)[7]

This is also a reason why the use by advanced countries' governments of R&D subsidies to firms may prove less effective as a way of supporting national output. This point was also developed by Gomory and Baumol (2009). Like Palley, they pointed out that in this respect the USA is in a condition of serious inferiority vis-à-vis China: lacking full independence from public authorities, Chinese corporations can be, and frequently are, compelled by their government to internalize Chinese national interests, while the US government cannot exert the same influence on its corporations.

But apart from technology transfers, there is a more general problematic issue that characterizes the contemporary open world economy, well summarized by former US Treasury Secretary Lawrence Summers (2008):

> In a closed economy anything that promotes investment in productive capital necessarily raises workers' wages. In a closed economy corporations have a huge stake in the quality of the national workforce and infrastructure. The situation is very different in an open economy where investments in innovation, brands, a strong corporate culture or even in certain kinds of equipment can be combined with labour from anywhere in the world. Workers no longer have the same stake in productive investment by companies as it becomes easier for corporations to combine their capital with lower priced labour overseas. Companies, in turn, come to have less of a stake in the quality of the workforce and infrastructure in their home country when they can produce everywhere. Moreover, business can use the threat of relocating as a lever to extract concessions regarding tax policy, regulations and specific subsidies. Inevitably the cost of these concessions is borne by labour.

Referring to the contemporary phenomenon of the fragmentation of the production of goods – a production that once took place in specific countries, but now is usually split into separate phases carried out in different countries within global production chains organized by large MNCs – Baldwin (2016, 2017) has spoken of the 'denationalization of comparative advantage', as nations no longer appear to be the natural unit of analysis in international trade. Instead of competition between countries, each striving to reinforce its comparative advantages, we now have competition between large firms, each trying to increase its competitiveness by recombining the different segments of its activity, split among a plurality of countries, and by exploiting the different sources of comparative advantage of each of them. In this new setting, Baldwin has argued, it is no longer certain that all participating countries gain from trade.

---

[7] See Krugman (1996a) for observations on the inappropriateness at the national level of policy advice contributed by company executives on the basis of their individual business experience.

A wide-ranging debate developed in the past that seems destined to continue forever: whether the growth of MNCs and the development of their activities on an increasingly world scale inescapably reduce the importance of the nation state. In his *Sovereignty at Bay*, Vernon (1971) was among the first authors to signal the danger and to discuss the problem. While arguments can be advanced both in support and against the hypothesis, it is beyond doubt that there is no longer a strict connection between the expansion of national firms and the expansion of the national economy. And the difficulty, pointed out by Baldwin, created by international trade theory continuing to refer to countries as the fundamental unit of analysis testifies to the reduced relevance, at least so far, of the nation state as the basic actor in international trade relative to the new powerful large MNCs.

* * *

When international trade theory recognized the importance of product differentiation and monopolistic competition in the 1970s and 1980s, it still largely continued to retain the 'representative firm' assumption, according to which all firms in each national industrial sector have access to the same basic technology, similar productivity levels and a similar degree of participation in international trade.[8] This assumption received a serious blow in the course of the 1990s, when a large mass of microdata on firms and plants became available, demonstrating the extreme heterogeneity of firms belonging to the same manufacturing sector, in terms of size, relative factor intensities, productivity and wages, and showing that these differences seemed to be associated with very large differences in the degree of firms' involvement in international trade. While the previous literature had highlighted the general positive effects of export activity, it was with Bernard and Jensen (1995, 1999) that a new line of research started to be developed, producing by the mid-2000s a specific body of international trade theory based on the recognition of firms' heterogeneity in productivity and involvement in foreign trade, centred on individual firm's characteristics and focusing on products instead of sectors: fundamental contributions were made by Melitz (2003) and Bernard, Eaton, Jensen and Kortum (2003).

It was found that in the USA, and also in other countries, export activity involved only a small fraction of industrial firms; that exporting firms were much larger in size, more capital- and skill-intensive, and showed significantly higher productivity levels than non-exporting ones; that exports were highly concentrated in a limited percentage of exporting firms; and that once a firm started exporting it tended to continue to do so. More recently, it was found that at firm level there is also a significant association between exporting activity and innovation, which was explained by

[8] It is this assumption, by the way, that for a long period limited the analysis by traditional international trade theory of the particular role of multinational firms in foreign trade. Dosi, Pavitt and Soete (1990) rejected the assumption and based their analysis of the relationship between technical change and international trade on the hypothesis of large differences between firms, even within the same country, in technological capabilities, technical coefficients (the amounts of factors' inputs per unit of output of a good) and product performance.

the fact that it is the firms operating in larger markets that can reach the sales volumes that justify incurring the high fixed costs of innovation.

All these features seemed to indicate that export activity is characterized by the high sunk costs (initial fixed costs that cannot be recovered if the activity is discontinued) of accessing foreign markets, so that within sectors only the most efficient firms can cope with such costs and reap the benefits of wider markets and further productivity growth produced by trade liberalization; while the increase in international competition owing to lower trade barriers and reduction of transport costs accelerates the exit of the least efficient firms from the market of a good.

Studies indicated that this within-industry reallocation of production and employment from low-productivity to high-productivity firms leads to an increase in aggregate productivity that represents a possibly more significant source of gains from trade than the traditional RHO welfare gains from specialization owing to factor movements from less to more relatively competitive industrial sectors. A second wave of microdata available in the late 2000s showed that high heterogeneity also characterized the more limited group of exporting firms.

Melitz and Trefler (2012), analysing in particular the effects of the 1989 USA–Canada free-trade agreement, concluded that trade liberalization produces three main gains: those due to increased product variety and economies of scale; gains in productivity at the firm level as a result of a larger market inducing firms to increase their efforts to develop innovations; and, possibly most important, productivity gains at industry level, connected to firm heterogeneity, produced by the shift of resources from low-productivity to high-productivity firms. But at the same time, they stressed that the positive overall effect on industries' productivity owing to the reallocation of market shares between heterogeneous firms also magnifies the generation of winners and losers among firms within an industry as free trade increases.[9]

* * *

If countries' and firms' interests can diverge, even more important are the differences between the interests of countries and individuals. Ricardian comparative costs theory and its free-trade prescription, which stress the advantages countries derive from specialization, imply that the trade advantages for a country are matched by equal advantages for its citizens (which is what makes it difficult to use the Ricardian framework to analyse the effects of trade on the distribution among different groups of citizens). As Palley (1998) remarked, comparative costs theory seems to introduce a 'representative individual' assumption, according to which all individuals in a nation are identical and share equally in the wages and profits connected with the activities in which their country specializes, while the hypothesis of full employment

[9] For reviews of the literature on firm heterogeneity see Helpman (2006, 2011), Bernard, Jensen, Redding and Schott (2007, 2012), Redding (2011), Melitz and Redding (2014). On large 'global firms' dominating international trade see Bernard, Jensen, Redding and Schott (2018).

allows any differentiated employment effect of trade on particular categories of persons to be ignored.

In the real world, the advantages of trade specialization are not shared equally among all citizens; in particular, given that firms' decisions are taken exclusively by management (the owner himself or his agent), the benefits in the form of higher profits or rents are often matched by wage losses for all or some groups of workers. Of course, international trade theory has long since found a solution to this problem in the theory of compensation: to a country's trade advantages in terms of higher overall national income potentially correspond advantages to all citizens if the benefits to individuals favoured by trade are higher than the losses to individuals damaged by it, since a compensation plan could be devised which would tax the citizens benefited to compensate the citizens damaged. The issue of trade loss compensation will be taken up in Section 12.3.1; it should just be noted here that adequate compensation plans have rarely been adopted in practice, while free trade can in fact cause significant wage and employment losses for large groups of workers.

3 Scale Economies

Adam Smith identified the origin of economic progress and of the benefit of international trade in the increase in labour productivity owing to the economies of scale consequent on the extension of the market and the higher degree of national and international specialization it allowed (Smith's contribution will be discussed in greater details in Section 8.1). On the contrary, the RHO model assumes constant returns to scale.[1]

Scale economies are the benefits, in terms of lowering the average unit cost of production of a good, that can be obtained by increasing the volume of production of the good. They may be due to the fact that larger volumes of production allow workers to concentrate on specific tasks and thus increase their productivity; or to the fact that larger volumes of production make it profitable to purchase more specialized, complex or technologically advanced machinery (or to introduce more efficient organization systems), thereby lowering the cost of each unit of the good produced; or to the fact that, once the investment in specific machinery (or any other kind of initial fixed expenditure) has been made, an increase in the scale of production allows the initial investment expenses to be spread over a larger number of units;[2] or to the advantages of geographical agglomeration – of having a large number of firms concentrated in given locations. International trade, by enlarging the extent of the market relative to an isolated national economy, allows greater exploitation of scale economies, thus providing advantages especially to the countries whose national market is limited by a small population and/or a low per capita income.

From a strictly technical point of view, increasing returns to scale occur whenever increasing the physical amount of productive inputs by a given percentage brings a larger percentage increase in physical production. But from an economic point of

[1] While Ricardo's principle of comparative advantage has been traditionally interpreted as being based on constant returns to scale, Ricardo actually never referred to constant returns in the chapter of his *Principles* devoted to foreign trade, while in the rest of the book he made frequent reference to diminishing returns to scale in agriculture (which in his time was the main sector of the economy). As indicated in Footnote 8 in Chapter 1, according to the new interpretation of Ricardo's trade theory, he was well aware of the possibility of traded goods being produced under non-constant returns, and formulated his principle allowing for that possibility.

[2] In the case of plants and machines, economies of scale owing to the spreading of an initial fixed investment over a larger number of units produced may not be distinguishable from the so-called economies of plant; that is, advantages that come from fuller utilization of existing productive capacity.

view, increasing returns can also be obtained whenever increasing the scale of production leads to lower unit costs by allowing savings in expenditures such as purchases of inputs (since orders of larger amounts usually allow higher price discounts), the cost of keeping stocks, distribution, advertising and R&D.

Cost savings may also derive from reductions in statistical risk, as the increase in the volume of production makes it possible both to forecast more precisely (as a result of the law of large numbers) the effective likelihood of certain events whose theoretical probabilities are known, and to have more possibilities for compensating diverging trends for different products, plants and places. For example, a firm may become multinational and operate in a large number of countries so as to reap the worldwide economies of scale that come from higher chances of compensating unfavourable market situations in one country with favourable ones in other countries. The very existence of the insurance industry is based on the possibility that its firms will reach a size permitting the exploitation of this kind of scale advantage. It is also a very important advantage in all the activities consisting of projects characterized by large initial investments, high probability of failure and very high profits in case of success (examples being oil research, pharmaceuticals and venture capital). It has been argued that the same consideration also justifies government support for big high-risk innovative projects: only the government has the resources necessary to invest in such projects covering a great number of different sectors, where it can be anticipated that success in some of them will produce sufficient gains to compensate for the inevitable failures in many others.

Scale economies can be distinguished between 'internal', which operate at the level of the individual firm (or plant), and occur when the unit costs of a particular firm decrease with the expansion of its production; and 'external', which operate outside the firm, and occur when the unit costs of a particular firm, although not decreasing with the expansion of its own production, decrease with the expansion of the production of the whole industrial sector (for example, because, in common with other firms of the same sector, the firm can take advantage of more efficient external facilities, inputs or services). External scale economies have a sector dimension (they can take place at the level of an industrial sector, of a group of sectors or of the entire industrial sector) and a geographical dimension (occurring at the level of a district, region, nation or even the world). Sources of external scale economies can be the advantages that come from within-industry specialization or from spatial agglomeration or from public intermediate inputs such as roads. Scale economies can be further distinguished between static, depending on the current level of production, and dynamic, which involve the passage of time and depend on the volume of past production.[3]

[3] Static internal economies of scale occur when, for instance, producing a larger number of units of a good allows a plant to use more efficient machines or (as in the famous example of Smith's pin factory) systems of labour division; or when the firm can spread fixed costs such as those for administration, R&D, distribution or advertising over a larger number of produced units. Dynamic internal economies of scale are obtained when, for instance, a larger volume of production allows a firm's management and workers to increase their productivity thanks to the more intense and more varied practice with

Increasing returns in manufacturing have been known by economists since Serra (1613) hinted at their importance in his treatise; they were at the centre of Smith's theory of development. Among modern economists it was Marshall who revived interest in the subject in his 1879 to 1890 works – at a time when manufacturing had become the dominant productive force in advanced countries – and introduced the distinction between internal and external scale economies. The subject was brought back to the centre of the economic stage by Young (1928), who was critical of Marshall's distinction between internal and external scale economies, and argued that the main economies that go under the name of increasing returns are part of a wider process of industrial development that could be better understood by referring to the original Smithian concepts of specialization, 'roundaboutness' of production methods and the extent of the market.[4]

The specific influence of increasing returns on international trade flows was recognized by modern economists long ago, for example by Nicholson (1897), F. Walker (1903) and especially Graham (1923). Nicholson remarked that increasing returns can create problems for the comparative costs theory; Graham showed that in the presence of variable returns a country could be damaged by free trade, and specialization might reduce its global output.[5]

---

working techniques; or when the greater experience gained by the firm through a larger volume of past production facilitates the improvement of its products or production processes. These economies are thus usually a function of total past production or of the distance in time from the moment production was started (as learning by doing may require time as well as practice). External static economies of scale at the industry level occur, for example, when the presence of a large number of firms producing textiles in a country permits the establishment of specialized assistance centres, which guarantee the immediate repair of national textile machines in the event of breakdown, thus increasing their productivity; or when in a tropical country the total volume of banana production allows the banana sector to reduce the cost of transport to markets by setting up its own fleet of special banana-carrying ships. An example of dynamic economies of scale at industry level is the establishment, once a certain level of textile production is reached in a country or region, of research centres for the study of textile materials and the improvement of textile machinery, leading in the fullness of time to greater innovation activity in the sector.

While scale economies refer to the decrease in the unit cost of production of a good when a larger number of units is produced, the term 'scope economies' refers to the fact that once a good is produced, marketed and distributed by a firm, the latter will see the costs of these operations sensibly decrease for a second, third (and so on) additional good that it decides to produce, as it can profit from the free or much cheaper cost of factors such as the establishment of brand name, channels of distribution and customers assistance, and knowledge of the market.

[4] On Young and scale economies see Lavezzi (2003) and Chandra (2004). The subtle differences between the concepts of economies of scale, on the one hand, and economies of specialization and division of labour, on the other, are discussed in Yang and Ng (1995). Here it is worth simply recalling that while scale economies refer to decreases in unit costs connected to an increase in the number of units produced, economies of specialization refer to decreases in unit costs obtained by organizing production (even of a given, fixed number of units) in a more roundabout way by having each worker or machine specialize in just one phase of the production process. Of course, the scope for specialization in different phases of the production process largely depends on the number of units produced.

[5] In his history of free trade, Irwin (1996) analysed the main contributions of economists since 1815

Graham took the case of two countries A and B producing in isolation two goods: watches – subject to increasing returns to scale – and wheat – subject to decreasing returns. Suppose that before trade A has a comparative advantage in wheat and B in watches; the opening of trade will then see country A increase its production of wheat so as to export part of it to country B in exchange for imports of watches from B, so that its domestic production of watches will diminish. Owing to economies/diseconomies of scale, country A will see an increase in production costs of both wheat and watches, as smaller and smaller quantities of additional wheat will be obtained by the application of equal additional amounts of productive factors, while in the production of watches the reduction in the number of produced units, in favour of imports, will also increase unit costs (the opposite occurring in country B). Graham concluded that the existence of variable returns to scale could justify the protection from import competition of sectors operating under increasing returns.

Ohlin himself, in his 1933 work, while specifying he was not strictly referring to increasing returns, stressed that specialization and large-scale operations can originate comparative advantages,[6] and considered them to be an important independent cause of trade after relative factor availabilities. Still, until some authors in the

---

to the study of scale economies and their effects on international trade, and devoted specific analysis to Graham's argument for protection in conditions of variable returns to scale.

Graham's article was strongly criticized at the time, but the possibility of welfare losses from trade in the presence of variable returns to scale he had advanced was generally conceded by trade theorists by the 1960s – see Caves (1967) – and was confirmed more recently by Ethier (1982) and Helpman (2011); see also Raffer (1994).

For Graham, manufactures are the typical goods produced at decreasing costs. He mentioned other important additional advantages for a country specializing in their production: manufactures enjoy a stronger long-run growth of demand relative to other goods and so better prospects of favourable terms of exchange; their production is particularly effective in promoting the improvement of skills; and since increasing returns lower the cost of production of industrial goods, manufacturers are compelled by the threat of competitors producing larger volumes and thus outselling them, to make continuous investment of their profits in extensions of their productive capacity (this last point, according to Kaldor (1980), had first been made by Marx). Given the advantages of industrial production, Graham went so far as to recommend protection of domestic industrial sectors not just as a temporary policy until these sectors gain enough strength to stand without support (as argued by List and the 'infant industry' argument), but as a permanent policy to keep activities in existence that are unable to withstand foreign competition on their own.

[6] For Ohlin (1967), this was a consequence of 'indivisibilities' in production processes: 'lack of divisibility makes production on a large scale more efficient up to a certain point than production in small quantities … As a matter of fact, the size of the factory or the establishment is very important. Only when fairly large quantities of certain factors and implements are used can the minimum cost combination be reached. This may be because the least unit of certain instruments is large, or because a larger unit is relatively more "efficient" than a smaller one. In short, so-called internal economies are the result of a lack of divisibility. External economies of production are often similarly connected with incomplete divisibility. For example, the advantages an industry derives from concentration in a certain locality are to some extent dependent upon the existence of a well organized labour market. If textile factories, for instance, were scattered over a large area, manufacturers could not be certain of finding instantly a sufficient supply of the special type of skilled labour they required' (pp.36–37).

1960s, and in particular Melvin (1969a), revived interest in them, scale economies were rarely the object of deep theoretical study as an autonomous cause of trade.[7]

A likely reason for this is that the existence of scale economies represents a serious blow to the standard RHO model (and to the mainstream economic theory associated with it). There is in fact an incompatibility between scale economies and competition, as Cournot had recognized as far back as 1838. Internal economies of scale, determining cost advantages for larger firms over smaller ones, encourage the creation of monopolies or oligopolies, thus contradicting the fundamental hypothesis of perfect competition on which the RHO model is based (which ensures that no single firm can influence the determination of the price of the good it produces; in Section 8.1 it will be shown how Smith, in his dynamic view of the economic process, was able to reconcile economies of scale and free competition).

An additional possible reason was advanced by Arthur (1990): increasing returns to scale, with the positive feedbacks associated with them (discussed in this section), introduce – as Marshall was probably the first to recognize and discuss – the possibility that the economic system moves not towards one optimum, but towards many possible and unpredictable equilibrium points, some of them suboptimal. Orthodox economists (but even Schumpeter, who was not) tried to avoid the analysis of phenomena leading to a significant number of possible equilibria, as the lack of a uniquely determined one was considered a negative, non-scientific result for economic research; while they also lacked the analytical tools, developed in more recent decades, for a rigorous treatment of scale economies and their feedbacks.

A third reason is that since scale economies have important dynamic effects (for example, learning by doing and stimulus to innovations and technical progress), when they operate market prices – on whose basis individual producers take their decisions – no longer provide correct signals on the growth and innovative efficiency of different lines of production, as underlined by Cimoli, Dosi, Nelson and Stiglitz (2006).

Sraffa (1926) pointed out that the escape from the contradiction between internal scale economies and the theory of price determination in free competition (on which the whole construction of economic theory was then based) devised by Marshall, with the introduction of the concept of external scale economies, was not acceptable. External scale economies, connecting unit-cost reductions to the volume of production of a whole sector of industry, allow for the existence of a plurality of small firms, each operating under the impression of producing under constant returns to scale, and therefore behaving as a price taker under perfect competition. But Sraffa argued that Marshall himself recognized the limited importance in real economic life of external scale economies. Given the empirical predominance of internal scale economies, Sraffa started instead to investigate the behaviour of firms operating

[7] Among the exceptions are Matthews (1949), Meade (1952) and especially Caves (1967). Caves analysed Graham's treatment of varying returns, as well as the insights provided on the subject by some economists between the 1930s and the 1950s.

under conditions of monopolistic competition, at the time a new area of theoretical research, but one that since the end of the 1980s would take central place in international trade theory (see Chapter 4).

Among external scale economies Marshall stressed those resulting from the development of industrial sector's firms connected with one another (in the sense of being at the same time both in competition and collaborating) and concentrated in the same locality. He advanced three main reasons – that continue to be relevant in contemporary economies – for the existence of important external economies in these clusters of industrial activity:

1. Specialized suppliers: in many sectors, production of a good requires specialized equipment or specialized services. A large and concentrated industry, instead of a small isolated firm, can create a market large enough to attract a wide range of specialized suppliers.
2. Labour pooling: a large and concentrated industry is likely to create a pool of workers highly specialized in the range of activities characteristic of the cluster, reducing search and hiring costs for each firm, as the danger is reduced of not finding, in case of need, the necessary additional workforce; while workers also enjoy the advantage of a reduction of risk, as in the case of dismissal by a firm they have more chance of finding another firm in the cluster that needs their services.
3. Knowledge spillovers: in a world where innovations are more and more critical in determining the success of firms, a large and geographically concentrated industry facilitates the sharing of productive ideas among workers and technicians in different firms, and makes it easier for firms to learn from local competitors by analysing their products. Particularly important is the informal exchange of information and ideas that takes place at the personal level, necessitating the physical contact and frequent meetings that only close geographical proximity can provide.[8]

[8] A particular case of external static and, especially, dynamic economies of scale at local industry level very close to Marshall's clusters is represented by the Italian 'industrial districts', peculiar territorial clusters of small to medium-sized, highly specialized, export-oriented firms belonging to the same sector – at the same time competing and collaborating with one another – whose strong points are: 1) a high level of trust among firms owing to their proximity and repeated exchanges; 2) a large availability of collective goods, such as social and economic infrastructure, formal and informal common procedures and codes, and synergies with other local institutions (universities, public administrations and credit institutions); 3) fast inter-firm circulation of information both on the best productive and organizational practices and on the evolution of the market for their products; and 4) large scope for common initiatives in fields such as input purchases, market research, sales and advertising, and workers' training. The Italian 'industrial districts' (and their connection with the Marshallian notion of industrial district) have been thoroughly analysed, from the late 1970s, by the Italian economist Becattini: see Becattini (2004).

The analysis of clusters has been the object of continuous investigation by Porter. Frequently referring to the experience of Italian industrial districts, he investigated the new characteristics, the points of strength and the vulnerabilities of modern clusters: see Porter (1998a) and, for a more synthetic analysis, Porter (1998b, 2000).

But there is another, possibly more important, reason why scale economies represent a serious blow to the RHO model. On the one hand, they destroy the very foundation of the Ricardian principle of comparative advantage that requires, to be operative and for trade to take place, and for producing clear forecasts on the pattern of trade once the latter is opened, that the two trading countries have stable different ratios between the efficiency of production in one good and in the other. In the presence of variable returns to scale, relative costs and prices of the goods before trade depend on the relative quantities of the goods produced, and thus on the relative dimension of the two countries and the relative intensity of consumption and production of the two goods in each country. After the opening of trade, the relative cost and price of the goods depend on the amounts of the goods produced in each country and the intensity of scale economies. On the other hand, scale economies destroy the HO justification for exchange in terms of the different initial relative supply of productive factors in the two countries, as scale economies can themselves create comparative advantages between two countries that are, before trade, absolutely equal in factor availabilities.

Suppose, following Melvin (1969a), that two countries have, in isolation, the same factors' supplies and are equal in all other economic respects, producing the same amounts of goods X and Y at the same prices. According to RHO theory, since the relative costs of producing the two goods are the same in the two countries, at the opening of the border between them no trade would take place. Suppose now that external scale economies at the level of the national industrial sector operate in the production of the two goods: if suddenly – owing to a marginal change in tastes or technology or for any other reason, even merely accidental – an increase takes place in one country in the demand and production of good X relative to the demand and production of Y, the operation of scale economies will lead that country to develop a specific comparative advantage in good X, making it profitable to start exporting that good to the other country in exchange for good Y (which at home will be more costly to produce because of the reduction in the number of units produced). The increase in the production volumes of goods X and Y respectively in the two countries, as a result of their initial export activity, will further strengthen, because of scale economies, the comparative advantage of each country in one of the goods, leading to more and more specialization and trade between them.[9]

---

[9] One interesting result can be deduced from Melvin's (1969a) analysis: in the case under consideration, in each country the increased employment of the factors used more intensively in the production of the good now produced in greater quantity will lead to an increase in the relative price of those factors. If this higher relative factor price is also associated with a higher absolute factor price and if there is factors mobility between countries, factors will tend to move to the country where their relative price is higher, leading to a change in the previously identical factor availabilities in the two countries. The final result will be that each country exports the good that is relatively more intensive in the relatively more abundant factors; but this superior factor availability would not represent the cause of trade between the two countries as in the RHO model, but rather be a consequence of the trade originated by increasing returns.

[continue on next page].

In this case it is scale economies that created comparative advantages that did not previously exist. But still more damaging to the RHO model is the fact that it is possible for economies of scale to originate and then reinforce trade flows between two countries in complete contrast to their initial comparative advantages in terms of factors availabilities.

Suppose we have two countries A and B. Both produce, at the same cost, good X under constant returns to scale. There is a second good, Y, whose production is subject to increasing external returns to scale (at the level of the national industrial sector). For any given amount of good Y produced, country A could produce it at a lower cost than country B. Clearly when trade is opened, country A's comparative advantage would be in the production and export of Y. But suppose now that to produce good Y country A has to start from scratch, because in isolation it did not produce this good in significant amounts, while country B, in isolation, produced large amounts of it and, thanks to scale economies, reached a low unit cost equal to price P. If country A started producing Y for the international market, the initial price it could offer would be higher than P, because with a low production volume A's unit cost would be higher than the unit cost of country B, despite the fact that, potentially, for any given amount of good Y, A could produce it at a lower cost and price than B.

So, if scale economies operate, there is no guarantee that it will be the right country – the relatively more efficient one in the production of a good – that will produce it. All previous discourse underlines the importance, in the presence of scale economies, of being, for whatever reason, the first producer of a good, even if other countries could potentially produce it more efficiently, as economies of scale tend to reinforce any initial occasional advantage.[10]

Purvis (1972) identified a similar case of mutual reinforcement between factor movements and trade, originated by an absolute technological advantage of a country in the production of a labour-intensive good. This advantage produces an export flow and allows for higher wage rates that attract labour from abroad; the case is discussed by Jones (2000, p. 6).

[10] A very similar argument – referred, however, to 'learning by doing' – had been advanced in defence of infant-industry protection by J. S. Mill in his *Principles of Political Economy* first published in 1848: 'The superiority of one country over another in a branch of production often arises only from having begun it sooner. There may be no inherent advantage on one part, or disadvantage on the other, but only a present superiority of acquired skill and experience. A country which has this skill and experience yet to acquire, may in other respects be better adapted to the production than those which were earlier in the field' (1909, p. 922). Gomory and Baumol (2000) have analysed the problem, supposing that firms are subject to internal scale economies and sunk costs of entry and that the same technology is available to all countries (see Section 11.1.3). Because of internal scale economies, each good is produced by a single country: the one that first started production and moved down the cost curve. This initial cost advantage then blocks all other producers, even if their cost curves lie below that of the initial producer. Multiple equilibria can be reached, depending on which country moves first; nothing guarantees that the equilibrium reached is the one ensuring maximum world production. If, for example, one country is the first to start production in a large number of sectors, it may gain economies of scale advantages in each of them that will keep out possible competitors; but the overall result will be productive inefficiency, as the scale economies the country can exploit in each of the sectors of its activity will

More generally, as highlighted by Arthur (1989, 1990, 1994), the localization in a given country of production and export of a good may find its explanation not in any original superiority of the country in the production of that good – possibly tied to the availability of given production factors or resources – but simply in a different dimension of the good's markets in different countries before trade is opened, in government support for initial production of the good, in a political or administrative decision (for instance of artificially keeping the exchange rate undervalued) or in a mere historical accident that caused the production of the good to be started in a country at an earlier date than in other countries. Much depends on who makes the first move, and how intensively. Once the superiority of a location for a given type of production has been established, scale economies (especially if reinforced by high sunk entry costs), phenomena of path dependence (which refers to dynamical systems in which earlier states of the system affect later ones) and hysteresis (the persistence of an event even after the initial causes giving rise to it have been removed) tend, over time, to reinforce the position of superiority of that location.[11] Most importantly, since initial production and international specialization in given goods is so self-reinforcing as to become often irreversible, not only the specific comparative advantages at the moment trade is opened, but also the decisions that originated those types of productions and specializations – and in particular the imposition of productive

---

be severely limited. If the country had concentrated production in a few sectors, allowing other countries to specialize in the others, a more efficient global pattern of production would have been obtained.

The analysis of Gomory and Baumol, as stressed by Palley (2008), highlights the large potential for serious conflicts between countries provided by increasing returns: since multiple equilibria are possible, each country will try to adopt measures to reach the equilibrium most favourable to itself. At the same time, these situations may, in principle, create the conditions for a cooperative effort by countries' governments to reorganize the structure of global production so as to reach a higher level of overall efficiency and welfare.

[11] Ohlin was well aware of the possibility that chance or historical accident could create comparative advantage, though he played down the empirical importance of the phenomenon, compared with the fundamental influence of factor availabilities: 'assume … a number of regions … their factor endowments and their demand are so balanced that the relative prices of factors and commodities are everywhere the same … no trade is then possible. As a matter of fact, in so far as the market for some articles within each region is not large enough to permit the most efficient scale of production, division of labour and trade will be profitable. Each region will specialize on some of these articles and exchange them for the rest. The character of this trade will be entirely a matter of chance if factor equipment is everywhere the same, for it doesn't matter whether a certain region specializes in one commodity or another, just as uniformly endowed individuals can with equal advantage specialize in any kind of work … The location of an industry in one region and not in another might simply be due to chance, the industry having gained strength in that particular region and having reached an efficient scale. Since it cannot profitably be carried on in every region because the total demand is too small, it tends to remain where it was first located. However … such cases … are probably not very important' (1967, pp.38–39); and 'It is evident that within limits a country may specialize in any one industry as well as in any other. Chance plays a significant part in determining the location of industry. An invention in a particular country may give rise to the manufacture of certain machines, whereas other machines are produced in other countries, partly as a result of inventions there. A different distribution of inventions would have caused a different location of production' (pp. 92–93).

choices even in a distant past as a result of colonial domination or other situations of power asymmetry – can emerge as powerful determinants of the long-term economic destiny of regions and nations.

The indeterminateness of the pattern of specialization under increasing returns leads to the attribution to mere chance of a large role in the explanation of the structure of international trade flows, and also opens up new horizons for historical research in the search for the origin of the present structure of these flows.

In the presence of scale economies, the same features of indeterminateness, unpredictability, possible *ex post* non-optimality of consolidated patterns, path dependence and hysteresis that characterize the location of production and exports also characterize the adoption of alternative technologies. Often the two phenomena are connected, as different technologies may be developed in different countries or locations. Moreover, in addition to static increasing returns to scale, it is a frequent characteristic of modern complex technologies that they display dynamic 'increasing returns to adoption', in the sense that the more widely they are adopted, the more experience is gained with them and the more improvements can be applied to them. Rosenberg (1982) called the phenomenon 'learning by using', citing as an example the improvements in aircraft design made possible by the accumulation of experience on and use of existing models. As a consequence, while there is no guarantee that it will be the superior technology that will survive in the long run, once a technology, even if originally inferior, is adopted and diffused, it will probably become the most efficient and profitable one thanks to successive improvements.

In conclusion, as Arthur (1989) remarked:

> the interpretation of economic history should be different in different returns regimes. Under constant and diminishing returns, the evolution of the market reflects only *a-priori* endowments, preferences, and transformation possibilities; small events cannot sway the outcome. But while this is comforting, it reduces history to the status of mere carrier – the deliverer of the inevitable. Under increasing returns, by contrast, many outcomes are possible. Insignificant circumstances become magnified by positive feedbacks to "tip" the system into the actual outcome "selected". The small events of history become important. (p. 127)

Among such circumstances, Arthur cited unexpected successes in the performance of prototypes (or early casually disappointing results from a potentially superior technology), previous personal experience or the mere whims of early developers and political circumstances; and referred to the choice between steam-propelled and petrol-propelled cars in the 1890s, and between light-water and gas-cooled nuclear reactors in the 1950s and 1960s.

An important aspect of scale economies – a phenomenon that is caused by them, but at the same time reinforces them – is the advantage that comes to early producers of a good from the fact that once they have chosen and introduced a standard (technological or of any other nature) – perhaps simply because it was more convenient for them given their specific conditions at the time – and it becomes established in their sector of activity, subsequent producers are often compelled to adopt it too, even if other standards would be technically superior and more profitable if only they could be imposed on all producers. The subject of standards (analysed in detail in Chapter 10) is becoming a central issue in our times, as the most dynamic products – such as the services connected to the Internet – tend increasingly to belong to sectors showing large-scale economies as a consequence of strong network effects (that is, the fact that the value of a good or service for an individual increases with the number of other individuals using the same good or service) and of networks marginal costs (the cost of providing the service to each additional customer) typically decreasing rapidly towards zero. Rifkin (2015) has analysed the phenomenon of zero marginal costs in contemporary types of production, holding that it has revolutionary consequences leading to a change in the very nature of capitalist economies.

Of course, while economies of scale (and other factors) tend to increase the competitive advantages of firms and countries that first introduce and develop a product, a sector of industry or a network standard, there may also be disadvantages in being 'first movers'. The firms and countries that first adopt a new technology, an organizational innovation or a new standard (all usually requiring considerable initial non-recoverable fixed costs) run the risk of seeing them soon superseded by better ones introduced by later innovators or of finding themselves isolated having introduced systems not adopted by other firms or countries (as happened with colour television). The very concept of catch-up in economic development by emerging countries is based on the advantages of being 'late movers': the possibility of exploiting a large stock of readily available technological and organizational innovations produced in leading countries; of choosing those that the experience of those countries has shown to be the most efficient and profitable; and of more easily introducing the most up-to-date ones, as this does not imply scrapping existing plants or changing established organizational systems.

* * *

Contrary to some of the other explanations of the basis of trade advanced in the 1960s and early 1970s (such as technology gaps), economies of scale lent themselves to rigorous theoretical analysis with the formal tools of orthodox academic economics. This explains why they became important for and were thoroughly investigated by international economists, gradually becoming part of standard trade theory. This development was largely thanks to the contribution of Krugman and other economists, who put scale economies at the very centre of their 'New Trade Theory' in the late 1970s and early 1980s (see Chapter 4). They thoroughly investigated, in particular, internal economies of scale, and connected them with the theories of trade based on product differentiation and consumers' desire for product variety, which had also been developed during the 1960s and early 1970s as an explanation for the unexpected post-World War II growth of intra-industry trade flows.

The rigorous formal models developed in the analysis of the influence of scale economies on international trade have permitted a precise examination of the trade patterns and welfare effects consequent on this phenomenon. However, very few generalizations are possible, since the influence of scale crucially depends on the specific assumptions employed in each model regarding a relatively large number of factors. The external versus internal nature of scale economies and the extent of their sectoral and geographical application have already been mentioned, while other basic factors regard firms' competitive behaviour and the competition strategies adopted, the nature (homogeneous or differentiated) of the goods, the existence and extent of barriers to entry into a line of production, and the integration or segmentation of national markets (markets are integrated when a good is sold at the same price in every market and producers consider the total demand for the good as the factor that determines the demand curve they face).

The analysis of the effects of scale economies on international trade is further complicated by the fact that scale economies usually do not operate on their own, but interact with other phenomena, such as technological progress and imperfect competition. Their importance, therefore, will become clearer in the course of this work as they will be repeatedly mentioned as contributing to other explanations of trade flows.[12]

[12] The empirical verification of the importance of scale economies in contemporary production and trade still faces considerable problems, so that clear evidence on the phenomenon is not available. Antweiler and Trefler (2002) attempted a calculation, referring to 71 countries over the period 1972–1992: they estimated that roughly one-third of goods-producing industries show constant returns to scale, one-third unclear scale effects and one-third increasing returns (in this group of industries an increase in factor inputs of 1 per cent appears to produce a modal increase in output of 1.1–1.2 per cent).

4 Imperfect Competition and Product Differentiation

In the 1960s and early 1970s, economists took note of the fact that the growth of international trade increasingly concerned not the exchange of products belonging to different sectors of production, as envisaged by the RHO model, but two-way flows between advanced countries of products belonging to the same sector ('horizontal' or 'intra-industry' trade). In their search for an explanation for the phenomenon they concentrated on scale economies, the prevalence in goods' markets of forms of imperfect competition, and technology gaps.

The analysis of imperfect competition is centred on the consideration of the economies of scale internal to the firm; it also moves from the rejection of the RHO model's hypothesis of no role for demand (as consumers' tastes and demand patterns are assumed in that model to be the same in trading countries). There are two main types of imperfect competition: oligopoly and monopolistic competition (a market configuration whose framework was developed in 1933 by Chamberlain in *The Theory of Monopolistic Competition*). Attention was thus focused on the influence on international trade of these two market structures, which appeared to predominate in the economies of advanced countries.

Increasing liberalization of trade has the general effect of widening the scope for competition among firms of different countries, and makes it very hard for national firms that have managed to establish a monopoly in a sector of the domestic economy to maintain that position of exclusive supplier. But at the same time there are forces operating at international level that favour imperfect competition in liberalized markets: 1) firms that wish to start export activity or extend their operations to new foreign markets generally must incur initial non-recoverable fixed investment costs (in part related to the collection of information on the new markets) and face much greater risks than those related to entry into the domestic market or the extension of activity to new regions of their country; 2) at international level differences in consumers' tastes are likely to be much wider than among different groups of national consumers, providing more scope for product differentiation; and 3) both transport and transaction costs are, as a rule, much higher at the international than at the domestic level, thus dampening the forces of competition. The effect of these factors can be so strong as to lead to possibilities of price discrimination (the adoption by a firm of different prices for the same product in different national markets). The sharpening of competition produced by the widening of the international market also creates strong inducements for the oligopolistic firms of different countries to aggregate at international level through mergers and acquisitions and through collusive agreements, which can lead to the formation at international level of oligopolies much bigger and more powerful than domestic ones (Vernon (1971) had already pointed to the typically oligopolistic nature of large US multinationals).

Oligopoly refers to the market structure in which a few large firms dominate the market for a good. It is characterized by: 1) concentration of the supply of goods in a limited number of firms that can modify either the price or the quantity of the good they sell, influencing, through their individual decisions, the market equilibrium; 2) barriers to entry into the market, such as scale economies, large initial fixed investments or other factors that create difficulties for new firms to start production; and 3) strategic interaction between the price and quantity decisions of each oligopolist and those of its competitors, since each firm takes its decisions aimed at profit maximization in reaction to previous decisions taken by rivals, and must anticipate rivals' reaction to its own decisions. Different equilibria can result from this type of competition; but, alternatively, firms may agree to maximize profit by adopting a common policy; that is, by colluding among themselves and reaching a 'collusive equilibrium'. The good produced by the oligopolists may be absolutely homogeneous (an example is petrol) or, more frequently, each oligopolist may somehow differentiate its product from those of its rivals, taking into consideration the specific demands of different groups of purchasers. While in perfect competition firms have to passively accept the price fixed by the market, the typical process of price formation under oligopoly is the addition by firms of a 'mark-up' (a profit quota) to production cost. Given the strategic nature of oligopolistic competition, game theory (the study of mathematical models of competitive behaviour among rational interacting agents) has proved to be the most appropriate tool for the analysis of oligopoly.

Monopolistic competition is instead the market structure in which: 1) there is a sufficiently large number of firms for each of them not to be able to influence the price of the whole market; firms' price decisions are no more interrelated, but depend on overall market conditions, so each firm can act independently of the actions of its rivals; 2) products are not homogeneous, as buyers have a preference for, and demand, specific brands or varieties of a good offered by different sellers; and 3) there are no or low entry barriers to new producers of close substitutes for the existing brands of the good (though fixed costs to start production may be the cause of scale economies). All this means that each producer has a measure of monopolistic power over buyers who prefer its specific brand, so that, within certain limits, increasing the price of the product over those of competitors does not eliminate it from the market, as happens under perfect competition.

Under monopolistic competition, the main effect of international trade on a sector is that of enlarging the market. As also happens in the case of an enlargement of the domestic market, there will be more firms competing monopolistically, and each firm will have the possibility of increasing the sales of its brand, thus reducing through scale economies the cost and price of its good; and consumers will derive gains from trade not only in the traditional form of lower prices of goods, but also through the availability of a much larger number of varieties from which to choose.

Since the advantages of international trade come from an enlargement of the market relative to the domestic one, at parity of other conditions they will be more important for small than for large countries, as the scope for increases in the measure of the enlargement will be by definition higher for the former than for the latter.

As for the availability of more varieties of a good, it must be noted that while for consumer goods it may provide in many cases only minor welfare improvements to the buyer (such improvements are often artificially magnified by advertising), it is especially important for intermediate and capital goods bought by firms for their productive activity: specific types of these goods, particularly fit for their production processes, may translate for firms into significant productivity or quality advantages.

At international level, one important, positive aspect of the operation of both monopolistic competition and oligopoly based on product differentiation must be underlined. In the Ricardian and HO theories, trade leads to national sectorial specialization, as countries concentrate on the production and exports of the sectors where they are relatively more efficient or where they more intensively employ the relatively more abundant production factors. This restructuring process between sectors may imply significant and painful adjustments, as the production of entire sectors will be abandoned or greatly reduced. In the case of international monopolistic competition and oligopoly, on the contrary, countries opening to trade will not see the closure or the drastic reduction of activity of entire sectors, but rather will specialize in the production and export of specific types of the same good, a process that will often take place within the pre-existing firms. The predominantly horizontal nature of the increase in trade between advanced countries in the post-war decades largely explains why wide-ranging liberalization initiatives were undertaken without any major complaint or polemic being raised about losses of jobs and displacements of firms and productive factors.

Ricardian comparative costs theory, based on pre-trade differences between the two trading countries in the ratios of the labour content of the two goods exchanged, practically ignored the role of demand. This can be a further explanation – in addition to the one indicated in Footnote 8 in Chapter 1 – of the fact that Ricardo, after establishing the limits for the exchange ratio between two traded goods to be advantageous to both trading countries, did not identify where exactly that exchange ratio would be located (as already indicated, it was J. S. Mill who solved the problem by pointing to the role of the countries' reciprocal demand for the product of the trading partner). The HO theory, explaining foreign trade on the basis of relative factor availabilities, reinforced Ricardo's supply-oriented position. It was the need to explain the increasingly horizontal character of post-war foreign trade flows of advanced countries that pushed some international economists to concentrate on the demand aspects of international trade and on the role of product differentiation.

Harrod (1933) had already observed that:

> commodities are apt to be somewhat specialized in character, differing in quality and detail of design according to the place in which the manufacturing process is carried out. These differences destroy the unity of the world market ... each type of product

> has its own price. The difference between such prices is often greater than the qualitative differences of the products might be expected to justify. (pp. 60–61)

In the years following the publication of Chamberlain's 1933 work, some economists started to investigate the possibility of applying the concepts of monopolistic competition and product differentiation to international trade, advancing in particular the idea that the existence of national tastes for specific varieties of goods could be the basis for international exchange (Caves (1967) reviewed these early contributions of the 1930s and 1940s). Kravis (1956) also pointed out that for some products (such as English woollens or Swedish furniture) the specific national origin can provide monopolistic advantages to the goods produced by certain countries.

A major contribution to the explanation of the unanticipated growth and concentration of trade in horizontal exchanges between advanced countries was provided by Linder's (1961) theory. Linder moved from the consideration that in a world of imperfect information entrepreneurs react to the opportunities for profitable activity of which they are fully aware, and these most likely originate from needs strongly felt in their national environment. In particular, whenever the production of a good is based on an innovation, the latter will almost always be the result of an effort to solve a specific problem of national society. In addition, if the entrepreneur were to start a production exclusively destined to the export market, he would not be able to access that pool of information, of critical importance in the first phases of a good's production, that only comes from strict and continuous interchange between producers and consumers. A large volume of sales in the domestic market is thus a prerequisite for successful export activity; an additional reason being the reduction in unit costs owing to scale economies that domestic sales make possible and that are important for competition in export markets – also, as underlined by Krugman (2008a), in order to overcome the disadvantage of usually higher transport costs in foreign than in domestic trade.

If a country's most exportable products are those first developed at home on the basis of a significant domestic demand, the goods most likely to originate a strong import demand in a country are also, according to Linder, those most demanded domestically. From all this, he concluded that a country's range of potential exports is the same as that of its potential imports, so that trade between two countries will be all the more intense the more their national demand structures are similar. If national income inside countries were equally shared among all citizens, the best indicator of demand similarity between two countries would be similarity in per capita income. But since income may be distributed inside countries very differently, it is similarity in the domestic distribution of income that, together with that in average per capita income, determines the degree of demand similarity, and thus of potential trade intensity, between countries.

But what will, in practice, determine the extent and the commodity composition of international trade flows between countries at a similar level of per capita income? For Linder, it is the same set of forces that determine trade within countries. As a result:

> When the entrepreneurs … meet each other on the international market, it is quite possible that they will discover that they can extend their market expansion paths into each other's territory while competing only with substitute and not with identical goods. The almost unlimited scope for product differentiation – real or advertised – could, in combination with the seemingly unrestricted buyer idiosyncrasies, make possible flourishing trade in what is virtually the same commodity. Ships bringing European beer to Milwaukee take American beer to Europe. The strong elements of *monopolistic competition* should be incorporated into trade theory as a trade-creating force … [In other cases] Advantages in the processing of raw materials in ample supply, technological superiority, managerial skills and economies of scale are perhaps the most important reasons why identical relative prices would be a mere coincidence and why some producers will be able to gain the upper hand over other producers of the same product. (pp. 102–103)

Linder's theory showed that trade between advanced countries with similar demand structures consists largely of the exchange of different types of the same good, each country enjoying a comparative advantage in the types of the product that most correspond to its own internal demand. But he did not go deeply into the reasons why in a country many consumers do not find satisfaction in the types of a good produced at home, demanding instead the types offered by foreign suppliers. It was the French economist Lassudrie-Duchêne (1971, 1972) who developed the concept of 'demand for difference' – which gives rise to two-way trade in the same goods – that is, the desire by a section of domestic consumers for varieties of a good different from those supplied by national producers.

He attributed this demand to two different causes. In the first place, in increasingly complex and sophisticated economies, consumers' needs are directed to particular types or varieties of the same products. Each differentiated good provides a group of specific characteristics, and it is unlikely that one good presents all the possible positive qualities, since the latter are usually incompatible (for a car, for example, fuel economy and ease of parking necessarily imply lower engine power, comfort and safety). The existence of differentiated types of the same good allows the consumer to choose the particular mix of characteristics that best correspond to his tastes or needs. In each country, because of scale economies and better knowledge of the domestic market, national producers will limit themselves to the supply of those types of a good that best satisfy the needs and tastes prevalent among domestic consumers. National consumers looking for different types of the good, more similar to those most common in other countries, will find it convenient to resort to imports of those specific types from abroad. But there is also another kind of demand for difference ('pure demand for difference'): that of domestic consumers who simply wish to distinguish themselves from the mass of national consumers and are attracted by the specific elements of originality, innovativeness, non-banality or exoticism found in the types or brands of a good produced by foreign firms or countries.

* * *

The working of oligopolistic markets has been formalized in a number of different models that differ on the basis of many possible fundamental assumptions (which in turn produce different results) regarding whether oligopoly applies to homogeneous or differentiated goods; which is the decisional variable (price or quantity) upon which firms are supposed to act; how decisions are taken by oligopolists (they may take them simultaneously, thus being unaware of rivals' choices, or sequentially, which implies reaction to rivals' decisions); whether national markets are segmented or integrated (in the first case firms can apply different prices in each national market; in the second they compete in a unified international market); whether collusive agreements (open or tacit) can be made among oligopolists; and the time horizon of the oligopolistic competition, the type and importance of entry barriers, and many other possible factors.

Despite the persistent and often increasing importance of oligopoly in the most important sectors of contemporary economies, international economists' interest in it, after some significant developments in the 1980s (briefly surveyed by Head and Spencer (2017)) by economists of what was later called 'New Trade Theory', declined after the first half of the 1990s. Oligopoly models were criticized for different reasons, the main one being the difficulty in adopting a general equilibrium framework (as was deemed necessary given the effects on the rest of the economy of the actions of large oligopolistic firms). Models that assumed market segmentation were also criticized because such an assumption requires that no arbitrage can take place (i.e. nobody is buying the product in the low-price market to resell it in the higher-price ones).

Since the end of the 1970s, international economists have increasingly concentrated, instead, on monopolistic competition, analysing trade in differentiated goods produced under internal scale economies, as they managed to find the analytical tools necessary to formally model this type of market, thus fully incorporating trade in these goods into academic trade theory and putting an end to the predominance in economic theorizing of the perfect competition model, opening the way to a more realistic trade theory. The first contributions were Dixit and Stiglitz (1977), Krugman (1979) and Lancaster (1979), while Helpman and Krugman (1985) developed a comprehensive treatment of the subject, which represented the core of what later went under the name of 'New Trade Theory'. Compared with oligopolistic competition, monopolistic competition presented a number of modelling advantages, the first being that in this case there is little scope for strategic interaction among firms. Concentration on monopolistic competition was later reinforced by the fact that it appeared to offer the tools for dealing with the increasing evidence of firm heterogeneity mentioned in Section 2.3; see Head and Spencer (2017).

As models of international monopolistic competition are now commonly presented in textbooks of international trade, we can simply refer here to the surveys by Krugman (1989) and Pomfret (1992) and to Neary's (2009) review of Krugman's contributions to international trade theory. It is important to note that the great significance that was attributed to 'New Trade Theory' is largely owing not only to the fact that it provides a solid theoretical foundation for horizontal trade in manufactures, but also and especially to the fact that the application of its concepts and models of imperfect competition to the field of tariff policy led to radical changes in traditional theoretical attitudes towards government intervention in international trade, leading to the development of 'Strategic Trade Theory'.

'New Trade Theory' economists, using the most up-to-date technical tools of the profession, suddenly demonstrated that in the world of imperfect competition that prevails in the contemporary world economy, government intervention (through the imposition, for example, of import tariffs or the provision of export subsidies) can often improve on free-trade outcomes. In markets with just a few firms and with restrictions to entry, where important rents are appropriated by producers, policies may be adopted that shift a large part of these rents from foreign to domestic firms; and in monopolistically competitive markets, trade policies can lead to an increase in domestic firms' output and number of varieties produced. This can be particularly desirable in the case of high-tech sectors and where important positive externalities are present.

The long-since established theoretical position of free trade as a superior policy was thus demolished. Of course, the desirability of intervention or non-intervention in practical cases depends on the specific circumstances of a given country (and particularly the likelihood of retaliation measures by its trade partners). Given the extremely uncertain empirical record in the field and the great difficulty, in any case, of translating theoretical arguments in favour of government intervention into practical effective strategic policies, the prevalent conclusion of these economists was that an extremely cautious attitude in advancing proposals of non-free-trade policies was to be maintained.

Two general limitations of 'New Trade Theory', acknowledged by Krugman himself, are worth stressing here. The first is that despite this theory having been hailed as a revolution in international economic theory, as observed by Scherer (1992) 'our substantive understanding of the relevant phenomena has not changed radically relative to the state of the art in, say, the 1960s. Much of the new work adds mathematical rigour and technical articulation to concepts that have long been known' (p. 22). Maneschi (2002), while concurring to some extent with this judgement by showing how most of the basic insights of 'New Trade Theory' had been anticipated by previous authors, credits that theory with having produced a real advance in economics:

> One of the strengths of the new theory is indeed that it can establish with precision results that were formerly intuited, but whose plausibility could not be confirmed, or previously unsuspected results. Beyond that, the tools of modern economic theory allow trade economists to create models that portray the functioning of economies of present-day complexity... (p. 250)

The second limitation regards the practical results (and thus the policy recommendations) that can be derived from the models of 'New Trade Theory'. The models of monopolistic competition, just as those of scale economies and oligopolistic competition, are based on a large number of different specific assumptions (regarding consumer tastes, technology, market structure, etc.) and thus provide few unambiguous general conclusions. As observed by Parrinello (2002):

> We conclude that the new theory enriches the theory of international trade because it analyses the role of additional causes of trade, but at the cost of increasing the number of factors responsible for the indeterminacy of the pattern of trade ... Then, if explanation of trade means prediction of the pattern of trade, progress by the new trade theory is very limited indeed. (p. 265)

Rodrik (2015) summarized the state of the art noting that 'Unlike the competitive model, which comes essentially in unique form, the number and variety of imperfectly competitive models are limited only by the researcher's imagination' (p. 68).

The mid-2000s have seen some revival of interest in oligopolist market structures: Neary (2003a) marked the beginning of this phase. It reflected the realization that the increasing role of big firms in international trade, highlighted by new empirical research, and the related greater importance of fixed entry costs could no longer be ignored. Evidence was also collected showing that market segmentation was a frequent phenomenon (since oligopolists typically also control the distribution channels of their products, imposing restrictions on wholesalers and retailers regarding resales abroad, thus preventing arbitrage). The revival was favoured by advances in modelling techniques that made it possible to overcome some of the problems of the previous generation of oligopoly models and to consider a larger number of possible firm structure configurations, although they also led to increased complexity and scope for very different results: see Head and Spencer (2017).[1]

Neary (2003a) proposed overcoming the technical problems inherent in attempts to incorporate oligopolistic models into general equilibrium analysis by assuming that in each sector with high barriers to entry only a small number of firms operate, exerting market power and engaging in strategic behaviour vis-à-vis other oligopolists in their sector; but he also assumed that a sector's oligopolists are not particularly important actors at the level of the whole economy and are thus not able to influence factor prices and national income, which they consider as fixed when taking their decisions. This makes it possible to avoid the intractable problems of previous models of oligopoly in general equilibrium, which assumed that oligopolistic firms that are large in their own sector are also large in the economy as a whole.[2]

---

[1] The alternate fortunes of the analysis of oligopoly in international trade theory highlights a basic problem in economics that will be taken up in Section 9.2: the tendency for economists to concentrate their attention and research on the issues that can be treated with the technical tools and the formal rigour that the profession considers essential for respectable economic research. This is an absolutely acceptable methodological position; however, it does not justify the tendency of economists to play down, and at times outrightly ignore – despite the fact that empirical observation indicates their crucial importance in real economic life – factors that cannot be exactly measured or rigorously modelled, or that in the course of the analysis lead to problems and configurations that existing tools find difficult to deal with. Maneschi (2002), with reference to the 'New Trade Theory', observed that 'While the latest theories score well in clarity and overall rigour, these advantages may have been purchased at the expense of properties that are not expressible in quantitative terms but are nonetheless important...' (p. 250).

[2] Neary (2003b) introduced in an oligopolistic model the interesting case of a country enjoying absolute advantage (an issue that will be discussed in Chapter 8). By absolute advantage he referred to the situation in which a country presents significant cost advantages (in the sense of a rise in labour produc-

Neary (2010) insisted again on the need to bring oligopolistic models back to the centre of the stage, taking advantage of the new possibilities of embedding oligopoly in general equilibrium and of endogenizing firms' entry into and exit from the market while maintaining the central role of a few large firms competing strategically, underlining the importance of incumbents' ability to make large investments (for example, in R&D) to discourage possible new entrants from trying to join the market. Head and Spencer (2017) have briefly surveyed a number of models that were developed following this renewed call by Neary to reinstate oligopoly in a central position; Neary (2016) himself developed a new model of oligopoly in general equilibrium.

* * *

Another important development of 'New Trade Theory' must at least be mentioned; it goes under the name of 'New Economic Geography'. Marshall and later Ohlin had been very interested in the problems connected with the location of economic activities, and important work – largely ignored by Anglo-Saxon economists – had been carried out from the 1950s onwards by Perroux and other French economists on the spatial structure of economic activities. However, economic geography and international trade, though directing their attention to the same phenomenon of diffusion versus agglomeration of economic activity – the former within countries and the latter between countries – maintained a strict separation. Economists and especially geographers had identified in scale economies and transport costs the basic determinants of firms' location; but the economics profession continued to refer to the perfect competition model, as it had not developed the theoretical insights necessary to analyse scale economies and imperfect competition in a general equilibrium framework, although that model was not particularly useful for the study of the spatial distribution of economic activities.

It was Krugman (1991) who opened the way to a strict integration between international trade and geography, building on some of his previous contributions and on the new developments in the analysis of scale economies, monopolistic competition and demand for variety. The starting point was the realization that increasing returns create an incentive to concentrate a good's production in a single location; and in order to minimize transport costs, it is a location close to the largest market that will usually be chosen for production, with the goods then exported to other national areas and foreign markets.

Once the analysis proceeded, it became clear that a number of other key elements are involved in the determination of the location of economic activities, and especially in changes in that location. While the basic forces of scale economies, both internal and external to the firm, and transport costs lead to the aggregation of activities in given locations (thus reinforcing the advantages of those locations through the increasing availability of infrastructure, the development of thicker markets for skilled

tivity) in all sectors of its economy. He showed how such a rise in absolute advantage in one country in all sectors leads both trading countries to reduce specialization based on comparative advantage.

workers and the synergies produced by firms' proximity), many other elements can intervene, from which opposite tendencies might derive.

Improvements in transport and communication reduce the advantages of spatial concentration of production; the agglomeration of activities in certain places tends to increase firms' demand for workers, thus pushing up local wages, so that keeping a location's economic advantage for firms depends greatly on the possibility of attracting workers from adjacent areas and other regions (in turn largely influenced by these workers' degree of mobility); the progressive agglomeration of activities in a place (especially a large city) tends to give rise to congestion costs, particularly as regards the cost of housing, traffic congestion and increased pollution. A point may be reached when a process of spatial diffusion starts to develop.

Given the many elements involved in these aggregation/dispersion processes, it is possible to build up an infinite number of complex models of the spatial configuration of economic activities, leading to very different results; while the empirical test of their explanatory power is also a very difficult task. On developments of the New Economic Geography see Neary (2001) and Ottaviano (2010); for a recent extensive survey of the whole subject of spatial economics see Proost and Thisse (2019); on the forces of attraction of cities, interesting observations are provided by Moretti (2012).

5 Technology

While it played an important role in the works of the classical economists, up to the 1960s technological progress was virtually ignored by international trade theory, which was based on the RHO model with given and equal technology in all countries.[1] For example, despite Ohlin's being a contemporary of Schumpeter, whose theory was centred on the role of innovations, one would look in vain in his *Interregional and International Trade* – even in the 1967 Appendix on contemporary trade theories – for a discussion of technology or innovations; the two words practically never appear in the text; only in Ohlin (1977) did he seem to have become aware of the gravity of this omission. The only important exception was the analysis by some international economists in the 1950s – largely stimulated by Hicks (1953), and surveyed by Caves (1967) – of the effects of technological progress on trading countries' 'terms of trade' (the ratio between the prices of exports and imports). That analysis confirmed J. S. Mill's mid-19th-century conclusion that a technological improvement in a country that lowered the cost of production of an exported good would worsen the country's terms of trade, to a greater or lesser extent than the cost reduction depending on whether the price elasticity of foreign demand was less or more than unity; but according to many possible specific assumptions, different results could be obtained.

The role of technology was disregarded because of the static nature of the RHO model, which concentrates on the demonstration of the gains from a better allocation of given resources when countries specialize according to comparative advantages. Modern economic life is instead characterized by continuing progress and innovations in products, production processes and organizational systems, which represent the main driving forces of competitiveness, productivity growth and development,

[1] The term 'technology' is employed in this section very loosely to indicate the complex of techniques, skills, methods and processes on which productive activity is based. 'Invention' or 'discovery' refer to an idea or principle that can potentially be exploited commercially but has not yet been applied concretely. 'Innovation' refers to the concrete application of an invention or discovery in the form of a new (or better) product or production process. Process innovations are mainly aimed at cost reduction, thus leading to a sharpening of price competition among firms, while product innovations are a way for a firm to create monopolistic advantages vis-à-vis competitors. The distinction between product and process innovations is not always clear cut: for example, a new system that allows hotel or taxi users to connect via the Internet with the providers of these services is a product innovation for the software firm that sells it and a process innovation for the hotels or taxis that adopt it.

and by governments' efforts to stimulate this innovative activity in all possible ways. In particular, governments in developing countries strive to promote, especially through transfers from abroad, the introduction and diffusion of modern technologies capable of changing their countries' comparative advantages, so as to allow them to produce and export more 'advanced' and rewarding products.

Some innovations represent fundamental technological breakthroughs that affect either a specific sector or – like the steam engine, electricity and the computer – many sectors of activity at the same time, but most represent improvements or refinements within existing basic technologies. In advanced economies, competition among firms, especially among the larger oligopolistic ones that have the necessary resources at their disposal, has increasingly been based not on price, but on the ability to introduce innovations. Ensuring a continuous flow of the latter constitutes for them a question of survival, to the point that the search for innovations has become a standard, almost routinized activity of contemporary oligopolistic firms, which devote large amounts of funds to investment in R&D; see Baumol (2002).

The rise of large oligopolistic structures has been favoured by the frequent strict association between technical progress and the economies of large-scale production. For example, the assembly line introduced in the 1910s by Ford was a technology that could be profitably adopted only for the production of hundreds of thousands of the same car.

While this chapter deals with the influence of technological innovation on trade, it must be remembered that many innovations of commercial and industrial importance have little connection with technological discoveries, R&D activity or learning processes, but instead relate to new business and entrepreneurial opportunities, examples being the discovery of a new market or a new product differentiation or marketing strategy (such as hire purchase or leasing).

Technology can move from one country to another in different ways. Apart from that which is freely available as it has become part of the common pool of human knowledge, it can be obtained primarily through trade, by importing the capital goods in which it is to a large extent incorporated. When it is protected by patents, it may be possible to buy them or the licence to use them under certain conditions. Imports of innovative products often make it possible to understand the technology on which they are based through 'reverse-engineering' (deconstructing the product so as to reveal its architecture, components and other basic features). But a more important transfer channel consists of direct investments by foreign firms, especially big MNCs that are in possession of many up-to-date technologies and may transfer them together with organizational, managerial and marketing systems and highly skilled personnel who can train local workers. MNCs' investments may thus not simply transfer technologies, but also help the host country to absorb them (as the mere possession of a technology does not imply ability to utilize it in production) and diffuse them among local firms (one possible diffusion channel being the movement to local firms of workers employed and trained by MNCs, or the establishment of independent firms by such workers).

Economic theory centred on the hypothesis of perfect competition, and international trade theory based on the RHO model, which refers to that hypothesis, has tended to avoid the analysis of innovations, since these are typically connected with the search for a monopolistic advantage – even if temporary – over competitors and to other aspects, especially dynamic ones, that contradict the perfect competition hypothesis (scale economies, the large role of uncertainty and risk, time-consuming learning processes, irreversibilities, synergies and continuous, largely endogenously generated technological progress). In addition, the introduction of technological progress and new products would deprive the comparative cost theory of its fundamental usefulness, namely its ability to predict trade flows on the basis of existing productivity gaps and factor availabilities.[2] But it is especially the very nature of technology – ambiguous and elusive, and therefore difficult to measure, as was explained in Section 2.1.3, and unpredictable as regards its effects (see Morozov (2011) on how many of the most important modern inventions evolved very differently from the early observers' forecasts) – that contributed to economists' difficulties in including it in their formal trade models. Rather, economic models of market transactions typically require reference to goods whose characteristics are known (or at least whose probabilities of having given characteristics can be estimated by trading parties). However, it is the dynamic aspects of modern economic life connected with innovations mentioned above that have attracted the interest of observers and policymakers in the post-World War II decades, when the importance of innovations and technology transfers for competitiveness and growth was fully recognized.

International economists, after some outstanding non-orthodox and formally rudimentary contributions centred on technology in the 1960s – the theories of the technology gap by Posner (1961) and Hufbauer (1966), and of the product cycle by Vernon (1966) – have not produced models or theories of comparable significance, in the sense of drastically advancing our understanding and interpretation of the dynamics and the effects on trade of technical progress and its international diffusion in today's globalized economy, despite the fact that this dynamics is increasingly shaping all aspects of our lives and countries' positions in the economic and political international hierarchy.

Important advances have taken place in the analysis of the relationship between technology and trade: the RHO model's hypothesis of production functions that are given and everywhere equal (that is, of instantaneous, free and universal availability

[2] Almost two centuries ago, Rae (1834) , a Scottish economist who had emigrated to America, published a book in Boston in which he stressed the role of knowledge, skills and technology transfers from abroad in producing technological advances that may allow a country to acquire competitive advantages in the export of goods at the expense of previous exporters: 'As there are no limits to the inventive faculty, so no community can assure itself that any commodity which it now produces and exports to some other community, may not come to be produced in that community, and so be no longer exported there … But while in the society B, the effects of the progress of invention would be thus beneficial, in A they might operate prejudicially' (1834, p. 304–305); see Maneschi (1998) for an analysis of Rae's contribution.

of technology) has been dismissed by international economists; the crucial importance of technical progress for growth and trade has been recognized and variables that try to take account of its fundamental role are currently included in trade models; the role of technology and technology transfers is at the centre of analyses of recent phenomena such as the development of international production chains. But, on the whole, technology appears to be a phenomenon that is difficult for economists to handle in a non-generic way, taking proper account of its many and complex aspects (one of the reasons being probably the extreme scarcity of international economists with a deep knowledge of the very different technological problems of the main sectors of economic activity); and it is the object of less theoretical debate and systematic analysis than many other, less important, issues of international economics. It is significant that in textbooks it usually gets short shrift – see, for example, Krugman, Obstfeld and Melitz (2014) – and when international trade driven by technology is discussed, basic reference continues to be made to the two theories mentioned above, now half a century-old and largely made obsolete by recent world developments, or to the thirty-year-old contribution of Dosi, Pavitt and Soete (1990).

Objective difficulties stem from the fact that technological knowledge and innovations – quite apart from problems of definition and measurement – are phenomena that present different, partly contradictory aspects, on many of which there is still no widely shared agreement. Crucial issues for the economic analysis of technology continue to be the object of debates, from the basic one of the relative role, in producing discoveries and innovations, of the genial individual, of team work and of stable R&D structures finalized to favour them; to the one regarding the motivations – an innate human curiosity for the working of the world around us, the stimulus of the search for ways to solve crucial practical problems or the prospect of financial gains from subsequent commercial exploitation – that lead to scientific and technological discoveries and innovations;[3] or those regarding the passage from a discovery to its practical commercial application in production and the channels through which an innovation, created by or available to a firm, comes to be diffused among the other firms of a country. Even the association between firms' R&D activity and economic innovations, taken for granted in economic discourse, has recently been subjected to critical analysis and qualifications (see Mazzucato (2013) and Hachem (2017)).

Another debated issue is the extent to which the transmission of knowledge requires personal physical interaction. While the contents of many patents are freely available whatever the country in which they were developed, and one would expect that following the ICT revolution the interchange of ideas among scientists and inventors can largely take place online, it seems that a lot of knowledge and stimuli to the development of innovations is acquired by scientists and inventors via the exchange of ideas and information that takes place through physical interaction and conversation both inside and outside the workplace, with colleagues living in the

[3] Referring to the pharmaceutical industry, Acemoglu and Linn (2004) found evidence that the extent of product innovation responds to the expected changes in the size of the market.

same area, as underlined by Lester and Piore (2004) and Moretti (2012). This is one of the reasons why cities – especially those where important R&D activities are concentrated – appear to provide special advantages for the diffusion of scientific and technological knowledge.

Crucial questions are also debated with reference to the international aspects of technology, especially those regarding technology transfers. They concern the relative importance of the different channels for these transfers; the domestic conditions necessary for a technology transferred from abroad to be absorbed by the receiving country, adapted to local conditions and diffused among domestic firms; and the role of MNCs in these transfers – see Keller (2004). On the experience of technology transfers, a considerable empirical literature has accumulated; but it appears quite difficult to extract general models from it, or principles going beyond lists of factors that have proved important to ensure the success of these transfers. As Hoekman and Javorcik (2006) observed, summarizing the results of a World Bank research project on global integration and technology transfer:

> Improving our understanding of how technology diffuses across borders is important in order to identify what governments can do through policies to stimulate international technology diffusion and its absorption in their economies ... The 'correct' policy intervention, if any, depends critically on the channels through which technology diffuses internationally and the quantitative effects of the various diffusion processes on allocative efficiency and productivity growth. Neither is well understood. Most of the empirical evidence is based on aggregate data or cross-sectional surveys and is subject to multiple interpretations. Case studies, while informative about the case at hand, are difficult to generalize. Hence policymakers have often acted on the basis of theory, anecdotes, or instincts. (pp. 1–2)

The difficulty economists face in dealing with the issues of technology – and particularly technology transfers from developed to developing countries – largely stems from the fact that the creation, application and diffusion of innovations and technological knowledge are not just technological problems. Rather, they are basically social problems, in the sense that they are the result of specific capabilities that are embedded in societies, as they are the product of educational and learning structures, scientific and technical institutions, firms' propensity to engage in R&D, accurately designed public policies and incentives and, more generally, an environment that stimulates change, emulation, progress and creativity. Of course, the size structure of firms and the degree and characteristics of competition between them are also crucial factors.[4]

---

[4] For instance, in Italy the prevalence of small industrial firms is considered to be an obstacle to the creation of basic technological innovations, which usually require large investments in R&D, while it has favoured the production of small 'incremental' innovations. At the same time, the peculiar characteristics of 'competition with cooperation' among small firms in industrial districts has been a fundamental channel for the rapid diffusion of innovations and best-practices among local firms.

It must be noted that the importance of technology and innovation in determining firms' compet-

It is difficult to collect information on all these aspects, even more to measure them, as many have a qualitative rather than a quantitative nature; it is just as hard to determine their relative weight in favouring the creation, application and diffusion of technology within and between countries, since they are all strictly interconnected. The difficulties are especially serious for international economists as information on foreign, especially developing, countries is less easily available or accessible.

One key problem that explains the largely unsatisfactory state of research on the influence of technological progress and innovations on trade and economic development is that while the issue is largely an empirical one, we lack satisfactory measures of countries', sectors' and firms' levels of technological advancement and production of innovations. These levels have to be estimated indirectly; but the indicators so far available (even if they could be calculated with the utmost precision) are not fully reliable. They are divided between those that, on the input side, try to measure the resources devoted to the technological and innovation effort, and those that, on the output side, try to measure the results of that effort. The former – such as measures of the amount or the share of total expenditure devoted to R&D, or the number or the share of the total labour force of researchers, engineers and other high-skilled personnel – do not allow us to determine whether the financial and human resources invested are efficiently and successfully utilized or not. The latter – usually measuring the patenting activity of firms and sectors – are biased by the fact that many innovations are not patented; and that while some patents regard fundamental technological breakthroughs, the majority concerns minor technological improvements, or may be applied for simply in order to discourage possible competitors from independently developing and using them (Mokyr (2018) underlies the fact that in 1997–2015 the number of patents granted in the USA increased by more than 5 per cent a year, five times faster than total factor productivity growth, which is commonly considered an indicator of technological progress).

A major improvement in the use of output indicators based on patenting activity has been made possible since the early 2000s by greater availability and detail of national patent offices' data on patents issued, and by the progress of computers in allowing classification and elaboration of these data. The US patent offices make it compulsory – and European offices optional – for those submitting a patent application to supply a list of the 'state of the art', in other words all previous patents and other sources of technological knowledge on which a new invention is based (in Europe, the patent examiners must in any case construct the list of references to so-

itive advantages, and the large external economies that characterize them, underline – as stressed by Mazzucato (2013) – the importance of the role of governments in acting as innovative agents in their countries, sustaining, directly and through incentives and financial assistance to private firms, education, human capital, basic long-term research and R&D activity. This point seems to have been widely recognized in recent years, in particular as a consequence of the digital revolution. For example, the *World Trade Report 2020* of the World Trade Organization (WTO 2020a) is entirely devoted to analysis of the policies that governments should follow to promote technological progress and innovation in response to the challenges posed by that revolution.

called prior art, as this is an important element in judging an invention's patentability). This has allowed researchers to develop a wholly new line of analysis of patenting activity based on patent citation. The latter makes it possible to reconstruct technological linkages between firms and between countries, as it identifies both the contributions of previous inventors to a given patented invention ('backward linkages'), and the new flow of inventions that a given one has made possible or facilitated ('forward linkages'). However, a lot of theoretical and practical problems must still be overcome for this information to provide a solid basis for the comparative analysis of national technological performances; a basic one being the different criteria and regulations applied by the patent offices of different countries (apart from the European ones, which have a common patent system). For a survey of the whole field of patent citation research see Jaffe (2016).

All the preceding considerations help to explain why on the issues regarding the relationship between technology and international trade – despite some important advances made possible by extremely enlarged and improved databases – we still seem to be left, on the one hand, with a multitude of individual case studies, which are difficult to generalize, and, on the other, with a multitude of theoretical models adopting widely varying assumptions, which inevitably lead to very different results (Grossman and Helpman (1995) have tried to provide a unified and synthetic formal theoretical framework within which different models and lines of research could be inserted).

* * *

Developing some observations by Balogh, Kindleberger and other economists in the years around 1950 – when post-war resumption of trade with the USA made Europeans realize the full extent of American superiority in producing and exporting new and more technologically advanced products – the technology gap and product cycle theories, produced in the 1960s, marked a watershed in economists' view of international trade (although it would take some time for them to obtain academic recognition). They showed that trade flows in manufactures, rather than being driven by the static comparative advantages of the RHO model, were responding to new dynamic forces, connected with the then exceptional dynamism of the US economy, which would remain at the centre of empirical and theoretical international trade research in the following half-century. For the first time, what really moves modern economic life – static and dynamic scale economies, rapid progress and unequal availability of technology, firms' investment in R&D, product innovations and improvements, forms of imperfect competition, international mobility of capital, knowledge and entrepreneurial abilities connected with MNCs' foreign investment and catch-up efforts by less advanced countries – were all taken into account (while still leaving some space for the traditional factor-proportions theory) to provide an explanation of trade that seemed at last to fit the reality of international exchange.[5]

---

[5] As Hufbauer (1970) pointed out, the main elements of the technology gaps and product cycle the-

A few years before, Kravis (1956) had formulated what can be considered the first 'new trade theory', advancing a rival explanation to the comparative costs doctrine, the 'availability theory', which anticipated elements that would be developed by other economists as distinct bases for trade, such as the introduction of new goods and product differentiation. According to Kravis, what governs trade is countries' domestic availability or non-availability of goods: countries export those that can be readily produced at home, while importing those not available. Non-availability could refer to the absolute impossibility of production (as, for instance, in the case of diamonds) or to the fact that an increase in domestic production of a good could only be obtained at a rapidly increasing cost (so that domestic supply is highly inelastic). The causes of non-availability could be lack of specific natural resources, technological inferiority vis-à-vis other countries able to introduce new or better goods, or a special attraction of domestic consumers to product varieties produced by specific foreign countries. An element of permanent or temporary monopoly was thus connected with the concept of availability.[6]

One aspect of Kravis's theory – the creation of new products as a result of scientific research – was brought to the centre of the analysis by Posner (1961), who concentrated on the dynamic developments that take place within an industry in the field of technological progress.

Posner considered the case of two developed countries A and B presenting basically the same characteristics, under the hypothesis of no international transport costs or other obstacles to trade. Suppose that in country A the synthetic fibre industry discovers a new, more efficient fibre, nylon, that is immediately used by A's tex-

---

ories had been somehow anticipated by Josiah Tucker as early as 1754; see Elmslie (1995) and Elmslie and Vieira (1999).

[6] The 'availability theory' has some connection with one fundamental point regarding the very validity of Ricardo's comparative costs principle: the latter is based on the hypothesis that, before the opening of trade, the two trading countries can produce the two goods exchanged and thus the domestic relative production costs of the two goods (be they in terms of labour incorporated, of total monetary production cost, or of opportunity cost) can be calculated. If a country cannot produce one of the goods, its cost cannot be determined (it can only be considered infinite), and so also the domestic relative costs of the two goods are not definable. This point has been stressed by Patnaik (2005): she argued that Ricardo provided with his principle the intellectual justification for the exchange, between advanced and developing countries, of tropical commodities for manufactures, (an exchange in fact forcibly imposed on subjected nations by colonial powers); but it was a principle indefensible in that case on the basis of its own hypotheses, as advanced countries located in temperate zones could not produce tropical goods. In our time the argument is possibly of even greater importance, as it applies to new goods connected with exclusive technological innovations (and so not producible by all countries), which represent a large, and the more dynamic, share of international trade.

Costinot and Donaldson (2017), noting that empirical research to test Ricardian predictions about patterns of trade on the basis of relative productivities in autarchy is impossible whenever a country does not produce one of the traded goods, developed an interesting methodology to overcome the problem in the case of agricultural productions. It is based on today's availability of millions of data on different crops' productivities under different climates and locations around the world, which allow the hypothetical productivity of any crop's production in any country to be estimated.

tile firms. Nylon will also be offered on the international market and after a period – called 'foreign demand lag' – B's textile firms will import nylon from A. Aware of the high profits that can be obtained by the production of nylon, and of the danger of their fibres being supplanted by nylon imported from A, B's producers of synthetic fibres will try to produce nylon at home. This can occur, after a period called 'imitation lag', through different imitation channels. One is an independent research effort by B's fibre producers; this effort will require fewer scientific abilities and financial resources than the original discovery in country A, as some of the characteristics of nylon production will have become known in B. A second channel may be the purchase by B's fibre producers of a licence from A's discoverer of nylon. A third one may be the establishment in country B of a subsidiary by A's nylon producers. As B's imitation effort leads to nylon production in B, imports from A will gradually decrease and then cease altogether. However, Posner pointed out that the length of B's imitation lag might be extended by the operation of scale economies, as country A, thanks to earlier production and export of nylon, may have installed large producing plants providing high static scale economies ensuring higher productivity and export competitiveness.

Hufbauer (1966) noted that the initial hypothesis of A and B being two equal countries with the same factor availabilities and prices must be modified; it may then be that the old factor proportions theory again has a role to play. Country B may have a relatively more abundant supply of labour than A and after some time, having mastered the technology of nylon production, may be able to start a flow of nylon exports to country A based on the advantage of lower unit labour costs owing to greater labour availability. One can presume that having more resources to finance research for new fibres, country A is more advanced and richer than B, and will thus also have a higher level of wages.

All the steps in the cycle of nylon production and export described above can be accelerated or delayed by a number of key variables, the most important being the technological ability and entrepreneurial spirit of B's fibre producers. But Posner stressed another point: even if, at the end of the cycle, B becomes the country that exports nylon, there are good reasons to expect that country A's fibre industry, having first discovered, produced and exported nylon, will enjoy such an advantage in terms of personnel and other resources devoted to R&D, and ability and experience in innovation activity, that it will produce a flow of further innovations in fibres or in a connected sector. This development will be favoured by the fact that there can be technological connections between one discovery and those following, in the sense that once a breakthrough has taken place on one front, further success on other fronts is likely to take place. In addition, complementarities in consumption will probably stimulate innovations in the products jointly demanded with those in which the initial discovery was made. All this led Posner and Hufbauer to the conclusion that while the individual new product will go through the phases indicated here, the sector of country A where the initial innovation has taken place, may, overall, register a relatively stable flow of new innovations and exports.

Empirical research demonstrated that the Posner–Hufbauer theory was a useful tool to explain the reality of growing flows of exports of new products from and between advanced countries in the 1960s and 1970s. The theory had some weak points, however. One might ask how far into the past one could go to identify in an initial innovation the explanation of technological disparities in a sector. Consumers and producers in country B can also be expected to gain from the experience with nylon a greater interest in – and develop better information channels about – discoveries and innovations occurring abroad, thus spotting them as soon as they take place, and to develop R&D facilities and organizational improvements so that they can more quickly set up national production and export of the new product. Posner also left unanswered the question of the reasons why a given new product can be expected to be first discovered and produced in a given country. But, most importantly, it was observed that in Posner's model the imitation lag was measured as the time lag between the date when the foreign product is first produced by a firm in the innovating and the imitating country, while the technological superiority of a country in a production is largely determined by the rapidity with which an innovation is diffused among all the firms within a given sector.

Vernon's (1966) theory of the product cycle can be considered an extension of Posner's theory. While Posner stressed the supply aspects of trade in technologically new products (the difficulty or onerousness for imitators of acquiring the knowledge necessary for their production), Vernon concentrated on the demand side for the explanation of why these products tend to originate in certain countries. He started from the hypothesis that all developed countries have equal access to technological knowledge, but this does not imply that they have equal possibilities of applying this knowledge to the development of new products. For this to occur, entrepreneurs will have to take upon themselves the risky task of incorporating specific technological knowledge into commercial products to be sold on the market. Drawing on concepts elaborated by Drèze (1960) and Linder (1961), Vernon argued that entrepreneurs will most likely realize – and react to – the possibility of applying a scientific principle to commercial production of a new product if they have at their disposal the easiest channels for communicating with possible consumers of the product. This ease of communication will largely depend on geographical and cultural distance; so that a country's entrepreneurs will most likely be aware of the scope for introducing new products with a strong potential demand in their national market.

Since the US market is characterized by a large percentage of high-income consumers and by a high cost of labour, it is to American entrepreneurs that new products directed to rich consumers and offering labour-saving services can be expected to offer the best sale prospects and thus to attract R&D resources and commercial production activity. Once production for the American market increases and the first export flows of the new products appear, it is likely that well-defined international standards for the product will have developed. As a product becomes 'mature', internal and then international competition will drive producers to concentrate on reducing production cost; and other industrial countries where the product can be manufactured at a lower cost (and where the best information on the domestic market is available) will then likely become the most competitive producers of the product, first satisfying domestic demand and later exporting to the American market.

While Posner's and Vernon's theories have been criticized from many points of view, their fundamental contribution is to have freed the analysis of international competition and specialization from the straitjacket of the static RHO model, where technology is given and freely available to and usable by all countries, no FDI takes place and the introduction of new products is excluded. In contemporary economies, technology develops more and more rapidly and competition between firms and countries is increasingly based on the ability to introduce new and more sophisticated products and production processes, an ability that appears to depend on three main variables: the deliberate investment effort in R&D, the accumulation of 'human capital' and learning by doing.

These theories concentrate on the demand and supply elements that give rise to technological innovations and, contrary to the hypothesis of perfect competition, on the monopolistic gains that – thanks also to the exclusivity granted for a certain period by patents – come from being the first to develop and produce new goods. Most importantly, they place at the centre of the analysis the contrast (but also the interconnections) between the dynamic forces that over time consolidate the ability of a country to generate innovations and diffuse them domestically, and those that, on the contrary, favour the transfer abroad of national technological knowledge. They also demonstrate that stable specialization patterns do not exist in the modern international economy: comparative (and absolute) advantages change with time as a product of a continuous innovation activity by more technologically advanced countries, and imitation and catch-up efforts by the others.

When Posner and Vernon developed their theories, a number of economists tried to address the same phenomena of technology gaps, trade in new products and product life cycles within a widened HO framework, by inserting in the latter, as factors of production in addition to, or substitution for, the traditional ones, some technology-related variables, such as the R&D effort or specific types of labour skills; see, for example, Keesing (1965, 1967) and Hirsch (1965). The critical deficiency of these 'neo-factor proportion' theories, as pointed out by Dosi, Pavitt and Soete (1990), is that they consider technological data as exogenous to the economic system, as given endowments on which, in each phase of its cycle, the producers of a good base their export competitiveness (while the R&D effort is a typical case, not of an endowment, but of the result of specific investment choices by firms and public institutions). In this way, little help is provided to understand the most important phenomenon: the dynamic process through which changes in technology and trade take place.

* * *

The technology gaps model developed by Dosi. Pavitt and Soete (1990) – who also took into account the progress in the analysis of trade in differentiated products and international monopolistic competition that occurred in the 1970s and 1980s – moved instead from the premises that:

> In most sectors… technology is generated endogenously; it is often firm-specific, differentiated and tacit in nature; and is practically, by definition, cumulative in development.
> Second, we reject the assumption that the generation of technology is independent of investment and production. In most sectors, it is strongly dependent on them.
> Third, the assumption that firms' technical choices are exogenously determined and optimal is rejected in favour of the proposition that such choices are generally discretionary and non-optimal, given the impossibility of foreseeing the nature and likelihood of all possible future technological and market developments … [Technology gaps reflect] International differences in innovative capabilities, in the sources and uses of innovations, in corporate strategies and institutional conditions… (1990, p. 9).

The validity of these premises has been largely confirmed. However, Dosi, Pavitt and Soete's specific model, which they applied to explain the trade performance of Organisation for Economic Co-operation and Development (OECD) countries, will not be examined here. Too long a time has passed since it was developed and too disruptive technological changes have taken place in the meantime: the data on whose basis their empirical analysis was conducted, results obtained and conclusions drawn, have probably changed so much that a comparable exercise carried out today would probably lead to different results and conclusions. There is instead one point that runs through their whole work, representing an important contribution that deserves to be underlined: their insistence that – as some authors had already pointed out (see Section 8.2.2) – in the analysis of international trade increasing importance must be attributed to the principle of absolute advantages. Dosi, Pavitt and Soete identify technology gaps between countries – especially those that refer to general technological capabilities – as a major determinant of absolute advantages for the more technologically advanced countries and argue that these absolute advantages are much more important than comparative advantages in determining exporters' international competitiveness and market shares (this point has been developed more recently in Dosi and Tranchero (2018)).

A fundamental characteristic of the Posner and Vernon theories was that they were largely developed outside the traditional framework of comparative costs theory, since the introduction of new products that cannot be easily and rapidly produced by other countries makes it impossible to apply Ricardo's principle; not only because, as indicated in Footnote 6, this principle cannot be applied to goods a country cannot produce in autarky; but also because it relies, to ensure trade balance equilibrium, on an adjustment mechanism based on price changes in the trading countries, while for new products price is not the fundamental competitive factor. Rather, the explanation of trade in new products seems to require reference to the concept of absolute advantage. Kravis (1956) was the first to highlight this aspect, pointing out that not only new products, but also many raw materials and other goods share this element of certain countries' exclusive ability to supply, which makes comparative costs theory inapplicable.

It may be recalled here that before the Industrial Revolution revolutionized transport with the introduction of railways and steamships, the physical obstacles to the international movement of goods were so great that, apart from short-distance trade between bordering or not too far away regions of different nations, only high-value (relative to volume) products, inexistent or in extremely short supply in other countries (such as silk, tea and porcelain from China, spices from South Asia, ivory from central Africa or sugar from the West Indies), could be the object of large flows of international exchange, as Smith himself underlined. For these exchanges absolute advantage or Kravis's 'availability theory' seem to offer a more adequate explanation than comparative advantages. One may speculate whether the absence in Adam Smith of the precise Ricardian concept of comparative advantage could be because in his time very little international trade was based on that concept.

Dosi, Pavitt and Soete started from the observation that, contrary to the hypotheses of the RHO model (and as will be explained in Chapters 6 and 7), labour unemployment is a typical characteristic of modern economies, and the adjustment mechanisms that in that model ensure the equilibrium between imports and exports and the rapid and costless movement of factors between different areas and sectors of the national economy operate rather weakly. For most sectors, firms' competitive ability depends on the absolute advantage produced by technological superiority, which allows them to gain wider shares of international export markets (and of the domestic one), thus providing a demand stimulus to activity and economic growth. Countries with overall superior levels of technological capability will, however, generally register higher wage levels, connected to the greater technological efficiency of their economies. Technologically inferior countries will have to base their export competitiveness on the availability of natural resources and, for industrial products, on the advantage – particularly important only in sectors not characterized by continuous introduction of innovations – of lower wage levels (but they found that in countries with superior overall technological ability, long-term increases in shares of international export markets often occurred in all or most industrial sectors); these countries' scope for economic growth will frequently be limited by the foreign exchange constraint, that is, the insufficiency of export receipts to finance essential imports.

While some other technology gap models, in addition to that of Dosi, Pavitt and Soete, were produced in the three decades after those by Posner and Vernon (they were described by Elmslie and Vieira (1999)), the characteristics of contemporary globalization have altered the basic mechanisms of the technological innovation/imitation cycles. Posner's and Vernon's theories had been developed mainly with reference to the imitation of new American products by advanced European countries; but just a few years after they had been formulated, Vernon himself noticed that a basic change had taken place, as the main European countries had largely overcome their position of technological inferiority vis-à-vis the USA, becoming in turn producers of new products and having their own MNCs. In the following decades the general innovator/imitator dialectic would continue to be central to the explanation of international trade competition; however, it would rather apply to all the main advanced countries with respect to the developing ones, whose characteristics are very different from those once typical of the European economies; and it would operate within a drastically changed context.

The fundamental difference is the shortening of imitation lags made possible by earlier and quicker transfer abroad of capital, technologies and highly skilled personnel in today's environment of offshoring and global production chains. Sharpston (1975) had already anticipated this development, but thanks to the ICT revolution it has progressed much more quickly and widely than one could imagine at that time. It may be said that the traditional concept of imitation lag itself has been largely superseded, as for new products the phase of physical production can at times be located from the beginning in technologically less advanced countries by the MNCs that manage contemporary global production chains and are increasingly concentrating on their more profitable 'core activities' preceding and following physical production (see Chapter 11).[7] But the progress of globalization and that of technology have modified the relations between technology and trade from many others' points of view as well. One aspect of those relations, concerning the process of international fragmentation of production – which has been investigated by Jones and Kierzkowski – will be analysed in Section 11.1.4.

[7] Sturgeon (2013) observed that 'Patterns of cross-border investment and trade based on product-cycles, where less developed countries receive older, *outmoded* products from more advanced economies (Vernon, 1966, 1979), are rapidly giving way to more unified global production systems and markets, with different countries specializing in specific aspects, or stages, of the development and production of *leading edge* goods and services' (p. 5).

Despite the obsolescence of the original model, the product cycle conceptual framework has continued to inspire more recent contributions; for example, Antràs (2005) developed a new version of Vernon's theory to explain how, owing to the incomplete nature of contracts, advanced countries' firms tend to move production to developing countries through wholly owned foreign affiliates in the first phases of the life of a good, and through contracts with independent local firms when the good has reached maturity.

6 Full Employment

Among the hypotheses on which the comparative costs principle and its free-trade policy prescription are based, that of the full employment of productive factors has been the object of heated debates in the last three decades.[1] This has been a consequence of the fact that, while the RHO model assumes that trade has no effect on the total number of jobs, growing rates of labour unemployment have characterized the majority of advanced countries in this period, when there have also been massive worldwide dislocations of productive and export activities. It was only natural that the question would be raised as to whether – and to what extent – these dislocations were responsible for the deteriorating situation of Western workers' employment. Stiglitz (2006), echoing an argument advanced by Keynes in 1930 (quoted in Section 6.2), has concisely described the problem we face, referring to US trade with China: 'Free trade advocates say that although jobs are lost, new opportunities are created. High-productivity/high-wage jobs replace low-productivity/low-wage jobs. The argument is persuasive, except for one detail: in many countries, unemployment rates are high and those who lose their jobs do not move on to higher-wage alternatives but onto the unemployment rolls' (p. 67).

Unemployment may be the result of long-term structural deficiencies of the economic system, as is often the case in developing countries, of persistent Keynesian insufficient demand or of transitional frictions in the movement of factors from declining to expanding activities in the national economy; but these causes may be interconnected. A basic hypothesis of the RHO model is that of perfect mobility of factors within individual countries, both between different parts of the country and between different activities – which implies that when a worker moves from one industry to another, he becomes immediately as productive as the workers already working in that industry; while in fact workers moving from one job to another often experience a loss of the value of their firm- and task-specific skills.

The rejection of the hypothesis of full employment of resources has a disruptive effect on the whole body of traditional trade theory and trade policy, opening the way

[1] The hypothesis of full employment has two implications. With reference to the pre-trade situation, it implies that no country can be led to enter (or scared away from entering) international trade by considerations connected to the goal of increasing the employment of domestic productive factors. With reference to the post-trade situation, it implies that the opening of trade cannot have any effect whatsoever on the level of employment of domestic productive factors.

for a completely different conception of the nature, goals and effects of foreign trade and of the mechanisms of trade balance adjustment. It implies that the Ricardian advantage in terms of welfare that the opening of trade produces to a country thanks to better allocation of resources – as the country concentrates on the activities where it is comparatively more efficient – could well prove inferior to the advantage that alternative non-free-trade policies could produce for the country in terms of growth and welfare consequent on the absorption of unemployed or underemployed resources into productive uses.[2] If there is unemployment of resources in the pre-trade situation, a country may produce and consume more goods by adopting measures to utilize the idle resources, without engaging in international trade at all. And *ex post*, if the opening of trade leads to job losses, the damage they represent might outweigh the trade gains, thus invalidating the conclusion that free trade is always beneficial. The existence of unemployment impacts on the very logic of comparative advantage, as this is based on the idea that free trade allows factors of production – considered as being always available in more limited amounts relative to what would be necessary to satisfy demand for goods – to be transferred from less productive to more productive uses. If factors are unemployed, more productive export activities could be undertaken without any need to transfer the factors from less productive ones.

More generally, the presence of idle production factors makes both the comparison of products' relative costs and the determination of the gains from trade problematic, as the relative costs of different goods are theoretically undefined; in fact, the 'opportunity cost' of one good in terms of another – that is, the amount of one good one has to sacrifice to obtain one unit of the other – may then be zero; see Prasch (1996).[3] It is true that the saving relative to autarky in terms of total labour hours expended in each of the two countries engaging in trade to obtain a given amount of the two goods remains the same even if there is labour unemployment. But it is a different situation when the work hours saved can be employed in the production of other goods that satisfy a country's needs, as opposed to when the work hours saved simply allow (or, more probably, force) some of its workers to substitute work with idleness. Full factor employment is also a necessary condition for the working of the RHO mechanism of adjustment of trade balance disequilibria, as this mechanism is based on changes in goods prices that if there is unemployment could be substituted by changes in employment and national product.

---

[2] While full factor employment is a necessary condition for the comparative costs principle and neoclassical theory postulates full employment of all factors, Ricardo himself, contrary to widespread belief, while assuming in his works that capital would always be fully employed, allowed for the possibility of labour unemployment in two specific cases: when the population grows faster than the economy, and when new machines are introduced.

[3] The fact that the absence of full employment makes the very identification of the gains from trade difficult, reinforces the argument of those such as Turnell (2001) who stress the importance of a commitment by governments to actively pursue policies designed to ensure the right to full employment as a necessary prerequisite for making accurate evaluations – and so taking the right decisions – regarding international trade liberalization initiatives.

The hypothesis of full employment regards not only workers, but also other factors. An excessive abundance of land and natural resources, leading to their unemployment, has been, especially in the past, a frequent occurrence, leading to the formulation of specific 'vent-for-surplus' trade theories, examined in Section 6.1. As for capital, if reference is made to this factor in the monetary sense, the very existence of savings not matched by equivalent investment is evidence of capital unemployment; but by ignoring the monetary aspects of the economy and thus equating trade with barter, the RHO model eliminates this problem altogether. With reference to capital in the sense of productive capital (plants, machines, stocks of raw materials and inputs, etc.), the same model excludes by hypothesis the possibility of excess productive capacity, which, on the contrary, is a frequent occurrence – according to some economists even a constant characteristic – of modern productive systems.[4] Ohlin himself considered excess capacity as one of the possible explanations of trade alternative to his factor-proportion theory, since the validity of the latter – attributing goods' relative prices in different countries to differences in relative factors availabilities – requires the equivalence of costs and prices, and excess capacity can lead a country to sell a good at a price lower than its cost (the other cases of non-equivalence of costs and prices identified by Ohlin were economies of scale and the existence of a risk premium for investment in a country, as risk leads to prices higher than firms' actual production costs).

6.1 The 'vent-for-surplus' theory

Adam Smith, in *The Wealth of Nations*, included among the great benefits of international trade the fact that it provides a vent for the surplus of the goods that a country can produce efficiently but does not absorb at home as domestic demand is already fully satisfied:

> When the produce of any particular branch of industry exceeds what the demand of the country requires, the surplus must be sent abroad, and exchanged for something for which there is a demand at home. Without such exportation, a part of the productive labour of the country must cease, and the whole of its annual produce diminish … It is only by means of such exportation, that this surplus can acquire a value sufficient to compensate the labour and expence of producing it. (Book III, Ch. V, p. 394)

The theory had a clear antecedent in Serra, who pointed out in 1613 that a way for states to obtain gold and silver from abroad was the export surplus, 'which occurs

[4] J. Robinson (1966a), to explain capitalist countries' drive for a trade surplus, argued that 'the capitalist world is still somewhat of a buyer's market, in the sense that capacity to produce exceeds what can be sold at a profitable price' (p. 9–10). M. C. Klein and Pettis (2020) report that in the US average used capacity in manufacturing industry went from 83 per cent in 1948–1979 to 80 per cent in 1980–1999 and 75 per cent since 2000.

when the commodities produced by the kingdom exceed the amount required for the needs or comfort of the inhabitants' (2011, p. 119).

Smith's 'vent-for-surplus' theory has generated a lot of misunderstanding. The idea that trade can allow the export of otherwise useless products was rejected by Ricardo, J. S. Mill and subsequent mainstream economists with the argument – implicit in the hypothesis of perfect competition with full employment – that it refers to a situation that cannot occur in the real world. Smith's expression seems to imply that the country is under some compulsion to produce the goods it exports, so that if domestic demand for them was fully saturated, if not demanded abroad they would either be produced and wasted, or would not be produced and the factors of production necessary to produce them would remain idle. The first possibility was considered totally irrational (it would seem that only a mistake in the forecast of demand might lead to production of unsaleable goods), while the second was excluded by the fact that, if factors of production were not demanded because of the lack of final demand for the goods in question, they would be employed for the production of other domestic goods for which there is still demand (J. S. Mill specifically stating that the substitution of previously imported goods would provide sufficient outlets). This argument was attacked by Williams as early as 1929: having rejected the Ricardian hypothesis of perfect movement of factors inside countries, both between locations and between different types of jobs (see Footnote 6 in Chapter 1), he held that the very historical process of international specialization – that is, the fact that countries' development has been based on progressive concentration and improvement of production for export in a limited number of activities – can make it impossible not only to revert to national self-sufficiency, but also to find acceptable alternative domestic activities to those closing down for lack of demand.

As mainstream economists continued to reject the 'vent-for-surplus' theory, attempts to rehabilitate it did not challenge the main argument directed against its general validity, but rather identified specific situations to which it could apply and be used as a useful tool to explain real trade flows. At the end of the 1950s, some international trade theorists recognized the possibility that productive resources might not be completely utilized before the opening of trade, but they basically referred not to labour, but to land. The few mentions of the factor labour referred exclusively to underdeveloped countries, where the presence of massive unemployment or underemployment could not be ignored. It was Myint (1958) who revived interest in Smith's vent-for-surplus approach, claiming that it could be usefully applied to explain the evolution of the structure of production and trade of underdeveloped tropical countries, characterized by a surplus of both land and labour, during the colonial period.[5]

A parallel model, called 'staple theory' (the word 'staple' indicating a resource-intensive commodity that dominates a country's economy), centred on a surplus of land

[5] See Findlay (1970) for a vent-for-surplus model based on Myint's argument; O'Brien (1984) argued that the pre-1913 experience of exports of primary products by Third World countries could best be interpreted in terms of 'vent-for-surplus' models. Lewis (1978a, p.21) had also referred to 'vent-for-surplus' export opportunities for underdeveloped countries.

or of specific natural resources, was developed from the late 1950s to the mid-1960s to explain the evolution of the Canadian economy; it was based on the works of Innis in the 1930s and 1940s and North in the 1950s.[6] Although doubts were raised by some scholars regarding its ability to fit the overall history of Canadian development, which was very diversified regionally, the 'staple theory' appeared useful for a more general understanding of the export-led development experience of important extra-European temperate areas where European people and capitals had moved to in previous centuries. In these sparsely populated countries, foreign demand allowed the exploitation of surplus productive capacity in some key primary commodities; and this export activity was the basis for the general national economic development, as it spurred investment and consumption in other sectors through the operation of forwards and backwards linkages. But it is clear that the notion could also be usefully employed to explain some important contemporary cases, such as those of oil-producing desert countries, in which no other activity could be carried out to obtain absolutely essential goods were it not for the role of foreign trade in giving value to an otherwise useless product.

An interesting 'vent-for-surplus' model was produced by Blattner (1973), in which the creation of an excess of productive capacity is the result of a specific strategy by firms operating in monopolistic or oligopolistic domestic markets to dissuade possible national competitors from entering the market. In the case of new entrants into such markets, cut-throat competition would ensue as incumbents would strive to expel them: product prices would drastically come down and larger quantities would be demanded by consumers. By keeping an excess of productive capacity, the monopolistic or oligopolistic firm would signal to potential domestic competitors that it is always in a condition to satisfy this possible increase in demand. As long as no other competitor tries to enter the market, the firm may find it profitable to use excess capacity to sell abroad, even if under cost, the additional amounts of the product it can produce.

In more recent times, Smith's argument has been taken up again. Elmslie and Sedgley (2002), on the basis of Smith's specific notion of 'productive' and 'unproductive' labour, have argued that when he said that without outlets in foreign markets 'a part of the productive labour of the country must cease', he did not mean that those workers would become unemployed, but that their productivity would diminish as they would be turned to less economically advantageous occupations. Two other contributions have focused on specific cases where the alternative to export would in fact be wasted production.

The first is the case of joint products analysed by Kurz (1992). He identified one particular point of Smith's vent-for-surplus theory that is unassailable by the traditional rejectionist argument. He noticed that in some of the passages discussing the

---

[6] See Caves and Holton (1959), Watkins (1963) and Caves (1965). More recent contributions are Neill (1991) and Findlay and Lundahl (1994). An early critic of the interpretation of Canadian development experience in terms of 'staple theory' was Buckley (1958).

vent-for-surplus function of foreign trade, Smith refers to joint-product processes of production (that is, processes in which the production of a good cannot take place without producing at the same time one or more other goods). One instance is when he speaks of hunters and shepherds providing themselves with food by killing animals, but by so doing also inescapably providing themselves with materials for clothing in excess of their own clothing needs. In these cases, foreign trade represents the only means that avoids having to throw away part of the goods produced as valueless. While Kurz makes a specific valid point, his argument that Smith's vent-for-surplus theory was basically developed with reference to joint products does not appear very convincing in the light of the many statements he made on this subject in *The Wealth of Nations*.

The second is the case of scale economies: Blecker (1997) advanced a new interpretation of Smith's vent-for-surplus notion – applicable, as in Smith's sentence quoted above, to all kinds of production, industrial even more than agricultural – arguing that it must be unified with his general theory of the benefits of international trade consequent on the enlargement of the market. Blecker argued that an industry that started to export, as a result of a historical accident or other contingent circumstances, could expect to reap progressively increasing cost advantages from scale economies if production could be progressively increased through the expansion of exports. But to achieve these productivity gains it must install surplus production capacity exceeding demand for its product in the domestic market and intended to be utilized for exports:

> Surplus productive capacity and absolute cost advantages necessarily develop together as a consequence of the opening up of foreign trade opportunities allowing for a greater division of labour... Interpreted in this way, Smith's trade theory conceptualizes the world economy as an integrated system in which the various national economies develop in a complementary fashion, such that producers in each country can reciprocally provide each other with different manufactured commodities in which they have absolute cost advantages along with surpluses that they must export. (p. 530)

More recently, the debate on Smith's vent-for-surplus theory has been reconstructed in detail by Schumacher (2015), who has advanced a new interpretation. He argues that the debate is the product of a total misunderstanding of the real meaning of some of Smith's passages in *The Wealth of Nations*, and that the theory has been built up by modern economists, starting with Myint (1958).

According to Schumacher, when Smith – who never himself used the expression 'vent-for-surplus' – employed the words 'surplus' and 'superfluities' to indicate that part of production that exceeds domestic demand and is exchanged through foreign trade for other goods subject to strong demand, he did not refer to overcapacity and idle resources that through trade can be exploited productively; he simply meant to indicate production carried out expressly to satisfy foreign demand. In this way, the country would obtain both the benefit of receiving highly desired goods in exchange for domestic products whose demand is already satisfied at home, and that of preventing the narrowness of the home market from hindering the division of labour in any particular sector, thus increasing productivity through scale economies and an increase in workers' abilities (a fundamental benefit from exports that was not considered by mainstream economists of the 19th century). An initial misinterpretation of some passages of Ricardo and J. S. Mill, in which the two economists criticized Smith for using words that could originate wrong readings of his position, gave rise to this misunderstanding, which then conditioned modern economists' interpretation of Smith's position; thus creating the myth of a Smithian 'vent-for-surplus' theory – of foreign trade making it possible for pre-existing unemployed resources and useless products to be productively exploited – which in fact he never formulated.

On the whole, Schumacher's argument appears convincing (and Blecker's position seems quite near to it). But if we accept his argument, another paradoxical conclusion can be drawn: as a result of that initial misinterpretation, a whole line of research has developed in modern times that, while contributing to the perpetuation of an erroneous reading of Smith's thought, has in fact produced very useful conceptual tools for understanding the economic problems and evolution of many countries particularly rich in natural resources and/or in labour.

We can add that part of the ambiguity of some of the theories derived from Smith's alleged vent-for-surplus argument may be clarified if we go back to a point already discussed in Section 2.1.1: the difficulty, in many cases, of distinguishing between the concept of good and the concept of factor of production. Smith spoke of foreign trade representing a vent for the goods, agricultural or industrial, produced by a sector of activity in excess of domestic demand. Myint's theory and the 'staple theory' seem instead to refer to a surplus of the productive factor land (or land and labour). Some of the confusion comes from the use of the term 'natural resource', which can be applied alternatively to the factor land (or its more specific subcategories) or to goods. Thus in the production of wheat, land is certainly a productive factor used (together with labour and capital) to obtain the final good. But when bananas, trees, mineral water, fish and minerals are produced spontaneously by nature and require only limited application of work (or work and capital) to collect them and transport them to the market, one can speak either of a good produced by nature or of a factor of production that contributes, with other factors, to making the final good available in the market.

The difficulty in attributing a natural resource to the category of goods or to that of production factors (land) seems to come from the fact that the choice depends ultimately on whether the degree of intervention of human activity (and capital) that must be applied to the original natural resource to make it ready for sale in the market is significant or insignificant. Unfortunately, it is difficult to establish a precise limit or measure of the degree of intervention that would allow the problem to be solved in the most common, intermediate cases.

6.2 Keynes and foreign trade

Apart from vent-for-surplus special cases, the theory of international trade has largely ignored the possibility of unemployment of labour and other resources. This is rather paradoxical, since as early as 1936 Keynes showed that involuntary (and not merely transitional) labour unemployment is a theoretical possibility, apart from being empirically a phenomenon all too frequently observed in real economic life.

The assertion that market mechanisms do not spontaneously lead to the full utilization of productive factors and the primacy of the goal of ensuring workers' full employment are at the centre of Keynes's theory. The Keynesian revolution produced a radical change in the perspective from which the whole process of national production is viewed, with fundamental consequences for international trade theory as well. Pre-Keynesian economics viewed the increase in a country's per capita product as the result of a resources-constrained process that consisted of combining and using all existing productive factors in the most efficient way: the free operation of market forces would ensure this result through competition and the signals provided by the changes in the prices of products and factors. Once this equilibrium of perfect competition with factor full-employment was reached, for a given number of hours worked by each individual in the year, an increase in per capita product could only be achieved by a greater effort of saving and investment, by more intense work and by the introduction of technical and organizational innovations (and, of course, by the efficiency gains from increasing international specialization). Keynes upset this view, arguing that the total volume of goods and services produced in an economy is determined by the strength of the demand, domestic and foreign, directed to the country's firms. An 'unemployment equilibrium' is possible, since productive resources can remain unemployed even for long periods if demand is not strong enough; and if market forces are not sufficient to guarantee full employment, the state must step in, providing the economy with the necessary additional demand through an increase in its own net expenditure (expenses minus taxes).[7]

---

[7] The reason why the market system is unable by itself to guarantee full employment is that the two fundamental prices in the economic system – those of money (the interest rate) and labour (the wage) – that according to pre-Keynesian theory would move so as to ensure equilibrium between the demand for and the supply of goods and factors at full employment – cannot reach that goal. In a depression, the reduction of the interest rate does not revive investment and income growth (quite apart from the fact that when the interest rate is already at a very low level there is by definition little space for further reductions). According to Keynes, investment is not so much responsive to interest rates as the result of entrepreneurs' 'animal spirits'; that is, of their decisions to invest on the basis of their expectations of future demand and profits. At the same time, the reduction of money-wages cannot ensure a demand for labour equal to its available supply: not only because workers tend to resist reductions in money-wages (even when associated with a lower price level), but also because if they did accept money-wage cutting, this would lower their consumption and consequently overall demand, pushing entrepreneurs to reduce investment. A lower price level associated with money-wage reduction, by increasing the real value of outstanding debt, would also impose a heavier burden on indebted entrepreneurs, further reducing their investment.

In this theory, therefore, a strategic role is attributed to net foreign demand (what is sold abroad net of what is bought from abroad) in contributing to the level of national activity and employment.[8] This explains why all countries strive to provide increasing foreign outlets to domestic producers (and to prevent foreign producers from

---

[8] In the Keynesian view of foreign trade as a component of demand, there is a point that deserves serious discussion. According to traditional expositions, Keynesian theory asserts that a country's income is the sum of consumption, investment, the balance between exports and imports, and the balance between public expenditures and receipts (the famous Y=C+I+(X-M)+(G-T) identity). Exports are viewed as an addition to domestic demand; they are exogenously determined, as they depend on other countries' import demand, which in turn is a function of their income level and rate of growth, wage levels and income elasticity (though in the longer run a country can obtain a higher export performance by improving and technically upgrading its factors and its products, adapting product mixes to international demand trends, etc.). Conversely, imports are viewed as a subtraction from domestic demand (implying that in the absence of imports people would direct the corresponding demand to domestic products). Until the process of globalization set in during the 1980s, this view could be accepted as an approximation to the real world as far as exports were concerned, though already long before Hufbauer (1970) had argued that 'A better procedure, in finding national export characteristics, would have been to use export *value added* ... for each commodity, rather than export *receipts* for that commodity, as the ingredient of national export composition. As M. Michaely and P. T. Knight observed, export receipts *minus* the world market cost of purchased inputs should ideally serve as the export composition vector' (1970, p. 156). But it seriously misrepresented the nature of imports. These can be divided into two distinct categories: imports of goods which are in competition with domestic production (if not imported, they could be produced – though possibly less efficiently – at home) and to which the Keynesian classification applies; and imports of energy products, raw materials, intermediate products, high-technology inputs or capital goods, not available at home but essential if the very production of the other goods is to take place. To view this second category as a subtraction from the demand directed to home producers seems hardly acceptable. It would follow that the foreign trade contribution to the demand directed to home producers in advanced countries should have been measured not just by net exports, but by the difference between exports and only those imports that do not represent external inputs essential for national production.

With the development of globalization, the spread of offshoring activity and the formation of global production chains, the whole Keynesian view of exports and imports has to be reconsidered. Exports, as traditionally recorded by customs data, no longer measure the demand that addresses itself to the production factors of the exporting country; the latter may import most of the components of its exports, so that the value of its exports may bear little relation to, and largely overestimate, the VA produced by its production factors. Imports, in their turn, increasingly consist of components or preceding production activities absolutely essential (as once were only raw materials) for profitable competitive exports to take place (see Section 11.2.1).

Another question pertaining to the Keynesian identity regards the independence of the different demand elements on the right side. It is common for each demand component to be considered in isolation, as if any variation in its value would determine a variation of the same amount in total income Y. If the identity is not considered in a merely accounting sense, however, the connections between the different components must be taken into consideration: Keynes himself stressed the stronger effect on income of an increase in investment relative to an equivalent increase in consumption owing to the mechanism of the multiplier set in action by investment. In the same way, it would be questionable to isolate the trade balance element, arguing that the introduction or elimination of trade barriers cannot influence income if the variation in exports and imports is expected to leave the trade balance unchanged. For example, the decision to reduce or increase, drastically and quickly, the commercial intercourse with foreign countries would in all probability have strong effects on the volume of investment.

supplanting domestic ones) and why, in order to gain an international competitive advantage, they try both to stimulate innovations leading to the introduction of new or improved goods and production processes, and to use all available means to lower production costs and final products' prices, often also resorting to special strategies aimed at keeping the rate of exchange of the national currency artificially low. By contrast, in the logic of the RHO model based on the full employment hypothesis, trade is simply a means to obtain goods that a country cannot produce or to exploit the productive advantages of specialization, and each country should strive to sell abroad, in payment for given volumes of goods imported, the minimum possible volume of domestic goods (that is, it should strive to sell its products at as high a price as possible).

The two very different perspectives – RHO and Keynesian – from which the national production process can be viewed explain some contradictions and misunderstandings frequent in the practical discussions of international trade problems. For instance, in order to expand a country's exports and limit its imports (so as to boost demand, and thus employment and income) national producers are continuously incited to increase competitiveness – that is, their capacity to offer their products in domestic and foreign markets at cheaper prices than foreign competitors. A successful response to this incitement would be reflected in the decrease of the ratio between the prices of national and foreign products. The opposite perspective is implied when problems of national 'terms of trade' (that is, the ratio between the price indexes of exported and imported products) are discussed, and the hope is expressed that these terms will improve: the advantage a country derives from trade is here measured according to the criterion of trying to sell abroad its products at the maximum possible price, while paying as little as possible for the imported products. The two contrasting perspectives also explain the contradiction of advanced countries frequently protesting against developing countries for taking unfair advantage of their very low wages to undersell producers of manufactures in industrial countries (allegedly an intolerable exercise of 'social dumping'), while they never happen to protest against those very low wages when the latter allow cheap imports of products such as bananas or coffee or minerals that cannot be produced in industrial countries.

When a country opens to trade, or when a new development changes the composition of the goods exported and imported, even if the commercial balance of payments remains in equilibrium (the monetary value of exports being equal to that of imports), it is likely that the 'employment balance of payments' (the balance between the number of workplaces created by exports and the number of workplaces lost because of imports) will change, because the labour content of one dollar of the goods exported and imported is almost always different. Since the 1980s, we have seen the virtual disappearance in many advanced Western countries of manufacturing sectors that produced simple goods (such as toys, textiles and apparel) employing large numbers of unskilled workers. These goods became the typical types of production and exports of developing countries in the first stages of industrialization and endowed with 'unlimited supplies' of unskilled workers ready to work at very low wages. Western industrial countries concentrated instead on the production of more 'advanced' goods and services requiring more highly skilled workers and saleable at much higher prices. This development was heralded by international economists as a new, mutually beneficial, international division of labour in line with the principles of comparative advantage and relative factor availabilities (to avoid problems of adjustment during the transition, advanced countries were exhorted to provide dismissed workers in 'traditional' sectors with assistance and incentives to retrain so as to rapidly acquire the skills required for employment in the more 'advanced' sectors). All this is fine as long as the hypothesis of the full employment of factors is maintained. In the real world, it is very likely that in the case under discussion the labour content, in terms of number of workers, of the goods exported by advanced countries to pay for an equivalent monetary amount of goods imported from developing countries, is much smaller than the labour content of the 'traditional' products previously produced at home and now imported, so that employment problems for advanced countries may ensue. Of course, if the new trade structure produces large benefits in terms of lower prices of the goods imported, people in advanced countries will use their increased purchasing power to buy more goods, part of which will be non-tradable goods and services that will create new employment opportunities for the workers dismissed as a result of the changes in the composition of imports and exports.

Gomory (2009) reminded us that we should be very cautious about certain kinds of discourse that we increasingly hear about comparative advantage. He referred to the advice offered to Japan that it should not worry if a growing number of its manufacturing sectors were being outpriced and displaced by emerging economies' low-wage competition: Japan, it was said, could well give up all its manufacturing activities, where its comparative advantage was evaporating, and concentrate instead on the activities, such as advanced research services, where its real comparative advantage now lies. This reasoning may very well work in a theoretical RHO world, where perfect competition rules and an individual producer or country has by definition unlimited scope for the sale of its products provided their price is competitive. In the real world, the situation is different: even leaving aside the problem of the 'employment balance of payments', if Japan were to give up all or most of its industrial production, it would need to import a huge amount of manufactured goods. In order to pay for these goods, it would need to offer the services of its advanced researchers in exchange; and in all probability, the international market for these services would not be large enough to absorb the huge amount of Japanese exports. Japan would thus be unable to pay for the importation of the manufactures it needs, and would have to drastically curtail its rate of growth so as to limit its demand for imports to the level of its export sales. Similar considerations have been advanced, with reference to the USA, by Gomory and Baumol (2013).

Although Keynes never developed a theory of international trade, he realized as early as 1930 that once the hypothesis of full employment is discarded, the whole logic of the comparative advantage principle and the consequent free trade prescription would collapse. In the 1930 Macmillan Report, discussing the proposal of eliminating British import duties on cars 'in order that we would stop the making of cars and make something else for which we are better suited', he noticed that the presence of high unemployment meant that 'the alternative for a time may be between producing motor cars or producing nothing' (Keynes 1981, p. 114).[9]

If full trade liberalization is allowed but unemployment is not ruled out, then any foreign product costing a cent less than the home-produced one will be imported, and this will produce a benefit to consumers in the form of a slightly lower price (owing to either greater productivity or lower labour wages of the foreign production); but if entire lines of activity are out-priced and have to close down and their workers and machines cannot find employment in alternative lines of production, the loss to the country will consist of all the income previously gained by the domestic factors of production that lose their employment (minus the small advantage of the lower prices of the goods now imported). As long as the 'tax' in the form of a higher domestic price imposed on the country's consumers is lower than the income lost under free trade by the labour and capital employed in activities unable to withstand foreign competition, a case for limiting imports could be advanced. Of course, the country protecting its home production will probably lose the possibility of expanding its exports to the foreign countries hit by its protectionist measures, as they can be expected to retaliate; but it all depends on specific situations. And in any case, particularly in developing economies, it may be that a country would be unable to find convenient foreign outlets for its products even if foreign countries were to keep their borders fully open (one such situation is mentioned at the end of Section 7.2).

From the empirical point of view, the experience of recent decades has strongly confirmed Keynes's assertion that involuntary unemployment, far from representing a possible temporary occurrence in the transition from one equilibrium to another, is a phenomenon that can be quantitatively very substantial and last for very long periods. And this not only in underdeveloped economies, where structural deficiencies and market distortions have always caused huge unemployment and underemployment of labour (and often of other resources as well), but also in advanced countries,

---

[9] Milberg (1994, 2002) argued that Keynes implicitly rejected the theory of comparative advantage. In fact Keynes did not accept the hypotheses on which Ricardo's principle is based (factor full employment and perfect domestic mobility of labour between different jobs and locations, Say's law – according to which supply creates its own demand - and the separation of the real and monetary sides of the economy), nor the operation of the mechanisms based on price changes (be they the price–specie flow, the movement of wages, or exchange rate changes), which in that theory ensure the re-equilibrium of trade balances (see Chapter 7). In Keynesian foreign trade theory – to which a fundamental contribution was made by Harrod (1933) – trade balance re-equilibrium relies on income changes.

A much discussed issue is whether Keynes was a free trader or a protectionist. This is because of the inconsistencies of his position on free trade: over the course of his professional life, he altered his views from initial full adherence to free trade to strong advocacy of protectionist measures in the early 1930s, and a more moderate position in favour of managed trade in his later years. This reflected his pragmatic approach to economic policy problems and the fact that, while recognizing the benefits of free trade, he wanted to avoid international policy considerations hampering the adoption of domestic policies directed to the primary goal of ensuring full employment. An exhaustive analysis of the issue has been provided by Cammarosano (2014); see also Irwin (1996) and Maurin (2013).

The book on Keynes by Davidson (2007) devotes considerable space to Keynes's views on international economic relations; it was commented on by Blecker (2009).

where the low levels of unemployment of the 1960s and 1970s are now remembered as a feature of a past 'Golden Age'. International economists, however, have been particularly reluctant to abandon the hypothesis of full employment (quite understandably, given the disruptive consequences of such a step). Most of them tried to push aside the problems Keynes raised, by holding that international trade is a field of economic analysis where one must start from the full employment hypothesis, because unemployment problems belong to the more general field of macroeconomics where one can presuppose that appropriate domestic monetary and fiscal policies are always in a condition to guarantee the desired level of employment.

The reality seems to be that national authorities usually do have some room for adopting policies to increase employment, but their action generally reaches objective limits (commonly, unsustainable balance of payments deficits, wage increases and/or inflation, and alarming levels of public debt) well before their employment objectives are attained; further problems may derive from the fact that the higher growth that monetary and fiscal policies might stimulate may require large additional inputs of higher-skill workers that may not be available among the unemployed. Stiglitz (2019), referring to employment problems created by innovations, while holding that 'The key is maintaining full employment. We can do this using fiscal policy… when monetary policy… fails to do the trick. Both monetary and fiscal policy stimulate aggregate demand, and with enough stimulus, the economy can always be restored to full employment', argues that there is a political problem: 'Blind ideology … may make undertaking sufficient fiscal stimulus politically difficult.' (p. 121).

In this respect, the stimulus to economic activity provided by exports seems to offer a number of possible advantages compared with an equivalent stimulus provided by other components of demand. First, exports directly produce receipts in foreign currency that finance, or help to finance, the payments abroad for the increased imports associated with a higher level of national income, thus preventing or postponing the emergence of balance of payments bottlenecks to growth. Second, while substantial increases in internal consumers' demand, if unemployment is not very high, normally imply – when viewed by the collectivity of national entrepreneurs – a corresponding increase in domestic wages and thus additional costs, exports represent a source of additional demand not directly connected to the perspective of an increase in production costs. Entrepreneurs' 'animal spirits' and propensity to invest are likely to be stimulated by this lack of association of future sales receipts with future increases in wage costs.[10] Third, exports – requiring the ability of domestic pro-

[10] When, nowadays, China is exhorted to modify its growth strategy centred on exports – a strategy that, given China's economic size, is creating problems for the rest of the world while seriously limiting the benefits from increased production for the Chinese population – in favour of one based on an increase of domestic demand, it is usually not considered that the latter strategy would likely imply large increases in wage levels and thus may not meet the approval of entrepreneurs.

A further, connected, consideration was advanced by Denis (1961) in his 'theory of pre-existing outlets', in which he developed a point originally advanced by Malthus in 1820. Referring to industrial countries, Denis held that entrepreneurs' expectations of export sales play a strategic role as a

ducers to withstand the intense competition ruling in international markets – exert a powerful stimulus on entrepreneurs to increase efficiency and to devise and adopt all possible technological and organizational innovations.

These advantages contributed, in developing countries, to the growing popularity of export-led industrialization strategies starting from the 1980s. But for these countries there was a further, more important, advantage in pursuing that strategy: they were often so poor that for most industrial goods no sufficient domestic demand existed to allow the profitable establishment and growth of their production (given the minimum scale they usually require): exports to advanced countries represented an obvious way to overcome this constraint.[11]

The globalization process that started in the 1980s, by making the entire world market available to the producers of any individual country (the share of exports in total demand has markedly increased almost everywhere), has apparently allowed producers to overcome the limits previously imposed by the volume of the domestic demand for their product. Therefore, for an individual country, the Fordist policy of supplying, through wage increases, domestic workers with the purchasing power necessary to absorb the goods they themselves produce can now be avoided (as would seem to be confirmed by the wage stagnation and cuts in social benefits found in some advanced countries and the slow rise of wages in emerging countries). But one should ask whether the same problem is not present also in our time, simply at international instead of national level.

Long ago, discussing the problems posed to advanced countries by imports from much lower unit cost emerging countries, Mead (1990) observed that 'to the extent that low wages in developing countries slow the rise of wages and employment in advanced countries, then the danger of international economic stagnation grows', and argued that:

---

stimulus to 'autonomous' investments (the investments that in Keynesian theory set the economy into motion, leading, through the mechanism of the 'multiplier', to further 'induced' investments). In order for entrepreneurs to make an initial decision to invest, there must pre-exist a prospect of additional demand for their products. Apart from technical progress (the introduction of new products or new production methods that would make it possible to out-price existing competitors and/or increase domestic consumption of the good), such a prospect cannot be induced by internal factors. The individual entrepreneur cannot hope that the additional income due to his own investment will be spent (as in the Ford's strategy of selling cars to its own workers in the USA of the 1920s) for the purchase of his own product. And a collective programme of autonomous investments on the part of a large group of domestic producers, which could be expected to increase the demand addressed to all of them through additional employment and without unduly raising wage levels, would be difficult to organize without more or less extensive state planning. In perfect competition, of course, the problem would not arise, as the individual entrepreneur could expect that the improvement in efficiency produced by his investment would make him more competitive so as to out-price other producers and sell any amount of his product; but Denis considered that modern industry is characterized by imperfect competition, where a slight reduction in price does not guarantee that customers will be taken away from competitors.

[11] The past experience, and especially the future prospects, of export-led growth strategies in developing countries have long been debated: see Felipe (2003), Mayer (2003), Blecker (2005b), Palley (2006b, 2011), Rodrik (2008), Blecker and Razmi (2010) and Sannassee, Seetanah and Jugessur (2014).

> low wages in developing countries contribute to a weakness of global demand and that this weakness in turn undermines political support for the multilateral free trade system … The increasing reliance on export-led growth strategies by developing countries without compensating policies to maintain global demand is in our view generating pressures that ultimately will close the markets on which export-oriented economies depend. (p. 37)

To face this problem of global demand insufficiency, Mead proposed that the implementation of agreements reducing trade barriers should be strictly tied to the adoption of generally accepted international standards of production for internationally traded goods that would lead to increases in wages and consumption in some producing countries, enlarging demand and markets; by standards, he meant rules for the relation of wages to productivity, for minimum wages and in respect of safety, social insurance and key rights of workers (taking into consideration, of course, the specific conditions of countries at different levels of development).

In more recent times, export-led growth strategies have been the object of reconsideration in the light of both the limited prospects of demand growth in advanced countries and the sharpening of competition for manufactured exports among developing countries as more and more of them have resorted to such strategies. The possible dangers of a 'fallacy of composition' have been pointed out: a decision to produce for export to advanced countries on the part of a single, marginal, developing country may be wholly justified, but when most developing countries rely on such a strategy for their growth, there might not be enough room for all of them to see their plans fulfilled. The result could be the formation of global excess capacity, and consequent cut-throat competition leading to export price deflation and worsening terms of trade for these countries. In this situation, one alternative strategy that would ensure maintenance of the advantages of international openness and competition would be for developing countries to rely on domestic demand more than on net exports, while taking initiatives to open their domestic markets more widely to one another, thereby significantly increasing their mutual (South–South) trade.

The theme of the contradiction characterizing the globalization process since the 1980s between, on the one hand, the efforts of all countries to force the export of their products to world markets by curbing wages and costs and offshoring to low-wage locations and, on the other, the lack of sufficient world buying power to absorb all the products produced, was taken up by some authors in the years preceding the global crisis of 2008. The mechanism that contributed to playing down the contradiction was based on the fact that the largest world economy, the USA – as the producer of the currency most widely demanded internationally for trade and financial transactions and as a store of value – could record growing trade deficits financed by foreign investment in its monetary and financial assets. This freed the USA from the balance of payments constraint that conditioned the economic policies of all other countries, allowing it to act as a 'buyer of last resort' at the global level. Of course, the huge US trade deficit was associated with negative effects on jobs in the tradable goods' sectors; but nevertheless, a high level of overall employment was maintained thanks to the increasing number of jobs offered by the non-tradable sectors (whose products must necessarily be produced at home, such as house and other buildings construction, restaurants, cleaning, teaching, hairdressers and doctors), which could expand thanks to the growth of expenditure financed by inflating debt.

Blecker (2005a) warned:

> the successful export-led economies (currently led by China…) put a constant drain on total world demand by failing to spend all their export earning on comparable amounts of imports from other countries. The US government tolerates this arrangement not only because production and outsourcing in low-wage locations have become so profitable for US MNCs, but also because this arrangement allows the US to finance its chronic trade deficits … without having to raise interest rates or depreciate the dollar … But the perpetual recycling of Asian net export earnings into the acquisition of American debt and the maintenance of an overvalued dollar cannot be a sustainable, longer-run equilibrium for the international payment system, and when this house of cards collapses, it may well take the global economy down with it unless measures are put in place to prevent a collapse. (p. 345)

One year before the outbreak of the crisis, Palley (2006a), noting that the contradiction indicated here had been papered over in the USA by the explosion of consumer borrowing in the wake of the deregulation of the financial market and the ensuing asset price boom, also forewarned that 'The problem is that such borrowing risks prove unsustainable if incomes are hollowed out, and that could stop the economic merry-go-round. If that stoppage produces an economic crash, globalization may crash, too'.

* * *

An extreme case of the problems that trade can create once we dismiss the hypothesis of full employment, is the paradoxical situation known as 'Dutch disease'. This is the situation that arises when a country, such as the Netherlands in the 1970s, suddenly discovers large oil reserves and starts to export oil (but the same problem can regard countries whose exports are concentrated in other precious raw materials). The rapid additional afflux of a massive amount of foreign receipts tends to increase the country's exchange rate, making the non-oil goods previously exported more expensive for foreign purchasers and thus undermining their international competitiveness; while foreign goods, having become less expensive in national currency, tend to supplant national tradable products in domestic expenditure. As a result, previous export and import-competing industries may gradually close down, generating unemployment, which is only partially compensated for by increased employment in non-tradable activities; while the oil-extraction sector, which now supplants export industries as a source of the foreign currency needed to pay for imports, creates, because of its specific technology, very few additional jobs.[12]

[12] Rodrik (2015) reminded us that the same situation might result as a consequence, not of an appreciation of the exchange rate, but of an increase in domestic wages. [continue on next page].

According to orthodox economic theory, the Dutch situation represents the maximum luck a country could hope for: as if it had suddenly discovered a large gold deposit, it can now give out just one resource at a very high price in exchange for practically all the goods it needs from abroad. On the contrary, taking a Keynesian perspective, the situation may represent a 'curse', as the country may experiment a sudden fall of the demand directed to the domestic producers of non-oil tradables and of the level of employment. In theory, also within a Keynesian framework, in such a situation it might be possible for the sudden increase in foreign receipts to be used to expand local incomes and demand. While a large part of this expansion would translate into increased imports – as the higher wages demanded by domestic workers would make the country's internationally traded goods uncompetitive – the demand for non-tradable goods and services might still grow enough to provide employment for a large part of the workers dismissed by other sectors. In practice, however – quite apart from possible mismatches in the skills required, limits to the consumption of non-tradables and the fact that many jobs in non-tradables sectors are likely to be unpleasant and low-skill ones unacceptable to locals – this possibility calls for basic changes in the country's institutional arrangements, as it is crucially dependent on how the oil income is distributed, and seems to imply large-scale state intervention, two issues that are extremely controversial politically.

While the Dutch disease situation had been recognized as early as 1835 by Longfield (see Maneschi (1998, p. 122)), and Vernon (1971) had remarked that 'The sustained existence of large raw-material industries in some countries tends to create an equilibrium rate of exchange that blights the possibility of competitive manufactured goods exports and handicaps local import-substituting industries' (p. 176), the problem attracted widespread attention by economists only after the 1970s Dutch experience. On the Dutch disease see Corden and Neary (1982), Corden (1984) and Brahmbhatt, Canuto and Vostroknutova (2010).

7 Trade Balance Equilibrium

Chapter 6 and this one have been separated because the hypotheses in the RHO model to which they refer regard two different economic phenomena: full employment and trade balance equilibrium (in this work the term 'trade balance' includes not only goods – which form the traditional merchandise balance – but also services, which appear in statistics as part of the wider aggregate current account balance). But the two phenomena are strictly connected: once the occurrence of unemployment is admitted, the effect of trade balance disequilibrium on the level of a country's employment becomes, as in Keynes's theory, a subject of the greatest importance.

As trade disequilibria must by definition be associated with corresponding transfers of international means of payments that finance them, the RHO hypothesis of equilibrium in trading countries' trade balances implies the hypothesis of absence of – or equilibrium in – international capital transactions. Therefore, relaxing the balanced trade hypothesis implies also relaxing the RHO hypothesis of no international movement of monetary and financial capital.

The possibility of running trade balance deficits for protracted periods has important economic consequences. As indicated by Autor, Dorn and Hanson (2016), with reference to the recent US experience of trade with China, such a possibility allows the country in which some tradable sectors are being displaced by the long-run increasing competitive ability of another country, to delay the necessary, often painful, reallocation of domestic resources towards other tradable sectors where the country is likely to be able to stand foreign competition, and shift instead resources towards non-tradable sectors. But the most important consequence of persistent trade surpluses/deficits is that they do not allow the comparative costs principle to operate fully.

Consider the following case, similar to the one analysed by Crinò and Epifani (2014). Suppose trade takes place, with many goods being exchanged, between a poor country ('South') and a rich one ('North'). We can assume that the South has a low average worker skill level and the North a high one. Suppose also that goods can be classified in increasing order of skill intensity (content of skilled labour relative to other factors). According to the comparative costs principle, we can expect low-skill goods to be exported by the South and high-skill ones by the North. And the separation point, in the goods' skill classification, between the lower-skill goods exported by the South and the higher-skill ones it will import from the North (that is the point determining until which goods' skill level it will be the South that exports a good), is the point where the value of the goods each country exports is equal to the value of those it imports. But suppose now that, for whatever reason, capital is transferred from the South to the North: a Southern trade surplus will be necessary for the overall balance of payments to be in equilibrium, which means that some higher-skill goods – those immediately beyond the previous separation point – will start being exported by the South, while the North will concentrate on the export of the highest-skill goods (one result is that the average skill intensity of exports will increase in both the South and the North – which, as noted by Crinò and Epifani, contributes to explain the growing wage inequality, in favour of more skilled workers, that appears to characterize both advanced and developing countries).

A likely mechanism that will produce the South's trade surplus is the depreciation of the Southern currency consequent on the capital transfer to the North and the connected increased demand for the Northern currency. This depreciation will lower the price of all Southern goods relative to their price in the North, to the point that some of the goods previously imported by the South will now be exported by it, as for Northern purchasers their import price has become lower than the domestic price. These new Southern exports respond to absolute advantages created by the currency depreciation, which cancel some of the Northern comparative advantages on which trade was previously based.

It is important to notice that the hypothesis of trade balance equilibrium is not only essential to ensure that the exchange of goods between countries takes place according to Ricardo's theory of comparative advantage, but is also necessary to support Ricardo's view of international trade as a form of barter, with money simply facilitating the exchange of commodities. The same vision of trade as barter and the postulate of 'money neutrality' (whereby money intervenes simply as a means to facilitate exchange, without any effect on the real economy) underlie the traditional separation in mainstream international economics between trade and finance, which leads to the exclusion of the effects of monetary factors from the analysis of international trade.[1]

The possibility of experiencing protracted trade balance disequilibria, and its effects, had long been neglected by mainstream international trade theory, but in recent decades has attracted the attention of a growing number of economists, probably as a consequence of the problems created by the persistent large trade deficits of the USA and surpluses of China (but Germany and Japan have also been running persistent

[1] J. Robinson, following Keynes, rejected this trade–finance divide; see Blecker (2005a). The view of international trade as barter, with the corresponding equality of the value of imports and exports, implies that money only acts as a means of exchange. But money also performs the functions of unit of value and of store of value; in this latter function it allows sales and purchases to take place at different times (but in the RHO model the time dimension does not exist). The option of making use of money in the future, setting it aside as savings, apart from creating problems of uncertainty (and thus of people's expectations) about money's future value, eliminates the equality between income and expenditure, introducing the possibility of income reduction and unemployment. At international level, it opens the way to the possible use of money by a country as a precautionary reserve to spend in case of future need, so that it no longer appears irrational for a country to follow the mercantilist policy of striving to expand exports and limit imports so as to accumulate a stock of international means of payment to be used should any balance of payments emergency arise.

trade surpluses). The USA, in particular, has uninterruptedly registered a negative balance of both trade in goods and trade in goods and services since 1976.

7.1 Trade balance re-equilibrating mechanisms

In a free market economy, for international trade to take place as envisaged by the Ricardian comparative costs principle, it is necessary that a country's comparative advantage in the production of a good (in terms, for instance, of labour hours necessary to produce it) translates into a lower absolute monetary market price for the foreign purchaser (relative to the domestic price of the same good). As was pointed out in Section 2.3, contrary to the situation of the two students in the example of Footnote 1 in Chapter 1 or of two countries with a state monopoly of foreign trade, international exchange is not carried out by two agents deciding to exchange a given amount of exported goods for a given amount of imported goods, the two flows balancing by definition as in all barter transactions. In a free market economy, foreign trade transactions are the result of purchases by a multitude of importers (firms or individuals) who limit themselves to comparing the absolute monetary prices of the good they want to buy, supplied by domestic and foreign producers, and choose the cheaper supplier, without any consideration of countries' comparative advantages or equilibrium between countries' total imports and exports. For the comparative costs principle to operate, a mechanism must therefore be at work between two trading countries, ensuring that the absolute monetary price of the good in whose production and export each country enjoys a comparative advantage is lower than the domestic price of the same good in the other country, and that the total value of the goods exported equals that of the goods imported. A number of such mechanisms have been relied on by trade theorists.

Before the 20th century, when money basically consisted of coins containing given amounts of precious metals (and of paper money exchangeable into those coins), economists relied on the 'price–specie flow mechanism' described by Hume in 1752 and founded on the quantity theory of money, according to which changes in the price level of a country depend on changes in the amount of money in circulation. Going back to the Ricardian example, if at the opening of trade the absolute money prices (in terms of given weights of gold) of both cloth and wine were higher in England than in Portugal, English consumers would start buying amounts of both goods from Portugal. The English trade balance would be negative and England would be sending more gold to Portugal to pay for its imports than it received from Portugal for its exports. The increased amount of money circulating in Portugal would drive up the price of all Portuguese goods, while the opposite would happen in England. At a certain point the absolute price of cloth, the good in whose production England was less inefficient relative to Portugal (that is, where English comparative advantage lies) would be lower in England than in Portugal and the Portuguese would start buying it from England, thus restoring equilibrium in the trade balance between the two countries.

Another mechanism, also based on the quantity theory of money, has traditionally been considered to be at work in modern inconvertible paper-money economies if countries maintain a rigidly fixed exchange rate of their currency with gold (as under the gold standard) or with another currency used as international means of payments (as was the case of the US dollar for advanced countries until 1971–1973). In the latter case, if a country's domestic prices, translated into dollars at the fixed exchange rate, increase for all or most goods more than the corresponding foreign prices, the country will import a larger quantity of goods from other countries and export a smaller quantity to them, experiencing – if previously the balance of payments was in equilibrium – an outflow of dollar reserves abroad. The opposite will happen in countries with dollar prices of their goods decreasing relative to those abroad. As central banks see outflows or inflows of gold or international money take place, they will react by adopting respectively a more restrictive or less restrictive monetary policy, so as to dampen or stimulate domestic demand and consequently lower the level of wages and prices in deficit countries and increase it in surplus countries. These changes will make deficit countries' goods more (and surplus countries' goods less) competitive internationally, increasing their exports and decreasing their imports (and vice versa in surplus countries), thus restoring trade balances equilibrium.[2]

A similar, but much more rapidly operating, mechanism is the variation of a country's exchange rate. In a fixed exchange rates system – the one established at Bretton Woods at the end of World War II, which lasted until 1973 – changes in exchange rates can take place only exceptionally, the typical case being that of a growing balance of payments deficit that ultimately, when the foreign exchange reserves have been exhausted, forces the authorities to devalue the national currency. In a system of flexible exchange rates, instead, the changes take place continuously, as the determination of the exchange rate is left to the day-to-day equilibrium between the demand for and supply of the international currency (the monetary authorities having only limited ability to influence the exchange rate by intervening in the market with sales or purchases of official reserves). If a country's costs and prices, translated into international currency, increase more than those of other countries and produce a trade deficit, the higher demand for the international currency to pay for imports relative to the supply by those receiving it in payment for exports will lead to a depreciation of the country's currency vis-à-vis the international one. This means that the prices of the goods produced by the deficit country will instantaneously decrease for foreign purchasers, while foreign goods will become more expensive for the deficit country's importers by the amount of the currency depreciation.[3] The deficit country's exports will increase and its imports shrink until trade equilibrium is restored.

---

[2] The mechanism of re-equilibrium through wage movements was stressed by neoclassical theory. Keynes did not exclude that money-wage reductions might lead to an improvement in the trade balance; but such adjustment may or may not take place, and in any case there might follow negative effects in terms of aggregate demand and unfair distributional changes.

[3] Just think of touristic services: foreign visitors arriving in a country whose currency has depreciated suddenly find all local costs reduced, in terms of their own currency, by the amount of the depreciation; while residents of the depreciating country going on holiday abroad will find a corresponding increase, in terms of their own currency, of all the prices in the foreign country.

A basic difference between, on the one hand, the mechanisms of price–specie flows and of monetary authorities' reaction in a rigidly fixed exchange rates system, and, on the other, the mechanisms of occasional exchange rate variations and flexible exchange rates, is that in the first two the correction of the trade imbalance is based on changes in the absolute level of all prices and wages in a country, a process that may be obstructed and distorted by many factors and that in any case will not be instantaneous;[4] while the other two do not rely on a change in the level of all domestic prices, but act only instantaneously – just as in summer, in order to start activities one hour earlier, an official summer time is often introduced instead of having the working hours of all national activities changed – on the ratio between domestic and foreign prices.

Unfortunately, however, the effects of depreciation usually do not stop here. When goods from abroad become more expensive, both producers using foreign inputs and consumers of foreign goods, if these products are not obtainable from domestic sources, will try to react to the increase in their costs and to the consequent lowering of real incomes by raising their products' prices and their wages, respectively. If they succeed, the resulting inflationary pressures are likely to lead to an increase in domestic prices and a loss of competitiveness of the goods exported, thus recreating the conditions for a new depreciation of the national currency. For a nominal depreciation (appreciation) of the exchange rate to produce a lasting correction of a country's competitiveness and its trade balance, it must represent a 'real depreciation (appreciation)'; that is, it must not be followed by corresponding increases (decreases) in the domestic price level relative to that of foreign competitors.

Exchange rate changes also have effects on the capital section of the balance of payments: if the deficit country has a stock of foreign debt (or other obligations) denominated in foreign currency, for the citizens of the country the depreciation of its exchange rate suddenly produces a corresponding increase in the value of this debt in terms of domestic currency; while it correspondingly decreases its value for foreigners if it is denominated in the currency of the depreciating country.

In this section, we have concentrated on the trade balance re-equilibrating mechanisms that operate through price changes. But for exchange rate devaluations to be successful in restoring external balance, it may be necessary that they be complemented by policies facilitating or reinforcing the automatic effects of devaluations on income levels and resource reallocation; since, as explained for example by Corden (1994), devaluations must produce both a reduction of aggregate demand (the external trade deficit itself signalling that total demand exceeds national output) and some

---

[4] The lowering of wages and prices through a decrease in the amount of money available in a country is a process that will develop only gradually and unevenly as it depends on many factors: the price-fixing power of different groups of producers and workers, the demand and supply elasticities of goods and factors, the degree of centralization in wage determination, the measure of money-illusion (the extent to which people only look at the nominal level of their remunerations and obligations instead of considering their value in real terms) and so on. A general reduction (increase) in prices and wages also has arbitrary distorting effects on domestic income and wealth distribution, as it increases (reduces) the real value of monetary incomes and outstanding debts fixed in nominal terms.

reallocation of production from non-tradable to tradable goods, so as to allow an increase in the supply of export and import-competing goods.

* * *

Devaluation lowers the price of domestic products paid by foreigners and increases the price of foreign products paid by residents – whose real incomes are thus reduced – at a stroke, in the expectation that these price changes will re-establish trade balance equilibrium.

The re-equilibrating mechanisms described so far in this section are not available when trade balance must be restored between regions of the same country (or between countries that have adopted the same currency, such as the euro area members), as they do not enjoy monetary sovereignty. In order to rebalance exports with imports, a region must rely on the so-called 'internal devaluation' mechanism (which in theory is available also to a country for restoring trade balance with countries having a different currency): the direct reduction – applied equally to internal and external customers – of the absolute price in domestic currency of the goods it exports (and of the goods that compete with imports) through a lowering of the nominal remunerations of the factors used in their production. This seems to be the only mechanism through which specialization according to comparative advantages could take place and restore regional trade balance, since for comparative advantages to operate, they must be translated into absolute price advantages visible to the purchasers of the goods. The problem is that at the level of a country's region this lowering of nominal remunerations faces two formidable obstacles. First, mobility of capital and especially of labour between regions, if not perfect, is very high and certainly much higher than at international level. Therefore, instead of letting their remunerations go down to the level necessary for comparative advantages to operate, capital and labour may decide to move to regions where their remunerations can be maintained at a higher level. Second, regions of the same nation are usually bound by common legal rules, trade union bargaining systems and other national practices that have a strong influence on the determination of factor rewards, making it impossible or hard to differentiate regional absolute remunerations to the necessary degree (just think of national minimum wages, national wage contracts and the linking of many financial incomes to the national interest rate).

In the case of nations adopting the same currency – for instance among euro area member countries – this trade balance adjustment through direct lowering of factor remunerations does appear, in theory, a possible alternative to the no longer available adjustment via exchange rate changes. However, 'internal devaluation', while it may cause the same deterioration in living standards as the negative change in terms of trade produced by exchange rate devaluation, will probably be perceived as more painful than the latter for psychological reasons (since it requires a reduction of the absolute level of wages and prices), and therefore is more likely to be resisted by workers and producers. In any case, the downward stickiness of nominal remunerations will cause the adjustment to take more time to take effect.

The basic difference between the correction of an external competitive gap vis-à-vis foreign countries via a change in the exchange rate and via 'internal devaluation' is that the first can be made at a stroke, through a simple decision by the national authorities (or, in the case of flexible exchange rates, through the mechanism of supply and demand of foreign exchange), with immediate and inescapable effects on all exporting and import-competing firms operating in the country and with all firms – both the less competitive ones unable to withstand foreign competition and those still quite capable of keeping themselves in the market – being accorded a sudden and equal price advantage in international markets. This will allow many uncompetitive firms to continue or resume exporting, and those that are still competitive to increase their profit margins and/or enlarge their international market shares (while all consumers of foreign goods and all producers relying on non-replaceable foreign inputs will be hit by the income loss and additional cost burden implied by the higher price of imports). On the contrary, correction via 'internal devaluation' leaves the responsibility for the correction to the individual initiative of each firm. The more productive ones, capable of withstanding foreign competition, will not need to make any change in wages, profit rates and prices. The remaining firms may well be aware of the necessity of reducing remunerations and prices; but while some of them may decide to make the correction, they may then try to delay the moment of the actual painful operative decision: some will implement it only gradually; some may still hope to maintain their market share without modifying their costs and prices. In any case, the scope for reducing wages and other remunerations only in the less competitive group of firms of an industrial branch or of the whole industrial sector is usually seriously restricted by the institutional and legal national wage-fixing rules and procedures.

Another psychological factor may make it easier to correct the loss of competitiveness of a country's products through variations in the exchange rate rather than through the direct lowering of factors' remunerations: the depreciation of the flexible exchange rate (or, in a fixed exchange rate system, the exhaustion of the official reserves) represents an irrefutable, visible-to-all, dramatic signal that a country is no more producing competitively and thus acts as an alarm bell, indicating that urgent measures must be taken to improve the mix or the quality of the goods or the technological or organizational level of the productive apparatus. Instead, the loss of national competitiveness that becomes apparent through a process of closures of existing firms, lack of establishment of new ones, increase of unemployment and a reduction in FDI, often takes place gradually and silently, without being raised as a problem until it is often too late, with no strong reactions or debates on the need to take urgent measures to improve competitiveness.

There is a further important difference between correction of a nation's competitive gap through exchange rate devaluation and through 'internal devaluation'. While the first automatically increases by the amount of the devaluation the nominal value in national currency of the external debts denominated in foreign currency, the second leaves their nominal value unchanged.

However, among regions of the same country (but not among euro area member countries at the current level of their political and social integration), other mechanisms are normally at work to reduce the economic and human costs a region must bear to restore trade balance equilibrium by 'internal devaluation'. Some of these mechanisms operate because of the existence of a national government responsible for all regions under its authority. One mechanism is national fiscal policy, through which part of the proceeds of rich regions' taxation can be transferred to the regions undergoing economic decline so as to contain the fall in living standards. Unemployment benefits and other direct or indirect subsidies may be provided to increase residents' incomes; special incentives may be offered to the rich regions' and foreign entrepreneurs to locate productive investments in, or direct their expenditures to, the regions in deficit or declining; infrastructure may be built by the central government to help such regions to increase their productive efficiency and competitiveness. A second mechanism is mobility of labour: as this is usually much higher across regions of the same country than across different countries (even in the absence of legal obstacles), it allows part of the labour force unwilling to accept job losses or cuts in incomes to move to other richer, more dynamic regions in search of better employment. In addition, specific government policies, not implying allocations of public funds, may be activated to direct or incentivize movements of factors towards or out of regions in deficit.

Of course, if a country registers a trade deficit, it means by definition that one or more other countries are registering a trade surplus; so the correction of the trade disequilibrium could take place through the initiative, not of the deficit country, but of the surplus country. The adoption by the latter of a mechanism of 'internal revaluation' would be much easier than the painful one of 'internal devaluation' just described: a surplus country would just need to favour increases in wages and other remunerations, in activity and employment, and in prices. Unfortunately, there are forces that tend to shift responsibility for trade balance adjustment from surplus to deficit countries. Deficit countries usually experience loss of competitiveness, reduction of activity and unemployment, and labour and capital emigration, and these factors at a certain point become unsustainable, making the adoption of radical adjustment measures urgent and inevitable. Instead, surplus countries are usually under no corresponding pressure to adopt expansionary measures to reabsorb their excess of exports over imports, since net external demand (unless the economy has reached its maximum productive capacity) is a welcome stimulus to activity and usually appears preferable to an increase in internal demand; while accumulation of financial claims on another country as a consequence of a positive trade balance, although not without dangers in the long term, creates no immediate problems to the surplus country.

7.2 Problems with re-equilibrating mechanisms

A first problem with the adjustment mechanisms discussed here is that, in order for them to translate comparative advantages into market price differences, they should only enter into operation in reaction to disequilibria in the trade balance. But suppose that items of the balance of payments – different from trade and from those capital movements that are specifically activated by the authorities to pay for difference between imports and exports – such as loans, foreign investments, emigrants' remittances, repatriated profits and foreign aid, are not insignificant or even become the overwhelming component in the supply and demand of international means of payments, as has been the case in the last decades. Then it can easily happen that the re-equilibrating mechanisms (in our times changes in exchange rates) that ensure a country's overall equilibrium in the balance of payments (the equivalence between the total supply of and total demand for international means of payment) do not correspond to – and may indeed move in the opposite direction to – those necessary to re-establish equivalence between exports and imports of goods on the basis of comparative advantage. As a result, trade surpluses and deficits, with their Keynesian positive or negative contribution to national product, may represent not just temporary disequilibria that will be corrected by changes in exchange rates, but a stable characteristic of an economy that may persist for a very long period of time without giving rise to any corrective force.[5]

A simple look at the reality of international economic relations shows that the hypothesis of trade balance equilibrium is empirically untenable: large and permanent imbalances in countries' trade accounts have been a common occurrence in modern history, all the more so since the 1980s.[6] Globalization, having led to practical freedom of international capital movements, has seen the volumes of these movements

---

[5] J. Robinson (1946) noted that in the presence of international capital mobility balances of payments may remain out of equilibrium for long periods. Modern neoclassical models have also been developed that allow for persistent (in some cases even 'permanent' or 'equilibrium') trade and current account imbalances; see Caballero, Farhi and Gourinchas (2008).

At a 1972 World Bank conference, H. G. Johnson (1973), discussing the economic prospects of developing countries, stressed the urgent need to reform the international monetary system so as to find a solution to the malfunctioning of the balance of payments re-equilibrating mechanisms, referring to 'the balance of payments disequilibria that result from a defective set of adjustment mechanisms ... The chronic deficits resulting from a faulty adjustment mechanism induce and are held to justify resort by advanced nations to such devices as 'voluntary' export restrictions, nontariff barriers to trade and controls on capital exports which interfere with the process of diffusion of economic development' (1973, p. 47). Unfortunately, the following fifty years would not see much reform on this front.

[6] In Italy for a very long period (from the late 19th century to the 1920s) large trade balance deficits were recorded that were financed largely by massive inflows of money from temporary and permanent emigrants abroad ('imports being financed by the export of people' as it used to be said). Kaldor (1980) pointed to the chronic trade surpluses already characterizing Germany and Japan by the time he wrote.

An interesting interpretation of persistent trade deficits in our days has recently been advanced by M. C. Klein and Pettis (2020). Developing arguments by Bernanke (2005) and Austin (2011), they argue that the huge and persistent Chinese (and, more recently, German) trade surpluses and, correspondingly, the huge US trade deficit – which are at the basis of the current inter-country trade conflicts – are not fundamentally the result of trade, in the sense of reflecting specific positions of national superiority and inferiority of countries in production capabilities and competitive advantages. This has been the traditional approach of international trade theory, which viewed trade disequilibria as the result of differences in the competitive potential of different countries, necessarily requiring corresponding movements of compensating capital. Rather, the main mechanism works the other way round: an unjust domestic distribution of income and wealth limits the consumption of the majority of the population of surplus countries through containment of wages, pensions and welfare state support (the latter factors explaining, more than cultural attitudes towards thrift and profligacy, the high saving rates in these countries); and when the opportunities for profitable investment at home are exhausted because of the limited domestic demand for consumption, capital is moved abroad (to the USA) and necessarily requires be-

become progressively a very large multiple of the volume of trade transactions. As a result, changes in exchange rates, instead of responding to the need to correct trade disequilibria, are determined primarily by financial transactions; and the latter are driven by a number of specific forces, different from those that determine commercial transactions, such as differences in interest rates and returns on investment, and also expectations, speculative waves and herd behaviour.

With very large and persistent international capital flows that allow a long-lasting disequilibrium between imports and exports, the translation of differences in comparative costs into differences in monetary absolute costs – directing consumers to purchase from each country the products in which it enjoys a comparative advantage – becomes impossible. And with unbalanced trade, the difference between the domestic and foreign prices of a good no longer provides the market signal indicating to firms the need to shift resources from uncompetitive to other more competitive products. Firms can think – often with good reason – that their product cannot stand foreign competition, not because of a real competitive inferiority, but just as a result of particular circumstances or policies that keep the foreign competitors' currency undervalued relative to the exchange rate that would balance trade. As they may consider these circumstances or policies temporary or artificial, and therefore liable to cease operating in the future, they may delay the shift of their resources (which would likely be irreversible) to more competitive lines of production.

The very existence of a persistent trade surplus means by definition that a country is exporting some goods in which it has no comparative advantage. In a flexible exchange rate system, persistent substantial capital inflows may keep a country's exchange rate (the price of its currency in terms of the currency used internationally for trade, say the dollar) higher than the one necessary to keep the trade balance in equilibrium, so that products in which the country has a comparative advantage present themselves on the international market as uncompetitive, starting from those whose comparative advantage is least. In the most extreme case, a country may end up in the paradoxical position of being undersold all round; that is, of not having a single good for which it is competitive, in the sense of being able to offer it on the market at an absolute price lower than that of foreign producers. In this situation, the reasoning, perfectly acceptable once we postulate equilibrium of trade balances, that there is nothing to worry about foreign countries becoming rapidly more competitive since 'if they export more and more to us, they will have to take more and more from us in exchange' no longer applies. And especially when the movements of capital (or other non-trade items) that prevent the exchange rate mechanism from re-establishing trade balance are, or are seen to be, due to specific deliberate decisions of foreign governments or big private agents,[7] the ground is ready for claims that 'they are rob-

ing balanced by huge trade surpluses. The overall conclusion, for the two authors, is that international 'trade wars are class wars' over domestic distribution.

[7] An example may be the policy apparently followed by China of favouring large scale acquisition of foreign firms and other foreign assets with the goal (among others) of helping to keep the exchange rate of the national currency undervalued so as to stimulate exports.

bing us of our jobs' to spread inside a country. And in such cases, as Blecker (2009) observed when referring to US trade with China, displaced workers cannot even take comfort in their jobs having been 'sacrificed on the altar of greater efficiency [produced by the operation of comparative costs]; rather, many of them lost their job due to mismanaged exchange rates as well as macroeconomic and trade policies that do not serve the national interest' (p. 33).

As far back as 1972, in an article in the *New York Times*, Samuelson lucidly identified the problem:

> American public opinion generally is of the firm conviction that America lacks comparative advantage in anything ... The academic economist must be aghast at this turn of public opinion. From the very definition of comparative advantage – repeat *comparative* – the economist maintains it is a logical impossibility for any country to lack comparative advantage in anything. To be sure, by the definition of what economists mean by an overvalued currency, if the dollar is overvalued, then fewer and fewer of our industries will be commercially viable in the comparative advantage sense.
> When that is the case the major premise of the free trader is denied: When workers are displaced from textiles, autos, you name it, it will not be because they've been sucked into a more efficient line of production, but rather that they are pushed into unemployment and onto the dole. (1972)

By way of conclusion Samuelson envisaged the possibility for the USA that 'It would become normal for us to enjoy an unfavourable balance of merchandise trade ... financed by our current invisible items of interest, dividends, repatriated profits and royalties.'

But a second problem with the adjustment mechanisms previously described is that, even if trade transactions were the only ones taking place between nations (with net capital movements only occurring for the purpose of financing trade deficits), their ability to operate in such a way as to restore balance of payments equilibrium is doubtful. As regards the price–specie flow mechanism, Marx had already observed in 1867 that an increase in the inflow of gold into a country, rather than raising the level of prices, would result in an excess of capital, leading to a lowering of the rate of interest and an expansion of credit. As Marx denied that capitalism normally ensures full employment, the availability in the surplus country of more money owing to gold inflows would lead to increased demand and increased production, thus generating a need for the circulation of a larger volume of money and preventing or strongly limiting the general increase of prices envisaged by the quantity theory (the opposite occurring in the case of a gold outflow).[8] Many later economists similarly rejected the simplistic connection between money inflows/outflows and the price level of a country. Harrod (1933) and particularly Keynes (1936) insisted that the main effect of an inflow/outflow of money would be a change in the interest rate, and if

[8] On Marx's view of the adjustment mechanism see Shaikh (1980) and Milberg (1994, 2002).

investments were sensitive to interest rates, the result would be an increase/decrease in investment, production and employment rather than in the level of prices.[9]

* * *

Apart from the price–specie flow – where trade disequilibria would set in motion spontaneous movements in the general price level, in opposite directions, in deficit and surplus countries – all the adjustment mechanisms listed here share the unfair asymmetry of adjustment initiative and adjustment burden that have been described with reference to 'internal devaluation', which allows surplus countries not to take upon themselves, nor even to contribute to, the correction of trade disequilibria. Just think of fixed exchange rate systems, where the exhaustion of foreign exchange reserves may force a country to devalue, while the progressive accumulation of reserves exerts little pressure on surplus countries (which can sterilize the possible inflationary effects of inflows of money) to appreciate their currency.

This asymmetry was at the centre of Keynes's theoretical thinking and practical policymaking, as he saw it imposing a pernicious contractionary bias on the international economic system. When, as World War II was approaching its end, he was charged with the task of advancing proposals for a new post-war international monetary and trade system that would prevent the disputes and conflicts that had plagued the interwar period, he put forward in 1944 a scheme that would compel deficit and surplus countries to equitably share the costs of adjustment. The scheme envisaged a mechanism of sanctions against countries experiencing stable trade surpluses and special credit facilities for countries in temporary deficit. Unfortunately, Keynes's plan had little success, as it was turned down by the USA: emerging from the war as the new hegemonic world power, the Americans worked for an arrangement that would guarantee them maximum freedom to follow their own monetary and trade strategies.[10]

While Keynes rejected, in the presence of persistent unemployment, any trade balance re-equilibrating mechanism based on prices or wages, he introduced a mecha-

---

[9] Keynes's opposition to free international capital movements was based on his belief that control of the rate of interest by national monetary authorities was an essential tool for a full employment policy. His disciple J. Robinson (1946) held that it could be doubted whether a decrease in interest rate in surplus countries receiving money inflows would have an effect on investments: first because such inflows could mainly affect the short-term interest rate and not the long-term one important for investments, and second, because investments may not be reactive to changes in interest rates.

Of course the increase in interest rates in the deficit country will tend to attract capital from abroad. Since these capital inflows can continue for protracted periods, persistent trade deficits will also be possible. But while these capital transfers will help cover the trade deficit, they will not by themselves produce the correction of the structural causes of the trade imbalance; the more likely result will simply be the creation of a problem of rising external indebtedness.

[10] On Keynes's proposals for the post-war international monetary order see Davidson (2007). A scheme that recalls Keynes's plan – called Macroeconomic Imbalance Procedure – was introduced by the EU in 2011 to prevent and correct excessive macroeconomic imbalances – including current account disequilibria – within the Union.

nism for the correction of trade balance disequilibria completely different from those on which the comparative costs principle is based, as it relied on changes, not in prices, but in national income and employment. As he considered a country's exports exogenously given and imports a fixed proportion of national income, a country with a persistent trade deficit will come to a point where, having exhausted all sources of external financing, it will be compelled to reduce its production and income to a level generating an import flow low enough to balance that of its exports. A surplus country, on the contrary, will see its income grow until the level of its imports rises enough to equal that of its exports (on the Keynesian mechanism of trade balance re-equilibrium see Machlup (1943)).

J. Robinson (1946) held that the income mechanism would be reinforced by a wage mechanism, as the growth in activity and employment in surplus countries would tend to increase their workers' wages, making its products less competitive, with the opposite occurring in deficit countries.[11]

As anticipated in Chapter 6, with the removal of the full employment and trade balance equilibrium assumptions and the introduction of the Keynesian adjustment mechanism, the whole nature of international economic relations changes. Trade no longer automatically ensures benefits to all participating countries with only possible inequalities in the way they are shared. It can now become either a mechanism for the transmission from country to country of powerful stimuli to growth and employment (as a country growing rapidly generates a demand for imports from other countries), or the instrument through which countries with insufficient levels of effective demand try to shift onto other countries the burden of unemployment by stimulating exports through fiscal incentives and other measures designed to increase their competitiveness. The effects of trade policy decisions are therefore no longer limited to extending or reducing the static benefits of international specialization, but influence – both directly through changes in import and export demand, and possibly indirectly through the influence of monetary inflows/outflows on interest rates – the level of activity, employment and welfare of a country and all its trading partners.

While traditional international economists conceive countries' growth as constrained by resources, which they postulate fully employed, and look at foreign trade as a way to increase income through greater international specialization according to comparative advantages, Keynes and his followers – reviving Smith's conception of trade and development – thought that usually countries' growth is not resource-constrained; rather they held that higher aggregate demand is the force that can push a country to fully utilize its resources and then to use more productively and increase these resources. In such a situation, countries will look to exports as the best way to enlarge the volume of demand, since export expansion also allows them to over-

[11] J. Robinson (1973) also referred to the wage mechanism as a way to save logically Ricardo's international adjustment mechanism based on prices without having to accept the quantity theory of money. In the case of near-full employment and trade balance equilibrium in a country, an increase in exports and consequent trade surplus would generate excess demand for labour, driving up costs and prices, thus reducing the competitive advantage of the country.

come the balance of payments growth constraint (the necessity of having international means of payment to pay for the higher imports connected with higher income levels);[12] so they are deeply involved in a competitive struggle to increase their international market share.

To avoid beggar-my-neighbour policies (such as wage cuts or competitive devaluations) that countries may adopt in this struggle, Keynes and his followers insisted on the necessity of higher levels of international cooperation and policy coordination so as to establish rules and mechanisms that would allow all countries participating in international trade to adopt more expansionary domestic policies, overcoming the limits posed by the balance of payments constraint.

* * *

Going back to the adjustment mechanisms operating through prices, it must be underlined that not only the price–specie flow, but also those mechanisms based on variations in exchange rates (exceptional variations of fixed exchange rates and flexible exchange rates) do not necessarily guarantee trade balance re-equilibrium (even in the absence of non-trade transactions). The effect of a devaluation in a country is to make imports more expensive for its citizens in domestic currency, so they will diminish the physical volume of their foreign purchases; while the prices in domestic currency of the goods they produce will now translate into prices in foreign currencies cheaper by the amount of the devaluation. Consequently, foreigners will increase their purchases and domestic producers will collect from the larger quantity of exports an increased amount in receipts, in terms of domestic currency. But as payments for imports will have to be effected in international currency, say dollars, using the receipts from export sales, let us see what happens to the trade balance in terms of dollars. The total import expenditure in dollars will certainly diminish, as imports are now more expensive when translated into national currency, so their quantity will be reduced. As for exports, if their price is fixed in terms of national currency their physical volume will certainly increase as they now become cheaper for foreign purchasers, but exporters will receive fewer dollars than before for each unit sold abroad: for the total value of exports in dollars to go up, their physical volume must increase by a percentage greater than that of the decrease in dollar prices owing to devaluation (that is, the price elasticity of foreign demand must be higher than 1). If this is not the case, the decrease in export earnings in dollars may be greater than the decrease in import dollar expenditures, and the trade balance may continue to deteriorate.

Alternatively, especially for standardized goods (such as raw materials) whose international price is determined on the world market, the devaluing country's exporters may continue to offer their goods to other countries at the prevailing international dollar price,[13] not expecting to sell additional quantities of the good, but receiving for

[12] On the balance of payments constraint see McCombie and Thirlwall (2004).

[13] In this case it is said that there is no 'pass-through' to foreign consumers of the advantage of de-

each unit exported a sum in national currency greater than before by the amount of the devaluation, thus realizing larger profits; but the country's total dollar export receipts will not increase, unless the greater profitability of exports pushes producers to a special effort to enlarge the physical volume of their sales in foreign markets. If imports consist of goods whose demand is not price-elastic (such as essential consumption goods or productive inputs not producible at home) the improvement in the trade balance may be too small to produce a significant correction of the deficit.[14] Overall, while theoretically the results of devaluations/depreciations on the trade balance are indeterminate, the experience of the last four decades seems to indicate that empirically their effectiveness in improving the trade balance is not certain. And while before 1973 the Bretton Woods system of fixed – and only exceptionally changing – exchange rates was held responsible for the misalignments of countries' price levels that produced trade disequilibria, the following period of flexible exchange rates has in fact seen these disequilibria grow in both size and persistence.

But there is a more fundamental criticism that can be levelled against all the traditional balance of payments re-equilibrium mechanisms based on the realignment of national costs and prices: they presume that a country can always increase the physical volume of its exports of the goods where its comparative advantage lies, if only it allows market mechanisms to lower sale prices down to the required level (the opposite happening in the case of price increases). This may take place through exchange rate devaluation/depreciation, a general lowering of the national price level or 'internal devaluation'. The problem with this presumption is that it often does not correspond to the working of the real world, for two basic reasons. The first is that in the contemporary economy, as is well known, both domestic and international competition are based not so much on price as on other factors, such as quality, reliability, technological superiority, brand attraction and so on (the basic role of non-price competition and technology in international trade was addressed in Chapters 4 and 5).[15]

The second reason, of great importance for developing economies, is that countries with severe trade deficit problems are very often poor countries with very low

---

valuation. The experience of recent decades shows that in practice partial pass-through is the prevailing practice in devaluing countries' export pricing.

[14] What precedes is summarized by the Marshall-Lerner condition, according to which a devaluation improves the trade balance of a country if the sum of the price elasticities of imports and exports is higher than 1. To what extent this condition is satisfied in practice depends on the specific situation of the devaluing country and also on the time horizon one is considering (as reactions to changes in prices of traded goods take time to produce their full effects).

[15] As Posner and Steer (1979) reported, 'There is another strand in the attack on the traditional exchange-rate mechanism. This is the suggestion that changes in cost or price competitiveness delay the true adjustment mechanism, or featherbed inefficiency and old-fashioned producers to the disadvantage of dynamic ones ... The implications are that a country faced with declining traditional markets and insufficient innovatory investment should concentrate on improving its rate of innovation, not on protecting (by lowering international real wages) traditional exporting trades. However, for that benign process to work there has to be a mobility of resources between activities and a responsiveness of innovators to the increased availability of these resources' (p. 144).

levels of productivity. If they open their borders to more competitive foreign products, many of these will be imported and easily supplant the corresponding goods produced domestically, with a benefit to consumers in terms of price and quality and a cost to the country in terms of factors of production losing their employment. Comparative costs theory tells us that the initial trade deficit will trigger one or more of the trade balance re-equilibrium mechanisms, producing, for the goods in which the country has a comparative advantage, a decrease in their international price and an increase in their export volume. But serious objections can be advanced here.

First, the reduction of domestic factors' real remunerations necessary to induce the required competitiveness of exports may imply for poor countries a wage level below the workers' physical survival threshold. Second, traditional trade theory presupposes that a productive structure is already in place in a country and that the correction of trade deficits simply requires adjustments in relative prices, while in fact the minimum economic, organizational and institutional framework necessary to allow unemployed factors of production to be utilized in, or switched to, additional or new export products (availability of entrepreneurs and skilled workers, responsiveness of economic agents to market opportunities, transport and communication facilities, distribution and advertising channels, banking institutions, legal system and a minimum of political stability, for example) may not exist, precluding the necessary supply response. Moreover, as underlined by Banerjee and Duflo (2019), even when the supply response is possible, problems of reliability, reputation and trust between producers and customers may hinder additional exports. Third, any product offered nowadays on the world market (and particularly on the advanced countries' markets) – unless we speak of raw materials – must satisfy certain minimum standards of quality, technology and safety that many developing countries are unable to meet (this point was stressed by Fitzgerald and Perosino (1999) and later by Bliss (2007)). As was often the case in the past with the USSR and the European communist countries, developing economies may prove unable to offer any single manufactured product on the international market that is acceptable even to the least demanding, poorest categories of consumers (especially in advanced and middle-income countries). In this situation, a country may end up being uncompetitive all round, and have as alternatives isolation (which guarantees a forced domestic outlet for low-productivity low-quality national products), drastic reduction of its growth rate so as to reduce imports to a minimum, large-scale emigration providing a constant flow of remittances to the population remaining in the country, or progressive accumulation of external debts.[16]

---

[16] The same factors mentioned here to explain why the export supply reaction envisaged by trade theory is likely not to take place in practice in the poorest developing countries also explain why international capital movements do not choose these countries as their favourite destination, despite the fact that in theory returns to the factor capital should be highest in the countries where this factor is in particularly low supply. Most capital moving to developing countries is directed to a small number of middle-income high-growth countries, where the conditions for acceptably normal productive activity are present.

8 The Return of Absolute Advantage

The preceding chapters have shown how international mobility of capital and trade balance disequilibria, factor unemployment, and imperfect labour mobility within countries can prevent, or greatly distort, the working of the adjustment mechanisms that would allow international trade to be regulated by the principle of comparative advantage (even a staunch supporter of free trade such as Irwin (2017) had to remind us, celebrating the 200 years since Ricardo's formulation of that principle, that 'many ancillary assumptions that economists take for granted – such as labour mobility, full employment, flexible wages and prices, balanced trade, and so forth – are needed for it to fully make sense' (p. 10)). Since the 1980s these conditions proved not to be particular or temporary deviations from normal economic life, but persistent characteristics of many national economies, frequently preventing the translation of countries' comparative advantages into absolute prices of their exported goods that are lower, for the purchasers in foreign countries, than those of the same goods these purchasers can buy from domestic producers. In addition, it has increasingly been realized that trade in new and high-tech goods and services – the most dynamic component of contemporary trade – does not respond to the comparative advantage principle, since many of these products cannot be produced at all by many countries and, in any case, are not demanded and exported on the basis of lower price, but fundamentally on the basis of other elements, such as better quality, superior technology and brand.

The comparative advantage principle was based on the difference in the domestic exchange ratio between cloth and wine in England and Portugal before trade: if 1 metre of cloth is exchanged in England for 1 litre of wine, while in Portugal it is exchanged for 5 litres, trade between the two countries will develop if obstacles to international exchange are abolished, because both parties will gain from it, provided it takes place at an exchange ratio between cloth and wine intermediate between the two domestic ratios. If the exchange ratio between cloth and wine before trade happens to be the same in the two countries, no trade based on comparative advantage can occur, as it would produce no advantage to any of the parties. However, international trade in modern market economies does not take place in the form of barter, but through the use of money. And different countries, contrary to what happens to regions of the same country (or to those European nations that adopt the euro), do not use the same currency, but different ones, independently managed, between which an exchange rate is established.

What happens is that each country exports those goods that, at the current exchange rate (determined by the many forces – trade flows being only one of them – that influence the overall demand for and supply of the national currency), have a price in international money, say dollars, lower than that of its competitors. This price will reflect to a large extent the cost of production (in real terms, that is in terms of a given bundle of basic goods and services) of a unit of the good in the country; a cost that, in turn, will be determined by the price (always in real terms) of the domestic production factors (having a given degree of productivity) employed for the production of the good. A major element determining the cost and price of most goods produced in a country is the cost of labour (referred, again, in real terms, to equally productive workers). Consequently, for many traded goods the unit cost of labour – the cost of labour per unit of output – will be a basic determinant of a country's international competitiveness.

In many countries, particularly developing or former communist ones, the unit cost of labour is much lower than in other countries. This can be because the national average real wage is kept at a survival level by a particularly low productivity of a large subsistence agriculture sector and/or by high unemployment and underemployment; or because – as happened in Eastern European countries, where capital and high-skill labour were abundantly available – the organizational deficiencies and the technological backwardness of the economic system led to an inefficient use of the workforce and other factors of production, and consequently to low real income per capita and real wages; or it may be because a country adopted a specific policy of containment of the real cost of labour. In these cases, it can happen that a country, once it manages to develop domestically or receive from abroad up-to-date technology and organizational and managerial systems, can offer at a very low price in international money – and thus enjoy an absolute advantage in the production and export of – a large number of goods, registering a persistent trade surplus. Another country, or other countries, will correspondingly register persistent deficits (at the limit, finding themselves outcompeted all round; that is, left without any good they can export), provided they can pay for imports with funds previously accumulated or received in the form of loans or capital inflows from the surplus country. But there is more than that.

It is very important to consider that if the monetary mechanisms that allow the translation of comparative advantages into lower prices for the foreign purchaser do not operate, not only does trade not respond to the principle of comparative advantages, but it may well take place in the particular situation in which, according to that principle, it could not occur because it would not produce to the trading countries any specialization benefit: when the two countries present, in autarchy, the same relative cost of the two goods. In this situation, it can well happen that the country with a lower general wage and price level will enjoy an absolute advantage in, and will export, both goods despite the absence of any comparative advantage.

The result of all the factors considered here is that we seem to be back to Adam Smith, as the determination of international trade specialization responds, to a large extent, to the same principle of absolute advantage that regulates trade within countries.

8.1 Adam Smith's theory of trade and specialization

Contrary to the Ricardian theory of comparative advantage, Adam Smith in his 1776 *The Wealth of Nations* applied the same principle that he used for domestic trade to explain the nature and benefits of foreign trade: the advantages of the division of labour obtained through the widening of the market for the goods a country can produce. While according to the RHO model it makes no difference what kind of goods a country specializes in, for Smith the scope for the application of the division of labour was much greater for manufactured goods than for agricultural goods; therefore, a country specializing internationally in manufactures would experience higher productivity growth than a country specializing in agriculture.

Referring to the famous example of the pin factory, Smith stressed the increase in the productive capacity of workers that comes from having each of them specialize in specific tasks of the production process of a good. He saw these advantages of specialization as flowing from three sources: the improvements in dexterity of each worker as he concentrates on fewer specific tasks; the saving of the time lost in passing from one type of work to another when the same worker has to perform different tasks; and the rise in productivity through inventions made by workers specializing in specific tasks.[1] Since the division of labour that allows static and dynamic increasing returns, and therefore economic growth, is limited for Smith by the size of the market, it follows that foreign trade, by increasing the number of potential purchasers of a given good and the maximum attainable scale of production, is a powerful factor contributing to greater national productivity and wealth.[2] But for Smith free

---

[1] A basic limit of Smith's analysis must be pointed out here. As Young (1928) remarked, 'It is generally agreed that Adam Smith, when he suggested that the division of labour leads to inventions because workmen engaged in specialised routine operations come to see better ways of accomplishing the same results, missed the main point. The important thing, of course, is that with the division of labour a group of complex processes is transformed into a succession of simpler processes, some of which, at least, lend themselves to the use of machinery' (p. 530). Blaug (1985) came back to this point, noting that when Smith speaks of the invention of machines, he gives the example of innovations dating back to the Middle Ages, but does not mention the basic innovations of his time that revolutionized industry. According to Blaug, the explanation for Smith's failure to anticipate the Industrial Revolution is the fact that it was only just after Smith's death that the machines incorporating the new inventions were introduced in factories, producing a sharp increase in industrial output (the issue had been the object of specific analysis by Koebner (1959)).

[2] A fundamental advance in the analysis of the advantages of the division of labour that took place after Smith was produced by Babbage (1832). He provided an insight that is extremely illuminating for the study of today's processes of international production fragmentation (discussed in Section 11.1.4). Babbage argued that 'any explanation of the cheapness of manufactured articles, as consequent upon the division of labour, would be incomplete if the following principle were omitted to be stated. *That the master manufacturer, by dividing the work to be executed into different processes, each requiring different degrees of skill or of force, can purchase exactly that precise quantity of both which is necessary for each process; whereas, if the whole work were executed by one workman, that person must possess sufficient skill to perform the most difficult, and sufficient strength to execute the most laborious, of the operations into which the art is divided.*' (1832, pp. 137–138). Babbage specified that after

foreign trade also has other important positive effects on productivity and growth (in addition to the possible vent it offers to goods or resources not demanded domestically, discussed in Section 6.1): it transmits knowledge and technology between trading countries,[3] reduces the scope for monopolistic practices and, by enlarging the area and strength of competition among producers, stimulates them to exploit the opportunities provided by economies of scale and specialization and to devise new and better products and production processes.[4]

G. B. Richardson (1975) analysed Smith's views on competition and the way in which, thanks to his dynamic conception of the production process, he managed to find compatibility between the two basic drivers of economic development – competition and increasing returns to scale – overcoming the problem, discussed in Chapter 3, of scale economies internal to the firm logically leading to monopolistic positions. According to Richardson, Smith was not worried – as Sraffa said of the economists

---

developing his analysis of the subject, he had discovered that the Italian economist Gioja had advanced the same principle in his *Nuovo prospetto delle scienze economiche*, published in Milan in 1815.

However, in addition to the size of the market that creates the conditions for an increased division of labour, another factor is necessary in Smith's theory for progress in productivity and economic growth to take place, namely the accumulation of productive capital, as the division of labour can only advance in proportion to the pre-existing capital accumulation. On this point, and more generally on the nature of Smithian growth, see Lavezzi (2003). R. Chandra (2004) recalled that there is no agreement among scholars on whether the division of labour or capital accumulation represents the central element in Smith's theory of growth.

Smith also stressed the importance of transportation efficiency in determining the size of the market. The latter would be larger the more efficient the transportation means, the higher the value of a good relative to its volume and the less perishable the good.

For an account of Smith's conception of the division of labour that is not so concise (and therefore inevitably superficial) as the preceding one see Groenewegen (1977).

[3] Quite prophetically, Smith remarked that although China was so large, populated and endowed with good communications that even in isolation it could establish manufacturing industries fully exploiting the division of labour, it would very much profit from international commerce, as 'more extensive foreign trade … could scarce fail … to improve very much the productive powers of its manufacturing industry … The Chinese would naturally learn the art of using and constructing themselves all the different machines made use of in other countries, as well as the other improvements of art and industry which are practised in all the different parts of the world' (Smith, 1961, Book IV, Ch. IX, p. 202).

[4] 'That by a more plentiful supply, to the great advantage and conveniency of the public, [competition] must have reduced, very much, the price of Indian goods in the English market, cannot well be doubted... The increase of demand, besides, though in the beginning it may sometimes raise the price of goods, never fails to lower it in the long run. It encourages production, and thereby increases the competition of the producers, who, in order to undersell one another, have recourse to new divisions of labour and new improvements of art, which might never otherwise have been thought of' (Smith, 1961, Book V, Ch. I, pp. 271–272).

Regarding competition, there is, however, a passage in *The Wealth of Nations* (Book I, Ch. IX, pp. 104–105) where Smith states that, taken as given the stock of capital of a country, the opening of new large trade opportunities (such as the acquisition of new territories or of new branches of trade) may produce a decrease in competition, since part of the existing capital would be shifted to these more profitable trade activities, reducing competitive pressure and increasing prices and profits in the old ones. Ricardo did not agree with this statement: see Depoortère and Ravix (2015).

of his time, clearly referring to Marshall – about scale economies leading to monopoly, because he expected competition to push manufacturers to seek out, develop and exploit the opportunities offered by scale economies and increasing specialization; and in the process new products, new implements, new production processes would continuously be developed, opening new fields to enterprise and competition (R. Chandra (2004), instead, pointed to the fact that Smith lived at a time when industrial capitalism had just begun and the size of firms was so small as not to raise worries about the possible development of monopolies based on scale economies). On the contrary, for equilibrium analysis based on the RHO model with given production techniques and given goods, increasing returns internal to the firm could only be expected to lead to concentration and finally monopoly. Chamberlain's introduction of monopolistic competition in different varieties of the same good made it possible to keep a degree of competition among producers, each subject to scale economies; but his theory retained a static character. According to G. B. Richardson, in a renovated Smithian perspective, with a huge market embracing the entire world, it might be envisaged that producers, not of goods, but of activities requiring specific capabilities, would have enough room to choose some subset of their activities so that specialization and interdependence rather than straightforward concentration would result from internal scale economies.

The positive dynamic effects of international competition on firms' performance highlighted by Smith have been considered of fundamental importance in recent decades – see J. D. Richardson (2001) and Baumol (2002) – and were particularly stressed by the advocates of contemporary globalization. They have certainly produced much larger advantages to trading nations than the static ones consequent on better allocation of resources owing to specialization according to comparative costs (which, according to the estimates of Costinot and Rodríguez-Clare (2018) for the USA, are more modest than commonly thought); this applies especially to the countries where strong monopolies and oligopolies had developed owing to the limited extension of the national market in sectors characterized by large-scale economies. However, as indicated in Section 9.2, after a first phase in which globalization led to increased competition, a tendency in the opposite direction seems to have been at work.

Strangely enough, the positive effects of international competition seem to have been overlooked by both orthodox post-Smith economists until recent decades – with the notable exception of J. S. Mill (see Mill (1909, p. 793)) – and by Keynes. For the former, there were probably three reasons. First, they postulated the existence of these effects through the very hypothesis of perfect competition: if competition is supposed 'perfect', it would be meaningless to analyse how it is made more or less strong by developments in international trade relations. Second, the hypothesis of given and everywhere available goods and productions techniques in the standard RHO model excluded taking account of dynamic factors, such as the Schumpeterian creation and diffusion of technological innovations fostered by competition (the development, since the 1980s, of the endogenous growth theory would very much change this perspective). Third, they believed in the comparative costs principle, which ensures that a country, whatever the level of its productivity and efficiency vis-à-vis other countries, will always find some goods to export in exchange for its imports (the goods where its relative inferiority is smaller): this, as indicated in Chapter 1, makes international competition, at the level of a country, a much less severe threat to production levels and employment than, at the firm level, the threat of an enterprise being eliminated by more efficient competitors. A possible fourth reason could be that, in RHO logic, specialization is basically determined by factor availabilities, and international competitiveness created by other elements has only a secondary role to play. Fagerberg (1996) argued that the point was not emphasized by neoclassical economists because their theory did not attribute much importance to trade as a growth-promoting factor and because gains from trade were considered once-and-for-all gains and found to be empirically limited.

As for Keynes, not only did he not dwell on the positive effects of international competition; in 1933 he even wrote in the *Yale Review* an article in favour of 'National Self-Sufficiency': 'I am inclined to the belief that ... a greater measure of national self-sufficiency and economic isolation between countries than existed in 1914 may tend to serve the cause of peace, rather than otherwise. At any rate, the age of economic internationalism was not particularly successful in avoiding war' (Keynes 1982, p. 237). He was referring not only to international trade, but also possibly even more to international capital movements. Apart from his conviction of the decreasing importance of the benefits of international specialization in modern times (which will be discussed in Section 8.2.1) this statement reflected, on the one hand, his concentration on the dramatic short-term economic problems of the 1930s, when greater self-sufficiency would have facilitated the pursuance of autonomous national monetary and fiscal policies to sustain employment; and, on the other, the experience of international trade both in the period of economic liberalism preceding World War I (when growing economic exchanges among countries did not prevent the conflict's outbreak) and, especially, in the years between the two world wars in which he developed his economic thinking. These interwar years were a period in which problems of competition in international trade produced the most serious negative effects, as they were one of the sources of the recurrent, acute international disputes and conflicts that finally led to the outbreak of World War II.[5]

These interwar trade clashes and the adoption of restrictive commercial measures by all developed countries also underlay the negative attitudes towards development strategies based on export expansion, widespread after the war among development economists and leaders of newly independent Third World countries. It was not un-

[5] In 1936 Keynes wrote in the *General Theory*: 'But if nations can learn to provide themselves with full employment by their domestic policy ... International trade would cease to be what it is, namely, a desperate expedient to maintain employment at home by forcing sales on foreign markets and restricting purchases, which, if successful, would merely shift the problem of unemployment to the neighbour...' (p. 382).

Keynes's 1933 article on 'national self-sufficiency' has been the specific object of one issue of *L'Économie Politique* (2006), in which French economists have reconsidered the article in the light of contemporary globalization.

reasonable at the time to anticipate little scope for relying on a revival of world trade and to refuse to entrust the process of economic development to outward-looking strategies whose success depended on advanced countries' unforeseeable trade policy choices. This consideration, together with the conviction that only the creation of modern industry could take Third World countries out of underdevelopment, led most of these countries to pursue import substitution policies. A balanced assessment of the experience with these policies – which was not so negative as commonly reported – is provided by Bruton (1998) and Rodrik (2001).

* * *

Smith managed, much more than Ricardo, to identify and shed new light on the dynamic aspects of development and trade (such as increasing returns, technological progress, learning by doing and enlargement of the scope of economic competition) that appear to have been at the root of the transformation of the world economy in the last two centuries, and particularly in recent decades, so he offers a much better guide to understanding today's ever-changing international economic environment.[6] Of course, he failed to formulate the principle of comparative advantage, although, as pointed out by Elmslie and A. M. James (1993), he once hinted at a mechanism very close to that principle when he mentioned the international exchange of manufactures against agricultural products.[7]

---

[6] Schumacher (2012a) has provided an extensive comparison of Smith's and Ricardo's theories of international trade, in which the differences between them are stressed. On Smith's foreign trade theory see also Blecker (1997) and Schumacher (2016a, 2020). In these last works, Schumacher advances the argument that when Smith emphasized the role of foreign trade in contributing to increase the size of the market, thereby allowing greater division of labour, he was not referring (contrary to Ricardo), to 'territorial' specialization, in the sense that countries could be expected to become exclusive producers for the whole international market of those goods for which they enjoyed absolute advantages (a situation, by the way, that would suffocate competition as each country would become a world monopolist in its most efficient types of production); this was how Smith's foreign trade theory was interpreted by subsequent international economists. Smith was referring to something different, namely to the 'mechanical' division of labour; that is, to the fact that a larger market allows producers to increase their production volumes and thus enlarge the scope for division of labour and specialization of workers in the production process that takes place inside the firm, and for greater diversification of national production. Schumacher reminds us that for Smith international trade, because of high transport costs, would involve, rather than agricultural and coarse industrial goods, relatively sophisticated manufactured commodities. Thus trade would predominantly regard rich, more industrially advanced countries, exchanging, in a highly competitive environment, fine goods in whose production they could exploit the advantages of specialization (but without international specialization taking place in different industrial sectors). Smith has been credited with anticipating modern theories of intra-industry ('horizontal') specialization and trade.

[7] In Book I, Ch. 1 of *The Wealth of Nations* Smith noted that, since scale economies were an important characteristic of manufacturing but not of agriculture, a rich nation usually has a much higher labour productivity in manufacturing than a poor nation, while in agriculture its superiority is not significant. In these cases the poor country can export agricultural products to the rich one, in line with the principle of comparative advantage. But the mechanism turning the poor country's comparative advantage in agriculture into an absolute price advantage is not, as later in Ricardo, the 'price–specie flow'. It

Greater adherence to reality of Smith's foreign trade theory is especially marked when one compares it with the highly restrictive hypotheses on which Ricardo's comparative costs principle is based. Smith did not postulate perfect mobility of factors (capital and labour) inside a country – either between different areas or between different employments – and total immobility of factors between countries.[8] Nor did he assume equilibrium in the trade balance or the working of an automatic adjustment mechanism such as Hume's price–specie flow, based on the quantity theory of money, described in Section 7.1 (see Schumacher (2016b) and Curott (2016) for a discussion of Smith's unclear position on Hume's mechanism). As to the level of utilization of productive factors, Smith did not accept Say's law (the principle that supply creates its own demand),[9] to which Ricardo and neoclassical economists adhered, and so did not postulate full factor employment. He did not see the level of production as constrained by resources, but rather, as later Keynes, by the level of demand, which is determined by the size of the market. International trade, by expanding the market for the goods in which a country has an absolute advantage, allows greater employment of that country's labour and capital, makes it possible to apply more productive production processes, increases workers' skills and stimulates inventions and technical innovations (for Ricardo, differences in productivity between countries do not change after they specialize). Since it gives rise to such dynamic gains, international trade was seen by Smith as a central element in the process of economic de-

---

is instead a mechanism based on the possibility for the poor country to overcome the slight inferiority in absolute agricultural efficiency through a small reduction of the agricultural worker's wage level. Maneschi (2009) also credits Smith with anticipating the theory of comparative advantage.

In the rest of his work Smith advances a general rule regulating international trade – the same rule that regulates the division of labour inside a country, or a region, or between individuals – according to which: 'If a foreign country can supply us with a commodity cheaper than we ourselves can make it, better buy it of them with some part of the produce of our own industry employed in a way in which we have some advantage' (Smith 1961, Book IV, Ch. 2, p. 478). This is basically the same rule as that called by Viner's (1937) the 'eighteenth-century rule' (p. 440) put forward as early as 1701 by Henry Martyn in the anonymous *Considerations on the East-India Trade*, according to which it is beneficial for a country to import goods from abroad whenever they can be obtained in exchange for exports whose production entails a smaller real cost than the production at home of the amount of goods imported (Maneschi (1998) noted that in fact the concept had already been introduced by S. Fortray in 1673). Ricardo also referred to this rule and incorporated it in his formulation of the principle of comparative advantage. Viner (1937) went as far as to declare that 'The doctrine of comparative costs is, indeed, but a statement of some of the implications of this rule, and adds nothing to it as a guide for policy' (p. 440). On the relationship between Ricardo's comparative advantage and the 'eighteenth-century rule' see Morales Meoqui (2012).

[8] Williams (1929) held that it was Ricardo's perfect domestic mobility of factors hypothesis, more than that of their international immobility, that was hardly acceptable at the time it was formulated. In the times of Smith and Ricardo (before the railway revolution), the state of internal transport in many countries made domestic movement of goods and factors more difficult than international seaborne movements between large economic centres.

[9] The principle was developed by Say in 1803, based on the belief that the incomes producers receive from the sale of their goods are immediately spent in the purchase of goods produced by other producers.

velopment of the countries producing manufactured products. Factors of production are not given and fixed exogenously, giving rise to international trade flows; rather, countries can increase their quantity and quality (even apart from movement from other countries, capital can be produced and workers can be educated and acquire skills),[10] so that the availability of factors is itself the result of international trade and development.

Smith's dynamic view of the trade–growth nexus was largely ignored by mainstream international trade theory until recently. The RHO model of comparative advantage enjoyed practically universal recognition as the centrepiece of trade theory and all previous contributions were viewed merely as building blocks of that model. In this distorted perspective, Smith's contribution was inevitably minimized, being reduced to the principle of absolute advantage – see Schumacher (2012b) – but in formulating this principle Smith, as indicated in Footnote 7, did not go much beyond the 'eighteenth-century rule' of 1701. Smith's view of the trade–productivity–growth nexus, in which trade endogenously leads to dynamic gains of technological progress and productivity growth, is incomparably more advanced and helpful in explaining modern world economic dynamics than the RHO model, which views productivity differences between countries in different activities, factor availabilities and countries' growth trajectories as remaining unaffected by international specialization, and, when taken into account, treats dynamic changes and technical progress as exogenously produced.[11]

Smith's theory, viewing trade and specialization as dynamic processes strictly connected to the unpredictable evolution of scale economies, technological progress and general economic development, made the future directions of trade flows more uncertain. The Ricardian, and even more the HO theories, with their static framework based on given resource availabilities and given technologies, had the advantage of allowing greater predictability of trade patterns. In Smith's theory, uncertainty also increased for another reason: considering foreign trade as an essential element in a process of development leading to progressive changes in the whole structure of the economy, his theory does not allow reversibility of decisions regarding resources allocation once a country has decided to open to international trade. On the contrary, in the RHO static world (with no economies of scale, no learning by doing, no

[10] The availability of labour is determined for Smith by the needs of production and capital accumulation: 'the demand for men, like that for any other commodity, necessarily regulates the production of men' (Smith 1961, Book I, Ch. VIII, p. 89). As capital accumulation normally increases labour productivity and the volume of production, it leads to greater demand for labour and therefore to wage increases; the resulting improvement in workers' conditions stimulates marriage and a larger number of children.

[11] Actually Ohlin, in the 1967 Appendix to his 1933 work, did recognize that 'international trade affects not only the use of the factors of production but also their *supply* – both quantities and qualities…' (1967, p. 313), but still his basic theory left this aspect aside. He also explicitly recognized that 'if one wants to examine how an increase in international trade – brought about through a radical reduction of the trade obstacles, for instance – affects the national income and factor prices, use of the proportions model and the 'terms of trade model' is not very fruitful. This is *a development through time*' (1967, p. 314).

technology changes, no fixed costs for starting or closing export activities, no time dimension), international specialization can be completely reversed at any moment, merely at the cost of losing the benefits of the better static allocation of resources it produces.

While stressing the beneficial effects of international trade and specialization, Smith, by holding that foreign trade is subject to the same logic as domestic trade, represented international trade as a competitive struggle in which there can be winning and losing producers (though he did not mention the possibility of countries as a whole losing from trade). This conception contrasted with that of Ricardo, who viewed free trade as a harmonious international division of labour based on comparative advantage, whereby all countries, no matter how low their level of development and productivity, are by definition competitive in some lines of production (those in which their inferiority is less marked).

What, according to Smith, determines countries' absolute advantage in the production of certain goods? It may be either natural or acquired elements. Among the first he cited soil and climate, as well as locational and communication advantages. He also underlined the importance of laws and institutions. But apart from availability of specific natural resources, it is the very process of the division of labour inside a nation that, by giving rise to higher productivity in the activities in which citizens have happened to concentrate in their historical development path, leads to different national specializations (which, however, may always change with time). These specializations are the basis for, and tend to reinforce, cost advantages in foreign trade; but it is trade itself that, by extending the market, creates new scope for improvements in productivity and technology and thus, in turn, for new international specializations. 'Natural' superior abilities of individuals, regions or countries in certain activities play a very small role in Smith's trade theory.[12] It is amazing how such a view of the division of labour anticipates the most recent trends in international trade literature that, while acknowledging the frequently random origin of countries' specializations, stress the importance of subsequent processes of path dependence, virtuous and vicious circles, technological trajectories and geographical concentration effects to explain the consolidation of these specializations.

To Ricardo, the explanation of the origins of absolute productive superiority of countries in given goods does not seem to be of great importance. What he was interested in was explaining the logic of the principle of comparative advantage (thus

---

[12] 'The difference of natural talents in different men is, in reality, much less than we are aware of; and the very different genius which appears to distinguish men of different professions, when grown up to maturity, is not upon many occasions so much the cause, as the effect of the division of labour' (Smith 1961, Book I, Ch. II, p. 19). Smith then goes on with the example of two people very similar to one another in their early childhood: the fact that one of them is educated to become a philosopher and the other to become a street porter and the practice by each of them of his job through the years lead each of the two persons to develop increasing productivity advantages over the other in his line of work. Had the two people been originally addressed to the opposite activities, they would have developed in time the same, but personally inverse, productivity differences.

showing the benefits of free trade) and demonstrating that the labour theory of value (according to which goods are exchange on the basis of the amount of work they incorporate), while regulating domestic exchange, does not apply to international trade: he simply stressed the fact that if the relative cost of production (measured in labour time) of two goods is different between two countries, given that capital and labour do not move across national borders, international specialization can take place under free trade and produce benefits for both trading partners even if one country produces both traded goods more efficiently than the other. For him, the differences in absolute as well as in relative labour productivities between two countries in the production of given goods seem to be exogenously given: 'the Ricardian theory is mute on a key ingredient: what causes labor productivity to differ across countries?' (Helpman (1998, p. 574)); Baldwin (2016) also noted that 'In Ricardo's conceptualization ... the national differences in competencies are assumed rather than explained' (p. 127). Ricardo did not specify which factors were responsible for them, beyond referring generically to 'each country producing those commodities for which by its situation, its climate, and its other natural or artificial advantages, it is adapted' (1951, p. 132). But the logic of Ricardo seems to locate these national differences in inherent pre-existing differences in the ability of countries' workers to make different goods (just as in our example in Footnote 1 of Chapter 1).[13]

Ricardo's statement quoted here has been interpreted as a reference to differences in natural conditions and in labour qualities and technology, despite the fact that he was almost silent on the origins of differences in technological levels. Since the RHO theory subsequently concentrated on differences in relative factor abundance as the basis for trade, while postulating availability of the same technology everywhere, it has become quite common to contrast the HO model based on 'natural' differences in relative factors abundance with an original Ricardian model based on differences in technology (that is, in production functions), although in Ricardo even these latter differences are presented as given characteristics of the countries, almost as if they

---

[13] Buchanan and Yoon (2002) stressed this contrast between the conception of Smith, connecting competitive advantages to workers' specialization independently of original individual capabilities (considered to be largely the same for all persons), so that every person could freely choose his specialization; and that of Ricardo, who based comparative advantages on innate differences in capabilities of different persons (or other trading units, such as countries), thus predestinating people to devote themselves to the tasks they are more adept at (in the same way as we can forecast that a very tall sportsman will specialize in basketball and a very lean one in trotting races), and making it possible to identify in advance the probable characteristics of international specialization. They pointed out that empirically trade flows are the result of a combination of the two different logics, and that the prevalence of one or the other has important effects on the problems posed by the contemporary globalization process. If countries' lines of activity nowadays can be easily supplanted by more competitive foreign products, implying more frequent transfers of workers to new jobs, then changes in the composition of trade flows consequent on the maintenance of open trade policies will prove much less difficult and painful for the individuals involved (and will raise far fewer problems of income redistribution among different groups of workers) if the individuals' efficiency is connected to the technical and organizational nature of the production process rather than to personal innate capabilities in specific activities.

too were the product of nature.[14] In this way, Ricardo was made the precursor of recent theories of international trade that stress the role of technical innovations and the dynamics of technological breakthroughs and catch-ups (discussed in Chapter 5), although one would find very little reference to these subjects in his trade theory.

One final but very important caveat, however, is necessary lest the contribution of Ricardo to economics and in particular to the analysis of the process of economic development should be underestimated or distorted. The comments advanced above in this section only refer to Ricardo's analysis of foreign trade in Chapter VII of his *Principles* devoted to this subject; and they apply even more to the Ricardian foreign trade contribution as it was inserted into the RHO model. But Ricardo was in fact deeply interested in the impact of international trade on the income distribution among classes, as it influenced capital accumulation and the rate of growth of the economy. It has been argued that the textbook Ricardian model is a misinterpretation of Ricardian trade theory, constructed in order to fit the latter into the RHO neoclassical model of international trade, and that that theory, and even the specific comparative advantage model in Chapter VII of the *Principles*, allow for alternative, more realistic and less static hypotheses, such as variable returns to scale and unemployment. Ricardo's insights have indeed been used since the 1980s by a number of economists to develop specific 'neo-Ricardian' dynamic models of trade and growth: see Maneschi (1992, 1998); on extensions of the Ricardian model see Costinot and Vogel (2015), Jones and Weder (2017) and Autor (2018).

R. Chandra (2004) has advanced, referring to Ricardo's limited analysis of the division of labour, an argument that may more generally explain why one finds Smith's theory of foreign trade much richer, more dynamic and extensively developed than that of Ricardo:

> in his preface to *The Principles* … [Ricardo] mentioned that he wanted to confine himself to aspects of political economy on which he differed from Smith. It is therefore possible that Ricardo did not develop the theme of the division of labor as an explanation for growth or international trade because he saw no reason to differ from Smith on this. While Ricardo may have thought of comparative advantage as an additional insight to the explanation of trade, the subsequent literature on the subject made it a focal point of trade. (p. 789)

[14] While for Smith the very act of trading – by enlarging the extent of the market and increasing the division of labour – sets in motion a virtuous mechanism of cumulative causation that improves learning, productivity and technological progress, in the Ricardian model specialization induced by trade does not alter the relative productivities of different activities inside and between countries.

Leamer (1984) noted that 'According to the classic Ricardian example, Portugal exchanges wine for cloth from Britain because Portugal is relatively efficient in the production of wine. The source of this comparative advantage was not Ricardo's concern, but it has been interpreted by many modern writers as "technological differences". This very superficial account of the causes of international trade seems to suppose that there are either biological differences between the Portuguese and the British that preclude each from emulating the productive techniques of the other or rather effective counterintelligence agents' (p. 36–37).

While Ricardo's principle of comparative advantages – his main contribution to foreign trade theory – was formulated in a static framework, there are significant references in his works to the influence of foreign trade on economic development and to the importance of technological progress. And there is also a particular dynamic aspect of trade that Ricardo underlined in Chapter VII of the *Principles* when he described two distinct types of gains from trade. The first gain, he wrote, is the traditional benefit that comes from the superior availability of goods produced by international specialization, which makes it possible to employ a lower amount of labour to obtain the same quantities of goods. Equally if no more important for him was a second, dynamic gain that a country obtains whenever the imported products consist of cheaper 'food and necessaries of the labourer': such imports, by lowering the cost of wages, allow the rate of profit to increase. As Ricardo considered the rate of profit the basic variable determining capital accumulation and the growth of the economy, but a variable subject to a declining trend because of diminishing returns in agriculture, the opening of the country to cheaper food imports imparted a strong beneficial stimulus to economic activity and development.

8.2 Recent revival of absolute advantage

8.2.1 Keynes's fundamental statement

In the early 1930s, while the Great Depression was ravaging the West, Keynes, despite his concentration on the problems of the moment, was able to look forward to the distant future and identify possible trends. Well known are his 1930 statements about the possibility for humankind – barring great wars or a population explosion – of envisaging in the not too distant future the attainment of the solution of the 'economic problem'; that is, of the objective of granting people a decent standard of living. He connected this possibility to the progress of science and technology, which had multiplied workers' productivity, and would continue to do so. However, for Keynes this would also imply the diffusion of a new illness, technological unemployment, as he thought that the pace at which ways to reduce labour utilization are devised surpasses the pace at which new types of productions are found in which labour can be employed – an issue that has returned to the top of the economic debate in recent years with the diffusion of digital technologies and the acceleration of automation: see, for instance, Ford (2009) and Brynjolfsson and McAfee (2011, 2014).

But in 1933 Keynes made another, fundamental statement. In the article on national economic self-sufficiency mentioned in Section 8.1, he identified a condition – increasingly characteristic of today's world reality – that according to the comparative costs principle would have progressively reduced the benefits of, and thus the scope for, international trade, but on the contrary has opened the way in the last four decades for massive trade flows based on absolute advantages. He argued:

> at a time when there were enormous differences in degree in the industrialization and

> opportunities for technical training in different countries, the advantages of a high degree of national specialization were very considerable ... But ... experience accumulates to prove that most modern mass-production processes can be performed in most countries and climates with almost equal efficiency (Keynes 1982, p. 238).

Modern societies are characterized by the large prevalence of consumption of manufactured goods vis-à-vis consumption of primary goods; at the same time, scientific progress reduces the use of natural raw materials per unit of GDP thanks both to the growing replacement of natural materials by artificial industrial substitutes and to technological improvements. In these conditions it could be expected that traditional international trade flows both of manufactured goods produced by advanced countries against primary products (highly dependent on the availability of specific natural resources or climates) produced by developing countries, and of primary goods against other primary goods – flows based on very large, sometime infinite, differences in relative domestic production costs in various countries – would become relatively less and less important (oil being the only significant exception). But at the same time, the scope for increasing trade flows of manufactures against manufactures would be restricted, applying comparative costs theory, by the very circumstance identified by Keynes: if modern industrial types of production – thanks to the transfer of knowledge and technology and advances in education – can be carried out in many different places with almost equal efficiency, relative production costs of any two manufactured goods inside a country will increasingly converge on those inside other countries, thus eliminating the very rationale for international specialization and exchange. For this reason, Keynes held that a greater degree of national self-sufficiency would not entail significant losses of efficiency gains and welfare, while – as already indicated – it would ensure a degree of isolation from the turbulent and unpredictable international economic environment of the 1930s and allow countries to pursue other desirable social objectives.[15]

Similar reasoning, a few years later, also led Robertson (1938) to forecast for the future a much diminished role for international trade relative to what he called 'the Great Specialization of the nineteenth century' based on exchanges of manufactures against agricultural products. This would result from a narrowing of gaps in comparative advantages among nations owing to the operation of three forces: proficiency in the arts of mechanized industry could not remain a monopoly of the group of nations that first learnt to use them; electricity was releasing factories from the need of prox-

[15] An additional reason Keynes advanced in the article for his advocacy of higher self-sufficiency – which would be validated by subsequent events – was the growing importance in people's expenditure and in national productive activity of non-tradable goods and services: 'Moreover, as wealth increases, both primary and manufactured products play a smaller relative part in the national economy compared with houses, personal services, and local amenities which are not equally the subject of international exchange; with the result that a moderate increase in the real cost of the former consequent on greater national self-sufficiency may cease to be of serious consequence when weighted in the balance against advantages of a different kind' (1982, p. 238).

imity to coalfields, opening the way for a more diffused location of manufacturing activities; the exploitation of virgin soils in the new countries seemed to be reaching its limit. Not only would this narrowing of the gaps in comparative advantages diminish the volume of foreign trade and the benefits produced by the remaining exchanges, but it would also create a situation in which small marginal changes in countries' production conditions could eliminate and reverse countries' comparative advantages, causing dislocations and distress for the individuals and communities engaged in export activities:

> the exchange of ice for coal between North Polia and Infernia not only yields a large measure of benefit to consumers, but is also likely to remain very stable, since a violent change in climatic conditions would be needed to disturb it. But the exchange of black shirts and red shirts between Fascia and Bolschevia is liable to ebb and flow in the most confusing fashion in accordance with minute technical changes. (Robertson 1938, p. 8)

For Robertson, the diminishing importance of world trade owing to the narrowing of the gaps in comparative advantages was likely to be associated with a further shrinkage owing to protectionist policies, as these would appear more necessary in view of the increased instability and insecurity of export activities and less costly in terms of foregone specialization benefits.

The great paradox of the post-war period until the 1980s was that this forecast was contradicted by the extraordinary growth of 'horizontal trade' in manufactures among advanced countries. Such trade could not be explained in terms of basic differences in production costs connected to the relative availabilities of basic productive factors, and it was for this reason that new trade theories were developed from the 1960s, based on new aspects of modern production: scale economies, product differentiation and monopolistic competition, and technological change.[16]

It is interesting to note that the penetrating observations by Keynes and Robertson on the reduction of inter-country differences in comparative advantage, which led the two economists to envisage less importance and higher volatility of comparative advantage and therefore less significant gains from international trade, have somehow been taken up sixty years later, in the very different context of contemporary globalization, by a staunch advocate of free trade, Bhagwati (1994), who developed the concept of 'kaleidoscopic comparative advantage'. He pointed out that in our 'Global Age' in which changes, especially technological ones, are taking place at an accelerated pace, firms in all countries are exposed to fierce competition from rivals in any part of

[16] Among the factors that explain why Keynes, Robertson and many other economists until the post-World War II boom were led to forecast limited development of international trade in manufactures is that they did not anticipate the crucial role played – especially in countries where high levels of economic well-being were reached – by product differentiation largely resulting from the massive increase and international diffusion of advertising and the growing importance of fashion in almost all sectors of consumer durable goods.

the globe, since capital can move to any place and the same technological knowledge and ability are spreading to an increasing number of countries. Just as in a kaleidoscope a little movement produces a completely different image, so in this environment a small change in the structure of the costs and prices of firms and countries abroad can suddenly wipe out a country's competitiveness, producing a very different configuration of comparative advantages. This new volatility of comparative advantage, while leading to higher efficiency of production and lower goods' prices, has the negative effect of systematically increasing industries and firms' uncertainty and vulnerability and workers' insecurity; workers risk the sudden loss of their jobs as a consequence of a small shift in conditions anywhere in the world and the moves undertaken in reaction to it by their employers. Overall, an increase in firms' labour turnover can be expected, with negative consequences for workers' wages.

Bhagwati also pointed out that this volatility represents a particularly serious danger for poor farmers in developing countries, as they may have shifted from subsistence agriculture to more profitable export crops only to see their products supplanted by the cheaper ones produced by more competitive rivals in another country. He stressed the importance of introducing policy measures to mitigate the effects of this increased risk for workers and farmers.

With the globalization of the last decades and the rapid emergence of new industrial economies, a new configuration of trade flows seems to be emerging. These flows (as was also the case with horizontal trade among advanced countries) are predominantly made up of industrial products and do not seem to respond to basic differences between countries in the domestic relative cost of production of different goods (reflecting, in turn, differences in the relative factor content of each good and in technology). These relative cost differences in the past were extremely significant for trade between advanced and developing countries, often almost infinite (as in Kravis's 'availability theory', mentioned in Chapter 5), since advanced countries could not produce tropical products or minerals not present at home, while underdeveloped countries had little ability to produce any manufactured product or tradable service competitive in the world market.

Nowadays, what seems to be happening is that – since production technologies and capital, following Keynes's and Robertson's forecasts, have become available almost everywhere (capital at a similar price) – the relative costs of different products inside each country are converging on those of other countries. Excluding of course primary commodities, the remaining fundamental divergence among countries regarding the availability and cost of factors is the developing countries' advantage in labour unit costs owing to the large supply of low-wage labour; an advantage that in past decades only applied to low-skilled workers, but more recently, with the rapid growth in the supply of more educated workers, also increasingly applies to more skilled labour. It is an advantage that – while still particularly important for low-skill labour-intensive products – extends practically to all manufactured goods (or phases of their manufacturing process), as well as to tradable services.

As the mechanisms ensuring the operation of the comparative costs principle appear not to work, trade flows seem increasingly to respond to lower absolute production costs. These lower costs, when produced by much lower labour unit costs in some developing countries, can apply to a large number of products belonging to all sectors of manufacturing, to many tradable services and, in some cases, to agricultural goods.[17] Absolute advantages of advanced countries seem to be restricted to a relatively limited (though highly profitable) section of goods and services requiring not easily transferable very high-level technology or skills, or superior organizational and marketing capabilities. Apart from labour unit costs (and levels of taxation), there are two other general absolute advantages influencing trade flows in a large number of goods and sectors: on the one hand, scale economies and geographical concentration of productive activities (both favouring world locations where economic activities have already happened to concentrate); on the other, the quality of the economic environment, represented by the institutional set-up, the availability of infrastructural facilities and the degree of political stability (all factors that have so far strongly favoured advanced countries, but are now also present in some developing ones).

As a consequence of these developments – together with other factors discussed in other chapters of this work – international trade economists, more than trying to explain why given countries export given goods, now try to explain why certain countries or locations seem to enjoy an absolute advantage for a large range of different products. This shift of the very object of analysis of international trade owes much to the theoretical contribution of Jones (1980, 2000), who showed that if a factor of production is internationally mobile (as capital and to a large extent technology in our time), the explanation of trade flows requires consideration not only of countries' comparative advantages, but also of their absolute advantages.

8.2.2 The rediscovery of absolute advantage

A long time ago, J. Robinson (1946) considered the possibility that one mechanism she had envisaged for trade balance re-equilibrium (the expansionary effect of an export surplus on employment, and therefore on monetary wages, increasing the price level and so reducing competitiveness and trade surplus) may not work as expected

[17] Sideri (1972) had somehow anticipated this development when he remarked that 'The old type of traditional division of labour, i.e. the specialization of countries along certain product lines according to the comparative advantage principle, still survives but is now being absorbed in a new kind of specialization which runs along factor-of-production lines … the countries that find themselves at the lower echelons of a highly hierarchical structure … are compelled to specialize in unskilled labour … Thus, an exchange of factors is replacing the exchange of goods, and more so vertically or "downward" than horizontally along the hierarchical structure of the international system … Against the main assumption of international trade theory, goods and factors have become more mobile except for unskilled labour' (1972, p. 384). But, writing before the emergence of China as an important exporter of manufactures, he still viewed the structure of international trade as basically centred on the dichotomy between a rising share of exchanges among advanced countries and a declining one between developing and developed countries.

and mentioned the possibility – which seems to fit to a large extent the Chinese experience in recent past – of a country with a large unemployed workforce (which would prevent large wage increases) recording a rise in productivity in its export sectors and becoming a competitive low unit labour costs producer of a large number of different products. This country would register a constant trade surplus based on absolute advantage, displacing jobs in other countries; as long as its wages did not increase more than its productivity, this absolute advantage would not disappear. In the same paper, Robinson noted that if capital moves internationally, it can compensate trade balance deficits, which can then persist for long periods, preventing the working of the comparative advantage principle. Two decades later, stressing the need for a reconsideration of traditional international trade theory, she took up the issue, arguing that 'The comforting doctrine that a country "cannot be undersold all round" was derived from the postulate of universal full employment' (J. Robinson (1973) p. 16).[18]

Just one year before, while the Bretton Woods fixed exchange rates system was collapsing, Samuelson (1972) , commenting – as already indicated – on the American conviction that the USA 'lack comparative advantage in anything', had recognized that an overvalued dollar might cause the sector after sector loss of US comparative advantage, with consequent unemployment; but he insisted that he still believed there existed a dollar devaluation relative to surplus countries' currencies that would permit the USA to have full employment under free trade. However, he did not exclude for the future

> a possibility that has some ominous overtones for the share of labor ... Under modern trends of comparative advantage, American management knowhow ... and American mobile capital may find that their most efficient use is increasingly to employ foreign labor as a substitute for traditional American activities ... The United States might in time become a headquarters economy ... It would become normal for us to enjoy an unfavorable balance of merchandise trade ... financed by our current invisible items of interest, dividends, repatriated profits and royalties. (1972)

A few years later, Kaldor (1980) also observed that 'On account of the dynamic effects of fast growth it is possible that a particular country's products become qualitatively superior, and hence preferred to those of another country, in all branches of industry' (p. 90). The fact that he and J. Robinson, two close collaborators of Keynes, focused attention on the role of absolute advantage in the explanation of trade flows was not accidental. As indicated in Footnote 9 in Section 6.2, although Keynes did not directly attack the principle of comparative advantage, implicitly he strongly rejected it. Strangely enough – given Keynes's lack of familiarity with Marx's work and complete difference of political views – the points he stressed in his refutation were substantially the same as those on which in the previous century Marx had based his

[18] For a general assessment of J. Robinson's contribution to the theory of international trade see Blecker (2005a).

attack against Ricardo's prerequisites for trade balance adjustment (curiously, also in his case without explicitly rejecting the principle of comparative advantage).

In 1980, Jones published a paper, already cited, in which he advanced the possibility not only of absolute advantages having a role in the determination of international trade flows, but also of the production process being broken down into several stages (with intermediate products representing distinct productive factors). His model was based on the premise that while some productive factors are internationally immobile, others are free to move to the most attractive locations in the world, which are those where some elements (he mentioned general superior technology and low levels of taxation, but one may think of low labour unit costs, institutions and infrastructure) most enhance their profitability. He stressed that absolute advantage would prove crucial in determining which country would attract the footloose factors:

> Although each nation can, by the law of comparative advantage, find something to produce, it may end up empty-handed in its pursuit of industries requiring footloose factors. Once trade theorists pay proper attention to the significance of these internationally mobile productive factors, the doctrine of comparative advantage must find room as well for the doctrine of 'relative attractiveness' where it is not necessarily the technical requirements of one industry versus another that loom important, it is the overall appraisal of one country versus another as a safe, comfortable, and rewarding location for residence of footloose factors. (1980, p. 258)[19]

In turn, the importance of this 'relative attractiveness' highlights the critical role that government action can play in influencing the factors that determine it.

A few years later, Brewer (1985) developed a Ricardian trade model – in which, however, the monetary and balance of payments dimensions were absent – showing that if international mobility of capital and rigidity of real wages are introduced, trade flows will be determined by absolute advantages, so that 'it is possible for a

---

[19] This point was further developed in Jones (2000), where he confirmed that when international mobility of a factor of production is introduced, the forces of absolute advantage may offset the forces of comparative advantage.

Interestingly, the basic argument in Jones's model and the fundamental relevance he attributes to location theory in determining the structure of international trade had been somehow anticipated by C. Frank (1973): 'The Heckscher-Ohlin view of comparative advantage … is still the basic intellectual underpinning of modern trade theory and the policy recommendations which stem from it. There is a growing concern that this type of trade theory is no longer relevant for analyzing trade problems and policies. The growth in the extent and speed of transport and communications has facilitated the growth of multinational corporations which operate with little regard to international borders. Capital is much more mobile than it used to be. Technology is transferred from country to country more rapidly, and the product cycle has become shorter. High-level management skills are no longer location specific and are applied without regard to borders … If we accept the reality of relatively free movement of capital and transfer of technology, then a quite different model of trade may be applied. The theory that one might use in analyzing this kind of world is more akin to location theory models' (1973, p. 63). Caves (1982), referring to capital mobility, had also concluded that 'In general, the more mobile are factors of production, the less does comparative advantage have to do with patterns of production' (p. 55).

country to be "undersold all round"', he also argued that his model 'provides a possible justification for the common complaint that foreign competition causes domestic unemployment' (pp. 177–178).[20] In the same year, MacDonald and Markusen wrote in favour of a 'rehabilitation of absolute advantage', referring to the problems of the optimal assignment of tasks to heterogeneous workers in a firm. They stressed the fact that workers' comparative advantages in certain tasks are not a good criterion for assigning them to different tasks when the level of their capabilities is very different in absolute terms relative to the differences in comparative advantage:

> [In a company] It is not persuasive that the employee with the highest comparative advantage in management should become president. Indeed, it is plausible that the presidency assignment will have something to do with absolute advantage; alternatively, a person with poor management skills will not be chosen even if he is relatively worse at every other task in the firm. (1985, p. 278)

The same reasoning can be applied to countries, particularly in the light of the growing importance of products' technological level: a developing country may have a strong comparative advantage vis-à-vis an advanced one in producing cars relative to producing computers, but if its absolute technological level is much lower in both productions we can expect the advanced country will export both goods.

In the same year as Jones's article appeared, Shaikh (1980), moving from a Marxist perspective, wrote a devastating article against Ricardo's principle of comparative costs, fundamentally basing his case on the argument, already examined in Section 7.2, that the trade balance re-equilibrating mechanisms do not work in the way envisaged by the adherents to that principle. The Ricardian principle was attacked head-on: 'the law of comparative costs is seen to be *impossible* precisely on its own grounds ... It is *absolute* advantage, not comparative, which rules trade' (p. 231) (years later, Shaikh (1991, 1996) would present formal versions of this model).

The starting point of Shaikh's (1980) model was a rejection of the RHO model's hypotheses of full employment and similarity across countries of production functions for given goods: he assumed that both technology and real wages are determined by local conditions. Real wages basically reflect national productivity, output growth, the level of unemployment and the relative force of workers and employers. On the basis of the levels of real wages and productivity, countries will produce goods at given real unit costs, on which domestic prices, expressed in national currency, will be based. He then assumed that there is international competition for tradable goods, not in the sense of textbook 'perfect competition', but in the sense that in any country of the world, producers of a given good have only limited room

[20] Developing Brewer's insights, Parrinello (2010) presented a model – with internationally mobile capital, possible unemployment, fixed real wages and countries using the same currency – to show that in a global market the rise and decline of countries can be explained by changes in absolute productivities and advantages prevailing over changes in comparative productivities and advantages.

for fixing a different price in domestic currency from the price prevalent on the international market (obtained by translating the price in international currency into domestic currency at the current exchange rate). In turn, the price prevalent on the international market will reflect the price offered by the world producer of the given good with both the lowest total (direct and indirect) unit labour costs of production and the ability to indefinitely expand the supply of the good (a producer he referred to as the 'regulating producer'). Producers with lower real unit costs will thus be in a position to offer lower prices in international currency, expanding their share of the world market for their good at the expense of less competitive rivals, more or less as happens for domestic market competition.

If a country with a trade deficit tries to restore trade balance by devaluing its nominal exchange rate, there are two possibilities. If workers resist the reduction in real wages induced by devaluation – a reduction consequent on both the higher cost in domestic currency of imported goods (items that might not be, or not fully, substituted by domestic production, such as food) and the necessity of compensating for the increase in production costs caused by the higher domestic price of imported raw materials – then the inflation resulting from the increase in their wages will nullify the effect of the initial devaluation (so that no 'real devaluation' occurs), and the external deficit will soon reappear. If, instead, workers accept the cut in real wages, competitiveness might be temporarily restored and the trade balance re-equilibrated in the short term, but at the cost of a painful reduction in living standards; while nothing guarantees that the increase in external competitiveness will produce a flow of additional export- and import-substituting activity sufficient to compensate for the negative effect of reduced internal demand on employment and income. But, more importantly, any trade balance correction will soon be reversed if the competing foreign 'regulating producers' increase their productivity at a higher rate than the devaluing country – as is to be expected if in the latter country devaluation and austerity are the only reactions to the trade deficit. Therefore, the only effective way to restore trade balance equilibrium in the medium to long term is by way of a modernization of the country's productive system sufficient to produce a narrowing of the gap in the rates of productivity growth between the country and its most efficient international competitor. Within such a properly devised modernization programme, an important role may be played by long-term foreign investment, as the latter – while providing funds to finance the trade balance deficit – has proved to be one of the best instruments for getting a country to adopt the most effective production technologies available in the world.

One reason for dwelling upon Shaikh's model is that his concept of 'regulating producer' seems to fit the recent experience of China, whose producers have managed to conquer positions of predominance in world markets for many manufacturing goods. This country (as, in prospect, India) has a huge population, a significant part of which is still to be absorbed into the modern sector of the economy, but has made a tremendous effort to increase the level of education of its citizens and the quality of its infrastructure, and has access to advanced technologies thanks to the large participation of foreign firms in its modernization effort. It appears destined, therefore, to have at its disposal for a number of years large supplies of labour, even at higher skill levels, enabling it to satisfy any increase in world demand for the goods in which it has reached (and will increasingly reach in the future) the position of absolute lowest-cost world producer.

Up to the early 1990s, the revival of the concept of absolute advantage was the work of just a few trade economists. Among them Culberson also deserves to be mentioned: in a series of books starting with Culberson (1984), he underlined how low wage competition in a world of massive trade deficits and capital movements impaired the working of the comparative advantage principle; (see Lutz (2008) on his contribution).

For traditional international trade theory, the theoretical possibility for a country to be 'undersold all round' was hard to accept, as it implied that free trade might not be the best policy for a country and that a different trade policy, aimed at overcoming the inferiority – or reconquering a previous advantage – in technical, institutional and other conditions, might be necessary before the country would be capable of sustaining free international competition. It was only in the following years that absolute advantage started to be more widely discussed. In all evidence this was connected with the emergence of China and other East Asian countries as major international exporters of manufactures in a growing number of sectors, and their registering persistent massive trade balance surpluses; and with the diffusion of offshore manufacturing facilities by advanced countries' producers, which led to increasingly widespread fears in advanced countries that an increasing number of lines of domestic production might progressively be supplanted by more competitive ones in emerging economies.

8.2.3 Institutional theories

Since the early 1990s, increasing attention has been paid by economists to a factor until then little discussed: the role of institutions in development and international trade (institutions are usually considered to include both the constitutional, political and administrative set-up of a country, and its laws, rules, social norms, traditions, practices and standards that affect the behaviour of its citizens and firms). By largely determining transaction costs, production costs and incentive structures, institutions have a strong influence on international competitiveness.

The role of institutions had long been recognized by economists. Adam Smith underlined the importance for development and trade of both public physical infrastructure and provision by government of intangible collective goods such as law, order, justice, weights and measures, stable money and even almost universal education. As for Ricardo, Parrinello (2002) held that 'the important feature of Ricardo's theory of international trade is that the institutional factor is a source of intercountry differences in the distributive variables which can explain the existence of comparative advantages…' (p. 259). Ohlin also stressed the importance of institutions in originating comparative advantages; though it is not clear whether he considered the institutional factor a specific additional factor of production or an element enhancing the productivity of the basic factors (land, labour and capital).

After Ohlin, international trade theory practically ignored the role of institutions. This was probably the effect of mainstream economists' reluctance – discussed in Chapter 9 – to take into account all the factors that could not be precisely defined and measured, despite their fundamental role in shaping economic life, since they claimed that their profession, alone among social sciences, had the 'scientific' character of physical sciences.

The basic factor leading to the great and increasing importance attributed to institutions since the late 1990s was the rediscovery of their crucial role by development economics, in the wake of the works of North (1990, 1991) (but he had produced contributions on the subject for many years before). Development economists, unable to identify the specific factors that cause economic development and explain why among countries with initially similar economic conditions and resources, some manage to trigger a process of industrialization and development, while others fail to get out of their state of underdevelopment, increasingly concentrated on the role of institutions in stimulating or obstructing development efforts.

This trend was strongly reinforced by the fact that in the late 1990s it was recognized that the ultra-liberalist development policies of the Washington Consensus (based on strict fiscal and monetary discipline, trade and foreign investment liberalization, minimum intervention of the state in the economy, drastic deregulation of economic activities, large-scale privatization of utilities and public services), which in the previous 10–15 years most economists had recommended – and international organizations such as the International Monetary Fund (IMF) and the World Bank had usually imposed as a condition for their financial assistance – to developing and ex-communist countries, had proved largely unsuccessful in producing the expected fast growth and development. It was acknowledged that economic liberalization policies adopted in advanced countries could not be simplistically transferred to countries lacking the basic institutional structures and the social norms and psychological attitudes necessary for a market economy to develop; elements that in advanced countries have formed in the course of decades (if not centuries) of industrialization and development, which evolve incrementally and cannot be created by the simple adoption of specific policy measures by public authorities. But it is these institutions that create the incentives for economic agents and determine production and transaction costs, thus conditioning the development possibilities of a country more than the mere availability of economic and financial resources.

Another factor that probably contributed to the rediscovery of the importance of institutions in international trade theory was the fact that some countries (China in particular) appeared to have reached a position of absolute advantage in the production and export of goods and services belonging to a number of different sectors. Attention was thus directed to elements determining a country's general superiority in many lines of production. Of course, lower labour unit costs represent the main element; but, as Jones (1980) had pointed out for the case in which there are production factors that can freely move internationally, some countries or specific locations may offer other absolute advantages. While he mentioned generalized technological superiority and lower taxation, it is better quality of infrastructure and institutions that immediately come to mind.

The analysis of institutions presents a lot of problems that complicate the debate on their role, as explained by H-J. Chang (2007). There is no generally agreed definition of them, so that different economists may refer to different types of institutions. Institutions are important in promoting development because they carry out important functions (such as coordination and administration, learning, stimulus to innovation,[21] redistribution and social cohesion). But the same functions can be performed by different institutions, as is frequently the case in different countries and, in the same country, at different times. Most institutions involve immaterial factors that are difficult, often impossible, to measure, so it is very hard to establish their importance on the basis of empirical evidence.

Mainstream economics has attributed great importance to secure and well-defined property rights (and to efficient judicial systems sanctioning their infringement), as they ensure investors will enjoy the fruits of their efforts. But property rights are provided by a large set of institutions (land and urban planning laws, inheritance law, tax law, bankruptcy law, intellectual property rights (IPR) law, etc.) and there is no objective criterion to aggregate them in a single indicator of an efficient property rights system. The latter is not necessarily the one that maximizes protection of property rights, as economic efficiency may require violation of established property rights, as happens with land reforms directed at eliminating obsolete and inefficient land tenure systems. While the importance of the protection of private property is usually emphasized, other forms of property rights may produce in some cases more efficient results. For instance, Coase and Wang (2013) recalled that a large part of the success of Chinese economic reform derived from the initial introduction of market discipline for 'township and village enterprises', which were a hybrid and uncertain form of property combining local government and de-facto private property; and concluded that 'the spectacular performance of township and village enterprises appears to run counter to a basic tenet in modern economics, which states that private property rights are indispensable to motivate entrepreneurship and discipline market behavior' (2013, p. 54).

While research on institutions has been primarily aimed at establishing their effect on growth, development and comparative advantages, these factors have also

[21] Dosi, Pavitt and Soete (1990) underlined the importance of institutions in fostering basic scientific and technological innovations. Contrary to what happens with incremental technical progress along trajectories defined by established paradigms, 'market processes are generally rather weak in directing the emergence and selection of radical technological discontinuities. When the process of innovation is highly exploratory, its direct responsiveness to economic signals is rather weak and … the linkages with strictly scientific knowledge are quite strong. Non-market organizations play an important role, providing the necessary conditions for new scientific developments and performing as *ex ante* selectors of the explored technological paradigm within a much wider set of potential ones … In the processes of search and selection of new technological paradigms, the institutional and scientific context and existing public policy are fundamental…' (pp. 243–244).

exerted a strong influence on institutions, so that the prevalent direction of causality is difficult to identify. H-J. Chang (2011) argued that historical evidence suggests that causality runs more strongly from economic development to institutions than in the opposite direction. He stressed that increased income levels and the requirements of new groups emerging from economic development create stronger demand for better-quality institutions; and, more importantly, that it is economic growth that provides the usually significant financial resources necessary to introduce and run them. He also reminded us that many of the institutions now considered as prerequisites for economic development were in fact introduced in today's advanced countries not before, but after development took place. He finally warned against the dominant discourse on institutions (similar to the past dominant discourse on policies to accelerate growth and development, which were later recognized as mechanical and superficial), according to which countries that need improvement in institutions should just introduce those that proved most efficient in advanced countries. But institutional change is not easy, as institutions are usually deeply embedded in societies, in their culture and customs (they are almost by definition introduced with the aim of being stable) and tend to develop with time an inner resistance to change; there is often a strict complementarity across institutions in different areas, so that institutional change in one area implies change of institutions in other areas; they usually require substantial economic costs; but, most importantly, institutions that have given good results in a country at a certain time may produce opposite results in another country with different characteristics or in the same country at a different time and in a different international context.

Nunn and Trefler (2014), in their review of the works on institutions as a source of comparative advantage, also underlined the strength of the reverse influence of trade and comparative advantage on institutions; and devoted a large part of the review to the analysis of historical cases, showing that one of the main factors through which the nature of the goods exported shapes domestic institutions, and thus influences long-term economic development, is which group of economic actors (such as merchants, entrepreneurs or large landowners) is enriched by trade and thus made more powerful to the point of being able to produce institutional changes favourable to its interests.

International economists have concentrated their analysis of institutions on some of them; see the surveys by Belloc (2006) and Nunn and Trefler (2014). Many of these works move from the concept of transaction costs, following a line of research developed by Coase since 1937 to explain why firms may prefer to keep a number of transactions within their organization instead of carrying them out in the market. They have stressed in particular – in addition to the question of limited and asymmetric information – the problems of contract incompleteness (the fact that contracts cannot cover all possible circumstances that can occur in the course of the contractual relationship, creating incentives for one of the parties to default) and imperfect contract enforcement (the lack of an authority compelling parties to fulfil their obligations). These two problems are particularly important at an international level, where there is a larger number of unforeseeable possible events and there is no supranational judicial authority. Given these risks and uncertainties, not only do personal relationships and repeated interaction, detailed knowledge of local conditions, and trust and reputation play a very important role in favouring international exchange, but the availability of efficient domestic contracting institutions can also represent for a country a specific comparative advantage in the export of goods for which contractual problems are particularly important.

Among institutional factors, one can be included that has proved crucially relevant for growth and development, particularly in developing countries: this is the availability of public officials in government, administration and public services with high levels of competence, autonomy, honesty and entrepreneurial spirit. Some economists have drawn attention to the key role of this factor: see Bardhan (1997, 2006), Bliss (2007) and more recently Milanovic (2019), while a survey of the economic analyses of corruption was provided by Aidt (2003). In particular, the corruption, patronage and favouritism of public authorities often represent the main stumbling block for poor countries that are attempting to emerge from underdevelopment. But they are a fundamental problem for middle-income and even advanced countries as well. In the latter countries, both the efficiency and international competitiveness of the economic system, and the very mechanisms of democracy can be undermined by forms – often subtle and indirect – of corruption aimed at the acquisition of citizens' votes, the appointment to public functions at all levels of individuals from specific family or political party groups instead of individuals chosen on the basis of competence, and the adoption by public authorities of measures favourable to the interests of restricted but powerful sections of the population.[22]

With regard to this subject, it seems that the most damaging among the negative consequences of Thatcherism and the post-1980 ultra-liberalist economic ideology has been that of spreading the belief that public authorities' inefficiency and corruption are problems without a solution – despite many experiences, in different countries, testifying to the opposite – that must be accepted as natural phenomena, so that their negative effects cannot be avoided. Consequently, the only possible way to

[22] In the course of this work, attention is repeatedly drawn to the negative effects on the correct working of the economy and the market produced in the USA by the use of economic power and financial means by big business to bend to its advantage the process of drawing up laws and regulations and applying them in practice. But similar distortions, produced by corruption or excessive improper influence of particular groups on public action, are found in other advanced countries. In Italy – one of the three large countries, with Japan and Spain, that in the first half of the post-war period managed to transform itself into a modern industrialized economy – the increased diffusion of corruption and favouritism in politics and public administration (together with, in some areas, infiltration of political and economic life by organized crime) produced a deterioration in the efficiency of government action, public services and public infrastructure that largely contributed, in the following period, to a persistent lack of productivity increases and economic stagnation. This risks leading the country to a new international record, this time negative: to represent the first case in history of a highly industrialized country degraded to the position of second-class economy, unable to take full advantage of the developments of modern economic technology and largely surpassed by an increasing number of economies that in the past were at a much lower development stage.

overcome the problem is a drastic reduction of all public intervention and the privatization, or outsourcing to the private sector, of all services that must necessarily be provided collectively.

On the contrary, what was needed – and economists' very limited contribution to the subject seems to represent one of the greatest failings of economics in the last fifty years – was an effort aimed at developing principles and mechanisms that can eliminate, or drastically reduce, those distortions in public action, since in practice one cannot conceive an economic system working without an efficient intervention and regulation by public authorities. But, especially, it was forgotten – or intentionally ignored – that it is impossible to carry out privatizations without establishing, for the private entities supplying the formerly public services, precise and severe rules and strict sanctioning measures for non-compliance. And that if a government or public agency is corrupt and inefficient, one must expect that, just as it is unable to directly supply public services efficiently, so it will be unable to establish effective rules for the supply of those same services by private entities, and to effectively sanction lack of compliance with such rules (the analysis by Crouch (2016) of the results of privatizations and outsourcing of public services to private enterprises in the UK and other advanced countries goes a long way to support this point).

9 Power in International Trade

9.1 The role of power in economics

Half a century ago, Rothschild (1971) edited a book entitled *Power in Economics* for the Penguin Modern Economics Readings series. In his introduction, he underlined the almost general disregard on the part of modern economists for the role of the exercise of power in economic relations, both domestic and international, despite the fact that the exercise of such power is widespread and very important in the real world and – though the visible part of it may just be the tip of a submerged iceberg – acknowledged by everybody. One of the wonders of modern economics is how incredibly little progress has been made in this field since then, apart from the further development of analyses – especially those initiated in the 1930s on imperfect competition – of just one aspect of economic power, namely market power (that is, market configurations violating the basic assumption of perfect competition among firms, allowing them to influence the prices and quantities of the products they sell). Widespread disregard for the more general aspects of economic power has continued to characterize mainstream economics, although in the most recent years a number of eminent economists have started to point to the importance of the issue. And the arguments advanced at the time by Rothschild to explain this anomaly now apply even more strongly – as he himself remarked when he returned to the subject in Rothschild (2002) – despite some important changes that have taken place in the meantime in the forms in which power impacts on economic relations.

Disregard for power aspects is particularly damaging for the understanding of international economic relations, because while inside countries – especially democratic ones – state authorities have long since intervened with laws and regulations to set some limits to the power of strong individuals, firms, groups and organizations to dominate weaker ones, no corresponding authority exists internationally. At this level, rules have only been agreed in a limited number of economic areas and have proved much more difficult to enforce. Just to give an example, while most advanced countries have introduced anti-trust laws, no corresponding legislation, apart from the EU, exists at international level.

Historians of the international economy have always recognized that the exercise of power in order to foster economic interests has been central in shaping the modern economic world. Just before Rothschild's book was published, Sideri (1970) analysed the history of commercial relations between England and Portugal – the relations that inspired Ricardo in his famous example of comparative costs – and showed the underlying interplay of trade and power in those relations. The following year, de Cecco (1971) provided a penetrating analysis of the British gold standard in which he showed how behind the myth of this impartial, automatic and smoothly working monetary mechanism ensuring international economic harmony operated the harsh reality of power relations based on Britain's tight control of the countries of its empire (notably India) and on its hegemonic position in the world economy. Among more recent works, Arrighi (2007) stressed the close connection that has characterized European economic development since the beginning of commercial capitalism in Italian city-states, between the search for power and military supremacy, on the one hand, and technological and industrial development, on the other; he argued that the Industrial Revolution as far as the production of capital goods is concerned, was largely a by-product of the European armaments race.[1]

In their history of the world economy in the last millennium, Findlay and O'Rourke (2007) concluded that 'For much of our period the pattern of trade can *only* be understood as being the outcome of some military or political equilibrium between contending powers', and discussing the 'Rise of the West' observed that:

> Plunder may not have directly fueled the Industrial Revolution, but mercantilism and imperialism were an important part of the global context within which it originated, expanding markets and ensuring the supply of raw materials. Violence thus undoubtedly mattered in shaping the environment within which the conventional economic forces of supply and demand operated. (pp. xix–xx)

Probably the greatest negative effect of plunder and violence in the history of the world took place when, starting with the discovery of America, they were exercised by European countries in other continents and proved crucial in fixing for the following five centuries the basic characteristics of Third World countries' insertion into the capitalist world economy.[2]

---

[1] The great contribution of states' military needs to the process of innovation is a constant in modern economic history. Reinert (2007) recalled that basic inventions for civil life originated as by-products of war, from canned food in the Napoleonic Wars to the mass production of weapons with standardized pieces in the American Civil War, burglar alarms in the Vietnam War and satellite communication in the Cold War with the Soviet Union. Nuclear energy, jet planes, lasers and computers were all developed thanks to state efforts motivated by military considerations. The relationship between power and imperialism, on the one hand, and technology (in particular military technology), on the other – a field of research pioneered by Cipolla (1965) – has been analysed by Headrick (1981, 2010).

[2] Adam Smith referred to this point when he observed: 'The discovery of America, and that of a passage to the East Indies by the Cape of Good Hope, are the two greatest and most important events recorded in the history of mankind … By uniting, in some measure, the most distant parts of the world, by enabling them to relieve one another's wants … and to encourage one another's industry, their general tendency would seem to be beneficial. To the natives, however, both of the East and West Indies, all the commercial benefits which can have resulted from those events have been sunk and lost in the dreadful misfortunes which they have occasioned … At the particular time when these discoveries were made, the superiority of force happened to be so great on the side of the Europeans, that they were en-

The great classical economists – Smith, Ricardo and Marx – were well aware of the importance of power asymmetries in the determination of the results of market transactions, both inside and between countries; they all had a 'conflictual' theory of distribution. In his *The Wealth of Nations* (1776), Smith described in detail the position of inferiority of workmen vis-à-vis masters in wage-fixing disputes, clearly showing that he did not attribute the results of those disputes to market forces, but to unequal power and coercion:[3] he charged the monopoly of colonial trade imposed by Great Britain with distorting the economic structure and diminishing the economic activity of the colonies and of Britain itself; and denounced the tendency of producers, whenever given the opportunity, to collude in order to limit competition and charge customers higher prices for their products. However, as Rothschild (2002) argued, two parts can be distinguished in Smith's *The Wealth of Nations*: in the first one – defending the emerging capitalist market society against the restrictions and regulations of the preceding feudal order – he showed how a competitive market economy could produce maximum efficiency. In the second, Smith discussed more applied and realistic subjects, and gave ample consideration to not strictly economic factors, in particular the power aspects connected with monopolies, producers' lobbies, superior bargaining leverage and capacity, and actions of the state.[4] Unfortunately, mainstream economic theory concentrated on the first part of Smith's work, basically ignoring his contribution in the second part, even if the importance of the power aspects in economic life has not decreased since his time.

Ricardo wrote his *Principles* with the main purpose of determining how national product is divided among classes: he viewed this division as a conflict among landowners, capitalists and workers, a conflict in which the role of power asymmetries was recognized as fundamental. In particular, he concentrated on the negative effects of landowners' monopoly of arable lands for economic growth and society's welfare,

---

abled to commit with impunity every sort of unjustice in those remote countries' (1961, Book IV, Ch. VII, p. 141).

[3] 'What are the common wages of labour depends everywhere upon the contract usually made between those two parties ... It is not, however, difficult to foresee which of the two parties must, on all ordinary occasions, have the advantage in the dispute, and force the other into a compliance with their terms. The masters, being fewer in number, can combine much more easily; and the law does not prohibit their combinations, while it prohibits those of the workmen ... In all such disputes the masters can hold out much longer. A landlord, a farmer, a master manufacturer, or merchant ... could generally live a year or two upon the stocks which they have already acquired. Many workmen could not subsist a week, few could subsist a month...' (Smith 1961, Book I, Ch. VIII, pp. 74–75).

[4] As for state action, it has become commonplace to identify Smith as the apostle of laissez-faire and of minimum government intervention in economic and social life. While this is not correct, as testified by his strong advocacy of public initiative in infrastructure and, especially, education, it must be considered that – as pointed out in a 1994 lecture by Bhagwati (1998) – his case for laissez-faire was strongly influenced by the fact that in his time government intervention, inefficient and socially undesirable (as it basically just served the interests of oligarchic groups), reflected the extremely limited extent of democracy: suffrage only covered a restricted class of property owners, and people such as Smith himself did not enjoy voting rights (as late as 1819, Ricardo entered Parliament by buying for £4,000 a seat representing a borough in Ireland, where he seems never to have set foot.)

since the increase in land rents owing to the extension of cultivation to less productive land would reduce, by raising food prices and consequently wages, capitalists' profits, which he viewed as the source of industrial investment and overall growth. And he clearly saw – as underlined by Nayyar (2007) – how the redistribution of incomes from rents to profits would be associated with a redistribution of political power from landowners to capitalists.

Marx went much farther in this direction, attacking the capitalist system itself for being based on a fundamental disequilibrium in bargaining power between workers and masters (because of the latter's exclusive ownership of the means of production), and the resulting coercion exercised against workers under the guise of consensual market transactions. At the same time, he underlined the brutal use of power on the part of the main European states to conquer and economically exploit large parts of other continents. On the whole, though, he took a favourable view of this last development, since he saw it as the instrument for the modernization of backward despotic regimes as a result of the introduction in their underdeveloped economies of the more advanced interpersonal relations, productive organizations, capitals and technologies of Western capitalism (see Warren (1980)).[5]

After Marx, power disappeared from mainstream economics. Two factors were basically responsible for this. The first was that Marx had shown the potential, politically revolutionary, effects of disclosing the power asymmetries hidden under formally voluntary economic contracts; as Galbraith (1983) stressed: 'The singular (and to many, the damaging) achievement of Marx was in persuading the working masses that this lack of power – this submission – was not natural or inevitable. Power could, in fact, be gained' (p. 170). The second, but interconnected, factor was the fact that the perfect competition model, in which there is no place for the exercise of power and where class differences do not exist (as every individual is the owner of a factor of production, be it land, capital or working capacity, on an equal footing – the original distribution of these resources being left unexplained) – became the only acceptable model to be used in economic theorizing. This meant that, apart from some non-orthodox economists, such as Rothschild and Galbraith, and some institutionalist ones, from Veblen (1920) to P. A. Klein (1987) (on institutionalist contributions see Samuels (1979)), the analysis of power remained confined to the Marxist camp,

[5] In the article 'The Future Results of British Rule in India', published in the *New York Daily Tribune* in 1853 (reproduced in Avineri (1968, pp. 136 and 138)), Marx wrote: 'the English millocracy intend to endow India with railways with the exclusive view of extracting at diminished expenses, the cotton and other raw materials for their manufactures. But when you have once introduced machinery into the locomotion of a country, which possesses iron and coals, you are unable to withhold it from its fabrication … The railway system will therefore become, in India, truly the forerunner of modern industry.' He concluded: 'The bourgeois period of history has to create the material basis of the new world – on the one hand the universal intercourse founded upon the mutual dependency of mankind, and the means of that intercourse; on the other hand the development of the productive powers of man and the transformation of material production into a scientific domination of natural agencies. Bourgeois industry and commerce create these material conditions of a new world…'

where at the level of international economics it gave rise to a long tradition of studies and disputes on imperialism.

One important exception to the mainstream silence on power in economics was the 1898 article in the *Economic Journal* by the Italian economist Pantaleoni on the possibility of introducing in the economic discourse the notions of 'strong and weak'; an article in which, however, he reasserted what had been in the previous half-century and would remain in the following hundred years the typical position of academic economists vis-à-vis power asymmetries. Coercion and violence, they admitted, may be at the basis of economic transactions. But since there is no objective, 'scientific' criterion for measuring and comparing the relative strength of the bargaining positions of the parties to a contract and the advantages they obtain from it, the only thing the economist can do is leave the entire question of power aside, taking as given people's preferences as expressed in formally voluntary contractual agreements: 'Contract is therefore based upon a presumption of parity of strength, even when and where parity does not exist, as is the rule' was Pantaleoni's conclusion (1898, p. 205).

The position of Pantaleoni and mainstream economists has been periodically criticized and attacked for more than a century by less conservative, and especially Marxist, opponents. Indeed, it is not difficult to establish a reasonable and fair principle to decide whether a market choice is really free, such as that proposed by Sandel (2012): 'Market choices are not free choices if some people are desperately poor or lack the ability to bargain on fair terms. So in order to know whether a market choice is a free choice, we have to ask what inequalities in the background conditions of society undermine meaningful consent' (p. 112). This is an application of the more general criterion by Wertheimer (1996) of fair market value as 'the price that an informed and unpressured seller would receive from an informed and unpressured buyer … on the market' (p. 230).[6] The issue of voluntary exchange versus coerced transactions has been the object of a penetrating analysis – conducted in the context of a critique of new institutional economics – by Palermo (2000), and in the last few years has been at the centre of discussions among philosophers debating the meaning and the causes of 'exploitation' in economic transactions (see Section 11.2.4).

In the field of international economics, Hawtrey (1930) was the first modern academic economist to devote a study to the interconnections between international politics and economics (leaving aside a 1919 work by Schumpeter that dealt strictly with imperialism; see Section 9.3), analysing the economic aspects of sovereignty; but he concentrated on the issue of nations' search for political and economic power

[6] Schultze (1977) had argued that 'If the income distribution is grossly unfair, the concept of voluntary decisions and unanimous consent is a charade; necessity is no less coercive for being economic instead of political' (p. 17). Feenstra (1998) observed that '… the "voluntary" nature of the employment relation is sometimes used as a justification for avoiding intervention. But this is surely incorrect! The fact that a worker would "voluntarily" continue in a job that exposed her to health hazards attests to her dismal alternative opportunities, and the complete absence of any bargaining power compared to the firm. This is precisely the situation where some institution (be it the government or a union) that can represent the interests of workers is called for' (p.45).

as a driving force leading to war. It was only in 1942 that Hirschman (published in 1969), writing during World War II, provided a systematic non-Marxist treatment of the issue of economic power in relations between countries.

Hirschman centred his analysis on those economic characteristics of two countries and their trade structure that tend to maximize the economic power of one over the other, basing his study on the detailed observation of the particular system of asymmetric commercial relations that Nazi Germany had managed to impose before and during the war on the countries belonging to its sphere of influence. He highlighted the importance of commercial policy as an instrument for exercising power over other nations, stressing the fact that the overall gains from trade of different nations do not only depend on the prices of the products after trade compared with the prices in autarchy – as taught by traditional economic theory – but also on elements of security/risk (such as concentration on certain products and certain countries of origin/destination) that determine the vulnerability of a country to a possible interruption of trade.

Of course, it was the specific atmosphere of the war under way that led Hirschman to this particular attention to power flowing from countries' different abilities to minimize the negative consequences of a sudden interruption of trade. But his general conclusion that 'international trade remains a political act whether it takes place under a system of free trade or protection, of state trading or private enterprise, of most-favored-nation clause, or of discriminating treatments' (1969, p. 78) is still valid in our times. Speculating on the future post-war international economy, he argued that the only means to eliminate this dangerous negative characteristic of international trade was:

> a frontal attack upon the institution which is at the root of the possible use of international economic relations for national power aims – the institution of national economic sovereignty … If we want to turn … from the sterile alternative between autarky and "economic penetration" to the achievement of international economic collaboration, the exclusive power to organize, regulate, and interfere with trade must be taken away from the hands of single nations. It must be transferred to an international authority… (pp. 79–80)[7].

The trade institutions and the organization of international trade established after the war were the product of debates in which Hirschman's proposal was a central element; unfortunately, they would only in small part represent its implementation.

However, Hirschman's work was rarely referred to in the following decades by mainstream international economists; the same happened with the contribution of

[7] Hirschman's attack against countries' sovereignty in the field of international trade was the expression of an opinion shared by some of his contemporaries in the light of the contribution of trade disputes to the outbreak of the war: Philippon (2019) cited the case of Jean Monnet, the spiritual father of the EU, who declared in 1943 that 'There will be no peace in Europe if States re-establish themselves on the basis of national sovereignty, with all that this implies by way of prestige policies and economic protectionism'.

E. R. Walker (1943) and with the analysis of the 'domination effect' developed by the French economist Perroux (1948, 1950), a precursor of contemporary theories of power (see Sandretto (2009)). Only in the field of development economics were the aspects of power characterizing the asymmetrical relationships between developing and developed countries taken into account by some authors. A thorough analysis of these aspects was presented by Sideri (1972), who concentrated on the role of technology in originating and perpetuating that asymmetry.

Interest in economic power dynamics revived somewhat with the Rothschild (1971) edition, mentioned above, of some of the studies published in previous years but largely passed unnoticed. In the 1980s two important contributions appeared, by Galbraith (1983) and Bartlett (1989). A number of studies have been produced in more recent years, such as Ozanne (2016), Skidelsky and Craig (2016), Zingales (2017), Mosca (2018) and Stiglitz (2019), indicating greater recognition of the power aspects in economics; although, overall, they do not seem to have managed to overcome mainstream economists' neglect of the subject.[8]

* * *

It must be recognized that the analysis of power in economics poses a number of problems, the first being the very definition of power and the distinction between 'economic power' and 'power in economic relations'; another being the difficulty of precisely measuring power. However, this is not, in itself, a valid argument for excluding power from economic theory, as serious problems of definition and measurement also apply, as stressed earlier, to many of the concepts on which economic theory is based, such as capital, factor of production, scale economies, technology and comparative advantage itself.[9]

When we speak of economic power, we usually refer to the ability of an economic

[8] Stiglitz (2019) points out: 'Look at a standard college economics textbook. The word *competition* is amply sprinkled through all of its chapters; the term *power* is reserved for but one or two. The term *exploitation* will likely be totally absent, a word long expunged from the conventional economist's vocabulary … Only recently have epitaphs like *exploitation* and *power* been used to describe what is going on.' (p. 239).

On works on economic power produced in the 1980s see Bardhan (1991). Among subsequent contributions – in addition to those just mentioned – one may cite Hirshleifer (1990), Cooper (2004), B. Roach (2007) (who concentrated on global corporations' power), Whalley (2009), Perelman (2012) and Palermo (2016).

In the field of international trade, an exception to the general disregard of the power aspects by contemporary academic economists was the work by Stiglitz and Charlton (2005), who stressed how power asymmetries damage less developed countries.

[9] Maneschi (1998) wrote at the end of his book on *Comparative Advantage in International Trade*: 'What can we conclude about the validity of comparative advantage as an explanatory principle of international trade? The first conclusion that emerges is that there is no agreement in the profession about the meaning of this term, which is used in a variety of different, often incompatible, ways' (p. 230).

Rothschild (1971) had observed that the concept of power in economics is no more elusive and ambiguous than the concept of disease in medicine; this, however, has not prevented medical science and medical practice from developing on the basis of this concept.

agent (a person, a firm, a nation, or a group or category of them) to impose, through the exercise – or the threat, explicit or implicit, of exercise – of economic coercion or through economic induction (offering monetary and other economic advantages or exerting psychological and intellectual influence, so as to make it desirable for the other party to behave as wanted by the more powerful one), its will on another agent, in the sense of driving that agent to behave in a way that is different from the way it would behave if it were free from any external pressure or influence. This power can be used to reach either an economic or – as, for example, is usually the case with economic sanctions – a non-economic result.

However, economic power does not need to be intentionally pursued or exercised through actions (in fact, it is most effective the less observable it is). The mere relative size of an economy (or a firm) counts: the importance of a country as a market for exports, as a source of specific imports or as a provider of finance or technologically advanced goods and knowledge to another country, may enable it to condition the other country's decisions (this power derived from relative size explains why coalitions of countries are critically important for conferring power against other parties). Power deriving from superior economic size is, of course, largely dependent on the degree of integration and interdependence between the parties, and the scope for the weaker one to resort to alternative sources or outlets for goods, production factors and technologies.[10]

When we speak of power in economic relations, reference is usually made, instead, to the ability of a country (or other economic agent) because of its superiority not only in economic but also and especially in military, technological, political, diplomatic or cultural terms, to impose on another one, intentionally or not, specific economic decisions or economic behaviour.

Different aspects of economic power can be distinguished (they are interlinked and tend to reinforce one another). In particular, one can refer to:

---

[10] There is one aspect of the importance of economic size in providing economic power that has been traditionally recognized and stressed by international trade theory: the determination of prices in the international market. All theorizing on this issue starts by separating the 'small country case', in which an individual country must take as given the price of a good established in the international market and this price is not influenced by its decisions or behaviour, from the case of a country whose size is such that its decisions or behaviour have an effect on the international price and market equilibrium.

The importance of economic size also explains why countries strongly integrated economically with a much larger one will find it extremely difficult – independently of any pressure exercised by the latter – to follow economic, monetary and exchange rate policies not consistent with those of the bigger partner.

A typical example of intentional exercise of economic power made possible by economic size is the US embargo applied since 1960 against Cuba. Any foreign firm not participating in it was denied the possibility of exporting to or operating in the USA; and given the importance of the US economy and its market, practically all the firms of the capitalist world had to comply, causing serious damage to Cuba. Had that embargo been declared by Guatemala or even France, these countries would have only damaged themselves.

- Market power: exercised in the market by an agent in order to influence the prices and quantities of the goods (or productive factors) bought and sold. This is the only aspect of power that has been analysed in depth by economists – as it represents a violation of their basic model of perfect competition – when they were compelled to recognize the realities of economic life, and it gave rise to an important theoretical literature on monopoly, oligopoly and monopolistic competition.[11] A very important determinant of this power (and increasingly so) is the exclusive availability of technological and organizational knowledge.
- General power: this influences all kinds of decisions taken by other economic agents (and by public authorities) through coercion, threat or inducements (that is, through sticks and carrots), or through the ability to deny competitors and customers access to the same information available to an agent or through mere size superiority or systemic significance (such as the control of key sectors of an economy). It is very important to consider that this kind of economic power may be connected not to the circumstances prevailing at the moment of a transaction or a decision, but to circumstances that occurred at an earlier time, when an economic agent acted in a way that prevented subsequent free choice by another economic agent. Bartlett (1989) developed the concept of 'event power' to indicate this power of determining conditions that will later force other agents to make coerced choices. One example would be that of a person digging a deep pit and filling it with poisonous snakes, then offering to sell a ladder to people who fell into the pit. That person would be exercising event power prior to the moment of the sale of the ladder. The ladder purchaser will certainly be willing to make the purchase, as the ladder will make him much better off, but it would be unacceptable to analyse his choice of buying the ladder without considering the previous exercise of event power that led him to that choice. Bartlett applied the concept to the process of originally defining and assigning property rights, noticing that the exercise of power and coercion in this process could only be excluded in the case of unanimous informed consent by all individuals affected by it; in any other case, someone must have had the power to compel someone else to accept those property rights against his will.
- Intellectual, cultural and reputational power: this involves the ability of an agent to influence the economic decisions of other agents through the diffusion of economic ideologies and arguments, the establishment of the intellectual climate of economic debate in public discourse and/or in the academic community, and in the set-up of educational programmes and university curricula, so that potential opponents can be persuaded to accept decisions and actions proposed by a party because they have been led to consider them as being in their own interest.[12] Gal-

[11] Firms' market power since the 1950s has been the object of empirical evaluation, with reference to the USA, by De Loecker, Eeckhout and Unger (2020) (see Footnote 42 in Section 9.4.1). Some interesting aspects of power in the theory of the firm have been investigated by Rajan and Zingales (1998).

[12] Patel (2009) has drawn attention to what is possibly the most shocking document one can find in the whole history of economic policy, which shows how strong – and devastating – the power of ideol-

braith (who in the 1950s had already analysed aspects of power in economic life) stressed in his 1983 book the importance of this 'conditioned power' that shapes preferences and interests of people to the point that they may not even realize where their real interest lies. Particularly important among the powers included in this category are the influence over mass media and the power exercised by firms over consumers through advertising and fashion-setting (which can reach the extreme of outright manipulation of people's perceptions and preferences).

- Technological and organizational power: this refers to an extremely important aspect of economic power, seldom discussed and highly underrated, namely the control over the directions of technological and organizational change, at the level of both individual firms and industrial sectors. Firm managers, particularly through control of investment, largely decide unilaterally the technology and the organizational structure and methods adopted by their firm; these choices determine the volume, location and bias in favour or against more intensive use of the various factors of production, and most other characteristics of firm activity. At sector level, through their investments and choice of specific directions of their R&D, firm managers collectively determine the changes in technology and organization in their sector of activity; in addition, they frequently organize to establish common initiatives in fields such as R&D, collaboration with universities and public research centres, and support and lobbying for specific government decisions and policies concerning technology.
- Power to shape the rules of the game: this influences or determines the institutional, legal and regulatory framework in which market transactions take place. As stressed, among many others, by Jacobs and Mazzucato (2016), 'It is not helpful to think of markets as pre-existing, abstract institutions which economic actors … "enter" to do business, and which require them, once there, to behave in particular ways. Markets are better understood as the outcomes of interactions between economic actors and institutions, both private and public' (2016, p. 18). At international level, this power concerns the definition, implementation and

---

ogy can be: the testimony before the US Congress investigating the origin of the financial crisis, delivered on 23 October 2008 by Alan Greenspan, chairman of the Federal Reserve (the US central bank) at the time of the outbreak of the 2008 global crisis. Greenspan had been an active follower of Ayn Rand, the author of a number of novels published between 1936 and 1957 in which she expressed an ultra-liberalist vision of capitalism, free enterprise and the free market. Greenspan shared this fundamentalist view of the free market – see his 1963 article against public regulation of private business 'An Assault on Integrity', included in Rand (1967) – a view that would strongly influence both economic theory and Western economic policy from the 1980s to the crisis. He admitted that his refusal to contrast the speculative financial bubble that finally originated the crisis was a consequence of his ideology of laissez-faire – held for forty years, but now proved flawed – which had warped his view of the working of the financial markets: he had believed that unfettered markets can do no wrong, as markets are by definition self-stabilizing. This admission may suggest an extreme and distressing interpretation of the origin of the crisis: the chief authority responsible for economic policy in the USA – the country whose economic policy largely conditioned those followed in the rest of the world – based his action on the tales of a free-market-fanatic writer.

control of the rules for trade, foreign investments, IPR, currency and finance (especially those governing the global economy); and the management or control of supranational economic institutions, as the exercise of power is greatly facilitated and legitimized (and more easily concealed) if it takes place through these institutions. There are different aspects to this power. A first and critical aspect is the power to control the agenda; that is, the power to decide the issues that have to be considered and discussed in each given situation. A second aspect is the power to impose one's own preferred alternative on an issue. This can take place through the already mentioned general use of sticks and carrots; through superior knowledge and intellectual authority and/or higher financial and human resources devoted to the study of a question and the preparation for meetings and conferences; but especially through lobbying efforts and exchange of favours with, and even outright corruption of, politicians, regulators and public officials. A third aspect is the power to determine the extent to which an existing law or regulation is applied in practice: this can be done by influencing the public financial appropriations destined to and/or the number, quality and appointment criteria of personnel assigned to checking compliance with and sanctioning disregard of a law or regulation.
- The ability to impose one's own standards, and especially technical standards, on other agents: within the preceding category, this is the type of power that has become particularly important in the contemporary world (it is the object of a specific analysis in Chapter 10). Another – but the two are often connected – is the power to control services and utilities (especially those based on networks) that are essential for the activity of a large number of or all other agents. In the past, many of these services, particularly when they conditioned the life and activity of all national agents, used to be supplied monopolistically by public authorities in a manner that could be controlled by citizens through the democratic political process. Today, most of these services have been privatized, which frequently allows the new owners to operate in conditions of practical monopoly or of oligopoly.

9.2 The origins of economic power and the reasons for its exclusion from mainstream economics

Where does economic power originate? There are different sources, again largely reinforcing one another. Apart from the possession of goods or productive factors that are essential or strategic – or even simply in short supply relative to demand – (already discussed in Section 2.2), the most important and widely resorted to are superior economic size and superior availability of financial means.

Economic size has already been mentioned. To a large extent, the power it confers is connected to the advantages of large-scale activity. A basic development of the economic globalization of the last thirty years has been the increase in economic size (in terms of assets and sales, not of employment) of large corporations, especially MNCs. The main argument for globalization advanced by its supporters was that elimination of trade barriers between countries would lead to greater competition and thus to greater efficiency. This tendency was indeed at work in the first phase of liberalization, when obstacles that previously prevented foreign producers from competing with domestic ones were eliminated. A major contribution to this increased international competition came from the fact that globalization allowed China (and some other developing countries) to become important, highly competitive suppliers in many markets around the world.

The tendency towards greater competition is still at work in certain sectors, but, overall (and particularly in the USA), it appears to have been offset more recently by an opposite one, especially as some firms in the ICT sector – where a limited number of network suppliers is unavoidable – have seen their markets grow exponentially and are now among the largest firms in the world.[13] Inside countries, firms increasingly decided – and were largely allowed by national antitrust authorities – to merge and create powerful national combinations so as to be able to withstand global competition. For example, the share of the total assets of US corporate firms accounted for by the top 100 firms went from 9 per cent in 1990 to 21 per cent in 2006 – see Brennan (2016) (however, Philippon (2019) does not find evidence of a significant increase in concentration in EU countries after 2000). But, more significantly, increasing mergers and acquisitions took place at international level, where – apart from the EU area – no antitrust authority exists. And many large firms that were not involved in these consolidation processes found ways to reduce competition through all sorts of alliances and forms of collaboration. The final result seems to have been a growing dominance of most global markets by – and increased political power of – oligopolistic and monopolistic giants. The full extent of these giants' economic power, however, is difficult to measure, because it has been greatly extended by their role as lead firms of global value chains (GVCs) (see Section 11.2); a role that allowed them to gain control of the entire production cycle of many goods even when their own resources and the activity directly carried out by them only modestly increased (or even, as happened with employment, greatly decreased).

Financial strength makes it possible to reinforce all the types of economic power listed earlier. In particular, it is the factor that contributes most to the basic element of power represented by a superior ability to wait; that is, to sustain temporary losses or lack of income in order to be able, in the longer run, to defeat opponents or to force counterparts to accept less favourable conditions in economic intercourse.

[13] On the US tendency to greater concentration, weakened competition, higher profit margins and no significant increase in operational efficiency (measured by the sales to assets ratio) since the late 1990s see Grullon, Larkin and Michaely (2019). For the same period, Gutiérrez and Philippon (2017) document the weakening of investment by US industries: they attribute it to greater industry concentration, in turn considered a consequence of higher entry barriers (produced by technological progress and reinforced by increased regulatory restrictions favourable to bigger firms) and possibly laxer enforcement of antitrust laws. On increased US corporations' profit margins see De Loecker, Eeckhout and Unger (2020), whose results are summarized in Footnote 42 in Section 9.4.1. On the tendency to increased concentration at world level, mainly through mergers and acquisitions, as a result of the development of global value chains see Nolan, Zhang and Liu (2008).

Smith referred to this power when, in the sentence quoted in Footnote 3 in Section 9.1, he spoke of the superior bargaining power of masters vis-à-vis workers. Another instance, fundamental in determining the results of the struggles between firms in situations of non-perfect competition, is the power of a firm to keep prices artificially at a level that does not cover costs for a period of time sufficient to make a possibly more efficient but financially weaker new competitor go bankrupt – so as to resume, after its exit from the market, prices that are much higher than costs (on this practice, called 'predatory pricing', see Bolton, Brodley and Riordan (2015)).

Financial strength also bestows power on nations (and large firms) by allowing them to keep larger stocks of raw materials and agricultural products to be used to minimize the effects of blockades or delays in the delivery of strategic goods (such as oil or food) or to influence the quotations of basic materials in international markets. It also confers power on firms by allowing them to build up and maintain idle productive capacity to be used in the event of unforeseen increases in demand or for strategic manoeuvres against competitors.

Of course, financial strength is closely related to the distribution of property, in all its forms ('power naturally and necessarily follows property' declared the famous American conservative politician and businessman Daniel Webster in 1820). But property is a very complex, not to say explosive, subject since, although it may represent the result of economic agents' successful activity in the market, it is to a large extent an attribute of an agent that precedes the agent's entrance into the market and largely determines the possibility of his reaching, in and through the market, particularly beneficial results. So that property's unequal initial distribution can be seen as a basic element creating an uneven playing field in the market's competitive struggle, thus producing not only unfair, but also economically inefficient results. Schutz (2011) showed how inequalities of personal income and wealth create unequal constraints that condition different economic agents' market choices. Long before, Meade (1964) had highlighted how 'An unequal distribution of property means an unequal distribution of power and status even if it is prevented from causing too unequal a distribution of income' (p. 39).[14]

At national level, one particular aspect of financial strength can be of critical importance, especially for developing countries: the availability of foreign exchange. As stressed by Raffer (1987), freedom of action for these countries is severely limited by the necessity of having a minimum of foreign exchange to import the goods

[14] Smith, while favouring the system of private property as the one most suited to promote economic growth, pointed out its negative effects in producing inequality: 'Wherever there is great property, there is great inequality. For one very rich man, there must be at least five hundred poor, and the affluence of the few supposes the indigence of the many. The affluence of the rich excites the indignation of the poor, who are often both driven by want, and prompted by envy, to invade his possessions … The acquisition of valuable and extensive property, therefore, necessarily requires the establishment of civil government … Civil government, so far as it is instituted for the security of property, is in reality instituted for the defence of the rich against the poor, or of those who have some property against those who have none at all' (1961, Book V, Ch. I, pp. 232 and 236).

(especially capital goods), specialized services, patents and licences that are essential for development (at times for survival), and that they are compelled to buy from abroad as they are unable to produce them at home even at a much higher cost. In order to get this essential minimum amount of foreign exchange, they are ready to accept prices for products they export or conditions for loans and foreign investments that they would straightaway reject if in possession of adequate stocks of foreign exchange.

After size and financial strength – and closely connected with them – the most important source of economic power is probably the unequal availability and distribution of knowledge (particularly technology) and information.[15] Already the Industrial Revolution, by creating more roundabout techniques of producing goods and turning people who previously produced at home most of the goods they consumed into specialized producers of specific parts of goods, had increased the complexity of products and productive processes; correspondingly it originated an asymmetry of power between sellers and purchasers owing to the difference in the amount of knowledge and information available to them for evaluating the good that is the object of a transaction, as for the average purchaser information would be more costly and often impossible to obtain. In contemporary economic life, knowledge and information are becoming ever more important, both because a growing share of consumption is devoted to goods and services providing – or strictly connected with – knowledge and information, and, more importantly, because the latter are increasingly strategic inputs in production processes, to which firms devote a large and growing part of their investment. The availability of more and better knowledge and information and/or the possibility of closing or reducing access to them by other economic agents is fundamental for firms both to gain an advantage over competitors and to keep consumers in a position of inferiority, as they may be unable to properly assess and compare the value of the products offered to them. J. D. Richardson (2000) observed that whenever markets work in an environment of imperfect or asymmetric informa-

[15] Although it may be difficult to draw the line between them, it is important to keep the role of knowledge separated from that of information. With the word 'knowledge', reference is made here to the availability of superior technological or organizational capabilities and skills and to the possession, and the possibility of exploiting, scientific and technological innovations. The most rewarding advantage for a firm (or a sector of activity, or a country) comes today from the production of widely demanded goods and services that competitors are unable to produce, or can produce only after a long period of attempts, or are forbidden from producing because they are covered by patents and licences. It is typically in the high-technology sectors that leading firms can exploit the advantages of the monopoly or quasi-monopoly that come from superior or exclusive technological and innovational capabilities. 'Information', on the other hand, is here meant to refer generally to that kind of knowledge that is not connected to specific technical or specialized education, training or research, but simply to the availability of news and data and to preferential or exclusive access to knowledge of facts that take place in the economy. It is thus easy to apply, reproduce and reuse. A firm may enjoy an information advantage over competitors because it has the means to finance subscription to a larger number of news agencies or more extensive or frequent surveys of public attitudes and characteristics. In the financial sector, the greater availability of, and access to, information is fundamental to success; but in this sector the boundary between information superiority and insider trading is often a thin one: see Cohan (2011).

tion, distortions are introduced in the market system that is based on the assumption of voluntary non-coercive transactions; and pointed to 'the awkwardness of calling uninformed "voluntary" transactions voluntary at all. And if "coercive" isn't quite the right word either, perhaps "exploitative" is, connoting the power of information advantage ... Imperfectly informed markets need regulatory support before they can become properly defensible...' (p. 119).[16]

Other fundamental sources of economic power are access to and control of the mass media (of critical importance whenever economic agents – particularly large corporations – want to induce the national government to take initiatives that benefit themselves, but are politically acceptable only if presented as beneficial for the entire nation); control of academic and research institutions; and cultural, academic and technological standing, reputation and credibility. Of course, superiority in personal and organizational abilities are of fundamental importance. But the exercise of power also has strong elements of hysteresis, in the sense that past history, tradition, customs, laws and political practices define the rights of bargaining parties to a significant extent and influence their behaviour and bargaining power even when the factors that originated them have long since disappeared. For example, in wage bargaining between trade unions and firm managers, apart from workers' productivity and supply/demand conditions, the determination of wages largely refers to what society at a given time and place considers to be a 'normal' wage.

It is also possible to view the exercise of economic power over a counterpart, and more generally the position of superiority in economic bargaining, in terms of a party's greater availability of options relative to another. These differences in the availability of options, in turn, are usually the consequence of the factors listed earlier (superior financial means, superior knowledge, etc.), but they may also be the result of strictly factual circumstances, as in the case mentioned by Vernon (1971): he noticed that in their confrontations with foreign MNCs, labour union leaders and host governments had a feeling of inferiority and dependence; and he connected this feeling to the objective circumstance that the MNCs, thanks precisely to the multinational character of their operations, have a number of choices – first of all the choice of moving their production to a different country – that their counterparts do not have. A very important instance of bargaining superiority owing to greater availability of options is the master/worker relationship, as masters not only enjoy more power because of the circumstances highlighted by Smith (see Footnote 3 in Section 9.1), but have the advantage of being the party that exercises unilateral control over the directions of their firms' technological and organizational change.

One last, extremely important source of power must be mentioned, which is rather special since it does not refer to any element of inherent superiority of an agent or group of agents: it is the asymmetry, pointed out by Olson (1965), between agents in

[16] Richardson recalled the well-known cases of markets for used cars and homes, where sellers know the real conditions of the good they sell, but buyers do not. In these cases, buyer protection regulation, compulsory warranties and anti-fraud legislation are necessary to have efficiently working markets.

the intensity of the interest they have in given collective or public decisions. Almost all collective decisions benefit some agents and harm others. These beneficial and harmful consequences, when concentrated on a limited number of agents, will likely be of critical importance for them, up to the point of determining the survival or the closure of their enterprises. These agents will therefore use all the means at their disposal to influence the collective decisions so as to reap benefits and avoid harm. Their counterparts, whose interest is opposite to theirs, may instead be large groups of agents (a typical example is consumers of large firms' products or of public utilities' services), each of them not critically influenced by a favourable or damaging decision because the amount of the individual benefit/harm may be of secondary or insignificant importance to them, or difficult for them to calculate, or they may be subject to the effects of the decision only occasionally. So it may not be worth their while to incur the cost and the inconvenience necessary, in the first place to obtain the necessary information, and then to get together and organize specific actions to try to bend the decision in their favour or to change the laws that prevent or hinder organized legal actions by large groups of agents (as is the case in many countries where class actions are not envisaged by law).

An interesting paradoxical point, stressed by Hirschman, may finally be mentioned: a country's economic power is, in a sense, inversely related to the gains it draws from trade, as the loss of them as a result of possible trade interruption by a counter-party weakens the country's bargaining power.

* * *

Why was the analysis of power excluded from mainstream economics? There are basically three reasons. The first is that power is not only an elusive and debatable concept, but it is also a concept that is very difficult to introduce and discuss in the type of formal, prevalently mathematical models that have become, not just the standard, but almost the only accepted, tools of analysis of mainstream academic economics. Power shares this characteristic with other, mostly intangible factors that are of critical importance in economic life, but have been ignored or have received insufficient attention from economists: most pertain to the psychological sphere, such as uncertainty, expectations, initiative, emulation, fear, non-calculable risk, trust, group and herd behaviour, non-pecuniary motives for economic actions (such as sentiments of fairness and solidarity), bounded rationality,[17] and entrepreneurship itself; others are of a different nature, such as institutions or knowledge, technology and innovation. The importance of these intangible factors was stressed by two non-orthodox economists, Keynes and Schumpeter, the most brilliant and innovative economic minds of the 20th century: Keynes put some of these factors – expectations, uncertainty, investors' 'animal spirits' – at the very centre of the mechanism of economic activity, while Schumpeter developed what is still the most illuminating conception of the en-

[17] The term refers to the impossibility for individuals to process unlimited amounts of data and their consequent restriction to limited information based on their own capabilities.

trepreneur's role and behaviour. Still, contemporary mainstream economics continues to practically ignore or downplay the aspects that it is unable to insert into its elegant formal models – or only represents them in a distorted or excessively simplified form when compelled to consider them – even if this means failing to provide an accurate explanation of fundamental economic phenomena (such as the role and motivations of entrepreneurs' activity).[18]

This attitude is to some extent merely the result of the force of tradition: economists taking inspiration from the abstract model of a competitive market economy of small firms provided by Smith in the first part of his work, in the closing decades of the 19th century developed economic theory – with a few exceptions – on the basis of a vision of economic activity as the spontaneous result of the choices of a multitude of individual economic agents all acting in the market, in conditions of perfect competition, as rational utility maximizers under constraints (these being only the general scarcity of resources and a given initial possession of personal wealth and capabilities; no account being taken of unequal power positions – which can strongly influence them – nor of the origin of the initial personal wealth); this process of maximization leading to a final optimal social configuration named general economic equilibrium.[19] But basically it is an attitude connected to the economists' pretence that, among the social sciences, economics is the only 'scientific' one.

In Western societies, from the 18th century onwards, the physical sciences made great progress and gained considerable prestige. Among the social sciences, only economics – through the use of measurable quantitative data and the application of mathematics and complex geometrical representations – seemed able to approach the methodological precision of the physical sciences and discover similar fundamental laws and principles. In reality, however, there are some basic insuperable differences between economics and the exact sciences, such as the almost total impossibility of carrying out controlled experiments in economics (especially as regards the macro-aspects); the fact that the very object of economic analysis, the behaviour of economic agents, is affected by their beliefs and expectations, and is thus subject to continuous change as a consequence of agents' learning from the experience of previous actions and events; and the fact that markets are not natural entities, but are fundamentally shaped by public policy choices, so that economics cannot be separated from politics. But in any case, for this claim to be justified, all aspects of

[18] Reinert (2007) observed that the very three main driving forces of capitalism identified by Sombart – the entrepreneur, the modern state that creates the institutions and the incentives that enable improvements in production and distribution for the benefit of the whole national community, and the mechanization of production with related technological improvements and innovations – were left aside by mainstream economics as they were hardly amenable to formalization.

[19] An example of this traditional attitude, and of the circular reasoning that underlies it, is Wolf's (1990) statement in his article in the *Financial Times* 'Some Myths about Economic Power': 'To have power, there must be a means of applying coercion. Relations in a competitive market are, virtually by definition, non-coercive. Unless private monopolies are involved, only governments can hope to turn economic means into effective forms of power. They can do so by buying arms; by buying influence; by manipulating trade; or by manipulating currencies'.

economic activity that could not be expressed through precise calculation, formulas or mathematical models, as is typically the case with power, had to be left aside and referred to other social sciences.[20]

This last argument calls for a digression. It has given rise to a debate on the tendency of recent decades only to regard as economics the analysis of economic phenomena through formal, usually mathematical, models. Resort to such models – as Rodrik (2015) reminded us in a useful book on the uses and limits of economic models – is fundamental to ensuring the clarity and consistency of the arguments advanced. Models make it possible to express in precise, non-ambiguous terms the hypotheses at the basis of an argument; they provide a rigorous framework within which specific hypotheses and explanations can be tested using economic data; unlike verbal expositions, they can show in a simple but rigorous way the degree of sensitivity of the conclusions of an argument to changes in the initial assumptions. But the use of models raises two fundamental issues.

The first regards the realism and the centrality of the assumptions. Since the aim of all economic theorizing, and particularly models, is to offer, at a high level of abstraction, a description of the fundamental mechanisms that operate in the real world, it is essential that the hypotheses on which models are built reflect the readily observable features of the real economy and that they manage to isolate, among the many variables that are involved in a phenomenon, those that have a critical, central role in determining the phenomenon. By the way, this book was born from the conviction that the hypotheses of the RHO model (and even the more realistic ones on which 'New Trade Theory' is based) do not adequately reflect modern economic reality, and that it would be of interest to present arguments advanced by economists starting from more realistic hypotheses.

The second issue has already been mentioned: it is usually very difficult to insert variables that reflect factors not amenable to quantitative expression in economic models – both in their initial assumptions and in their inner working: such factors, therefore, tend to be either completely eliminated from the analysis or just mentioned in passing. When these factors are of primary importance in determining economic behaviour and economic events (and, as Einstein is said to have observed, 'Everything that can be counted does not necessarily count; everything that counts cannot necessarily be counted'), two serious negative consequences follow. The first is that essential determinants of economic phenomena are omitted, so that the explanation of the phenomena examined is, at best, only partial. The second consequence is more devastating, as it distorts the whole evolution of economic theory. Once economists realize that in the academic world – and especially in academic literature – only formally elaborate modelling is considered to constitute serious economics, they will shy away from those economic subjects and issues where the fundamental

[20] Moreover, some economists have argued that since the methodology of modern mainstream economics is the only one having 'scientific' character, other social sciences should also try to adopt it. Such 'economic imperialism' has been strongly criticized by, among others, Rothschild (2008).

factors involved are not amenable to precise quantitative expression. They will, on the contrary, concentrate on those subjects and issues offering maximum scope for the development of elegant presentation, formal refinement and use of advanced testing techniques, even if they are of secondary or minor economic significance. The result will be the building up of a seriously distorted theoretical edifice, whose parts will be out of proportion with their effective empirical significance; a distortion that will also produce negative educational effects as it will inevitably be transmitted to the teaching of economics.

This explains, for example, why, in the field of imperfectly competitive market configurations, monopolistic competition based on product differentiation and scale economies – for which advanced modelling instruments have been developed – has been from the mid-1970s the object of detailed analyses on the part of international economists; while the larger phenomenon of oligopoly, which presents more problems of formal modelling, has attracted much less attention despite its great importance in contemporary economic life. Another example was advanced by Krugman (1990) in the introduction to his book: he argued that Smith, rather than Ricardo, had clearly identified some very important factors giving rise to, and following from, trade, such as scale economies. These factors were ignored or minimized by mainstream economics for a long time because of a lack of advanced mathematical instruments with which to model them, and were only recently rediscovered by 'New Trade Theory' economists when those instruments became available. The long dominance of Ricardo over Smith (of comparative advantage over scale economies), Krugman concluded, was thus simply down to economists' search for 'the perceived line of least mathematical resistance' (p. 3-4).

More debatable is Krugman's position on the issue of models: he has argued – see Krugman (1993) – that all theoretical thinking consists of some kind of modelling, that economics is essentially a collection of models, and that broad insights need to be expressed in model form if they want to have any influence. He does recognize, as in the previous paragraph's example, the distortions that the tendency of economists to emphasize what they know how to model can create, but he still strongly supports the insistence on formal modelling.

A second reason power was left out of mainstream economics is of an ideological nature. Since the last part of the 19th century, when a strong capitalist class had consolidated and a powerful socialist movement argued that workers were not receiving wages corresponding to the full value of the goods they produced, the approach to economics of the classical economists, Smith, Ricardo and Marx, centred on the study of the factors (particularly power conflicts) that determine the distribution of incomes among the different classes of economic agents participating in the production process, was abandoned; and an alternative approach, marginalism, strictly centred on individual economic agents' choices, was developed.

The theories of the classical economists were based on the labour theory of value, according to which the value of a good was identified with the labour time necessary for its production; a theory (discussed in Section 9.3.2) that involved a lot of difficult theoretical and empirical problems. With the marginalist revolution, the position adopted by economists to solve (or, more properly, to set aside) the problem of goods' value – a position that would be held up to our times – was the theoretically and empirically more simple, and politically very convenient one, of measuring the value of a good by the price it fetches in the market on the basis of the law of supply and demand; supply and demand determined, in their turn, by the subjective choices, based on intensities of desires, of individual utility-maximising consumers and producers who operate in a static world of scarce resources. The basic underlying hypothesis was that perfect competition rules in the economic system, leading to a harmonious general equilibrium where every economic agent receives an income exactly corresponding to his contribution to the market value of the good created by the production process. In this system, there is no possibility of establishing an objective measure of value different from the market price, and exploitation cannot exist as no one can receive 'unearned income' (since, in a circular reasoning, we receive an income because we are productive, while the proof that we are productive is the mere fact that we receive an income for our services).

The weak point of this ingenious theoretical construction is that, while the owners of factors of production receive the 'just' remuneration for the services of their factors, it remains a mystery how the initial distribution of resources takes place. But this is not a secondary issue. On the basis of this distribution, some people happen to have capital and land (both in very different amounts) to contribute to the production process, while others, for lack of alternatives, can only offer their work; some people happen to have great wealth and a high income they can use for investment or consumption, while others can only spend for consumption the miserable wages they receive. In the words of Kay (2003):

> The obvious problem is that the value people attach to particular goods or services is the result not just of how much they want those goods or services, but also how much money they have. Mr Saito did not put the extraordinary value of $82.5 million on *Portrait of Dr Gachet* because he was uniquely devoted to great art but because he was extraordinarily rich. The legitimacy of market values as weights depends on the legitimacy of the income distribution that gives rise to it. (p. 177)

Mainstream economists of the last 150 years have set aside the problem by taking the initial distribution of resources in a society as given and not belonging to the field of economic analysis (the issue was relegated to sociology, at most to economic history). In this way, they avoided the discussion – where the analysis of power aspects would have been unavoidable – of how that distribution has come into existence and whether it is legally, politically, economically and morally justified. They limited themselves to underlining the utmost importance, for an economy to function properly, of a clear and stable framework of property rights; basically ignoring that, as underlined by Kay (2003), these rights 'are socially constructed, and can be defined in many ways and allocated among individuals, households and firms in many ways' (p. 317).

A third reason is of a more practical nature, as argued by Rothschild (1971):

> The disregard of power aspects is greatly helped by the fact that concentration on the mechanics of economic and market adjustment within a given framework enables the economist to avoid the detailed occupation with facts which powerful social groups prefer to keep under a cloud of uncertainty. This desire for secrecy is in itself a real and objective difficulty ... With power, however, the discovery of truth is not only difficult, it can also lead to clashes with entrenched interests. Thus the social scientist is faced with difficulties ... At its worst, the economist facing this situation turns apologist by covering up existing power relations behind an impressive barrage of "economic necessities" and "economic laws". But one can escape this dilemma without running into trouble by concentrating on those aspects of the economic scene in which power relations are unimportant or can be taken as exogenously given. (pp. 11–12)

Later, Rothschild (2002) stressed the fact that mainstream economists' reference to the Smithian model of perfect competition among small firms, the consequent support for free markets and minimum state intervention, and the neglect of issues of distribution among classes and groups with unequal power positions all provide strong support for those groups that hold and exercise superior power; groups that can exert a powerful influence on economists' careers, external appointments and funds for research.[21]

Galbraith (1983), in turn, argued that economists' silence on power aspects was not only a condition for the application in economic theorizing and teaching of refined geometrical and mathematical tools that require the assumption of free market competition; but it was also a particularly efficient instrument for social conditioning, that is for exercising the 'conditioned power' mentioned earlier, in order to hide the reality of the dominant power of big corporations in contemporary economic life: 'power is served in many ways and ... no service is more useful than the cultivation of the belief that is does not exist' (p. 137). However, he was optimistic for the future: he argued that at the time he wrote, this conditioning power was proving less and less effective, as it was becoming obvious to everybody that it collided too much with reality. Developments in following decades would prove that his optimism was unwarranted.

9.3 Imperialism and unequal exchange

In no other aspect of international economic intercourse was the exercise of power at the same time so fundamental, so evident and so universally acknowledged as in the

[21] One may wonder, with Rothschild, why extremist pro-market economists, according to whom state action must be reduced to a minimum because politicians are just personal utility maximizers looking for vote-maximization or appointment to higher office (when not for maximum personal enrichment by whatever means) never regard economists as utility maximizers looking for maximum prestige and career opportunities rather than for 'truth'.

On the conditioning power of powerful business groups over economic (but also non-economic) researchers, experts and regulators see Zingales (2012).

relationship between colonizing and colonized countries. Violence and plunder were the forces that practically without exception allowed the initial establishment and the subsequent perpetuation of colonial relationships.

Since the very birth, with Adam Smith, of modern economics, economic relations between leading European countries and their overseas colonies have been the object of specific analyses and heated debates by economists. In *The Wealth of Nations*, Smith devoted a specific chapter entitled 'Of Colonies' to the issue. Ricardo also had a chapter 'On Colonial Trade' in his *Principles*, in which he basically agreed with Smith's negative view of the colonial institution, although he admitted that trade with the colonies could be regulated so as to confer on the mother country more benefits than under free trade. Marx put relations between dominant capitalistic industrial countries and colonial/peripheral areas at the centre of his view of the development of capitalism, but he died before producing, as he had planned, a detailed study of international economic relations, and did not even sketch a theory of imperialism;[22] so his ideas on the subject (discussed by Brewer (1980)) were differently interpreted by his followers, originating sharp controversies. From the middle of the 19th century until the end of World War II, the issue attracted little attention by mainstream economists. Keynes was also silent on the subject; while Schumpeter showed a keen interest in it, to the point of writing a study on imperialism in 1919 (translated into English in Schumpeter (1951)), but concentrated his analysis on its sociological and psychological aspects, leaving aside the economic ones. In response to the Marxist authors who identified imperialism as the highest phase of capitalist development, he played down the importance of economic motivations for the phenomenon, arguing that the colonialist and imperialist drive is not the product of capitalism, but of pre-capitalist, atavistic irrational aggressive impulses to war and conquest; impulses that with capitalism and the spread of market relations would gradually disappear (he again criticized Marxist theories of imperialism in Schumpeter (1942), but without providing any personal contribution to the issue). So the analysis of the economic relationships between industrial countries and underdeveloped areas was almost exclusively left to Marxist economists,[23] who developed their theories of imperialism between 1900 and 1920.

Things started to change after World War II, when the condition of underdevelopment in which the majority of world populations lived was at last universally recognized as a central problem in world politics and economics: with the colonial system

---

[22] Hirschman (1976) noticed that, strangely, Marx did not even take up the economic theory of imperialism that Hegel – a personality who strongly influenced his whole work – had briefly formulated in 1821 in *Philosophy of Right*. This theory, which anticipated those developed at the beginning of the following century by Hobson and Rosa Luxemburg, stressed the insufficiency of domestic consumption to absorb current production in more advanced countries and the consequent drive to seek markets in foreign lands.

[23] Apart from the case of Hobson, discussed in Section 9.3.1, as a partial exception one may point to Graham (1923), who stressed the advantage of specialization in manufactures rather than in primary products, as a consequence of the already mentioned differences in returns to scale in the two sectors.

starting to break up and the Cold War developing, the possibility could be envisaged that newly independent countries might adopt, as had happened with China, the socialist model of the USSR: in fact during the 1960s, on the basis of the results of the 1930–1960 Soviet experience, that model seemed to offer the highest potential for rapid exit from underdevelopment through industrialization.[24] Post-war research on underdevelopment, its causes and cures was thus carried out not only by Marxists and other non-orthodox economists, but also by many other economists – of very different ideological and economic convictions – belonging to the academic world, leading to the creation in the course of the 1950s of a specific branch of economics called development economics.

An early, basic contribution to this new branch was provided by Arthur Lewis (1954, 1955), who produced extremely useful insights on the determination of countries' wages and prices and on the factors responsible for what appeared at the time as a tendency to the worsening of underdeveloped countries' terms of trade (that is, the ratio of the average price of the products they exported to advanced countries to the average price of the products they imported from them).[25] At the time, his insights did not attract the attention they deserved; but in the early 1970s the issue became a topical subject and for a decade originated heated debates within the left following the publication in 1969 of Emmanuel's *Unequal Exchange*, in which it was argued that advanced countries – and their working classes – exploit Third World countries through the mechanism of import and export prices. Lewis further developed his analysis of the terms of trade between industrial and tropical countries in the second half of the 1970s, providing interesting new insights that were discussed by economists at the time, but were then left aside in the following three decades (when Emmanuel's work also seemed to have been gradually forgotten). It is only in more recent times that the subject of 'unequal exchange' seems to be re-emerging – although in very different terms – as a consequence of the growing importance in the world economy of GVCs and the connected problem of determining how, within these chains, the prices of final goods are formed in the successive stages of their production and distribution (see Chapter 11).

[24] This conviction was not only deep-rooted in supporters of socialism and shared by many Third World leaders; though today the fact seems to have been completely forgotten, it was also widespread among Western politicians and economists opposed to Communism, who, consequently, nourished deep political worries.

[25] In the debate on the terms of trade between underdeveloped and advanced countries, given the respective specializations of the two groups of countries at the time and the data then available, economists mainly referred to the terms of trade between primary and manufactured products. For recent evidence on the terms of trade for primary products versus manufactures from 1865 to 2009 see Ocampo and Parra-Lancourt (2010); on the terms of trade for developing versus developed countries from 1980 to 2014 see UNCTAD (2016).

9.3.1 Theories of imperialism

Since the end of the 19th century, the need was widely felt among left-wing economists for the elaboration of a theory of capitalist imperialism (that is, of a theory of the asymmetrical economic relationships between capitalist industrial centres and colonial and semi-colonial periphery, the former aiming, in the words of Blaug (1985), at 'political and economic control over backward areas to guarantee the home country an outlet for idle savings and surplus manufactured goods in exchange for strategic raw materials' (p. 259)). By that time, new developments in the international economy – related to what is now called the 'first globalization' – had taken place that modified the economic landscape compared with the times of Smith, Ricardo and Marx. The main new phenomena that students of imperialism identified and on which they concentrated their attention were the acceleration of the geographical spread of capitalism, with a scramble for colonies and inter-imperialist rivalry, especially between old and new industrial countries; the importance and rapid growth of capital exports by capitalist centres; the development of monopolies, cartels and trusts in advanced countries; the growing importance in these countries of finance capital and its fusion with industrial capital in huge national interlocking groups; and the difficulty of finding domestic outlets for massively increased industrial production.

From 1902 onwards, theories of imperialism were advanced. As they have been the object of extensive surveys and critical expositions – see Kemp (1967), Owen and Sutcliffe (1972), Brewer (1980, 1999) and Griffin and Gurley (1985) – only a short summary of them will be presented here.

The initial contribution was provided by a non-Marxist English economic heretic, J. A. Hobson. In 1902, he wrote *Imperialism: A Study*, a work that strongly influenced subsequent Marxist theories of imperialism; but he was also a precursor of the Keynesian theory of employment, as Keynes himself underlined. Hobson held that the advanced capitalist states were driven to conquer and occupy new lands by the necessity of finding outlets abroad for the capital and goods that capitalists could not place at home; the reason for this drive was that the productive power of modern industry required the continuing opening up of new markets and areas of investment, but the domestic 'mal-distribution of consuming power' prevented the absorption of goods and capital within capitalist countries. Imperialism was the inefficient result of an economic system that concentrated in the hands of the 'possessing classes' more purchasing power than they could consume or invest at home. This oversaving could be eliminated, according to Hobson, by a political change in the income distribution system, so as to make the excess of purchasing power flow to workers in the form of higher wages and to the community in the form of higher taxes on the more wealthy to be spent to satisfy social needs.[26]

[26] Hauner, Milanovic and Naidu (2017) have found empirical support for Hobson's theory with reference to belligerent countries in the years preceding World War I. [continue on next page].

In the following fifteen years, Marxists produced their basic works on the economic theory of imperialism. In 1913, Rosa Luxemburg, a Polish-German thinker, published *The Accumulation of Capital*, in which she developed Hobson's insights into a complex (and heavily criticized) theory of the necessity, if capitalist accumulation was not to come to an end, of finding outlets for growing industrial production in exports to non-capitalist areas. In 1910, a fundamental contribution had been provided by the Austrian Rudolf Hilferding in *Finance Capital*. He underlined the importance in industrial countries of the rise of the joint-stock company since the last decades of the 19th century, a development that led to a huge concentration of capital in the hands of the managers of a few large companies. He argued that this had produced in industrial production the replacement of free competition by monopolistic structures such as cartels and trusts; and that this process of concentration in production was associated with – and reinforced by – a second fundamental development, namely the growing connection between industrial and banking capital, with the second dominating the first, so that the system could go under the name of 'financial capital'.

In *Imperialism and World Economy*, written in 1915, the Russian Nikolai Bucharin took up Hilferding's new insights and stressed the contradiction between the concentration and centralization of capital inside each industrial country, and the drive of national capital to expand outside national borders. At international level, while growing interdependence required the formation of supranational aggregations and monopolies, such a development found an obstacle in the different interests and strategies of individual states and national capitalist groups. The result was increasing international rivalry, leading the capitalist system to war and breakdown. In his famous pamphlet *Imperialism, the Highest Stage of Capitalism*, written in 1916, Lenin drew on Hobson, Hilferding and Bucharin, producing a synthesis of their theories that enjoyed great popularity all over the world.

The works of Hilferding, Bucharin and Lenin have been the object of widespread criticism, starting from the fact that they tended to attribute to all industrial countries some characteristics that were more typical of the German experience. However, they did identify and stress – apart from the growing importance of foreign trade and international capital movements – one fundamental aspect of the dynamics of capitalism since the last decades of the 19th century, namely the rise to dominance of the large corporation and the diffusion of monopolistic and oligopolistic practices; a development that creates a lot of problems for traditional economic theory, built on the premise of free competition. In fact, in the 1930s academic economists started to acknowledge changes in firms' competitive behaviour, producing new theories based on the notions of imperfect and monopolistic competition and developing the study of the modern large corporation. In the first decades after World War II, it was the

An interpretation of the contemporary economic relationship between the USA and China in terms of Hobson's theory of underconsumption leading to imperialism, has been advanced by Austin (2011): paradoxically, in this case it is China that plays the role of the 'imperialist' country, using the USA as a vent for its excess savings and commodities.

analysis of oligopoly that would make significant progress; while the role of the large corporation and monopolies in contemporary capitalism would be the object of two important works by unorthodox economists: the Marxists Baran and Sweezy (1966), and Galbraith (1967).

In the following decades, attention concentrated on the nature and operation of MNCs, since these were universally recognized as the leading actors on the international scene, in particular with reference to the two basic developments of the last thirty years: offshoring and GVCs. But new insights on the role of the big firm inside industrial countries were limited: to some extent, one may speculate, this may be because of the dramatic changes produced by the ICT revolution in firms' technological and organizational set-up, and because the consequences of these changes are still extremely uncertain, especially as regards the effect on the size of firms, since it is still impossible to assess whether they will lead to an increase or a decrease in the importance of scale economies in production and distribution.

As for the theory of imperialism, in the forty years after World War I no major new development was registered, probably as a consequence of the lack of debate in left-wing circles in the intellectually stifling atmosphere of the Stalinist period. But it is important to remember that Marx's belief in the progressive role of Western capitalism's penetration in peripheral areas had been reversed since 1928 by the international communist movement and left-wing economists, who argued that this penetration caused underdevelopment rather than development.

A new contribution based on this last insight was produced by the Marxist economist Baran (1957). Concentrating on the problems of underdeveloped countries (most of which at the time had not yet achieved political independence), he argued that forcible penetration by Western capitalist powers into these countries did not release in them the productive forces of capitalism, leading to the creation of modern industry and the abandonment of pre-capitalistic forms of economic organization. The development of capitalism in these countries did not follow the same trajectory as in the advanced countries that industrialized later than England. Rather, the particular conditions of the incorporation of colonial areas into the capitalist system created specific obstacles to capitalist industrialization and condemned these areas to persistent underdevelopment. While emigrants from Western Europe who had moved to temperate lands of white settlement (uninhabited or made such by extermination of natives), unencumbered by feudal traditions, established capitalist societies and – once they managed to overthrow the mother country's domination – freely proceeded on the road of accumulation and development, in peripheral areas where European mass settlement was not possible, the situation evolved in a very different direction.

In these last societies, where feudal or other pre-capitalist cultures and economic practices prevailed, Europeans, from their initial penetration, engaged in plunder, extermination of natives, seizure of slaves and colonial subjugation aimed at extracting maximum short-term gains from the exploitation of mineral and agricultural resources – one extreme instance of such devastating European intervention being, in modern times, the Belgian Congo under King Leopold's rule (1885–1906), as illustrated by Hochschild (1998); but even the record of the more 'enlightened' British colonial rule is tragic, as Tharoor (2017) reminded us with reference to India. While Western rule introduced some changes that stimulated capitalist development, such as the expansion of trade, the introduction of more advanced technology and the provision of some transport infrastructure, other prerequisites for the development of capitalism were blocked by colonial powers. All through the colonial period, these powers appropriated the colonies' surplus (the difference between production and necessary consumption), which might have been used for capitalist accumulation, and through prohibition or commercial policy prevented the development of local industry, while handicraft was destroyed by the competition of manufactures from the advanced Western powers. The economy of the colonies and semi-colonies was mainly in the hands of foreign capital and foreign enterprise, interested in the extraction of profits to be sent back home rather than in the development of local capitalism. In agriculture, feudal landowners prevailed, with little interest in modernization of their estates. The local bourgeoisie of merchants engaged in trade, commodity speculation and moneylending – the class that in Western countries, together with some artisans, had given impulse to capitalist accumulation, turning into a class of industrial and financial entrepreneurs – was unable to extend its role beyond parasitic subservience to foreign capital and enterprise. The state, which in all the cases of Western (and Japanese) capitalist development had exercised a key role in supporting industrialization – through the protection of new industries from foreign competition, the provision of essential infrastructure and education, and other initiatives – was in the hands of colonial administrators systematically hostile to the growth of local manufacturing industry. The final result of all this was the permanence of the colonial and semi-colonial periphery's backwardness.

These ideas of Baran, and specifically the notion that monopoly capitalism and imperialism in advanced countries and economic and social backwardness in underdeveloped ones were strictly connected, would be at the basis of a revival of left-wing theories of imperialism in the late 1960s and 1970s. While a number of economists contributed to this revival (among them Arrighi, Furtado, Cardoso, Dos Santos and Amin), it was A. G. Frank's (1967) 'dependency theory' and Wallerstein's (1979) 'world-system' perspective, that enjoyed the widest popularity in left-wing circles. These two authors moved from the premise that capitalism must be analysed as a global exchange system that allows world centres – thanks to their stronger state machine, economic resources and monopolistic powers – to expropriate the economic surplus of peripheral areas. In contrast to Marx and his followers, who characterized capitalism as a specific mode of production born with the Industrial Revolution (free labourers selling their labour power to capitalists who monopolize ownership of the means of production), they identified capitalism with exchange, and so dated its birth back to the first long-distance commercial initiatives of Italian city-states in the 13th–16th centuries. While the metropolitan centres would move with time from Italian city-states to Portugal and Spain, then to Holland and England and finally to the USA, the metropolis–periphery exploitative relationship would never disappear. Peripheral areas, deprived of their potential investment funds, and most of them also of political sovereignty, would be unable to start a development process and would remain, with few exceptions, in a state of dependence that would lead to the formation of a local ruling class subservient to metropolitan powers and whose interest would be the perpetuation of their own country's underdevelopment.

Frank and Wallerstein, while introducing some elements of novelty with respect to Baran's analysis, lacked a systematic theoretical structure, employed debatable terms and concepts, and tended to make unwarranted generalizations. Not surprisingly, they were the object of severe criticism – see, for example, Lall (1975), Brenner (1977), Brewer (1980) and Barratt Brown (1999). But above all, as will be argued in Section 9.4.2, they were contradicted by the developments of recent decades, when some former peripheral countries – China in the first place – managed to escape, through industrialization and exports of manufactures, the 'development of underdevelopment' to which, according to those authors, they were inexorably condemned.

A major contribution to the revival of the issue of imperialism in the 1970s came from the publication of a very controversial book on 'unequal exchange' by Emmanuel (1969), which will be the object of Section 9.3.2. Debates on imperialism continued among left wing economists in the 1980s, but thereafter the issue, while not falling into total oblivion, appeared to lose much of its interest and no particularly significant contribution was made. Probably this reflected the political and ideological shock produced in left-wing circles, on the one hand, by the sudden, inglorious and totally unforeseen meltdown of the USSR (with its European communist satellites) and, on the other, by the equally unforeseen epochal development represented by the Chinese economic miracle, which took place within a framework of increasingly capitalist economic institutions and policies.

The world scene of the last thirty years was characterized by the widespread adoption, on the part of developing countries (especially the more dynamic ones) of new development policies based on greater resort to market institutions, huge foreign investments by advanced countries' MNCs and exceptional growth of manufactured exports. This new economic environment, and the contemporaneous ICT revolution, led to the massive transfer of manufacturing activity from advanced to developing countries, and in particular to the formation of a new kind of international division of labour, based on networks managed by MNCs, producing parts of manufactured goods in different countries to be assembled in a final location. These GVCs will be examined in Section 11.2; the analysis of their structure, their hierarchical organization and, especially, the division of the final value of the goods among participants in the chains have been the object of increasing study by economists, leading in some instances to a revival of concepts and interpretations connected with the theories of imperialism.

9.3.2 The problem of unequal exchange

The central issue in the economic relationships between advanced and developing countries is the determination of the terms of trade between the products exchanged by the two groups. In fact most of the power asymmetries (military, political, technological, economic) between the two groups – which led to the imposition of colonial and semi-colonial rule and the distortions that this rule produced in the economies of the second group – and the existence of the latter's 'exploitation' by advanced countries, should find ultimate expression in the prices of the products exchanged. It is these prices that reflect the characteristics of the supply of and demand for the products exchanged; characteristics which in turn are the result of the overall economic structure of the two groups of countries and their interrelationships.[27]

This problem is basically an extension to all the products exchanged between the two areas of the problem of the determination of the exchange rate between wine and cloth that Ricardo tried to solve as soon as he had established the comparative costs principle. As was explained in Footnote 8 in Chapter 1, he easily identified the range of the wine/cloth exchange ratios that in his famous example would make trade advantageous (compared with autarchy) to both Portugal and England; but did not enunciate a rule that would determine where exactly, within that range, the exchange ratio would be fixed; J. S. Mill advanced in 1844 a solution that involved 'reciprocal demand curves' and abandoning the labour theory of value. Mainstream economists in the following one hundred and eighty years or so clung to that solution, but did not devote much effort to investigating the underlying forces that determine the shape of the supply and demand curves for the products exchanged (just as they failed to investigate the forces that led to given shapes of the supply and demand curves for work in domestic wage determination). For them, as long as the act of exchange was voluntary and the determination of the prices of the products exchanged was left to the market and not imposed by force, there was very little for the economist to say on the subject.

The concept of unequal exchange was clearly present in Adam Smith, when he discussed the exchange of products between town and country in *The Wealth of Na-*

---

[27] The problem of unequal exchange refers to the prices of products exchanged and the remuneration of the factors employed in their production in trading countries. However, if one is interested in the more general inequality of the gains trading countries derive from exchange, once it is realized that the RHO model's hypothesis of full employment in trading countries is seldom observed in the real world – especially when developing countries are considered – it is clear that analyses limited to products' prices become unacceptable: employment – and other – benefits and losses owing to trade can be highly significant and must be taken into account. In Section 6.2 it was remarked that in the case of balanced trade, the employment gains that trading countries derive from exchange may be very different (since the employment activated in a country by the export of one dollar of a good can be very different from that activated, in the country where it is produced, by the import of a dollar of the good received in exchange); but the scope for inequality in employment gains is greatly widened by the frequent cases of unbalanced trade and the operation of absolute advantages. Inequality in the employment effects of trade explain why in advanced countries complaints are frequently heard about losses that trade with emerging economies – while improving terms of trade – produces in many sectors for workers displaced by low-wage competition.

Unequal gains from trade can also flow from other factors and operate in the opposite direction: for example, in trade between advanced and developing countries, the advantages of acquisition of technological knowledge incorporated in the products exchanged are usually very high for the latter group and non-existent for the former.

tions. Referring to the incomes of town workers and of their employers, he noted that 'Whatever regulations, therefore, tend to increase those wages and profits beyond what they otherwise would be, tend to enable the town to purchase, with a smaller quantity of its labour, the produce of a greater quantity of the labour of the country' (1961, Book 1, Ch. X, pp. 139–140). This is possible, he explained, because producers concentrated in a town can easily combine together to apply monopolistic practices against countryside producers scattered over large areas; in addition, he pointed out that towns, frequently situated on the coast or on navigable rivers, can buy their supplies of agricultural products from many alternative, even far-away, suppliers, while producers in the countryside have no corresponding possibilities in their purchases of towns' products and services.

Marx based his whole theory of capitalism on the notion of 'exploitation'. Like Smith and Ricardo, he believed in a labour theory of value: the value of a product is given by the number of work hours (of a given average quality and efficiency) necessary – directly, and indirectly through the application of labour to the production of capital goods and other inputs – to produce that product. As the capitalist class has monopolistically appropriated the whole mass of the means of production, workers have no choice but to accept an unequal exchange: they must sell the power of using their working capabilities to a capitalist for a certain number of hours – say ten a day – and receive in exchange a wage that corresponds to the value of the labour necessary to produce the worker himself; that is, to the number of work hours necessary to produce the goods that represent in their society the necessary minimum for workers' subsistence and reproduction. This necessary minimum requires for its production a lower number of work hours – say seven – than that furnished by the workers to the capitalist. The surplus value, corresponding to the difference of three hours between the labour power sold by the workers and the labour incorporated in the wage they receive, is the measure of their exploitation.

Marx did not believe in Malthus's theory of population, according to which any increase in the availability of food would be followed by an increase in population, which would bring income and consumption back to the subsistence level. But he held that in order to safeguard their profits and make sure that workers' wages are kept at subsistence level despite the spread of industrial production, capitalists – apart from trying to extend the number of hours of work supplied by each worker – strive to increase workers' productivity by introducing labour-saving technical innovations and new machinery into production processes. In this way they can ensure the continuous existence of an excess of labour supply over demand (the 'industrial reserve army').

Of course Marx's theory is not as rough and simplistic as synthetized here. But this seems to represent its basic core, and it appears both to make sense logically and to reflect the reality of workers' shameful exploitation in the first phases of industrial capitalism. The problem with Marxist notions of value and exploitation is that they raise a number of unsurmountable difficulties at both the theoretical and the empirical level. Apart from the problems that will be indicated below in this section, no satisfactory procedure has been found to reduce different kinds of work and different skills to a common unit of measure; nor to determine the value in terms of work hours of land, minerals and other non-reproducible factors and products; the direct and indirect labour content of both the goods produced by the workers and the goods on which they spend their subsistence wages, is practically impossible to calculate. What we can observe and measure are only wages and prices of products; and although intuitively one may sense that prices should in the long run reflect somehow products' direct and indirect labour content, the practical difficulties and the theoretical complexities of deriving prices from values (the famous 'transformation problem') have proved impossible to overcome, thus leaving the whole construction of Marxist economics without a solid foundation.[28]

The difficulties with the Marxist labour theory of value appear even more unmanageable when, from the national context in which Marx developed his analysis, one moves to the international context. Here one is faced with two basic additional conceptual problems. The first is the apparently unsolvable one of establishing the very meaning of the 'international value of a good' exchanged between different nations. Is it the average number of labour hours necessary for the production of the good in the exporting country? Or in the importing country? Or in the average of the two trading countries? Or in the average of all countries of the world producing – or exporting – that good?[29] The problem has become more and more serious with time, as in all countries the share of imports and exports in gross national product has continually increased, especially in the last fifty years. Ricardo was well aware of this problem, and came to the conclusion that while the labour theory of value applies to the exchange ratios between goods within a country, it does not apply to goods exchanged internationally; and, as already mentioned, it has even been argued that it was largely to prove this point that he developed the theory of comparative costs.

The second problem concerns the determination of the value of the labour necessary to produce the worker himself; that is, the value of the goods necessary to ensure the survival and reproduction of the worker. This value, according to Marx and all his followers, is not exactly the same everywhere, not only owing to differences in the amount and characteristics of goods that, given local conditions, are needed for survival, but also to the fact that a historic element – which reflects the past evolution of wage levels, traditions, habits and shared values – contributes to determine what in each country is considered as the 'minimum necessary' remuneration of the worker.[30] These differences were not so great up to the middle of the 19th century,

[28] See J. Robinson (1966b) for a critique of Marx's economic theory. Schumpeter (1942) concluded that 'For economics as a positive science... which has to describe or explain actual processes, it is much more important to ask how the labour theory of value works as a tool of analysis, and the real trouble with it is that it does so very badly' (pp. 23–24).

[29] Barratt Brown (1974) observed: 'It is possible in any single country to talk about socially necessary labour-time because there is a norm for technical conditions of production from which deviations are not very great, but between countries the idea of an average world-wide socially necessary labour-time in production has very little meaning, as the wide range of wages and productivity [in different countries] ... indicates' (p. 239).

[30] This point had already been stressed by Smith: 'By necessaries I understand, not only the commodities which are indispensably necessary for the support of life, but whatever the custom of the coun-

when, after all, the miserable average real wage of an English worker was not so much greater than that of an Italian or even an Indian worker. But since those times, wages in advanced countries have progressively increased, as industrial activity grew at very high rates, workers formed trade unions that managed to ensure continuous improvements of wages and working conditions, and from the last decades of the 19th century welfare states started to develop, with an impressive extension and geographical diffusion after World War II – so that the 'minimum necessary' remuneration must now cover a relatively large number of basic needs. In underdeveloped countries, instead, the subsistence wage has grown, on the whole, at a much slower rate.[31] The wage differences in absolute terms between the two groups of countries have become so incredibly large that since the 1980s they have led to a huge transfer of manufacturing activity from advanced countries to developing countries. According to some authors, these differences represent the basic mechanism of exploitation of the latter countries, in particular within contemporary GVCs.

But there is another, more basic problem with Marx's theory that – even if all the problems so far indicated could somehow be solved – makes the very reference to labour content in the analysis of unequal exchange and exploitation inadequate in the context of the capitalist system as it has evolved since Marx's times and more particularly in the last forty years. Already towards the end of Marx's life (he died in 1883), the main productive forces at the basis of capitalist development had ceased to be the traditional factors of land, labour and capital. As was explained in Chapter 5, the dynamics of capitalism in modern times depends increasingly on the progress of scientific knowledge and on the systematic application of that knowledge to productive activity in the form of innovations and technological improvements; two phenomena that are strictly related to the accumulation of human capital in all its forms and to the resources that are devoted to scientific and technological research. The

---

try renders it indecent for creditable people, even of the lowest order, to be without' (1961, Book V, Ch. II, p. 399).

[31] This has not meant that the overall standard of living of the workers in today's developing countries (even the poorest ones) has also progressed very slowly: on the contrary, as stressed by Deaton (2013), general conditions of life have greatly improved in the last hundred years in these countries. But this improvement, rather than the increases in subsistence wages, basically reflected the introduction and diffusion of important scientific discoveries and technical and social innovations and practices produced in advanced countries, particularly in the medical field – so that basic measures of well-being for developing countries nowadays show much higher levels than those recorded by today's advanced countries when they were at comparable levels of development. Thanks to the adoption of public initiatives in sanitation and water supplies, chemical war against disease-bearing pests, large-scale vaccination and new medicines, the most important indicator of living conditions – the number of years a person can be expected to live – has increased dramatically: as reported by Deaton, in 2005–2010, people over ten years old in less developed regions of the world could expect, according to the United Nations, to die at the age of 66, as against 42 in 1950–1955. Other important improvements were represented by the introduction of school systems extended to all or most of the population; the adoption of better modes of transport; the availability (which GNP measures can incorporate only very imprecisely) of better-quality products and new ones, increasingly cheaper, such as plastics, radio and TV, mobile telephones and computers.

contribution of this 'knowledge and technology factor' to the growth of production is extremely difficult to measure, but it certainly renders obsolete the descriptions of the production process developed by classical economists in terms of the traditional factors of production.[32]

Of course, this is a criticism that can be addressed not only to Ricardo and Marx, but also to most economists up to our days, as they largely continued to refer to these traditional factors of production. The problem is that only Marx made the economic exploitation of labour by capital the central point of his economic theory as well as the foundation for a revolutionary political movement charged with the mission of reshaping the whole economic and social structure of the world. However, as stressed by Mason (2015), it is a testimony to the depth of Marx's insights that already in 1857–1858 he was aware of the additional difficulties introduced by the new 'knowledge and technology factor', though he did not incorporate it in his main work. He wrote in the *Grundrisse* (which would remain unpublished until a century later) that the productive power of machines such as the cotton-spinning machine, the telegraph and the steam locomotive was 'out of all proportion to the direct labour time spent on their production, but depends rather on the general state of science and on the progress of technology, or the application of this science to production'.

* * *

After Marx, the labour theory of value was abandoned by non-Marxist economists. The value of goods was calculated on the basis, not of some intrinsic value, but of market wages and prices; that is, the total monetary cost of the factors of production used to produce them and the forces of demand. But the problem of unequal exchange did not disappear. At international level it resurfaced, in the form of debate on the long-term movements of Third World countries' terms of trade, in the decades after the end of World War II.

The issue was raised by Prebisch (1950) and Singer (1950), who managed to bring it to the attention of international economists (on their work see Guillermo Peón (2004) and Brolin (2006)). They argued that there was a tendency for Third World countries' terms of trade to deteriorate chiefly for two reasons: first, primary commodities, then these countries' main export products, are characterized by lower income elasticity of demand than manufactures, their main import products; second, while in industrial countries productivity gains translate into increased wages for workers, in underdeveloped countries they translate into lower export prices, to the benefit of foreign purchasers. This is because of the market power of producers and workers in industrial countries, which allows them to keep a high level of wag-

[32] As early as 1827, List, in his pamphlet *Outlines of American Political Economy* published in Philadelphia, had advanced his conception of development based on industrial activity, in which he stressed the crucial role of 'capital of mind', by which he meant something not very far from the contemporary concept of human capital; it included the general level of education of a country's population, the entrepreneurial initiative, the attitude to work, and the level of capabilities and structures of government and public administration.

es, even in unfavourable cyclical phases; while in underdeveloped countries this is not possible, owing to workers' low bargaining power and the limited presence and strength of trade unions.

But it was W. Arthur Lewis who provided, between 1954 and 1978, a new fundamental contribution to the terms of trade issue – a contribution that was developed without reference to the labour theory of value, but only to the free market determination of wages and prices when countries are at very different levels of economic development. This had the advantage of freeing the debate on the mechanisms of unequal exchange from the polemical and moral arguments on the wickedness of colonial and imperialist powers (however justified these arguments may be) that frequently characterize theories of imperialism, connecting instead those mechanisms to the mere working of the market forces of opportunity costs.[33]

9.3.3 Lewis's theory

Lewis presented the core of his argument in 1954–1955. He attributed due importance to the factors responsible for economic growth having taken place in some areas of the world but not in others that at the time and later on were stressed by development economists: the availability of capital, entrepreneurship, education, technology, institutions, relative political power of different social classes, colonialism and so on (see Lewis (1955)); but he concentrated on another point. In his famous article (1954), discussing the expansion of exports by underdeveloped countries, he advanced the fundamental general principle that the wage (in real terms) that people in these countries will ask for and receive for working in any sector of an economy, is basically determined by the compensation or the wage (measured in quantity of food) they can obtain working for the same number of hours in the traditional subsistence agriculture sector where the overwhelming majority of the population finds a living. If in this sector farmers get a very low income because average labour productivity (physical output per man) is very low – owing to overpopulation in the countryside, unfavourable climate or soil conditions, primitive agricultural technologies or any other reason – they will accept work in other sectors of the economy provided they are paid a wage slightly higher than the alternative income they would get by continuing to work in the countryside. This is the reason why they are willing to go to work at very low wages in plantations and mines producing for export. These low wages lead to the low costs and low prices of export products, mainly to the benefit of the final consumers in advanced countries. Any increase in the productivity of workers in plantations and mines does not benefit these workers, as they will continue to be paid little more than the previous wage, since their only alternative is to go back to

[33] Lewis (1978b) discussed extensively, and on some points agreed with, the arguments advanced by the authors of theories of imperialism; but he employed such arguments mainly to better explain the historical origins of what he considered the basic market mechanism determining terms of trade, and to show how colonialism aggravated and consolidated the negative effects of its working.

the low-productivity subsistence agriculture sector. Nor does it normally benefit the capitalist investing in plantations and mines, as Lewis postulates that the capitalist's profit is determined not by the level of productivity in his specific production, but by the general international rate of profit on capital (in theory a country might obtain an increase in the price of its export products by subjecting them to an export tax, but this would require an agreement among all the countries producing the same products to apply a similar tax: a condition difficult to satisfy in practice, though OPEC oil price increases in the 1970s could be cited as a case in point).[34]

From all this, Lewis drew two main conclusions. First, that in underdeveloped countries modern capitalist enterprises in manufacturing and export sectors could be started by taking advantage of the possibility of paying worker wages only slightly above the very low wage in traditional agriculture; this movement of farmers from the land to other activities would not cause any significant reduction in total food production, as the workers who moved first would be those working in the worst agricultural locations, where their productivity was consequently almost zero. Second, that the most important economic goal in these countries, if they wish to improve their international terms of trade,[35] is not to increase the productivity of export sec-

---

[34] In more technical terms, Lewis developed a model with one factor of production (labour), two countries (a tropical one and a temperate advanced one) and three goods (a first good, say rubber, that can be produced only in the tropical country; a second one, say steel, that can be produced only in the temperate advanced country, and a third one, say wheat, representing food in general, that is produced in large quantities in both countries). Suppose that in the tropical country 1 unit of wheat is exchanged for 6 units of rubber, while in the advanced country 1 unit of wheat is exchanged for 3 units of steel. As wheat is produced in both countries, its international price must be the same in both. As a consequence, the international exchange ratio between rubber and steel – apart from fluctuations owing to short-run changes in demand or supply – will be 6 units of rubber for 3 units of steel (equivalent to 2 units of rubber for 1 unit of steel). If the tropical country doubled its productivity in rubber production, so that at home 1 unit of wheat would exchange for 12 units of rubber, the international exchange ratio between rubber and steel would move to 12 units of rubber for 3 units of steel (equivalent to 4 units of rubber for 1 unit of steel), so that the tropical country would see its terms of trade deteriorate by half, all the advantage of the productivity increase going to the rubber consumers, almost all located in the advanced country. If, instead, the tropical country managed to double its productivity in food, then, as rubber producers could go back to the now doubly productive agricultural subsistence sector, their wages in rubber production, and so the rubber price in terms of wheat, would have to double if they were to be kept working in the rubber sector: 1 unit of wheat would thus have to be exchanged no longer for 6 units of rubber, but only for 3. As a consequence, the international exchange ratio would move to 3 units of rubber for 3 units of steel (equivalent to 1 unit of rubber for 1 of steel), producing for the tropical country a doubling, in its favour, of the terms of trade.

It must be stressed that Silvio Gesell – an eccentric personality defined by Keynes in the *General Theory* as an 'unduly neglected prophet', whose monetary theory he much appreciated – had clearly formulated in his 1916 *The Natural Economic Order* the principle at the base of Lewis's theory: 'The wage of the average worker is equal to the fruits of labour of the average cultivator of free land, and is wholly determined by such fruits. Every change in the fruits of labour of the cultivator of free land influences wages, regardless of whether such changes are caused by technical improvements, by scientific discoveries, or by legislation' (Gesell 2012, p. 73).

[35] The notion of a country's terms of trade that is usually employed, and that can be calculated relatively easily from the available empirical data, is the ratio between the index of the prices of products

tors, but the productivity of the agricultural food sector. If this is done, the wages of

---

exported and the index of the prices of products imported, known as the 'commodity terms of trade'. It is essential to note that since all terms of trade indexes are calculated as ratios of export and import price indexes equal to 100 at a chosen base time, and are themselves expressed as indexes equal to 100 at that time, they can only measure improvements or deteriorations in the relationship between export and import prices of a country between time periods; they cannot tell us anything about the advantage, fairness or 'equality' of the exchange ratio between exports and imports at the base time or at any other point in time.

If one is interested in the variation that changes in export and import prices produce in the remuneration of production factors employed in traded goods, the proper index to refer to is the 'double factorial terms of trade', which corrects changes in the commodity terms of trade for changes in the productivity of a country's export sector and of the foreign sector producing the country's imports. This index, unfortunately, is extremely difficult to construct in practice. Conceptually, it measures the changes in the physical quantity of domestic factors embodied in a country's exports that are given in exchange for one unit of foreign factors embodied in its imports. When one wants to refer to the movements of the terms of trade as an indicator of changes in the fairness, 'equality' or degree of exploitation of exchange transactions, this correction for productivity changes in trading countries seems necessary. And this is indeed the notion of terms of trade employed by Lewis (and also by Emmanuel). If one is instead interested in calculating the improvement in the welfare of a country produced by trade, the proper index to use is the 'single factorial terms of trade', which corrects the changes in the commodity terms of trade only for changes in the physical quantity of domestic factors embodied in exports that are given in exchange for one physical unit of imports.

To understand the reason for the correction obtained by referring to double factorial terms of trade, suppose that between two periods, all other conditions remaining unchanged, a technological discovery takes place in the world and can be freely applied to the production of the only good a country exports, increasing the physical productivity of the factors employed for its production; in all probability market forces will lead to a reduction in the world price of the good. If thanks to that discovery a, for example, double quantity of the export good could be produced with the same quantity of production factors and at the same time the international market price of this good was reduced by half, the country's commodity terms of trade would register a 50 per cent deterioration; but the remuneration received by the factors of production for their services would remain the same, and so would the single and double factorial terms of trade. However, a difficult conceptual problem would remain: the preceding argument is perfectly acceptable in the case of an increase in the productivity of factors employed in exports that is due to an innovation that 'just happens' and costs nothing to the country applying it. But if the productivity increase is due to an innovation that the exporting country has obtained as a result of a specific domestic technological effort (or investment of funds) or to an intensification of the work effort of the workers in the export sector, equity would seem to require that the country should obtain a specific exclusive benefit for those efforts.

Given the extreme practical difficulty of measuring at a point in time the quantity of production factors a country employs in the exports it gives in exchange for one unit of foreign factors employed in its imports (that is, a measure corresponding to the concept of double factorial terms of trade), one is left with the difficult task of finding alternative criteria to judge the fairness of international exchange. As his model includes only one factor of production, namely labour, in a late work Lewis (1980) referred as a criterion to 'the just principle of equal pay for equal work ... It would be fair if, given two people with equal diligence, intelligence, and equal work, these two people were paid the same' (p. 27). This seems to correspond to an equal real wage for performing a similar task with the same level of personal productivity. But since in the real world not only labour but other factors as well must be considered, one would have to solve the problems connected with the separate estimate of their respective contribution to productivity change in the trading countries. And there are further problems: for example, suppose two people, one working in an advanced country, the other in a developing one, perform a task with

workers employed in the export and other sectors, and the price of their products, will rise *pari passu*.[36] It is important to note that, although overpopulation in the countryside is usually associated with low agricultural productivity, as the amount of land available to each farmer may be too small, the cause of low wages is not the excess of population per se, but the low level of agricultural productivity. If, for instance, tomorrow in Bangladesh new seeds were discovered that multiplied yields in subsistence agriculture by ten, all other conditions remaining the same, agricultural real wages and consequently real wages in every other sector would also be ten times as high; but the excess of available agricultural workers might remain unchanged (of course, in the longer period the development of other lines of production made possible by the increased income and demand of now richer farmers would absorb part of the agricultural labour surplus).

Although the basic elements of Lewis's theory were clearly delineated in his 1954–1955 works, the specific model he developed in the 1954 article – the one that enjoyed great popularity among economists – was basically a closed-economy model centred on 'unlimited supplies of labour'; and the part of his theory relating to international terms of trade went largely unnoticed. In his later works, Lewis (1969, 1976, 1978a, 1978b) concentrated instead on this second issue, extending his analysis to explain the historical evolution of the terms of trade between exports of industrial and tropical countries, and developing the open-economy version of his model.

He recalled that by the middle of the 19th century, England's agricultural productivity far exceeded that in the rest of the world and in particular in the tropical areas; an advance that had been a pre-requisite for the Industrial Revolution to start and then to progress. But Lewis stressed that at that time an additional mechanism

---

equal personal productivity; it would seem that fairness requires they receive the same real wage. But if the developing country suffers from inferior efficiency in other aspects of the production and distribution system (for instance because of inadequate transport facilities, or larger distance from ports), one may reasonably argue that lower remuneration of workers (and of other production factors) is necessary to compensate for these elements of inferiority.

The issue of fairness in international exchange is further complicated by the likely contrasts between the criteria that might be adopted to ensure greater fairness in exchange at international and national levels respectively. The application of the equal pay for equal work criterion at international level would cause developing countries to record a large increase in the wages of workers producing exports (whose price would rise correspondingly). But these wage rises would in all probability conflict with the criterion, aimed at reducing domestic inequality among members of the population (and made effective by competition in the labour market), of keeping wages in all sectors not too distant from the average national level (in turn reflecting the average level of productivity of the economy). To solve the contrast, authorities should apply a special tax to the increased wages of the workers in the export sectors, distributing the proceeds to the whole population.

[36] Strictly speaking, this argument applies to the aggregate of underdeveloped countries that can produce a given export good. If a single underdeveloped country managed to increase its productivity in food production, that would raise its agricultural and average wage, but would not increase its export price unless it is a large exporter of the good and other countries with low productivity in food production cannot expand the export of the good to an extent sufficient to replace the country's export supply.

connecting wages to agricultural productivity set in at world level, which worked through emigration.

In the second half of the 19th century, a very large number of people (some 50 million according to Lewis) left Europe, mostly bound for the countries of temperate settlement (North and South America, Australia and New Zealand, South Africa); and a not dissimilar number left China and India, going mainly to the tropics to work in plantations, mines and construction. The motivations that moved these two streams of people set the terms of trade between tropical and temperate commodities. Asians came from countries where agricultural productivity, and consequently wages, were very low, so they were willing to go abroad to work for wages that were slightly higher than their domestic wages, but still miserable. Europeans, too, expected to be paid higher wages in new settlement countries than those they earned on the land at home; but in Europe agricultural productivity had reached levels that were several times higher than those of Asia, and so wages were also much superior. Europeans, therefore, only moved to lands whose conditions (in terms of climate, soil quality, availability of land per man and, later on, degree of mechanization) meant they could expect to reach levels of agricultural productivity and wages higher than in Europe; while Indians and Chinese were ready to move, to work in plantations and mines, to any land where agricultural productivity and wages were just slightly above the extremely low domestic level. So, if Europe and its industry needed large amounts of basic commodities that only the new lands of temperate settlement could provide, such as Australian wool, they had to pay prices for them that would allow the producer to reach an above-European standard of living. For tropical commodities, on the contrary, it was sufficient to pay a price that would allow the workers to reach an above-Indian standard of living. Lewis could therefore conclude: 'If tea had been a temperate instead of a tropical crop, its price would have been perhaps four times as high as it was. And if wool had been a tropical instead of a temperate crop, it could have been had for perhaps one-fourth of the ruling price' (1976, p. 16).

Since the difference in wages, related to differences in productivity in the food sector and in the characteristics of emigrant flows, caused an unfavourable exchange ratio for tropical products versus temperate products (temperate settlement's agricultural products and European manufactures), the opportunities for development that international trade presented to the two groups of countries were very different, and the international division of labour that was established set them on diverging trajectories: high productivity in food production, high wages and high export prices provided European advanced countries and the British-populated countries of temperate settlement with both the means to invest in the continuous progress of education, infrastructure and capital goods, and the local market demand necessary to start the industrialization process; so that they increasingly specialized in the production and then in the export of manufactures, while tropical countries specialized in tropical agricultural and mineral commodities. With time, this division of labour became more and more difficult to modify, as it was reinforced by a number of additional factors and by the operation of vicious/virtuous circles: the competitiveness of advanced countries in manufactures increased and so did the effort necessary for latecomers to catch-up; imperial powers' policies set obstacles to dependent and semi-dependent countries' industrialization; and politically independent peripheral countries frequently proved unable to develop a modern entrepreneurial middle class, strong enough to take political power away from conservative agricultural interests.

Moreover, in the second part of the 19th century, the transport revolution drastically lowered the costs and increased the speed of intercontinental merchandise movements, producing a massive increase in the export of primary commodities from the periphery to industrial countries, which made the industrialization process appear less urgent in producing countries. At the same time, according to Lewis:

> the speed of this adjustment created an illusion: it came to be an article of faith in Western Europe that the tropical countries had a comparative advantage in agriculture, when in fact, as Indian textile production soon began to show, there were much greater differences in food production per head than in modern industrial production per head as between tropical and temperate countries. (1978b, p. 200)

and:

> European economists have been telling the tropical countries ... that their comparative advantage lies in agriculture, but this seems not to be true. Anybody can learn the skills of manufacturing, and both capital and entrepreneurship are highly mobile. But agriculture depends on natural environment, and it is by no means obvious that the tropical environment is better suited to food production than the temperate environment. (1976, p.153)

These arguments – while supporting Keynes's fundamental statement quoted in Section 8.2.1 on the possibility for all countries to reach levels of efficient production of manufactures – are basically those that have led some critics (Reinert (2007) being an example) to identify in Ricardo's comparative costs principle the ideological tool used to justify colonialism: that is, to provide a moral defence for maintaining countries in the condition of producers of raw materials only, while all the advanced countries that industrialized in the 19th century were careful not to follow Ricardo's theory of comparative advantage and free trade until they had become competitive producers of manufactures.

Lewis's theory of unfavourable terms of trade for the products of underdeveloped countries does not depend on – although its effects may be reinforced by – other negative mechanisms that are likely to be at work. One is the possibly less dynamic effects on growth of the production of raw materials compared with the production of manufactures already discussed in Section 2.2. Another is the different elasticity of the demand for raw materials and manufactures included in the Prebisch and Singer argument mentioned in Section 9.3.2. A further one, also part of Prebisch and Singer's argument, connects unfavourable terms of trade not with specific negative characteristics of the products exported by underdeveloped countries, but with the characteristics of these countries' economies, which do not allow workers – by contrast with what happens in advanced countries – to obtain, thanks to organized trade union action, high wage levels. Lewis stressed this last point, although he concentrated on the roles of low productivity in food production and the unlimited supply of labour.

While he favoured industrialization because he saw limited scope for increases of raw materials exports to absorb the surplus population released by low-productivity subsistence agriculture, Lewis's main point was that as long as the problem of the concentration of the working population in food-producing agriculture and the low productivity of food production was not solved, any movement to new export products, and specifically manufactures, would not improve the terms of trade, but simply add low-wage exports of manufactures to low-wage exports of primary products. He anticipated that the drying-up of advanced countries' reservoirs of unskilled low-wage workers, owing to near full employment and zero population growth, would push these countries to invest in manufacturing activities in low-wage countries and to import industrial products from them. He held that the process had started in the 1960s, and drew attention to the fact that by 1975 already one-third of developing countries' non-oil exports were manufactures.

Lewis also stressed the fact that terms of trade were not unfavourable for all agriculture: Australia, New Zealand, Denmark and other countries have become some of the richest countries in the world by exporting agricultural products to advanced countries. He shared the position of the Canadian historian Harold Innis who wrote in the 1930s about the importance of primary products' exports as an engine for growth. In contrast to the 'dependency school', popular in the 1970s, Lewis pointed out that in their first phases of development the British-populated countries of temperate settlement were highly dependent on exports of wool, meat, wheat and other primary products to industrial countries:

> If dependency made the temperate settlements among the richest countries in the world, why would it have made the tropics poor? It was, in the first place, the unfavourable factorial terms of trade that kept the tropics poor. Also their failure, unlike Australia, to use their increase in wealth as a basis for some industrialization. Some who failed owed this to their colonial status; but in truth, self-governing East and Central Europe and self-governing Latin America were just about as defective in this respect as the colonial states. (1976, p. 150)

Emmanuel (1969) would stress the same point: 'the colonial pact did not have in itself a large immiserizing effect, if it did not associate with low wages in colonized countries' (p. 293 of the French text). The USA, after all, continues to represent the largest world exporter of agricultural products and the largest world importer of manufactures without complaints being heard about unfavourable commodity or factorial terms of trade.

Lewis's theory can be criticized for a number of simplifying hypotheses and debatable points, the first being his treatment of labour as the only factor used in the production process, which allows him to argue that the differences in real wages (in terms of food) between two countries are determined by the relative productivity of their food sectors (Findlay (1981) developed a North-South terms-of-trade determination model with two factors, labour and capital). These critical comments cannot be discussed here - reference can be made to Myint (1964, 1976), Bruton (1980), Lal (1983), Ranis (1984), Raffer (1987), Hunt (1989) and the more recent retrospective evaluations of Lewis's theory by Alam (2004), Brolin (2006) and Gollin (2014). But in any case, his theory appears to deserve being re-examined and further developed because, despite the almost half a century that has passed since it was formulated, it may represent one of the keys to the explanation of the nature and causes of asymmetries and inequalities in the advantages that today the different actors involved seem to gain from participation in GVCs. Paradoxically, while it is agreed that the most important issue in contemporary world economics and politics is the gap between advanced and developing countries, few economists have shown an interest in deeply investigating how the prices of products exchanged between the two areas are determined.

9.3.4 Emmanuel's unequal exchange

Emmanuel seems to have been the only economist who fully realized – and explicitly acknowledged in his *Unequal Exchange* (1969) – the importance of Lewis's theory of wage and price determination and the break it represented with mainstream economic theory. A number of common points characterize the theories of the two economists. Both argued that product prices are determined by wages and assume that profit rates are equalized at world level. Both identified the concept of unequal exchange with the double factorial terms of trade, and connected the terms of trade between advanced and underdeveloped countries, not to specific characteristics of the products exported by the two groups of countries (raw materials against manufactures), but to the kind of country (high wage or low wage) from which the products originated. For both it was necessary, for unequal exchange to take place, that the products exported by one group of countries not be produced by the other group (otherwise a tendency would set in to equalize their prices at an intermediate level that would strongly reflect the wage level in the countries that produce the overwhelming part of the total supply of, and/or can expand the production of, a given good – which is why advanced countries have discontinued the domestic production of standard textiles and apparel). The two economists also shared a not unfavourable attitude towards foreign investment in underdeveloped countries, because of its possible important contribution – especially in the form of technological transfers and the acquisition of labour and managerial skills – to the development of these countries. But Emmanuel identified the cause of unequal exchange in a mechanism totally different from that of Lewis.

Lewis's theory was based on the determination of countries' wages by productivity levels in subsistence agriculture, that is by a technological factor endogenous to the economic structure of the country. For Emmanuel, instead, wages are delinked from productivity, whether in the food-producing or in any other sector. Labour cannot be considered a commodity, whose price is determined by market conditions; on the contrary, wages are basically an independent national variable, in the sense of being, if not totally exogenous, 'pre-determined' as a result of power relations between workers and owners of other production factors, although they are historically connected to the level of development, the traditions and the specific political and institutional evolution – especially as regards the power of trade unions – of each country (Lewis (1954) himself had recognized the existence of such a conventional element). For Emmanuel, the outcome of negotiations between workers and employers 'depends to a large extent upon the relation between what the workers are demanding and *what society regards, in a certain place and at a certain moment, as the standard of wages*. It depends on a certain *level of attainment*, which is itself the result of past struggles and evolutions' (1969, p. 156 of the French text). He argued that, labour being basically immobile internationally and capital mobile (so that the rate of profit tends to international equalization), product prices basically reflect the independently fixed price of labour, which represents products' main cost component. A large set of particular conditions has historically allowed workers in advanced countries to obtain high levels of wages – with positive effects on development thanks to the enlargement of domestic markets for industrial and other products and the stimulus to use highly productive capital-intensive technologies – while conditions in underdeveloped countries led to a perpetuation of low wage levels and restricted domestic markets. As a result, an exchange of high-price against low-price products has been taking place between the two areas, whereby the workers of advanced countries exploit the workers of the Third World.[37]

This unequal exchange undermined, for Emmanuel, the international solidarity of workers and their common fight against capitalist exploitation, on which Marxism and international workers' movements had based their hopes of changing the world (in fact, lack of international workers' solidarity was dismally demonstrated in 1914 by the failure of socialist movements' attempts to prevent working classes' acquiescence to the fanatical nationalistic calls to participate in World War I; and before and after that time, as Lewis had pointed out, by the steadfast opposition of the working classes and their trade unions in all relatively advanced countries to the immigration of workers from low-wage countries). Given this conclusion, it is not surprising that Emmanuel's book raised, in Marxist and left-wing circles, heated reactions, producing 'unlimited supplies of commentary' (in the words of Brolin (2006), who surveyed them): indeed, it is not easy to find other economic works that gave rise, in just a few years after their publication, to a comparable number of critical contributions.

Another important point of contrast between Emmanuel and other left-wing economists was the possible progressive role for Third World development attributed by Emmanuel to FDI and multinationals. In this respect, Emmanuel joined Warren – see the exchange between Warren (1973) and Emmanuel (1974) – another heretical

---

[37] Emmanuel also advanced the argument that it was possible for workers in advanced countries to obtain relatively high wages without reducing the rates of profit of capitalists to unsustainable levels, precisely because capitalists could offset the higher cost of workers with the benefits of the lower cost of raw material inputs imported from underdeveloped areas as a result of unequal exchange.

voice on the left, who in the 1970s resumed Marx's view on the overall progressive role of Western powers in introducing capitalism and industrialization into underdeveloped countries; a view that, as already indicated, had been reversed since 1928 by the international communist movement and left-wing economists. Emmanuel's position on this issue was, however, less optimistic than Warren's, since for Emmanuel the volume of foreign investment flowing to Third World countries was not large enough for its positive effects to set in motion a process of capitalist development.

No further space will be devoted here to Emmanuel's theory, not only because its main points have been the object (together with other theories of unequal exchange) of a number of expositions and discussions – see Brewer (1980), Raffer (1987), Brolin (2006), Lichtenstein (2016) – but because it is a theory that presents serious contradictions and a lot of highly debatable points. These problems stem to a large extent from the fact that, wanting to present himself in the left-wing debate on unequal exchange as a follower of Marx, Emmanuel adopted in his arguments Marxist concepts (the first being Marx's labour theory of value) and Marxist schemes, but then frequently referred to Ricardian, Sraffian and other tools of analysis, so that his arguments are confusing even to the expert reader. One is led to understand why, in a devastating critical assessment of Emmanuel's book, Salvati (1971) could go as far as to consider it a theoretical mess and attacked its main arguments, only leaving it the merit of reproposing Lewis's important insights on the inequality of international exchange between advanced and underdeveloped areas. In fact Lewis's theory, based on very simple, precise and empirically well-grounded arguments, appears much superior to Emmanuel's, which is based on the questionable consideration of wages as an independent variable and encumbered and complicated by the resort to formal Marxist schemes abandoned by the generality of economists because of their unsolved theoretical problems and the empirical difficulty of applying them to the real world.[38] Still, one must recognize Emmanuel's contribution in underlining the im-

[38] It was argued earlier that Lewis's theory represents in fact a theory of unequal exchange. It is worth noting that neither in his 1954–1955 works nor in those of 1976–1978 did Lewis ever refer to the terms 'unequal exchange' (in the latter works he never even mentioned the name of Emmanuel, despite the fierce debates that had raged in the previous years on his book) or 'exploitation' or even simply 'unfairness' in international exchange, strictly limiting himself to the neutral technical expression 'unfavourable terms of trade'. He probably wanted to avoid even the slightest association of his theory with those, prevalently Marxist, that were then fashionable on the left, because of the discredit this association would have produced for his theory in academic economic circles. Even so, Brolin (2006) considered it likely that the surprising lack of influence of Lewis's theory of the terms of trade on the dominant paradigm of development economics was because the association was in fact widely felt, despite all his efforts to prevent it. It took specific questions posed by an interviewer later for Lewis (1980) to finally disclose his position on unequal exchange. He admitted that there was exploitation by advanced countries of labour and raw materials of less developed ones, but argued that it took place through the impersonal working of free market forces and reflected the low agricultural productivity and the excess of labour supplies in less developed countries' food production sector. He said that he considered the resulting free and competitive determination of commodity prices grossly unfair, as fairness would require (as already indicated in Footnote 35) that people with equal capabilities, diligence and work effort be paid the same wage everywhere.

portance of developing the analysis of the fundamental question of unequal exchange and in widely publicizing, contrary to Lewis and thanks to the debate raised by his work, an issue that in previous years had been insufficiently analysed.[39]

9.4 Changes in economic power asymmetries and conflicts

9.4.1 Changes at national level

In advanced countries, in the three decades following the end of World War II, the basic class conflict between capitalists and workers that had been at the centre of the visions of Smith, Ricardo and Marx became much less acute, while the class of large landowners completely lost its earlier power. The condition of workers, after more than a century of fights for basic economic and social rights, greatly improved thanks to general economic growth, to Keynesian policies aimed at full employment and to the development of a welfare state that almost everywhere provided all, or the majority of, the population, with health care, education and other basic services. Education provided an important opportunity for social advancement; the working class became highly diversified, with different groups identified by different skill levels; there was an increase in the proportion of white-collar and self-employed workers (as growth led to the prevalence of the services sector in total GDP and, especially, employment); while generally class distinctions became less significant with the development of mass consumption, mass education, and mass information and entertainment. The power of large industrial corporations continued to grow, but found a counterweight in the increased power of organized labour and often of the state. Inequalities in the distribution of wealth and income, although still significant, were considerably reduced.

These trends in advanced countries have largely disappeared or been reversed since the second part of the 1970s, with the growing diffusion of the neoliberal ideology and the economic policies derived from it, strongly reinforced by Thatcher and Reagan from 1979–1981 (see Krugman (2007d) on the development of that ideology in the USA). The new policies aimed at freedom of international movement of goods and capital; reduction of state intervention in the economy, of public regulation and of taxation; privatization of public services and utilities; abandonment of government full employment policies; and cancellation or reduction of many workers' rights and related irrelevance or much decreased power of trade unions. Stiglitz (2019) recounts

[39] While the concept of unequal exchange in Lewis and Emmanuel basically refers to unfavourable terms of trade produced by inequality of wages between developed and underdeveloped countries, another interpretation of the concept attributes instead unfavourable terms of trade to the more general difference in bargaining power resulting from the unequal monopolistic power of exporters in the two groups of countries (owing, in turn, to markets for industrial products being less competitive than those for raw materials). See Sutcliffe (1972), who credits A. G. Frank (1967) with developing this interpretation.

how in the USA 'the power of workers has been eviscerated' (p. 54); already in 2006 Samuelson had stressed (in Sha and Hughes (2009, p. 34)) that 'globalization has almost completely emasculated trade unionism'; for Stansbury and Summers (2020), the declining bargaining power of the workers is the key explanation for the American falling labour share and workers' worsened conditions; see also Kreuger (2018).[40] In the course of this period the progress of technology and automation, and especially the ICT revolution, made large groups of workers redundant in both manufacturing and services (for example, in banking). Very important in determining a worsening of workers', especially low-skilled industrial workers', conditions (both wages and trade union activity and other basic rights) was the growing resort – and even the simple threat of resort – by advanced countries' corporations and even middle-sized firms to the offshoring of production to low-wage emerging countries (domestic subcontracting, especially in the USA, also greatly increased); moreover, with the growing separation of firms' decision-making centres from the physical location of production activity, firms felt less and less responsible for (and interested in) workers' conditions and wages.

The final result was a drastic reduction of workers' power and voice, as the very large firms that used to concentrate hundreds of thousand workers progressively shed more and more of them (Davis (2016) spoke of 'the vanishing American corporation'; he was right with reference to the corporations' once gigantic size in terms of employees, but not if one refers to their power and turnover). Security of employment and remuneration largely disappeared; and 'flexible' and other precarious forms of dependent and formally independent employment spread through all sectors. Workforces were increasingly isolated and fragmented, 'consisting of privileged insiders, with access to a wide range of benefits and forms of security, surrounded by a motley assembly of "contingent" workers, some working in the same premises, some working locally in other places, some in other parts of the country, and some "overseas"' (Standing 2007, p. 49); thus they lost the sense of belonging to the same group and sharing common interests.[41]

[40] In the present work, the negative effects produced by the diffusion of the Thatcher–Reagan neoliberal ideology and connected economic policies are repeatedly pointed out. Still, in historical perspective, a more nuanced reading of the Thatcherian 'conservative revolution' may be advanced: see the brief assessment of that experience in the book by the writer-journalist-historian Amin Maalouf (2019). He stresses the disastrous effects of the neoliberal ideology in producing social drift and sometimes 'obscene injustice', and especially in establishing a culture of mistrust and denigration of public authorities, whose interventions in economic life were represented as encroachments from which citizens had to defend themselves; but credits it with favouring the first large-scale transmission by Western capitalism of know-how and dynamism to important countries with different cultures, making it possible for many developing countries to follow a new road that might lead them out of underdevelopment.

[41] Weil (2014, 2019) has brought to public attention the phenomenon of the 'fissured workplace', which has created in the USA a dual labour market. Large corporations have progressively concentrated on their more profitable 'core' activities, outsourcing large parts of the production process abroad and transferring the burden of employing the mass of the lower-skill and, increasingly, middle-skill workers to smaller domestic companies of contractors, subcontractors and franchisees included in their supply

Median workers' wages (more indicative than average wages, as they measure the wage of the worker who has half of all workers earning less than he does and half more) grew much more slowly, if at all; and labour's share of GDP shrank, as the benefits of continued productivity increases (the latter, however, became progressively lower since the 1970s, apart from a temporary revival in the USA in 1995–2005, which reflected the introduction of ICT technologies) were concentrated more and more in the hands of the owners of share capital and technology, professionals with high-level skills and managers of corporations and financial institutions.[42] At the same time, in many countries the education system appeared to have lost its previous capacity to act as a strong source of equality of opportunity, and positions of superiority and inferiority in the income distribution were increasingly transmitted from one generation to the other. Inequality in the distribution of income and wealth, as pointed out by Piketty (2013), Atkinson (2015), Stiglitz (2015) and more recently the participants in a Peterson Institute conference – see Blanchard and Rodrik (2019) – increased dramatically (with differences among countries), contributing to worsen the vicious circle between superiority of financial means and ability to influence the

---

chains. These companies, operating in highly competitive markets with reduced profit margins, usually pay extremely low wages, do not provide the benefits and training typical of the large corporations, and can easily avoid compliance with workplace laws and regulations.

On the economic, social and psychological effects of job insecurity in the USA see Uchitelle (2006). A distressing description of the degradation of the conditions of the American working class – of the less educated white part in particular – has recently been provided by Case and Deaton (2020).

[42] Note that the share of national income represented by the traditional forms of capital (monetary capital and ordinary plants and machinery) also seems to have shrunk, as indicated by the fact that return on risk-free capital (government debt or bank current accounts) has gone down since the 1990s, while the price of capital goods relative to other goods has decreased. It is the share of income represented by the profits of large firms that has greatly increased, thanks to the rents from high technology, patents and brands, but especially growing market power connected to higher entry barriers and lax antitrust legislation and enforcement.

De Loecker, Eeckhout and Unger (2020) have analysed the evolution of US firms' market power by estimating their mark-ups (the measure of how much prices exceed marginal costs) on the basis of firm-level data for all publicly traded firms (they found that their results are confirmed for the universe of manufacturing, retail and wholesale trade firms included in the US census). They have calculated that aggregate mark-ups, relatively stable between 1955 and 1980, increased sharply in the following period, from 21 per cent in 1980 to 61 per cent in 2016. Only in part was this due to the rise of overhead costs (from 15 to 21 per cent of total costs); they estimated that the average profit rate (total sales minus all costs, as a share of sales) rose from around 1 per cent in 1980 to 8 per cent in 2016. They found that the increase in average mark-ups was almost exclusively the result of an exceptional rise in mark-ups of the firms already at the top of the mark-ups distribution, which increased their shares of the market, while the median mark-up remained unchanged. They also found that the increase in average mark-ups was not the result of changes in the firms' industry composition as it took place within all industries.

De Loecker and Eeckhout (2018) tried to analyse mark-ups throughout the world, using data for 134 countries. They found large increases in firms' mark-ups in North America and Europe, and the smallest increases in emerging economies in Latin America and Asia. Evidence on increases in mark-ups (mostly explained by increases for the already high-mark-up firms) in advanced, but not in emerging, countries for publicly listed and privately held firms has also been presented for the 2000–2015 period by Díez, Fan and Villegas-Sánchez (2019).

political and cultural milieu to obtain laws and regulations more and more favourable to the most powerful and wealthy. To prevent workers from reacting to this situation, and at the same time to ensure a satisfactory level of aggregate internal demand, in the USA public authorities increasingly resorted to consumption and expenditure support through unchecked credit expansion, feeding an unsustainable spiral that finally exploded in the 2008 global crisis.

While the general trends indicated above characterized almost all Western advanced countries, they were much more marked in the USA, pointing to specific features of the American economy and society that set this country apart from those of Europe, Japan and even Canada. If it were true, as is commonly argued, that globalization and technological progress are responsible for the deterioration in the conditions of US citizens – and of the working class in particular – then other advanced countries, that have equally been exposed to these disrupting forces, should have recorded, contrary to what happened, equally serious negative developments. Philippon (2019) has summarized the main features of the US economic and political system that may account for the different evolution.

* * *

In the long period from the Industrial Revolution until the 1980s, in which advanced countries' economies were based on industry, the central conflict of power was the one between masters and workers. In this conflict, despite fundamental improvements in workers' rights and conditions, power was in the hands of the employers and the concept of worker exploitation never disappeared. In the following decades, the drastic contraction in big industrial firms' employment, the reduction (because of automation and offshoring) of production workers relative to workers engaged in logistics (delivery, transport , stock management, etc) and services, the increase, in some countries, of self-employment and employment in very small firms (both in traditional service activities and in the professions and other specialized high-skill activities) have led the basic workers versus masters conflict to take on new, differentiated and often confused forms; it appears to have lost its centrality in economic and political life, paradoxically in the very period that workers witnessed a significant deterioration of both their economic conditions and civil rights.

As for confusion, one has just to consider that with the advent of globalization and the spread of international production chains, production processes have been largely fragmented and dispersed among a plurality of firms and countries (see Chapter 11). Intermediate products are often produced by different economic agents (advanced countries' national producers, MNCs' foreign subsidiaries, emerging countries' large domestic producers and small enterprises), to be completed or assembled in a final location (so that countries' exports recorded in trade statistics largely represent products and components manufactured elsewhere). The prices at which they are traded at each stage are difficult to trace, and in any case are usually established by the lead firms controlling the production chain – firms that often limit themselves to research, marketing and management activities – on the basis of their specific strategy (frequently just to minimize taxes or to meet standards of minimum VA percentage content fixed by national authorities to grant producers a number of benefits). The effective nationality of the lead firms may be hard to assess, as they often have legal seat, fiscal seat and production or research facilities located in different countries. Higher productivity in a firm, as measured by VA per employee, may reflect not improved effort and performance by the workers or better management and organization of the firm, but simply increases in profits owing to lower prices of inputs and components imported from low-wage countries. Sturgeon and Gereffi (2008), possibly the most prominent scholars of international production chains, observed that 'many important industries are becoming globally distributed and now co-evolve in elaborate and ever shifting cross-border ecosystems that make unclear where control and competitive advantage truly lie' (p. 3). In these conditions, it is not easy to determine who is producing what part of the final product, at what cost and price and where, and so who is being exploited and who exploits other participants in the production chain.

At the same time, as just indicated, in many advanced countries, in the prevalent situation of high unemployment, the proliferation of new typologies of precarious, underpaid but formally independent work often serves to mask the reality of continued exploitative relationships: what was once the clear relationship between master and worker now increasingly consists of a service provided by a supplier to a customer (in many low-wage service sectors where remuneration is based on results, firms spare no effort to convince their employees that they are 'entrepreneurs'); and sometimes the worker, with the diffusion of subcontracting, may even find it impossible to identify his real employer. Most importantly, with the growing complexity of modern industrial societies where technological progress and knowledge play a larger and larger role, there is no way to distinguish the contribution to production of these factors from that of the traditional production factors of land, labour and capital. It is also impossible to establish how much of the monopolistic rents accruing to firms from the production of new goods is the result of R&D activities financed by producing firms and how much is the result of basic and applied research carried out by public institutions, financed by citizens' taxes and freely available to firms.

The very identification of 'capitalists' has become problematic: with the increase of workers' savings – especially those connected with pension plans – investment funds and pension funds have become the most important investors and financial operators, so that often the same people benefit as savers and investors from the exploitation of themselves as workers. And, of course, the same workers exploited at home as producers may be the beneficiaries, as consumers of cheap foreign products, of a much heavier exploitation of developing countries' workers; Western workers, for their part, complain that they are the victim of 'unfair' trade with poor countries, whose extremely low standards in wages and working conditions, leading to unsustainable competition, are held responsible for their loss of jobs and stagnant wages. Finally, the very traditional distinction between domestic and foreign producers has been blurred, as the latter may be the subsidiaries of a national MNC and the former the subsidiaries of a foreign MNC.

Other forms of power asymmetry have instead become important, in which individuals appear in a position of inferiority not as workers but as consumers (making a mockery of the very concept of consumer sovereignty). In recent decades, there has been a significant increase in the share of total activity of industries and services presenting intrinsically monopolistic characteristics. Especially in countries where the defence of consumers is extremely limited and supervision by public agencies does not exist or is particularly inefficient, large private domestic and foreign firms in sectors providing essential services (traditional utilities and services that have been privatized, and new network services connected to the ICT sector) can exploit their monopolistic or oligopolistic position by exercising power over a mass of individuals without any possibility of bargaining, coerced to accept any condition they impose for their services,[43] and, on top of that, subjected to endless intrusions into their personal life with unsolicited advertising initiatives (the coercion of buyers and other counterparts of large corporations is discussed, with specific examples, by Reich (2015);[44] see also Crouch (2016)).

It used to be said that under modern capitalism people's lives are reduced entirely to consumption, and that collective action – owing to the much restricted scope for intervening in the political sphere – can also only regard people as consumers (as witnessed by the increasing importance, especially in the USA, of consumers defence associations, firms' extreme care for customer satisfaction and strengthening of class actions). Even this is no longer true: with the advent of e-commerce, customers are completely isolated and price discrimination (charging different prices for the same product to different groups of customers) has reached the extreme limit. Thanks to the information large corporations extract from our use of the computer and the mobile phone to deal with them, they can know everything about our habits, needs, paying capacities and so on, so as to tailor the price they charge for their product to each individual. This is stressed by Lynn (2010):

> from one airline seat to the next, the prices delivered via digital means may vary immensely … the asymmetry of power is complete. In such a relationship, the public no

[43] The phenomenon of consumers' lack of defence has reached extremes that appear ridiculous, but are unfortunately very serious: network service providers, for example, request customers to allow them to use cookies and other devices for the collection and utilization of confidential personal data (for purposes that customers are not in a condition to control). Customers are asked whether they accept these devices, but usually only the affirmative answer is allowed in practice, as otherwise they are denied access to a service that is often absolutely necessary for them to work, obtain essential information or lead a normal social life. Since usually no competing providers of the service are available – and when they are, they usually impose the same condition for their service – consumers appear as subject to a form of coercion (many would speak of blackmail) that does not seem to accord with the concept of free and voluntary market transaction.

[44] In this book, the author seems to have abandoned the idea, set out in Reich (2007), according to which globalization was accompanied by a lowering of technical entry barriers in many sectors, thereby reducing the importance of scale economies. He had argued that this, together with trade liberalization, had led to a marked increase in competition among producers and greatly increased the power of consumers relative to corporations.

> longer has any idea of what it, as a whole, must pay for any particular item. In other words, the various members of the public no longer have any interests in common. In the digital world, the mob is atomized. There is no public. (pp. 55–56)

It is interesting to note that a power of coercion over consumers can often be exercised by 'New Economy' giants even when the consumer is a government or a public entity or a large firm in another sector. Such actors, when in need of a giant's services, may initially be able to choose a supplier on the basis of competition among possible candidates. But once one supplier firm has been chosen and has installed the necessary infrastructure, and the actor has adapted its internal organization to this infrastructure, it may realize that it has been locked in by the firm. In following years, it may be unable to switch to a different supplier (and consequently will have little bargaining power over the conditions of subsequent contract renewals), since suppliers have at their disposal the means to make any such change extremely costly – and in any case the switch would imply difficult organizational changes. These switching costs are connected to the growing importance that standards and networks – which will be discussed in Chapter 10 – have acquired in the modern economy.

More generally, within advanced countries, the power of large enterprises in industry, services and finance (and of a few very wealthy individuals) has grown relative not only to that of workers and consumers but also, and perhaps more significantly, to that of their own state. Bakan (2004) advanced a different argument: it is true that corporations have become much more powerful, but this does not mean that the power of the state has been reduced: simply, the state has lost its ability to act in defence of the public interest (in particular as regards the environment, consumers and workers) and has increasingly used its power to further the interests of corporations. In any case, it is a fact that the state has proved less and less capable of acting as an impartial umpire (willing and able to sanction monopolistic and oligopolistic positions and other market abuses); has largely abandoned the role of regulator of private economic activity in the interest of the entire nation, increasingly devolving the setting of the rules of the game to producers themselves (particularly in the financial sector) through so-called self-regulation; and has let its own agenda be increasingly dictated by the specific interests of big business.

This loss of independent domestic power by the state – so that instead of having surveillance of the market by the state we have surveillance of the state by the market – was fostered by its need to adopt a more business-friendly attitude both to offset competition from other countries in the attraction of foreign investment and to prevent transfers of productive facilities abroad by national and foreign firms producing in the country (such transfers have become increasingly easy for firms as they moved from the production of manufactures requiring large physical investments, to that of immaterial goods and services – such as call centres – requiring much less physical equipment and fixed infrastructure). It was accentuated by states' precarious financial conditions, as a number of factors led to the narrowing of the tax base and therefore to the increase of state budget deficits despite radical cuts to public services. Among these factors are a system of taxation that is increasingly favourable to the corporate sector and the wealthiest individuals; the growing role in economic production both of gigantic firms connected to the ICT sector and its largely immaterial networks, and of value chains covering the whole world (two developments that make the identification of where VA is created extremely difficult); the expansion of e-commerce and digitally downloaded products, which complicates or prevents the recording of transactions and the levying of taxes; the general difficulty of identifying the economic agents operating via the Internet and the place where their transactions take place; and the scope offered to the wealthiest and most powerful actors to drastically reduce or practically avoid taxation by exploiting 'financial havens' (see Section 9.4.2).

The USA, more than other countries, has been characterized by the increased power of big business, a power that comes from different sources and manifests itself in different forms. The very economic scale of large US MNCs and financial institutions gives them a great power vis-à-vis the state and other economic agents, and grants them a central role in moulding public opinion and shaping the directions taken by the economy and non-business institutions – as was acutely pointed out long ago by M. D. Reagan (1963) (for a more recent discussion of the rising power of US big business relative to the state see Rothkopf (2012) and Stiglitz (2019); for the UK see Crouch (2016)). They lead the world as owners and producers of technological know-how and innovations; their largely monopolistic position in this area helps them to consolidate their position of world leadership. But it is in the first place the huge concentration in their hands of financial resources derived from profits in domestic and international activities that has allowed them to obtain increasing advantages in the political, ideological and mass-media fields. And these advantages, in turn, have helped them to pursue and achieve a further increase in their economic power, especially by influencing the process of setting the rules of the economic game: a vicious circle that has cost US society a heavy price in terms of the deterioration of the mechanisms of democracy, as explained by authors with different political positions such as Hertz (2001), Krugman (2007d), Crouch (2011, 2016), Stiglitz (2012, 2019), Zingales (2012, 2017), Reich (2015, 2020) and Case and Deaton (2020), who have also advanced proposals to redress this unfair and dangerous situation.

In the USA, corporate and financial giants, thanks to their foundations' massive funding of think tanks, research centres, universities and specialized journals (see Krugman (2007d) and Mayer (2016)), have been able to practically monopolise, until the 2008 crisis, the academic and intellectual economic discourse; and have engaged experts in all fields to provide advice and assistance to parliamentary and government authorities and public agencies. They have propagated and popularized their extreme pro-market ideology through their direct and indirect control (made possible by practices such as addressing advertising spending only to information media supporting their views) of newspapers, television channels and other sources of information. But, most importantly – as documented, among others, by Philippon (2019) – by taking advantage of politicians' need for massive financial funds for election campaigns and other political initiatives; by building up a massive lobbying system; and by developing a practice of exchanging advisory and top managerial positions between public entities and large private corporations, they have managed to introduce laws and regulations that systematically tilt the workings of markets in a direction favouring their interests against those of workers and the public (it is easy to see how thin is the boundary between these practices and outright corruption). This explains why antitrust legislation and enforcement have largely been abandoned, environmental and safety regulations reduced, rules limiting workers' and trade unions' rights severely augmented and penalties for corporate crime (extremely lax relative to those regarding other crimes) seldom applied. At the same time, intellectual property defence has been greatly reinforced, the taxation of corporations, their managers and the very wealthy made lighter than the taxation of workers' incomes, and the use of money to obtain favourable public decisions largely legalized, to the point of substituting the 'one man one vote' mechanism of democracy with one that looks as if it is based on the market principle of 'one dollar one vote'. A milestone in this evolution was the 2010 Supreme Court decision in the *Citizen United v. Federal Election Commission* case, the final point of a process whose stages are outlined by Rothkopf (2012), according to which – contrary to the principle that political rights are bestowed on people and not on artificial legal entities – corporations are considered as people under the First Amendment and as such have the right to exercise 'free speech' and support candidates in elections through anonymous financial contributions.

* * *

In all countries, but especially in the USA, the increase in the economic and social power of big business has also been the consequence of the fact that, in order to create new opportunities of profitable investment for corporations, more and more fields of human activity, for centuries kept by law or tradition outside the economic sphere (culture, arts, museums, scientific speculation, sports, health, education, defence, security, even interpersonal relations) have been progressively included in the market sector and reduced to the status of mere producers of merchandises, sold with the assistance of the usual mass marketing techniques, and whose value is exclusively measured by their market price.[45] And when these activities are not themselves directly bought and sold, they are increasingly used as instruments and opportunities for promoting the sale of traditional mass consumption goods, as happens today on television with continuous advertising interruptions of films and cultural and politi-

[45] Mason (2015) sees the beginning of this tendency in the marketization of leisure that took place in the first two decades of the 20th century. Indeed, more than a century ago Veblen (1909) pointed out how 'The modern economic situation is a business situation, in that economic activity of all kinds is commonly controlled by business considerations … Indeed, so great and pervading a force has this habit (institution) of pecuniary accountancy become that it extends, often as a matter of course, to many facts which properly have no pecuniary bearing and no pecuniary magnitude, as, for example, works of art, science, scholarship, and religion. More or less freely and fully, the price system dominates the current commonsense in its appreciation and rating of these non-pecuniary ramifications of modern culture' (1909, p. 631).

cal debates (and tomorrow we can expect, given present trends, with similar interruptions in university lectures, presidential addresses and religious services). Even the atavistic respect for small children, which in the past led to their being excluded from commercial exploitation, has been abandoned, as they have proved to be the most effective targets for advertising campaigns and messages. This extension of the market to all aspects of human activity has been acutely analysed by Kuttner (1996) and later criticized by Sandel (2012). It has been met with resistance in most societies, including some other advanced countries, where different value hierarchies predominate, and represents one of the basic negative points of contemporary globalization.

Another aspect of the same phenomenon of compulsive marketization of all aspects of life is the tendency – favoured and sustained in particular by large US corporations, especially in international fora where new rules are established – to extend patents, licences, copyrights and brands to all kinds of physical objects and expressions, and even to immaterial phenomena. Human and animal genes, plants, folk practices and traditions can already be patented and exploited commercially – or one can expect they will very soon be allowed to be (Stiglitz (2006), for instance, reported that in India some yoga positions have been the object of patents). Demands increase for inclusion in the UNESCO World Heritage – now largely considered the equivalent of a brand, with a huge potential for commercial exploitation – not only of monuments, parks and geographical areas, but also of centuries-old technologies and traditional music, dances, recipes and so on. On present trends, it would seem that a future can be envisaged in which payment for IPR will be imposed for singing a tune while walking in the street, or for resorting, when playing football or other sports with friends, to particular moves, techniques or strategies devised by some brilliant sportsman.

But even where traditionally non-economic activities and services have continued to be excluded from market transactions, their provision has increasingly been devolved, particularly in the USA, to the non-profit and 'humanitarian' activities of big corporations and ultra-rich individuals. As states and local authorities found that – because of the fiscal privileges, subsidies and tax avoidance loopholes granted to such economic agents – they are short of funds to meet their citizens' demand for educational, cultural, sports and welfare services and for aid to poor countries, it was the corporate and the high-income personal sectors that intervened to provide for a significant part of the initiatives in these fields (for which they can claim large fiscal benefits). Their action can be more effective than the corresponding one carried out by public authorities, as it is not slowed down by political disputes, bureaucratic procedures, conflicts of competence and national boundaries. This development provides corporations and the super-rich with new opportunities for strengthening their public image and for imposing their own priorities and values, often narrowly focused on their commercial interests. So it further restricts the field of operation of accountable democratic public choices – 'Today Microsoft puts computers in our schools; will it tomorrow determine what our children learn?' Hertz (2001) wondered – while it can be exploited as a way of obtaining ever more favourable treatment from public authorities in normal economic activity.

9.4.2 Changes at international level

In the course of the last forty years, fundamental changes have taken place in the geography of world economic power. The Chinese economy, despite the still huge gap in per capita income with advanced countries, has recently overtaken the USA as the largest economy in terms of total GDP (if calculated at parity of purchasing power). The importance of India's economy has also increased enormously thanks to high growth favoured by exports of advanced services. A significant number of emerging countries (Brazil, Turkey, Indonesia, Mexico, Thailand, Vietnam and South Africa) have become important centres of industrial activity, and the first four have also greatly increased their political power. Russia, after the difficult, dramatic period following the fall of the USSR, has regained its status of important economy and, most notably, has seen its political and military power largely restored; but its economy is more and more based on the production of raw materials and fuels, while its export of agricultural, manufacturing and advanced services' products (apart from those connected with the military sector) continues to be of scant importance in world trade. The advanced countries as a group have seen their economic weight decline because of slower growth. This has largely been the inevitable result of the high standard of living already reached in the course of previous decades; in part it reflected the consequences of the 2008 worst post-war global crisis. All these changes in the relative economic power of nations have been accompanied by, and often reflect, changes in the power of different groups of economic agents, in the factors giving rise to economic power asymmetries and in the relative importance of different aspects of economic power.

In the last fifty years, military power and sheer violence – which, as already pointed out, fundamentally shaped the network of international trade relations in past centuries and determined the modern configuration of countries' economic positions – were less and less resorted to (or threatened) in order to obtain economic advantages. Wars and violent conflicts are still frequent among the poorest developing countries, but they mainly stem from ethnic and political controversies, although these are often intermingled with economic issues (typically the control of precious natural resources such as oil or metals).[46] Between advanced nations, after the experience of the two world wars, resort to military conflict for economic (or other) reasons, has been abolished, thanks to political agreements and to the establishment of economic and other international rules, and of supranational institutions charged with their application. In Europe, where contests between the main countries originated those tragic wars, the former enemies have become members of a political and economic union.

[46] Unfortunately, the increase in population and the worsening of the climate and of the environment may lead in future to more frequent conflicts – especially between poor countries – connected to the ownership of natural resources and especially to new conflicts over the use of basic resources such as clean water, which in the past, if available in a country, could be consumed without creating problems for neighbouring consuming countries.

Military initiatives and participation in coups d'état by developed countries against small, and sometimes even middle-sized, developing countries have continued up to recent years. But direct application for economic reasons of extreme military violence of the type resorted to by Britain in 1839 – when it opened war against China to compel its government to eliminate the ban on opium imports so that the British could sell Indian opium (in addition to Indian cotton) to China and import tea in exchange – would probably be impossible and would certainly misfire today.

In our times, the use, or the threat of use, of military means to reach economic goals (such as safety of or increase in oil supplies) has overall proved to be scarcely effective, as demonstrated in the cases of the Iranian revolution in 1979 and of the Iraq invasion in 2003. There are two basic reasons. First, the exceptional postwar improvement in economic conditions of the citizens of advanced countries and the growing complexity of modern military technology make resort to war both unpopular and extremely expensive in these countries. Therefore, parliaments seldom approve unlimited military operations, usually setting strict limits to the number of soldiers and the level of financial resources involved. On the contrary, the exercise of military force, to be credible and effective, must reach a very large 'critical mass' and appear potentially limitless. Second, experience has shown that even when the conquest of foreign territories by leading countries' modern armies can take place relatively easily, keeping the conquered territories under the control of the occupiers and/or their local allies is extremely difficult and expensive (in part because technological advances have made guerrilla warfare and especially terrorism both cheaper and more harmful). As a result, inter-country controversies, especially those between advanced states and between advanced states and the more economically powerful emerging states, tend to be resolved by peaceful bargaining, in which the more powerful parties can make use of the various, especially economic, not openly violent instruments of power at their disposal.

The most notable power change at international level seems to regard the relationships between countries and powerful private foreign economic agents (specifically large MNCs and large financial firms). The increase in firms' concentration in the last thirty years has already been mentioned in Section 9.2; with international flows of goods, investment and technology almost completely liberalized, large MNCs have become more and more important in the world economy, as their size has grown continuously in terms of the resources they control, directly and indirectly (in terms of the number of their workers the opposite has occurred); and a handful of these MNCs have become the almost exclusive masters of the New Economy. With their decisions to locate productive facilities in one country instead of another, large MNCs decide which country will benefit not only from their investments, expenditures and employment creation, but also and especially from their technological and organizational know-how and from the opportunities they provide for the transmission and local advancement of skills. Because of their bargaining power, MNCs can set one country off against another so as to ensure their investments and activity enjoy the most favourable conditions in terms of taxation, environmental regulation and labour standards.[47] The increase in their power has been much favoured in recent years by the direct relationships they have developed with formally independent local firms in other countries within the new system of GVCs (see Chapter 11). This system has allowed them to reach a centralization of world production and capital that goes much beyond what can be calculated on the basis of conventional measures of firm concentration.

At the same time, since many governments are facing problems with external indebtedness, the power of the institutions that have managed to concentrate among themselves the activities of collecting and investing world savings (international banks, other big financial firms, institutional investors and rating agencies) has also greatly increased. They can now, in a few seconds, send or withdraw huge masses of funds to or from a country, sufficient in critical times to trigger the country's default or currency devaluation, or to save the country from them. As a result, the destiny of governments often appears to depend more on the marks assigned to them by the markets than on the votes they get from the electorate. And, in turn, the electorate shows decreasing interest in participating in elections, as most political parties are compelled to propose similar policies in their programmes – those most likely to be approved by international investors and institutions; while the parties that claim to aim at restoring national economic sovereignty are mostly populist ones, making use of ultra-nationalist propaganda and demagogic economic arguments, and seldom proposing serious reform action. The popular disillusion with national politics, together with the sense of uncertainty, insecurity and confusion produced by the process of globalization, has strongly reinforced – or given rise to – the search for stronger identities and ties at the local level, often leading to the creation of powerful movements calling for regional independence.[48] The basic problem is that while glo-

[47] Half a century ago, in his book on MNCs, Vernon (1971) argued that 'Sovereign states have legitimate goals toward which they try to direct the resources under their command. Any unit of a multinational enterprise, when operating in the territory of a sovereign state, is also responsive to a flow of commands from outside, including the commands of the parent and the commands of other sovereigns. Moreover, the multinational enterprise as a unit, though capable of wielding substantial economic power, is not accountable to any public authority that matches it in geographical reach and that represents the aggregate interests of all the countries the enterprise affects. As long as these two issues remain unsolved, the constructive economic role of the enterprise will be accompanied by destructive political tensions' (p. 240). He ended the book with the conclusion that 'Nations cannot put off much longer some joint understanding over the conditions when subsidies and tax concessions were appropriate in the international movement of industry ... The basic asymmetry between multinational enterprises and national governments may be tolerable up to a point, but beyond that point there is a need to re-establish balance' (pp. 270–271). Despite this point having been reached long ago, significant international initiatives to tackle the problems he had identified have not been undertaken. A similar proposal was advanced by H. G. Johnson (1973) when he argued that to promote wider world economic development, there was a need for a reform of the international monetary system (to ensure smooth balance of payments adjustments), for progress in world trade liberalization, and 'Thirdly, there is the need to devise some sort of international code governing relations between the national state and the multinational corporation' (p. 49).

[48] Already since the early 1990s, the strengthening of such sentiments of more locally restricted identity and solidarity had been attested by the breaking up into a multiplicity of national countries of

balization has increased insecurity and inequality, it has also reduced governments' ability to respond to these developments.

The power of MNCs and large financial intermediaries vis-à-vis foreign countries is strongly reinforced by the backing they manage to obtain from their own governments and from the official international institutions that these governments largely control. While states appear more and more reluctant, by themselves, to take strong international initiatives of any kind, large corporations and financial firms have at their disposal huge amounts of funds and a lot of channels of personal contact that can be used to influence decisions by parliaments and governments. So they can easily obtain the additional support of their state's power for their private initiatives and decisions.[49]

One final development must be mentioned: the phenomenon of 'financial havens', a typical example of both the absurdity of contemporary international economic arrangements and of the power of some economic actors to influence the behaviour

federal states such as the Soviet Union and Yugoslavia, or by the split of Czechoslovakia into two separate nations. It must be noticed that in recent decades the 'death of distance' connected to the ICT revolution, and trade and capital liberalization, have made it possible to overcome some traditional limits imposed by geography on smaller-size countries – first of all the competitive disadvantage of the limited extension of national markets for goods and production factors. This, together with the formation of supranational entities such as the EU, strongly incentivized the creation of more geographically limited national states and the spread of regional independence movements.

[49] One may cite the case of the accident in the US chemical giant Union Carbide's plant in Bhopal, India, in 1984 – the worst industrial accident ever recorded, which caused the death of around 22,000 people and chronic and debilitating illnesses to around 100,000 – see Amnesty International (2004) – when US authorities refused to cooperate with the Indian government in the latter's efforts to bring Union Carbide top executives to trial.

An example of the tendency of MNCs to dictate the rules of the international economic game is provided by the negotiations for the Trans-Pacific Partnership signed in 2016, but then aborted because of lack of ratification. As reported by Stiglitz and Hersh (2015), MNCs fought to have a clause inserted in the agreement according to which if the authorities of a country introduced or changed laws and regulations causing harm to a foreign firm, they have to indemnify the firm for the corresponding loss of income; the clause would apply even in the case of laws and regulations introduced for safety and health reasons. A clause of a similar nature was included in the North American Free Trade Agreement's Chapter 11, as pointed out by Stiglitz (2006). Clauses of this kind, depending of course on the stringency of their interpretation and application, may practically reduce governments to the status of passive captives of MNCs, which would dictate environmental, safety, health and, at the limit, monetary and fiscal legislation and policies to most governments, drastically curtailing national sovereignty and the working of democratic institutions.

In more recent years, US trade policy appears to have moved away from active engagement in multinational institutions (basically the World Trade Organization) and multinational initiatives, in which less powerful countries can band together to defend their interests, to increasing negotiation of bilateral and regional agreements where – particularly in dealing with developing countries – they can fully exploit their huge negotiating superiority. This has allowed them more and more frequently to require trade partners to accept the investor-state dispute settlement mechanism; that is, the right for foreign corporations to sue the host government before a private arbitration body, instead of domestic courts, to obtain compensation for damages brought about by the introduction of regulations and policy change (see Rodrik (2018c) and Elliott (2019)).

of national and international authorities in their favour. The number of states that derive a benefit from offering individuals and corporations (and often criminal organizations) very limited or zero taxation of their activities and banking secrecy is extremely restricted. Most countries, especially among the important ones, are, on the whole, severely damaged by the scope for their citizens and firms operating in their territory to escape taxation by locating their legal seat and depositing their capital in offshore centres (just as they are damaged by the registration of their merchant fleets and large private ships in some accommodating small countries). A serious common initiative even by just the few most important countries could easily put an end to or drastically reduce these practices, as has been demonstrated in some recent cases (such as the rapid abandonment by Switzerland of its legendary strict banking secrecy as a result of pressure by the USA and other countries).

Zucman (2013), after providing first estimates of the huge loss to states' finances produced by financial havens, advanced reasonable proposals to stop or at least significantly limit their activity. But the prospects for the adoption of such measures remain uncertain, despite some very important progress registered since the 2008 global crisis and particularly in the last few years – as a result of a more responsible attitude of the authorities of the main advanced countries – especially through ambitious, and apparently successful, initiatives carried out by the OECD and the exchange of information among taxation and banking institutions (see Section 12.3.4 for the new trends in this field).

The point is that if capital is free to move to offshore centres, it is not because of the 'unrestrainable forces of globalization' or the modern technology that allows it to be moved to any point in the world 'at the click of a mouse'. It is because governments – and specifically those of the few most important countries – decided not to control or regulate such centres, and allowed them to operate, sometimes using methods bordering on piracy, in small islands disguised as independent countries or autonomous territories. Or, as Zucman explained with regard to Luxembourg, it was because the authorities of the EU, having abstained from seriously trying to stop that country, which changed from a small nation into a mere offshore platform, from 'commercializing its own sovereignty … [through] the sale to multinationals throughout the world of the right to decide their own rate of taxation, regulatory constraints, and legal obligations for themselves' (2013, p. 87) (just as the same authorities allowed Malta to practically sell its EU passports to foreigners for 650,000 euros).

The reasons for this passive attitude are quite clear: a few important countries, such as the UK (and to some extent even the USA) act as financial havens relative to other countries. The City of London and Wall Street gain considerable advantages from the existing situation and exert pressure on their governments not to take serious action in this respect; and these countries' ambiguous position with regard to common initiatives against financial havens is in turn an excuse for other countries not to take strong measures. In the EU, the economies of the Netherlands, Ireland, Luxembourg, Malta and Cyprus, although representing 23 million people against the area's total population of around 450 million, are heavily dependent economically on their status of financial havens and are in a position, given the present EU rules on unanimity in decisions regarding sensitive subjects such as taxation, to block serious efforts to put an end to these shameful practices. Then, in some countries politicians themselves are among the beneficiaries of the banking secrecy and tax evasion opportunities provided by financial havens. But the most important explanation is that powerful corporations, organizations (including criminal ones) and individuals derive enormous benefits from the existence of these centres, and have at their disposal very effective means to induce governments and politicians not to take serious action that would damage them.[50]

* * *

In parallel with the strengthening of the international power of the big private corporate agents, a new and unanticipated phenomenon has started to develop, one that dampens that tendency (as power is not an absolute concept, but typically a relative one): an increase in the bargaining power of the governments of some large emerging economies in their confrontation with big MNCs to obtain improvements in their position in the new international division of labour that is taking place within GVCs

[50] In the words of Stiglitz (2019), 'It would be an easy matter to close down these fiscal paradises. All that would be required is to cut their banks off from the US financial system unless they agreed to transparency and other regulations that apply to US financial institutions ... the difficulty is the politics, the influence of the rich who will do what they can to keep their "benefits". Our banks and those in Europe helped create these fiscal paradises as part of their "services" to rich clients and themselves' (pp. 85-86).

With reference to the practices of corporate tax avoidance by MNCs, two additional possible reasons were advanced more recently to explain why governments and tax authorities, despite some important initiatives in recent years, were not active in trying to put an end to such practices (mainly consisting in shifting profits to affiliates located in fiscal havens through three channels: manipulation of the prices of intra-group' imports and exports; charging artificially high interest payments on loans from affiliates in fiscal havens; locating in these affiliates intangibles, such as proprietary trademarks, patents and copyrights, then used by other group firms against payment of a royalty whose real value is impossible to ascertain). Durst (2019) argued that the governments of all countries wish to attract investment by foreign companies because it benefits employment and growth, and to this end offer reduced corporate taxation. As governments face political resistance, in the form of charges of being too generous to MNCs, if they explicitly increase fiscal benefits beyond a certain point, they simply grant additional advantages to foreign MNCs by tacitly permitting them to move profits to fiscal havens.

Tørsløv, Wier and Zucman (2018) pointed instead to a problem of perverse incentives for the tax authorities of advanced countries. They observed that in the current international tax system the main advanced countries have comparatively high levels of corporate taxes, but paradoxically their tax authorities concentrate on fighting international companies' profit-shifting from their high-tax countries to other relatively high-tax ones, rather than profit-shifting to fiscal havens. They noted that in the present reinforced OECD system of information exchange and tax authorities' cooperation among member countries, it is much more likely that success will be obtained in the fight to defend their tax bases from shifting to other main countries than to fiscal havens. This is because information on profits booked abroad is much more easily obtainable from other OECD high-tax countries than from fiscal havens; because companies are unlikely to oppose transfer price corrections that lead to profit shifts from one high-tax country to another, while they will use all possible means to prevent the shift from a fiscal haven to a high-tax country; and because of an efficient tax dispute resolution procedure that has been agreed among OECD countries, but not between them and fiscal havens.

that are restructuring the whole system of world production. As will be explained in Chapter 11, MNCs, taking advantage of advances in ICT, have been able in recent decades to fragment production processes – from the initial creation and design of a good to its delivery to the final consumer – into a series of stages (or tasks or components), characterized by different mixes of productive factors and technological and organizational skills. Each stage is allocated to the country or region that ensures the most profitable production (in terms of technical efficiency versus cost). Some emerging countries – China is the most important case – have shown that large developing countries supplied with basic infrastructure, educated workers, saving capacity and especially government authorities that are competent, determined, far-sighted, relatively honest and caring for the improvement of the economic conditions of their populations have the power to impose on advanced countries' MNCs conditions for their participation in the latter's value chains that favour the upgrading, in terms of technology acquisition and learning, of the stages assigned to them; and that this participation can be used as a central element of a strategy of overall national economic development.

In this respect, the extraordinary experience of China's growth miracle has delivered a tremendous blow to the beliefs of both extreme right- and left-wing economists as regards the possibility for developing countries to catch up with advanced countries within the framework of the contemporary globalization process dominated by the economic power of the USA and the international economic institutions largely under its control. Neoliberal economists have been preaching since the 1980s, with incredible success until the explosion of the 2008 crisis, a gospel – the so-called Washington Consensus – according to which the only way for developing countries to overcome their economic backwardness was to allow an unrestricted opening of their economies to foreign trade, FDI and foreign capital; to let markets freely determine the directions of economic activity; to drastically reduce all state intervention in the economy by privatizing public services and abolishing or minimizing public regulations. They recommended – and international organizations often imposed – these reform policies without paying any serious attention to their concrete implementation and their pacing and sequencing, although these had proved to be decisive factors in determining the failure or success of reforms; nor to the fact that the very markets that were to solve all economic problems were frequently absent in developing and former communist countries. China's (and India's, as previously other Far East nations') economic success, on the contrary, has come without respecting these rules, rather while directly contrasting with them – as underlined by Lin (2012), at the time World Bank Chief Economist.

On the opposite side, left-wing 'anti-imperialist' economists had instead excluded the possibility that a process of catching up by developing countries could take place through participation in the movement towards a more open international economy that culminated in the current globalization process. For decades, they had presented MNCs from advanced countries and their direct investments in the Third World as the wicked of the story, the symbol of Western imperialism and exploitation. And to a large extent they had been right, as MNCs' investments in developing countries until the 1980s were still, as in colonial times, concentrated in agricultural and mineral raw materials; and to defend and extend these investments, MNCs had actively participated in or had induced their governments to organize or support direct military interventions, coups d'état, physical elimination of insufficiently subservient political leaders, separatist wars, not to speak of widespread resort to intrigue and corruption (see, for example, Litvin (2003) or the bestseller by Perkins (2004)). These economists had attacked the analysis of Warren (1973, 1980), a heretical voice on the left, who had expressed (together with Emmanuel, as already pointed out) a relatively positive judgement on the experience of introduction of capitalism in underdeveloped countries and, in contrast to the then fashionable dependence theory, had argued that in post-colonial times foreign investment by multinationals in the Third World, because of the technology transfers that usually accompany it, represented a key opportunity for countries seriously aiming at economic modernization and industrial development.

The majority of left-wing economists did not understand the fundamental changes in power that the world economy underwent from the early 1980s; in particular, they underestimated the importance of the changes that had taken place in some important developing countries as a result of the experience accumulated in the course of post-independence industrialization attempts and of the new interest on the part of MNCs for the growing ability of these countries to participate competitively as producers of manufactures in MNCs' production chains. China, in particular – thanks, on the one hand, to the attraction exerted by its unlimited supplies of relatively educated low-wage workers and massive potential domestic market and, on the other, to the determination and bargaining skills of its leaders and their clear vision of the economic goals to be pursued at each stage – managed to extract from foreign investors conditions that increasingly favoured the technological and qualitative upgrading of its manufactures, making its participation in the globalization process the centre of its surprisingly successful development strategy.

The other great power change at international level is the one connected with the fixing of standards and the role of networks, which will be the subject of Chapter 10. A key effect of the ICT revolution has been the rise to predominance, among MNCs, of those belonging to the ICT sector itself. They have managed to develop sufficient power to be able to condition the action of governments, not only in smaller countries – as was the case with some traditional large MNCs in the past – but also in large countries. And since until recent years those dominating at international level were almost all US corporations, their increasing power also favoured the predominance of the US government over those of other foreign countries. But at the same time they have developed in every country in the world a power vis-à-vis consumers and other firms such as was seldom exercised before by private corporations.

10 The Battle of Standards and Networks

10.1 The role of standards

Among the different aspects of economic power, increasingly significant in today's world economy is the power to fix the rules of the economic game. And among these rules, those regarding standards are particularly important, as they greatly influence at domestic, but especially at international level, the success of firms (both those that are involved in the creation of standards and related infrastructure and those that make use of the standards or produce goods and services based on them) and the location of production activities. Therefore, unequal power in influencing the establishment of standards is a source of serious distortions of national, but especially international, market competition.

Problems related to standards stem from the fact that, as stressed by Kay, 'There is nothing in the organization of a market economy that guarantees a good, or any, solution to standards issues'; but despite that, he noticed that 'these markets usually work, often through regulation or government-sponsored agreements; sometimes through spontaneous order emerging in the marketplace; occasionally through the success of the products of one particular firm' (2003, p. 252). In all cases, however, the process through which standards emerge creates considerable scope for the exercise of power, so that one can agree with Busch (2011) that 'in our modern world standards are arguably the most important manifestation of power relations' (p. 80). The power conflicts over the fixing of standards can take place among economic agents within a country, across different countries, or involve at the same time different agents and different countries. Here the centre of interest will be the last two cases.

The word 'standard' has different meanings. In a broad sense it can refer to all the rules of the game that discipline an activity, be they political, economic, technical or cultural (as the decision of an international body to use certain languages as official languages for its meetings and documents) or of whatever other type. In a stricter economic sense, the word refers to the basic regulations of an economic activity (for instance, in the field of labour, those fixing the maximum duration of work, the minimum age of workers, the minimum wage or the powers of trade unions). In a still stricter sense, it refers to technical standards – to technical specifications of goods and services, software, infrastructure and networks, usually established with the purpose of reducing transaction costs and making it possible for a larger number of operators to produce and/or use them (some technical standards respond to other goals, such as safety, health, defence of the environment or better consumer information).[1] They are the key factors permitting the interoperability and interconnectability of goods, components, systems and networks.

As argued by Busch, the advantages of specialization and division of labour described by Adam Smith in his pin factory example are based on standardization, which allows complex production cycles to be fragmented into specific tasks that can be easily performed by workers as they do not require previous acquisition of special skills. In the last two centuries, two strictly connected forces have been driving the movement towards standardization within and across countries: radical improvements in the means of transport and communication, and the advantages of specialization and scale economies. At international level, in the decades following the 1830s, railways and then steamships made it possible for the first time to move massive amounts of goods and huge numbers of people between countries and continents. Later on, the telegraph and the telephone made it possible to transmit information almost instantaneously from anywhere in the world to any other point. These advances opened the way for a huge increase in international trade and corresponding increases in productivity through the exploitation of comparative advantages and scale economies. But for this potential movement of goods, people and information to take place at a low cost and in a short time some basic common technical standards had to be established in all the participating countries for both the new means of transport and communication, and the old national systems of measuring, weighing, paying for goods and so on. For information on the history of standards see Russell (2005) and Ping (2011).

The authorities of the most advanced countries were aware of the need for such harmonization if the 'first globalization' (we refer to the 1870–1914 period, though some authors anticipate the initial date by one or two decades) was to take place. While imposing uniformity of standards in the domestic economy proved relatively easy, since the state had the legal power of intervening in this field, at international level the problem was rather complex. All through the 19th century, governments organized a series of international conferences aimed at reaching common rules and specifications. Many of these conferences were successful, leading to the establishment of international standard-setting organizations, as happened in the fields of telegraphy (1865), meteorology (1873) and postal services (1874); others failed (such as the one on navigation convened by the USA in 1889); common rules were established on patents and on copyrights respectively by the 1883 Paris Convention and the 1886 Berne Convention, and on carriage of goods by rail by the 1890 Berne Convention.

In the monetary field, it must be recalled that in 1867, 1878, 1881 and 1892 the authorities of the major independent countries of the world (whose money was made

[1] These technical standards are not discussed in this chapter, but they are of great importance in international trade as they can represent non-tariff barriers that have a major influence on trade flows, and run the risk of being used as hidden protectionist measures. For a discussion of these non-tariff barriers see UNCTAD (2018).

of precious metals and of notes freely convertible into them) met in a series of conferences to reach an agreement on a single monetary standard. The world's main countries were divided at that time into a majority with a bimetallic standard (with both gold and silver coins in circulation, mostly at the compulsory exchange rate of 1:15.5), Great Britain (and Portugal) with a gold standard and the other countries with a silver standard. The last three conferences were meant to lead to an agreement based – given the scant world supplies of gold – on the adoption of the bimetallic standard; but, primarily because of British opposition, a final consensus was never reached. From the mid-1890s – thanks to large discoveries of gold in South Africa and to British economic, commercial and banking pre-eminence – the gold standard, centred in London, became de facto the standard for international monetary and financial transactions, but each country maintained its own domestic monetary system. From the mid-1860s to the 1890s, France, Italy, Switzerland, Belgium and Greece were united in a bimetallic Latin Monetary Union that unified the characteristics of the member countries' coins and some monetary rules.

Even the adoption of international labour standards – so that improvements in working conditions and worker rights in different countries would not find obstacles in worries about international competitiveness – became the object of a conference on international labour legislation held in Berlin in 1890. The issue would be taken up again at the Versailles Conference in 1919, leading to the inclusion in the peace treaty of basic labour principles and rights, and to the creation, in that same year, of the International Labour Organization (ILO); see Kapstein (1999).

In the field of product standards, it was often the main private producers or their organizations that tried to reach, at national and international levels, agreement on the basic standards for their products. In some cases, the establishment of common standards took place without involving any discussion or conflict, as the firm that made a new discovery or innovation or first developed a product managed, thanks to its initial adoption of a standard and its leading position in that field, to impose its standard on – or to have its standard spontaneously adopted by – later producers (as was the case, discussed later, of the typewriter keyboard).

Both public and private attempts to establish common standards often failed. Especially when different countries or main producers or utilizers had already gone a long way using their own specific standards, agreement often proved impossible (or was not even attempted), or was reached without including all interested parties. For instance, weights and measures, railway gauges, driving on the left or right and currencies were never unified even among the main countries and still represent a considerable hindrance to international economic relations. Perhaps the most ambitious, and failed, attempt at standardization was the proposal by a Polish individual, L. L. Zamenhof, in 1887 to introduce Esperanto, a simplified international language that would have overcome what has represented in human history the greatest obstacle to international intercourse in all fields. For product standards, the paradoxical case of the domestic electrical outlet plug can be cited: despite representing a minor element, of negligible monetary value, and despite electric domestic appliances being among the most internationally traded products, the International Electrotechnical

Commission has classified 15 different types of plugs that are at present currently in use worldwide (even within the EU, different plug standards are used).

In other cases, a common standard could only be reached after a long period of time and often thanks to special or chance factors; as happened with one of the recent basic transport innovations, the standardized container, which in the course of decades had to overcome a series of obstacles before finally seeing the light: Levinson (2006) recounts its history. It is very important, however, to distinguish between standards that differ among nations but can be translated from one to the other without major difficulties and costs, as with weights and measures, and those that cannot in any way be made commensurable, such as driving on the left or right.

Although a large body of empirical economic research on standards is not yet available, in recent years the importance of standards, and specifically of international standards – to which in the past economists had not paid particular attention (Kindleberger (1983) being a significant exception) – has been the object of an increasing number of analyses, which have underlined the large contribution they make to the progress of productivity and overall economic growth. There is a review of them in Swann (2010a).[2]

Swann, and then Blind (2013), analysed the channels through which standards foster innovation, productivity, competition and consumer welfare, though they also indicated some possible negative effects. It has already been mentioned that standardization was essential to exploit scale economies and to allow the division of labour and specialization on which the Industrial Revolution was based; later on, it produced great benefits through the exploitation of network externalities. In addition to making the exchange of goods and information possible in the first place, standards reduce transaction costs, sparing producers both from the need to inquire about other regions' and, especially, foreign countries' specific standards, and the expense of adapting products to those standards. In the early stages of development of a technology, they contribute to achieving focus, cohesion and critical mass. They codify and diffuse state-of-the-art and best practices at low cost among producers and foster competition between and within technologies, thus stimulating innovation. By reducing uncertainty and risk, they incentivise firms' investment in the development of new products.

The very process of standard-setting serves to accelerate the production and diffusion of innovations, as experts who meet in standardization committees share knowledge on products and production processes and gain some indication of competitors' future plans; such exchanges of both direct and tacit knowledge would normally find an obstacle in the secrecy necessarily imposed on researchers and technical personnel by their firms. Most important in recent decades has been the fact that by strictly defining the characteristics of products and their components, standards permitted the extraordinary growth of production offshoring and its diffusion to distant coun-

[2] According to Cebr (2015) – a study commissioned by the British Standards Institution – standards contributed over 37 per cent to the annual labour productivity growth of the UK economy over the period 1921 to 2013, and over 28 per cent to the annual GDP growth.

tries and even to smaller firms, thus increasing the efficiency of international production chains and allowing developing countries to participate in these chains with consequent opportunities for technology transfers and growth. On the role and effects of standards in global production chains see Kaplinsky (2010) and Aerni (2013).

Common standards, particularly product standards, also greatly benefit consumers. They lead to lower product prices, as they intensify competition and innovation and allow easy comparison of the price and quality of products. They considerably reduce consumers' risk of being locked in to a product with a specific producer's standard that may be rapidly superseded by a similar product based on alternative technologies; so they favour the purchase of innovative products as soon as they are offered on the market. Finally, they benefit consumers and other economic agents by reducing the risks connected with imperfect and asymmetrical information, as they guarantee that products conform to precise sets of characteristics. This last function also contributes to overcoming problems of 'adverse selection' – the phenomenon that occurs when economic agents offering products of superior quality have no means of signalling this quality to purchasers, so that suppliers of lower quality products can sell at the same price as suppliers of high-quality ones; consequently, the latter try to get the price corresponding to the real value of their product by selling through channels external to the market (a typical example of the phenomenon is the problematic determination of the market price of second-hand cars).

There are also possible negative effects of standards. Consumers may suffer from the reduction of variety that standards produce by definition (but since standards facilitate the compatibility and interoperability of constituent parts, they may allow consumers to choose the favourite product for each component). Instead of fostering competition, standards, especially for products based on networks, may reinforce monopolies, as the standards proposed by the most advanced and strongest parties have a greater chance of being adopted internationally. While a problem with standards is that their general acceptance and definition through the traditional standard-setting procedures implies a costly and usually long process, there is also the opposite danger that a standard may be fixed at too early a stage, preventing the development and adoption of a more efficient alternative standard.

Two basic general characteristics of standards must be stressed. The first is that they have a double nature, since they can operate both as instruments of international cooperation, allowing wider beneficial economic intercourse to take place with mutual advantage between nations, and also as instruments generating conflict when directed to obtain advantages at the expense of other nations through the exercise of pressure or coercion to adopt them, or when used as artificial devices for isolating a country from external economic exchanges. They can often determine whether producers and markets are united or separated, thus creating or eliminating the possibility of international competition and favouring or preventing the exploitation of scale economies. Before the international standard for containers was adopted, transport firms that used a given standard were exclusive suppliers of the markets of the countries whose transport infrastructure adopted that standard; at the same time, for all bulky goods, national producers enjoyed an unfair competitive advantage over foreign ones, as the latter had to pay much higher delivery costs owing to differences in transport standards between different countries; and finally, without the introduction of the international container, the technological revolution (and consequent reduction in costs) that has taken place in transport through the automation of operations and infrastructure would not have been possible.

Standards seem to have an ambivalent effect on the volume of trade, because, on the one hand, the unification of systems', networks' and products' characteristics, by eliminating a factor of artificial protection, enlarges the potential market for producers; but, on the other hand, they can cause cost increases in order to comply with international or export market standards and thus lead to higher prices and lower competitiveness that limit export possibilities (a problem particularly significant for developing countries that have to overcome many obstacles to comply with international standards mainly set by advanced countries). This would explain why Swann's (2010b) thorough survey of the empirical literature led him to conclude that while compliance with standards seems on the whole to have a positive effect on the volume of international trade, frequent exceptions call for caution in drawing definite conclusions. More specifically, he showed how the effect of standards on countries' innovative activity, productivity and growth (which in turn largely determine export performance) depends on the specific nature of the standard, the kind of product to which the standard applies and the characteristics of the producing countries.

The second characteristic of standards is that they are subject to strong path dependence, since later adopters' decisions depend on the decisions of previous adopters, and hysteresis, in the sense of endurance in time because, since continuous investments are usually made in the infrastructure they require, the more time passes, the more a change from one standard to another (even if a more efficient one) creates a lot of practical difficulties and implies the loss of all or most of the funds already invested (and of the specific skills developed) in the superseded standard. Inertia and tradition also contribute to standards' endurance over time.[3] The result is that enormous power is obtained by those who first introduce a standard and manage to have it adopted by an initial number of users and/or producers. Famous in the field of product standards is David's (1985) example of the typewriter keyboard layout standard, which won universal adoption because it minimized the likelihood of keys sticking on manual typewriters. In more recent times, when that problem disappeared, more efficient keyboard layouts (in terms of typing speed or learning costs) could have been introduced, but the market proved to be locked in (and continues to be so even with computer keyboards) to the initial inferior standard because no producer has taken the initiative of going against a century-and-a-half-old practice given the uncertainty about the possible reaction of customers and competitors, and thus about

[3] Clocks produced in the last 500 years have hands moving 'clockwise' around the dial, as this is the convention that has emerged by tradition, so that we would consider insane any clockmaker producing a clock that moves in the opposite direction. But at the beginning that choice was not so incontrovertible: one can still see in Florence's 15th-century cathedral a clock with a dial by Paolo Uccello whose mechanism moves hands 'counter-clockwise'.

the benefit of moving first. Path dependence and endurance in time also give rise to one of the advantages of standards, namely predictability, as they allow producers and users to expect that a standard, once agreed upon, will probably be maintained and respected for a considerable time by all accepting parties (although technical progress and the introduction of new products may impose the early adoption of new standards). It also frequently happens that once a standard is defined, the customers who adopt that standard find themselves locked into an exclusive relationship with the initial provider of the standard product or network. The fact that the adoption of a standard has such long-lasting effects explains, of course, why 'standards wars' tend to be particularly fierce.

10.2 Standards wars

The setting of international standards takes place as a rule at conferences or meetings where each government, or, more commonly, national (private or government-controlled) standard-setting body, or group of national firms advances its proposals. Unfortunately, there is another power asymmetry here: a general tendency for producers to be over-represented and for final users and other non-commercial interests to be under-represented in the participating national bodies.

The choice of an international standard is based in the first place on technical considerations, as it is in the interest of all parties to maximize the efficiency of the new common standard. But just as important is the fact of having been the first to devise and adopt a standard in a given field of activity and to have taken the initiative of establishing a de facto international standard. Of course, specific national interests, buttressed by the specific powers of each nation, also play a major role in producing the final decisions. In sum, the process leading to the adoption of a standard can best be represented as a coordination game where all the participants have an interest in reaching a common solution, but do not agree on what the solution should be. It is a field where the most fruitful tools for analysis seems to be provided by game theory.

Among the basic factors that determine the interests and thus the position of a country regarding the fixing of standards, the following must be mentioned. The first factor is the specific factual situation of the country regarding the issue under discussion: for example, if the choice of a standard for the limit of territorial waters were under discussion, one would expect that countries where important oil or gas discoveries have been made in their waters will try to have territorial waters extended as far as possible; while countries without domestic oil or gas resources will take the opposite position, so as to be allowed to search for them near the place where offshore oil or gas have already been found by other countries. The second factor is the amount of investment that a country has already made in a standard. As previously pointed out, if the alternative standards under discussion are very different, it is likely that the adoption of one standard will imply the loss of all the investment made to develop and diffuse the others. A third factor, when the choice of a standard implies the choice of a specific technology produced by a specific firm, is the nationality of the developers of standards, as each nation can be expected to try to support the standard produced by its own firms. A fourth possible factor may be mentioned: as one of the reasons for the search for an international standard is to allow all producers to access and compete in the entire world market for a product, nations or firms that doubt their ability to withstand full international competition may try to prevent the adoption of a common standard by insisting on other countries adopting their own, technically less efficient one. The overall conclusion is that as every country will tend to fight for the adoption of the standards it favours or has already introduced, the final outcome will be the result of the use by each party of all the bargaining power instruments at its disposal.

The process of standard setting (in the rest of this section, the discussion will refer to technical standards) has been made more complex by a recent development. While in the past it was customary for firms in high-technology sectors to design and develop new products in their R&D departments and then to proceed to their manufacture, one of the aspects of the general contemporary process of production fragmentation has been the frequent separation (in the semiconductor and pharmaceutical drug sectors, for example) of the knowledge-based design step from the manufacturing step, the two being carried out by separate specialized firms. The fact that the two types of firm often follow different business models and have different objectives may create difficulties in the committees of standard-setting bodies where the experts from the two groups must work in strict collaboration; see Layne-Farrar (2010).

Standards wars typically see firms or alliances of firms contending for the national or international adoption of their alternative standards; in the case of international standards, national governments are also involved as supporters of the domestic firms' positions. These wars are particularly fierce in the ICT sector because, as explained in Section 10.3, most of its products are characterized by strong network effects and consumers place a high value on product compatibility. Moreover, a specific characteristic of network industries is their tendency to 'tipping'; that is, the fact that once a technology has managed to reach a critical mass of users, it tends to dominate the whole market.

Standards wars have been the object of analysis by Shapiro and Varian (1999) (see also Stango (2004) and Egyedi (2010)). They examined three historical examples of conflicts over standards in the USA (those concerning railway gauges, direct versus alternate current in electric systems and colour television), drawing from them, and also from more recent cases, a number of general lessons on the 'art' of standards wars. They identified some critical assets that determine strength in such conflicts: control over an installed base of loyal or locked-in customers; possession of patents and copyrights controlling valuable new technology (and especially technology allowing the owner to produce – and to prevent competitors from producing – new goods compatible with older ones, so that purchasers of the new product will not have to scrap all the products or infrastructure connected with the previous technology); ability to innovate, which, among other things, conditions a country's/firm's possibility to develop an alternative technology to the one patented by a competitor; capability to manufacture the products involved in a standards war at a low cost;

strength in complementary products, as the expectation of large profit streams from sales of related products in the case of victory in a standards war strongly motivates producers and firm's financers; and reputation and brand name, which are fundamental in all markets – especially network markets – where the role of expectations is very important, as previous successes and a trusted brand will convince consumers that the product sold is the best and will be the one prevailing in the event of a standards war.

Shapiro and Varian also pointed out the critical importance of some strategic moves: one is pre-emption, or being the first to develop a product, as longer experience will allow greater progress in the learning process and in the exploitation of scale economies, and thus lead to cost advantages.[4] Another key move is the formation of strong alliances with other producers, suppliers of inputs and complementary products, and consumers, so as to increase the group's overall bargaining power. As in military conflict, the availability of these assets and strategies is important not only because it provides the strength to win a standards war, but also and especially because it shows competitors how costly a war would be for them, thus pressuring them to accept a truce or negotiations on terms favourable to the owner of these assets and strategies.

Standards wars may have beneficial effects by making the emergence of a superior standard possible and (as with military wars) by compelling contenders to make special material and intellectual efforts to devise superior products and solutions to critical problems. More likely, however, they will prove to be very costly for both contending parties and society at large.

Standards wars, especially when protracted in time, imply a waste of resources and their distraction from employment in the development of new products and technologies. They lead to a stalling of investment by both producers and customers reluctant to spend unrecoverable amounts on what may soon prove to be the losing standard. When they do not end with the defeat of one party (and connected losses by the defeated of financial investments and high-level skills and experience accumulated in the losing standard), they usually imply a socially damaging fragmentation of standards, as each party will probably manage to impose its own standard in its national market (in the case of conflicts between giants from different nations) or on its share of customers, but without certainty that it will not be superseded in the

---

[4] 'First-mover' advantages have been stressed by Scherer (2010, 2015), who considers them, on average, much more important than patents as spurts to investment in technological innovations: '"first-mover" advantages … include the head-start that innovators usually have over imitators and the opportunity to earn supra-normal profits during this period; the extension of that head-start through resort at first to product and then production process secrecy; the opportunity to advance down learning curves and hence reduce costs during the head-start period; the reputation advantage that accrues to those who are perceived by consumers to have pioneered a product innovation, permitting the retention of sizeable market shares and premium prices despite imitation; and the fact that imitators often have to spend nearly as much on R&D as innovators but typically capture much smaller market shares over which to amortise their R&D costs' (2010, p. 22). A similar opinion was expressed more strongly by Moser (2013) on the basis of evidence from economic history.

future by the competing standard. Another possible negative effect of standards wars (one that, however, may also occur for other reasons) is premature standardization: as the stake in the conflict is the acceptance by formal bodies or by the market of the predominance of a firm's standard, the winning firm will resort to all possible means to obtain that acceptance as rapidly as possible, without allowing the necessary time for possibly superior standards – or refinements of its own standard – to be developed and tested.

This explains why firms that are faced with the prospect of prolonged financial costs and possible outright elimination from the market in the event of defeat tend to look for a peaceful solution before a conflict explodes or for an early truce once it has started. Often, rivals find ways to cooperate to establish common standards; or weaker contenders recognize their position of inferiority and accept the opponent's standard predominance, making use, where possible, of adaptors, converters and other devices allowing connection of their products with the winning party's standard, or trying to carve a niche in the market where their standard may still be demanded. Such survival policies may allow the firm to keep a presence in the market in the hope of future success in introducing new products.

10.3 The privatization of standards and the ICT sector

The growing mobility of people, merchandise, capital and especially information made possible by recent technological advances makes it more and more difficult for national governments to control and regulate the economic activity that takes place within their borders. Imposing national standards very different from those already prevailing abroad in taxation, banking and financial activity, product safety, intellectual property, communication networks and so on is generally impossible unless a country is ready to isolate itself from the rest of the world, giving up the advantages of international economic, political and cultural intercourse. One has to agree with Cairncross (2001) that governments will have no other choice than to cooperate more than ever before, both with one another to establish common standards and with the private sector, since the latter has been provided by the progress of technology with increasing opportunities to escape national regulations imposed on it against its will. Although great advances have been made by governments in the introduction of internationally agreed rules and standards, these advances continue to find an obstacle both in the difficulty of reaching agreement (especially when almost universal agreement is necessary) and in the delay that inevitably characterizes public authorities' realization of – and reaction to – innovations in technology and other changes taking place in the modern world. In some cases, faced by the difficulty or impossibility of establishing common rules and standards, governments will have no alternative but to agree on mutual recognition of national ones, as happened in the EU with regard to banking from the late 1980s until the 2008 global crisis.

Product standards (which cover basic characteristics such as safety, materials employed, environmental effects, interoperability, interconnectability, quality and performance) were mainly set by producers themselves or by private technical bodies at the level of national sectors until the 1980s; international standards were not common. The exceptional growth in international trade and the technological revolution of the following decades greatly increased the cost of incompatible national product standards; as a consequence, there was rapid growth in international standards. They were, and continue to be, mostly produced by international private standard-setting organizations, with membership restricted to private national standard-setting bodies (but in a few cases also governmental or government-regulated entities); see Mattli and Büthe (2003) and Büthe and Mattli (2011). The basic principles that officially guide the activity of these organizations are openness (all interested parties should be free to participate), balance (between the interests of different participant categories) and consensus (which does not mean necessarily unanimity, but qualified majority decisions, taken after all participants have been given a chance to present their arguments). The standards produced are usually voluntary (though those regarding safety, health, environment and consumer protection often translate into formal government regulations), but tend to become mandatory in practice, as firms face difficulties and additional costs if they decide to follow different standards.

This process of delegating the regulation of product standards to private international bodies is part of a more general trend that also applies to other categories of standard. It is supported by firms and other private actors on grounds of greater efficiency and lower cost compared with public regulation. Governments, for their part, have not opposed this development, as they lack sufficient financial resources, technical experts and the capacity and flexibility necessary for early identification of problems and speedy procedures to find their solution. This privatization of international standards regulation is viewed with particular favour by MNCs and large, internationally competitive firms, as they are interested in the rapid establishment of uniform international product standards that will extend their market to the whole world, while they are more capable of influencing the standard definition process.

However, this development raises a number of serious problems. Büthe and Mattli have stressed the fact that the international standardization process is a highly political one, typically characterized by the exercise of power; a power exerted in this case not so much by states, as by national private standard-setting bodies and by firms enjoying the largest market shares. Kennedy (2006) has argued, however, that it is useful to look at the 'battle of the standards' as a conflict between competing industrial coalitions, not necessarily identified on the basis of nationality.

Büthe and Mattli have recalled that private international standard-setting bodies, financed as a rule by private-sector stakeholders, are not subject to public oversight nor to disclosure obligations on the discussions leading to the adoption of a standard, so that very little information is available to either the public or researchers on the working of the standard-setting process. Most importantly, they observed that the representation of stakeholders in these processes is extremely unequal and leads to serious biases and negative distributional effects. Global private-sector standard-setting bodies that exclude governments' participation and are usually dominated by big business inevitably tend to support industry interests at the expense of those of the public. Their greatest failing is the restricted, often practically inexistent, room they provide for consumer participation. Two top global product standards bodies (the International Organization for Standardization, ISO, and the International Electrotechnical Commission) allow just one international consumer organization to be represented, without voting rights, in their technical committees; and even this only at their discretion. They do not provide any financial assistance to the participation of consumer representatives, so potential involvement is limited by consumer associations' shortage of funds. Private standard-setting bodies do not seem to welcome active participation in their committees by consumer representatives: the latter appear to be invited just to show that all stakeholders are represented and are not expected or encouraged to make a substantial contribution to the standard-fixing process. All these circumstances have led a number of observers to criticize the trend towards delegation of the responsibility for standardization (and for other global regulations) to private international bodies as a move towards a world order devoid of democratic transparency, accountability and legitimacy, and contrary to the traditional principle of counterbalancing the excessive influence of business interests in the public arena by giving more power to other private and public agents.[5]

An even more worrying and highly debated recent development regarding the tendency to privatization in national and international standard-fixing is the increasing role played, particularly in the US ICT sector, by the practice of standardization by consortia or private forums – see Schoechle (2009). These are clubs of usually financially very strong firms that work together informally to produce standards in rapid reaction to new market developments, outside traditional formal standard-fixing bodies, which they accuse of following principles and procedures that are exceedingly complex and difficult to implement, and that excessively delay the definition of standards. Consortia may also provide their members with the services of branding, testing, certifying and marketing new products; the general phenomenon of technology and patent sharing arrangements is discussed by Baumol (2002).

* * *

The most important reason for the exceptional growth of the importance of technical standards in recent decades is the fact that the goods and services that have registered the biggest increases in consumption and investment have been those con-

[5] Büthe and Mattli have also examined the different general approaches to standard setting in the USA and Europe, which are the product of the different economic and business histories of the two areas. They consider the European system of product standardization – centralized, hierarchical, coordinated, regulated, subsidized, and inclusive, while the US system tends to present opposite characteristics – to be more effective, other things being equal, for the purpose of influencing the process of setting new formal international standards, as it allows national producers and other stakeholders to obtain more timely and diffused information on proposed new international standards and to ensure a more unitary and effective representation of national interests. They attribute this advantage to the fact that the prevalent institutional model of European national product standard-fixing systems is complementary to – in the sense of better fitting with and thus more easily coordinated with – the model that characterizes contemporary international standard-fixing institutions.

nected with ICT and produced by the giants of the New Economy. Compared with traditional goods, these products have special characteristics: they do not incorporate materials that are destroyed by the act of consumption, they do not degrade with use, their consumption by a person does not prevent their consumption by other persons, and, being based on easily transmittable information, their producers must defend themselves from imitators through forms of monopoly, such as patents and copyrights or by imposing the purchase of their related products to those wishing to use them. But the most important characteristic of such goods and services is that they are typically dependent on networks and are characterized by large network economies; the latter refer to the fact that with the increase in the number of users, two things happen.

On the one hand, their cost goes down: in many cases the marginal cost, the cost of one additional unit, may be practically zero, thus impairing the very operation of the market price system (where, in perfect competition, the price of a good is equal to the cost of the least efficient supplier remaining in the market). On the other hand, the utility of the product for the user – and the entities, such as advertisers, that use the network to promote their products – increases with each new user (just as a century ago the utility of buying a telephone increased with the number of people that also had one). As a result, they represent the typical products whose producers, once they have managed to establish an initial advantage over competitors, have great opportunities to become monopolists in their sector – see Rifkin (2015) for a general discussion of the issues posed by ICT networks and the tendency for ITC products to zero marginal cost. This is why the ability to influence the adoption of the standard for a product, and especially for a network, is of critical importance for producers. This ability will be largely determined not so much by superior competitiveness and technological efficiency as by a producer being the first mover, thus benefiting from network economies. Countries and big firms are particularly interested in this battle of the standards as products based on networks typically have a market that extends to the whole world, while the networks, once established, tend to allow their providers to behave like monopolists or, at worst (for them), oligopolists.

In the ICT sector, more than in others, a new fundamental problem is creating difficulties for the standardization process, exacerbating standard wars, with potentially negative consequences especially for the development of latecomer countries. While patents are subject to IPR,[6] so they are a typical private good whose licence (the con-

[6] This work does not discuss the problems connected with IPR (which cover patents, copyright and brands). However, since today's international competition is largely based on technology and innovation, the IPR discipline has a crucial impact on the diffusion of technological knowledge, on the degree of competition between firms and countries and on countries' economic development and catch-up possibilities.

Patents and other products of intellectual creation are increasingly the object of international trade (with firms often specializing in their production, as noted in Section 10.2); but trade in them has a special characteristic not present in trade in physical goods or in other services: 'When two parties are

cession to other entities of the right to manufacture, use, or sell one's own invention) can be refused by the owner or sold at a price, standards have traditionally been a public good, made available to all producers, consisting of documents where all the details of the standard are minutely specified. As they contain a substantial amount of knowledge in codified form, they represent, as already indicated, an important instrument for the diffusion of knowledge within and between economies. However, in recent years, as standards – and especially network standards – have seen their technical complexity grow, they have increasingly required, as a condition for their definition and for their operation, the availability of a large number of patents; and the owners of these 'essential patents' can, and often do, use them as an additional important strategic weapon in standard wars, to impose their own standard, or to

---

negotiating over some physical product, the owner of the product can threaten to take it away at any time if the other party does not live up to his end of the bargain. If … a restaurant does not pay its suppliers, those suppliers stop delivering to the restaurant. Intellectual property cannot, however, be "taken away"; once an idea has been shared, it cannot be unlearned' (Layne-Farrar 2010, p. 41). IPR protection is the mechanism that should allow trade in IPR or in goods covered by IPR to take place, as it gives the right to sue for unauthorized use of intellectual property and obtain enforced collection of licensing fees. But there is always the risk that recourse to this mechanism will prove not to be fully effective, take a long time and involve high legal costs that not all producers can afford.

From the 1980s onwards, a marked trend can be observed – originating in the USA and progressively followed by other advanced countries (the main producers of innovations) – towards both domestic and international reinforcement of the defence of patents and copyrights to an extent that cannot be justified by the alleged goal of stimulating innovation activity and dynamism of the economy, but rather mainly reflects the power and lobbying activity of existing, especially large, producers interested in maintaining and extending their monopolistic positions against possible new competitors. IPR protection can now be obtained for minor or very generic innovations, the time period of protection has been widely extended (even retrospectively) and the fields of human activity where protection can be obtained have been enlarged. The result has been a dramatic growth in the number of patents demanded and obtained in the last decades, without any apparent consequent acceleration in inventive activity.

A growing number of economists have expressed strong criticism of this development in the IPR system, especially as it seems to create serious handicaps to developing countries, as pointed out by Bhagwati (2004), Stiglitz (2006) and Pasinetti (2007). It has been stressed that, historically, some of the countries that made important contributions to innovation had no patent system or only a very limited one; that even today a large number of important innovations are not patented; and that the present IPR protection system does not seem to contribute to spur innovation, but rather to hinder it – see Moser (2013). This last charge finds support in the practice of big corporations of applying for a huge number of minor and generic patents with the sole purpose of preventing competitors from developing innovations (already Schumpeter (1942) had pointed out the social waste produced by firms' 'buying up of patents in order not to use them' (p. 80)); and in the spread of agreements among big producers to share among themselves all their patents, thus reinforcing the position of the group against external competitors. This negative judgement is shared by economists with different ideological views: see, in addition to the authors mentioned above, the very strong position of Boldrin and Levine (2008) and Baker (2016), but also Lynn (2010) and Mazzucato (2018). Already long ago World Bank Vice President for Special Programs Ismail Seragelding (1998), referring to research in biotechnology, complained that we had entered a period when scientific 'breakthroughs that are coming are for the first time driven by proprietary science' and thus subjected to highly restrictive patents of long duration, while previously it had been especially public international and national research institutions that contributed to scientific discoveries, considered a public good to be made freely available to everybody.

prevent or delay the development of given standards, or to extract excessive royalties for incorporation of these patents in standards; see Ernst (2013).[7]

The patents owners' market power conferred by these possibilities may lead to the adoption of standards that are technologically inferior but less dependent on the goodwill of the owners of essential patents to allow their use in standards at a reasonable price. Although formal standard-setting bodies require that owners of essential patents make them available to all interested parties on 'reasonable' terms as a condition for a standard to be adopted, there is wide scope for different interpretations of the word 'reasonable' and for opportunistic behaviour on the part of the owners of essential patents; the latter may in the end refuse to take part in the standard-setting process, trying to impose de facto standards based on their own patents. A possible solution to this problem – see Gibson (2007) – could be the early identification of the patents involved in the competing standards under discussion for a final choice; and before this choice is made, all interested holders of essential patents should officially declare whether and at what precise conditions they are ready to license their patents to all potential users.[8]

One of the main reasons for the success and increasing role of private consortia in standard-fixing is that these bodies manage to solve the problem of patents included in standards. As stressed by Schoechle (2009), 'consortia are in a good position to deal with and manage this increasing problem by forming patent pools and/or licencing authorities, capping royalty obligations on standards, negotiating with IPR holders from a position of strength, and enforcing IPR disclosure policies among their members' (p. 164). He admitted that consortia standardization is a reality that needs to be recognized and incorporated into the global system, but argued that this cannot take place by simply legitimizing their present practices, which result in dangerously

[7] While the ownership of essential patents is a very important asset for a firm as it conditions the possibility to establish a standard based on them as a formal international one, the value of a patent (as of any other IPR asset), essential or not, is in turn largely influenced by its being or not included in a formal international standard.

[8] The issue of the inclusion of essential patents in standards has been in the 2000s at the centre of a standards war, which attracted large attention, between China and the USA on the adoption of an international security standard for wireless devices; see Gibson (2007). In 2003, China had tried to introduce at home its own mandatory national standard, WAPI, which it wanted to be adopted internationally despite there already being a widely accepted formal international standard, approved by ISO in 1999. The USA insisted on the respect of the WTO's Agreement on Technical Barriers to Trade which requires that in case a relevant international standard already exists, countries must use it as a basis for mandatory national standards. Apart from advocating the application of an exception in that Agreement for cases of national security requirements, China countered that mandatory adoption of existing international standards is unfair, as these standards do not respect the required criteria of being open, accessible and fair to all potential participants. In particular, they frequently impose large costs on developing countries – which often have not participated in the process of definition of the standards – especially in the form of payment for patents and other intellectual property they incorporate. The Chinese WAPI standard was submitted in 2010 to a vote within the ISO for possible adoption as a new international standard, and rejected. The following year, the Chinese government cancelled the WAPI project, without, however, formally withdraw the mandatory WAPI standard for the domestic market.

tilting the system towards the most powerful players. Instead he proposed intervening by reforming IPR laws and enforcing antitrust laws.

The general issue of proprietary standards – that is, private standards established by individual firms and frequently protected by IPR, which may become de facto standards for a whole sector (Microsoft is an example) – was also discussed by Aerni (2013) with special reference to the food sector and to the role of standards in the working of GVCs. He argued that these private de facto standards, which do not apply the principles of openness, transparency and consensus that should guide standardization, may at times facilitate innovation and trade, but may also actively block them to increase the profits of the standard-owning firms.

* * *

China provides an illustration of the problems, and inevitable contradictions, that a large emerging country faces in trying to develop a national policy aimed at ensuring progressive technological sophistication, modernizing the domestic standards regime and playing a key role in setting world standards.

In this regard, in a very interesting article, Brunnermeier, Doshi and H. James (2018) have pointed out the striking similarities between the contemporary economic and technological competition between China and the USA, and that which took place between autocratic, state-centred Germany and liberal free market Great Britain in the last decades of the 19th century – also a period of globalization and radical technological innovation. Regarding leading-edge sectors (at the time radio telegraphy, now ICT) and connected standard-setting issues, they stress the parallelism, in the two cases, between the problems, attitudes and strategies of the old and established leader and those of the emerging power.

Chinese leaders understand that we are at a historic turning point in the international economy, where the ICT revolution imposes the establishment of new world standards that, owing to hysteresis, will probably remain unchanged for decades once agreed upon. In recent years, they have made increasing China's influence in international standard-fixing a policy priority and have taken active part in the cooperative international effort to establish new standards. Understandably, they would like to have their national standards adopted worldwide; and given China's huge present, and especially prospective, market size both in terms of producers and consumers (so that it will represent a large share of any future world market), the point may well be reached in the not too distant future where China's decision on a standard and its domestic implementation will leave other countries with no choice but to adopt it themselves.

Suttmeier, Yao and Tan (2006), who analysed Chinese problems – and inconsistencies, probably largely reflecting different interests and opinions among domestic actors – in defining a position on international technical standards, argued, as some other observers, that despite a rapid growth of resources devoted to R&D, on the whole China did not register a particularly brilliant record of autochthonous technological innovation. They ascribed this result to a prevalent attitude of the country's exporting firms of largely relying on transfers of technology from abroad. Chinese insistence on developing its own standards on the basis of national R&D abilities, using the large domestic market as a springboard in the hope of seeing other countries adopting them, may not work; other countries may agree instead to adopt one of their own, possibly more technologically advanced, standards. This would probably lead to the opposite result of Chinese standard isolation, as its national standards would probably be incompatible with the more widely adopted foreign ones, jeopardizing the progress of China's integration into the world economy and the international competitiveness of its products (and in fact the Chinese effort to develop national standards could alternatively be interpreted as a strategy aimed at protecting its large domestic economy from full international competition).

Other observers, however, on the basis of more recent evidence, have expressed a much more positive judgement of Chinese technological advancement. Wei, Xie and Zhang (2017) have underlined the great increase in recent years in human and financial resources invested in science and technology; in the share of firms' expenses for technological progress devoted to in-house improvement relative to those used for importing and digesting foreign technologies (which went, respectively, from 20 and 78 per cent in 2000 to 84 and 11 per cent in 2014); and in the results from the innovation effort (measured by the number of patents registered in the USA by Chinese applicants and of citations of Chinese patents – granted by the Chinese patent office – by all patent applicants in the USA). It is a fact that in more recent years increasing worries have been manifested in the USA about Chinese progress in some of the most promising new technologies, such as the Internet of Things and 5G networks.

Breznitz and Murphree (2013), analysing China's technology standards policy, stressed the fact that after their first unsuccessful attempts (as in the WAPI case) at having their own specific standards adopted internationally (and even in the domestic market), the Chinese have somehow modified their strategy. According to them, the Chinese development of domestic standards and the attempts to have them applied internationally should be viewed as mainly aimed at having these standards taken into serious consideration and tested by the market. Ultimately it is the result in terms of wide adoption of Chinese standards by producers in domestic and international markets that will be decisive in determining the success of Chinese technology and production, more than their formal adoption as domestic or international standards. The two authors point to the decisive importance, for Chinese producers, of standards having superior performance and competitive capacity in the market: Chinese authorities find obstacles to imposing on producers located in China, foreign and domestic, the adoption of standards that the latter do not consider capable of ensuring success in selling more products. They argue against the widespread representation of Chinese standards policy exclusively in terms of 'techno-nationalism' and protectionism, since among the Chinese authorities themselves – in a political system characterized by fragmentation and competition among different bureaucracies – there is no unified consensus on imposing a policy of Chinese standards at all costs.

The two authors attribute instead great importance to the successful Chinese efforts to study, and gain a deep knowledge of, the process of international standard-setting, in which they are taking an increasingly active part, challenging US leadership and practices. They see the Chinese activity in international standard-setting as centred on the purpose of establishing an international discipline favouring low prices for patents and other intellectual property, especially as regards those incorporated in international standards; and they consider the increasing understanding of, and familiarity with, the formal rules and practical procedures of the standardization game by Chinese representatives in standard-setting bodies as the main threat to American hegemony in this area (aggravated by the likely united front of Chinese and European representatives).

As for the Americans, they have an interest in international agreements on standards (as on many other issues) to be concluded as soon as possible. At present, they are by far the leading world power in technology and innovation and also in politics and economics: any agreement concluded at this time would inevitably largely reflect their strategies and their interests, allowing them to preserve or set the standards most convenient for them. If it proved impossible to reach common positions on standards in current negotiations, agreement would have to be put off to a future date, when in all probability a more powerful China – in technological, economic and political terms – will have much greater bargaining power when trying to impose its own standards on the world.

That world power relations in international standard-fixing are changing is also demonstrated by the current experience, in the field of corporate taxation, of the Base Erosion and Profit Shifting (BEPS) initiative launched in 2013 by the OECD (the organization representing the wealthiest countries of the world, which also has tried in the post-war period to coordinate – with the main purpose of avoiding double taxation – national tax systems at international level), aimed at establishing common criteria for the taxation of MNCs' foreign activities (see Section 12.3.4). In the past, international tax standards were basically the product of the initiatives and interests of a few advanced countries, with the USA in a dominant position. This time, instead, the OECD initiative was set in motion by the G20 group of countries in response to a largely shared opposition to the unacceptable tax privileges of large, predominantly US, MNCs, particularly in the digital field. The basic stimulus to the initiative seems to have come from the main EU countries (also interested in putting an end to the role of fiscal haven played by some smaller EU members), but the emerging economies of China, India and Russia, together with a very large number of developing countries and international organizations, are taking part in the work of the groups charged with formulating recommendations for changes in corporate tax law.

10.4 Worries about the giants of the New Economy

Given the importance in modern economic and social life of the networks provided by the big corporations of the New Economy, it is not surprising that their operation is everywhere a source of major concern for governments, and especially for citizens, because of a number of basic issues that public authorities have been unable – but often simply unwilling – to solve. But no less crucial are the consequences of these deficiencies for the proper working of the market system, which requires transparency and a level playing field in firms' domestic and international competition.

There is a contradiction between the private status of these – foreign, for most countries – corporations and the nature of public utility and/or the critical public importance of the services they provide in a country – a contradiction that once again highlights the position of power inferiority not only of individual citizens and firms, but also of their national authorities, vis-à-vis the big private MNCs that manage fundamental networks (a 'new feudalism', as some observers have called it).[9] On the one hand, these services are often produced in conditions of practical monopoly or oligopoly by private corporations who can impose, through unilateral contracts, unfavourable conditions on their domestic and especially foreign customers (their activity not being subjected to strict and easily enforceable national or international regulations). On the other hand, these corporations provide services essential for the life of citizens, firms, communities and governments: for example, many private transactions, financial operations and administrative acts take place online, and often online payment or online submission of documents is imposed by law. Logic would have it that if citizens are compelled by public authorities to make use of a network provided monopolistically or oligopolistically by private agents, those authorities should strictly regulate the conditions for citizens' access to, and use of, that network. And if such regulation proves impossible, they should in some way be transformed into a public service.

The enormous economic power of today's network giants allows them to condition the domestic and international activity and competitiveness of firms. Just consider search engines providing users with lists of producers of goods and services: a normal searcher looking for a product will concentrate on the first twenty or thirty producers listed; very seldom will he examine the fiftieth or the hundredth. The order of presentation is thus of critical importance for the success of a producer; but the weight attributed to each of the many criteria that search engines declare to take into account in producing ranks is unknown and in any case hardly controllable by the user. The network also exercises a crucial role in the provision of advertising, as advertisements tend to move more and more from traditional mass media to the Internet, where the number of viewers is increasing exponentially and, most importantly, messages can be easily directed just to the people identified as the most likely to be interested in the products advertised. But the criteria and policies followed by network providers in the acceptance, management and pricing of advertising are not fully open to scrutiny and control by customers, citizens or public authorities.

The Internet with its platforms is in a condition to produce fundamental changes in the power relationships between economic counterparts, again at both domes-

[9] In a particularly critical assessment of today's prevalent, basically private, standard-setting procedures – but also more in general with reference to the ability of big firms to condition the development and use of innovations, ideas and intellectual debates – some authors (see Travis (2000), Boyle (2003) and Schoechle (2009)) have instead argued that we are experiencing a process of digital and standards enclosures parallel to the land enclosures that took place in Britain in the 16th–19th centuries.

tic and international level: between firms and their customers and between different groups of firms or individual producers. Consider, for example, the relationship between hotels and their customers: once, the individual customer had little bargaining power vis-à-vis the hotel (especially one belonging to an important chain) over the price of a room; today, popular platforms acting on behalf of millions of customers have managed to extract from hotels extremely low prices that in some cases may not even allow them to cover the cost of the service. While once the customers of any restaurant, hotel or resort, and the purchasers of any product, faced with a disappointing performance of the good or service, could in practice only react by ceasing to buy from their particular supplier, now they can publicize their complaints on a platform all over the world, with good chances of compelling the supplier to change his ways (of course, this tool is also dangerously open to abuse). In addition, entire categories of producers, as is now happening in some places with taxi drivers, can see their income and bargaining power drastically reduced overnight by the introduction of a new network development such as Uber.

A different, but possibly more serious, problem comes from the de facto possibility for the private owners of these networks to penetrate citizens' life, accessing their most confidential information and utilizing it for commercial – and hypothetically also political – purposes (of course, the risk of improper or illegal intrusion into network systems to collect information on citizens' private sphere also exists for 'deviated' government agencies). And especially as providers of online services to firms, governments and public entities, they might access both firms' internal and external information flows and confidential public documents and state secrets. Their power over public authorities and firms is reinforced by the fact that both depend on them for the provision of essential network services frequently without an effective possibility of resorting to alternative suppliers.

The exclusive availability on the part of network owners, and firms to which they transmit or sell their information, of extremely detailed data on people's habits, preferences, needs, political and cultural tendencies and so on represents a powerful means to distort in their favour the operation of market competition. Since they are the only ones in possession of perfect knowledge of their current and potential customers, they can direct precise offers of products to the right person at the right moment. Any firm competing with them or trying to enter their market will be in a position of inferiority, lacking comparable information on customers' characteristics.

Worries about possible misbehaviour and abuse of monopolistic positions are not just hypothetical: it has frequently been the case that giants of the New Economy have been caught infringing systematically even some of the few existing national laws and regulations, particularly in the fields of taxation and antitrust. And, just as happened with some giants of the financial sector caught acting illegally, they have shown themselves ready – in order to avoid long trials with unforeseeable results, but in all cases damaging for their public image – to negotiate fines with domestic and foreign authorities. Such fines are apparently huge, but are really tiny if compared with the profits illegitimately obtained; so that, rather than a deterrent, they have often represented an invitation to continue illegal practices. Serious action against these giants by US authorities is unlikely: apart from the fact that they are mostly American and can therefore effectively influence their national public authorities, it has to be considered that it is the USA that obtains from their activity most of the advantages in terms of taxes paid, high-skill jobs created, income produced and positive image at international level for the economy they come from. Serious action could be expected from the EU, as it pays dearly for the Web giants' misbehaviour; but unfortunately the problems faced by the EU in adopting common initiatives on important issues are well known. In any case, given the importance of networks in modern economic life, this is an area where major international disputes – in which different countries' differences in economic and political bargaining power prove decisive – have emerged and can be expected to intensify in the future.

A different problem has arisen in more recent years with the development of social networks and the spread of a multitude of new sources of news and information. This is not the place to discuss the issue of 'fake news', whose destabilizing effects have been experienced on many occasions, nor that of the devastating effects for the life of individuals (but also of firms) that messages and other material posted on social networks can produce. But one issue is worth mentioning: who is going to be assigned the task of establishing – and monitoring the observance of – the rules that regulate messages, news and information that appear online? There seems to be a dangerous tendency to leave that task to the giant network corporations themselves, who would thus further advance their independence from governments and public authorities, deciding autonomously the contents of what people read and see online, with possible important economic effects (the decision by the main US social networks in January 2021 to close President Trump's blogs has at last highlighted the critical relevance of this development). Unfortunately, with the exception of an unprecedented EU initiative launched in 2018 (the EU Code of Practice against Disinformation, agreed with the main online platforms and advertising associations, aimed at improving platforms' transparency and proper information), that tendency does not seem to be opposed by governments, who find it convenient to leave to private corporations a task that is, both technically and politically, extremely difficult, expensive and controversial. The result is that fundamental decisions on the information people can diffuse and receive – of critical importance for the very working of democratic life, but not less important for the proper working of market competition risk being devolved to private entities that have huge direct material interests in the issue.[10] At a higher, more general level, worries have been expressed about the fact that a few social network giants nowadays behave – as if they were public authorities – as controllers of the largest part of the sphere of collective debate, something that a private firms should not be allowed to do.

[10] It has been reported, for instance, that the giants of the Web employ thousands of workers in low wage countries to clean the texts posted on the net of contents that are indecent, offensive or otherwise improper. It would seem, however, that the precise criteria adopted for the screening are not fully disclosed, leaving wide room for discretionary judgements.

But in a longer perspective, possibly the greatest danger that trends in the ICT sector point to seems to be the monopolistic or oligopolistic collection of national and international data of all kinds by the big corporations of the New Economy. They started to collect data on their users and consumers mainly to improve the targeting of their marketing policies. But then they realized they had accumulated a huge trove of data and information that, reorganized and classified according to new criteria, could be re-utilized for different, more profitable purposes: scientific and social research, security, insurance and so on (not excluding use for gaining advantages in political contests). They are now strongly pushing for the early establishment of agreements with governments and other public institutions – taking advantage of the latter's frequently difficult financial situation – to obtain the right to use the latter's stores of largely confidential data and information for research and other purposes in exchange for investments in projects and initiatives of public interest.[11]

Agreements of this type open the way to two kinds of extremely dangerous developments. In the first place, there are the devastating consequences that might follow from ICT giants not scrupulously respecting the anonymity and confidentiality restrictions agreed to in such contracts; a possibility not so far-fetched given that governments and regulators do not seem to have the ability – or often the will – to access the firm-specific technical information that would allow them to check firms' effective compliance with contractual engagements (as the 2018 Facebook–Cambridge Analytica scandal has shown). In the second place, if – as seems to be happening – a few giant corporations end up establishing a private monopoly and subjecting to their conditions and prices other institutions', firms' and individuals' access to the empirical statistical and informational base essential to research and activity in many fields, they may prove to be in possession of the means (as 'information is power') to direct this research and activity in certain directions and not in others, thus adding a further threat to freedom of research and fairness of market competition.[12]

---

[11] An example of this kind of development is the agreement, which caused strong polemics in Italy in 2017, signed the previous year (without the text being publicly disclosed) between the short-of-funds Italian government and IBM for the establishment in Milan of an important research centre (involving an investment of about €150 million). Apparently the Italian government was to give IBM, in exchange, the entire statistical patrimony of health data on the 10 million population of Lombardy, for purposes of scientific research (a generic term that may apply to many different activities) and with a guarantee of data anonymity. Probably as a result of the polemics it aroused, the initiative – which found legal support in the recent, not unambiguous, 2017 European Law (17G00180), but would have required the approval by the Italian Data Protection Authority – does not appear to have gone ahead.

[12] More recently, attention has been directed specifically to the importance that collection of large data sets provided by network users represents for the progress of research on artificial intelligence. Exclusive possession of essential data by a few private monopolists would jeopardize research in this field by public institutions and other private entities; leaving a few big firms, already very active on this front, the power to establish the lines of development of research and secure exclusive appropriation of all the economic gains from discoveries and innovations in what now appears as the area of science most promising for the future because of the many possible fields of application of theoretical and technological advances.

The monopolistic power and especially the huge profits enjoyed by ICT giants – largely thanks to particularly low rates of taxation and the de facto scope for tax elusion and evasion – appear all the more unacceptable when one recalls that this sector is the one where, to a larger extent than in others, the fundamental discoveries and innovations that allowed later developments in the field by these giants were produced by public research or by projects financed by public authorities using taxpayers' money. Common sense would suggest that if a government provides money and takes the financial risk connected with an innovation, it should also receive part of the profits produced by that innovation, when successful, and/or have a say on how those profits are employed. Mazzucato (2013, 2018) has stressed this point, advancing practical proposals such as allowing public agencies to retain equity or royalties in technologies produced with their financial support; or requiring that firms receiving public support for innovation reinvest the profits obtained into productive activity rather than use them, for example, for speculative share buy-backs.

* * *

Given the monopolistic power and the distortions that characterize both the formal status and the practical behaviour of the giants of the New Economy, one is led to wonder how we can explain the fact that no fundamental reaction, or request for national and international regulation of their activity and control of their operation, has come from the public or (apart from recent developments regarding taxation) from public authorities.

The latter probably tended to shy away from directly taking autonomous initiatives in this field because of a mix of reasons: the prevailing ideological tendency for a general reduction of state intervention in the economy; the increasing financial constraints they have been subjected to; the lack of technical expertise and specialized personnel; the awareness of the extreme difficulty of finding satisfactory and politically widely supported solutions; and the direct and indirect influence of the big corporations whose power and profits would be seriously curtailed by the introduction of serious rules regarding their activities.

But probably the most important reason was the fact that networks' and online platforms' sphere of operation and customers span the world because of the particular, immaterial nature of their products and the complexity of their structure, so that efficient regulation and control of their activity would also have to be exercised at the supranational level according to internationally agreed criteria and rules applying to most, if not all, countries. But given the ICT giants' concentration in just a few countries (and particularly the USA), their crucial role as networks allowing contemporary economic and social life to take place, and the huge power that their monopolistic positions ensure in many fields, national authorities hold very different positions on the issue of their regulation and control. Therefore, little supranational discipline of their activity can realistically be envisaged for the near future, apart from taxation issues, where surprising progress seems to have been made in 2021 (see Section 12.3.4). Of course, it would be very important if common positions on the issue were reached at least at the EU level, as they could represent a base for future wider international agreements.

As for the lack of significant reaction by the public, apart from the asymmetry of interests pointed out in Section 9.2 (in this case between a few ICT firms having a huge stake in the way the sector is regulated and hundreds of millions of individuals having only a marginal personal interest in the issue, and so less likely to mobilize to put pressure on national and international authorities to get regulation favourable to them), the basic explanation seems to be the huge economic and political power achieved by these giants, which has convinced a large part of the public that no realistic possibility exists of changing the rules of the game they have imposed. But two other factors also seem to have contributed.

The first is ideological: from the 1990s, when the ICT revolution took off, a whole mythology developed about the new characteristics of the Web, which despite having been successively largely disproved, left a strong imprint in the mindset through which people look at it. This mythology of the Web concerned the potential beneficial effects of the new technology, which was heralded as going to produce not only – as it did – huge economic advantages for society, but also the diffusion of knowledge and information, and, most importantly, a revolutionary strengthening of direct democracy: for the first time in human history, free public political debate, in which every citizen had the possibility of participating, could take place at all levels and everywhere. Unfortunately, since the start of this century these expectations have been largely disappointed and a very different reality appears to have prevailed regarding the relationship between the Internet and democracy, providing support to the less optimistic forecasts of Morozov (2011).

The mythology also concerned the apparently revolutionary features of the innovation process in ICT technology, which characterized some basic ICT products created in the first phase of its development: innovation was presented as the product of the activity of a mythical figure, the young smart individual working in isolation in his garage, without the financial backing and the huge research facilities of big corporations or public institutions. But starting from those early discoveries, the world's biggest (in terms of market value) and most powerful monopolistic/oligopolistic companies have developed; so that today the most likely choice by the smart isolated young inventor would be to sell the patent for his innovation to an ICT giant.

The second factor is connected to the lack of user charges for many Web services, which allows everybody, without restrictions owing to personal characteristics or income conditions, to access a basic tool for economic, social and political life: the providers of Web services could thus be presented as benefactors, motivated by the goal of furthering human progress and freedom. In the first years of the Internet revolution, this mythology probably reflected genuine enthusiasm by most observers for its first surprising results and expectations of huge positive effects that would follow from them. As time passed and the reality of the world of the Internet proved to be very different from the expectations, it is not unreasonable to think that the mythology continues to be divulged mainly through public relations and advertising initiatives by the Web giants. In any case, people appear to be very sensitive to the argument that requests for regulation and control of Web giants by public authorities on behalf of Web users may push the providers to charge for all the services offered.

People seem to forget two facts: first, that huge profits are reaped by Web giants from the services freely supplied to the public, through the payments they charge for advertisements and services provided to other firms; and second, that the free Web services are already paid for by users through the compulsory provision, without any remuneration or possibility of negotiating its conditions, of data and information on all aspects of their habits, preferences and most personal characteristics, which can produce large revenues for the service suppliers through both direct utilization and sale to other firms. Rather, it should be pointed out that this exchange is economically a highly unequal one because of its asymmetric, distorting effects on competition, both domestic and international. The information that network users obtain from the Web is made freely available to any person in the world and therefore cannot be the source of any exclusive competitive advantage to an economic agent that makes use of it. The economic value of the information that Internet giants obtain from users is, on the contrary, extremely high, since, appropriately re-elaborated, it provides them with an exclusive asset they can directly exploit or sell to specific economic agents that can use it to obtain advantages not available to their competitors.

* * *

If so much space has been devoted to the ICT revolution, it is because it has produced a shake-up of the entire structure of international production and trade in goods and services, such as did not follow from basic technical innovations in the previous hundred years. The transport and communication revolution of the last decades of the 19th century allowed unprecedented massive movements of people across continents and caused a disruptive change in commodity trade flows, but it did not simultaneously subvert the way production and work in all sectors were carried out; and only had marginal effects on the exchange of services, which continued to be provided basically at the local level. Other fundamental innovations – electricity, the internal combustion engine and motorization, domestic appliances, radio, cinema and TV – did have radical effects on people's ways of living, modifying the hierarchy of goods and introducing new ones in consumption patterns, and also affected the location and organization of manufacturing within countries; but their effects on international production and trade basically consisted of a different composition of the goods produced and exchanged. In the case of the ICT revolution, changes in production technologies (which, however, as shown by Gordon, have not produced a long-lasting productivity acceleration in advanced economies),[13] and in the sectoral composition of

[13] See Gordon (2018) and Gordon and Sayed (2020). Gordon basically attributes the pronounced overall slowdown in productivity after the early 1970s in both the U.S. (with a temporary revival in 1995-2005) and in Europe to a diminished impact of innovation on productivity, playing down the effect of reduced investment.

Phelps (2015) also points to innovation as the factor responsible for the slowing down of productivity growth in the advanced countries. He attributes this to a reduced innovation effort by society as

consumption and production took place at the same time as – and were strictly interconnected with – changes in international flows of direct investment and technology transfers; thus speeding up the processes of acquisition and loss of comparative advantages by countries and regions, and radically transforming the whole international structure of production and trade. The time available for countries and firms to react and adapt to these changes was drastically reduced. The geographical area directly involved by the changes extended to all regions of the world.

---

a whole, as a result of a distorted system unable to introduce the necessary stimuli to inventive activity: on the one hand, current economic theory wrongly suggests that innovation can be incentivized, through the market price system, by merely economic stimuli; on the other, a large part of the workforce is excluded from active participation in society as it is relegated to underpaid routine activities offering no opportunities for self-fulfilment and stifling imagination, creativity, entrepreneurship and innovation.

11 Offshoring, Fragmentation of Production and Global Value Chains

The RHO model refers to a world where, apart from raw materials, only final products are traded. Although the exchange of special parts or components of goods had taken place in the post-war period among advanced countries, until recent decades most international trade in manufactures concerned final consumer and investment goods. So it is not surprising that in the theory of international trade the exchange of intermediate products was for a long time treated as a secondary issue, if not just as a theoretical curiosity. Surveying international trade theory, Bhagwati (1964) argued that the exclusion of intermediate goods represented one of its major limits; and in the course of the 1960s some international economists, such as Vanek (1963), Amano (1966) and Melvin (1969b), developed pioneering theoretical analyses of trade in inputs. But it was only from the 1990s onwards that interest in the subject widened, as empirical data confirmed that a shift of international trade towards intermediate products was well under way and that production processes were increasingly fragmented into phases, tasks and components located in different countries. The RHO model's assumption of production of final goods only could therefore no longer be accepted.

The acknowledgement of the new reality had important consequences for international trade theory, as increasingly the object of the analysis of exports moved from the 'good' to the 'input' or component of the good or to the 'phase' or specific 'task' in its production process. An important theoretical contribution was made by Jones (2000): long interested in the subject, in this work he summarized his efforts to extend the traditional corpus of international trade theory to encompass international trade in inputs (he also made a major contribution to the extension of traditional trade theory to international movements of factors of production).

The increasing role of trade in intermediate products has important implications for the monopolistic competition theory of international trade (discussed in Chapter 4), as some elements on which that theory was based do not apply to these products. The theory was mainly developed to explain the fast growth of horizontal trade among advanced countries in manufactured goods destined to final consumers in the post-war decades. Many elements typical of monopolistic competition – such as desire for variety and differentiation, tastes, product appearance and design, and fashion – have little role to play in the sale and export of intermediate products. The latter, as it also happens in the case of final capital goods, are destined not to final consumers, but to manufacturers, for whom these elements, mainly related to psychological attitudes, are almost irrelevant: manufacturers are expert, well-informed buyers, choosing intermediate goods and components on the exclusive basis of their price, reliability, productivity and technological level. Competition on both price and quality appears paramount in such trade. However, some elements of monopolistic competition and diversification, such as products' real (and not just advertised) differentiation and the ability to supply customer-tailored products, also strongly influence trade in intermediate goods. These elements of differentiation are of crucial importance for manufacturers, as the availability of specific varieties or models of an input, particularly fit for their production facilities or the specific type of their final product, translates into higher competitive ability and profits.

The impact of trade in intermediate goods has been revolutionary. Together with the moving abroad of the entire production cycle of many goods by some firms of advanced countries and the autonomously generated acquisition of industrial abilities by many developing countries, the fragmentation of the production of most goods into components produced, and phases largely taking place, abroad has transformed the whole world geography of economic activity. It had fundamental effects on the level, and especially the sectoral, geographical and labour composition, of jobs in both advanced and developing countries. It changed the very organization of the firm through the increasing diffusion of global production chains. It contributed considerably to the emergence of important new industrial countries, regions and locations, posing serious problems for the advanced countries, regions and locations where the activities offshored, or in any way now performed abroad, were previously concentrated.

11.1 Offshoring, fragmentation and trade in tasks

11.1.1 Offshoring[1]

Lewis (1976) had argued that in advanced countries the end of population growth and the attainment of full employment, with consequent labour market tensions,

[1] For simplicity, the term 'offshoring' will be employed in this work as a very general term referring to the performance by a firm of whole or parts of the production cycle of a good in a foreign country (that is, a country other than the one where the headquarters of the firm are located), or to the acquisition by a firm of intermediate inputs, previously produced in its country, from foreign subsidiaries or foreign independent firms. The term 'outsourcing' will instead be used when intermediate inputs, components or phases of the production process are acquired by a firm from external suppliers either domestic or foreign.

Offshoring typically refers to transfers abroad of existing activities and the opening abroad of new activities by national firms. For offshoring to produce the negative effects at home (in the first place the alleged subtraction of jobs) on which most debates on the subject concentrated, new activities and intermediate input purchases abroad should be included in the concept only if they would have taken place at home had offshoring not been feasible. As it is practically impossible to make such a distinction, reference is made to all new activities and intermediate input purchases abroad by national firms.

opened the way to three reactions, all of which took place as he expected (the first two being already under way in his time). The first was the substitution of many low-skill activities by machines (and the introduction of domestic mechanical equipment to allow women to enter the labour market). The second was the granting by advanced countries of immigration permits to emigrants from underdeveloped countries, so as to meet labour shortages. But as this was bound to create opposition for social and cultural reasons, a third phase was to be expected: large-scale investment in low-wage countries by advanced countries in manufacturing activities for export. Of course Lewis anticipated the possibility that this development, by itself, while helping to moderate the problems of population explosion and unemployment in the Third World, would simply add low-wage exports of industrial products to low-wage exports of primary products, without allowing these countries to break out of the basic problem of unfavourable terms of trade. As already indicated, to solve this problem he envisaged only one course of action: to increase productivity in food production, so that higher wages would have to be offered in other sectors, including the export sector, to attract workers from the countryside. Lewis had witnessed the initial stages of the transfer of manufacturing production to developing countries. The phenomenon had been favoured by the establishment by a number of these countries of 'industrial export processing zones', small territorial enclaves where foreign investors could locate industrial activities for export without being subject to many of the national regulations on economic activity (especially in the fields of taxation, profit repatriation and worker conditions) and where efforts were made to provide firms with modern infrastructure not generally available in the rest of the country.[2]

The transfer of manufacturing activities to less developed areas had been the object of economists' analyses since the beginning of the 1970s – for an early one see Ádám (1971) – and by the middle of that decade Sharpston (1975), referring to 'international subcontracting', produced a detailed analysis, on the basis of empirical evidence already accumulated, of the scope of offshoring, the explanations for it and its main effects. He defined subcontracting, which could cover products, components or processes, as 'all export sales of articles which are ordered in advance and where the giver of the order arranges the marketing' (p. 93); subcontracting gave developing countries the possibility of producing manufactures for export despite their lack of an organization capable of covering the marketing aspects of export production (outlets, brands, advertising, market research and design), which often entail high initial investment costs and present large-scale economies. Sharpston also stressed another beneficial aspect of subcontracting for developing countries, namely access to foreign markets, which at that time was a serious problem for emerging economies: developing a point already made by Helleiner (1972), he remarked that while in the case of direct exports of final products by developing countries both firms and trade

[2] An early analysis of export processing zones (an institutional arrangement still widely adopted in developing countries) was provided by Fröbel, Heinrichs and Kreye (1977); for an assessment of these zones' past experience up to the 2000s see Milberg (2007) and Milberg and Winkler (2013). For interesting observations on their role in the Chinese post-1978 reform strategy see Coase and Wang (2013).

unions in advanced countries would lobby for measures against imports (as happened with textiles), in the case of international subcontracting by advanced countries' producers only the unions would do so, as subcontracting firms would greatly benefit from that trade (in fact, in the following decades the global tendency has been for tariff barriers to be lowered much more markedly for components and intermediate products than for final ones).

Since the times of Lewis, in the majority of developing countries, despite technological advances in agriculture, the 'unlimited supplies' of labour produced by the population explosion in the second part of the past century have allowed only limited increases in farmers' productivity and incomes and, consequently, in wages in non-agricultural sectors. In advanced countries, on the contrary, while problems of unemployment surfaced again, wage levels managed to keep the relatively high levels reached in the post-war decades. This led to serious problems of international competition for this group of countries, as in the period a gradual abolition of tariffs and other obstacles to trade started to be extended from exchanges between advanced countries to trade between them and developing countries; at the same time, capital movements were also largely liberalized, while the end of the Cold War in 1989–1991 meant that exports – and other forms of transfer – of advanced technologies to practically any country in the world found much lower obstacles in political and military considerations. But in this period, two other epochal developments took place that would transform the initial transfer of some manufacturing and services to developing countries into a huge geographical redistribution of the whole apparatus of world industry (and, partly, services): the first was the meltdown of the Soviet communist bloc and the gradual opening of communist China to the market economy, while India abandoned its policy of substantial isolation from the world market; the second was the ICT revolution.

The first development had the effect of extending the capitalist market economy to practically the whole planet. It resulted, as stressed (above all) by Freeman (2005, 2008a, 2008b), in the doubling of the working population in the capitalist world; the addition concerned predominantly workers at very low wage levels and (with the exception of the USSR and Eastern Europe) low-skilled, but satisfying the minimum conditions for being employed in modern productive activities thanks to the coming to fruition of the huge effort of basic education carried out in previous decades. The addition to the world stock of capital and technology was, on the contrary, relatively modest: a lot of capital goods in former communist countries were simply scrapped as they did not reach the minimum standards required in the new capitalist market environment; while no technological contribution to production for the market could be provided by the very poor countries and – apart from sectors connected to the military – by the countries of the former Soviet area. As a result, a shock was registered in the world market in the relative availability of the factor labour (especially unskilled labour) vis-à-vis the factors capital and technology (according to Freeman, the world capital–labour ratio fell to around 60 per cent of what it would have been if China, India and the ex-Soviet bloc had remained isolated); which translated, thanks to the second development, into a shock to its relative price, weakening in particular the bargaining position of workers in advanced countries.

A revolution in the relative world availability of factors had also been at the basis of the first globalization that had taken place between 1870 and 1914. At that time, it was a change that occurred in the relationship between land and the other factors of production, as the diffusion of railways and improvements in transoceanic shipping allowed the agricultural (and mineral) products of the whole American continent and other far-away areas to become available for sale to Europe and the rest of the world, causing a sharp reduction in their relative price and serious problems for European agricultural producers.

The ICT revolution, which was accompanied by progress in merchandise transport owing to the container revolution and the decline in air transport costs (see Hummels (2007)), made it possible to transfer and exchange information, technological knowledge, capital, goods and services even over long distances at low (sometimes near zero) cost and, for information and financial capital, in real time; thus providing opportunities to organize, coordinate and control at any location economic activities taking place anywhere in the world.[3] This allowed inclusion in the world labour market of huge labour supplies that had previously been inaccessible because they had required geographical proximity; now these labour supplies could join up with capital and knowledge and technology transferred from advanced countries.

While all previous industrialization processes had required long periods of time for the gradual development of capital accumulation and especially for the creation, absorption and diffusion of knowledge and technology, now these factors could be easily and rapidly obtained from abroad, allowing developing countries to acquire in a few years the ability to produce manufactures competitively – or at least cover some stages of manufacturing production – that would otherwise have required decades to develop domestically. This new economic environment drastically accelerat-

[3] Baldwin (2006, 2016) speaks of a revolutionary 'second unbundling' produced by contemporary globalization, which has opened the way to 'the great convergence' in economic conditions between advanced and developing countries. While the first globalization based on steam (by which he refers to the entire period from the 1820s to 1914), revolutionized transport, making it possible to separate the location of production from that of consumption, the second globalization based on ICT has revolutionized the transmission of knowledge and information around the world, allowing the international separation of factories producing inputs or parts of a given product, as it made it possible to provide any country with technological know-how and to coordinate economic activities at a distance.

One consequence of the ICT revolution was to make globalization much more disruptive in terms of both speed and scope (as it also transformed many non-tradable goods and, especially, services into tradable ones) than the first 1870–1914 globalization. S. S. Roach (2009) underlined that the new high speed of economic changes, connected to much more rapidly progressing technology, creates problems in the application of traditional trade theory predicated on a much more sluggish pace of technological evolution. Many reactions and adaptations envisioned by trade theory – typically the redeployment of labour from one activity and location to another – require a much longer time than that allowed by contemporary continuous economic change.

ed the tendency already at work from the 1970s for industrial production to increase in developing countries as a consequence of the transfer of some manufacturing activities from advanced countries.[4]

Some firms from advanced countries, producing labour-intensive traditional manufactures such as apparel and shoes, offshored the whole production cycle to new low-wage locations in developing countries (thus reinforcing these countries' autonomously developed ability to produce industrial goods); but the general tendency was for big firms of advanced countries – and with time also for medium-sized ones – to locate in low-wage countries (by establishing subsidiaries, subcontracting to local firms or forming joint ventures with the latter) those phases of the manufacturing process where labour was the main input and tasks were simple and standardized so that they could be easily performed by unskilled labour. In some developing countries that had managed to upgrade their workforce skills and in Eastern Europe, where educated and more skilled workers had been formed in the communist period, the activities offshored included more complex tasks requiring more qualified workers.

The offshoring of production phases, or specific components, of a good to developing countries opened up new possibilities for their exports, industrialization and development. As Baldwin (2016) explained (developing a point highlighted by Arndt and Kierzkowski (2001) in their Introduction with reference to the firm, but originally advanced for the individual by Babbage in 1832 as indicated in Footnote 2 in Section 8.1), when all phases of the production cycle take place domestically, a country's competitiveness in a final product is a sort of average of its competitiveness in each phase. It is usually difficult for a developing country to present, or to create, a comparative advantage in the export of a manufactured good, as this frequently involves some specific production or distribution phases for which there is limited availability of the necessary factors of production and which may require huge investment outlays (examples are R&D, complex technology, particular labour skills, marketing and post-sale assistance networks). On the contrary, the country may present, or more easily create, a comparative advantage in those specific phases of a good's production cycle that require factors of production abundantly available domestically.

Furthermore, the know-how required for a single production phase can be ac-

[4] As Ozawa (2019) observes, 'Emerging markets exhibit "endowed" comparative advantages in their relatively abundant-factor intensive goods, i.e., labor-intensive manufactures and/or natural resources. Neoclassical trade theory assumes that emerging countries can capitalize on them both immediately and autonomously once they open up for trade. The reality is, however, that they are usually incapable of doing so because critical joint inputs are unavailable, and institutional support is inadequate – in such inputs as technology, access to export markets, trade finance, marketing skills, and trained labor. In the past, these necessary inputs were locally sought through aspiring economies' own efforts under … infant-industry protection. However history shows that such efforts often failed. In an age of globalization, however, expeditious help comes from MNEs [multinational enterprises], especially those from the advanced world, which can immediately provide all the joint inputs and supports. MNEs do not just *supplement* comparative advantages fully, but also, more importantly, *amplify* their strengths through superior capabilities' (p. 198).

quired and absorbed much more easily by a developing country than the know-how required for the entire production cycle. At the same time, firms from advanced countries are more ready to transfer the technologies necessary for specific phases of production as they do not risk creating a competitor for their final product.

Finally, there is an important scale economies advantage: each phase of production (or each specific component) of a good normally presents a minimum scale of production to cover its costs and is subject, up to a maximum point, to increasing returns. The production of the final good is thus conditioned by the minimum scale and by the importance and dynamics of scale economies in each phase or component. If the production cycle is fragmented into phases or components, a country that cannot reach the scale necessary for competitive production of the final good can limit itself to those phases of production or to the manufacturing of those components for which it can reach (sometimes by supplying a plurality of makers of the final good or producers of different final goods that all incorporate a given multi-use component) the minimum necessary – and possibly also the optimal – scale of production. All the difficulties listed here, that in the past developing countries trying to industrialize through export-led policies would have had to overcome, also go far to explain why most of them followed instead - with limited success - industrialization policies based on import-substitution.

The fragmentation of the process of production and distribution into phases thus liberates the developing country's comparative advantage in a specific phase of a good's production from its comparative disadvantage in other phases, allowing the country to enter rapidly into manufacturing production and exporting. In this way, the products a developing country can profitably produce and export are no longer limited to the simplest final ones, such as apparel or toys, but can extend – without covering the whole production cycle – to a very large number of more complex products. Fragmentation can also benefit advanced countries: in the case of overall loss of competitiveness by domestic firms in given sectors, it makes it possible to avoid the complete dismissal of activity, as firms can concentrate resources on the more sophisticated and rewarding ones where they continue to enjoy a comparative advantage, leaving most or all physical production activity to developing countries (other advantages of fragmentation for developed countries are discussed in Section 11.1.4).

The phenomenon of offshoring also had important theoretical consequences. In one sense it represented the inversion of Adam Smith's original concept of specialization, which reflected what had happened at the beginning of the Industrial Revolution. As transport and communication were very slow and expensive at the time, the reaping of the benefits of the division of labour required concentration of workers in a single place, the factory, where they could specialize in different tasks. Only in this way was it possible to ensure efficient coordination of different operations and the swift passage of intermediate goods through subsequent production phases. In recent times, with improvements in transport and the ICT revolution, the benefits of the division of labour have been obtained through an opposite process: as tasks can be separated in time and space, they are allocated to the specific places or countries best suited, in terms of comparative – but especially of absolute – advantages, to perform them; the coordination function being provided by a centre that can increasingly be located even at a great distance from the production facilities.

Offshoring led to a change in the very object of analysis of international trade theory, as it moved the whole logic of the RHO model – and of the models produced after it – to a different level: trade and its explanations, rather than to the production of specific goods, now applied to specific tasks performed and specific intermediate goods produced. This opened new fields of theoretical work: the analysis of fragmentation, trade in tasks and GVCs.

Of course, the entire issue of developing-country competition in manufacturing and services based on extremely low wages rests on the premise that this huge gap between the wages of advanced and developing countries reflects an effective gap between the unit labour costs of production (that is, labour costs divided by labour productivity) in the two areas; in other words, that lower wages in developing countries are not simply compensating for lower labour productivity. For a long time in the past, the opinion that the huge international differences in wages in manufacturing and tradable services simply reflected huge differences in worker productivity in these activities was widespread among economists. In more recent times – as the educational level of developing countries' workers has greatly improved and other complementary factors that in the past kept these countries' worker productivity very low (capital, technology, specialized skills, physical and institutional infrastructure) have increasingly become available, domestically or from abroad – most economists have come to realize that, in line with Keynes's fundamental statement, in manufacturing and tradable services the inferiority of developing countries in labour productivity has largely reduced, if not been eliminated, so that the large gap in worker wages between developed and developing countries (excluding the most backward ones) produces a large gap in unit labour costs.

This gap is created – as pointed out by Lewis – by countries tending to have a relatively unified national wage level, which reflects the average worker productivity in the entire economy. But since worker productivity in developing countries is particularly low in agriculture – which in many of them represents the largest share of total employment and provides a huge reservoir of unemployed or underemployed workers – many of these countries register, in manufacturing and services, very low wages despite having reached a worker productivity not much lower (sometimes even higher) than that of advanced countries.[5]

[5] More than forty years ago, Sharpston (1976) argued that 'At its lowest, labour productivity in developing countries for international subcontracting operations seems to be about 60% of developed country levels … in certain cases … as much as 30% higher … The key reason why productivity may be higher in a developing country is that jobs suitable for international subcontracting are often low-grade, low-paid jobs in developed countries; but relatively well-paid and highly desirable ones, in a developing country. As a result, an employer in a developing country can pick and choose his work force … Labour productivity differentials in favour of the developed country – where they exist – have little effect in eliminating the vast differential in wages' (p. 334).

Fifteen years later, it was Mead (1990) who stressed the same point, referring to new evidence available and particularly to the results of research by former US Secretary of Labour Ray Marshall, accord-

11.1.2 The debate on offshoring

Between 1980 and the mid-1990s, as offshoring became more widespread and visible, while the real wages of low-skilled Western workers decreased or stagnated – leading to growing inequality in workers' incomes and reductions in the share of labour in GDP – a debate developed in advanced countries, especially in the USA where the phenomenon appeared to take place particularly fast. It regarded the possibility that competition from manufacturing exports of low-wage developing countries could depress the level of wages of less-skilled workers (and in perspective also of skilled ones) in industrial countries. It started to be envisaged that what traditional trade theory had advanced as a positive, equitable, long-term effect of trade (although conditional upon extremely restrictive assumptions), namely the equalization of relative and absolute prices of factors in trading countries, might turn, in the new environment created by globalization, from a merely extreme theoretical hypothesis into a real nightmare scenario: since the working population of advanced countries amounts to only a small fraction of that of developing countries, by the principle of communicating vessels the equalization of the price of labour envisaged by the theory would take place at a level much nearer to the wages of poor countries than to that of rich ones. Nayyar (2007) observed in this respect that 'It is ironical that the same factor-price equalization theorem, which was placed on a pedestal because it implied that free trade is equitable, is now pulled down to demonstrate that free trade cannot do anything as wicked as equalize wages across countries' (p. 79).[6]

Let us try to explain briefly the concept of factor price equalization. In the RHO model with two countries, two goods and two factors, at the opening of trade each country will export the good that incorporates, compared with the other good, a larger content of the factor more abundantly available and therefore cheaper, relative to the other factor, at home than in the other country. Since in each country trade increases the demand for the factor more intensively contained in exports, with the development of trade this factor will gradually command a progressively higher price (the opposite occurring for the factor more intensively contained in the good imported), until the relative price of the two factors, and therefore of the two goods, will be the same in the two countries. At this point, no country will have a comparative advantage in one of the goods and trade will stop. As long as the two countries do not specialize completely (in that case only one good would be produced by each of them), with free trade the price of the traded goods will be the same in the two countries; but if the prices of the goods are equalized, the absolute remuneration of the

ing to which in the developing countries of the Southern hemisphere in 1980 wages were 25 per cent of those in the advanced North, but levels of productivity 65 per cent.

[6] The question of the possible depressive effect on the employment levels and the wages of Western low-skilled workers of the competition from manufacturing exports of low-wage countries had been the object of debate since the early 1970s; but it started to become a central issue of trade theory and international economic policy a decade later.

On the difficulties of determining the effects of trade on wages see Deardorff and Hakura (1994).

factors employed for their production will also be equalized (a similar result would be reached if the factor relatively more abundant in one country, say labour, were gradually to migrate to the other country). Factor price equalization is based on very strict assumptions, in particular no complete specialization (which requires that factor availabilities in the two countries are not too dissimilar), the same technology in the two countries and perfect mobility of factors within each country from the production of one good to the production of the other.

An article by Freeman (1995) under the threatening title *Are Your Wages Set in Beijing?* faced the issue squarely, with a critical summary of the results of the debate that had taken place on the subject among economists in previous years. On the one side were those who believed in the tendency to factor price equalization and feared that in a global economy the wages and/or employment of low-skilled workers in advanced countries would be driven down by the competition from low-wage workers in developing countries. On the other were those who considered the equalization of factor prices as a mere theoretical possibility, of minor practical relevance: since internationally traded goods and services imported from low wage countries represented a very small percentage of the total amount of goods and services produced in the majority of advanced countries, their prices could not determine the level of wages in the entire domestic economy.

Freeman's article was, and still is, very useful in pointing out the extreme complexity of the issue, which, apart from theoretical problems, can lead to very different conclusions since it involves a large number of variables whose values depend on factual circumstances. Unfortunately, while conclusions can only be drawn on the basis of clear and reliable empirical evidence, there are both controversies on the proper methodologies to be used in empirical tests and a shortage of precise, detailed and reliable data on which tests can be based.

As for the theoretical problems involved in the issue, two are particularly important. One is the question of whether, to argue for a negative influence of developing countries' low-wage exports on the wages of unskilled workers in advanced countries, one needs to show that imports of traditional goods from developing countries by advanced ones have reached significant shares of domestic consumption; or, as underlined by Freeman and other economists, the mere threat of importing such goods and especially of offshoring their production to developing countries is sufficient to force low-skilled workers in rich countries to accept wage reductions even in the absence of any trade (a powerful argument, but one that cannot be supported empirically as it concerns a psychological phenomenon for which no measure is available).

The other is the difficulty of establishing whether the decrease in the wages of unskilled workers in advanced countries has been mainly caused by imports (or by the threat of imports) from low-cost countries – as argued by Wood and Leamer – or by technological progress, which in modern times has been characterized by an overall unskilled-labour-saving bias – as argued by the majority of economists, including Bhagwati, Lawrence and Krugman (for references on the controversy see the bibliography in Krugman (1995)). The two causes are actually largely interconnected, reinforcing one another, as stressed by Wood (1994) himself when he observed that competition from low-labour-cost developing countries leads to a loss of jobs either directly through loss of markets, or indirectly through advanced countries' innovation effort in response to this competition, leading to the adoption of automation and other labour-saving technologies. After all, if call centres' jobs had not moved from America to India, in all probability they would not have remained in America but would have been substituted by a larger resort to automated electronic response systems by American firms. And if imports from developing countries cause a lowering of wages in advanced ones, this is because technological advances in transport and communication have made offshoring possible and developing countries' acquisition of technologies previously held exclusively by advanced countries has allowed them to develop competitive lines of production for export.[7]

While minimizing the direct negative effect on wages in advanced countries of trade competition from developing ones, Bhagwati and Dehejia (1994) underlined another effect of changes in trade under globalization that might have been a source of declining wages in advanced countries: the increased volatility of trade flows in response to even small sudden changes in different countries' and locations' competitive advantage (the kaleidoscopic comparative advantage already discussed in Section 8.2.1). On the one hand, volatility drastically reduces firms' interest in investing resources in training workers, upgrading their skills and providing them with benefits whose cost is only justified in a longer-term perspective, since sudden changes in relative competitiveness may compel firms to fire some of their workers or move production (or phases of it) to other countries, or even stop their activity altogether. On the other hand, by producing higher labour turnover, volatility also reduces workers' incentive to accumulate skills at the workplace, as these may not be transferable to different jobs; and since non-transferability of skills may be higher for less-skilled workers than for those who are more skilled, the former are also probably less inclined to use search-period spells between jobs to make the often expensive invest-

[7] Autor, Dorn and Hanson (2015) have advanced first answers to the problem of untangling the effects of trade and technological progress on US employment and its composition, coming to the conclusion that the US areas most exposed to trade shocks were not those most exposed to technological shocks. Referring to the 1990–2007 period and using data on the employment structure (broken into the three categories of production and clerical routine jobs – those most subject to computerization and thus to automation – , manual-task-intensive jobs and abstract-tasks jobs) of 722 local markets covering the entire continental USA, their analysis points to a large difference in the consequences of trade and technology, whose impact shows little overlap across either time or geographical areas. They found that: 1) while trade (measured by the penetration of competing imports from China) was associated with significant negative aggregate employment effects, automation of routine tasks was not; workers with less than college education were those most affected by trade, but only slightly by technological change; 2) while technology affected areas more specialized in routine occupations by producing losses of routine jobs (both in manufacturing and other sectors) that were largely offset by increasing local manual and abstract jobs, trade competition had a negative effect on all occupational groups in manufacturing; 3) in manufacturing the impact of trade increased from the 1980s to the 2000s, while the impact of technology, which had been particularly strong in the 1980s, declined; outside manufacturing, on the contrary, the impact of technology increased over the three decades.

ment of effort and money required for the acquisition of new skills. The two authors also stressed another consequence of increased volatility of trade flows: a growing demand for 'fair trade'; that is, for the international harmonization of labour, ecological and other standards so as to ensure a level playing field where countries and firms cannot arbitrarily change competitive conditions through a lowering of these standards (the issue will be discussed in Section 12.3.3).

Freeman's (1995) conclusions were very cautious: given the difficulty of empirically establishing the influence of trade with developing countries on the immiseration of US low-skilled workers, it could not be argued that such trade had been the main cause of the phenomenon. However, there was a possibility that Western wages might be 'set in Beijing' in the future; but this would not exert much influence on the wages of low-skilled workers as the latter, whatever had happened in the past, were increasingly finding employment in non-traded services in advanced countries, while manufacturing sectors based on unskilled work had already been largely abandoned or scaled down.

Overall, in the first phase of the offshoring debate an optimistic position tended to prevail among economists (see, in addition to Freeman and Bhagwati, Krugman (1995, 1996b)). It was based on the conviction that most of the negative developments affecting less-skilled workers were caused by technological progress rather than by trade; that competition from developing countries appeared to be limited to low-skill lines of production; and that displaced workers' adjustment would be relatively easy as workers losing their job in specific sectors would find work in expanding export sectors elsewhere. In short, although trade with these countries might damage the wage conditions of low-skilled workers in advanced countries, the latter would increasingly specialize in more profitable high-skill products or production phases, while taking advantage from the import of low-cost manufactures and components produced by unskilled workers in developing countries.

From the first half of the 2000s, the debate took a new turn, as both offshoring and the quantity and quality of developing countries' export activities increased, thanks also to the greatly enlarged supply of skilled labour as a result of the heavy investment in higher education undertaken by these countries in previous decades. Most importantly, while in the past super-exporting developing countries had been few and not particularly large (the 'Asian tigers': South Korea, Taiwan and Hong Kong), they now included more countries and, in particular, giants such as China, which in 2001 entered the WTO (China WTO membership had a relevant effect on its exports to the USA, not because it reduced the already very low US import tariffs, but because it gave the Chinese the very important guarantee that no tariffs could be raised in the future). China represented a basic new challenge for international economists: for the first time they were faced with the possibility of analysing in practice the impact of a large trade shock.

At the theoretical level, in the same years the contributions of Gomory and Baumol and of Samuelson (see Section 11.1.3) provided support for a less optimistic attitude, as they cast doubts on the prevailing opinion about the benefits of offshoring and free trade in a world characterized by large inter-country transfers of technology and production methods. They pointed out that conflicting interests could develop between trading countries and that negative terms-of-trade effects might cause welfare losses to advanced countries or drastically reduce their previous gains from trade with developing ones.

With the entry of China onto the world export scene, worries spread among economists, including eminent ones, as they realized that, fulfilling Wood's (1995) forecasts, low-wage countries' competition not only had become extremely important in quantitative terms, but also had started to extend from traditional industrial sectors to higher-skill goods and tradable services that cut across all sectors (and these services were increasing in number as advances in ICT tend to transform many non-tradable services into tradable ones).[8] As a result, a depressing influence would also be exerted on the remunerations of more qualified workers, since this development reflected the drastic reduction of the monopoly rents that advanced countries had enjoyed in the previous two centuries thanks to their exclusive access to knowledge, technology and highly qualified labour. More than that, China was not only acting to reduce the gap with rich countries by rapidly adopting their superior technology, but was itself actively advancing the frontier of technology as it saw the advantages of becoming a leader in high-tech sectors.[9]

An important development in the debate came from S. S. Roach (2003), chief economist of Morgan Stanley. He argued that 'global labour arbitrage' was irreversibly operating in the now open and unified world economy, characterized by excess supply of products and consequent increasing competition. Unable to raise prices, firms in developed countries were desperately looking for ways to reduce costs. As labour represented the main component of production costs (some 80 per cent), and wages in countries such as China and India ranged between 10 and 25 per cent of those of comparable domestic workers, 'offshore outsourcing that extracts product from relatively low-wage workers in the developing world has become an increasingly urgent survival tactic for companies in the developed economies' (p. 6). The basic

[8] Already some decades earlier H. G. Johnson (1973) had indicated the likely effects of the abolition of technological and political barriers to trade and investment: 'If … there were no barriers to the free movement of goods, one would expect production with a new technology to locate itself in regions with the lowest cost of factors of production; and if capital were free to move, these would be the regions with the lowest labor costs' (p. 45).

[9] Freeman (2008b) stressed the importance of developing countries' investment effort in higher education and research, advancing a 'critical mass' argument: developing countries, in particular China and India, 'have moved to the technological frontier because success in high-tech fields depends on the absolute number of scientists and engineers, rather than on the relative number of science and engineering workers that belong to the overall workforce … Put differently, there is an economy of scale in research, development, and innovation that enables large populous countries to reach the scientific and technological frontier. China and India can have a large footprint in high tech because they will have many highly educated scientists and engineers, not because they approach the advanced countries in science and engineering workers per capita … The low wages in these large populous countries, moreover, makes them formidable competitors for an advanced country because it gives them a potentially large cost advantage in attracting investment centered on research and development' (pp. 175–176).

contradiction of the global economy was that while low-cost developing countries had managed, largely thanks to the MNCs' offshoring activities, to enter the supply side of world trade, their demand response was lagging behind: what was necessary was action on their part to push up domestic demand, particularly private consumption, whose level was still extremely low, thereby putting an end to America's role of chronic net importer from the rest of the world. But while Roach advocated dollar devaluation to speed up the reduction of the growth of US imports and the increase in its exports, he anticipated that the global rebalancing would take quite a long time, as the lack of a basic social safety system (health, pensions and unemployment insurance) in a country such as China inevitably pushed the population to set aside a considerable part of its increased income as precautionary savings.

Another source of considerable concern was the forecast by Blinder (2006) that, as a result of advances in telecommunications and developing countries' entry into the global economy, offshoring of an increasing number of service sector jobs by advanced countries could be expected to add to the offshoring of manufacturing jobs. He advanced estimations of the number of total US jobs that might be offshorable, corresponding to some 30–40 per cent of the total 2004 US workforce; more detailed calculations led him to reduce that estimate to 22–29 per cent in Blinder (2009). He underlined that his figures did not refer to jobs that would actually be offshored, but just to those at risk of being transferred. Even more worryingly, he pointed out that 'offshorability' applied equally to skilled and non-skilled jobs, as work positions under threat could not be correlated with either workers' wages or educational levels.

Of course, one has to consider that while offshoring – just like technological progress – causes the loss of many jobs in advanced countries, at the same time it creates new jobs and new exports that can compensate, or even more than compensate, for the losses: lower product prices owing to higher productivity and cheap imports increase people's buying power, allowing them to buy more goods produced domestically, thus activating employment; and firms, thanks to the profits from offshoring, can invest more resources in new initiatives and new lines of production at home[10] (see also Pa-

[10] Dickens and Rose (2007), for example, argued that employment in the USA in recent decades actually tended to rise in line with the supply of workers; and that after the early 1980s US unemployment was on a decreasing trend despite a strong rise in the share of imports in GDP. They also pointed out that since the majority of jobs at risk in Blinder's estimates were service jobs, the impact of their possible loss would be less disruptive than the loss of manufacturing jobs had been in the previous period, since it would not cause the closure of whole plants or industries and would not be geographically concentrated, so that no overall devastation of specific areas or cities would be produced. In a 2007 conference at the WTO, Bhagwati (2009) also argued that network services are the sector where US comparative advantage is greatest, and that job losses in call centres offshored to India were more than offset by increased exports of more rewarding high-skill, high-value professional services.

Evidence on the impact of Chinese manufacturing imports on US employment has been produced by Acemoglu, Autor, Dorn, Hanson and Price (2016): they estimated that imports from China between 1999 and 2011 (the period of the big surge in Chinese exports) were directly responsible for about 10 per cent of the reduction (the latter amounted to 34 per cent) of manufacturing employment; but if indirect inter-industry effects are also considered, the impact on manufacturing almost doubles, and there were

nagariya (2007) for a critique of Blinder's thesis). However, Ford (2009), analysing the specific characteristics of new computers – in particular their incredible and increasing speed of operation – concluded that in all probability the largest part of existing jobs, both in less and in more skilled activities, are likely to be superseded in the not too distant future by computer programs; so it would be urgent for economists to devise possible solutions to the problem of widespread excess of manpower relative to available jobs. He expected that the only jobs likely to survive are those that require hand–eye coordination and reaction to the unforeseen, abilities that computer programs find very difficult to develop; and these jobs can be found in both highly skilled and less-skilled activities.[11] For a general attack on the forecasts of dramatic negative effects of technological progress on employment see Milanovic (2019).

The new, less optimistic, American attitude in the mid-2000s on offshoring and competition from developing countries' exports found expression in Freeman's contribution to a 2006 Conference, published in Freeman (2008b), where – after recalling the great importance he attributed to the 'great doubling' of the population of global workers – he advanced a much more worrying perspective than the one he had envisaged in 1995: 'I favour the argument that the increased supplies of skilled labor in low-wage countries will squeeze highly skilled as well as less-skilled U.S. workers' (p. 162). In the very long run, factor price equalization would probably take place without great losses for the USA as continued social and technological progress in China and India would allow equalization to be reached through their wages progressively reaching the US level thanks to improved productivity; however, this development could be expected, in the best of cases, to take some 30 years for China and 40–50 years for India. The big problem was what would happen to wages in advanced countries during the transition.[12] He saw the well-being of workers in the

also significant employment reductions outside manufacturing. Autor, Dorn and Hanson (2016), have analysed the impact of the same 'Chinese shock' at the local level (subdividing the USA into clusters of counties with the commuting structure for a local labour market) and have found that – contrary to the popular view of the US labour markets as highly fluid and flexible – declines in local employment caused by Chinese import penetration were significant and persisting, as they were not offset either by sectoral reallocation or by labour migration to other areas.

[11] One may add that even part of these last services are at risk, in the sense that although they require personal contact, they may be 'indirectly offshored' by having the customers in advanced countries move – thanks to cheaper and quicker transport facilities – to a developing country where they are delivered by local suppliers. Of course, this does not apply to restaurants or hairdressers, but certainly can involve plastic surgeons or dentists and even homes for the elderly.

[12] Blinder (2007) after recalling Keynes's remark in 1923 that 'Economists set themselves too easy, too useless a task if in tempestuous seasons they can only tell us that when the storm is long past the ocean is flat again' – while accepting the argument that the loss of jobs in all US services that do not require physical proximity may be offset by an increase in new service jobs, pointed out the very serious transition problems for unemployment, wages and aggregate demand that this adjustment would imply. This was because the new position in which service jobs would return to or surpass the previous level would only be reached through a long and disruptive process of huge job losses and huge job gains: 'we do foresee a massive transition as millions of workers are rudely reallocated by the market mechanism. Unfortunately, the vast majority of trade theory pertains to the analysis of full-employment equilibrium

latter countries as basically depending on the overall result of the influence of positive factors – the likely higher growth of productivity in advanced countries owing to more highly educated workers and the lower prices of goods produced by low-wage countries – and of negative factors – labour market pressure from foreign low-wage workers, worsening terms of trade, loss of comparative advantage in high-tech sectors. Freeman concluded: 'While U.S. wages will not be set in Beijing, how workers fare in China, India, and other rapidly developing low-wage countries will become critical to the position of labor worldwide' (p. 162).[13]

Krugman, in his analysis (2008b) and in his newspaper articles (2007a, 2007b, 2007c) also presented a very different, much less optimistic, picture (relative to his position in the mid-1990s) of the trade relationships between developing and advanced countries. Abandoning the hectoring tone of the articles collected in Krugman (1996b) towards economists and politicians expressing worries about possible negative effects of low-wage countries' competition, he argued that a basic change had taken place since 1995. First, advanced countries' imports of manufactures from developing countries had become a significant phenomenon (by 2006, for the USA, trade in manufactures with these countries had exceeded the value of trade with advanced countries). Second, while previously it had been anticipated that competitors in developing countries (then the 'Asian tigers') would soon see a rise in wages, thus dispelling the fears of their exerting low-wage competition, now 'the rise in the average wage of U.S. trading partners relative to the U.S. level – has gone into reverse' (2008b, p. 108), as new important exporters, particularly China and Mexico, had come on the scene. Third, the exports of developing countries had come to include more sophisticated products; in particular, the largest increase in imports from them was registered in non-traditional and high-tech sectors (although he thought that this development was largely the result of a statistical distortion, as it probably simply reflected the growing participation of developing countries in the international production cycle of high-tech goods as producers of the simpler components and tasks). Contrary to his positions in the 1990s, he now admitted – looking at the US persistent trade deficit – that the traditional trade theory's assumption of trade balance equilibrium was not acceptable and that trade deficits can have an influence on the demand for and the price of factors.

In this situation, Krugman could argue:

---

states and has little or nothing to say about either unemployment or transitions. Too often, economists simply label certain things as "transitional costs" and then proceed to ignore them' (pp. 8–9). He pointed out that the issue of whether service offshoring is 'big deal or business as usual' is a crucial one, since in the first case a variety of policy responses may be called for.

[13] Two possible transition scenarios were described by Freeman (2008a): a good one, in which China and India rapidly close the gap in technological competence and wages with the advanced countries; and a bad one, where they 'develop enclave economies in which only their modern-sector workers benefit from economic growth while the rural poor remain low paid and a sufficient threat to the urban workers that wages grow slowly … To add to the nightmare, huge within-country inequalities in China, India, and other countries produce social disorder that creates chaos or gets suppressed by a global "superelite" … The bad scenario resembles some recalcitrant Marxist's vision of global capitalism' (p. 5).

> In fact, it's hard to avoid the conclusion that growing U.S. trade with third world countries reduces the real wages of many and perhaps most workers in this country … Trade between high-wage countries tends to be a modest win for all, or almost all, concerned … By contrast, trade between countries at very different levels of economic development tends to create large classes of losers as well as winners … It's often claimed that limits on trade benefit only a small number of Americans, while hurting the vast majority. That's still true of things like the import quota on sugar. But when it comes to manufactured goods, it's at least arguable that the reverse is true. The highly educated workers who clearly benefit from growing trade with third-world economies are a minority, greatly outnumbered by those who probably lose. (2007c)

A few years later, Van Reenen (2011), drawing on more up-to-date data, summarized the main trends in wage and skill distribution in the advanced countries in the post-1970s period. He found that between the late 1970s and the early 1990s the sharp increase in wage inequality was largely due to an increase in the demand for skilled workers that outstripped their supply and was connected with technological developments, which created a large divide between the wages of unskilled and skilled workers. From the early 1990s to 2008, inequality continued to increase, but at a slower rate and reflecting a different development, namely a 'polarization' process. The ICT revolution, which had previously affected unskilled manual routine jobs, in this period mainly reduced the jobs and wages of skilled routine workers (such as clerks and bank tellers) in the middle of the wage distribution; while it had no effect on the position of unskilled manual workers – now concentrated in service jobs (such as child care, restaurant meals, cleaning and nursing) that robots and computers are unable to master – and continued to increase the efficiency and wages of the most skilled and educated workers.

As for the debate on whether technology or trade were the main drivers of wage inequality, Van Reenen (2011) observed that up to the mid-1990s economists' prevalent position in favour of the role of technology was largely conditioned by their use of data preceding China's export offensive. And taking up Wood's (1994) speculation that increased trade competition from developing countries might spur in advanced ones technical change (the latter replacing routine tasks, while increasing the efficiency of high-skill tasks), argued in favour of the conclusion – suggested by the empirical work of Bloom, Draka and Van Reenen (2011) – that 'Chinese imports do seem to be having an important effect on demand for skill, but this is mainly through their impact on technological change rather than directly' (Van Reenen, 2011, p. 20).

After the 2008 global crisis, the great debate on offshoring largely subsided (for a survey of the effects of trade on inequality see Harrison, McLaren and McMillan (2011); Goldberg (2015) collected relevant essays on the issue - regarding both advanced and developing countries - published in the previous 20 years). The main reason seems to be that in the first years after the crisis, economists' attention concentrated on its effects. Probably the big wave of substitution of low-skilled labour with offshoring had largely come to an end. In any case, the debate that had taken place had led most economists to agree on the existence of a problem, previously denied or minimized, of negative effects of offshoring on important sections of the workforce. And after 2017, it was President Trump's boastful protectionist initiatives that monopolized the public debate on international trade.

11.1.3 Gomory and Baumol's and Samuelson's theoretical contributions

Two important works by Gomory and Baumol (2000) and by Samuelson (2004), while not directly referring to offshoring, contributed to the dramatization of the general issue of developing countries' export competition. Their arguments were all the more worrying as in both cases they were developed under the hypotheses of full employment and trade balance equilibrium: the fact that these hypotheses are hardly acceptable only adds to the problems for advanced countries that these authors pointed out.

Gomory and Baumol produced an interesting, innovative analysis of trade relationships between countries. They abandoned the traditional representation of international exchange in which all trading countries always reap specialization gains and an optimum equilibrium point is reached in which each trading partner produces the goods at which it is naturally best. They developed a model where a considerable number of goods exchanged are considered, produced under significant scale economies and high sunk costs (non-recoverable fixed costs) of entry. They also assumed complete specialization (the goods of each industry being produced by only one of the trading countries; they argued, however, that their main conclusions also applied to the case of industries shared between countries), resulting from initial production that occurs in one innovating country, frequently as a simple consequence of historical accident. This implies the possibility of an inefficient division of production activities between the trading partners, in the sense that a situation might occur in which an improvement in overall productivity could be obtained if the two countries simply exchanged one production activity for another. They demonstrated that in this more realistic setting, considerable 'zones of conflict' in international exchange exist in which one country only gains at the expense of the other by taking over the latter's lines of production, while overall welfare gains may either increase or decrease.

In particular, they showed that:

> an industrialized country will benefit if a *very underdeveloped* trading partner acquires new industries and generally improves its productivity ... until that partner reaches a level of development that enables it to play a more substantial role in the global market place. Usually this level of development is still very substantially lower than that of the industrialized country ... After this point acquisition of more industries by the newly developing partner *becomes harmful* to the more industrialized country. (2000, p. 4)

The underlying reason for these results, so different from those derived from the traditional RHO model of international trade, is that, as a consequence of the large-scale of operations required, the difficulties of entry, and the possibility of changes in countries' ability to produce, the situation is no longer that represented by the Ricardian wine and cloth example:

> Today there is not one uniquely determined best economic outcome based on natural national advantages. Today's global economy does not single out a single best economic outcome, arrived at by international competition, in which each country serves the world's best interests by producing just those goods that it can naturally turn out most efficiently. Rather, there are *many possible outcomes* that depend on what countries actually choose to do, what capabilities, natural or human-made, they actually develop. These outcomes vary in their consequences for the economic well-being of the countries involved. (p. 5)

Once one of the possible outcomes materializes, 'Any such position once arrived at, whether deliberately or by the purest accident of historical events, does not break down overnight. Market forces will preserve it because of the difficulty of entry for new competitors in such an industry' (p. 7).

However, patterns of industrial dominance in modern industries are not unchangeable:

> in the modern world it is possible for many countries to learn the skills involved in making a product, and then to practice those skills until they approach the capability of the world's productivity leaders. The skills and know-how of large, multinational corporations enable them to set up shop … almost anywhere in the world … If the new workers learn to perform these skills as productively as the world leaders, and if their wages are lower than those in other countries, then the unit cost … will be lower … than elsewhere … The same outcome can occur by means other than the stimulus of multinational corporations. Any means of learning will do. (pp. 9–10)

As Hughes synthetized in the Introduction to Hughes and Sha (2009):

> Gomory and Baumol stressed the ability of countries to invest in ways that would shape and change their comparative advantage. In contrast to the 19th century world where factors of production – often land and labor – were relatively fixed and did not flow easily between countries, 21st century national policies could guide the development of new comparative strengths based on investment, research and development, and education. (p. 2)

One consequence of this possibility for countries to create and modify their comparative advantages in an environment of increasing returns and rapid and substantial technological progress is for Gomory and Baumol a much increased fragility of international specialization equilibria (again Bhagwati's concept of 'kaleidoscopic comparative advantage'): 'While superiority based on natural advantage provides stability in the industries where such advantages exist, industries whose method of operation can be learned and that do not require huge entry costs are subject to rapid changes in their competitive positions as new countries acquire the know-how and become competitors' (2000, p. 42).

The two authors pointed out in particular that scale economies can create trade conflicts between countries as their national incomes converge. In a world composed of just two trading countries (of not too dissimilar a size in terms of labour forces), with each industry taking place in either one or the other country (complete specialization), each country gains by retaining or taking over from the other as many industries as possible, since in this way it can capture a larger share of total world income and higher wages for its workers; but this applies only up to a certain point, beyond which its national income decreases because of a loss of efficiency. This loss is caused by the fragmentation of the country's production factors among too large a number of industries, so that in each of them it is impossible to reach a volume of production allowing full exploitation of scale economies. So if country A starts from having almost all world industries, it will benefit if country B, producing very little of world income, increases the number of its industries, allowing A to reduce its excessive number of activities and to reap in each of them gains from scale economies. However, beyond a certain point the acquisition by B of additional industries will start to cause losses to A. As for total world income, it will be maximized when the number of industries (supposed of similar weight) is equally split between the two countries, allowing full exploitation of scale economies, and will decrease as one of the countries manages to increase the number of its industries, with the reduction becoming particularly significant when a very large share of industries comes to be concentrated in one of the countries.

But to make sure that the beneficial balanced division of industries takes place – and, at this point, that each country concentrates on those industries where it is relatively more efficient – would require specific intervention by the countries' governments, cooperatively establishing the industries to allot to each partner in order to ensure fair gains for both of them from the higher overall efficiency and income thus obtainable: it cannot be expected that the free market mechanism based on independent decisions by private firms will spontaneously lead to this result (another example of the conflict of goals between firms and countries discussed in Section 2.3).

* * *

A particularly shocking event – both for mainstream trade economists and for public opinion on the benefits of trade liberalization – was the publication by Samuelson (2004) of an academic article in which he highlighted the possibility that developments in free trade might in fact produce a loss of welfare for one of the trading countries.

The fact that trade, because of the particular inelasticities of export demand and supply, might lead to 'immiserizing growth' of a heavily export-based country – that is, to progressive reductions in its income as a consequence of unfavourable changes in the terms of trade when it increases the productivity and volume of production of an export good – had been pointed out by H. G. Johnson (1954, 1955) and especially by Bhagwati (1958); but for decades this possibility had been considered by international economists as no more than a theoretical curiosity. Now Samuelson, a legendary authority on international trade theory, applied these old theoretical insights to the analysis of the effect on today's advanced countries of developing countries' manufacturing catch-up: he presented a formal analysis showing that, even under favourable demand elasticities, free trade between an advanced country such as the USA and a rapidly innovating developing country such as China might in fact lead to changes in the comparative costs and terms of trade that would cause the USA to lose part or all of its previous gains from trade, so that, in the limiting case, it might as well revert to autarchy.

The reason for this result – in the two-country example developed by Samuelson in which, on the basis of comparative advantage, the technologically more advanced country, the USA, exports good 1 to China in exchange for good 2 – is that an invention or technological advance (or mere imitation) by China, allowing it to reach efficiency in the production of good 1 that previously it had been unable to produce competitively and had had to import from the USA, can eliminate the comparative advantage the USA had enjoyed until that time. So:

> after the invention … comparative advantages have been emasculated – for the reason that now, in every place, $\Pi 1/\Pi 2$ [the relative US productivity of labour in producing goods 1 and 2] and $\pi 1/\pi 2$ [the relative Chinese productivity of labour in producing goods 1 and 2] … [are] now equal … Each place can now do as well in its new autarky as it can do under free trade. (Indeed under free trade rules, no one is any longer motivated to specialize geographically; there is no need or advantage in doing either exporting or importing.) (2004, p. 141).

The argument seems to be a reassertion, after seventy years, of Keynes 'fundamental statement' (see Section 8.2.1) that led him and Robertson to forecast a decreasing importance of international trade in economic life.

Samuelson's overall conclusion was that he had demonstrated how in the game of 'the roulette wheel of evolving comparative advantage in a world of free trade' – again a concept recalling Bhagwati's 'kaleidoscopic comparative advantage' – 'sometimes free trade globalization can convert a technical change abroad into a benefit for both regions; but sometimes a productivity gain in one country can benefit that country alone, while permanently hurting the other country by reducing the gains from trade that are possible between the two countries' (p. 142). In the latter situation, however, he warned against recourse to protectionist measures, as 'free trade may turn out pragmatically to be still best for each region in comparison with lobbyist-induced tariffs and quotas which involve both perversion of democracy and nonsubtle deadweight distortion losses … In this millennium … "Tariffs are the breeder of economic arteriosclerosis"' (p. 143). He argued that Gomory and Baumol (2000) had reached his results, but basing their argument on scale economies; and concluded that the negative competitive pressures produced on US lower-middle-class wages by developing countries' cheap exports – analogous to the pressures that would have been produced by mass migration from these countries to the USA – were the effect of the loss of the American workers' monopoly of access to superior US capital and scientific, engineering and managerial know-how. To some extent, a similar process had already taken place after World War II in favour of Western Europe and Japan; but now, with giants such as China and India entering the industrial (and services) global economy in the new environment of the ICT revolution, the phenomenon was much more threatening.

Two different, interconnected arguments, not very clearly distinguished by Samuelson in his article, appear to contribute to his conclusions. The first is the materialization of the forecast by Keynes and Robertson that industrial capabilities would spread in modern times to a larger and larger number of countries, so that relative efficiency in the domestic production of different goods would become increasingly similar among countries; this reduction of comparative cost differences would progressively lower the gains from trade to the point of eliminating countries' interest in engaging in international exchange. For developing countries, the reduction in the gains from trade would be compensated by the advantages of higher productivity of their production and consequently of higher living standards, and by the lower vulnerability caused by overcoming the concentration of exports in a few raw materials to be exchanged against essential manufactured goods. But for advanced countries, the loss of trade gains would not find any compensation.

The second argument refers to the terms of trade; that is, to the division between trading countries of whatever amount of gains the exchange produces. As a result of Chinese progress in the production of good 1 – the good that previously only the USA could produce efficiently and export – its world supply is much increased and the USA, having lost its monopolistic position in the good's production and export, will no longer be able to sell it to China at a particularly favourable exchange ratio against good 2 (whose world demand and price would probably be much higher as a result of Chinese income and wage growth), so that a deterioration of America's terms of trade could be expected.

It is important to remember that Samuelson's arguments were developed under the hypothesis of trade balance equilibrium. If that hypothesis is dropped – as seems necessary in the case of the real persistent trade disequilibria of the USA and China, and as Samuelson (1972) himself had envisaged long before – one comes to another, much more worrying, conclusion. Even if, following Samuelson's argument, equality of comparative advantages in the two trading countries was reached, so that there would be no reason, in the RHO framework, for exchange between them, a massive Chinese export flow to the USA could develop, based not on comparative but on absolute advantage: since the price of almost all goods is, thanks to lower unit costs, much lower in China than in the USA, China would export both goods 1 and 2 to the USA.[14]

[14] Panagariya (2005) did take into consideration the possibility of a continuing overall US trade deficit caused by an excess of US imports over exports in trade with China, but played down the seriousness of such an eventuality by arguing that there are only two conceivable alternatives. The first is that the Chinese accept to export indefinitely to the USA more than they import from them, which according to Panagariya would be a very convenient situation for the USA, as it would allow their citizens to permanently raise their living standard by consuming the excess of Chinese goods imported over the goods exported to China. But it may be objected that this would put the USA in a dangerous situation, as the Chinese could always abruptly stop the accumulation of dollars consequent on their

While Gomory and Baumol's book was almost ignored by the majority of economists (see Brandly (2007) for an extremely negative review), Samuelson's contribution was the object of many critical comments, especially since it had been largely interpreted as a rebuttal of the widely publicized claims about the large benefits for the USA and other advanced countries that globalization, free movement of goods and factors, and offshoring would produce: see Bhagwati, Panagariya and Srinivasan (2004), Panagariya (2004, 2005), Dixit and Grossman (2005), Mankiw and Swagel (2006) and Bhagwati (2009). While all critics recognized the validity of Samuelson's theoretical analysis, and of his conclusion that it is possible for a country to be damaged by free trade, serious objections were advanced on empirical grounds, minimizing the effective importance of the points he raised and of the likelihood of some negative developments he anticipated for developed countries (Bitzer, Görg and Schröder (2012) confirmed empirically the possibility that an advanced country may be damaged by the outward diffusion of domestic knowledge, but could not judge whether an alternative no-trade situation would represent an improvement).

It was argued that countries' terms of trade are the result of changes in the overall demand for and supply of the individual products traded, and these changes are influenced by many different factors and can lead to very different results; the pessimistic outcome envisaged by Samuelson being only an extreme among many possible ones. In any case, the available empirical data did not point to any post-1990 deterioration in America's terms of trade; if anything, it was the excessively low prices of imported goods that created problems for the US economy.[15] It was observed that Samuelson's argumentation could not be applied to the much discussed offshoring of services to India, as this was not a case of a previous US export being superseded by Indian competition, but of a non-tradable domestic US service that the ICT revolution had transformed into a tradable one in which India presented a comparative advantage. And this new increasing tradability of services represented one of the points of strength of the USA, as it already enjoyed a large comparative advantage in the

trade surplus, with possible unforeseeable negative consequences for the dollar exchange rate; or could use the funds corresponding to their surpluses for continuous acquisition of strategic US firms and infrastructures to the point of placing the USA in a situation of dependence vis-à-vis China. Moreover, Panagariya's argument only considers the traditional RHO rationale for export activity (exports as the means to obtain imports), excluding any relevance of the Keynesian rationale (exports as a contribution to aggregate demand and national income). The second alternative is that one day the Chinese will use the assets they have accumulated as a consequence of their surpluses to finance a deficit in trade with the USA: in this case the current US trade deficits could be interpreted as the simple result of a specific inter-temporal choice of the trading partners. While there are few signs that the persistent US deficit is the result of a specific American choice (unless whatever trade balance is registered is by definition classified as such), it must be considered that, again, it would be up to the Chinese to decide the moment – not necessarily convenient for the USA – when their huge accumulated surplus would be spent.

[15] One may add that even if its terms of trade were to deteriorate, this may not by itself represent a negative development for the USA, since what determines an increase or decrease in a country's welfare is the movement of single-factorial terms of trade, which measure the physical amount of domestic factors of production incorporated in the exports exchanged for a given physical amount of imports (see Footnote 35 in Section 9.3.3).

supply of the most sophisticated and technologically advanced services and a large surplus in the balance of services trade. It was also argued that the ability of China and India to provide the necessary supplies of top-level skilled workers in high-tech sectors was subject to serious doubts. And it was pointed out that Samuelson's article, by concentrating on the simple hypothesis of a Chinese catch-up with an unchanging US technology, did not consider the particular ability of the USA to originate continuous flows of innovations that recreate superior productivity and wage levels and positions of technological monopoly (an ability that can derive considerable support from developing countries' supplies of cheap components and collateral services).

The most important objection, however, seems to be another: it could reasonably be forecast that the developing countries growing most rapidly will become more and more similar to today's advanced countries (in particular as regards wage levels) and that the OECD countries' post-war experience will repeat itself. As happened first with European countries, then with Japan and more recently with Korea, trade induced by differences in factor availabilities (which in Samuelson's argument, as in those of Keynes and Robertson, would lead to a progressive fading away of the gains from trade and thus to a lower interest in trade between China and the USA) would be substituted by horizontal trade. The latter is a much less disrupting kind of trade, as it does not lead to the elimination of entire industrial or service sectors. This objection seems to point to a not unlikely development. Baldwin (2016) argued that the tendency for trade with developing countries to shift from cost-competitiveness based on wage gaps to cost-competitiveness based on firm-level-excellence 'driven by extreme specialization that allows firms to become the low-cost supplier in particular varieties of intermediate goods … is already underway … I believe this will continue' (p. 294). However, the huge dimensions of China and India – with their reservoirs (very large in the case of India, now much reduced in the case of China) of cheap workers and still low levels of agricultural productivity, which may exert a restraining influence on the tendency of fast growth to increase workers' wages – added to the extraordinary speed with which transformations take place in today's world, suggest that their full development as leading protagonists on the world economic scene may not produce the same effects as the gradual addition of much lower-sized new industrial European and Asian economies in the post-war period.

11.1.4 Fragmentation and trade in tasks

From the first half of the 1990s, international economists increasingly devoted attention to one of the effects of the second globalization: the 'disintegration' or 'fragmentation' at the world level of the production process of many goods. The greater ease of trading and communicating produced by the ICT revolution and the growing liberalization of trade and capital movements allowed big MNCs, capable of organizing operations on a world scale, to split the production of goods into separate blocks, phases or components, each carried out where its production cost is lowest, to be completed or assembled in a final location.

The benefits of fragmentation are much higher than those produced by traditional sectoral specialization. Just think of a Belgian consumer buying an Italian car: in the past he could benefit from the price reduction, relative to a hypothetical Belgian car produced in autarchy, consequent on the Italian comparative advantage in car production. Now he can benefit not only from the Italian sectoral comparative advantage in cars, but also, since the Italian producer imports many car inputs or components (batteries, tyres, etc.) from the world least-cost suppliers, from the comparative advantage of each of the latter in the production of a specific input.

The phenomenon of fragmentation, which started to become widely visible at the end of the 1970s, had been anticipated by some far-sighted observers. Long ago, when the first globalization was just beginning to take shape, Chevalier (1851) had pointed out that a manufactured good could go through many successive processing phases, taking place in different countries, before reaching the final seller. More than a century later, Caves (1967) – pointing out that Nurkse in the mid-1930s had applied the analysis of separate stages of manufacturing in his study of international capital movements – observed that:

> The production functions assumed in international trade models are restrictive ... also because they telescope a series of production processes into one. Any number of stages of production become combined in a single production function ... But a real difficulty arises if these intermediate goods move in international trade with as much freedom as finished products. At the very least, dealing with this possibility requires describing the production structure of a particular country not in terms of the products created but in terms of the activities engaged in. (p. 147)

He went on to credit R. Robinson (1956b) with implying that comparative advantage analysis must run in terms of activities and not final products.
G. B. Richardson (1972, 1975) again highlighted the possibility that:

> the production of any one commodity is undertaken not by any one firm but by very many firms each of which specializes in a particular phase or stage of the process. It will for this purpose be convenient to regard firms as undertaking *activities* rather than making and selling products... (1975, p. 355)

At the same time, Helleiner (1972) pointed out, with surprising foresight, that:

> A new phenomenon of rapidly increasing importance is the "putting out" to developing countries of unskilled labour-intensive processes, "midway" in the production process, by international vertically-integrated corporations ... In some instances these processes consist of components manufactured from local materials; in others they involve further processing of imported inputs which are then re-exported. It may well be that in such "processes" rather than in "industries", as conventionally thought of, lies the immediate industrial exporting future of the Third World; but export enclaves could develop, within which multinational firms purchase cheap labour and outside of which little impact is registered ... The prospects for this type of development depend, in

> large part, upon the tax treatment by the developed countries of these manufactured imports. As long as import duties are levied only upon the foreign value added and are kept low they should be bright. The multinational firms engaged in these activities will, for the first time, act as strong interest groups in the markets of the rich for liberal tariff policies such as these. (pp. 75–76)

At a conference in 1976, Ohlin (1977) himself stressed that:

> The factor proportions should evidently refer to each stage of manufacturing (production) which can be kept separate from other stages that are to some extent handled by other firms or productive units. This is necessary if the analysis is to explain trade where different stages of production are situated in different countries. (p. 31)

It was especially a book by Fröbel, Heinrichs and Kreye (1977), whose English translation appeared in 1980, that threw light on and directed the attention of economists to 'the new international division of labour' under way. Based mainly on an extensive empirical analysis of case-studies relative to German industry, the work represented an early exposition of the modern fragmentation theory – to which Sanyal and Jones's (1982) model of trade in intermediate products would provide the theoretical underpinning – that would open the way to the development of the contemporary literature on GVCs.[16]

Basic advances in the analysis of fragmentation were produced by Jones (1980) and later by Jones and Kierzkowski (1990), Jones (2000), Jones and Kierzkowski (2001a, b); the main contributions to fragmentation and trade in tasks theory were summarily surveyed by Baldwin and Robert-Nicoud (2007).

The comparative advantages of a country in a given fragment of production of a good can derive from the superior relative availability of the factors most intensively used in that fragment, from superior productivity in the performance of that fragment, or from other advantages such as better geographical position or the presence of collateral facilities or infrastructure required for that specific fragment.

Of course, the possibility of fragmenting internationally a good's production into phases and the number of these phases depend on the specific characteristics of its production's technology and the incidence of transport and other trade costs of moving intermediate products across countries; but other particular elements can determine the number, location and structure of individual fragments This explains the very different degrees of fragmentation and the variety of sectoral and national fragmentation models that we observe in practice.

For instance, in their analysis of the world automotive industry, Sturgeon, Van

[16] In line with the position prevalent at the time among left wing economists, the book's authors drew the conclusion – which would be clamorously disproved by the Chinese development experience – that 'After decades and centuries of underdevelopment of the so-called developing countries the recent export-oriented industrialization of these countries offers but faint hope that the living standards and conditions of the mass of their populations will undergo any substantial improvements in the foreseeable future' (English translation, 1980, p.7).

Biesebroeck and Gereffi (2008) and Sturgeon and Van Biesebroeck (2011) underlined some distinctive characteristics of this sector. Pressure for local content by national political institutions and public opinion – largely connected to the central and symbolic role of automotive production – chiefly contributed to keep final vehicle assembly, and much of the production of parts and car design activity, close to end markets (which, given the development of new important final markets, has produced a greater international dispersion of assembly facilities). The world structure of the industry, where few very large producers are engaged in fierce competition, has prevented joint initiatives to establish world industry-level standards. In turn, a lack of common standards for parts and sub-systems has slowed down the development of powerful independent suppliers working for a plurality of car producers; and has heightened the need for close relationships between lead firms – and their foreign affiliates – and foreign independent suppliers to facilitate the exchange of uncodified information and tacit knowledge.

As a result, the automotive industry has maintained strong national and supranational regional productive structures. Within this general framework, however, new possibilities are opening for those developing countries that manage to achieve high quality standards, introduce advanced technology and acquire design capabilities. Some of them may develop a role – or enlarge their present one – as regional final assembly hubs; others, proximate to important advanced countries, can specialize as just-in-time suppliers of parts within regional trade blocks; only the ones with very large domestic markets, such as China and India, can attempt to enter the world market as important producers and lead firms in the industry.

As for variation in national fragmentation models, one may point to the distinctive pattern that characterizes German industry. Sinn (2006) tried to explain the peculiar situation of Germany: the largest goods exporter in the world at that time, enjoying a huge trade surplus, yet showing overall economic stagnation and considerable unemployment or underemployment of its labour force. He attributed this condition to the country's role of 'Bazaar economy'. Industrial workers' hourly wages were the highest in the world, owing to excessive trade union power and too generous incomes provided to the unemployed by unemployment payments and the welfare state, so that industrial firms were unable to stand international competition in the new globalized world, and even in domestic services demand could not expand because of increasing labour costs and prices.

The solution found by German industrialists in all sectors was that of massively transferring labour-intensive production activities to low-wage countries, especially the near Eastern European ones, and henceforth concentrating on the downstream production stages and the most sophisticated functions (design, engineering, marketing and distribution) where the productivity of German highly skilled workers and technicians could compensate for their high wages. In theory, the industrial workers released from offshored activities should have moved to higher-value jobs, producing a better international division of labour. In practice, Sinn underlined that the alternative to the jobs dismissed – as Keynes had observed for the British auto industry in 1930 – was not more valuable new ones, but unemployment (early retirement and welfare state payments) and the underground economy. Germany's exports were huge (both in quantity and value), but the VA in Germany represented a decreasing share of their price. As the quantity of the goods exported continued to grow, total exported VA also increased, remunerating capital and work skills of increasingly sophisticated technological level. Firms managed to maintain competitiveness, but workers, apart from highly skilled ones, did not.

* * *

Jones and Kierzkowski drew attention to two important issues. The first regards service links. Fragmentation, they stressed, is not costless: as the blocks of activity into which production can be fragmented generally do not take place close to each other, and may be separated not only by space but also by ownership, it is essential that efficient services be provided to ensure the connection, coordination and control of the different production blocks (services, as has been said, provide the glue that holds supply chains together). These service links comprise transport, telecommunications, insurance, quality control, accounting, management coordination and so on; many of them serve the economy as a whole and represent public goods; so they are frequently provided by the state, which makes it imperative to improve their efficiency by minimizing red tape and eradicating corruption of public employees. Most service links exhibit high initial fixed costs and large scale economies that are more important than in production activities (which contributes to the optimal degree of fragmentation being dependent on the size of the market); some links regard networks, whose specific problems have already been discussed. The cost of service links has been lowered by technological improvements, a reduction of regulations, a decrease of international trade barriers and of differences in standards. This has strongly reinforced the tendency to fragmentation, overcoming the opposite forces, mentioned in Chapter 4, that promote increasing agglomeration of economic activities.[17]

Fragmentation and service links considerably complicate the analysis of comparative advantages: not only do the latter now apply to a much larger number of products (all those produced by each fragment of the production cycle), but the comparative advantage of different production blocks and the competition among countries and locations do not simply depend on superior efficiency in production, but on superior efficiency in the provision of service links as well.[18]

---

[17] Kimura (2013) has analysed the fragmentation/agglomeration dialectic with reference to the development experience of East Asian countries that are now trying to make the difficult transition from middle-income to developed country. Most of these countries followed an industrialization strategy based on various forms of fragmentation by MNCs and participation in MNCs' international production chains. As they developed a significant core of industrial activities, they started to enjoy the increasing advantages of agglomeration, so that their industrial structure became more stable and they gained extra time to improve it, thus upgrading their position within GVCs.

[18] Golub, Jones and Kierzkowski (2007) conducted, with favourable results, a first test of the proposition that the institutional environment and the availability, quality and cost of service links are of basic importance – in addition to traditional competitive advantage measured by unit labour costs – in determining developing countries' success in attracting offshoring of manufacturing activities from

Jones and Kierzkowski stressed the fact that for international fragmentation of production to take place reliability in the timing of shipments is essential (but the time dimension is even more important in the other services that ensure the coordination of the production cycle). When the production cycle is fragmented, it is the weakest fragment that conditions the performance of the whole cycle. This leads us to underline more generally the central importance that the timing of economic activity has come to assume in our globalized economy (and not only at the international trade level: think of 'just in time' systems at the base of contemporary logistics). This importance has in fact been increasingly recognized in recent years, as for example by S. S. Roach (2009) and Friedman (2016). As globalization offers unprecedented opportunities for productivity gains from relocation and the reshuffling and restructuring of economic activities, but also entails high economic and human costs to carry out the necessary adjustments, the time required for the transition to new equilibria represents a key factor. As a consequence, policies (particularly in the fields of education, retraining and the labour market) serving to ensure the maximum adaptability to change of the economy and the workers have become extremely important.

Unfortunately, with the exception of Keynes and his Cambridge followers, time is an aspect that has been largely ignored by economic theory in general – as Reinert (2007) observed, 'Only in economic theory does it take the same amount of time to grow a tree as to cut it down'(p. 177) – but particularly by international trade theory because of the central position it attributed to the RHO model.[19] The latter is a

advanced countries. Interestingly, they also found that service links appear to be more important than education in explaining whether a developing country participates in global manufacturing activity.

Fort (2013) analysed the factors leading US firms to fragment production among different locations (both domestic and foreign). She found that plants' use of communication technology is the most important factor associated with both offshoring and, especially, outsourcing to other domestic firms. She reported that the share of US firms fragmenting production domestically is 13 times higher than the share that offshores, and stressed the importance, for the effectiveness of plants' communication technology, of suppliers' ability to receive and process electronic communications. Wage differences and distance to suppliers are significant, but much less important factors associated with fragmentation. The same author further analysed the relationship between technology and fragmentation in Fort (2017), where the particularly strong influence of the adoption of communication technology on the extent of domestic fragmentation was confirmed, so that more fragmentation at home could be envisaged as an alternative to fragmentation abroad.

[19] Melvin (1990) underlined economists' lack of attention to the time dimension. He noted, in particular, that while international economists had tried to take into consideration, on the supply side, changes in technologies in the course of time, they had paid no attention, on the demand side, to such changes in consumers' tastes and preferences.

Another important exception to international economists' limited interest in the role of time is Deardorff (2003), who examined the importance for trade of time and speed and the consequent need to take time into account when calculating the costs of trade. He argued that short reaction times in production and distribution have become a basic competitive factor in contemporary economies, where changes in economic variables and in economic decisions take place with increasing speed. Production in advance of actual demand is not only very expensive because of the cost of keeping inventories, but it is also extremely risky, as market conditions are subject to sudden, unforeseeable changes (particularly where

theoretical construct unfit to analyse dynamic processes: the time dimension, and consequently the very factors underlying economic change (such as learning processes, innovation, entrepreneurship, risk and uncertainty, credit, and endogenous capital accumulation), are completely absent in it; so that problems and dislocations caused by the transition from one equilibrium to another are ignored and economic choices and changes take place instantly and are freely reversible (of course, as mentioned at the end of Section 8.1, much effort has been deployed by some economists since the 1980s to modify the RHO model so as to extend it to dynamic contexts).

Leamer (2012) has taken up the issue of the lack of the time dimension in the HO theory. He has stressed that timing determines the extent of the validity of the HO theory: while at a point in time we may conceive of countries' specializations as the result of their factor availabilities, in the longer run these availabilities, apart from minerals and land, can be created and changed; and the effects of the HO principle (such as the tendency for trade to increase the domestic price of more abundantly available factors, to the point of leading to international equalization of their prices) crucially depend on the time it takes to shift factors from the production of one good to another; but both changes in factor availabilities and intersectoral movements of factors may be so slow that their effects may be swamped by technological changes taking place in the meantime.[20]

The second important issue analysed by Jones and Kierzkowski (2001b) concerns the horizontal aspects of vertical fragmentation. MNCs are aware of, and would like to profit from, the advantages that specific foreign locations enjoy in the production of a particular new block of a good's production cycle. But against these advantages

---

tastes and fashion influence demand). This puts a premium on firms' ability to wait for the appearance of demand for a product and then producing it instantly to order. Speed of production and distribution is strongly influenced by the available infrastructure (much of it inevitably public) and by government efficiency in bureaucratic procedures (Sharpston (1976) had already pointed out that bureaucratic barriers – in addition to bad transport infrastructure and language and cultural differences – artificially add intangible 'administrative distance' to merely geographical distance in hampering trade).

Strangely enough, political theory seems to have recognized the importance of time in our modern societies more rapidly than economic theory. Scheuerman (2001, 2004), noted that with the accelerating pace of technological progress and social change and the heightened tempo of everyday life, instantaneousness and simultaneity have become central features of our societies. He pointed out that in this environment the traditional time-consuming democratic mechanisms and procedures of the political process and the very equilibrium of constitutional powers can no longer be maintained. He also advanced a proposal for reform of the institutions of liberal democracy in the light of the contemporary acceleration of change, so as to preserve their basic normative and institutional core.

[20] The prevalent disregard for time in economic analysis has become more and more unacceptable as the time perspective has been increasingly recognized as a critical dimension of both basic economic concepts (just think of the notion of 'learning by doing') and of economic agents' decisions. Attention has especially been attracted in recent decades to the dangerous tendency, since the early 1980s, to 'short-termism' in the time horizon adopted in evaluating the profitability of activities, projects and innovations by asset-holders, investors and managers, particularly in financial markets. The disastrous effects of this tendency have come to full light with the 2008 global crisis, which seems to have led to some reconsideration on the part of managers of the policy of concentrating almost exclusively on short-term shareholder value. On the issue of short-termism see Haldane (2016).

must be weighed the costs – usually considerable and largely fixed – of setting up the additional production block and the service links (regarding communication, transport, accounting, coordination and control) necessary to integrate it into their GVC. If the new block produces specific materials, components or other intermediate products or tasks that can be employed in a plurality of end products and sectors (as happened with computer chips and batteries), the new block's market can expand considerably and the fixed costs can be spread over a much larger volume of production. The same applies to an even greater degree to the service links that need to be activated for a new fragment of the production process to be outsourced abroad: if they can also be employed – and service link technology is seldom sector-specific – to allow additional fragmentation of production blocks for other goods or sectors, their cost will be much reduced, and greater stimuli imparted to investment aimed at their technological improvement and innovation. Naturally, for new production blocks or service links to be employed in the production of different goods or sectors, important investments and R&D efforts may be required (and stimulated by the new profit prospects) in redesigning and standardizing them.

Jones and Kierzkowski also pointed out another positive effect of fragmentation on technological improvement, which regards the adoption of already existing best technologies. They noted that the application to production of the most up-to-date available technology capable of producing important cost benefits tends to be delayed by a general human attitude of reluctance to modify established work practices, and most strongly by the resistance of workers, researchers or others who are deriving rents from previously acquired knowledge. This resistance can be much more easily overcome if an additional shock takes place, creating conditions that make people feel change can no longer be postponed or unavoidably producing changes of personnel. Mergers and acquisitions are examples of such shocks, and this is an important reason why they may lead to improvements in firms' efficiency. Fragmentation represents another possible shock, and by adding its efficiency gains to those associated with the application of a more productive available technology, may make it possible to overcome the obstacles to the latter's adoption.

* * *

One basic issue raised by international fragmentation regards the decision by firms in advanced countries managing the whole cycle of production of a good (usually large MNCs) between resort to ownership ties (subsidiaries or other connected foreign entities) or to market transactions with local independent firms, for the supply of intermediate inputs. Theoretical analyses of these choices have been provided by Antràs and Helpman (2004), Helpman (2006), Antràs and Rossi-Hansberg (2009) and Antràs (2016). Here it is important to observe that in a first phase the fragmentation process took place mainly within the confines of the MNCs: in command of global production networks, they moved phases of their production or manufacturing of specific inputs to subsidiaries or connected firms located in the countries where these activities could be undertaken at the lowest cost. But soon the subcontracting of phases or specific components to local independent producers abroad through arm's-length transactions started to spread, becoming in more recent years the predominant typology of offshoring (at the same time intermediate forms of relationship between lead firms and suppliers have also multiplied). These transactions take place in the open international market, differentiating themselves from traditional market transactions only in that they usually involve expectations and relations of trust, connected with repeated exchanges and long-term relationships, and the sharing of some information by subcontracting firms that provide instructions and precise specifications to suppliers. They allow MNCs, on the one hand, to overcome some inevitable resistances of vertically integrated firms to continuous changes in products and production locations and to process innovations; on the other hand, MNCs are able to exploit their strong oligopolistic position as purchasers of intermediate products whose supply is subject to strong competition among many local manufacturers in different countries. This input sourcing in the open world market through subcontracting to independent local firms appears generally more advantageous to MNCs when it concerns activities that don't need to be retained within the firm's organization as a condition to benefit from rents and monopolistic/oligopolistic positions.[21]

Direct transactions in the market, relative to the establishment of subsidiaries, allow MNCs to concentrate on the core activities where their specific exclusive advantage lies. They make it possible for MNCs to eliminate the large expenditures related to capital investment in manufacturing and the locking up of capital and other resources in production phases where developing countries have a comparative advantage. They allow MNCs to transfer large part of the risks and responsibilities of

[21] The literature discussing MNCs' choice between organizing the production cycle within the corporation itself or through markets has traditionally centred on two main factors. The first is transaction costs: transactions within a large corporation may be more efficient than those taking place through the market because they require fewer formalities and take advantage of better communication channels; because the corporate head office has more and cheaper information about its own subsidiaries and affiliates than can be collected through the market when dealing with independent partners; because *ex post* control and adjustment are likely to be easier and more accurate when they take place within the same corporate structure; and especially because the contracts in which market relations are incorporated are unavoidably incomplete (that is, they cannot envisage all the possible circumstances and points of controversy that may arise in the course of the contractual relationship). Some of the transaction cost advantages that come from having the whole production cycle take place within an MNC have been drastically reduced by the revolution in ICT and transport. On the contract incompleteness issue in relation to firms' internalization/externalization choice see Antràs (2005) and Antràs and Rossi-Hansberg (2009).

The second factor is the exclusive property of 'strategic' immaterial assets (technologies, know-how, organizational innovations, brands, knowledge of and long-standing relations with suppliers, customers, public authorities, etc.) that MNCs have accumulated in the course of their activity and that represent the source of most of the gains they derive from the organization and management of the entire production cycle. Only some of these assets, such as patents, copyrights and brands, can be protected by legal instruments from possible acquisition and use by other entities; and even in these cases protection may not be 100 per cent effective. The probability that some of these assets will fall into the hands of, or in any way become available to, external entities or competitors is much higher if market relations with external suppliers are entertained than if all phases of production take place within the MNC. When an MNC deals at arm's length with suppliers it normally establishes relations of collaboration and channels of mutual information that inevitably result in some confidential knowledge leaking to the supplier.

production activity to external suppliers;[22] they can produce large cost reductions as local independent firms - and those to which the latter, in turn, subcontract part of the activities – have usually much wider scope than MNCs for avoiding respect of local regulations on wages and work conditions and environmental standards; and they provide maximum production flexibility. Changes in products, production processes and locations of production can be undertaken more rapidly, as they do not imply the losses (and the resistance by endangered individuals and communities) connected with dismissal or conversion of directly owned production facilities and with firing or retraining firms' own workers. The consequences of temporary reductions in the volume of production caused by cyclical changes in final demand can be shifted to outside producers, while sudden increases can be satisfied by activating additional external suppliers. Direct transactions in the market also have the advantage of avoiding any blame – which could be very damaging for an MNC's image – for accidents or unacceptably low wages and working conditions of people employed in production. At the same time, high-technology firms in advanced countries can more easily transfer to a local supplier in a developing country the specific bits of specialized knowledge necessary for the production of the specific part or stage of the final product they subcontract, since it is not likely that by doing so they favour the establishment of a competitor for their final product.

Transactions in the market also offer advantages to local firms in developing countries. They can maintain their relative independence, while avoiding the risks and problems of upstream activities (design and R&D), downstream activities (outlet networks, branding, advertising, market research, customers' assistance) and overall coordination activities, for which they usually lack the necessary, often large amounts of capital, specialized knowledge and skills, and organization. Another advantage is that through subcontracting they can obtain the same favourable treatment regarding access to developed countries' markets that would follow from hosting MNCs' subsidiaries, as also in this case MNCs will have an interest in lobbying for free imports into their developed country of the inputs they need. Finally, and most importantly, this arrangement may allow developing countries to familiarize themselves with modern manufacturing methods and to receive technical assistance, quality control services and sometimes even capital, thus developing a comparative advantage that can be exploited for the sale of their inputs to other MNCs or for improving skills and technology that they can then apply to other, more sophisticated lines of manufacturing production.[23]

---

[22] As pointed out by Lynn (2005), a strong critic of outsourcing and global production chains, 'Unfortunately, most of these suppliers, which are under near-constant pressure to cut their costs, have responded quite naturally by outsourcing much of their own work to other companies farther down the chain. And so on. The result, when outsourcing has spread widely and deeply enough through any industrial system, is that many responsibilities are not so much shifted from one company to another as from one company to no company' (p. 11).

[23] Sturgeon (2013), noticing the growing importance of intermediate forms of international sourcing arrangements that do not fall precisely into either the category of intra-group trade nor in that of arm's-

* * *

One extreme, but rapidly increasing form of fragmentation deserves mentioning: the 'factoryless firm'. This is a firm, located in an advanced country, that limits its activity to some key tasks related to, but not directly involving, physical manufacturing – which is outsourced to other domestic and, more and more frequently, foreign firms – and thus does not employ any industrial workers. It is a typology of firm that had somehow been envisaged half a century ago by Samuelson (1972), when he spoke of the USA as moving towards a mere 'headquarters economy'; and started to be considered a concrete possibility by manufacturing experts in the early 1990s. But it was only in the 2000s that its emergence was taken into consideration by economists: Curzon Price (2001), for example, drew attention to this new kind of firm that 'Increasingly, in developed countries ... manufactures nothing at all directly, but contracts out all but its innermost core competence. It is a pure service entity' (p. 91). Their typical work consists in the pre-production activities connected with the design and engineering of the goods they sell; in the coordination and control – directly or through providers of manufacturing services – of the production activities carried out by other firms; in the fixing of the prices and quantities of goods; in the performance of post-production activities such as marketing, branding and logistics. Apple is an example of this type of firm, which is quite common in the semiconductor industry. These firms pose difficult problems of classification: in US statistics they were included until 2017 in the wholesale sector, although they did not implement, as traditional wholesalers do, the intermediation of goods between producers and retailers or consumers, but a number of tasks that used to be undertaken by the manufacturing firms themselves. From 2017 they have been moved to the manufacturing sector.

Factoryless firms have only recently been subjected to specific analysis – see Bernard and Fort (2013, 2015, 2017) and Bayard, Byrne and Smith (2014) – especially because statistical classifications of economic activities did not allow (and still make it very hard) to identify them precisely and calculate their weight in terms of VA and employment and evaluate other important characteristics (types of workers, wages, productivity, import and export activity, etc.). Early research indicates that their involvement in production and international trade is significant and rapidly increasing (for semiconductors it was estimated that these firms cover about one-quarter of global sales). The fact that these firms perform tasks that in the past used to be undertaken by manufacturing firms themselves may help – together with the increasing externalization of services such as cleaning, canteens and surveillance that also used to be performed by manufacturing firms' employees – to explain to a significant extent the reduction of the share of manufacturing in total GDP and employment

---

length trade, identifies a trend towards increasing similarity in sourcing arrangements: 'In essence, external international sourcing arrangements imbue inter-enterprise trade with characteristics similar to intra-group trade: better control from the center, higher levels of bi-lateral information flow, tolerance of assets specificity, and a harmonization and immediate integration of business processes that increase the potential for foreign activities to substitute for activities performed at home' (p. 5).

registered in recent decades in advanced countries (on the increasing difficulty of establishing a distinction between the activities carried out by the manufacturing and service sectors see Fontagné and Harrison (2017)).

A debate has developed over the issue of whether some fundamental activities of the factoryless firm – design, R&D, improvement and innovation of products and processes – require, in order to be efficiently carried out and to progress, the existence of a large base of manufacturing allowing a constant interchange with people engaged in the physical production of goods in plants located nearby, as argued, for example, by Helper, Krueger and Wial (2012) and Bonvillian (2012) in their advocacy of the necessity of a strong manufacturing sector to ensure the general dynamism of the US economy; or whether recent advances in communication technology and transport make it possible to externalize manufacturing activities to any part of the world without significant losses of efficiency and innovative capacity in the activities that remain at home.

* * *

The analysis of fragmentation and offshoring has been carried one stage further by Grossman and Rossi-Hansberg (2006, 2008), who provided a formal framework for the analysis of task trade; that is, trade not in specific goods, but in specific tasks that are part of the production cycle of a good (or of a number of goods that may well belong to different sectors) and can now be performed in different locations and countries whenever transferability is technically possible and lower trading costs make the transfer profitable (on the characteristics of tasks that make them more or less suitable to be transferred to distant locations see Blinder (2006) and Levy and Murnane (2006)). The fragmentation approach tended to view the production process as a cycle made up of different specific phases, each of which could be located in a different place, and fragmentation was modelled as a discrete choice. The trade-in-tasks approach instead stresses the continuum of tasks, whose organization is subject to constant change.[24]

An important contribution by Grossman and Rossi-Hansberg is their analysis of the effects of offshoring on wages in advanced countries. Previously, the debate on offshoring had centred on the claim, inspired by the factor price equalization theo-

---

[24] Unfortunately, so far it has been very difficult to collect evidence on the precise extent of trade in tasks. There is not only the well-known general problem that trade occurring within MNCs is subject to special reporting requirements that offer considerable scope for the manipulation of transfer prices. The specific problem (which also hampers the collection of data on the international transactions of factoryless firms) is that trade in tasks increasingly refers to non-material activities implying no physical movement of goods across countries' boundaries; so that it is not registered on documents collected by customs houses, but has to be largely estimated indirectly through specific surveys. However, recent availability of new databases has allowed a start to be made on empirical work on specialization based not on the nature of the goods traded but on the sets of tasks carried out by workers producing different goods. A pioneering analysis of functional specialization in trade was provided by Timmer, Miroudot and de Vries (2019), who identified the contribution to VA exported and countries' comparative advantages of four basic functions: fabrication, R&D, marketing and management.

rem, that this practice leads to a reduction of the wages of less-skilled (and, in the future, also of more skilled) workers, and on the expectation of a deterioration in the terms of trade as a result of the loss of the science and technology monopoly. Grossman and Rossi-Hansberg argued that in fact offshoring could produce an increase in the wages of advanced countries' low-skilled workers.[25]

They pointed out that the effect on these wages of improvements in technology that allow greater diffusion of offshoring can be broken down into three basic components. The first is a labour supply effect, caused by more offshoring, which leads to the release of domestic labour employed in the tasks that are transferred abroad. The second is a terms of trade effect – conditional on the offshoring country being an important producer of a product – created by the fact that offshoring will probably alter, at initial world market prices, the relative incentives to vary the volume of production in both the unskilled and skilled labour-intensive sectors; thus leading to changes in the composition of output that will cause adjustments in the relative prices of the goods, and therefore in the relative remuneration of factors used to produce them. The third is a productivity effect, which has been largely overlooked in the offshoring debate. It results from the fact that when there is an improvement in the technology of offshoring, making it cheaper to perform the most low-skill tasks abroad, the low-skill labour force remaining at home will concentrate on the tasks where its productivity is highest; and the firms that use this labour most intensively will get the highest cost savings as they enjoy an increase in the productivity of the remaining workers. These gains, analogous to those produced by higher productivity owing to technological progress, induce them to expand their production relative to firms that use other kinds of labour more intensively, thus increasing, after the initial reduction, the demand for this type of labour, leading in the longer period to an increase in its wage. This productivity effect, according to the two authors, can easily prevail over the possibly negative first and second effects of task trade on wages. It must be underlined that the cost-reducing effect of the decrease in the cost of offshoring is not limited to the firms that can now resort to this practice, but also applies to firms that have already offshored some activities, as the latter can now be carried out at a lower cost.

Grossman and Rossi-Hansberg's model has been criticized: see Taylor (2006), Milberg and Winkler (2013) and Coe and Yeung (2015). It has been pointed out that in their model, as in most trade models, full employment is assumed; that they say nothing on the effects of offshoring on the countries that get the offshored jobs; that their model, based on two factors, skilled and unskilled labour, practically ignores – again as do the majority of recent trade models – capital, and consequently the problem of firms' profits and their utilization, which is of fundamental importance if one wants to assess the consequences of offshoring on innovation and economic growth.

---

[25] Jones and Kierzkowski (2001a), referring to unskilled labour, had also come to the conclusion that 'However reasonable it sounds to suggest that should a country lose the labor-intensive fragment of production to foreign competition, real wages will suffer, this need not be the outcome' (p.27).

What seems to have been forgotten in many economists' analyses of offshoring and GVCs is the lesson of Ricardo on the centrality of profit and accumulation in the capitalist economy; after all, his advocacy of free trade was based on the positive effect that it would produce by increasing profits, which would be reinvested in economic activities, leading to faster growth and development.

Analyses of fragmentation and trade in tasks represented an important advance for international trade theory, and formal models to analyse the issue have been developed by Jones and Kierzkowski, Deardorff, Grossman and Rossi-Hansberg, Baldwin and Robert-Nicoud; see Baldwin and Robert-Nicoud (2007) for references. Baldwin and Robert-Nicoud (2010) have also analysed how theoretical developments of trade in tasks can be integrated into standard trade in goods theory. However, less progress seems to have been made in deriving from these contributions unambiguous conclusions on the effects of these phenomena on production, trade, prices and different skill groups' wages.[26] This is hardly surprising: as also happened with the debates on offshoring discussed earlier, in the analysis of fragmentation and trade in tasks many possible starting hypotheses and many variables are involved, so that, according to the specific hypotheses and the specific values of the variables taken into consideration, models can produce very different results.

The present work does not cover the trade policy aspects of theoretical analyses of international trade. But one basic policy consequence of trade in tasks must be underlined: just as the search for optimal trade policy has led to different tariff treatments of final goods and intermediate goods, so trade policy should now move to take specific tasks as its target. Of course, the fact that a growing part of trade concerns non-physical activities and tasks creates serious difficulties for the authorities charged with enforcing the applicable rules and taxation.

11.2 Global value chains

11.2.1 Structure and problems of GVCs

As researchers realized that trade in intermediates and international fragmentation of production had become major features of economic activity, they started to investigate how this new system was organized and managed. They pointed out that the distribution among countries of the different phases, tasks or components into which the production of a good was fragmented and the organization, coordination and control of the entire process were, as a rule, the work of a big and powerful MNC located in

[26] Two empirical works adopting a theoretical framework based on Grossman and Rossi-Hansberg (2008) have been produced by Wright (2014) and Wolszczak and Parteka (2015). The first, using US data for 2001–2007, provided overall support for the trade-in-tasks model, in particular for the significant size of the productivity-enhancing effect. The second, based on a wide panel of European countries and manufacturing sectors for 1995–2009, suggested the possibility of a negative effect of offshoring on European manufacturing employment, concentrated on low-skilled workers.

a developed country. What usually happened was that such a 'lead firm' would move from producing a good at home, to offshoring some phases of its production (typically the most simple and unskilled labour-intensive) to low-cost developing countries; and then to organizing a complex production chain (that is, all the activities going from conception of a product to its delivery to the final consumer and disposal after use), in which the manufacturing process was increasingly located abroad, while the lead firm concentrated on upstream activities (such as product design and R&D), downstream activities (marketing and distribution) and the overall management of the chain. It was estimated that MNCs produced 33 per cent of world output in 2014, and were coordinating some 80 per cent of global trade: see Cadestin, De Backer, Desnoyers-James, Ye and Rigo (2018) for data on MNCs activity and their role in GVCs.

Offshored activities could either take place in plants abroad owned by the lead firm, giving rise to intra-firm activity within the MNC, or outsourced to independent or quasi-independent foreign producers through inter-firm exchanges in the market (the factors influencing this choice were analysed in the preceding section). The form of the chain could be that of a 'snake' (in which the processing of intermediates must take place in sequential stages until final assembly), or a 'spider' (in which components produced in different places are sent directly to a final location for assembly), or a mix of the two, or a more complex 'web' form. As for the nature of the lead firm, Gereffi (1994) drew attention to a second type of chain that had developed, which was organized and managed not by a producing firm, but by a large retail firm. The latter would take no part in direct production, but would basically order specific products from foreign suppliers, control their quality on behalf of final consumers and provide for all the marketing and retailing activities.

Gereffi, Humphrey and Sturgeon (2005) stressed the central importance of the way the chain is governed, and identified three main types of value chain governance (apart from the extreme cases of governance through mere market relations and through direct hierarchy). In 'modular value chains', the most market-like type, suppliers produce goods or services according to the purchaser's specifications, taking full responsibility for the technology used, which often consists in generic machinery that can be employed to satisfy the orders of a wide customer base. In 'relational value chains' – where tacit knowledge must be exchanged because it is impossible to codify specifications, transactions are complex and suppliers have high-level capabilities – the mutual dependence between supplier and customer is regulated through reputation, family and ethnic ties, lower spatial distance and mechanisms that impose high costs for contract violation. 'Captive value chains' are characterized by small suppliers' dependence on larger dominant customers; frequently the lead firm exercises a high level of monitoring and control over suppliers, who face significant costs if they decide to switch to new customers. Key variables in determining which type of governance is adopted are the complexity of the transactions, as more complex ones require greater interaction among participants in the chain; the codifiability of transactions, meaning the degree to which suppliers can receive and act upon information and specifications from firms ordering their products thanks to widely known and used codification schemes; and, of course, the degree of competence of suppliers.

International production chains have been given different denominations, such as global commodity chains, GVCs and global production networks. These names refer analytically to slightly different concepts, progressively elaborated as the phenomenon of production chains evolved through time – see Bair (2009). As stressed by Milberg and Winkler (2013), the GVC approach – associated with the pioneering notion of 'value chain' developed by Porter (1985) – emphasizes the ownership, governance and power structures within each link and across the links of the chain, the upgrading possibilities of supplier firms and the distribution of VA along the chain:

> The main focus of the GVC framework is the governance of the supply chain, including the nature of contracting with suppliers, the degree of sharing of technology, the extent of entry barriers along the supply chain, and the ability of firms to "upgrade" within the supply chain by moving into aspects of production generating higher value added per worker. (2013, p. 17)

For simplicity, the term GVC will be used in this chapter to refer to international production chains in a general sense.

The development of GVCs was particularly rapid in the 1990s and 2000s (up to the 2008 crisis). Although they have extended to include most countries in the world, they remain extremely concentrated in a few areas, the most important being the East Asian region (where they first developed at the initiative of Japanese investors) and the Eastern European countries.

Trade in intermediate goods and services, according to the World Bank (2020), went from some 40 per cent of world trade in 1990 to over 50 per cent in 2007. But that share appears to have declined slightly in the following years. This may have reflected the reduced participation in GVCs by China, which had previously relied largely on them in its export strategy. It seems that this, in turn, is an effect of the great economic advance of the country in recent years, which has allowed its big manufacturing firms to increasingly resort to domestic suppliers for more technologically complex or sophisticated inputs and components previously imported from advanced countries and other foreign specialized producers; the issue is discussed by Aichele and Heiland (2019).[27]

GVCs have been the object of specific analysis by economists since the 1990s, and basic contributions have been associated with the names of Gereffi, Sturgeon, Kaplinsky, Milberg, Feenstra and Kierzkowski. As GVCs gradually became the dominant mode of international trade, a huge literature developed on them (for an extensive survey up to 2013 see Park, Nayyar and Low (2013); more up-to-date surveys

[27] Gaulier, Sztulman and Ünal (2019) advance the argument that the evidence of a moderately increasing share of intermediates in world trade in 2002–2008, followed after the 2008 crisis by a downturn in 2011–2016, may be largely the effect of the measurement of trade flows in monetary terms. They calculate that taking account of price effects, both the share of intermediate goods and that of the specific 'Parts and Components' aggregate in total world trade in goods recorded a modest but steady rise over the 2000–2016 period, with no sign of downturn after the crisis.

are Coe and Yeung (2019) and Kano, Tsang and Yeung (2020)) and they have now found their place in textbooks on international trade. Therefore, we refer the reader to general works such as Paus (2007), Bair (2009), Milberg and Winkler (2013), Coe and Yeung (2015), World Bank Group et al. (2017, 2019) and Ponte, Gereffi and Raj-Reichert (2019); the latest trends in GVC evolution are synthetically analysed in McKinsey Global Institute (2019) and Antràs (2020), and more extensively in World Bank (2020). We will instead stress the change of perspective that this strand of the literature has imparted to international trade theory and highlight some important issues that have emerged from the debates on GVCs.

Milberg and Winkler (2013) quite rightly criticized the models prevalently used by economists until that time to analyse the phenomena of offshoring and international production chains for being based on the assumption of full employment and for neglecting capital, as they were focused on the skilled/unskilled labour dichotomy. But the central point of their critique was that these models refer – with extensions and modifications to take account of some modern developments – to the RHO theory of comparative advantage. They argued that these models:

> have conceptual, historical and ethical limitations that generally fail to capture the broader institutional context – including corporate strategies, labor market segmentation, buyer-supplier asymmetries, and government regulations – which are keys to understanding the social welfare and economic development consequences of globalized production. Profits, their sources and their uses, have largely disappeared from the analysis, despite their centrality in determining the international division of labor and in driving the dynamic gains from offshoring. As a result of these shortcomings, economists have ceded the academic voice in the debate over offshoring – to sociologists and geographers, experts in management, development studies, labor relations and, yes, to journalists and popular writers. Economics, it would appear, has been outsourced to the non-economists. (p. 5)

More generally, one may observe that the most important element that is missing or only superficially analysed in many economists' contributions is the power relations that develop within GVCs and which to a large extent determine their structure and economic effects (this, by the way, is one of the reasons why so much room was devoted to the phenomenon of economic power in Chapter 9).[28]

[28] Kaplinsky (2000) had already argued that 'Because value chain enquiry spans different economic branches and sectors, effective analysis requires the participation of different disciplines ... Moreover, since power is a key component of governance, and trust is critical to enhanced inter-firm cooperation and new forms of work-organization, there is a simultaneous need to draw on the insights of political science and sociology' (p. 17). The scarce attention paid to the issue of power continues to be considered one of the main weaknesses in GVC economic analysis: see Chor (2019) and Dallas, Ponte and Sturgeon (2019). In the latter work, the three authors have tried to provide a conceptual framework for the analysis of power aspects in GVC research.

Milberg and Winkler also stressed that, as already pointed out above, many of the theoretical models of offshoring are open to highly divergent results (one of the reasons being that they are strongly influenced by the specific institutional arrangements of various countries), so that the determination

The diffusion of GVCs has drastically changed the international trade landscape: instead of the interchange of final goods, we now observe, across national borders, complex, interconnected flows of final goods and services, inputs and components, specialized personnel, capital, technologies and know-how. Correspondingly, interdependence among countries has significantly increased. Trade (and other economic) policies adopted by individual countries participating in GVCs now have much greater consequences for other countries, as they impact with multiplicative effects on foreign upstream and downstream producers in the chain. The same happens with supply chain disruptions and with unforeseen shocks taking place at any point in the chain, in particular with sudden changes in the final demand for GVCs' products. For example, a drop in final demand pushes firms to delay orders and run down inventories, amplifying the fall in production all along the chain of upstream producers, as seems to have occurred during the 2008 global crisis.[29] Risk seems to have increased with the development of GVCs, making supply chain risk management a central task of lead firms: since a growing number of firms participate in a global chain, the visibility and transparency of their activity decreases, while the number of points in the chain where disruptions can take place increases.

In this new global environment, many of the basic concepts on which international trade theory had been based since the time of Ricardo have largely lost their significance and usefulness. Take imports and exports: already half a century ago, Hufbauer (1970) had argued:

> A better procedure, in finding national export characteristics, would have been to use export *value added* ... for each commodity, rather than export *receipts* for that commodity, as the ingredient of national export composition. As M. Michaely and P.T. Knight observe, export receipts *minus* the world market cost of purchased inputs should ideally serve as the export composition vector. (p. 156)

But it was only with the diffusion of fragmentation and GVCs that things started to change. Production fragmentation implies, on the one hand, that if a country is exporting a good, that does not mean that it has a comparative advantage in the production of that good: the country may be simply covering the role of final assembler of a good whose components have all been imported from other producing countries. As intermediate goods may cross national borders several times, the value of international export flows tends to be inflated by double (or triple or more) counting. This

of the gains from offshoring is left to empirical research. They noted that such research in this field seldom managed to overcome serious statistical and methodological problems; and even when it did produce precise and widely accepted results, these could usually be subject to different evaluations and interpretations.

[29] See Cattaneo, Gereffi and Staritz (2010). Kimura (2013), however, while recognizing that a massive macro-shock taking place anywhere in the world and affecting part of the production network will be transmitted to the whole value chain, argued that in these cases 'private firms make every effort to minimize a shock and keep production networks working well', suggesting that 'production networks may rather work as a macroeconomic stabilizer against shocks' (pp. 379–380).

is why the analysis of the products that a country exports is now being substituted by the analysis of the VA that has been contributed by the country to the final price of the products it exports. And comparative advantage, as already indicated, should be calculated on the basis of the relative costs in autarchy, in different countries, not of specific goods, but of specific tasks or production phases (or components).

On the other hand, a country may import certain products or components in order to be able to competitively produce a good or a good's fragment or production phase in which it enjoys a comparative advantage, and the imported good may incorporate inputs that the country had previously exported to the country from which it now imports. Therefore, the traditional Keynesian treatment of export items as a simple addition to – and import items as a simple subtraction from – the aggregate demand of a country has become superficial and often misleading (as was pointed out in Footnote 8 in Section 6.2). In this new logic of looking at trade in terms of VA, a country's bilateral trade with another country loses most of its meaning, as trade disequilibria vis-à-vis a country from which imports are received may simply reflect disequilibria that have developed vis-à-vis third countries that produce most of the components or production phases incorporated in the goods imported; and the stimulus to domestic demand imparted by exports may not be originated by the demand of the country to which the exported good is sent, but by the final demand of another country located at the end of a long international chain.

Even Ricardo's criterion for the determination of comparative advantage finds problems in being applied to a world where trade is dominated by the exchange of inputs and by GVCs. Comparative advantage, according to that criterion, is established by comparing relative costs of producing final goods in each of the two trading countries under autarchy, and the gains from exchange are greatest when these relative costs diverge the most. In a world of production fragmentation – just as happens with new goods – such a comparison is very frequently impossible, as in a country production of some intermediate goods or production phases may not conceivably take place at all in autarchy (the problem, mentioned in Footnote 6 in Chapter 5, was discussed, with reference to fragmentation, by Baldone, Sdogati and Tajoli (2007)).

The traditional theory and policy of protection and those of the exchange rate have also become obsolete – or at least must be applied much more selectively – in a world economy where the relevant variables are not exports and imports but exported and imported VA.[30] Protection of national sectors and currency devaluation no longer simply favour the international competitiveness of national producers, but may cause

[30] The definition of a country's exchange rate itself needs to be changed: the variations in a country's exchange rate have been traditionally defined and calculated as the weighted average of the variations of its exchange rate vis-à-vis the currencies of each of its main trading partners, the weight assigned to each bilateral exchange rate variation being the share of the total trade of the country that takes place with that partner. Now the shares should be calculated not on the basis of imports and exports, but on that of VA imported from and exported to each country. On the fundamental changes in the calculation of exchange rates that must be introduced once one refers to VA traded instead of gross trade values see Bems and R.C. Johnson (2015).

serious problems because of the higher prices of imported inputs and components, which represent a large share of the final value of the goods produced and exported. The identification of the countries that compete with national products (and against which the adoption of protectionist measures might be under consideration) requires extreme care: as just pointed out, foreign countries that export final goods that compete with national products may in fact be simply final assemblers of the goods they export, the real competitors being third countries from which the exporting country imports inputs and components (R. C. Johnson (2014) highlighted some changes in traditional international macroeconomic perspectives that must be introduced in a world of GVCs and briefly referred to protection and exchange rate policies). In this new environment, the traditional alignment of the interests of advanced countries' national firms and workers in support of protectionist and exchange rate measures directed to defending national production activity has broken down, as national GVC lead firms' profitability may be sustained by the import of low-cost intermediate or final products, so that trade unions may be left alone in trying to defend workers' jobs at home (this may largely explain why US initiatives aimed at pushing China to revalue its currency so as to contain the US trade deficit, while repeatedly advocated, have in fact never been seriously put into practice).

GVC theory has also contributed to intensify a change, already under way, in the concept of the gains from trade. Just as some economists had distinguished in the past static and dynamic gains from exports, now it was observed that for developing countries that have been integrated into GVCs, static benefits from better allocation of existing factor resources appear rather limited, given the power of lead firms to impose low prices – and consequently low factor remunerations – on their suppliers. What has become the key issue in assessing whether participation in GVCs is beneficial for a country is instead the potential dynamic advantage that the country can reap in terms of upgrading: a notion, as observed by Milberg and Winkler, that is by itself anathema to the old international trade tradition based on the RHO model, as it implies a refusal to concentrate on exploiting existing comparative advantages and, instead, an effort to create new ones.

* * *

Despite continuous changes, the evolution of GVCs continues to be characterized by the persistence of an asymmetric market structure. On the one hand, global lead firms, which in most sectors appear to have reached very high levels of concentration (mainly through mergers and acquisitions), continue to show a pronounced ability to maintain pricing power. Their strategy has been to focus more and more on their core activities where their monopolistic or oligopolistic advantages (largely deriving from exclusive ownership of patents, brands and other intellectual property) are the greatest, while drastically reducing costs by progressively transferring physical production and its connected risks to suppliers at home and abroad. In this way they have managed to keep high mark-ups over costs and high levels of profits, even when part of their advantage has been passed to final customers in the form of lower prices. Li and Miao (2018) attribute this increase in mark-ups, and the connected rise in firm concentration, to the greater possibility of the already bigger and more productive firms to take advantage of the cost savings from the import of cheaper intermediate products. On the other hand, competition among suppliers is becoming more and more intense, leading to falling firm mark-ups in the developing countries increasingly involved in GVCs: the evidence on this contrasting evolution of firm mark-ups in developed and developing countries is reported in World Bank (2020); see also Footnote 42 in Section 9.4.1.

However, among suppliers in GVCs there has often emerged a group of first-tier suppliers, who have managed – by upgrading their production capabilities and/or by concentrating, mainly through mergers and acquisitions – to improve their bargaining position vis-à-vis lead firms, getting much better prices for their products and more favourable conditions regarding transfers of technology and know-how, while they have increased their power vis-à-vis their second-tier domestic and foreign suppliers. The growing role of these suppliers – in large part located in advanced countries – who have often managed to represent, at different key points of the supply chain of many different industries, global giants with strong bargaining power, has been highlighted by Nolan, Zhang and Liu (2008).

Milberg and Winkler (2010, 2013) have argued that in advanced countries, but particularly in the USA, the potential dynamic role of GVC lead firms – and more generally of all non-financial corporations – in the global economy has been significantly reduced by the phenomenon of financialization: only a limited quota of the larger profits from offshoring and reduced cost of inputs and from technical progress and innovation are recycled into the domestic economy through investment in physical and immaterial capital and in R&D, which would lead to increased productive activity and labour demand and ensure the long-term ability of the economy to generate innovations and higher productivity (the traditional justifications for capitalists' search for higher profits). Since the early 1980s the share of the US corporate sector's productive investment in both national income and profits registered a marked reduction, and the same tendency appears to characterize other advanced countries – as confirmed by Gutiérrez and Philippon (2017), who attribute the decline of investment in the USA primarily to the increase in concentration and connected lower competition (see Footnote 13 in Section 9.2). Corporations have instead increasingly followed the policy of returning their net gains to their shareholders through higher distributed dividends and share buybacks, and/or of investing them in financial assets and particularly in mergers with and acquisition of other corporations, or takeovers of new dynamic small enterprises threatening to become in the future serious competitors, whose owners can hardly resist the offer of a high price.[31] As already indicated, since the 2008 global crisis managers

[31] Corporations' financial investment was motivated by the higher returns that financial and speculative assets seemed to ensure in comparison with productive investments; by the fact that mergers and acquisitions made it possible to gain control of competitor firms or to create more powerful producer groups; and especially by the goal of maximizing shareholder value – in the short-term perspective that until the 2008 global crisis increasingly characterized investment – through distribution of dividends

seem to have reconsidered the policy of concentrating almost exclusively on short-term shareholder value, but whether this will lead to an abandonment of that policy still remains to be seen.

Two issues are fundamental in the analysis of GVCs. The first regards the distribution of gains among the different participants in the chain, and will be the object of Section 11.2.3. As explained by Kaplinsky (2000), in a world where manufacturing capabilities have rapidly spread to more and more countries, intensifying competition among producers, these gains largely take the form of rents (defined as advantages connected with the possession of attributes that can be protected from competition) that accrue to those participants in the chain that are in a position to exploit entry barriers. These rents are increasingly concentrated in the intangible segments of the value chain. Specialized skills and technologies, exclusive possession of patents, copyrights and brands, superior organizational and managerial skills and financial resources, knowledge of and long-time relations with suppliers and customers are the main assets that – together with superior power and market distortions – cause potential competitors to face obstacles to entry into the most rewarding segments of a GVC and to the creation of new GVCs competing with existing ones. With GVCs becoming more and more complex and difficult to coordinate, lead firms have secured increasing rents from their activity of GVC governance.

The second issue regards the scope for developing countries to upgrade their economic and social conditions through their firms' participation in GVCs. Economic upgrading refers to firms' moving up the production chain of a given product to more rewarding phases requiring higher skills, or moving to produce different, more sophisticated products in the same or in other GVCs by developing the ability to perform more complex activities or production phases that allow them to increase their bargaining power and obtain more VA per unit of productive factor employed. It implies raising the productivity, quality and flexibility of production and the skills of workers through better organization and the application of more advanced technologies. Different aspects of economic upgrading have been identified: product upgrading, which implies moving to higher VA products in a given chain; functional upgrading, the move to more technologically complex stages of the production cycle (as from product manufacturing to product design); and intersectoral upgrading, the change from one GVC to another in a different sector that permits a higher remuneration of production factors. But upgrading can also occur in the form of a deepening of a firm's capabilities within a given segment of the GVC.

By social upgrading, reference is made instead to workers' wage levels, working conditions and rights (such as the right to strike and to establish and join trade unions). To a large extent, economic upgrading seems to represent a necessary (but not sufficient) condition for social upgrading. But the latter, and in particular workers' rights, can often be simply imposed by state regulations, as it frequently does not

---

and share buy-backs. On the causes and consequences of allocating profits to shareholders, and buy-backs in particular, see Lazonick (2014).

imply significant additional costs (in the case of the right not to be discriminated in job offers on ethnic, religious or political grounds it would rather lead to higher efficiency and lower costs). To avoid social upgrading becoming an obstacle to international competitiveness, it has been suggested that a labour standards clause could be included in WTO trade negotiations; of course, labour standards should be fixed at different levels for countries at different stages of economic development (labour standards will be discussed in Section 12.3.3).

Firms' participation in GVCs is no guarantee of their economic upgrading. It may instead produce downgrading by blocking a participant – particularly a less developed country lacking the skills and capabilities required for production in the more 'advanced' and profitable stages, tasks or components of GVCs – in an unfavourable and gradually deteriorating position in the chain, with production limited to the lowest-VA segments.

High strategic abilities on the part of firms vis-à-vis the strategic behaviour of GVC lead firms appear necessary for upgrading, since normally a basic conflict of interest characterizes the relationships between lead firms and their suppliers. Lead firms try to externalize all non-core activities, concentrating on the exploitation – and trying to avoid any loss – of their immaterial and intellectual assets; but some leakages of these assets from lead firms to their suppliers unavoidably take place. Other participants in the chain, wishing to upgrade their activities, pursue the opposite goal of maximizing those leakages, so as to gain access to some at least of the factors that are key to a successful upgrading strategy.

Sako and Zylberberg (2019) have analysed the strategies that suppliers can try to pursue in order to upgrade their position within a GVC and secure a larger share of the value produced by the latter; avoiding in particular being locked into a position of 'captive' participant with only the lead firm as customer. They stress the importance of suppliers' efforts to upgrade through strategies of technological innovation; but it is essential that such innovation cannot be easily imitated by competitors. The existence of a working IPR regime is important in this respect, as is the supplier's availability of complementary assets such as complementary technologies, distribution channels and logistics networks.

In these conflicts of interest between lead firms and other participants in GVCs – beyond the basic bargaining strength connected with each parties' objective position as exclusive or attractive provider of production factors, markets, or specific inputs and technologies – a key role is played by the public authorities of developing countries, as the Chinese experience has clearly demonstrated. To make fruitful participation in GVCs and upgrading by national firms possible, it is not only essential that they provide the physical, educational and institutional infrastructure necessary to develop indigenous technological learning abilities (in countries that first decide to follow a policy of development through participation in GVCs, the authorities also have to take the critical decision of choosing the most profitable and promising entry point into a GVC). Even more essential is their role in providing the sophisticated bargaining abilities required to make GVC lead firms grant conditions more favourable to domestic participants in the chain and to the upgrading of their activities.

These bargaining abilities largely depend on the degree of competence, honesty and identification with their country's development goals, of the national leadership.

The notion of contrasting interests, and consequent power struggles, between lead firms and their suppliers – just as more generally among the participants in GVCs, all trying to appropriate a larger share of the overall value produced by the chain – should not, however, be overemphasized. The great heterogeneity of GVCs and the different specific contexts and circumstances in which they operate allow for not infrequent cases where it is in the interest of the lead firm – particularly in a longer-term view of the GVC's sustainability – to help suppliers and other partners in foreign countries to acquire or consolidate positions of technological advantage and to avoid squeezing them in negotiations over prices.

The concept of upgrading is apparently clear and uncontroversial; however, as happens with many economic concepts, a more in-depth examination shows it to be ambiguous and debatable. Tokatli (2013) has analysed the issue and the criticisms that have been addressed against the use of the upgrading notion. He has stressed that for a manufacturing supplier firm in a developing country, entering into a new higher-VA activity in a GVC does not guarantee that the additional VA will be captured. As often happened in the apparel industry with the design function, an activity, new for the manufacturer, may have been discontinued by the buyer simply because of the decreasing gains and increasing risks associated with it.

The notion of upgrading has typically been referred to a unidirectional process of improvement of production and enlargement of the range of activities, but firms in GVCs may actually pursue a much more complex strategy. They may be upgrading, downgrading and backsliding at the same time, according to the different situations that characterize different products, markets and competitors, branching out in many directions and 'wearing multiple hats' (as an example, the same firm may supply a large retailer or a famous firm with apparel marketed under the buyer's brand, while selling analogous products under its own brand in less sophisticated markets).

But the most serious problem with the notion of upgrading is that it has been mainly developed with reference to firms from developing countries participating in GVCs, and it is not clear to what extent it can be extended to the region or country to which the firms belong. The problem (already discussed in general terms in Section 2.3) is of crucial importance for developing countries that have often based their whole development strategy on domestic firms' participation in GVCs. In fact, upgrading by a firm belonging to a GVC does not guarantee upgrading for the whole region or country where it is located. As the literature on export processing zones pointed out decades ago, the critical element in these export-oriented activities is their ability to impart stimuli to the rest of the economy, avoiding the creation of a mere modern enclave isolated from a surrounding backward economy. Nothing ensures that an upgrading firm contributes to other firms' upgrading: the opposite may even be the case, as higher productivity by a firm may sharpen overall competition compelling other producers in the same sector to reduce workers' remuneration or to exit the market.

11.2.2 The progress of empirical research on GVCs and trade in value added

For a long time, the empirical analysis of GVCs and their effects on participating countries has found obstacles in statistical and methodological problems, as not only the framework of international trade theory, but also the whole system of national and international collection and elaboration of statistical data was based on the consideration of the final good as the fundamental object of analysis – and not its production phase, task or component. As late as 2008, Sturgeon and Gereffi, pointing to the scientific inadequacy and the predominantly merely ideological nature of the debate on globalization, could rightly observe:

> There is a reason that the globalization debate remains so impoverished. The data that economists use to argue their position, one way or another, are outmoded. They are based almost entirely on assumptions of unitary national economies trading finished physical products at arms-length. The shift to services and services trade, digitalization of business processes, the spike in intermediate goods trade, and the "compression" of development in places like China and India – all either symptoms or enablers of global value chains – have changed the rules of the game, and our data regime has not kept up. (2008, p. 29)

The following years were marked by a revolution in empirical research on international transactions that allowed a start to be made on giving practical content to the new fundamental concepts, definitions and categories that had been elaborated, and put at the centre of their theoretical analyses, by international economists. The digitalization of import and export data recorded by customs and the additional statistical data collected and processed by official national authorities on the basis of other sources, such as banks and international investors, has provided information on the new aspects of international trade and investment. But great progress has been achieved especially by researchers and research institutions in improving old databases and creating new ones, so as to extract from them a lot of empirical material providing information on the new characteristics of trade and on GVCs in particular. As a result, the scientific level of the economic debate on GVCs and on other issues raised by globalization has greatly improved, although much work is still called for – first of all in the field of trade in services – to obtain an adequate empirical foundation for debates on international trade. Interesting analyses based on the data produced by the application of the new statistical sources and methodologies, are contained in the article collections by Mattoo, Wang and Wei (2013), Amador and di Mauro (2015) and Banca d'Italia (2016). A description of the main results produced by GVC research has been provided by World Bank Group et al. (2017, 2019), while Antràs (2020) has presented an updated synthesis of the 'state of the art' in GVC research from the conceptual point of view.

Two lines of empirical research appear to have produced remarkable advances. The first, of crucial interest for macroeconomic analysis, is the reconstruction, largely based on input–output tables, of countries' trade flows in terms, not of traditional imports and exports, but of VA exported and imported. The second, fundamental for microeconomic analysis, is the collection and elaboration of firm-level databases providing information on the characteristics of firms taking part in foreign trade and specifically in GVC activity. This is a line of research that will make it possible to greatly improve the study of the heterogeneity of firms involved in foreign trade, which since the late 1990s has become an important new field of international economics (a third line of research consists of case studies of specific GVCs).

The new developments largely concern statistical and methodological techniques, which remain outside the scope of the present work. Still, their importance is such as to warrant a brief reference to them (for specific analyses see R. C. Johnson (2018) and Ahmad (2019); for an updated, easily readable exposition of the basic concepts, problems, and main research initiatives in VA trade – together with a specific study of the UK position – see Cambridge Econometrics (2020)).

Information on the location of VA, and particularly of profits, in GVCs is only partially available (there are also difficulties in the collection of data on the ownership of firms and productive assets). This is a problem that affects not only GVCs, but also more generally the determination of VA incorporated in all goods exported by domestic firms and sectors. Quite apart from participation in well-structured GVCs managed by lead firms, economies have experienced up to the 2008 global crisis a large increase in the import content of the goods produced and exported, so that the data on the value of the exports of goods belonging to given sectors or product categories collected by customs (gross exports) give a highly distorted measure of the VA incorporated in exported products; that is, of the contribution (measured by the remuneration received) of domestic factors to the final value of these products. But the recorded value of countries' imports may also incorporate the value of inputs that the same countries had previously exported to those from which they now receive the goods.[32] Moreover, the data recorded by the customs do not specify in which sectors of an economy the different categories of imported goods are used as inputs, or whether they are directly destined to final consumers or investors; and do not indicate whether the goods exported to given countries are used for final consumption or investment in those countries, or just as inputs for products sold in their domestic market and for those exported to third countries.

The VA incorporated in a country's exports of given sectors or subsectors – just as the sectoral and geographical breakdown of a country's imports and exports among all the countries that, respectively, contributed to their production or made use of

[32] These problems of VA determination also deeply impact on the measurement of corporations' size and, consequently, of the degree and the tendencies of concentration of production in different sectors of the economy. In a country, the weight of a corporation in a sector is frequently measured on the basis of the value of its sales relative to the entire sector sales. Since with the fragmentation of production there can be little correspondence between a corporation's sales value and its VA, it is the latter that appears to be the proper measure of the corporation's weight, which should then be compared with the VA of the whole sector to which it belongs to obtain measures of concentration. Of course, since reference to sales value still gives a measure of the importance of a lead corporation as a controller of its whole GVC, sales continue to represent a fundamental indicator of a corporation's' importance and power.

them along the production chain – must then be indirectly estimated. The problem is particularly serious for services, as the determination of their VA and its attribution to specific service categories is a very hard task; in particular, it is very difficult to collect reliable information on the high-value and largely immaterial services provided by GVC lead firms. The importance of services increased very much in recent decades, so that their share of the total value of world trade in goods and services was estimated by WTO (2020b, p. 10) to have reached 23.6 per cent in 2019.

To solve many of these problems, research institutions of different countries and/or international organizations have launched programmes of international collaboration aimed at the construction of detailed national input–output tables according to common definitions and criteria.[33] These comparable tables can then be linked together, splitting each country's imports and exports of each sector among different countries of origin and destination on the basis, in the first place, of the data on bilateral trade transactions recorded in gross terms by the customs. The linking of the national tables makes it possible to obtain tables referred to larger regional areas or (aggregating under the heading 'rest of the world' the countries for which national tables are not available) to the world as a whole; the final ideal target being complete and detailed world input–output tables. It would then be possible to determine each country's (and its sectors') backward linkages – that is, all the previous international passages of their imported inputs through the entire production chains; and forward linkages – that is, the successive uses of the products a country exports by all the countries located further down the production chains.

The main limits of these international initiatives, apart from the general one regarding services, are the lack of national tables for many countries, the difficulty of producing data according to common definitions and criteria, the limited level of product disaggregation that can be reached (as international tables cannot be more detailed than the least disaggregated national table they include) and the inevitable recourse to often unrealistic 'proportionality assumptions' to overcome the non-availability of information on many relevant elements that must be recorded in the tables (one may have to assume, for example, that country A's steel imports from countries B, C and D are all allocated to the different steel-using industrial sectors of country A in the same proportions as steel produced in country A is allocated to these sectors).

Apart from input–output analysis, other statistical innovations are the digitalization of customs forms (which has allowed the extraction of totally new information from their data) and the predisposition of new databases and new indicators, mainly

[33] National input–output tables, first developed by Leontief in the 1930s, have been largely used in advanced countries in the post-war period. They are basically matrices that show in monetary terms (at current prices or at the prices of a base year), on the input side, the origin (a domestic sector or import from abroad) of the products directly consumed or invested, or used as inputs, by domestic sectors; and, on the output side, the destination (final consumption, investment or use as input by other domestic sectors, or export abroad) of the output of each domestic production sector. For a description of input–output tables and an overview of the international projects under way to construct global or inter-country input–output tables see Remond-Tiedrez and Rueda-Cantuche (2019).

at the micro-level, throwing new light on the involvement and position of firms (as illustrated by Bernard and Moxnes (2018) for firm-to-firm trade networks), MNCs and countries in GVCs, and the connected aspects regarding the employment content of trade, measures of international competitiveness, MNCs' activities, trade policy design and so on. The collection of micro-level information also faces serious problems. For example, in many cases it requires the collaboration of firms and so is conditioned by firms' readiness to provide data they may consider confidential and whose collection implies loss of time and considerable effort on their part; while some important data may be unknown to the firms themselves, as is the case for the determination of the country of origin of many inputs that firms buy from wholesale suppliers and distributors without caring to inquire whether they are produced domestically or imported from abroad.

Some interesting results of these empirical analyses of GVCs may be mentioned. Examining the VA content of trade, R. C. Johnson (2014) estimated that for the world as a whole VA exported went down from about 85 per cent of gross export value in the 1970s and 1980s to 70–75 per cent in 2008. The percentage in this last year varied sharply across countries (for the 20 top exporting countries, from 50 to 90 per cent, with most of the advanced countries recording values between 70 and 80 per cent). It was much higher for services than for manufactures; so that while in terms of gross export value manufactures contributed 67 per cent to total world exports and services only 20 per cent, in terms of VA exported, the contribution of services (41 per cent) even slightly exceeded that of manufactures (39 per cent).

OECD 2018 estimates, as reported by M. C. Klein and Pettis (2020), indicated that Chinese gross exports overstate exports in terms of VA by some 30 per cent, and US gross exports by about 20 per cent (for imports the percentages are, respectively, 30 and 16).

Banga (2014) estimated that 67 per cent of world VA exports created under GVCs in 2009 accrued to OECD countries (the figure was about 9 per cent for both Germany and the USA, 5 per cent for Korea and 4 per cent each for Japan, the UK and France); the share of China was about 9 per cent; in total those of Russia, India, Brazil and South Africa amounted to 5 per cent; those of the main emerging East Asian exporters to 11 per cent. The rest of the world, which includes the large majority of developing countries, only had a share of 8 per cent, confirming the high geographical concentration of GVC export activity.

New calculations have shown that since the 1990s, despite a massive increase in both the physical volume and the gross value of developing countries' manufactured exports, the VA incorporated in these exports has grown at a modest rate. This is largely because, merely as a result of the intensification of fragmentation of production in GVCs, the share of imported inputs in these countries' exports has greatly increased. But it may also reflect a shrinking of the share of the total value of the goods produced by the chain that is obtained by low-wage manufacturers for given manufacturing activities as a consequence of increasing cut-throat competition among suppliers and the lower bargaining power of low-wage manufacturing firms and countries vis-à-vis GVC lead firms and other participants from more developed countries.

Analysing the manufacturing production activities carried out within GVCs by 40 developed and developing countries (covering some 85 per cent of world GDP), Timmer, Erumban, Los, Stehrer and de Vries (2014) estimated that between 1995 and 2008 the share of capital (defined in the broadest sense, as the difference between gross VA and labour income) in the VA of these activities seems to have increased not only in advanced, but also in emerging economies, where it was already very high at the beginning and wages remained relatively low in the course of the period. In both groups of countries, the share in VA of high-skilled labour greatly increased, while the shares of middle- and low-skilled labour went down significantly. Together, capital and skilled labour registered an increase in their share of manufacturing VA from 55 to 63 per cent.

More recently, Pahl and Timmer (2020), on the basis of data for the manufacturing sector of 58 countries (of which 38 were developing ones) covering the 1970–2008 period, found that both countries' and industries' higher degrees of participation in production for exports within GVCs are associated with higher labour productivity growth (this effect being larger the further a country is from the productivity frontier). But they did not find any evidence of higher participation being associated with higher employment growth (even when taking into account the indirect effects on employment in non-manufacturing activities); concluding that GVC participation is a mixed blessing at best, and that economic upgrading through such participation is possible, but far from automatic.

11.2.3 The distribution of value added in GVCs

In a market economy, the contribution of any economic entity (individual, firm, sector, region or country), that is the value of what it produces, is measured by the monetary VA of its production. VA is the difference between the sale price of a product and the cost of acquired inputs (raw materials, intermediate products and other inputs); it typically includes wages, profits, rents and depreciation; GDP, obtained by summing the VA of all national producers, is the value of what an economy produces. The theoretical underpinning of this accounting convention is the idea that the working of the free market and its mechanism of perfect competition ensure that the evaluation of a product or of a factor of production expressed by its price measures its contribution to the economy and its true value.

In GVCs, the contribution of each participant – and the gains it obtains from participating in the GVC – is also measured by the monetary VA produced by that participant; and the contribution of a participant relative to the contributions of other firms or countries taking part in a GVC is measured by the percentage that its VA represents in the total VA produced by the entire chain. The measurement of the VA in a GVC is not an easy task, as it presents a lot of difficulties, mainly of an empirical nature (as illustrated in the preceding section). But there are major logical and theoretical problems as well.

A common misunderstanding that adds confusion to the debates on this subject must first be dispelled. It is commonly believed that the VA produced by a firm also measures the benefits the firm derives from its productive activity, so we often hear incitements to firms to move towards the production of goods with higher VA and to increase the percentage that their VA represents in the total VA produced in the entire cycle of production of a good. Such incitements make little sense: as for the latter, the percentage of the total value of a product represented by a firm's VA has, by itself, little economic meaning. For example, if a manufacturing firm produces luxury teapots it will probably employ the same quantity of its productive factors, will obtain the same absolute amount of VA from its activity and the same benefits from production, irrespective of whether the teapots are made of silver, gold or any other metal; but the percentage of the final teapot price that its VA represents will be extremely different in the three cases: for a gold teapot the final price will reflect the enormous value of the raw material employed, the opposite being the case for a steel teapot. More generally, there is no reason why it should be more profitable for a firm to participate in a GVC as a receiver of a large share of the total VA produced by the chain than to participate in many GVCs as a receiver, in each of them, of a small share of the chain's total VA.

As for the former incitement, just as in order to determine the profitability and the economic health of a firm, one must look at the profit it obtains per unit of monetary capital invested, more than at its total absolute profits, if one wants to measure the advantage that a firm derives from participation in a GVC, rather than the absolute VA obtained, one should measure the VA obtained from the employment of each unit of labour, capital and any other factor of production (of given quality and productivity). If, for example, employing for one week one unskilled worker and the capital represented by a drill costing $50, firm X produces $200 of VA, while firm Y produces only $100, one can say that firm X produces double the VA per unit of factors employed compared with firm Y, and so obtains benefits double those of Y (in fact, this is what people usually have in mind when they improperly speak generically of maximizing a firm's VA). Unfortunately, measuring VA per unit of factors employed is a daunting task (it requires overcoming the same difficulties as those involved in measuring the conceptually analogous 'factorial terms of trade', discussed in Footnote 35 in Section 9.3.3), because of the problems in collecting data on the use and cost of factors so that each factor is allocated the share of the total VA that corresponds to its contribution.

A major qualification applies to the preceding discussion. So far, when speaking of a firm's VA and its gains, reference has been made to gains, measured by VA, obtained by all the factors of production employed in the firm. Maximization of the firm's VA per unit of productive factors employed is certainly the goal of those that take part in the firm's activity, considered as a group. But in a market economy the goal of a private firm is a different one: it is the goal of its owners and managers, which consists in the maximization of the part of the VA that represents the return on capital invested and on managers' entrepreneurial activity (from the point of view of salaried managers, also of the part representing their salaries), and this usually implies an effort to minimize workers' wage bill.

When reference is made to a country, and not to a firm, these arguments apply only in part. Contrary to the firm's goal of maximum return on capital and entrepreneurial activity, the basic economic goal of a country is the maximization of the sum of all its firms' VA, that is of its GDP. If the national production factors are fully employed, a higher GDP can only be obtained by increasing the VA per unit of factors employed by the firms that make up the economy (that is by increasing factors' productivity). But if the national factors of production are partly unemployed, an increase in GDP can also be obtained through the simple increase in total VA obtained by favouring the establishment of new firms and the employment of additional factors of production in existing ones so as to increase their activity.

The crucial problem in GVC analysis is that what one would like to measure is whether the percentage of a GVC's total VA that a firm or country obtains from participation in a chain represents a fair remuneration for the activities of the factors employed – for the 'real' contribution of the firm or country to the total VA of the chain. Here one bumps again against the problem that was discussed when trying to define the meaning of 'fair terms of trade' in the exchange of goods: the problem of finding a measure of a good's (or a good's component's) 'real value'; that is, a value having an objective existence independent of the price it fetches on the market. The classical economists – Smith, Ricardo and Marx – all adhered to a labour theory of value: they basically related the value of a good to an objective element, reflecting the level of scientific, technical and organizational progress reached by a society – represented by the cost of production as measured by the quantity of direct and indirect labour (of given quality) employed for the good's production.[34] The insuperable theoretical and practical problems of employing this notion of value, especially when dealing with modern economies based on knowledge and technology and largely involved in international trade, have been discussed in Section 9.3.2, and explain in part why the concept was abandoned by non-Marxist economists in favour of the marginalist concept of value identified with market price. This identification of the productive contribution to national wealth with the receipt of an income excludes the very possibility of countries, social classes, firms or individuals, capturing value created by other producers.[35]

---

[34] Smith actually exposed at least two different theories of labour value of a good. One, like those later developed by Ricardo and Marx, is based on 'labour embodied' – that is, on the amount of labour time necessary to produce a good. The other is based on 'labour commanded': it makes the value of a good dependent not on the amount of labour embodied in it, but on the amount of labour that the good can purchase (so that the value of a good depends on the level of workers' wages). On this point see De Angelis and Harvie (2008): in their article, these authors also try to apply a notion of 'labour commanded' to get a measure of foreign investment that indicates the real amount of labour resources that the investment makes it possible to mobilize.

While the issue cannot be discussed here, it must be pointed out that labour theories of value, like all theories trying to establish the 'real' value of a good, also have to solve the difficult problem of establishing which working activities are 'productive' – that is create such 'real values' – and which are 'unproductive': on the issue see Baran and Sweezy (1966), Harvie (2005) and Mazzucato (2018).

[35] As stressed by Mazzucato (2018), it also has the effect of ignoring or underestimating the contribution to value creation of many government activities that greatly increase the efficiency of private

In GVC analysis, establishing on the basis of objective criteria the 'real' or 'intrinsic' value of a good and then seeing how monopolistic positions and other market distortions, differences in bargaining power, and temporary disequilibria between demand and supply cause the price of the good to diverge from its value, would overcome the basic problem that mere reference to VA leaves unsolved: the distinction between increases in VA that result from higher creation of value through larger or better application of – or application of higher-quality – factors of production or through superior technological or organizational structures and capabilities, and increases in VA obtained by simply appropriating value created by other producers thanks to the previously mentioned distortions.[36] It is the same point that led J. Smith (2016) to conclude that GDP is falsely labelled, as it does not measure what is domestically produced by the firms operating in a given national economy, but also includes the share (positive or negative) of the value of other countries' product that

---

producers but are made available to them free of charge or at a fraction of their cost, as they are not sold in the market at a price reflecting the interplay of supply and demand.

[36] A simple example can show both the substance of, and the difficulty of finding a solution to, this problem of measuring the 'real' contribution of each participant firm or country in a GVC. Suppose that in the production of a shirt, sold in the market to the final consumer for $100, the following VA is registered by firms A, B, C and D – located in four different countries – taking part in the GVC: $30 is received by A for overall chain management, R&D, design, brand and marketing; $50 by B for manufacturing the shirt; $10 by C for transport and distribution; $10 by D for retail sale. Suppose now that – the final price of the shirt remaining at $100 and nothing else changing – a lower-cost manufacturing firm B* is found in another country where workers' wages and working conditions, at parity of labour productivity, are so low that the VA of manufacturing falls to $20 (alternatively one could think of firm B being compelled, by the threat of losing its client, to lower its wages and profits so that its VA is reduced to $20). Suppose that now A is found to produce VA of $50 instead of $30 and D $20 instead of $10, while the VA produced by firm C remains at $10. In any conceivable 'real terms', it is evident that the contribution of the manufacturing firm (and its country) to the overall chain has not changed; simply, wages are much lower in the new manufacturing location (or wages and profits have been reduced in the original manufacturing firm). Equally, the contributions of A and D have not changed at all in any 'real terms'; simply, these firms (and their countries) have managed to appropriate a larger share of the final price, at the expense of the share going to the manufacturing firm (and its country). Intuitively, one is led to conclude that firms A and D (and their countries) are somehow draining wealth from (or 'exploiting') the manufacturing firm (and its country). But in practice the data specified here are very difficult to collect; and in any case to speak of 'exploitation' in the new situation would depend on the possibility of classifying the original arrangement as 'non exploitative', which is a very hard task.

In general, economists have avoided any open discussion of the problem of appropriation by more powerful firms or countries of VA created by other firms or countries, although they have frequently shown they are aware of the existence of this phenomenon. Often this recognition seems to be implicitly indicated by the linguistic expressions they use. For example, Morgan Stanley's chief economist S. S. Roach (2003) argues – as already quoted in Section 11.1.2 – that 'offshore outsourcing that extracts product from low-wage workers in the developing world has become an increasingly urgent survival tactic for companies in the developed economies' (p. 6); and Antràs and Rossi-Hansberg (2009) report that an important 1986 contribution by Ethier showed that when MNCs do business at arm's length with other firms, their 'headquarters cannot always devise a contract that ensures ex post efficiency and extracts all surplus from their contracting partners' (2009, p. 55).

these firms manage to capture. Unfortunately, the now huge literature on GVCs has devoted very little effort to tackling this fundamental problem.

The problem is that value is an extremely ambiguous and nebulous notion: 'Even among capitalist firms, the production of value can be perceived differently', recognize Coe and Yeung (2015, p. 35); the slippery nature of the concept of value and the differing meanings of the word employed by GVC researchers have been analysed by Havice and Pickles (2019). So far, no one has been able to propose an acceptable criterion for determining the 'real' value of a good. Mazzucato (2018) does not even attempt to advance a criterion. Coe and Yeung try to generically connect the notion of value at the same time to the classical-Marxist concept of surplus value and to the concept of rent produced by superior organization, exclusive technological know-how or by dominant monopolistic or oligopolistic positions. But they offer little help in finding a solution to the practical problem of measuring value. J. Smith (2016) also states generically that 'By "value" we mean both Marxian notions of surplus-value and more orthodox ones associated with economic rent' (p. 271), but again does not provide any guidance on their practical calculation (and in any case the insuperable limitations of a labour theory of value have already been mentioned). Stiglitz (2019) declares that his purpose is to 'explain the true source of the wealth of nations, distinguishing wealth creation from wealth extraction. The latter is any process whereby one individual takes wealth from others through one form of exploitation or another' (pp. xiii–xiv), and then acutely identifies the many different forms through which exploitation of workers and consumers takes place; but he does not advance any indication as to how it might be calculated.

The most important element that prevents, in practice, the distinction between creation of value and mere appropriation of value created by others is that, contrary to traditional theory based on perfect competition, the search for monopolistic rents is not just a distortion of normal economic activity but represents a fundamental element of modern economic life. But while some monopolistic rents are the result of mere subtraction of income from other economic agents, others are the result of activities and innovations that may bring them (and certainly society) large benefits. The very progress in the standard of living in industrial countries since the Industrial Revolution is a consequence of the increase in productivity originated by the fact that entrepreneurs – eager to prevent the fall in profits resulting from perfect competition – have exerted all possible efforts to introduce improvements and innovations in products and production processes, not easily or rapidly imitable by competitors, that, while producing a benefit for society, at least for a certain time can provide them – by law (as with patents) or de facto – with a monopolistic advantage, and thus produce extra profits; and governments (starting with Venice, where patents were invented at the end of the 15th century), to incentivise this socially beneficial innovative activity, have officially granted innovators the right to monopolistically exploit their inventions for a given number of years. But monopolies and rents may also be pursued by firms through other practices that reduce the welfare of the rest of society, such as illegal but hard to identify actions, exploitation of loopholes in legislation, lobbying and pressuring (or direct and indirect payments to) politicians to introduce laws and regulations granting them special privileges and advantages, or artificial creation of barriers to prevent competitors from entering their market. The problem is that it is hardly possible to establish precisely the borderline between socially advantageous, or in any case justifiable, monopolies and rents, and those that simply represent exploitation of other, less powerful agents (the sharp dispute, referred to in Footnote 6 in Section 10.3 on the usefulness, for the purpose of stimulating innovation, of the present legal rules on patents and copyrights, is originated by many economists' conviction that these rules only in part serve the purpose of rewarding, and thus stimulating, innovation, while to a large extent they represent simply a means for firms to extract additional undeserved payments from the users of the innovation).

But even if that distinction could be made, another problem would remain, namely that there are some fundamental factors of production that we all recognize as greatly contributing to higher productivity and general progress, but whose amount and contribution, as already indicated, are unmeasurable. First among them are the intangible assets that increasingly represent the basic source of rents and profits for GVC lead firms: the provision of essential specialized technological knowledge, or the ownership of brands that contribute to the success of the product of the chain, or the ability to organize, manage and control the whole GVC.

In passing, the example in Footnote 36 represents an extreme case: usually, when a GVC lead firm manages to find cheaper manufacturers, the price of the product to the final consumer is reduced; that is, the lead firm transfers part of its cost advantage to the final consumer, so as to increase the total number of customers and to avoid attracting new competitors. This means that if 'exploitation' of the manufacturer is taking place, final consumers, largely located in advanced countries, are among the 'exploiters'. In fact, it is thanks to low-cost imports that the level of consumer prices in advanced countries has practically stopped rising since the end of the last century and inflation no longer represents a substantial problem there. And the reduction of the price of many items of consumption is one of the mechanisms that – together with the development of credit and the increasing employment of women – has allowed the middle and lower classes in those countries to slightly improve or maintain their standards of consumption despite the stagnation or decrease in their monetary incomes.

Of course, the VA produced by the manufacturer in a GVC will tend to shrink simply as a consequence of technical progress: if freely available technology allows new, more efficient production methods or processes to be introduced, the working of competition will cause a reduction in the price of the good and in the VA of the manufacturing activity in the chain, without any manufacturer being 'exploited' as a consequence of that reduction.

One of the difficulties in the search for a notion of the real value of a good in the context of GVCs regards, in particular, the creation of value by the labour that materially manufactures a good or component or provides a service in the production cycle. What we know from a firm's accounts is simply the VA produced by each unit of labour it employs – which is measured by the wage the firm pays to the worker – but what we would like to know is whether this wage corresponds to the real contribution of the worker to the price of the final product sold to the consumer, or whether some part of that contribution is appropriated by other participants in the chain. Only in the first case would there be no exploitation of the worker and its wage could be defined as 'fair'. The problem then is to find a way to establish whether the wage paid to the worker is a fair one or not.

One criterion for the definition of the fair remuneration of the worker's contribution to the value of a good could be that referred to by Lewis (see Footnote 35 in Section 9.3.3) according to which a good's price should be such that the employment of a unit of labour of equal quality and productivity would be remunerated, in real terms, equally everywhere. If the same amount of labour gets a different remuneration in different countries, one might argue prima facie that in the international exchange of products some firms and countries are exploiting others (however, differences in the remuneration of equal factors in different countries may be required to compensate for general elements of inferiority of certain countries, such as a lower quality of physical and institutional infrastructure or higher transport costs owing to an unfavourable geographical position).[37] While for some factors, such as a firm's intangible assets, it is impossible or very difficult to make a comparison of remunerations in different countries, it would appear that for labour such a comparison can be made, although it would involve serious problems of conversion of currencies to a common unit and comparison of the cost of living in different countries (but, after all, MNCs do make such comparisons whenever they have to decide in which countries to locate production and other activities).

While the equal pay for equal work criterion may appear excessively demanding, it also appears hardly acceptable to apply the minimalistic criterion according to which the fair value of a good (or component or phase of production in a GVC) would correspond to the price of the good that would allow the producing firm to remunerate the factors that contribute to its production, and specifically labour, at the same rate as those factors are remunerated on average in its country (the criterion advocated by Tolles (1957) that is mentioned in Section 12.3.3). This is the criterion to which MNCs usually refer when, accused of exploiting local workers, they point out that in their factories located in developing countries, wages and working conditions are better than those currently provided by domestic firms (not to speak of those prevalent in the agricultural and the 'informal' sector of the economy, where a large part of the population is employed). It is, however, a criterion that simply refers to the traditional concept of value as measured by the market price (in this case the average market price of labour in each country), and provides no help in determining whether in a GVC part of the value produced by one participant is appropriated by another.

[37] Product prices ensuring equalization of the remuneration, in real terms, of identical workers in different countries may solve problems of fairness in international exchange, but they would still leave unsolved the problems of fairness in the ratios between the remunerations of labour and capital.

All this discussion will certainly remind the reader of the theory of unequal exchange based on good's labour content, discussed in Section 9.3.2; the issue is basically the same. Although that theory was dismissed as unconvincing because of the many problems it left unsolved, it must be recognized that the issue is a real and fundamental one, even if there appears to be no satisfactory solution for modern GVCs either.

The problem under discussion has an important connection with the concept of – and the policies leading to – economic upgrading, analysed at the end of Section 11.2.1. Two different, though strictly interconnected, aspects of economic upgrading were mentioned there. On the one hand, there is the effort to move to activities, stages of production, alternative GVCs, that provide a firm (or a country) with better opportunities to increase its technological know-how, its workers' skills, its organizational abilities, in the expectation that the higher productivity consequent on this effort will allow it to obtain a larger amount, or a superior qualitative/technological level, of products from the same resources and consequently a higher VA per unit of factors employed. On the other hand, there is the effort to prevent the increase in a firm's VA made possible by the higher level of productivity from simply being appropriated by the lead firms or other participants in the chain in the form of lower prices for the firm's products. Although firms' enhanced abilities connected with the first effort would probably also include superior strategic and bargaining skills, nothing guarantees that a firm that enters a new, higher-VA segment of GVC activity will not continue to see part of that VA captured by another participant in the chain. Coe and Yeung (2015) also underlined the possibility that upgrading processes present a zero-sum element: if a firm upgrades its activities, but all firms performing analogous activities also upgrade theirs, competition will probably erode any possibility for the firm to obtain VA gains from its upgrading efforts.

11.2.4 The determination of 'fair' labour remuneration

The space devoted to the problems connected with the identification of where, along the GVC, VA is actually 'created' is also justified by the fact that the general issue of determining where economic activities producing VA are precisely located has been brought to the centre of the international debate by the ambitious Base Erosion and Profit Shifting (BEPS) initiative in the field of corporate taxation launched by the OECD in 2013 (this is discussed in Section 12.3.4). Its purpose was to thoroughly reassess and harmonize the body of international tax laws to prevent MNCs' artificial profit shifting across affiliates located in different countries (that is, the practice of making profits produced by the activity in a high-tax country formally appear as produced by an affiliate located in a very low-tax country or in a tax haven, so that the profits would be taxed there); and also to establish common rules for the taxation of profits from digital services provided by MNCs. The immaterial and highly complex nature of networks and digital services based on them – plus the additional complication that a large part of the value of many of these services is created by the activity of, and the provision of information by, consumers themselves – makes it extremely difficult to identify the 'real' VA at different stages and locations of the production process, and consequently to determine the tax base for the taxation of corporate profits and the jurisdiction entitled to collect taxes.

While lack of consensus among the main countries compelled the OECD to partly scale down the initial plan of a basic reassessment of international corporate tax law, the organization did manage to convince the participants in the initiative (the OECD members and a large majority of developing countries) to accept the basic general principle it had proposed, namely that profits should be taxed 'where substantive activities generating the profits are carried out and where value is created' (OECD (2016), p.1). As a consequence, by a strange paradox, the issue of the determination of the 'value' of a good or service, which had been relegated to extremely complex theoretical discussions among a few left-wing economists, was suddenly brough to public attention by the BEPS initiative; the latter – triggered by a request by the G20 group of countries – was organized and managed by the tax experts of the OECD, an organization representing the advanced countries (and certainly attracted considerable interest from the tax law advisers of the world's top MNCs), probably not familiar with the intricacies of value theory.

By using the expression 'value creation' – which had been widely employed, mainly with reference to conventional VA, in GVC analysis – the OECD probably only wanted to refer to the need to put an end to MNCs' unacceptable practice of disguising profits clearly produced by activity in one country as produced in another low-tax country or a tax haven, where in fact neither physical nor immaterial activity was taking place. It employed the expression 'value creation' rather generically: its precise content was never clearly defined, and in practice different countries could give it the meaning that appeared most convenient to them.[38] Lennard (2018) was quite right to stress that:

> One risk of the current emphasis on "value creation" as the foundation stone of this new taxation edifice is that if there is no consensus on what it means, then any consensus based on the term will be seen through different lenses, with the consequent possibilities of an uncertain investment environment and double taxation or even double non-taxation. (p. 60)

What presumably was not anticipated by the OECD was that the introduction of the term 'value creation' as the central element of the whole initiative would give new life to that search for a concrete measurement of 'real VA' that had been recently pursued without practical results by the economists mentioned in Section 11.2.3.

[38] As Morse (2018) observed, 'Allocating taxation in accordance with value creation is meant to match tax jurisdiction with some "real" location of a corporation's activity. But this does not make the meaning of value creation clear. Value creation might refer, for example, to one or more of the following factors: employee location, sales location, location of production capacity, location of management or location where capital is raised. What value creation is *not* is more clear: income should not be allocated to a jurisdiction where a corporation has only a paper presence' (196).

The OECD, by reiterating the validity of the long-since-established 'arm's length principle' (according to which the products sold by one MNC's affiliate to another within a GVC or in any other intra-MNC transaction must be attributed, for taxation purposes, the market price the product would fetch if the same transaction were carried out between independent firms), indicated that it was simply seeking to reconstruct the conventional VA that would have been recorded at each step of a GVC if genuine market transactions had taken place. But in the course of the debates originated by the initiative, some new positions regarding the measurement of products' value emerged, stimulated by the analysis of the equity and justice aspects of the issue; and an interesting proposal was advanced to introduce a new concept of labour's fair value.

Another paradox is that this new line of research on value creation was not the product of the effort of economists, but mainly of philosophers and tax-law experts, two categories from which one would not expect significant contributions to the development of economic theorizing (but research and public debate on GVCs was also initiated not by economists, but by sociologists, geographers and industrial relations experts). Philosophers had conducted a heated debate on the issue of exploitation and its possible meanings and causes since the mid-2000s, when the phenomenon of developing countries' 'sweatshop factories' (that is, firms characterized by abysmally low wages and working conditions) were brought to public attention in advanced countries, particularly in the USA, by the media and by anti-sweatshop movements. The OECD initiative contributed to enlarging the debate on value creation, involving tax experts in it, and in recent years a large number of contributions have been devoted not only to the economic, but particularly the ethical aspects of the issue.

Christians (2018) attacked the notion that income should be taxed 'where value is created' as misleading and finally divisive: she observed that it wrongly conveys the idea that it is possible to precisely fragment geographically the final income obtained by the sale of a good produced by a GVC into the different values contributed by each firm, on the basis of neutral, merely 'scientific', criteria; so that each national jurisdiction can then tax the share of the good's final price assigned to its territory. Christians pointed out that such geographical fragmentation cannot be carried out on the basis of any objective or 'scientific' criteria, since the final income produced by the sale of the good produced by the chain is the result of a cooperative effort involving many complex interactions and interdependences among participating firms (this is a typical case of the value of a final product being higher than the sum of the value of the different components and activities contributing to its production). Instead, one should recognize that the criteria followed by different national tax authorities to divide among themselves, for taxation purposes, the income produced by the final good's sale are the result of political compromises, which have significant distributive effects (and which inevitably reflect differences in bargaining power).[39]

[39] Christians recalled that the four economists (Bruins, Einaudi, Seligman and Stamp (1923)) who produced in 1923 the report to the League of Nations on double taxation which set the basis for all sub-

Christians also noted that if, for purposes of taxation, the basis for the determination of where value is created in a GVC is the conventional VA (reflecting market prices) obtained by the participating countries, as proposed by the OECD, then the unfairness of the division between advanced and developing countries of the income obtained from the final sale of the goods would also apply to the division of the tax base between the tax authorities of the two groups of countries – most of the total VA continuing to accrue to the advanced countries providing the high-skill services upstream and downstream of physical manufacturing performed by developing ones.

In a subsequent article, Christians and van Apeldoorn (2018) – professors of Tax Law and Philosophy, respectively – taking as given the OECD core principle that countries should tax the income that can be attributed to them on the basis of value creation, have tackled the issue of distinguishing effective value creation from mere appropriation of value created by others. That distinction, they point out, hinges on the concept of a product's fair market value, and they note that in the course of the BEPS project, quite often reference had explicitly been made to the concept of 'fairness' in allocating corporate profits to different national jurisdictions for taxation purposes. They propose a new operative criterion for the definition of fair labour remuneration, which could be immediately and easily applied in practice for taxation purposes; and point out that if workers' activity in MNCs' affiliates located in developing countries were fairly remunerated, the price and the VA of the components produced – or of the production phases performed – by these countries would be much higher than those calculated on the basis of market wages and prices. Correspondingly, the tax bases to which each country hosting an affiliate of an MNC applies its tax rate would be much greater for the developing countries where the manufacturing or service-producing affiliates are located. In other words, if the market wages and prices are lower than the fair ones, the difference can be attributed to an unjust appropriation by one party of a share of the value created by another, that is to exploitation; and then, the OECD principle of allocating MNC profits among countries on the basis of the effective value creation requires that the value created by a country but appropriated by another, be assigned, for taxation purposes, to the first (even if its workers continue to be underpaid). In this way, at least, the government of the country where worker exploitation takes place would recover in the form of increased tax receipts part of the value that has been subtracted from its workers.

At this point, the problem would shift to the definition and calculation of the fair value of workers' activity to be compared with market wages effectively paid to them. To identify this fair value of labour, Christians and van Apeldoorn start from the observation that there is ample agreement by courts and law scholars on the fact that for a market transaction, and the price it leads to, to be proper or fair, certain conditions must be fulfilled: the parties to the transaction must not be 'related' (that

---

sequent developments in the field of international taxation, while underlining the need to share between countries the tax base produced by common economic activity by locating the source of the various income streams, were aware that this operation could not be carried out on the basis of scientific criteria and concluded that it would be largely a question of political feasibility.

is, must not belong to the same corporation or multinational group), must have adequate information on the facts regarding the transaction, must fix the price by negotiation and mutual agreement after ample time to find alternative counterparts and, most importantly, 'If coercive conditions exist such that one party or group systematically suffers a disadvantage against the other, it is clear to everyone that prices will not reflect market value' (p. 12): the requirement that parties must not be compelled to transact was discussed in Chapter 9 on economic power; it is the same principle that justifies antitrust authorities' intervention in the case of monopolies and represents the basis of labour law.

The two authors point out that basic United Nations' covenants on human rights voted for by practically all nations in the world establish the right of workers to wages and working conditions allowing them and their families to lead a dignified existence. They then define exploitation as follows:

> system-wide advantage-taking that occurs because workers are, within a given market, unable to command wages that would sustain their lives in accordance with what is generally accepted as their minimum or basic human right. Exploited workers may choose to accept work under such conditions, since all other alternatives may in fact be worse. However, their choice is compelled in the sense that they would not have accepted these conditions if their human right to a living wage had been fulfilled. (pp. 21–22).

In these situations market wages must be considered unfair; and the prices of goods produced by systematically exploited workers cannot be said to reflect fair market value.

The problem then hinges on the possibility of calculating, in different countries, the amount of the living wage (the wage allowing the satisfaction of essential needs). It may appear that such a calculation is an excessively complex and speculative exercise. But existing tax regulations already require firms belonging to an MNC group to routinely carry out much more complex and speculative exercises: for instance, when these firms are called on to apply the arm's length principle to transactions with related parties, they have to calculate what the market price of those transactions would be if the entities were independent parties; and these calculations often regard transactions for products or services for which no corresponding market transactions exist, but whose price must be abstractly constructed on the basis of complicated hypotheses. In the case of living wages, the data necessary for their calculation already exist. Two international organizations periodically provide measures of the living wage – defined as the wage sufficient to afford a decent standard of living – in different world locations (and these measures reveal that in low-income countries there is a very large gap in many industries between the prevailing wage and the one that should be paid if a living wage were to be ensured; for instance, in Dacca, Bangladesh, the first is only half the second for garment workers).

The notion of fair wage proposed by Christians and van Apeldoorn appears to be a reasonable and easily calculable one, providing, at least for the labour component, an acceptable notion of fair VA to be used for tax-base assessment purposes, and a more realistic alternative to the equal wage for equal work principle. It is based on the premise that work remuneration must everywhere allow a decent standard of living; but acknowledges that this minimum standard must not only satisfy essential biological needs (as is the case with the stricter notion of subsistence wage), but also includes some needs connected with the specific development stage and the particular features of each location (for a detailed description of how one of the available living wage indicators is calculated see R. Anker and M. Anker (2017)). Although devised to reach a better allocation of MNC groups' tax base, it may represent an interesting criterion for the measurement of the real value of the contribution of the workers in the different countries participating in a GVC (of course the problem would remain of evaluating the contribution of the owners of other factors of production, who may also be unfairly remunerated in GVCs because of a position of inferiority in bargaining with lead firms or other participants).

However, this notion seems unable to provide an answer to one objection (which also applies to many other situations when one tries to satisfy the UN human rights principle that workers' wages and work conditions must allow the worker to lead a dignified life). Frequently in developing countries, especially the poorest ones, because of adverse geophysical conditions and underdeveloped material, technological and institutional infrastructure, the productivity of economic activities (and often that of the individual workers themselves) is so low that, given the competition in the international market, these activities can only be carried out without losses by domestic or foreign firms if they pay wages and provide work conditions lower than those allowing workers a dignified life. The only choice confronting these countries then appears to be the one between producing in sub-human conditions or not producing at all. In this case, the purchasers of these poor countries' products do not seem to be unjustly appropriating part of any conceivable real value produced by the poor countries; the latter, rather than being the victim of exploitation, seem to suffer from their limited availability of resources or from their inability to extract from their resources the same real value obtained by their competitors, and therefore must compensate by a lower remuneration of their workers (and other factors of production) for other elements of inferiority of their economies (or a lower productivity – relative to some competitors' average – of the workers themselves).

Van Apeldoorn (2019) explicitly considers this possibility of employers being objectively unable to offer jobs at living wages, so that attempts to impose these wages by law would only damage a country's possibility of increasing, or even just maintaining, activity and employment; and defines this condition as 'structural exploitation' (since according to his definition exploitation takes place whenever workers are compelled to offer their labour at less than a living wage). When such a situation occurs, he argues that the human duty to provide assistance to people unable to secure for themselves a minimally decent existence creates an obligation on the part of advanced countries to transfer resources to poor countries so that the latter may guarantee their workers that basic human right. This position – like the one that bases the duty of advanced countries to transfer resources to poor ones on the obligation to compensate them for the damages produced by an unfair international economic order built and so far managed by advanced countries in their exclusive interest – is certainly defensible. But it seems to move the whole discussion of exploitation too much from the economic to the moral sphere to be of great help in the task of finding operative criteria for measuring unfair value capture among participants in GVCs.

In practice, however, much more frequent than the preceding case is the one where wages and work conditions in developing countries do not allow workers to lead a decent life, not because they or their economic systems are unable to produce, with wages fixed at a living wage, saleable goods for the international market; but only because the low bargaining power consequent on their abject poverty and lack of alternatives compels them to voluntarily accept a remuneration below the living wage to which they are entitled as a basic human right. These workers are capable of producing efficiently and do create value, but part of that value is unjustly appropriated by the purchasers of their products or services through unfairly low market prices, obtained by profiting from their pressing needs and/or by threatening to move production or shift orders to other, more compliant, locations and producers. This is the basic reason that leads van Apeldoorn to attack the OECD interpretation of the principle of taxing income where value creation takes place, which identifies the proper or fair value of a good or service with its arm's length market price: 'These workers capture too small a portion of the value in GVCs in the sense that they would have commanded higher prices had they been able to refuse to work on unjust terms' (2009, p. 174).

This last case (remunerations much lower than the real contribution of workers to value creation) also appears to apply to the majority of sweatshop enterprises typical of poor developing countries, which have reproposed the old dilemma that led J. Robinson (1962) to the paradoxical statement that 'the misery of being exploited by capitalists is nothing compared to the misery of not being exploited at all' (p. 45). Economists, overall, have not devoted much effort to analysing in depth the issue of sweatshops. With few exceptions, they have made little progress from the arguments of Krugman's article 'In Praise of Cheap Labor' (1997), taken up by Bhagwati (2004), Wolf (2004) and Powell (2014a, b), that poor countries' low productivity level – and not the alleged wickedness of MNCs – is the reason for the existence of sweatshop enterprises; and that MNCs in these countries provide greatly sought-after employment opportunities, contribute to economic growth and modernization – the only factors that in the final analysis allow the condition of extreme poverty to be overcome – and offer significantly better wages and work conditions than local firms; providing, in sum, jobs that represent a great improvement over alternatives available to workers. Krugman also observed – on the basis of arguments reminiscent of Lewis's – that even if campaigns in advanced countries in favour of decent wages and working conditions for the workers employed in sweatshops managed to achieve their goal, this would not change the miserable conditions of the majority of poor countries' populations, employed in subsistence agriculture and other low-productivity activities or unemployed; producing only a privileged aristocracy of workers employed by MNCs and their direct supplier firms, isolated from the rest of their fellow citizens.

Few dissenting voices have come from economists to contest these arguments, which pointed to the uselessness of anti-sweatshop campaigns conducted in advanced countries. Elliott and Freeman (2001) presented a balanced assessment of the results produced by these campaigns: though conscious of their limits and contradictions, these authors indicated some significant results that such campaigns had helped to achieve. Miller (2003) attacked Krugman's defence of sweatshops, stressing the fact that it was debated among economists whether the introduction in developing countries of some basic labour standards could really have the negative results on employment and export growth alleged by sweatshop supporters (the issue of what could be done to improve the conditions of sweatshop workers largely coincides with the one – which is the object of Section 12.3.3 – regarding the desirability of introducing international labour standards); and that the empirical evidence for the apparel industry in poor countries showed that the introduction of living wages would not produce cost increases for final products such as to lead to reductions in the level of worker employment. C. Barry and Reddy (2006) stressed instead the fact that the apparently inescapable dilemma between sweatshops' miserable conditions and the advantages of increased employment and export and growth opportunities that they produced could be overcome by changes in international trade rules. These rules should be reformed so as to reward the developing countries that introduce improvements in basic labour standards – and to penalize with exclusion from preferential treatment and other trade benefits those that continue to violate them – so as to eliminate the competitive advantage produced by the maintenance of shameful work conditions. The idea was further developed and revamped in C. Barry and Reddy (2008), where they presented a well-articulated framework (described in Section 12.3.3) that takes into account specific objections advanced by critics against a project of 'unimposed' linkage between higher labour standards and trade – plus financial – benefits.

It is instead among philosophers that since the mid-2000s the issue of the miserably low wages and working conditions of workers in developing countries has given rise to a heated debate and a large number of academic contributions on the moral acceptability of the phenomenon of sweatshop enterprises and more generally on the concepts of worker exploitation and 'voluntary' transactions. This interest on the part of philosophers has certainly been greatly stimulated – apart from the crucial relevance in today's world of the problems connected with poor countries' industrialization and development and the large space that the media have devoted to the appalling conditions of sweatshops in poor countries – by the peculiar, contradictory nature of the sweatshop phenomenon. A phenomenon that appears to – and in many ways does – represent unfair or evil behaviour towards other human beings, but at the same time is considered beneficial by – and produces effective improvements for – these same beings (the apparent need, in other words, to do bad in order to do good), provides the best raw material for analyses and ethical debates a philosopher could dream of.[40] As these contributions cannot be discussed here, only some hints of their contents will be given.

[40] Incidentally, in a recent contribution Carabelli (2021) discusses Keynes's methodological approach to the process of economic policy decisions, including those involving 'tragic dilemmas'.

A useful general analysis of the main concepts of exploitation (a term generally identified with some notion of taking unfair advantage) that have been proposed is provided by Ferguson (2018); see also surveys by Snyder (2010) and Zwolinski and Wertheimer (2016). Most of these concepts have been developed in opposition to the laissez-faire approach to economic power that characterized economists from the 1870s onwards and reproposed more recently by some strongly pro-market-choice philosophers (a basic contribution being that of Zwolinski (2007)), providing arguments against anti-sweatshop campaigns. These pro-market philosophers do not see anything morally wrong in voluntary labour market transactions (defined as transactions between uncoerced informed parties, where coercion only refers to threats of immediate wrongful harm), whatever their conditions, on the basis of the argument that if a firm abstained from entering the transaction, the worker would lose the opportunity to obtain a job that he considers as producing superior benefits relative to any available alternative. At the same time, the respect for individuals' autonomy and liberty, which find their expression in labour market choices (including the worker's choice of giving up basic worker rights or accepting unsafe jobs), even when these choices are severely restricted by economic necessity, leads pro-market philosophers, as a rule, to consider it impermissible for the law to introduce legal prohibition of contracts for sweatshop labour.

Unfairness or exploitation has been identified either with worker remuneration that implies an 'unequal' division of the mutual gains obtained by the combination of labour with the firm's capital, or with a remuneration lower than a given absolute measure (such as a living wage, covering the worker's basic needs). The unequal division, in turn, can be identified with reference to the difference in labour content of what is exchanged, in the tradition of Smith and Marx; or with an unfair division of the total 'consumer's surplus' the parties derive from the exchange; while Wertheimer (1996) identified it in a wage different from the one the worker would have received in a hypothetical fair market environment (defined as one where the parties to a transaction are 'informed and unpressured'). Wertheimer's criterion, while acceptable in theory, is not of great help in practice, as the fair market value may either refer to the theoretical market price of perfect competition, in which case there would be no problem of a division of gains from the exchange (as every party would simply have to accept the market price identified by the point of intersection between the market's demand and offer curves); or to the actual market price in the absence of unfair circumstances, which would raise the problem of agreeing on the meaning of this last expression once again.

Some authors have connected exploitation with the notion of taking advantage of past injustice, which places the worker or a poor country in a position of vulnerability that greatly reduces their bargaining power. The term 'previous injustice' can be interpreted more or less extensively. It can lead to the concept of 'structural injustice' or unfair background conditions, which can be referred to the past evolution of property rights, the structure of the world trading system or the effects of colonial history. While these past developments can be the basic reason for the present vulnerabilities of countries and individuals, there is a problem of establishing how far back in history one can go to identify past injustices and which, among the innumerable injustices that have taken place in the past, can be objectively considered as important to explain present conditions of worker and country vulnerability.

The concept of the living wage as a fair remuneration has been based instead on the notion of the general duty of people to respect the dignity of other human beings and their basic human right to a decent standard of living, and not take advantage of vulnerability that is caused by their lack of better opportunities. Alternatively, it has been based on the concept of treating other people as ends and not as merely means; or on a general duty of beneficence, or solidarity towards other human beings unable to cover their basic needs, which requires – whenever it is reasonably possible – altering the terms of exchange so as to help them to reach that minimum level of needs satisfaction. However, it can happen – as pointed out earlier in this section – that the living wage may be too high for a firm to obtain any gain from hiring a worker; while, on the other hand, the contribution of a worker may be so great that simply paying him the living wage would be clearly unfair and exploitative.

12 The Emergence of New Industrial Competitors and Advanced Countries' Response

12.1 China's (and other developing countries') economic success

In the post-war period until the 1980s, among countries with significantly large populations, only Japan, Italy and Spain managed to join the group of industrially advanced Western countries. By the 1980s, some new manufacturing exporters had appeared in East Asia – South Korea and two small economies, Taiwan and Hong Kong – challenging the advanced countries' industrial monopoly, but their weight was too small to make any substantial difference to the overall structure of the international division of labour. The picture changed dramatically from the 1990s onwards, with the emergence of a huge new manufacturing exporter, China, and a huge new services exporter, India, while some other large developing countries – such as Brazil, Mexico, Turkey and South Africa – became important new manufacturing centres (see Nayyar (2013) on developing countries' catch-up).

The Chinese growth record has been spectacular: from 1978, when a new outward-oriented economic and political strategy was introduced, until 2019, its average yearly growth rate was about 9.5 per cent; only in three years, all before 1991, did it go below 6 per cent, the figure it has been converging onto, from 10.6 per cent in 2010, in the following decade of unavoidably lower rates. In per capita terms the average annual growth was around 8.4 per cent; so that with a population that increased only from 972 million in 1978 to 1,434 million in 2019 (from about 22.6 to 18.4 per cent of the world population), its share of world GDP (calculated at purchasing power parity) went from about 2.3 per cent in 1990 to more than 17 per cent in 2019. China's share of world exports of goods, less than 1 per cent in the late 1970s and still insignificant (2.5 per cent) in 1993, reached 13.6 per cent in 2020: see Coase and Wang (2013) for very interesting observations on China's economic reform and the strategy followed by the Chinese leaders that made such a performance possible; the 40-year developments in China's trade, foreign investments and global production sharing have been analysed by Ju and Yu (2018).

The Chinese economic success is without precedent in history: for the first time, a country of huge territorial and demographic size – and, moreover, subjected for more than a century, despite formal independence, to colonial domination and exploitation, and then for thirty years to a communist experience that ended in disaster – managed, in just a few decades, to get out of underdevelopment (at least in most of its regions). It seems to represent the fulfilment of the forecast advanced a century ago, with incredible clairvoyance, by the theorist of imperialism Hobson:

> It is at least conceivable that China might so turn the tables upon Western industrial nations, and, either by adopting their capital and organizers or, as is more probable, by substituting her own, might flood their markets with her cheaper manufactures, and refusing their imports in exchange might take her payment in liens upon their capital, reversing the earlier process of investment until she gradually obtained financial control over her quondam patrons and civilizers. (1938 [1902], pp. 329–330)

In the last hundred years, the only other attempts at a comparable project of overcoming underdevelopment were those of China itself under Mao in the thirty years after the 1949 success of the communist revolution and of the Soviet Union after the Revolution of 1917. The former ended with the Cultural Revolution that raged from 1966 to 1976, causing the paralysis of the state organization and of the economy, severe damage to the country's infrastructure and productive apparatus and the killing of from 0.5 to 2 million people.[1] The Soviet Union's experience, after raising high expectations of successful industrialization given the exceptional progress achieved between the 1930s and the 1960s, also ended up in – happily enough, bloodless – failure. And the new Russia also proved unable in the decades following the transition to a capitalist economy to produce a major transformation and modernization of its productive structure: neither a modern agriculture, nor any advanced non-military industrial or service sector competitive at international level emerged; although the extremely favourable evolution of the price of raw materials on which the economy continued to be based allowed a significant (but extremely unequal) improvement in the standard of living of its population.[2]

[1] Despite this final conclusion, some aspects of the communist experience between 1949 and 1966 seem to have contributed to the establishment of the preconditions that allowed the successful implementation after 1978 of economic reforms. Jacques (2009), after recalling that under Mao China achieved an impressive growth rate (of 4.4 per cent per year in 1950–1980, more than doubling GDP per capita), argued that during the first phase of communist government the groundwork was laid for industrialization and modernization, and that social advancement was even more outstanding. Spence (2011) pointed out that 'China, turned to communism … perhaps sowed the seeds of its future rise by educating the vast majority of its people' (p. 29) and 'swept away residual elements of class and caste dating back to the days of the empire and transitional republic … eliminating concentrated ownership of land and other assets … That made it unlikely that policy would be dominated by formerly wealthy special interests' (p. 107). And Coase and Wang (2013) recalled that 'To its credit, a revisionist view has brought to light the hidden or overshadowed continuity between Mao's economy and post-Mao reform. By this process, China's economic achievements during Mao's era have been duly recognized' (p. 6). As stressed by Daokui Li (2019), between 1949 and 1979 progress in education and infrastructure allowed Chinese life expectancy to go from 35 to 66 years, adult illiteracy from 80 per cent to 23 per cent and gender equality was achieved in elementary education (see also the synthetic assessment of the 1949–1976 economic experience in Brandt, Ma and Rawski (2014), a work identifying the characteristics of Chinese society that have shaped the evolution of its economy from the 14th century to present times).

[2] The failure of the new Russia's economic modernization, just as its failure to establish a truly democratic political regime, stemmed largely from the chaotic way in which the transition from communism to capitalism was organized and carried out in the very first post-Soviet years after 1991 by the

A direct comparison of the paths towards a capitalist economy followed by China and Russia cannot be made given the great differences between the two countries'

---

new Russian political rulers, whose paramount objective was the quick and definitive elimination of the Soviet economic and political system. Both they and their domestic economic experts had no experience, and most of them not even an idea, of what a capitalist economy implies. And they had to manage the transition in desperate circumstances, when the country and its strongly centralized economy had just been dismembered into a number of separate independent nations and all its financial resources had been exhausted (while the country was burdened with a massive foreign debt vis-à-vis Western countries).

But a major role in leading the new rulers to a disorderly transition path that jeopardized the subsequent process aimed at economic modernization seems to have been played by Western economic advisors (both individual economists and international economic institutions) to whom, in their desperate situation – and contrary to the policy followed by Chinese leaders – the new rulers turned for guidance and advice. Those were the years in which many economists and the most influential international economic institutions had become uncritical advocates of the ultra-liberal policies of the Washington Consensus. And although they had little or no direct experience of how the Soviet society and its economic system worked in practice, foreign advisers – the most influential ones acting in the ambiguous guise of transactors representing at the same time, in a confusion of roles, the US government, the Russian authorities and private interests, as highlighted by Wedel and S. Chandra (2004) – managed to convince the new Russian rulers to follow their prescriptions, which were the same for all countries in the world irrespective of local conditions and especially of national histories and traditions. These prescriptions were formulated and implemented without considering the critically important timing and sequencing of steps in their adoption; and played down the importance of the many elements (first of all the existence of a state capable of ensuring the rule of law) that are a condition for a market system to work.

Apart from the very severe physical sufferings of the population in the first reform period (testified by a drastic fall in life expectancy such as seems never to have taken place in peacetime in an industrialized country in the last eighty years) and the psychological shock of seeing their once powerful and respected country dismembered and humiliated at international level (the indelible memory of that humiliation largely explains the Russians' support for Putin's ultra-nationalistic policies in later years), the most serious negative result was that the implementation of the programme of fast privatization of almost all Soviet firms that the authorities were led to adopt turned into what is probably the greatest robbery ever recorded in history.

In a few years, a small number of 'oligarchs' managed to get hold of a large part of the nation's precious natural resources and of the economic wealth accumulated during decades of work by Soviet citizens, a development that would negatively condition the whole subsequent evolution of the Russian economy and society. A highly critical judgement of the Russian 'shock treatment' transition strategy was expressed at the time, among others, by Bhagwati (1994) and Murrell (1995); see the later contributions by Black, Kraakman and Tarassova (2000), Stiglitz (2002), Desai (2005) and, for an opposite view, Zhuravskaya (2007); for a more general recent assessment of the Russian economic transition and differences compared with that of China see Guriev (2019).

As for the political leaders of Western countries (the USA in particular), they probably understood that a different economic course had to be followed if the Russian economy was to move towards effective, sustainable capitalist growth and modernization, a course that required as an essential pre-condition, given the conditions of the new Russia, a massive Western initiative of financial and technical assistance on a scale not inferior to that of the US post-war Marshall Plan for Europe. But at that moment, the most urgent priority of Western policy seems to have been to get rid once and for all of the threat of a militarily and politically powerful Russia that might, after all, revert to some kind of Soviet regime. And, as the Chinese experience was to confirm, it is difficult to contribute to an independent country's effort to build a strong, dynamic economy without that effort also leading to an increase in the country's political and military power.

situations. But it must be stressed that from 1978 Chinese rulers – by contrast with those of post-Soviet Russia, who hastily imposed from above a model of capitalism imported from abroad – followed a home-made strategy based on the gradual and carefully sequenced introduction of reforms adapted to their specific national conditions, which were first experimented in limited areas and, if successful, extended to the whole country (see Lin (2012) and, especially, Coase and Wang (2013)).

What has made the progress of China (and, looking ahead, of India) so important for the world is the country's gigantic size. China is the most populated country in the world (India is now almost on a par with it; together, the two countries represent 36 per cent of the world population); the reduction, already indicated, in the Chinese percentage of the world population from 1978 to 2019 was the result of the drastic lowering of the birth rate per woman produced by the exceptional progress in the standard of living and by the measures of birth control introduced by the government since 1973.[3] Given China's size, while the economic success of any other country (apart from India) could only marginally or modestly affect the rest of the world – as happened in the recent past with the 'Asian tigers' – China's success has inevitably produced a fundamental change in the very structure of the world economy. Even if the Chinese success were an exception among developing countries (which it is not,

[3] The importance for population growth containment of the Chinese authorities' switch in 1979 from a policy of birth control on a voluntary base to a strict compulsory one-child policy – quite apart from its other negative consequences, illustrated by Fong (2016) – is denied or minimized by some observers (see Zhang (2017)); but it seems that the new policy did contribute to facilitate the attainment of the exceptional per capita GDP growth in the following decades (see Wei (2015)).

In the light of the very serious problems that the past rapid decrease in population growth is now creating, and will continue to create, for the Chinese economy (the main one being the aging of the population, producing a drastic reduction of the percentage represented by people of working age), it may be concluded that policies of birth control in poor developing countries are not a good recipe for long-term economic development. This conclusion would ignore – or at least unjustifiably play down – the most critical problem for poor countries trying to get out of the vicious circle of underdevelopment through a self-sustaining process of rapid industrialization. The greatest difficulty faced by these countries is the initial effort required to trigger the process and ensure its advancement in the initial phases. As a large number of obstacles have to be overcome to this end, it is extremely helpful if the country can avoid the additional burden of a difficult demographic situation in which a considerable part of the available resources must be allocated to the maintenance and education of a large number of young children. The Chinese economy did actually take advantage during the critical industrial take-off period from the very favourable age structure of its population obtained by the reduction in birth rates. Since with the passage of time this favourable demographic situation is inevitably reversing, serious negative effects will in all probability ensue for the future growth rates of the economy. But the problems that will be created by a possibly drastic growth reduction will then regard a population that will have come out of the state of dire poverty, managed to build its basic infrastructure and reached relatively high levels of basic and higher education, so that it will suffer much less from lower growth rates than an economy at subsistence levels. Of course, to the preceding economic argument in favour of birth control, the moral one can be added concerning the desirability of giving birth to a large number of children many of whom would be condemned to hunger, illness and death in their infancy by their parents' and the country's lack of resources.

An interesting analysis of past and future Chinese development – and connected problems for advanced countries – in terms of demographics has been advanced by Goodhart and Pradhan (2017).

given the economic performance of India and other important economies), it would not represent a case of 'exception confirming the rule' but rather of 'exception making the rule'.

One factor that largely explains China's success is the relatively high and unexpected level of efficiency, honesty, organizational ability, careful choice of strategies and priorities, and highly pragmatic approach that, on the whole, the economic leaders of China, totally lacking experience of the working of a capitalist system, showed in managing the transition to a market economy. It is a fact that some serious mistakes were made; that changes in the course of reform were at times imposed by new or previously not recognized circumstances; and, most importantly, that – as argued by Coase and Wang (2013) – some fundamental steps to a market economy took place as a result of developments that leaders had not expected or had even expressly declared they wanted to avoid; while on a couple of major occasions when the whole progress of reform risked being reversed, only a lucky coincidence of circumstances seems to have saved it. Still, results showed that Chinese leaders proved surprisingly right in most of their decisions; and, more importantly, when this was not the case, they freely discussed (within the ruling group) possible alternative strategies, allowing even strongly dissenting opinions to be expressed and following the principle of choosing the final course of action on the basis of factual evidence.[4]

Of course, it was the strict control of the country and its population that they maintained through monopoly of political power and at times drastic use of repressive measures, which allowed them to obtain from the Chinese masses – in exchange for the tangible, unexpected, exceptional improvements in living standards and the new position of power and prestige the country visibly reached at international level – substantial acceptance of the political limitations they imposed and support for their reform measures. It is an 'implicit contract' that may, however, prove dangerous in the future for Chinese rulers, as other priorities (in the first place ecological ones, of which they seem to have recently become conscious) or unforeseen circumstances may impose a change to the 'growth at any cost' policy followed until now. Not to speak of the possibility that totally new developments (such as technological innovations allowing manufacturing production to take place anywhere in the world at very low cost) may threaten the very role of China as the 'factory of the world' on which the whole Chinese development strategy has so far been based.

Chinese, Indian and some other developing countries' fast growth in the last three-four decades has produced at world level the greatest income redistribution

---

[4] The ability of Chinese leaders was greatly underestimated by most Western observers and economists. In particular, the superficiality of the majority of US assessments of Chinese economic developments was at a similar level to that shown in the case of the Russian transition to capitalism. Autor, Dorn and Hanson (2016, p. 4) mention how, just before the Chinese export offensive on Western markets began, the forecast for the following 25 years of the *Wall Street Journal* of 23 June 1989 placed China among the growth-laggard developing economies, pointing to the 'stultifying bureaucracy of hard-line communism'. It is no wonder that US. economists and politicians were caught unprepared when, in the course of the 1990s, Chinese goods started flooding the US market.

ever experienced, apart from the one that took place as a consequence of Western countries' Industrial Revolution, which, in the course of a much longer period, created income gaps between developed and underdeveloped countries that progressively widened until three-four decades ago. For the first time, a substantial part of the world population was taken out of the most abject poverty: some 450 million people in China and India in 25 years according to Little (2008) and some 650 million in 'upper-middle-income' countries around the world in just about 25 years according to Baldwin (2016), while Stiglitz (2019) advances the figure of more than 740 million in China alone in 40 years. In addition, countries that, even after gaining full independence from colonial powers, had no voice at international level because of their economic and cultural underdevelopment – although many of them had given a large contribution to civilization in the past – have become important protagonists on the international scene, regaining political weight and taking an active part in international organizations and other fora where previously decisions of basic interest for the entire world were exclusively taken by a small number of advanced countries.

It is a fact that to a large extent this extraordinary economic progress has not taken place in the conditions of political freedom, improved domestic income distribution and generalized social progress one might have hoped for or reasonably have expected on the basis of the experience of Western countries, where economic development was accompanied, at least in the long run (but, for colonial powers, only for the citizens of the mother country), by significant political and social advancement. Still, it is an achievement that should have been welcomed in advanced countries as it represents a key step on the road to the fulfilment of a goal that for more than a century was shared in the West by the working class movements and by most other sectors of the population.[5] The former had steadfastly called for improvements in the conditions of workers in all parts of the world and for the end of colonialism, imperialism and economic exploitation of the Third World; the latter had also found it increasingly unacceptable that there was a growing gap between a small part of the world where a decent standard of living was assured and a much larger part where people continued to live in conditions of abject poverty, both shameful and dangerous.

As for the danger that abject poverty represents in our times, one has just to look at the intolerance, fanaticism and even terrorism to which economic frustration has led in some regions of the Islamic world, or to the devastating effects of disorderly migration from poor countries in terms of resurgence of racism and xenophobia in advanced countries – in both cases a consequence of the failure of national economic policies of a number of developing countries to produce significant improvement of living conditions – to imagine the nightmarish situation in which we would find ourselves today if giants such as China and India, with their much larger populations, geographical dimensions and armaments, had not managed to emerge – or, in the

[5] Samuelson (2004) observed that even if the spread of knowledge across national boundaries were to eliminate (à la Keynes-Robertson) comparative advantages and trade, this would be the consequence of such a positive development that 'humanity ought to deem such a result to be good rather than bad, even if it exacts some price from the erstwhile most productive geographical place' (p. 142).

Indian case, at least to provide first signs and well-founded expectations of approaching emergence – from their condition of deep underdevelopment.

12.2 Advanced countries' reaction

Quite surprisingly, the economic progress of successful developing countries – of China in particular – has instead been predominantly met in advanced countries only with fear and anxiety. That progress basically reflects the West's loss of the world monopoly of capital, knowledge, technology, specialized skills and education (especially higher education), which made it possible for industrial countries to dominate the world economically, politically and militarily for a long period; it also reflects the fact that where advanced countries managed to keep part of this monopoly, the technological advances in transport and communication allowed their major enterprises to associate it with the 'unlimited supplies of labour' of developing countries. The Western monopoly had been established in the Industrial Revolution, but in fact had its origins in the European technological and economic superiority connected with the scientific revolution of the late 15th to 17th centuries. The loss of this monopoly unavoidably implied for its population a reduction of benefits and significant costs of adjustment to the new situation. And the loss of privileges derived from rents and monopolies (whether justified or not) and of the connected leading positions at world level has seldom been accepted by the losers without bitterness and resentment.

Another feature of recent developing countries' industrial progress that has contributed to this negative reaction of both people and the media in advanced countries has been stressed by Palley (2018). Rejecting the traditional reference to a first 1870–1914 globalization and a second one still under way, which started after World War II and accelerated from the 1990s, he identifies a specific 'third globalization' that took place in the latter period, after the second ended in the 1980s. The first two globalizations were aimed at increasing international trade so as to reap the benefits of larger outlets and specialization, producing significant improvements for the workers in advanced countries. The trade benefits were basically connected, in the first case, with the opening of new markets for the agricultural products and raw materials of emerging overseas economies, exchanged against European manufactures, thanks to improved and cheaper transport technology; in the second, they stemmed mainly from the large increase in intra-industry trade among advanced countries. By contrast, the globalization that started in the 1990s was driven by a process of relocation of a large part of the advanced world's – especially the USA's – industrial apparatus to developing countries. It was stimulated by MNCs' search for the higher profits obtainable by associating their capital, technology and specialized skills with the low-cost labour supply of developing countries. Increased trade was simply the consequence of this relocation, which, together with the threat of further offshoring and automation, made it possible for large industrial Western firms to drastically reduce the number of industrial workers and, especially, the bargaining power of domestic workers; as testified by the large decrease of labour's share of national income to the advantage of capital.

Still, it has been amazing to see how the West's negative reaction to developing countries' advancement confirmed the definitive loss, after the campaigns against the war in Vietnam and apartheid in South Africa, of the last shreds of the spirit of international solidarity of the peoples, and specifically the working classes, of Western countries;[6] and represented the refusal to acknowledge that China (as some other emerging economic powers) has simply started to regain the position to which it was destined by its demographic and geographical size and by its exceptional economic and technological advances in the centuries preceding the European scientific revolution. Economists, too, largely concentrated their debates about the rise of new industrial powers on the negative consequences for developed countries' workers, devoting much less attention to underlining and discussing the importance and the effects of this development for the workers of emerging countries.

Faced with this epochal transformation of the world economy, many observers in advanced countries have directed their attention to points of secondary importance, typically noting how the penetration of Chinese goods in their countries, particularly in its early phases, involved mass-marketed low-price low-quality goods frequently drawing advantage from unfair or even illegal practices, such as imitating and counterfeiting Western products or producing them with little respect for technological patents and copyrights, and in some cases outright smuggling. Forgetting the fact that – as highlighted in an interesting article written by Rapp (1975) well before the new Chinese export strategy took form – this is the typical aggressive competition strategy followed by economic latecomers to penetrate markets exclusively dominated by well-known high-quality long-since-established producers; as happened in the first half of the 17th century with northern – specifically English – competition in manufactures at the expense of the then leading manufacturing power, Mediterra-

[6] Mason (2015), Walzer (2018) and Milanovic (2019) recall the likely reasons for this development. Walzer reminds us of Marx's mistakes in assuming that 'workers have no country' and that they share the same material interest in the overthrow of capitalism, of whose exploitation they are all victims. In fact workers demonstrated very strong national loyalties. And their material interests proved to be all but coincident, so that the only possible basis for international solidarity could be a moral duty to help other people undergoing oppression, sufferance and deprivation. But with the spread in all the capitalistic world of the mass consumption individualistic model and ideology, moral arguments are not going to produce much effective action. Mason recalls another of Marx's mistakes: the presumption that the working masses were longing for revolutionary action to overthrow the capitalist system; while they demonstrated that what they were really pursuing was simply a more survivable form of capitalism, which in the West they managed to obtain. Milanovic, pointing to the movement away from uniform economic conditions among poor people regardless of nation – which took place from the second half of the 19th century – stresses in particular the rise in the West of a strong welfare state, which appears increasingly unsustainable in the face of developing countries' trade competition and large immigration flows. To these reasons, one can add the shameful end in 1989–1991 of the Soviet Union (and its communist satellites), which had always claimed to be the upholder of workers' international solidarity (all too often only to mask under that label the reality of imperialistic interventions abroad).

nean Venice.[7] Morris (2012) pointed out the similarity between contemporary Chinese practices and those followed by the USA in the 19th century to catch up with British technology. While Brunnermeier, Doshi and H. James (2018), recalling that all latecomers managed to close the 'technology gap' by a mixture of theft, imitation and investment in education and basic science, have drawn an impressive parallel between today's Chinese-American economic competition (and the American reaction to it) and that which occurred at the end of the 19th century between the old dominating power, Britain, and the new rising power, Germany.

In historical perspective, the shock of China's and other developing countries' entrance as major protagonists onto the world economic stage, and of the economic dislocations associated with this development, seems to have been absorbed by advanced countries without excessively traumatic effects (just compare them with the effects of Germany's emergence as an industrial power and its catch-up with European leading economies, which largely contributed to originate the two world wars). Even the outburst of the 2008 global crisis did not produce significant protectionist measures. In most of the advanced countries, the already modest growth rates only temporarily turned negative, and when this happened it was in essence the effect of the crisis. The latter was largely produced by domestic factors in the USA, and can only indirectly be related to the radical changes that took place in the international division of labour. It was only in 2018, when the crisis had long since been overcome in the USA, that President Trump started his protectionist offensive against China.

* * *

Some factors can help to explain, though not to justify, the negative reaction of developed countries to the advance of China and other developing countries.

That advance was characterized by surprising speed: just consider that the Chinese share of world manufacturing exports, after only marginally increasing from 1.2 to 1.9 per cent between 1984 and 1990, sped up in the following years, reaching 18.8 per cent in 2013. Most of the advanced countries, as already pointed out, were very

[7] Rapp argued that it was aggressive competition in the European and Near-Eastern established markets, and not proximity to the new overseas Atlantic ones, that explains the manufacturing success of North-West Europe and the corresponding decline of the previously dominant Mediterranean centres: 'all the competitive characteristics of the industrial exports brought to the Levantine market by North Atlantic producers (led by England) in the first half of the seventeenth century were designed … to supplant the preexisting southern merchandise. To overcome the Italian industrial hegemony a consistent policy of cutthroat pricing was employed. This was made possible by the lower cost of labor in the developing North, by an absence of ingrained, restrictive practices, and by state support (rather than heavy taxation) of exports. Further, a "new retailing" emerged. The new competitors recognized the virtues of selling cheap and to accomplish this old ideas about quality went by the boards. The result was a range of vastly cheaper products for sale in the South. In order to insure that these goods would compete fully with southern manufactures northern producers faithfully imitated the style and brand markings of goods that were well-established in the marketplace, to the extent that this could be done without added cost. Counterfeit and smuggling went hand in hand with these practices. This combination of tactics bears strong resemblance to other historical instances of trade rivalry…' (1975, p. 521).

slow to understand the significance of the change that was taking place and consequently the need to adopt economic measures to minimize the harmful effects of the newcomers' export activity (and to explain to their own populations that after five centuries of Western countries' colonial rule and two centuries of industrial predominance over developing countries, things were at last rapidly changing).

Apart from an attitude of ignoring problems because of political idleness and limited intellectual ability, a major contribution to this result came from the uncritical stance of most economists and politicians towards offshoring and globalization and their possible negative effects; an attitude that had its roots in the traditional, almost religious, reverence of economists for the free trade principle, but also reflected the success of the massive ideological offensive of ultra-liberalists who managed to spread the gospel of the Washington Consensus, illustrating the wonders that would be produced by totally free movement of goods and capital in the new globalized economy. At the same time, the adoption of serious measures helping the workers damaged by offshoring and trade to cushion the shock found an obstacle in the unwillingness of the main beneficiary of the new developments, big business, and of the wealthiest part of the population, to contribute to the additional public expenditure these measures would have required.

As regards the speed of change produced by innovations, Baldwin (2016) recalled the striking difference between the few decades it took for the ICT revolution to go from the first inventions in the 1960s–1980s on which it was based to their applications to practically all productive sectors and for their spread to the whole world between the 1990s and the 2000s, and the corresponding time it took the previous great technological revolution, that of the steam engine, to apply to a large number of sectors (railways, in the first place) and to reach all countries. The first steam engine in commercial use – for pumping water out of coal mines – appeared in 1712, the first working steam locomotive in 1804; the big advances in land and sea steam transport started in the 1820s–1840s and continued, reaching almost all countries, in the course of that century. The acceleration in the production of technological innovations and in the changes they produce in both connected and different fields has also been underlined by Friedman (2016).

It also seems that in many advanced countries the effects of the abolition of obstacles to imports from developing countries agreed at international level were seriously underestimated (in large part because few anticipated the ability of Chinese producers to export), [8] so that significant measures to prevent disruptions and hardship for

[8] Stiglitz (2019, p. 80), while observing that in the international trade negotiations of the late 20th. century "...the global rules of the game were tilted – not against, but in *favor* of the United States and other advanced countries at the expense of developing countries... we secured strong intellectual property protections... We've succeeded in forcing countries to open up their markets to our financial forms...", argues that "It's true that American workers have been disadvantaged... But that is partly because American negotiators got what they asked for: the problem was with how we managed globalization and with what we wanted – trade agreements simply advanced corporate interests at the expense of workers in both developed and developing countries." (those were the years in which big American

the damaged parties were not adopted. In this respect, it can be recalled that Adam Smith himself had warned of the danger of over-fast trade liberalization:

> Humanity may … require that the freedom of trade should be restored only by slow graduations, and with a good deal of reserve and circumspection. Were those high duties and prohibitions taken away all at once, cheaper foreign goods of the same kind might be poured so fast into the home market, as to deprive all at once many thousands of our people of their ordinary employment and means of subsistence. The disorder which this would occasion might no doubt be very considerable. (1961, Book IV, Ch. II, p. 491).

More recently it was another free-trade advocate, H. G. Johnson (1973), who warned:

> If the advanced countries are effectively to open their markets to imports from the less developed countries, it will be necessary for them to devise both domestic adjustment assistance programs and safeguards against disruption of domestic markets, production and employment by too-rapid acceleration of specific categories of exports from the less developed countries. Both are necessary and complementary… (p. 48)

Resorting to adjustment assistance alone, he observed, would unjustly put the whole burden of compensating the victims of changes in comparative costs on the shoulders of importing countries only.

What seriously worsened the situation in advanced countries, contributing to the delay in both the recognition of the problem and the adoption of measures to minimize its effects, was the fact that offshoring to and massive imports from the new super-exporters coincided in time with (indeed were, as indicated in Section 11.1.2, strictly interconnected with) the ICT revolution. It was thus quite hard to understand whether the difficulties faced by advanced countries with reference to less-skilled workers' wages and jobs were a product of automation and technological innovation or of new countries' trade competition. In any case, the adoption of measures often found obstacles in the difficulty of predisposing specific programmes of sectoral change and restructuring economic activities, as innovations and technological progress have proved to be increasingly unforeseeable, often producing their most important effects in sectors apparently very distant from those where they initially take place;[9] while international trade changes also depend on the different development abilities of an increasing number of countries that have entered the international market. These abilities to become – or resume after a period of decline the role of – major players in the world economy

corporations, having experienced the advantages of offshoring, pressed for the rapid elimination of all restrictions on international investment and trade).

[9] However, as Stiglitz (2019) observes with reference to the neoliberal opposition to industrial policy based on the argument that 'governments shouldn't pick winners', 'the reality is that every successful country has had an industrial policy: much of the US's policy was embedded in the Defense Department … In any case, all governments have to make long-term decisions about designing education systems and infrastructure, and these have to be based on a vision of where the country is going' (p. 336).

depend on the convergence, at times merely random but always hardly foreseeable, of economic, political, social and natural circumstances.

* * *

In China's case, a number of considerations suggest that the largest part of the shock to advanced countries inevitably produced by its exceptional growth performance and massive and rapid entrance on the international trade scene, may be already behind us.

In the first place, as indicated in previous chapters, up to the 1980s Western countries were isolated from the huge masses of people in the rest of the world by transport and communication obstacles and by the drastic political division of the world into capitalist and communist areas (while India followed a policy of limited integration into the world economy). When all these barriers suddenly disappeared, Western countries were faced with the fact that these masses in the rest of the world – thanks to the major earlier efforts by their governments in the fields of education and basic infrastructure – had reached the minimum standards required for employment in the production of at least the less-skilled industrial and modern service exports. Since the disrupting effects of this epochal change seem, in the case of China, to have largely petered out (though a few hundreds of millions of poor rural workers may still be available for low-wage work in industrial cities), it can reasonably be expected that in the future much less traumatic effects – and more diffused among all groups of workers – for advanced countries will result from further Chinese economic progress. Many observers, Goodhart and Pradhan (2017) in particular, argue that in China demographic changes have put an end to the 'unlimited supplies' of workers (and to other conditions that contributed in the past to high rates of growth of output and exports), as a consequence of the drastic reduction of birth rates and the rapid ageing of the population. They also exclude the possibility that in the next few years the possible 'new Chinas', India and Africa, may take the place of China as world economic powerhouses, because of their lack of adequate administrative infrastructure (and, in the case of Africa, of human capital).

Second, the Chinese economic miracle was the result of a series of fundamental reforms that radically changed the economic and social structure of the country. Now the great change has already taken place, the new socio-economic set-up of the country seems to have found a degree of stability and no programme of comparable future radical reforms appears to be under consideration by the political leadership. The exceptional growth of the past forty years has largely reflected a process of reallocation of the country's labour force from low-productivity farm activities to much higher-productivity manufacturing. As this reallocation has been accomplished, future productivity growth will have to rely on technological and organizational innovation directed to increase productivity and the upgrading of existing activities.

Third, in the new environment of globalization, the ease of transferring technologies and know-how – previously one of the biggest obstacle to developing countries' economic progress – increased dramatically, especially through MNCs' foreign investment and participation in GVCs. China was able to rapidly exploit the huge backlog of technologies that had not been available in the country before because of objective obstacles, of its own policy of economic isolation and of Western constraints on technology transfers on military grounds. That backlog seems to have been largely absorbed by China and the technological gap with the West drastically reduced even in a large number of high-tech sectors. Therefore, the further technological progress necessary to eliminate the remaining gap and then to keep China at the level of (or overtaking) continuing Western technological advances will have to rely more and more on indigenous progress at the scientific and technological frontier, and may thus proceed less rapidly than in the past.

Finally, the recent deceleration of China's exceptional rate of GDP appears destined to continue (exports cannot in any case maintain their previous growth rates, as the Chinese share of world merchandise exports has now reached over 13 per cent – from 2 per cent in 1990 and by far the largest in the world; and the growth rate of world trade has significantly slowed since 2008). Chinese leaders seem to have become conscious in more recent years that the country must devote a smaller share of its resources to investment and export and more to consumption, as it has to satisfy a huge domestic demand for pensions, health and other social services. In the future, limits to growth will come from the shrinking of the labour force (the absolute size of the population age cohort of 15–60 years started to decrease in 2012), produced by the demographic developments mentioned in the preceding section, which will reinforce the tendency, particularly marked since 2011, for wages to accelerate (so that by 2016 real manufacturing wages were fourteen times the level of 1980); all observers agree that China is already no more a very low-wage country.

Authorities also seem to have recognized at last that they have to take strong measures to reduce the still very large geographical differences in living standards and the macroscopic inequality of personal incomes and wealth, and to safeguard the environment, which has seriously suffered as a result of the policy of 'growth at any cost' followed in past decades. In turn, the introduction of new goals in development policy may create a new problem: one of the keys to Chinese success has been the use of meritocratic criteria within the Communist Party and the administration for appointments and careers of officials at all territorial levels; these criteria made basic reference to the rate of growth of their area. The introduction of new goals in development policy will probably make it more difficult to establish precise criteria for the assessment of officials' performance (a problem that adds to the one of officials' corruption, which has apparently been increasing in recent years[10]).

* * *

[10] The issue of corruption in China is analysed in Milanovic (2019), as it is a key element in the development strategy followed by technocratic-authoritarian governments aiming at fast growth, which this author considers, in present world conditions, to be the only existing version of capitalism alternative to the liberal capitalism of the USA and Western Europe.

The characteristics and future prospects of the Chinese meritocratic model of society have been described and discussed by Bell (2015).

As regards the possible effects of the rise of China on, and the lessons its experience offers to other developing countries trying to narrow the gap that separates them from advanced economies – a subject much less debated than the consequences for advanced countries – a general consideration is that both Chinese and Indian growth acceleration definitively confirmed a result that had been gradually recognized after the 1970s by development economics: that the gap does not so much depend on lack of domestic savings and capital accumulation (the factors stressed by Marxist and early post-war development literature) as on the low level of knowledge and technology, educational standards and industrial skills of countries, and on the insufficient development of infrastructure and of some institutional factors. Among the latter, a key role appears to be played by the quality and autonomy from specific interest groups of political leaders and top public officials; and particularly by their strategic and bargaining abilities in both bilateral relations with advanced countries and big MNCs, and in multinational fora where the 'rules of the game' for trade, foreign investment, IPR and standards are established. After independence, China and, to a much lesser extent, India recognized these points, as witnessed by their great efforts to improve the coverage and quality of education at all levels and by China's policy, after 1978, of requiring MNCs and other foreign investors to transfer technologies and train the local workforce as conditions for their operation in China.[11]

While the export success in manufactures of China and some other developing countries gave rise, particularly in 2000–2008, to a boom in world demand for oil and other mineral and agricultural raw materials that greatly benefited developing countries exporting primary products, a basic issue is whether the Chinese export success will make it easier or more difficult for other developing countries to follow the manufacturing export-oriented development strategy adopted by the 'Asian tigers' and then by China itself. In the past, pessimists pointed to the increasing difficulty some developing countries faced in expanding, or even maintaining, their sales of low-skilled manufactures in the final markets of advanced countries in the face of Chinese competition. Optimists, instead, forecast the repetition in the Chinese case of the 'flying geese' sequence, highlighted by Akamatsu (1962), that characterized East Asian export experience in the post-war period, according to which countries that start export activity concentrating on simple low-skill low-cost products tend to abandon their initial

[11] The policy, on the part of developing countries, of mandating joint ventures and other forms of local collaboration with MNCs instead of the establishment of wholly foreign-owned subsidiaries, so as to maximize technology transfers and leakages to domestic firms, runs the risk, according to some economists, such as Hoekman and Javorcik (2006), of not achieving the desired effect. It would appear that technologies transferred by MNCs to wholly owned subsidiaries are of a newer vintage and higher value than those licensed or transferred to joint ventures and partially owned affiliates. The imposition of licensing or sharing technology may not only produce the transfer of lower-quality technologies, but also may reduce the inducement for MNCs to invest in a country altogether. MNCs seem, instead, to be much keener to transfer technology abroad to their local suppliers ('vertical transfers'), as in this case it is less likely that the transfer would lead to future direct competition in final products with the transferring firm. Of course, this is an area where the relative bargaining power of the contracting parties largely determines the final result.

specialization with the progress of development and to switch to export sectors that are more technologically advanced or more sophisticated; thus leaving new space to less developed exporters in the advanced countries' markets for simpler products.

The answer to this question depends on many factors regarding the nature of the products exported and the characteristics of both their supply and demand. It seems that in the first phase of China's export offensive, when it flooded export markets with low-price and low-quality simple products, its superior competitiveness may have caused some damage to those developing countries whose exports were concentrated in the same sectors as China's (for example, Mexico); and. that the upgrading of the structure of Chinese exports and the increase of Chinese wages in the country's regions where the bulk of export activity was located is opening up new spaces for other developing countries' sales in the markets of advanced countries, and in the Chinese market itself. But as many new developments have taken place in more recent years, any forecast is highly uncertain. As noted by Baldwin (2016), the 'flying geese' sequence has been disrupted by the fragmentation of production and the formation of GVCs, which made it possible for China to rapidly acquire export competitiveness in some high-tech sectors in the same development phase in which observers had expected the country to remain concentrated on 'traditional' sector exports. In any case, it would seem that so far China's rise did not, on the whole, cause serious shocks for other, especially poor, developing economies, as evidenced by their overall positive record of growth and exports in more recent decades.

A worst-case future scenario could be conceived in which China, while switching to the export of more sophisticated and technologically advanced products – possibly even those at the very frontier of technology – would continue to enjoy an absolute advantage in 'traditional' products. As remarked before, there is still in the peripheral regions of the country a minority of the total population – but, given the size of China, representing some hundreds of millions of people – of poor countrymen available for low-wage employment in the manufacture of these products, which may thus continue to flood world markets.

On the other hand, a different scenario may be envisaged considering that, given the size of China and the average level of the income its population has already managed to reach, a huge market may be opening up in the country – in addition to the markets of advanced countries that until now represented the main outlet for developing countries' exports – for the export of 'traditional' goods by the economies still in the initial phase of the transition to the production and export of manufactures.

One further important question regards the large group of very low-income developing countries, the majority located in Africa. The Chinese, both because of their very recent experience of managing to get out of similar conditions of abject poverty, and because of the enormous potential in terms of people, capital and technologies they can now deploy given their size, could activate in these poor countries a complex of new economic initiatives on a scale sufficient to significantly improve their development chances. Indeed, in the last years, mainly driven by the search for sources of raw materials, China has massively intervened in Africa and some Asian countries, offering its technical and financial assistance and promoting and carrying on activities not only in the fields of agriculture and mineral extraction, but also in the building up of basic infrastructure facilities. The recent New Silk Road initiative is an example of the huge infrastructural projects that China is going to undertake, which could also produce large gains for some of the least developed countries.

Another field where China can give an invaluable, increasing contribution to the cause of both low-income and middle-income developing countries is that of multinational negotiations on trade, investment and IPR. In the past, developing countries used to have little voice in these negotiations because of their lack of weight in world trade and GDP, their frequent political and economic dependence on industrial countries, their limited financial resources and their much lower level of technical and bargaining ability; it was advanced countries that usually had the upper hand, imposing on the really important issues the choices that were more advantageous to themselves. The recent rise of China, together with that of India and other important developing countries (and of Russia), has radically changed the situation. Now the interests of middle-income countries are increasingly represented in international economic and political fora, and these new protagonists can often defend the interests of less powerful low-income countries, as on many issues (such as patents and copyrights) they hold similar positions and can establish common fronts vis-à-vis advanced countries.

12.3 Possible responses by advanced countries to changes in trade and technology

International economic developments connected with the process of globalization since the 1980s (changes in countries' and regions' comparative advantages, increased tradability and exchange of services, offshoring by national firms and the formation of GVCs, the advent of new powerful trade competitors, etc.) have represented such a major change in the world economy that they would in any case have created problems of adjustment for advanced countries. But these problems were particularly aggravated, as pointed out particularly by Baldwin (2016), by some specific, largely interconnected, characteristics of those developments, which were mentioned in preceding chapters but which it may be useful to summarize here:

- High speed of change, which hinders intervention to facilitate adjustment, as it can make the very analysis of the phenomena and consequently the measures proposed or adopted to deal with them, rapidly obsolete.
- Low predictability and controllability of changes, so that individuals, entrepreneurs and public authorities face extreme uncertainties and risks regarding long-term investments (such as, for the first of these categories, the choice of education and connected future jobs; for the second, the decision to move parts of the firm's activity abroad or to enter new markets; and for the third, the building up of infrastructure or the framing and implementation of educational reforms). In addition, governments' ability to control the direction and timing of economic developments has been drastically reduced by the liberalization of international

movements of goods, services, capital, patents and so on; by the severe restraints on initiatives in many fields (such as industrial policy) by international rules allegedly intended to increase free competition; by privatizations and the restricted scope for intervention in the economic sphere and for action to curb big business's superpowers (for example, they have practically no say in the developments of networks, despite the latter's increasing role of 'public good'); and by their decreasing level of technical competence as a result of the diminishing financial and especially human resources allotted to them.

- Extreme volatility of changes, as comparative advantages have the kaleidoscopic characteristics highlighted by Bhagwati, with consequent extreme vulnerability of workers and owners of other factors of production.
- Individuality of the consequences of change: while the changes that occurred during the first globalization (1870–1914), such as the transport revolution, had effects that tended to apply to large, relatively easily identifiable categories of people and firms (in that case, the majority of agricultural producers in Europe), the changes produced by contemporary globalization typically hit, in an almost random manner, specific sub-groups of individuals belonging to wider categories (for instance workers or professionals whose specific product or service is made transmissible via a network by unforeseeable advances in communication technology). In this situation, faced by developments they cannot control, individuals are left without any defence, as solidarity among workers based on community of interests dissolves, while trade unions lose power as a consequence of their members being fragmented and divided by contrasting interests and demands. The final result is a growing feeling of isolation that deepens the anguish, uncertainty and insecurity produced by the possibility of losing one's job or the level of wage attained, in an environment where the social insurance principles at the base of the welfare state appear to be evaporating.
- Strict interconnection of changes in international trade with changes in technology (the latter also seem to share with trade the characteristics listed above). But even when the two changes are independent of one another, their consequences, and the reasons why these consequences are so disrupting for people in advanced countries, are largely the same. The two basic problems that both phenomena give rise to concern the availability of employment and the level of workers' wages, and the difficulty of making long-term choices as regards education and connected future jobs. Leaving aside the second problem, the first one seems to be largely due to distortions and asymmetries in the way both the gains from trade and those from technical progress (the main forces allowing continuing GDP increases in advanced countries) are divided among groups of the population. In this situation, most of the proposals for solving or reducing the problems produced by one or the other of the two phenomena also apply to the people damaged by, or vulnerable to, either of them.[12]

[12] One last point, underlined by Rodrik (2018a), may be added, which explains why in more recent

At the beginning of our century, when the problem of increased competitive pressure on advanced countries as a result of globalization and the emergence of major low-wage exporters became a serious concern for Western economists and politicians, Sweden's trade minister Pagrotsky (2000) attacked US conventional wisdom, according to which European employment and growth problems were the consequence of inadequate incentives, inflexible markets and suffocating levels of taxation; so that the prescription Europe should follow was to abandon its old-fashioned welfare state and instead imitate the USA. He pointed out, referring to his country's good record of growth and employment, that, on the contrary:

> The Swedish example shows that the supposed contradiction between social protection and a flexible economy is, if not false, at least greatly exaggerated. An ambitious public sector can be part of the solution, rather than part of the problem. The challenge is not to dismantle the European model, but to modernize it so as to provide Europe's citizens with security in support of change, instead of security against change.

In a similar vein, De Grauwe (2001) pointed out that empirical evidence contradicted the common 'race to the bottom' view, according to which social security spending in rich countries is put at risk by globalization since it raises labour costs for firms, inducing them to offshore production to low-costs countries. In fact, data showed that in general it was OECD countries with high social spending that had high scores in competitiveness rankings. Competitiveness and productivity, he explained, largely depend on the quality of human and social capital; and a workforce's education and skills, ability to innovate and identification with the economic system are all greatly improved by a high level of social spending – the only condition being that it is carried out by a responsible government following strict criteria of efficiency.

Developing the same line of argument, Milberg and Houston (2005) observed that two basic kinds of reaction to developing countries' export offensive could be envisaged on the part of advanced countries. One was the attempt to maintain or recapture competitiveness through cost cutting – basically, reductions in workers' wages and benefits and in small-scale producers' remuneration, which involved giving up many workers' rights won as a result of long and painful struggles – and a drastic downscaling of the welfare state, reducing the provision of public services and social security that had been progressively introduced in previous decades. The other was the attempt to defend competitiveness and continuous recreation of monopolistic advantages through the introduction of new products and production processes, concentration on high-quality goods and productivity increases, all to be obtained thanks to the development and application of innovations and technological improvements and to the upgrading of workers' skills. This would allow increases in profitability and in wages and

---

years further trade liberalization initiatives have met with increasing unpopularity in advanced countries. The ratio between the costs (in terms of the worsening of distribution) and the net gains owing to lower market distortions produced by tariff reductions tends to increase as the liberalization process applies to progressively lower tariffs.

working conditions, and the maintenance of the basic provisions of the welfare state. Innovations, rapid productivity growth and flexibility would be stimulated (as workers would be more ready to accept them) by cooperative labour relations, by stronger, more centralized trade unions and by better working conditions; but especially by reinforced social insurance and assistance by the state, which would prevent the increased volatility of comparative and absolute advantages, and the resulting vulnerability of jobs, from translating into increased economic insecurity for workers. The danger of following the first strategy was that it could easily degenerate into, and intensify, the race to the bottom envisaged by critics of globalization, whereby countries would compete in offering producers lower and lower requirements in the fields of taxation, respect for the environment and workers' wages and rights.

According to Milberg and Houston, on the basis of the evidence up to the late 1990s, both the 'low road' and the 'high road' to successful international performance had been followed by advanced countries, with varying results. As for the feared race to the bottom, they pointed out that on the empirical evidence of the phenomenon there was considerable debate, so that no definite conclusion could be drawn on the issue.[13]

Considering the developments that have taken place in our globalized world in the last two decades, one gets the impression that on the whole things have not fundamentally changed, and that advanced countries, apart from the Scandinavian ones, did not pursue with steadfastness and determination either the first road or the second. Rather, they seem to have let the tendencies pushing along the 'low road' ('retreat of the state', scaling down of the welfare state, drastic reduction of workers' and trade unions' power and, later, the effects of the 2008 global crisis) operate, and only introduced some measures to avoid the worst excesses connected with that road.

As regards the race to the bottom, the more recent evidence also seems to confirm Milberg and Houston's conclusion. What is certain, however, is that the fear of 'regulatory arbitrage' by firms has been a powerful factor restraining governments' action to impose the more demanding environmental, labour and taxation standards deemed desirable for the improvement of the welfare of the national community. Rodrik (2016a) has strongly objected to this development, proposing that countries should be allowed to place restrictions on foreign transactions in order to prevent regulatory arbitrage.

In the last few decades, the conviction has spread among economists that the increased speed, unpredictability and volatility of changes under globalization call – if the latter is to obtain the acceptance and support of workers needed to avoid halting

[13] It seems that in advanced countries a structural change has drastically reduced the likelihood of a race to the bottom in labour conditions (which remains a problem for developing countries): in the last decades of the past century almost all of them followed a strategy of progressively abandoning the lines of production, and especially the phases of production, where the availability of low-cost unskilled labour (or the disregard for environmental pollution) represented the fundamental competitive advantage. In all of them non-price competition – especially that connected with technological innovation – has become more and more the critical factor determining international trade competitiveness.

or reversing it – for major public measures to assist workers damaged by trade and technological changes. More recently, a number of theoretical and empirical studies – for example, Piketty (2013), which, though not belonging to the dominant Anglo-Saxon literature, managed to achieve a surprisingly wide diffusion – have highlighted the more general unacceptably distorted distribution of income and wealth in advanced countries and the unfairness of the way in which gains and losses from trade and technical progress are shared among groups of the population. With the danger that, in the absence of intervention, it may not be possible to resist demands for protectionist policies, the application and diffusion of technological advances may be delayed, and the development of extremist and demagogic nationalistic political reactions may not be contained.

However, while economists advanced many interesting proposals, few concrete public initiatives followed. Primarily this was because of the dire conditions of most countries' public finances; the steadfast opposition of those people and business groups who would have to shoulder most of the financial burden of such initiatives or give up unjustified privileges and advantages, but who hold the resources – capital, technology and high-level skills – most easily transferable abroad in our globalized world; and the fact that after the outbreak of the 2008 global crisis, the attention of people, authorities and economists (and public funds) shifted away from the trade and technology issue to concentrate on the dramatic consequences of the crisis. And when attention for the issue resumed, the political response in the USA, with the Trump presidency, consisted in protectionist initiatives against China that seemed to offer scant hopes of providing real solutions to the problems – while they led other countries to concentrate on trying to avoid being involved in the moves and counter-moves triggered by the American trade offensive, which for the first time in the post-war period risked the origination of a generalized trade war.

Among the proposals that have been advanced and debated, those listed in the following sections appear worthy of examination. When the contemporary process of globalization was just beginning, practically the only intervention that – following a long tradition – economists envisaged was monetary compensation of workers damaged by trade liberalization. As industrial countries started to see their less-skilled manufacturing activities lose competitiveness and move to developing countries, it was widely argued that the response should be a large effort of education at all levels, an increase in R&D expenditure, an upgrading of workers' skills and programmes of retraining and assistance for the people who had lost their jobs. It was also proposed that negotiations should take place at international level to establish minimum common standards for workers' conditions and rights, environmental protection and taxation, both to ensure a more level playing field in trade competition and to prevent possible races to the bottom for those standards with damaging effects for all trading countries.

But later, the increasing competitiveness of some developing countries even in higher-skill lines of production and the persistent worsening of advanced countries' distribution of income and wealth led a growing number of economists to think that the problem could not be solved just by stronger action on the fronts mentioned.

While initiatives on these fronts can make a contribution, they argued, what is really necessary, especially since the effects of trade and technology are strictly interconnected, is a major change in the very mechanisms through which the benefits of both trade and technical progress are distributed among holders of different factors of production and groups of the population.

12.3.1 Compensation and retraining of trade-damaged workers

According to Ricardo's comparative costs principle, trade and specialization bring benefits to all trading countries and their inhabitants. The principle, as explained in Section 2.3, extends to trading countries the same logic that applies to two individuals exchanging two goods. But as countries are composed of a large number of individuals performing very different economic activities and holding very different interests, while most decisions on exports or imports are taken, independently, by firms and not by individuals or governments exchanging two goods (or bundles of goods), it is inevitable that changes in production connected with the opening up of trade cause losses to some groups of citizens in the trading countries.

The whole current theory of economics and economic policy is based on the Pareto efficiency principle exposed by the Italian economist Pareto in 1895, according to which the only criterion for defining an economic situation 'superior' to, or 'more efficient' or 'more beneficial' than another is that it brings an addition to the welfare of some members of a community without causing a loss of welfare to any other member; therefore any policy measure that changes a situation is economically justified only if it satisfies that criterion. The problem is that in the real world any change or policy measure inevitably causes losses to someone and thus fails to satisfy that criterion.[14]

---

[14] Since it takes any initial situation as given and imposes an extremely demanding condition for its change, Pareto's criterion has been attacked as a subtle political instrument in defence of the existing economic order, in particular of any unjust distribution of income and wealth that may occur in a society. In a country with a slave economy, for example, the abolition of slavery, by severely damaging slave owners, would represent a violation of Pareto's criterion, leading to an economically 'inferior' situation. Even Irwin, a strong advocate of free trade, recognized that 'The criterion is biased in favor of the status quo, which itself need not be equitable by some standard' (1996, p. 188).

As a guide to economic policy, Pareto's criterion can be seriously misleading: Deaton (2013) has attacked the criterion for its narrow perspective, arguing that its 'mistake is to apply the principle to only one dimension of wellbeing – money – and to ignore other dimensions, such as the ability to participate in a democratic society, to be well educated, to be healthy, and not to be the victim of others' search for enrichment. If an increase in top incomes does nothing to reduce other incomes but hurts other aspects of wellbeing, the Pareto principle cannot be called on to justify it' (p. 214). Only on the basis of a narrowly utilitarian logic can it be argued that any unjust harm caused to people can be adequately compensated *ex post* through a monetary payment. In the case of loss of a job, for instance, the payment of a sum equal to the previous wage might adequately compensate the worker for the economic damage suffered, but it is debatable whether any additional payment could compensate for the loss of the basic right to work and of the dignity conferred by the working activity.

To get out of the impasse, recourse was made to the principle of compensation originally formulated by J. S. Mill in 1825: a change or policy measure is beneficial and justified if the members of the community gaining from it could provide full monetary compensation to the members damaged by it and still find themselves in a better situation. However, it has become current practice among economists to interpret this principle in terms of potential compensation: a change or policy measure is beneficial for society if those who gain from it could *potentially* compensate the losers. Consequently, while the principle of compensation has been applied to judge whether a policy measure is economically justified, it has never been requested, as a condition for the measure to be introduced, that the compensation envisaged by the principle be actually paid to the losers. Samuelson (2004) pointed to the unacceptability on ethical grounds of the principle of compensation as applied by international economists.[15] Blinder (2007) was more categorical, arguing that trade liberalization cannot represent a Pareto improvement unless the losers are actually, not theoretically, compensated. Baumol, in 2006 – see Sha and Hughes (2009) – went as far as to declare: 'imagine a case in which those economists who say that trade is always beneficial are right … If one-tenth of the workforce nevertheless were seriously injured, it is clearly a crime against humanity not to take measures to compensate them adequately' (2009, pp. 34–35).[16]

Compensation of workers damaged by trade poses a number of theoretical and practical problems. At the theoretical level there are two main difficulties. The first regards the principle of compensation in general and the impossibility of separating investment and production decisions from measures affecting distribution. If a policy measure has an overall positive effect on national efficiency and welfare, but while benefiting a group of people or firms it also produces losses for other groups, it is usually argued by economists that the measure should be adopted so as to reach

---

[15] 'treating all people in each region as different *homogeneous* Ricardian laborers … inhibits our grappling with realistic cases where some Americans (capitalists and skilled computer experts) may be helped by what is decimating the real free-trade wage rates of the semi-skilled or of the blue-collar factory workers … Contemplate a scenario where Schumpeter's fruitful capitalistic destruction harms a really sizable fraction of the future U.S. population and, say, improves welfare of another group and does that so much as to justify a calculation that the winners could be made to transfer some of their gains and thereby leave *no* substantial U.S. group net losers from free trade. Should noneconomists accept *this* as cogent rebuttal [of anti-free trade positions] if there is no evidence that compensating fiscal transfers have been made or will be made? … The economists' literature of the 1930s – … to say nothing of earlier writings by J.S. Mill, Edgeworth, Pareto and Viner – perpetrates something of a shell game in ethical debates about the conflict between efficiency and greater inequality' (pp. 143–144).

On Pareto gains from trade see Facchini and Willmann (2001); on the difficulties of achieving these Pareto gains through redistribution in a dynamic setting see Willmann (2004).

[16] On the debate on the compensation principle see Irwin (1996).

An argument has been advanced by ultra-liberalists against the very concept of trade-damaged compensation: since for them any obstacle to totally free trade is by definition a tax (measured by the loss of the gains from trade) imposed by its beneficiaries on the rest of society, the fact that the obstacle is eliminated by liberalization, producing a loss to previous beneficiaries, cannot be considered the cause of a damage that should be compensated, but simply the abolition of a previous unjustified privilege.

a better allocation of resources and the connected superior national welfare. If the distributional consequences are considered as patently unfair, it will then be up to the political process to introduce taxes on the economic agents advantaged by the measure so as to finance a lump sum transfer to compensate the losers. It has been objected, most strongly by Baumol (2002), that:

> The concept of lump-sum transfers as a mode of redistribution that can preserve economic efficiency unscathed is … a legend … Akerlof (2000) comments that applied economists are well aware that, generally, lump-sum transfers are simply not possible. I certainly agree. More than that, even most pure theorists must know this in their hearts. But this does not stop them from using this mythical device in their formal writings to focus exclusively on allocative efficiency, assuming away the implications for distribution. (p. 143).

The concept is a legend because members of the groups benefited by the policy measures 'will soon learn that their economic activities – those that contributed to their pre-transfer wealth or income levels – also condemn them to the role of transfer payer … Clearly this is an incentive to the payers to cut back on the activities that force them into that position…' (p. 145).

The second difficulty concerns the justification for compensation of trade-damaged economic agents. In principle, compensation could be justified on two grounds. First, it could be argued that no one should be damaged by events that do not depend on their choices or behaviour, and if that happens society (or the agents unjustifiably benefited by the event, if they can be identified) should compensate them. Apart from the extreme degree of national solidarity that the criterion would imply, it would extend to so many possible causes of damage that their identification in each case would be exceedingly arduous, so that it would be much more practical to substitute compensation for damage from a specific cause (such as trade) with a form of general coverage for all possible undeserved misfortunes, such as basic income and health insurance provided by the state. A second justification – the one advanced when trade-damaged compensation programmes were introduced – is that losses produced by trade (contrary, for example, to those produced by technical progress or by the normal working of firms' competition) are usually a consequence of specific trade liberalization agreements that governments voluntarily decide to underwrite because of the overall benefit they represent for their country. But this criterion is not convincing: apart from the difficulty of discriminating between damage resulting from specific trade agreements entered into by governments and damage produced by import increases reflecting improved foreign competitiveness within the framework of long-since-existing trade agreements, there are many discretionary decisions of governments, such as restrictive monetary or fiscal measures, that produce unjustified losses to some people but, because of an established tradition, are not considered ground for requests for specific compensation measures.

Rodrik (2018a), trying to explain why job displacement and income losses caused by trade have been singled out for requests for public action (while technological changes and other factors, producing much greater harm to some groups of the population, have not been the object of equally strong demands), advances a different explanation, which also accounts for the increasing requests for the introduction of international labour standards. He holds that popular opposition is not aroused by inequality per se as by inequalities that are perceived as unfair because they violate fundamental domestic norms or social understandings. People who have long seen competition in domestic labour markets regulated by laws or social arrangements so as to prevent certain unacceptable excesses (such as child labour or lack of minimum safety in the workplace) deeply resent the harm caused by low-cost imports from developing countries in which these extreme conditions seem to be considered normal and acceptable; such trade is seen as distorting the rules of the trade game, thereby undermining the basic social contract that regulates advanced countries' societies.

At a practical level, the main difficulty of applying the principle of compensation to trade is that it is difficult to clearly identify the victims of trade liberalization (often the damaged sectors are not only the ones directly experiencing import competition, but also those supplying them with components and inputs); to determine the extent of the damage and the appropriate compensation; and especially to attribute damage to trade rather than to other causes – such as technical change, an unfavourable evolution of demand due to cyclical factors or changes in tastes, and competition among firms – which frequently represent concomitant factors of worker displacement. In addition, as stressed by Rodrik (2018a), compensation can be very costly, and both the increase in taxation it requires and the mechanisms used to provide assistance create behavioural distortions that may produce significant welfare losses. But he considers that the main difficulty with compensation is political, and regarding credibility and time consistency. As explained in Rodrik (2011), governments, and exporters who are going to reap substantial gains from a trade agreement, in order to have the agreement approved or at least not opposed by prospective losers, promise *ex ante* to compensate them for the damage they may suffer. But such promises are not fully credible: once the agreement has been signed, governments and exporters will lose interest in seeing the assistance programme really carried out. This is why among the measures proposed to deal with the inequalities created by trade some economists included the requirement that when a trade agreement is expected to bring benefits greater than the losses of the damaged groups, the agreement should be approved only if a mechanism can be envisaged that makes it certain that compensation will materially be provided.

The real reason why compensatory assistance programmes for trade-impacted workers, firms or communities have been introduced is that they are considered the instrument to overcome the opposition of those expected to be damaged by trade and foreign investment liberalization agreements considered beneficial to a country as a whole.

It is in the USA that trade-damaged compensation and adjustment assistance has been an especially important issue and has given rise to important government programmes. This is because import penetration has been a particularly shocking experience for the country, both because until the recent globalization its economy, given its size, had been much less open than those of all the other advanced countries, and because of the persistent US lack of a general safety net that in other advanced countries has been provided to workers and citizens by the welfare state. US trade-damaged compensation was introduced in 1962 as part of a trade liberalization package, while trade adjustment assistance programmes, centred on measures for workers' retraining, were introduced with the Trade Act of 1974; later Acts, starting from 2002, modified, extended and ameliorated the assistance provided.

America's long experience with programmes of trade adjustment assistance has been extensively analysed – see, among others, Kletzer and Rosen (2005) and D'Amico and Schochet (2012) – and has largely been judged rather negatively. Blinder (2007), for example, considered this assistance 'miserable', as the resources devoted to it were too limited (and consequently it was not generous enough to those damaged and could only cover some of them), it was badly designed, and provided more assistance than adjustment. Autor, Dorn and Hanson (2016) – concentrating on the US reaction to the 'Chinese shock' – pointed out the very limited effects of assistance in contrasting the unemployment and depression of US industrial communities hit by Chinese import penetration. Rodrik (2019) also referred to the limited effectiveness of US adjustment assistance, which he attributed to politicians having little incentive to fund it adequately or to make sure it was working well. The lack of advocacy of greater assistance resources on the part of economists and politicians may also have been partly because it would have implied admitting that gains from trade liberalization are not as large as commonly claimed.[17]

12.3.2 Upgrading through education, skills advancement and R&D

For many years until the beginning of this century, as low-skilled workers appeared to be the main victims of the emerging countries' increased exports, it was argued that advanced countries' international competitiveness could only be maintained by more rapidly shifting production and exports towards high-tech, high-quality goods and services. To obtain this result, a massive effort to improve the general level of the population's education, upgrade the skills of the workforce and accelerate the introduction of technological innovations through increased R&D was deemed essential.

[17] It may be thought that the rationale for the adjustment assistance of trade-displaced workers should also be applied to firms, entrepreneurs and owners of capital damaged by trade, and some US programmes do indeed also apply to firms and communities. It must be considered, however, that entrepreneurs and capitalists, unlike workers, have as a central object of their activity – for which they receive a specific remuneration, profit – the assumption of risk, and therefore should not be insured against the effects of wrong decisions, unfavourable events or bad luck. They also have, in the event of difficulty in maintaining their business, much greater possibilities and means to deal with the transition time from one activity to another, while workers seldom have enough income or wealth to provide for their basic needs during the transition or to invest in the new skills necessary to find another job. In fact the basic reason for firms and communities having been included in US programmes seems to have been that of preventing their lobbying for protectionist policies.

Much stressed, particularly in the USA, was the urgent need to increase the quality of primary and secondary education and to open access to university to the part of the population that could not afford it (the mechanism of student loans does not appear to have produced the expected results). The effort to spread education among all sections of society was also deemed essential to contrast more generally the increasing income and wealth inequalities. Equal, if not more, importance was attributed – in the light of the increasing uncertainty as to the kind of jobs that will be available to students when they enter the labour market – to the change in attitudes and skills that education should try to develop in young people. More than specialized knowledge and skills, it should favour the acquisition of flexible skills and general abilities that can more easily be transferred from one type of job to another, such as adaptability to change, problem-solving, use of imagination and creativity, interest in innovations and ability to interact with other people and take part in team work.

Government initiatives also appeared particularly urgent in the field of worker training and skills acquisition. In the new environment of offshoring and labour force reductions, firms' concentration on 'core-activities', sudden changes in countries' competitive advantages and accelerated worker turnover, characterising contemporary globalization, big private firms had largely abandoned the interest in investing in training and upgrading the skills of their workers they had had in the past, when they could expect their employees to spend their whole working life with them. As for increased public and private R&D, its crucial role was clear from the fact that it underpins technological progress and innovation, which in turn represent the main drivers of U.S. international competitiveness.

Unfortunately, it does not seem that, overall, the USA and most other advanced countries have launched particularly significant initiatives on these three fronts (while some emerging countries have been rapidly progressing in these respects). Public budget difficulties, aggravated by the 2008 global crisis, and the unwillingness of politicians to raise corporate and personal taxation to collect the necessary additional financial resources, are probably the basic explanation. But even in the absence of these obstacles, the current state of world economic activity suggests that these initiatives will be less effective in terms of defence of employment and wages than they were in the past.

While it is essential to raise educational levels, the definition of governments' policies in this field finds obstacles in the inadequate knowledge of the influence of different educational systems and practices on students' abilities and on their success in future working activity; and, more crucially, in the unpredictability of the directions of future technological progress and of different countries' advancement abilities (the latter determining the strength of foreign competition and the likelihood of production being relocated abroad). The difficulty, already mentioned, for government industrial policy to predict which lines of production have more scope for the growth of markets and exports in the future is largely paralleled by an analogous difficulty in the field of education policy. While once it could reasonably be expected that more and better education was the key factor ensuring employment and higher wages, now the latter largely depend on the degree of jobs' offshorability (in turn, a function of the extent to which jobs require a personal interface) and automation progress, both of which are quite hard to forecast. This difficulty also strongly impacts on the decisions of individuals and families regarding education, as private investment in this field is equally restrained by the extreme uncertainty on the gains it will produce in terms of future job availability and remuneration. In a few years, new offshoring possibilities (which now seem to apply equally to skilled and non-skilled jobs), developments in automation, biases of technology against or in favour of given factors or skills, and changes in other countries' competitive advantages may subvert the expectations people have today with regard to education.[18] More generally, labour market developments have increasingly led Americans and peoples in many other advanced countries to lose faith in education as the basic means of economic and social advance. And in any case, as observed by Gomory and Baumol (2009), 'improvements in education are unlikely to be so profound that they turn out Americans who are more productive than the three or four Asians who can be hired for the same wage' (p. 550).

Similar considerations apply to worker training and skills upgrading. While, as indicated, firms have largely lost interest in efforts to develop these activities at the workplace (and the best training takes place within a firm that has already hired the worker), workers themselves have shown diminished interest in devoting time and resources to such activities: in the present environment of volatile specializations they face the risk that investment to acquire new abilities will not help them to find a new job, since, once acquired, they may again be made obsolete by new developments in offshoring or technology.

As for R&D, it was remarked in Section 2.3 that with high mobility of capital and technology, and production offshoring, there is no longer any guarantee that private R&D expenditure and government funds devoted to basic public research and to incentives for corporate R&D will result in more production and employment at home, rather than in cheaper labour locations abroad. Gomory and Baumol (2009) have proposed, in this respect, that the USA should adopt a new, more direct policy. Just as Asian countries make it more profitable for foreign corporations, through tax and other incentives, to relocate – and create jobs in high-VA (per unit of factor employed) production activities – in their countries, the USA should introduce similar incentives, applying differential rates of corporate taxation with special rebates for firms that retain or increase jobs in such activities at home. They also pointed out that the close linkages between universities and corporations – once considered a basic factor of strength of the American economic system as they allow more rapid translation of innovative ideas into practice – may also have lost much of their effectiveness with the globalization of corporate activity, as they may simply lead to

[18] There is one important respect in which the possible contribution of investment in education to the welfare of a country and to that of an individual differ. When citizens, having acquired certain educational qualifications or skills, do not find employment, these qualifications and skills become useless for their country, but they may be profitably employed by their individual owners if they manage to move to another country.

a more rapid spread of US innovations abroad, increasing foreign, rather than US, high-tech lines of production and jobs.

12.3.3 Labour (and other) standards

From the end of World War II to the beginning of the 1970s, in developing countries, a pessimistic outlook was widespread as to their export growth potential and the evolution of their terms of trade with advanced countries. Trade was largely seen as a threat, as it tended to consolidate the traditional colonial division of labour based on their comparative advantage in raw materials and advanced countries' comparative advantage in manufactures. Strangely enough, from the 1980s it was the advanced countries that increasingly worried about the negative consequences of trade with developing countries, as the latter's growing competitiveness in manufactures and services was seen as a threat to the employment and wage levels of their less-skilled (and later even skilled) workers.

By a similar paradox, the issue of exploitation of low-wage workers and countries by firms and consumers of advanced countries – which was discussed in earlier parts of this work – has often been taken up in recent decades of progressively liberalized trade, by firms, workers, trade unions and even governments of advanced countries, and transformed, through a complete inversion of perspective, into a question of 'unfair competition' by developing countries based on unacceptably low labour – and environmental – standards: Daly (1993) spoke of 'reverse imperialism' caused by free trade. So we seem to be faced with a crime – unfair international trade relations – whose author and victim exchange their roles according to the observer's point of view.

The reason for this contradiction was explained in Section 6.2. Observers refer alternatively to the traditional theory of perfect competition (where unemployment is excluded by assumption) at the basis of the RHO model, which leads to the best of trading worlds for a nation being seen as the one in which it sells its exports at the highest price and buys its imports at the lowest; or to Keynesian theory, with its need for stimuli to effective demand so as to reach full employment, in which the maximum volume of net exports, induced by superior competitiveness and low price, is the goal of foreign trade, as it produces increases in demand, production and employment.

The question of unfair labour standards (which refers to wages and other conditions of work, such as working hours, worker rights, trade union activity and child labour) is not new. Basic labour rights and principles were included in the 1919 Versailles peace treaty and represented the basis for the establishment of the ILO, an international tripartite body made up of representatives of labour, business and governments set up in the same year. The issue of developing countries' competition based on low wages was discussed in the post-World War II period by Tolles (1957). He argued that underdeveloped countries' wages could not be considered unfair as long as they corresponded to the prevailing domestic wage level in those countries. That level was very low because those countries' average labour productivity was also very low owing to the small amount of capital and other factors of production per worker (Lewis's not too dissimilar explanation was discussed in Section 9.3.3).

Three decades later, as US manufacturing industry started to seriously suffer from the price competition of imports from newly industrialized countries, based on their rapid productivity growth accompanied by very limited wage increases, Mead (1990) – as mentioned in Section 6.2 – argued that only the expansion of domestic demand in those countries and a narrowing of the gap in unit labour costs between them and advanced countries could prevent recourse to protectionist measures by the latter. He proposed that international labour standards should be introduced for internationally traded goods to compel the new competitors to increase wages in line with productivity, improve work conditions and respect key worker rights.

The eminent World Bank ecological economist Daly (1993) recalled that increased competitiveness imposed by global competition can be pursued by reducing costs by increasing efficiency, or by lowering standards for pollution, wages and labour conditions. In the second way, firms increase their profits by transferring to the rest of society, or groups within it, the burden of negative ecological and social externalities, whose costs should instead be internalized. This is the reason why countries fix, with laws and regulations, environmental and labour standards (such as minimum wages) for their domestic economy. Unfortunately, there are few such rules at international level, and many countries – in particular developing ones – tend to fix their standards with a view to stimulating exports and attracting foreign investment. Instead of leading to increased efficiency, this practice risks giving rise to a race to the bottom that ends up by damaging all countries.

Daly argued that countries with higher standards should be allowed to introduce tariffs corresponding to the costs that foreign firms save by externalizing them through low standards. Such tariffs would not represent a totally new practice: The General Agreement on Tariffs and Trade (GATT) rules allow countries to impose restrictions on imports of goods produced by foreign prison labour (a practice probably less damaging and morally more acceptable than child labour or uninsured risky labour), and international rules allow the application of anti-dumping restrictions against imports whose prices do not fully cover production costs or are lower than the domestic price in the exporting country; in such costs, environmental damage and losses of community welfare are simply not included. According to Daly, countries should be left free to fix their own domestic cost internalization rules; but when they sell to a foreign country they should play by that country's rules, paying a tariff sufficient to eliminate the advantage of lower standards; otherwise they would be forcing the importing country to accept a lowering of its more stringent national standards.

Daly reiterated his position, with clarifications and extensions, in Daly and Goodland (1994), where it was stressed that countries not applying regulations that allow full internalization of environmental and social costs cause not only a static international misallocation of resources, but also a dynamic distortion of comparative advantages. Given the critical importance of scale economies and the competitive advantage of being an early producer of a good, a country that starts to produce on the basis of not accounting for external costs can gain an unfair initial advantage relative to competitors internalizing these costs, which allows it to become a major competitive producer of a good although initially it does not present any objective comparative advantage in it.

But on the issue of unfair standards, other economists have expressed different ideas. The issue was taken up in particular by Bhagwati. In the same issue of *Scientific American* in which Daly's article was published, Bhagwati (1993b) argued that differences between countries in environmental standards are perfectly natural: different countries will probably have different trade-offs between environmental and other standards (for instance, minimum nutritional or health standards for the population); and even if they pursue the same environmental objectives they may choose, according to the specific national situation, to reach the goal by attacking different causes of environmental pollution and therefore impose different standards on different industries (or more or less strict standards to the same industry). In conclusion – apart from the cases where reference can be made to universal values, such as basic human rights – he viewed the opposition of environmentalists and other groups to unregulated trade as a way to impose their own particular values on other countries that may not share them. In addition, to allow values that are not universally accepted to intrude on free trade would open the way to an endless succession of demands for international trade agreements to include specific standards regarding any aspect of human activity. Finally, the criteria for the practical determination of the right amount of tariffs necessary to eliminate foreign social and environmental dumping would be extremely difficult to define and highly controversial (this, however, to a large extent also applies to the anti-dumping tariffs that countries are presently allowed to introduce).

As for labour standards, Bhagwati (1998) argued in his 1996 Prebisch Lecture that diversity of labour practices and standards mostly reflects different economic conditions, cultural values and analytical beliefs and theories, so that it is difficult, apart from extreme cases, to equate them with universally accepted basic human rights. He advanced the example of worker participation in corporate decision-making, certainly an element of economic democracy, which is highly valued and specifically regulated in countries such as Germany, but largely disregarded in the USA (even the basic right of organization of trade unions and the right to strike find much less popular support and legal enforcement in the USA than in Europe).

Bhagwati also squarely faced the issue of child labour, arguing that it is an extremely complex one and that, just as with the prohibition of this practice inside countries, the outright exclusion from international trade of products obtained from child labour might simply damage developing countries without contributing to eliminate the practice. Child labour is a product of poverty, and frequently the only alternative to it is either children's starvation or prostitution and criminal activities, rather than school attendance. The analysis of available empirical evidence by Edmonds and Pavcnik (2005) would largely confirm Bhagwati's arguments: child labour is basically a result of the parents' need for additional income; public authorities of poor countries do not have the means to enforce the official prohibition of the practice, just as they are usually unable to enforce compulsory school attendance. While the problem can only be solved by economic development that increases parents' incomes and countries' financial means, in the short term – apart from the elimination of the worst abuses – the problem could be attenuated by improving the quality of schooling, so that the prospects of future higher earnings connected with better education could push parents to renounce the income from children's work; by having governments covering the direct expenditure for school attendance; and especially by devising programmes of public cash transfers to poor families conditional on their sending children to school (such as were introduced in Brazil, apparently with positive results).

The general impression one gets from the 1990s debate on labour standards – see Stern (1998) – and also other standards is that Bhagwati's arguments on the logical unsoundness and the practical impossibility of imposing uniform standards on all countries when there are abysmal differences in their economic conditions do have a valid foundation (uniformity of standards is probably a realistic goal to pursue among advanced countries; but what is of interest to labour standards' advocates is overcoming the huge difference in standards between advanced and developing countries). But some basic labour standards – such as the ILO's 'core labour standards' (freedom of association and right to collective bargaining, prohibition of forced labour, non-discrimination in employment and elimination of the worst forms of child labour) should be enforced irrespective of the specific conditions of individual countries; after all, they mostly regard worker rights that would have no major impact on the developing countries' competitive advantage of low labour costs. To this end, a reformed ILO, enjoying effective regulatory and sanctioning powers (the latter is currently almost non-existent), would appear the most logical solution. But given the practical unlikelihood of such a development (so far many governments, including that of the USA, have even refused to ratify fundamental ILO Conventions), a reasonable solution could be the one, proposed by Elliott and Freeman (2003), of the ILO retaining responsibility in determining labour standards and monitoring countries' compliance with them, while devising a mechanism to empower the WTO to apply sanctions in the event of violations of the core labour standards that influence trade.[19]

On the issue of labour – and other – standards, the majority of economists until recent years seemed to have sided with Bhagwati's critique of the efforts to include standards in WTO trade negotiations, since such inclusion, given the differences in priorities among countries, would probably just bog down negotiations. There were, however, dissenting voices. J. D. Richardson (2000) argued that multilateral trade negotiations are not going to produce results without an enlargement of the base of

[19] As the end of World War II was approaching, it was envisaged by the American and British victors that the post-war international economic order would be centred on three institutions: the IMF, the World Bank and an International Trade Organization, which would be concerned with the problems of labour and trade. This latter never saw the light of day, and a narrower entity, the GATT, was charged with the discipline of tariffs and trade; so international issues concerning labour were left to the ILO, whose powers and efficacy were severely constrained: see Kapstein (1999).

their beneficiaries, so that the inclusion in these negotiations of some additional issues, which he called 'market-supportive', would contribute to, rather than hamper, their progress (after all, the WTO had already broadened its traditional trade issues when it produced the Agreement on trade-related IPR, in which a large measure of discretion by individual countries was allowed). He proposed expanding the negotiations to cover competition policies (concerning cartels, mergers and anti-competitive behaviour), technology policies (such as changes in WTO agreements on IPR and trade-related investments to ensure a wider diffusion of technology) and labour policies (specifically those regarding freedom of association and collective bargaining). This would at the same time increase the effectiveness, stability and sustainability of the market system, generating a new wave of gains from trade (estimates of gains from further traditional trade liberalization are rather modest) and widely disseminate those gains within and between countries, thus bringing support for the negotiating process from nascent and small businesses, workers and their unions, and technology users.[20]

The debate on labour standards continued in the following two decades, which witnessed two important developments. One is that clauses related to the respect of basic labour rights were increasingly included in international trade agreements, although on a piecemeal basis and largely in very general terms. The other is that a number of distinguished economists expressed, or moved to, positions favourable to the inclusion of 'social clauses' in international trade relations.

For example, Krugman (2007a), abandoning his more optimistic mid-1990s position, admitted that 'Fears that low-wage competition is driving down U.S. wages have a real basis in both theory and fact ... Trade still isn't the main source of rising economic inequality, but it's a bigger factor than it was'. He stressed that reduced demand – and therefore lower wages – for US less-skilled workers were influenced by the competition from low-wage countries and that 'cheap consumer goods at Wal-Mart aren't an adequate compensation'. And while not expecting labour standards to have a significant influence in improving American workers'

[20] A specific proposal by Richardson in the field of labour was the liberalization of agency services for workers. As part of the general liberalization of services it is promoting, the WTO should allow foreign organizations (trade unions in the first place) to offer their services regarding collective representation and bargaining, workplace safety monitoring, grievance and dispute settlement, training and employee assistance, and so on. This would contribute to alleviating a number of market failures in labour transactions, limiting practices that border on coercion and creating effective countervailing market power to that of employers. In Richardson's vision, this development, while extending the traditional domestic competition among unions to the international arena, would promote a degree of international coordination in unions' initiatives; it would also emphasize global worker solidarity, by allowing similar workers in different countries to collectively modulate competition among themselves in the same way as unionized workers of the same firm or sector do domestically. Richardson's proposal could in fact represent a first step towards overcoming one of the basic factors that have allowed globalization to be organized by, and to work to the primary advantage of, international big business; namely, the almost total absence of internationally coordinated trade union initiatives designed to ensure that a larger share of total trade gains from globalization go to the workers.

wage situation, since the new foreign competitors had wages so low as to continue in any case to represent a small fraction of the US ones, he concluded by recommending strengthening the social safety net and: 'let's have strong labour standards in our pending trade agreements…'. For his part, former Treasury Secretary Lawrence Summers (2008), noticing that not enough serious consideration had been given to the possibility of raising standards through global cooperation, argued that 'While labour standards arguments have at times been invoked as a cover for protectionism, and this must be avoided, it is entirely appropriate that US policymakers seek to ensure that greater global integration does not become an excuse for eroding labour rights'.

More recently, Rodrik (2018b) reminded us that globalization is not an irresistible force of nature, but largely the result of human action, as it is consciously shaped by the rules agreed by national authorities; that it has been pushed too far by ultra-liberalizers, who have managed, in the interest of big business, to have it arbitrarily extended to an excessive number of activities beyond trade; and that it has so much limited countries' national sovereignty that we must recover part of the latter, since the inequalities and consequent domestic social disintegration produced by globalization risk triggering protectionist and populist reactions. He argued in favour of introducing labour standards in WTO regulations. Countries damaged by trade partners' 'social dumping' should be allowed to introduce trade-restricting measures as is envisaged for the case of traditional dumping practices. He made a convincing case for countries' right to introduce such measures by defining trade as 'unfair', and representing social dumping, whenever competitive advantage is obtained through the violation of basic worker rights in exporting countries.

More debatable, as it involves a lot of complex and highly controversial issues, is Rodrik's argument that safeguard clauses, which allow countries to restrict access to their domestic market, should also be granted whenever such access threatens to undermine the domestic social bargain – that is, the basic rules of the economic game that have historically come to represent the institutional framework of a country's economic and social relations. Clearly, in advanced countries this social bargain includes wage levels and other benefits (such as those regarding the number of holidays or the limits to overtime) that do not constitute basic worker rights (they significantly differ from country to country) but cannot be restricted without creating serious social disruption in the countries where they have long since been established. Rodrik's defence of the national social bargain seems to contradict another of his arguments, namely that 'In the specific context of trade with developing nations, what should be of particular concern for labor advocates is not low wages or labor costs per se, to the extent that those reflect labor productivity or alternative employment opportunities' (2018b, p. 4). Clearly, the expression 'alternative employment opportunities' refers to Lewis's concept of wages (determined by the prevailing low level of productivity in the large subsistence agriculture sector), and to the Tolles (1957) criterion reported at the beginning of this section, of wages being fair in a country whenever they correspond to the 'prevailing domestic wage level'. The problem is that the greatest threat to advanced countries' social bargains seems to come from the fact that the very low average national level of productivity and wages of some developing countries keeps down the wages in their manufacturing and service industries where labour productivity is not significantly lower than that of advanced countries.

An interesting contribution to the issue of labour standards that deserves to be mentioned is the proposal by C. Barry and Reddy (2008) to introduce labour standards in multilateral trade negotiations through a direct link between improvements in these standards by developing countries and the provision of special trade advantages and financial assistance to them by advanced ones. The proposal would favour the adoption of higher labour standards by creating incentives to reach that goal, especially by eliminating the danger that by adopting higher standards in isolation a country might experience a damaging loss of international competitiveness (which is at present the reason, if not for races to the bottom, at least for the lack of significant advances in labour standards in many developing countries). The proposal is structured so as to overcome all the main objections traditionally raised against the idea of linking labour standards to trade agreements, and two of them in particular: that such linkages would produce a welfare loss for the developing countries' workers whose conditions they are meant to improve; and that they represent an imposition of rigid labour standards on those countries through the threat of trade sanctions in case of non-compliance.

The proposed general scheme – whose specific characteristics should be determined on the basis of what will result in practice to be the arrangement most likely to obtain the support of a sufficiently large number of countries to make it viable – envisages that the progress of a developing country towards the adoption of a minimally adequate level of wages and working conditions (such as those corresponding to ILO core labour standards) would be a condition for the country to obtain the benefit of increasing access for its exports, over the existing level, to the markets of advanced countries. As the adoption of higher labour standards may imply unsustainable increases in costs and lower competitiveness for these countries' firms, the proposal establishes that in these cases significant financial assistance would be provided by advanced countries – through various possible mechanisms – to the firms of the countries taking part in the scheme.

While compliance with some core labour rights would be expected from all countries regardless of their specific situation, some room for flexibility is provided in the proposal, as the latter relates the degree of the required improvement in labour standards to the level of development and other circumstances of each country. Finally, to overcome the objection that the application of labour standards might create an isolated aristocracy of workers in export industries of developing countries, the proposal envisages that the respect of labour standards ensuring more favourable access to the markets of advanced countries must apply not just to workers in export industries, but also to the workers in all the other economic sectors of the country.

12.3.4 Tax harmonization

Bhagwati (1998), while rejecting the case for inclusion of ecological and labour standards in international trade negotiations, argued that the basic tools employed by countries (and state governments in federal countries) to attract capital to their jurisdictions is not the offer of the right to pollute freely, but the offer of substantial tax breaks and of land grants at very low prices. He anticipated that a race to the bottom was indeed likely to take place in fiscal standards through competitive reductions in corporate tax rates.[21]

A tax race to the bottom is commonly expected to result in inefficiently low tax levels, causing under-provision of public services and diminished scope for redistribution policies; it would also reinforce the shift of the tax burden from mobile production factors (capital and highly-skilled labour) to immobile factors (less-skilled labour and real estate) and consumption. However, the empirical evidence on such a race to the bottom having taken place continues to remain mixed (though the existence of competition in corporate taxation appears largely confirmed). It is an established fact that a general tendency to significant decreases in statutory corporate tax rates has characterized the post-1980s period – from 49 to 24 per cent between 1985 and 2018 for the world average (with a decrease in the USA in just 2018 from 35 to 24 per cent) according to Tørsløv, Wier and Zucman (2018). Research has also indicated that increased international capital mobility puts downward pressure on countries' corporate tax rates; and that, in turn, lower corporate tax rates are associated with higher levels of FDI, which would confirm the importance of the level of taxation as a factor attracting FDI. But it has also shown that traditional arguments on the negative effects of high tax rates on FDI are based on assumptions that may not always correspond to reality; and, most importantly, that in attracting FDI the advantages of agglomeration of economic activity and provision by government of good physical and institutional infrastructure largely match those related to a more favourable tax treatment (but paradoxically, the very cost of attracting FDI through lower tax rates reduces the resources available for infrastructure improvement; see Yamin and Sinkovics (2009)); while the offer of particularly attractive natural resources or the presence of a large domestic consumer market can strongly reinforce the bargaining power of a developing country vis-à-vis MNCs. On the preceding points see

[21] The issue of fiscal competition for the attraction of multinational investment has been under discussion for decades. For instance, Vernon (1971) concluded that 'Some kinds of "artificial" factors … ought to be prevented from providing the basis for a major decision on the part of multinational enterprises. Others, however, should be subject to international agreement … Nations cannot put off much longer some joint understanding over the conditions when subsidies and tax concessions were appropriate in the international movement of industry' (p. 270). More recently, Summers (2008) argued that 'the US should take the lead in promoting global co-operation in the international tax arena. There has been a race to the bottom in the taxation of corporate income as nations lower their rates to entice business to issue more debt and invest in their jurisdictions. Closely related is the problem of tax havens … It might be inevitable that globalization leads to some increases in inequality, it is not necessary that it also compromises the possibility of progressive taxation'.

Garretsen and Peeters (2006), Karmakar and Martinez-Vazquez (2014) and Owens and Zhan (2018).

That differences in the taxation of goods can have effects on trade flows was pointed out by Ohlin in the 1950s and reiterated in Ohlin (1977); Melvin (1970) presented a model explaining how such differences (both in the tax rates applied to goods and in the collection of the tax at the producer versus the consumer level) can give rise to specific comparative advantages for a country. When the international movement of people and capital was limited by capital controls and by technical obstacles to transport and communication, analysis of trade distortions owing to differences in fiscal standards attracted limited interest from economists and mainly regarded differences in the taxation of goods. With capital liberalization, transport progress and the ICT revolution, attention shifted to differences in direct taxation of firms, persons and property as they can variously influence trade, FDI and movements of other capital, highly skilled workers and rich people. For example, Jones (2000) stressed that 'intercountry differences in [factor incomes] taxation take a first-order importance in affecting patterns of production and trade if there exist any inputs that have a choice of country in which to locate' (p. 20).

Differences in corporate taxation are probably not a major factor of advantage in trade and competition for the attraction of FDI between advanced and developing countries, given the huge differences in labour costs between the two groups. But they represent a significant competition-distorting factor in trade and FDI attraction among advanced countries, especially within the EU, where many other standards and regulations have been unified or co-ordinated. And they are an even more important factor in competition among developing countries, which frequently base their development strategies on FDI. In both cases, these corporate taxation differences may indeed lead to a dangerous, and in the end damaging for all, race to the bottom in applying tax rates and fiscal incentives particularly favourable to holders of capital, technology and specialized skills.

It is quite natural to look at differences in taxation – in particular corporate taxation – as a distorting factor that hinders the level playing field necessary for free competition, and to identify economists arguing for their international harmonization as promoters of a more equitable and efficient trading system. This is probably right: tax harmonization is aimed not only at avoiding, through common tax rates, unfair competition and possible races to the bottom, but also at simplifying the comparison of national tax regimes and their compliance by investors and entrepreneurs through the adoption of uniform definitions, standards and mechanisms applied by different countries in tax policy (for example, establishing common criteria for the determination of corporate tax bases; that is, the amount of profits to which tax rates are applied),

Nevertheless, the issue is highly debatable and confusing.[22] Some economists deny

[22] This seems to be largely because taxation has an extremely complex nature, having multiple, frequently incompatible, functions, so that a balance must somehow be struck between different possible objectives, such as providing an equitable mechanism for sharing the expenditure for public services; incentivizing economic actors to invest, innovate and increase efficiency, and to abstain from activities and

the advantages of tax harmonization. Advocates of tax competition argue that lower taxes in a country simply indicate that the country is more efficient than others in providing public services, and that this is a competitive advantage that a country should not only be allowed, but also encouraged to exploit, like the advantage of more efficient workers or more efficient physical and institutional infrastructure. Others argue that different levels of taxation usually reflect differences in the extension and quality of services that citizens – to improve the efficiency of production, or to ensure a higher standard of living, or to guarantee egalitarian access to essential services by every member of society – freely decide to produce and/or finance collectively instead of having them bought privately by individuals in the market. But if the citizens of a country decide to have more or better public services or larger financial transfers to poor members, that has nothing to do with distortions in international competition: it is up to the country's citizens to decide whether they can allow themselves such services and transfers (in the same way as higher ecological or labour standards), knowing that this may negatively influence international competitiveness.

However, the issue is more complex than this. Taxes are not intended to only cover expenditure for the desired level of services or interpersonal transfers: some countries, other things being equal, must charge higher taxes because they are burdened with interest payments on a large public debt incurred in the past to build necessary infrastructure or simply inherited from previous generations (which in turn may have dilapidated the money, or used it in failed projects, or for payment of war expenses or war reparations imposed on them). Or they may have a particularly unfavourable demographic structure that generates higher expenses for pensions or for education. While some countries can apply extremely low tax rates because the government is the owner of important resources (such as oil) that it can use to finance public infrastructure and services, there are countries that have to charge higher taxes than competitors simply because they need more funds to compensate for particularly unfavourable geographical or climatic conditions; these conditions inevitably require, to obtain the same level of infrastructure as other countries, much higher public investment expenditure (just think of the cost of building a road network in a mountainous country or of maintaining that network in a very cold one). Does the concept of com-

---

behaviour that would produce negative externalities; creating the conditions for equality of opportunity among individuals (and firms); and operating a redistribution of the benefits and losses produced, without any justification or with inequitable effects, by the activity of the economic agents in the market.

A comparison comes to mind between taxation and punishment for crimes: the latter, like taxation, seeks to satisfy different goals, such as punishing people for wrongdoing, thus providing some psychological relief to the victims and discouraging people from committing crimes by showing them how painful the punishments are for breaking the law; isolating dangerous individuals from the rest of society, so that its members can conduct their lives without fear; and re-educating criminals and gradually reinserting them in social life so that, at the end of their prison term, they may take on activities and ways of life useful and riskless for themselves and for society. The kind of punishment most fit to reach one goal – just as happens with taxes – may well be incompatible with the one most fit to reach another. Thus one should not be surprised that discussions on both crime punishment and taxation are so heated and frequently inconclusive.

petition on a level playing field imply that tax harmonization would confer an unfair advantage to the countries not having to cover these additional costs? The issue is further complicated by the fact that a higher level of public services, while requiring a higher level of tax rates, can raise the productivity of production processes, and so (as is frequently the case in Scandinavian countries) may not have any negative effect on international competitiveness.[23]

The differences in economists' opinions on tax competition versus tax harmonization largely reflect opposite ideological views on the nature and role of government. Arguments in favour of harmonization are usually based on a view of government as a 'benevolent' entity, which collects taxes and uses them to provide citizens, as efficiently as possible, with the public services they demand. The opposite position, developed by the 'public choice' school (associated with James Buchanan), moves instead from a totally negative view of government as an entity representing the personal interests of public officials, who pursue the goal of tax revenue increases in order to maximize the size of the public sector and so of their own rents (in terms of money and/or career advancement, power and prestige). From this perspective, competition among countries to attract and retain increasingly mobile investors and entrepreneurs through lower taxation is seen as a powerful instrument to compel politicians to deliver only those services that are really demanded by their citizens and to do it at the lowest possible cost. While the first 'benevolent' government position seems to put too much faith in public officials' lack of personal interest, the 'public choice' position appears unacceptable in its rejection of the possibility that public officials may in fact entertain a genuine interest in citizens' welfare and in ignoring the role of democratic institutions – free elections and free media in the first place – that in any case create powerful incentives for public officials to take citizens' well-being and demands into account.

* * *

The issue of tax harmonization underwent a fundamental revival in the last decade mainly as a consequence of two connected developments. On the one hand, following the outbreak of the 2008 global crisis, almost all advanced countries experienced fiscal shortfalls that made it difficult to provide social assistance just at the time it was most needed, and public attention focused, more than before, on MNCs' long adopted practices (indicated in Footnote 50 in Section 9.4.2) which allow them to shift profits from high-tax countries where they are earned, to very low-tax countries or fiscal havens where apparently little business activity is carried out, but where the corporation earning the profits has established its residence. On the other hand, in recent years the issue of the New Economy's giants – among the largest and most profitable world corporations – being able to largely or completely escape taxation in the

[23] Two contributions discussing problems of tax harmonization in the context of the contemporary integration of economies and liberalized capital movements are Baldwin and Krugman (2000) and Rodrik and van Ypersele (2001). For a general review of arguments for and against tax harmonization see Karmakar and Martinez-Vazquez (2014).

countries where they operate has increasingly been of interest to media and economists, leading, particularly in the EU, to a strong public reaction.

In 2013, as mentioned in Section 11.2.4, in response to a request by the G20 group of countries, the OECD launched the ambitious BEPS initiative – in which developing countries and international organizations were also invited to participate, and actively did so – to investigate and propose common solutions to the problem of profit-shifting, and also to tackle the tax problems of the digital economy (whose products' VA is very difficult to localize), envisaging the possibility of a major reassessment of the whole body of international corporate tax law (the EU, for its part, had been active since 2001 in advancing proposals for the harmonization and simplification of member countries' tax systems).

The initiatives of the OECD and the EU were indicative of a new attitude of governments on the issue of corporate taxation and fiscal havens, and led to a number of important advances in the direction of greater harmonization, coordination and transparency of tax systems (one of the most important results being the much increased exchange of information among tax authorities and between them and banking institutions). But the hopes for a fundamental change in international tax laws came up against the reality of a lack of consensus among the main countries.[24]

On the problems created by the digital economy, in particular, a sharp contrast divided the countries that feel these problems can be tackled by small adjustments within the framework of existing international tax arrangements and those that think a major change in the international tax treatment of digital activity is called for. The issue is of fundamental importance (and highly complicated) because the digital revolution has not only created a wholly new sector of firms specialized in this activity but has also deeply penetrated the way production is carried out in practically every other sector. A clash developed in more recent years especially between the USA, home to most of the world's giants of the New Economy that in the past have reaped huge profits from the lack of any international tax regulation of digital ac-

[24] Among the many solutions that were proposed for the corporate taxation of MNCs, two are worth mentioning: first, a corporate minimum tax, to be applied to gross revenue (that is, turnover; taxation based on that aggregate is already applied by a number of developing countries) and then divided among countries where the corporation operates on the basis of an agreed formula. Such a tax, despite its drawbacks (it may impose the payment of taxes on corporations not recording any profit), would have the advantages of simplicity and efficiency: it would eliminate all the complex problems regarding deductions from income and tax avoidance through profit-shifting (on the proposal see Durst (2019). The second proposal was some form of formulary apportionment; this kind of approach was advanced by the EU Commission in 2011 for the EU area. It envisaged the consolidation of MNCs' profits within the entire EU and then the apportioning of the tax base to different EU members according to a formula based on indicators of activity (turnover, wage bills, employees and physical capital); each member country would then be free to subject its share of the tax base to the tax rate it considers most appropriate (this is analogous to the system applied in the USA and Canada for state-level corporate taxation). A similar formulary apportionment system (based on employees, assets, sales and users) was among the methods recommended by the OECD in 2019 for allocating taxing rights on part of MNCs' profits generated by cross-border digital activities.

tivities and stand to lose them if any serious discipline is introduced; and the EU countries, which represent the group most damaged by the lack of regulations, while their degree of political unification – even if largely incomplete – provides them with a bargaining power much superior to that of individual countries.

The overall result until 2020 was that the OECD had to scale back its original goal of redesigning international tax law in the light of the new realities of our times, advancing instead proposals for reform (originally expected to be definitively agreed by 2020) on some of the most critical issues, and producing recommendations that a very large number of countries have been implementing, although very selectively. Problems were further complicated by the introduction in 2017, by the Trump administration, of an extensive reform of the US corporate tax system and later by the American decision not to subscribe to some of the BEPS proposals, and then, in 2020, even to suspend participation in talks on crucial aspects of the digital economy taxation project.

Since 2015, as the BEPS initiative appeared to make little progress, particularly on the issue of taxation of digital services, the UK, France and Italy, as well as Australia, India and Israel, decided to apply, until a final agreement was reached, unilateral national measures of taxation of these services. The OECD, acknowledging its failure to reach a common accord on the issue, gave its approval – provided certain criteria were respected – for the interim adoption by individual countries of any of the possible solutions it had advanced in its documents. The danger was that as more countries enacted their own piecemeal provisions, the hope of ever reaching a consensual arrangement was fading further, with MNCs facing increasing uncertainty, compliance costs and risk of double taxation; see Gianni (2018).

Following the change in the US administration, a surprising result was suddenly announced in London on 5 June 2021: the countries of the G7 group (the four largest European countries, the USA, Canada and Japan) agreed to support the OECD initiative and committed 'to reaching an equitable solution on the allocation of taxing rights, with market countries awarded taxing rights on at least 20% of profit exceeding a 10% margin for the largest and most profitable multinational enterprises … We also commit to a global minimum tax of at least 15% on a country by country basis.' (G7 Finance Ministers & Central Banks Governors Communiqué, London 5 June 2021). Less than a month later, India and China had also entered into the agreement (of course, its implementation will take a number of years, as many important technical details will have to be defined).

Even apart from this recent unexpected success, the importance of the BEPS initiative must not be underestimated: it is the first attempt to produce, within a relatively short time, a large revision of an international tax system established between the 1920s and the 1940s; it includes all the important countries of the world and a very large majority of the others (the total number of countries participating in the initiative is 139); for the first time developing countries are fully represented, with some of them playing an active role; and it is at the centre of political and public attention and debate, contrary to previous work on tax changes that took place within restricted groups of tax experts. Institutional mechanisms and international agreements fostering tax cooperation increased drastically, producing a fundamental improvement in the international exchange of information and in transparency in the field of taxation.[25]

12.3.5 Distribution and redistribution of the national gains from trade and technical progress

A growing number of economists have become convinced that instead of, or in addition to, trying to compensate and assist workers adversely affected by trade and technology, a fundamental attack should be made against the economic and political mechanisms and practices that in advanced countries, and particularly in the USA, lead to a distorted distribution of trade and technology benefits and in general to growing inequalities of income and wealth between different groups of the population. These distortions are both unacceptable from economic, political and moral points of view, and dangerous, as they can easily lead to an escalation of protectionist demands and to negative populistic political reactions.[26]

---

[25] The issues of tax competition and recent developments in the reform of corporate tax systems cannot be discussed in this work. The issue of the taxation of MNCs and the technical details of the related debate were the object of the essays edited by Pogge and Mechta (2016). For a synthetic description of the progress of the BEPS initiative and the developments it has triggered in the field of tax competition see Ault (2019); interesting contributions are Keen and Konrad (2013), Tørsløv, Wier and Zucman (2018), Lennard (2018), Durst (2019) (who analyses, in particular, international tax problems from the developing countries' perspective), Fuest, Parenti and Toubal (2019) and J. Li, Bao and H. Li (2019a, b). For the specific issues pertaining to the taxation of the digital economy and intangibles in general see OECD (2013, 2018, 2019), Lennard (2018), Grinberg (2019) and Hadzhieva (2019).

The work of Tørsløv, Wier and Zucman (2018) is of particular interest since it provides up-to-date quantitative estimates of MNCs' profit-shifting from developed countries, based on new databases. The share of corporation tax that non-tax-haven developed countries lose because of profit-shifting to financial havens is estimated to be close to 40 per cent of the profits MNCs produce outside the country where the parent company is located, the EU being the prime loser from this shifting (the effect being a reduction of overall EU corporate tax revenue around 20 per cent). The authors also try to correct the data for GDP, balance of payments and corporate capital income, including in these aggregates the figures corresponding to MNCs' profits shifted to fiscal havens, which are not considered in the data for these aggregates produced by national accounts statistics. The effect of the correction is quite significant: for instance, European capital's share of corporate VA is estimated to have increased since the early 1990s twice as much as estimated on the basis of national accounts. It is found that MNCs' profit-shifting is a practice common to all sectors of activity and not limited to ICT sectors, and that it takes place predominantly through manipulation of intra-group transfer prices and the offshoring of intangibles, while intra-group interest payments are much less important. As for the countries most affected by profit-shifting, about 35 per cent of the total profits shifted come from the EU non-tax-haven members, 30 per cent from developing countries and 25 per cent from the USA.

[26] From the economic point of view, inequality and the forces that have intensified it appear increasingly damaging to the working of the market system itself. They lead to a loss of potential efficiency gains; reduce the creation of resources and distort the allocation of existing ones; prevent market signals from indicating the types of production that would most improve the welfare of the majority of people; and reinforce asymmetries of power, information and access to technological knowledge, that

Economists have also increasingly come to recognize – see, for example, Reich (2015), Baker (2016), Stiglitz (2019) and Case and Deaton (2020) – that those mechanisms and practices are not the consequence of natural economic laws or inescapable market logic, but simply the result of a general deterioration of political life and of the working of democracy, connected with the increasing disparities of power among economic actors. In other words, the problem of inequality appears to be of a political, more than an economic, nature; accordingly, the solutions should be searched for in the political rather than the economic sphere. And the idea is increasingly spreading that it is the basic social contract among government, workers and business that should be refounded so as to adapt it to the new realities of technological progress and international trade.

The difficulties we are confronted with today were anticipated by some forward-looking economists. More than half a century ago, Meade (1964), referring to the progress of automation, identified what is still largely the core of the problem: 'The question we should ask is: What shall we all do when output per man-hour of work is extremely high but practically the whole of the output goes to a few property owners, while the mass of the workers are relatively (or even absolutely) worse off than before?' (p. 26). To provide possible answers, he advanced, without going into details, a number of suggestions (see Footnote 31 in this section) that to a large extent correspond to the main proposals advanced in the last few years, which are briefly discussed in this section.

---

reduce potential growth. From the political point of view, they contribute to a reduction of constitutional rights, a lowering of the standards of integrity of political representatives and public officials, and a general deterioration of the political process and of democratic life, as the latter appears more and more based on the principle of 'one dollar one vote'.

People have realized that the results of economic globalization are very different from those that fervent advocates of free markets and minimum state intervention in economic life declared it was leading to. They saw how the alleged free market was based on abysmal inequalities in starting conditions (in terms of income, wealth, education and information) among players of the economic game and that the rules of the game were rigged in favour of the rich and the powerful; and that the result has been a further increase of inequality, stagnation or worsening of wages and economic conditions, much higher insecurity and finally the worst economic crisis since the 1930s – not to speak of the negative externalities of economic activity, threatening the ecological equilibria of our planet. Even those who were ready to accept the logic of the perfectly competitive market have thus been led to abandon trust in and support of the market in general, which in turn produced further negative effects on the working of market mechanisms. This increased awareness of the economic situation might have represented a very positive development if it had led people to demand changes that could eliminate the market distortions listed here. Unfortunately, people appeared to be more prone to support demagogic proposals to improve their current situation through apparently simpler solutions in terms of protectionist barriers, or a generic fight against financiers and multinationals plotting against the people, or the identification of foreign immigrants and minorities with the origin of all economic difficulties.

On populist reactions to the increased inequalities produced by globalization see Rodrik (2018a). The lack of more constructive political reactions, as argued by Rodrik (2016b), can be basically attributed to the greatest weakness of the left in recent decades: the inability of its economists and political leaders to provide a politically popular and economically sound programme of transformation of capitalism and globalization according to the needs of our times. All too often, instead, they uncritically accepted the widely trumpeted arguments and policy recipes of market fundamentalists.

In their contribution to a 1972 World Bank conference on the development prospects of the Third World, at a time when globalization was just beginning, H. G. Johnson (1973) and C. Frank (1973) foresaw the basic problems that increased international integration would create for advanced countries. Johnson observed:

> technological lags among nations may reflect the existence of barriers to the free movement of goods, capital and labor, rather than anything inherent in the nature of technology itself. If, for example, there were no barriers to the free movement of goods, one would expect production with a new technology to locate itself in regions with the lower costs of factors of production; and if capital were free to move, these would be the regions with the lowest labor costs. (p. 45)

In his comment on Johnson's paper, Frank pointed out that:

> The free movement of capital and technology … implies complete factor-price equalization in the long run … Of course skill differentials may persist and keep wage rates higher in the United States than in other countries. But … skill levels will have to increase much more rapidly in the United States if United States workers are to maintain the same relative rate of growth in worker incomes. It also means that other ways of redistributing income may have to be found. If a free and competitive economy will shift the relative returns in the United States in favour of capital, we must find ways of giving workers some share of the increased returns to capital, that is ways in which labor can share more equitably in gains from trade. (1973, p. 64)

As for possible measures to pursue this goal, he argued:

> While adjustment assistance might mitigate the losses in income and welfare for workers who lose their jobs as a *direct* result of import competition, it does very little to redress the deterioration of labor's perceived bargaining position with multinational firms and the general tendency for downward pressures on returns to labor relative to returns to capital. There are ways in which labor's complaints might be met. Most important are full employment policies, manpower training programs and measures for income redistribution. (p. 67)

Unfortunately, H.G. Johnson's and C. Frank's insights were almost ignored at the time and did not have much effect on international economists' thinking; the policy measures proposed by C. Frank, apart from some – scarcely effective – action on manpower training programmes, were not adopted.

Twenty years later, when the first results of globalization became visible and started to be discussed among economists, it was the most eminent journalist of the *Financial Times*, Samuel Brittan (1993), who took up the issue. Noticing the changes under way in the world economy (increasing economic weight of developing countries, shift from manufacturing to services in advanced economies, offshoring to developing countries, increasing gaps in wages and employment conditions between low and high-skill Western workers), he concluded:

> The challenge is to find non vindictive ways of redistributing income towards the losers, it is to find methods of redistribution that do not assume that all income belongs to the state, it is to find methods of redistribution which do not destroy the gains from trade and technology, while compensating those who would otherwise lose out from change.

The problem is that after more than a quarter of a century we still do not see any beginning of serious concrete action to meet that challenge.[27] Interestingly, a decade before, when the design of Thatcherian privatizations was under discussion, Brittan (1984) had provocatively advanced the proposal that the shares of the companies to be privatized, instead of being sold on the market, should be freely distributed to the population on a strictly equalitarian way, so that income from capital would supplement people's income from work.

One had to wait until the mid-2000s, when the US debate on offshoring took a more pessimistic turn, to see the development of a consensus among economists about the seriousness of the increase in income and wealth inequality in advanced countries and the urgency of devising mechanisms to redistribute to the factor labour part of the huge benefits that trade, offshoring and technical progress (and the enormous scope for tax avoidance) produced for owners of capital, technologies and for some very high-skill sections of employee labour (such as the managers of big corporations). Although Samuelson (2005) pointed out that even at that time many economists continued to show little interest in the problem of the distorted distribution of the gains from trade, proposals were more and more frequently advanced regarding possible interventions to resolve the problem.

Six main lines of action have been proposed, which are briefly described in this section. To them may be added the revival of the proposal, already advanced by Keynes in 1930, of fighting unemployment by sharing among all workers, through a drastic reduction of weekly work hours, the limited human-work requirements of modern automated production (but such sharing would also require strong redistribution mechanisms in favour of workers, as the wages corresponding to reduced work hours would not provide the minimum compensation necessary for a decent standard of living). Almost none of these proposals are mutually exclusive and some are conditional on others being adopted. Really significant results could probably only be obtained if some of them were jointly implemented. The need to adopt a plurality of policies to tackle the problem of increasing inequality in advanced countries was also the conclusion Blanchard and Rodrik (2019) arrived at after presenting an interesting summary of the results of a conference on inequality held the same year at the Peterson Institute.

The problem about these proposals has not so much to do with their economic logic, their operational structure or the technical difficulty of implementing them in

[27] Taking up the issue 13 years later, Brittan (2006) argued that, given the increasing mobility of other factors, the only really immobile factor of production that should be taxed to finance compensation of workers damaged by globalization is land, by which he meant 'pure space, which is commanding higher and higher returns because there is so little of it in favoured locations'.

practice (after all, most of them have already been experimented in some countries and important lessons can be drawn from these experiences). The main problem is instead the difficulty of widely publicizing these proposals and how to produce an awakening of citizens' democratic conscience so that they become aware of the urgency of these actions, and how to find ways of organizing citizens' initiatives that can lead to the proposals being included in the political agenda.

Two of these proposals (a more comprehensive safety net and universal basic income, UBI) directly entail – as is also the case with trade-damaged compensation measures, especially if properly designed and applied – an increase in taxation for the wealthiest members of the population in general and/or for the groups that unjustifiably gain from trade and technical progress at the expense of other groups. However, the necessary increase in tax receipts would not so much require higher rates of taxation and a reinforcement of tax progressivity as the simple cancelling of loopholes in fiscal laws and regulations, and the abolition of the scandalous resort to fiscal havens.

The other proposals are more in line with Stiglitz's (2019) insistence – based on an argument developed by Hacker (2011) – that the problem of rebalancing power between the owners of different factors of production or groups of the population through the elimination or drastic reduction of both the precariousness and the vulnerability of some of them, should not be treated as a problem of redistribution of the gains from trade and technical progress, but as a problem of an originally distorted distribution of these gains, calling for major changes in the political and economic structure of our societies. The difference between the two approaches is not of secondary importance, but goes directly to the root of the problem.

As stressed by Stiglitz, it is not so much that in modern economic life some production factors or some economic agents originate most of the advances in productivity, and a moral concern for equality and social justice dictates that the fruits of those advances should be more widely distributed. Rather, what usually happens is that productivity advances are (or appear to be) the products of the activity of some economic agents and factors, and not of others, because specific political and power mechanisms – which he analyses in detail – produce a distortion of the rules of the economic game and an infringement of basic constitutional principles: 'Inequities are created in the very process by which incomes get generated, as firms exercise monopoly and monopsony power or as they exploit others...or as they discriminate against the vulnerable or those of particular races or ethnic groups' (Stiglitz 2019, p. 198). Such mechanisms, for instance, make it possible for the principle of equality of opportunity to be systematically violated, so that through better education or family and business connections certain social groups have a disproportionate probability of reaching the top or the more rewarding positions in society. There is nothing inherent in the working of the market system that dictates that corporate managers should be paid exorbitant salaries without relation to the results of their activity; or that the benefits of innovation – very often resulting from publicly funded research – should be monopolized by private firms through patents and other IPR for unjustifiably long periods on the basis of a legal discipline resulting from firms' lobbying and other forms of pressure over politicians and regulators.[28]

Intervening directly on the distribution mechanisms would make it possible to largely avoid redistribution through taxation, which has two negative effects. The first is the practical difficulty of making people pay the taxes they are called upon to contribute, as tax evasion and tax avoidance (the specific use of existing legal regulations so as to avoid or reduce the amount of taxes to be paid), especially in certain countries, are widespread. The second, and the more important one, is a psychological consequence of taxation. Many people, once they receive given incomes on the basis of market transactions, consider them as the just reward for their contribution to overall wealth creation; and see the taxes on those rewards, beyond what is necessary to contribute to a minimum of public services they themselves make use of, as unjustified subtractions of part of their income for redistribution purposes whose rationale and goals they do not share. If the pre-tax incomes people receive were the result of an originally more equitable distribution process, *ex post* redistribution could be drastically reduced. This point had been made by Hacker (2011) and Reich (2015); the latter author observing that everybody clearly sees the visible, increasing redistribution of income from the rich to the poor carried out by government through taxes and transfer payments; while few are aware of the invisible, much larger redistribution in the opposite direction that is carried out by the anonymous workings of a market largely rigged in favour of the most powerful economic agents, who have managed to fix the rules of the market game. Case and Deaton (2020) have recently taken a much stronger position: 'We do not think that taxation is the solution to rent-seeking: the right way to stop thieves is to stop them stealing, not to raise their taxes ... We need to correct the process, not try to fix the outcomes' (p. 12).

The six main lines of action proposed are as follows:

1. *Macroeconomic policies for full employment.* General macroeconomic management should sustain demand and ensure full employment, as C. Frank (1973) suggested. An economy working at or near full employment is the most effective insurance for workers losing their job that another, not much inferior, will be found. Displaced workers, unemployed people and those first entering the labour

[28] Blanchard and Rodrik (2019) distinguish policies to reduce inequality in a way slightly different from Hacker and Stiglitz, identifying three different categories: 'pre-production policies' (such as provision of health care, education and inheritance/estate taxes) which influence the endowments with which people enter the labour market; 'production policies' (concerning the minimum wage, job guarantees, industrial relations and labour laws, economic activity regulations, innovation and antitrust policies), which affect the main aspects of the production process; and 'post-production policies' (such as progressive income taxes, wealth taxes, transfers and social safety nets), which redistribute income and wealth.

O'Neill (2020) has shown the logical difficulty of clearly separating income pre-distribution from income *ex post* redistribution: the existing structure of taxes collected and benefits and services paid out by the government are part of and shape the market arrangements that define economic agents' rights and determine their possible actions and bargaining power.

market would thus not be compelled by economic necessity to accept whatever wages and work conditions are offered them; and the reduction of insecurity and connected anguish would largely eliminate the workers' generalized resistance to change that is produced by uncertainty.

These goals inspired advanced countries' macroeconomic policies in the first post-World War II decades and contributed to the unprecedented economic and social progress of that 'Golden Age'. Subsequently, a series of factors contributed to a much reduced engagement by politicians and economic policy managers in the fight against unemployment and wage stagnation: the disappearance of the communist threat, which had made governments give priority to full employment and continuing improvement of the conditions of their working masses; the possibility for domestic firms, in the new globalized economy, to find outlets for their products in foreign markets and to offshore to low-wage countries large parts of their production; the greater ability of families to support members, especially young ones, not finding a job or losing one; and the objective limitations to macroeconomic management resulting from increased inflation, swelling public debt and reduced scope in the new, more integrated world economy for independent national macroeconomic policies.

Milberg and Winkler (2013) recommended in particular the adoption of measures to increase domestic real investment, which in the USA and other advanced economies has registered a marked deceleration in recent decades in connection with the move towards financialization (the phenomenon was discussed in Section 11.2.1). C. Frank had proposed cancelling taxation rules favourable to investment in offshored production facilities and compelling firms shifting production overseas to bear part of the costs of the training and relocation of domestic workers displaced by the shift; Milberg and Winkler, among others, advanced more specific suggestions, adapted to contemporary conditions. They are aimed not only at eliminating unjustified taxation advantages for corporate profits from offshore investment and activity, but also, and especially, at restoring corporate managers' policy of reinvesting profits in the firm to ensure its growth through increased productivity and innovation, producing long-term gains for all the parties involved in its activity; drastically reducing the use of profit for financial operations, mergers and acquisitions, redistributions to shareholders and share buybacks, designed to increase share value in the short run.

Under the heading of macroeconomic policies – despite its very different nature – one may also include the demand, already advanced half a century ago by H. G. Johnson (1973), for a reform of the international exchange rate system. Since other obstacles to, and interventions distorting, trade flows have been significantly reduced, improvements in exchange rate mechanisms have become relatively more important. With comparative advantages having become more kaleidoscopic – that is, more subject to sudden changes as a result of even small movements in relative competitiveness – the lack of smooth and efficient exchange rate adjustment mechanisms and exchange rate manipulation can have disrupting effects on trade flows. Exchange rate policies directed at keeping the national currency undervalued have been used by some countries to gain unjustified competitive advantages at the expense of competitors; or they have been introduced as a temporary measure for whatever other reason, but owing to the operation of scale economies and hysteresis have produced permanent losses to competitor countries (since once a line of production has to be closed in a country as a consequence of the superior competitiveness of another one artificially produced by a temporary exchange rate devaluation, the production terminated cannot be later resumed, as reversibility of investment and closure decisions does not occur in the real world). In a 2006 panel discussion, Prestowitz – in Sha and Hughes (2009) – proposed that negotiations should take place within the WTO to ban the use of currency manipulations, just as it had been agreed for export subsidies. He noted that such manipulations not only allowed some countries to artificially sustain their export competitiveness at the expense of other ones, but also had the additional effect of stimulating investment by foreign corporations in their countries – with its infusion of technology and skills – by making it cheaper: 'by maintaining … undervalued currencies, they not only export products, but they effectively import factories' (p. 40).

2. *Reinforcement of antitrust discipline.* Much stronger antitrust action has been advocated to contrast the formation of monopolies and oligopolies in many sectors, especially in the USA where such action has been severely weakened by the political initiatives of corporate interests. In the USA, the latter managed to have an extremely restrictive theoretical concept of antitrust action adopted by legislators and judges, and very lax enforcement of existing antitrust rules. US antitrust action, as stressed by Stiglitz (2019) – who also indicates the specific areas where reform of current legislation is particularly urgent – is not directed at preventing concentration of economic power from leading to excessive political influence. The authorities' intervention, following the ultra-liberalist ideology of the Chicago School – according to which economies are naturally competitive, so that monopolies can only be temporary and action against them is unnecessary and counterproductive – is conceived as strictly limited to cases of blatant restraint of competition and price abuses in a short-term static perspective. Particularly strong antitrust action should be envisaged for concentrations and anti-competitive practices in the field of information and knowledge, as both in the sector of mass media and in those of academic publishing and IPR – that is, the markets for ideas, where absolute freedom is essential as they concern products with goals and influence that go way beyond those of ordinary products – particularly damaging effects are produced by monopolies and oligopolies.

   As pointed out in Section 9.2, globalization has allowed new scope for international competition, and the ICT revolution has given medium and often even small firms access to production processes and sales channels that in the past were only available to firms producing on a large scale. But at the same time, in many sectors globalization has created the need for a much larger size of firms to ensure they can competitively produce and sell at world level. This has caused a marked increase of entry barriers and the formation of gigantic groups.[29] Overall, globalization and the ICT revolution, especially by allowing the creation of GVCs and favouring the explosion of merger and acquisition activity, appear to have led, most clearly in the USA, to a higher degree of corporate concentration, the reinforcement of existing oligopolies and monopolies, and the creation of powerful new ones.

There is also another reason for this trend towards concentration: new high-tech sectors in particular require massive availability of funds and resources to reach a critical mass in R&D activity and in other functions. This is largely because the impossibility of forecasting the occurrence (and the effects) of innovations makes it necessary for firms to promote a large number of lines of research (both within and across sectors) so as to be confident that success in at least a few of them will produce large profits, compensating for the inevitable losses in all the research and innovation initiatives that end up in failure.

Given this trend towards concentration among large firms at both the national and international level, a more severe antitrust discipline appears essential, especially in countries where it is most deficient (for example, in the USA more than in the EU). But since with globalization competition is increasingly taking place at the level of the world market, even more necessary would be international antitrust action against MNCs' restrictive business practices, and in particular against the monopolistic behaviour of GVC lead firms, favoured by the huge asymmetry of bargaining power between them and their suppliers. Unfortunately, no supra-national authority exists for fixing rules ensuring competition and sanctioning monopolistic behaviour in the international market, and it is not to be expected that any significant international antitrust discipline will see the light of day in the near future, given the marked differences in national views on this issue.

3. *More voice to workers and their representatives.* Many consider it essential to rebalance power between workers and their employers in advanced countries not only by restoring basic worker and trade union rights and eliminating through macroeconomic policies the chronic excess of unemployed workers over available vacancies, but also and especially by more generally increasing the voice of labour, which at all levels and in all spheres has been overwhelmed by that of big business. This has been largely a consequence of the loss of power by trade un-

---

[29] The contradictory consequences of the ICT revolution for corporate concentration and competition are exemplified by the effect it had on consumers' and firms' information flows On the one hand, it allowed consumers to go online for instant and free information on products, sellers, prices and previous customers' evaluations, which they would never have accessed in the past; and it allowed small firms to collect an enormous amount of information on markets, competitors, prices of inputs, customers, export possibilities and so on that in the past was available only to very large firms. On the other hand, it has created a disastrous divide between the large majority of firms and a few gigantic corporations or groups that monopolize the collection, and thus the distribution, of huge masses of data on all aspects of people's economic and non-economic lives; the unequal availability of these data creates asymmetries of information between firms that greatly distort competition.

ions, which in the early post-war decades successfully managed to promote workers' interests and demands.

Starting in the 1980s, a number of developments, reinforcing one another in a vicious circle, have weakened trade unions in all advanced countries; and particularly in the USA and the UK, where the attack on organized work (favoured by the latter's excesses and mistakes) became a specific declared objective of the new ultra-liberalist governments of Thatcher and Reagan. Major changes took place in the structure of production of advanced countries, away from manufacturing – which implied large concentrations of workers in factories and had a long tradition of workers' trade union militancy – towards services, where usually workers are widely dispersed and isolated and have more differentiated interests, so that trade unions have always been more difficult to organize. Automation proceeded rapidly. There was massive recourse by firms to offshoring and, for the activities remaining at home, to the threat of offshoring them. In some countries an offensive was successfully carried out by employers and big business to have practices violating basic worker and trade union rights both within and outside the workplace (such as agreements among firms not to employ workers leaving one of them) declared legal or tolerated in practice; Kreuger (2018) illustrates some of these practices adopted by US firms, often through tacit forms of collusion. To these factors must be added the deficiencies and mistakes of trade unions themselves, such as their scarce ability to devise organizational changes and strategies for workers' action adapted to the new technological conditions of modern working activity (for example, they tend to be organized by sectors, but the development of trade in tasks and GVCs would require a different structure); and in many countries their inability to undertake initiatives to tackle the dramatic phenomena of limited workers' rights for part-time and other precarious workers, and of massive youth unemployment. The final result has been a loss of efficacy of their action, at the same time an effect and a cause of drastically reduced membership and connected financial weakening (for proposals to increase the voice of workers by strengthening trade unions see Andrias and Rogers (2018) and Tucker (2018)).

The voice of workers has been drastically reduced at all levels, as Hira and Hira (2005) pointed out with reference to the USA, but the tendency has been common to most of the advanced countries (on reduced workers' voice see Hyman (2018); on the different concepts of voice developed by students see M. Barry, Dundon and Wilkinson (2018)). In many countries fear of job loss, trade union weakness and the overall diminished bargaining power of workers have reduced individual and collective freedom at the workplace, where workers may even be afraid to express their views and denounce abuses for fear of being blacklisted; while managers care less and less about their employees – reduced in numbers and liable to be fired at any time following the introduction of new automated devices or the sudden offshoring of parts of the production process – as they have to concentrate their efforts almost exclusively on maximizing shareholder value. Even worse is the situation of the growing mass of part-time, semi-autonomous and precarious workers not covered by the legal rights and safety nets of normal workers. In the EU, the 2002 Directive introducing a general framework for improving workers' information on their firm's activities and establishing bodies and procedures for the consultation of workers and dialogue between them and employers, finds obstacles to its effective application. Hickland, Cullinane, Dobbins, Dundon and Donaghey (2020) illustrate with case studies how companies in the UK and Ireland managed to circumvent the Directive and maintain 'employee silence'.

There is a scarcity of worker-oriented think tanks, while big business has plenty of money to fund – directly and through its foundations (see, for the USA, Mayer (2016)) – research, studies, conferences and debates on issues of its own choice by personalities of its own choice, whose results it can widely publicize. Big corporations' influence is particularly important, especially in the USA, in universities, to which they contribute with substantial funds and scholarships, and offer many other forms of collaboration; consequently, they inevitably exert, directly and indirectly, a strong influence on students' curricula, teachers' appointments and the choice of research subjects. The influence on research directions is becoming all the more marked as research is dependent on the availability of empirical data, of which in many fields the giants of the New Economy are becoming the exclusive owners, and can thus decide to which institutions and researchers – and at what conditions – their databases will be supplied.

Even more overwhelming is the voice of big business in the sphere of the media: not only does it control large part of newspapers, magazines, and TV and radio channels, but it can also strongly influence all the others, as they are dependent on advertising revenues from large firms. In this way, it can choose the issues and establish the intellectual climate in public discourse. The activity leading to public policy decisions includes a large number of committees and meetings in which workers' representatives participate only marginally. Government offices that represent workers' interests are frequently starved of funds and personnel; for example, in many countries, under the pretext of reducing budget deficits, public agencies charged with controlling the respect of, and sanctioning non-compliance with worker wages and safety and health regulations are left without the resources necessary to seriously carry out their tasks (see, for the USA, Weil (2014)).

But most striking – in a globalized world dominated by exchanges between countries of goods, capital, technology and ideas, and thus increasingly necessitating the definition of international rules for these exchanges – is the lack of workers' voice at international level, although they are the main victims of the disruptions caused in advanced countries by international trade and investment. This applies not only to the IMF and the World Bank but to other international organizations as well, while on labour issues the ILO – in whose activities trade unions are institutionally entitled to be represented – has continued to be a scarcely significant entity because of its insufficient regulatory and sanctioning power.

In international negotiations on trade, foreign investment, patents and IPR, and the fixing of technical standards – that is, where the basic discipline that determines present and future economic life is established – labour representatives' presence, just as that of consumers, appears to be scarcely significant. National delegations to these negotiations are dominated by representatives of business interests – see Rodrik (2018c) – and by politicians and public officials who all too often look at the national interest from the perspective of the business community and big national MNCs. The presence of workers' representatives is scant, not welcomed, and in any case scarcely effective because of trade unions' lack of adequate financial means and consequently of personnel and experts capable to match the competence and confidential knowledge of firms' conditions and strategies, of those representing corporate interests. A similar situation prevails regarding the voice of labour in the international entities responsible for the implementation of and compliance with international agreements and rules and for sanctioning their infringement. Therefore, the current structure and mechanisms of international institutions should be modified so as to ensure labour has a voice in international arrangements corresponding to its weight in the economy and in society and to the losses it has suffered as a consequence of trade and investment liberalization. Measures should also be taken to ensure that labour representatives in international institutions and fora have sufficient means, in terms of financial support, information availability and technical competence, to make their participation authoritative and influential.

Most disappointing is the action of workers and trade unions as regards the reinforcement of worker solidarity and the coordination of worker demands and action at international level, which particularly within GVCs would be essential to further the interests of labour of all participating countries.[30] As noted by Kapstein (1999), 'This inability of labor to articulate common international goals means that it is harder for multilateral organizations to understand and respond to its concerns. Contrast this with the case of mobile capital, which can state with great clarity its demand…' (p. 161).

Contrary to what happens with ecological and other movements, common action is not only absent between workers of advanced and developing countries, but extremely rare among workers of advanced countries. Even within the EU, the effort to reinforce ties among citizens of member countries has achieved very little progress in the field of worker action and organization (despite the existence since 1973 of a European Trade Union Confederation and since 1994 of a European Works Council, which brings together employees of EU multinational companies). Big corporations, on the contrary, share much the same international perspective and interests, have more financial, intellectual and organizational means at their

[30] That international solidarity and common action is essential for the working class when confronted with the phenomenon of offshoring was underlined by Marx (1867) in the years when British jute industrial production was being relocated to India: 'in many cases national associations have become powerless: a study of the struggle waged by the English working class reveals that, in order to oppose their workers, the employers bring in workers from abroad or else transfer their manufactures to countries where there is a cheap labour force. Given this state of affairs, if the working class wishes to continue its struggle with some chance of success, the national organizations must become international'.

disposal, and can much more easily coordinate initiatives and lobbying activities (also owing to their more limited number). It seems as if Marx's predictions on the working class's international solidarity and common action putting an end to the power of capitalists have in fact materialized, but in the opposite direction.

4. *A more comprehensive social safety net.* Most economists have by now come to the conclusion that a much stronger system of basic welfare guarantees for workers is essential to increase their domestic intersectoral and geographical mobility, so as to produce a more favourable attitude on their part towards change and innovation, leading to the greater labour market flexibility required by an increasingly competitive and changing international market. In strict terms, a more comprehensive social safety net does not represent a redistribution of income: its purpose is not to give workers part of the income from capital, technology or intellectual property, but to provide economic security, that is a form of insurance for workers, who are exposed to a high and increasing risk of being damaged by trade and technological progress. It would go a long way towards eliminating the anxiety, uncertainty and sense of precariousness that – possibly more than stagnant or reduced income – has caused a worsening of workers' living conditions. The measures that have been proposed are highly heterogeneous, but a coherent programme including a number of them could be highly effective in enhancing worker security, reducing the cost of transition from one job to another and easing the moving in and out of the labour force. They include the following:

   - Provision by governments of free education, training, health assistance and other basic services, so that unemployment or wage reductions do not imply, for the worker and his family, a lack of means to pay for these services; this would also help to reduce business costs (employers now provide some of these services), thereby restoring or increasing firms' competitiveness.
   - Portability of benefits (pensions, health insurance policies, etc.) now supplied by the employer and lost by the worker in the event of job loss or change of employer;
   - Measures to promote mobility from declining to expanding locations (such as the insurance – already provided in some cases by employers in the USA – to cover losses on housing sales for workers relocating out of declining areas).
   - Substantial and long-term unemployment benefits and forms of wage insurance. An example of the latter is the insurance, proposed by Baily, Burtless and Litan (1993) and redefined by Kletzer and Litan (2001) (see also Kletzer (2003)), that provides for the payment for up to two years from the time of the loss of a job – but paid from the moment a new one is accepted – of a substantial part of the difference between the wage earned in the lost job and that in the new one, so that displaced workers would be encouraged to promptly accept a new job even if it meant a lower wage than the previous one.
   - A government role as employer of last resort: the assurance for workers that in the event of inability to find – or loss of – a job, government would step in

to directly provide employment in public works or social services; (but see Kriesler, Halevi and Setterfield (2020) for a negative assessment of the ability of this measure to ensure the maintenance of full employment without unlikely fundamental institutional changes).

5. *Universal basic income.* In more recent years, an increasing number of economists have proposed the introduction of forms of UBI. The proposal, first advanced by Thomas Paine in 1797 and revived by Meade (1964), envisages that every adult citizen should receive for all his life an unconditional cash transfer sufficient to cover basic needs, without any obligation to engage in a working activity. Its economic rationale is that since a large part of the income produced in a country is the result of a collective national effort (past and present) to build up public infrastructure – both productive (physical, educational and scientific) and social (trust and cooperation) – and of the use of national natural resources, a fraction of this income should be given back to the community by distributing it equally among all citizens.
UBI would have two main effects that would lead to a revolutionary enlargement of individual freedom. First, work would become a matter of personal choice: people would be able to accept the jobs offered to them only if they considered them to be suited to their abilities and aspirations, or decide – in exchange for a lower standard of living – to reduce the time spent working, or even to stop working altogether, so as to devote themselves to other activities of their choice; for the first time in human history man would be freed from the obligation to work in order to satisfy basic needs. Second, by eliminating in labour contracts the element of coercion represented for most workers by the fact that the refusal to accept – or the loss of – employment would imply lack of income to provide for vital necessities, UBI would strongly increase workers' bargaining power vis-à-vis employers in labour market transactions, largely reducing the importance of market inequalities. In addition, being equally distributed to all adult citizens (with account taken of dependent children), UBI would strongly enhance equality among household members, as it would increase the bargaining power of the most vulnerable ones (housewives, the elderly and those with disabilities).
UBI would eliminate the problem of providing income to people displaced by trade and automation, making it possible both to achieve the much-needed increase in economies' productivity through the acceleration of robotization, technical progress and trade liberalization, and to eliminate many tiring or unpleasant jobs. It would solve the problems of the increasing number of people with autonomous, semi-autonomous and intermittent jobs, who are often not fully covered by existing social protection systems. By providing a secure steady flow of income to satisfy basic needs it would also stimulate risk-taking, entrepreneurship and investments with highly uncertain results (including those in human capital).
A basic operational advantage of UBI is that it would replace most of the existing schemes of means-tested assistance to the poorest section of the population, thus eliminating large administrative expenses, the necessity of complex controls

of people's effective eligibility for benefits and the inevitable perverse incentives and abuses in their application. It would also remove the social stigma connected with receiving public assistance and the practical problems that often prevent the poorest sections of the population from applying for and obtaining the assistance they are entitled to receive.

There are three, largely connected, main obstacles to the adoption of UBI. The first is political, as it would produce a radical change in existing power and freedom equilibria between poor and rich in favour of the former. The second is financial, as it implies substantial increases in public expenditure over that now devoted to the various forms of assistance that it would replace and, consequently, higher taxation of the wealthiest. The third is ideological: it goes against a deeply ingrained principle of our societies, namely the centrality of work (though these societies passively accept that some members, thanks to inherited wealth, lead a comfortable life without ever working).

Work is not only a source of income to cover basic needs, but also an essential element of human dignity and of social inclusion since it involves relationships with other workers and participation in the common effort to improve a country's economic, social and cultural conditions. This has come to represent a psychological obstacle to UBI, as for many people their own identity and sense of existence is strictly linked to their jobs. UBI would thus not solve all the problems connected with unemployment. But there is also a widespread conviction that social aid should be based on reciprocity, so that benefit recipients should gain the right to this aid by trying in all ways to look for and show themselves ready to accept any available decent work offer. The fact that UBI is unconditional conveys the idea of unearned assistance, implying that some persons should be taxed so that others may choose to remain idle. This last eventuality, related to the possible disincentive inherent in UBI to engage in active job search is, however, scarcely likely. That workers, even if provided with an income to satisfy basic needs, would still look for a job allowing them to satisfy the growing demand for non-essential goods and services, is testified by the intense efforts deployed by workers just earning living wages to increase worktime and search for better-paid jobs.

UBI would not remove the need to provide additional benefits for people with special needs (such as those connected with serious illness or disability). And while its replacing many existing assistance schemes would produce a large overall change in income distribution from the wealthiest to the poorest and middle sections of the population, it could also lead to a reduction of the benefits granted to some of the poorest groups on which existing assistance schemes are focused.

For all these reasons, UBI has never been fully introduced, and not even experimented with to a significant extent or for a sizable length of time. Experiments have been carried out in some countries (Finland, for example) in limited forms, as regards the percentage of the population covered and especially the amount of income assigned (usually only a fraction of what would be necessary to cover basic needs).

A fundamental economic effect of the introduction of UBI, of central interest for international trade, is that by largely supplementing labour income it could allow advanced countries to keep workers' wages at a low level, thus improving the competitiveness of many lines of production that at present are inevitably moving to low-wage developing countries. This could have both positive and negative consequences: many jobs could be saved, but – as happens with low market wages in general – a powerful stimulus for entrepreneurs to switch resources to higher-VA (per unit of factor of production) activities would be reduced. Disputes about unfair competition may also develop, both between advanced and developing countries, and among advanced ones if they did not all introduce UBI schemes or introduced schemes providing different levels of benefits; and such schemes may even run the risk of being considered as state subsidies to firms. Similar problems would be raised by the proposal, advanced for Germany by Sinn (2007), of paying a state subsidy to unemployed workers who accept low wage jobs, so that they would prefer working to receiving unemployment payments (Phelps (1997) had already proposed such wage subsidies for the USA, but to be paid to employers). But UBI could also have the opposite effect of increasing market wages, as workers would not be compelled by the necessity of satisfying basic needs to accept whatever wage or working conditions were offered to them.

The debate on UBI has been made particularly difficult by the fact that when economists and politicians speak about it, they usually refer to different definitions and concepts of UBI, which leads to large differences in the characteristics of the UBI schemes they propose to introduce in practice. Additional difficulties stem from the fact that since most economists consider the introduction of a full UBI scheme impractical, they propose the introduction of limited schemes, to be gradually extended with time, that supplement, rather than replace, existing forms of assistance and are thus hard to compare).

The very purpose of UBI is unclear, which makes it difficult to compare estimates of the ability of different schemes to succeed. Most proponents seem to consider UBI to be basically directed at poverty alleviation, in which case analysis should concentrate on evaluating its possible results relative to those produced by the existing or alternative systems of assistance to the poor. But this comparison is not easy, as social assistance programmes also generally aim to help and incentivize assisted persons to look for and find a job, which is not a specific aim of UBI schemes. Others concentrate on UBI's effect in re-equilibrating power relations between workers and other sections of society; yet others stress instead the liberating effect of the possibility of refusing undesired types of work or even work altogether (or doing a job that the market does not remunerate with a living wage, even if it has a high social value). It is significant that while some consider UBI as a way to slow down the tendency towards automation by pushing workers to accept low-wage jobs that, by themselves, are not sufficient to provide a decent standard of living, others see it as a way to allow and stimulate an acceleration of automation and the elimination of low-productivity jobs (and further progress in trade liberalization), since it would ensure the workers who are the possible victims of these developments do not risk losing the means to satisfy basic needs. For a general review of the problems of and the debate on UBS see Gentilini, Grosh, Rigolini and Yemtsov (2020); see also Van Parijs and Vanderborght (2017), OECD (2017), Ghatak and Maniquet (2019) and Hoynes and Rothstein (2019).

6. *Profit-sharing and 'social dividend'.* As incomes produced by economic activity are increasingly derived from – and therefore allotted to the owners of – capital and technological and organizational knowledge, it has been argued that traditional trade union policies directed at improving workers' incomes by raising wages are ineffective, and even counterproductive, as they may further reduce firms' competitiveness and accelerate the offshoring of activities to low-wage countries and automation. Instead, it is incomes from those factors that should be more equally distributed among all participants to the production process through profit-sharing with workers or with the government that would then distribute these profits, directly or through better public services, to all citizens.
   Allocation of part of the profits to governments would be justified by the fact that the latter make a large contribution to firms' innovations by funding the greater part of basic scientific research and providing financial backing and incentives to many innovation activities of private firms. As the risks and costs of research are largely socialized, logic would have it that governments should have a share in – or a say in the use of – the rewards from successful innovations. Mazzucato (2018) has advanced proposals such as allowing public agencies to retain equity in firms or royalties in technologies for which they provided funding; making loans to firms income-contingent (that is, repayable on the basis of future income), as is done for students; or conditioning public support of firms to the subsequent reinvestment of profits in production. Reich (2015) instead proposed giving each citizen a share of all intellectual property awarded by the patent office, so that everybody would gain from the application of innovations.
   Profit-sharing usually refers either to the allocation of some of a firm's profits to its workers or to the distribution to workers of some of their firm's shares so that they may receive in the form of capital income some of the gains obtained by the firm. The proposal that workers should receive part of their wages in the form of shares of the firm they work for, or in other forms of sharing their company's profits, goes back to the 19th century. Profit-sharing and employee stock ownership started to be introduced by US corporations in the 1880s. In Europe, in the first decades after World War II, the introduction of profit-sharing schemes was mainly viewed as a response to communist parties' and left-wing trade unions' attacks against capitalist labour relations. The idea was that workers sharing in the profits of their company would give up or moderate the attitude of outright confrontation against 'masters', and would increasingly identify with their company and develop a sense of ownership and of teamwork. At the same time, it was expected that profit-sharing schemes, by introducing a direct economic interest on the part of workers in the success of their company, would stimulate them to make stronger personal efforts in their working activity, leading to increased productivity.

Although profit-sharing schemes, in some cases encouraged by specific legislation, spread – unevenly – among Western countries and grew rapidly from the 1970s onwards, they have generally remained limited in the extent of the workers covered – in most European countries some 10–15 per cent of workers for profit distributions and some 2 per cent for the distribution of companies' shares (see Welz and Fernández-Macías (2008)), but an important exception is the USA – and, especially, in the share of workers' total income and wealth that such schemes represent. It is in the USA that in the last few decades forms of profit-sharing (in the wider sense of part of workers' remuneration being connected with their company's profits) have spread significantly, to the point of covering about half of all employee workers (but with large differences between sectors).
On the whole these schemes appear to have had a positive effect on productivity; an effect that seems to depend to a great extent – like their other positive outcomes, such as an increase in worker satisfaction – on the simultaneous adoption of other workplace policies that empower workers (participation in decisions, reduced supervision, etc.). However, apart from exceptional cases such as the shares distributed by some Silicon Valley high-tech firms, profit-sharing schemes appear to have represented only a very small part of workers' remuneration. They have therefore not produced a significant redistribution of companies' profits to workers, nor reductions in overall inequality (also because the lowest-paid workers are the group least covered by such schemes). On the experience of profit-sharing schemes see OECD (1995), Kruse, Freeman and Blasi (2010) and Fibírová and Petera (2013).
Until recent times, the interest in these schemes of economists (with exceptions such as Meade and Weitzman), politicians, trade unions and workers themselves has been rather limited. It would seem that the schemes are more akin to forms of payment by result applied at work-team, plant or firm level, than attempts to shift a significant part of the benefits produced by capital, technology and knowledge in favour of workers. But in recent years, interest in profit-sharing seems to have revived in connection with the evidence of protracted worker wage stagnation despite continuing increases in labour productivity and corporate profits, and the consequent search for ways to redistribute income from owners of capital and technology to workers. A renewed, broad-based use of profit-sharing schemes – which in the USA have instead seen reduced support by the government since the end of the 1970s – as an important means of contrasting income and wealth inequalities has been advocated by some economists, such as Blasi, Freeman and Kruse (2017) and Milanovic (2019); this last author also proposes the introduction of other measures to contrast the increasing concentration of capital ownership, such as a more favourable treatment of equity ownership for small and medium shareholders – and a less favourable for big ones – and the application of significant inheritance and wealth taxes.
Of course, to produce important results in the reduction of inequalities in income distribution, the schemes would have to be applied to most, if not all, employee workers and represent a large percentage of their income and wealth. But this

development is not likely to meet the approval of corporations: not only would it cause a significant reduction in profits going to shareholders and managers; but it would also imply either the sharing with workers' representatives of confidential information on real profitability that managers may not like to disclose, or the attribution to workers of a significant percentage of ordinary shareholder rights (so far in the USA employee-owned shares, with the exception of stock market companies, do not normally imply full voting rights).

Important schemes of employee ownership of the stock of their company would also produce large inequalities among workers, as successful companies would distribute much more wealth than less successful ones, and self-employed and unemployed workers would not take part in these schemes. But a more worrying consequence would be the large risk workers would run by having too much of their wealth concentrated in the shares of their company: should the latter close down or experience serious difficulties, they might not only lose their source of income, but also a large part of their wealth. Considering all these problems, it seems that in the fight against inequalities, schemes such as a form of UBI mostly financed by taxes on firms and rich individuals would represent a much simpler and less risky project than a large-scale scheme for workers' ownership of their firms.

There are, however, other schemes that may in a very wide sense be included under the label of profit-sharing, although they could more properly be called 'social dividend' schemes. They have a different nature from those discussed above (to some extent they may be considered forms of UBI), as they do not envisage worker participation in the profits or capital stock of the firms they work for, but the distribution of a social dividend; that is, the acquisition by all citizens of increasing shares of the capital of – or the income produced by – firms in the economy as a whole (an example is Brittan's (1984) proposal, mentioned earlier in this section, of sharing the property of the capital of corporations to be privatized equally among all citizens).[31]

These proposals have been advanced by economists of different political tendencies. Left-wing economists have drawn inspiration from the debate that starting in the 1930s developed on the social dividend; that is, an addition to wages that

[31] Interest in these schemes led to a reconsideration of the proposals – covering forms of profit-sharing, UBI and social dividend – advanced by Meade in works that go from the 1930s to the 1990s: see Van Trier (2018). Meade (1964), envisaging that as a result of automation the proportion of national income that accrues from earnings would be greatly reduced, held that a large part of people's income should come from property, while work would become more a matter of personal choice. He thus proposed to move to a more egalitarian economy by way of a large pre-distribution of capital (through a major extension of free education, strong progressivity of inheritance and wealth taxes, diffusion of profit-sharing schemes in companies and home-ownership incentives), so that every citizen would benefit from capital returns and increase not only his income, but also his private wealth. In later works he also envisaged the enlargement of public ownership of capital through the creation of institutions similar to contemporary sovereign wealth funds (the latter are state-owned funds investing in real or financial assets usually with the receipts from the export of state-owned oil or other natural resources).

in a democratic socialist society should be distributed to all citizens as a share of the surplus produced by publicly owned capital and technology; the main contributions to that debate, discussed by Van Trier (1989, 2018), came from Lange, Lerner and Cole. More recent proposals were examined by Marangos (2004).[32] From very different political positions, 'social dividend' proposals have been advanced in the USA, based instead on the aim of countering income and wealth inequalities not through taxation and dependency on the state, but through a more even distribution of capital ownership, so as to make every citizen an investor obtaining profits from his investments to supplement whatever income is received from work or other sources. For example, it has been suggested (see Ashford (2010)) that an interest-free loan should be granted annually to all citizens by a reformed banking system (to be repaid with part of the income produced by the investments, and covered by credit risk insurance), so that people could invest in a dividend-bearing stock portfolio of qualified companies that carry out productive activities. It has also been argued that trade unions should not represent workers as labour workers only, but also as capital owners, taking part on their behalf in companies' decisions.

[32] Standing (2006) looked with favour on the setting up of Community Capital Grants, a sort of social investment fund (akin to those proposed by Meade), through which a significant part of the income produced by capital and technology would be indirectly distributed among the population. The scheme envisaged that a sizable part of firms' profits should be used to contribute to form a fund, intended to benefit not only the workers of a firm, but also outsiders in the local and the national economy. For Standing, the fund could be split into a part to be invested inside the firm, and another to be used for infrastructural and skill-development projects meant to benefit the community outside the firm; and since he proposed that the fund's managers, democratically elected, would sit, with voting rights, on the firm's board defining the firm's investment strategies, there would be an important change in corporate governance, with the introduction of major elements of economic democracy.

Concluding Remarks

As a conclusion to this work, a few final considerations can be advanced regarding two general issues. What overall judgement can we give about the large increase in international trade of recent decades? And what has been the role of international trade theory and international economists in identifying and interpreting world trade changes while they were taking place and in providing analyses and explanations for them once they became well-established features of the international economy?

The growth rate of world trade in goods and services has been very high in 1990–2019 and surpassed GDP growth. It was the result of the further progress of trade liberalization; the entry into the capitalist market of a large part of the world previously isolated from it; the increase in developing countries' exports consequent on their industrialization process, offshoring by advanced countries, development of trade in intermediate products within GVCs and growth of South–South trade; and the fact that many non-tradable services became tradable thanks to the progress of ICT. To some extent, however, increased trade simply reflected the statistical effect of high growth of recorded gross exports associated with the increasing share of imported inputs and components, while in terms of VA exported the increase was significantly smaller.

It cannot be denied that the growth of international trade has produced large benefits for societies. More than the static ones deriving from better allocation of resources as a consequence of the specialization envisaged by the Ricardian theory incorporated in the RHO model, it is the dynamic ones, related to the extension of the international market and originally underlined by Adam Smith, that have been very important. They reflected the greater scope for scale economies in an enlarged market and the much increased competition for many goods and services in terms of both price and innovation, between firms of different countries, which translated into large benefits to consumers in the form of lower prices and a much wider variety of goods. But particularly large were the benefits deriving from the exceptional stimulus to technological progress and growth that international trade provided to many important developing countries that based their development strategies on the favourable dynamics of world trade, with results of great historical significance.

These dynamic trade gains cannot be precisely measured or estimated, because their influence mixed with that of other concomitant factors. And because conventional calculations of the effects of trade liberalization and trade growth can provide estimates of price and income effects produced by a better allocation of resources, but bump up against insurmountable difficulties when they try to estimate the dynamic effects, in terms of stimuli to productivity growth and innovation, that – when other necessary factors are present – can trigger the process of fast self-sustaining growth. In any case, it is a fact that for the first time since the Industrial Revolution, thanks to policies centred on opening to trade and foreign investment, a large proportion of the world's population, which since those times had been consigned to underdevelopment and abject poverty, has managed to reach acceptable standards of living in the course of just a few decades.

But the growth in international trade, has also produced, particularly in advanced countries, significant negative effects. Contrary to the optimistic initial forecasts by the majority of economists on the trade gains that – directly or through the 'trickle-down' effects of the gains accruing to the main beneficiaries – would have been shared by all citizens, the division of the benefits from increased trade has been extremely unequal. So much so that since the early 2000s, a growing number of economists have had to acknowledge (or stop pretending to ignore) that in general trade produces benefits for some groups of the population, but also losses, often significant, for others. However, while the conviction spread among economists that this asymmetry of trade effects called for the adoption by the state of major compensation and adjustment assistance measures for the people damaged, little attention was paid to the fact that in practice such measures were adopted only to a very limited extent, and in many countries a serious discussion about concrete programmes on a scale able to provide a solution to this problem (and to the connected one of the negative effects on workers of technical progress) has not yet begun.

The unequal effects of increased international trade are not limited to different groups of individuals. Firms, too, have been very differently affected by trade liberalization: it can be argued that the greatest contribution of the recent new line of international trade research centred on firm heterogeneity, mentioned in Section 2.3, has been that of highlighting not only the positive effects that involvement in export and import activity produces on firms' productivity, profitability and growth; but also the very diverse possibilities that different types of firm have to overcome the obstacles to entering and developing this activity and the resulting large asymmetries in firms' progress, productivity, mark-ups and market power.

In the 1990-2019 period of sustained trade growth, income inequalities among countries, on the whole, came down significantly, so that an overall decrease in income inequality seems to have been registered at world level for all individuals (that is, considering the whole world population as belonging to a single country); but inequalities within countries, both advanced and developing, increased. In the latter group of countries, these growing domestic inequalities did not in general prevent improvement, in some cases very relevant, in the incomes and living conditions of all groups of citizens. In advanced countries, on the contrary, they were frequently the result of huge income growth for the restricted group of the richest citizens, while for the rest of the population slow growth or substantial income stagnation was registered, in some countries with a reduction in absolute terms for some medium to low income groups. Of course, it is very difficult to establish to what extent this worsened income distribution should be attributed to international trade and how much to the – probably predominant – effect of technical progress and the unequal distribution of its benefits. But certainly the way the globalization process was managed by international institutions and the main Western countries was largely responsible for these results, as pointed out by Stiglitz and Rodrik.

The history of the last two decades of the 20th century was marked by two major events that have provided fundamental lessons in the field of international trade. The collapse of the USSR and its satellites showed to what extent the absence of domestic and, especially, international competition among firms can lead to inefficiency, bureaucratization, lack of respect for basic consumers' demands, absence of stimuli to productive activity and to the development and diffusion of innovations. However, the Chinese and Indian experiences of exceptional economic growth – which continued well into the first two decades of the new century – have demonstrated that the introduction and diffusion of market mechanisms capable of overcoming those distortions, and the opening to international trade and investment, do not require, but rather advise against, the adoption of that free market lacking rules and limitations whose miraculous effects were extolled by ultra-liberalist champions.

* * *

The majority of international economists continue to refer to the Ricardian principle of comparative advantage, though introducing important changes in the framework of the RHO model to take account of some new contemporary economic realities. This book has tried, on the contrary, to emphasize the increasing role that absolute advantages play today in international trade competition, so that the latter is getting more and more akin to the competition that takes place inside countries.

This is owing to, on the one hand, the frequent inapplicability to the real world of some basic starting hypotheses of the comparative advantage model: many goods, especially high-tech ones whose share in international trade is rapidly increasing, are not the object of price competition, but are produced only by a few specific countries or big firms on the basis of the exclusive possession, often reinforced by monopolistic or oligopolistic practices, of technological and organizational advantages; persistent worker unemployment is widely diffused, not only in developing countries but in advanced countries as well; massive chronic disequilibria (at times aggravated by exchange rate policies) characterize the trade balance of the major trading countries; and production factors of different countries present different degrees of mobility both internationally and domestically (between different geographical areas and between sectors of activity). On the other hand, the traditional internal and international mechanisms that should re-establish equilibrium in trade balances, so that countries' comparative advantage in certain goods translates into lower absolute monetary prices of these goods for foreign purchasers, do not operate or do so only to a very limited extent (the tensions in US–Chinese relations in the last two decades, largely related to trade balance disequilibria, have contributed to highlight this problem).

To recognize that many basic hypotheses of the RHO model are not, or are no more, acceptable as approximations of reality and that international trade increasingly responds to absolute advantages, sometimes covering a large number of sectors (as the constraint of balancing exports with imports no longer applies), leads to attribute a key role to countries' general elements of competitive advantage. These may still consist of abundance of a traditional production factor, as in the case of cheap labour; but increasingly reflect other determinants, such as favourable geographical location and/or previous concentration of economic activities; superior physical, educational and institutional infrastructure and political stability; greater technological and innovational ability and effort; predominance in standards and networks; and, particularly in developing countries, availability of political leaders and public officials with high levels of competence, autonomy, honesty and pragmatism.

Thanks to 'New Trade Theory', scale economies and their effects on the geographical concentration of economic activity in given locations, and monopolistic competition through product differentiation have been incorporated into the body of mainstream international trade theory, putting an end to the one and an half century-old monopoly of the perfect competition model. But international trade theory has been unable to provide satisfactory answers to other key challenges presented by the concrete developments of the international economy.

It does not seem to have produced an analysis of the role of technology in international trade up to the central role it plays today in shaping the dynamics of growth and trade; in particular, it has insufficiently recognized, until the very latest years, the novelty and the key importance of networks and international standard-fixing and their consequences for international competition. Only to a very limited extent – thanks to the recent efforts of a few eminent economists – have the power aspects that largely shape international economic relationships begun to be considered. In this respect, a positive effect – probably the only one – of the dramatic deterioration in US–Chinese trade relations produced by Trump's initiatives has been that of having finally made it evident to everyone how power aspects are strictly connected to, and largely determine, the structure of international trade and investment; and how important are the position, and the conditioning power, of supremacy in international networks and standard-fixing.

In Section 6.2, reference is made to Keynes having introduced a wholly new conception of foreign trade. The RHO model, based on the hypotheses of full employment and trade balance equilibrium, viewed exports exclusively as the means to obtain from abroad a certain amount of goods at a lower cost (in terms of units of the exported good given in exchange) than they would have cost if produced at home, Keynes, instead, viewed them mainly as an additional component of demand (and imports as an element reducing demand), which would help increase a country's production, employment and income. While contemporary macroeconomic theory has incorporated into its framework basic elements of the Keynesian perspective, international trade theory still largely works within the framework of the RHO model, simply modifying some of the specific assumptions of the model that are in sharp contrast with the reality of contemporary international exchange (it is significant that most analyses of foreign trade one finds in textbooks or in books addressed to non-specialists are conducted on the assumption that trade balances are in equilibrium, and when the effects of trade on employment are analysed, they are limited to the consequences produced by a changed factor composition of the products exchanged). The persistence of this dichotomy between the two conceptions of foreign trade is the source of many disagreements and misunderstandings in the debates on international trade issues, particularly those connected to offshoring.

From the 1980s to the 2008 crisis, many international economists – in the USA probably a majority – uncritically supported the generic and superficial prescriptions of the ultra-liberal ideology of the Washington Consensus, of indiscriminate deregulation and privatization (which, mechanically applied to developing and transition countries, led to disasters such as the Asian crisis of 1997 and Russia's disorderly transition to capitalism after 1991). As a consequence, for a long time they basically supported – with some exceptions, such as Rodrik and later Stiglitz – the thesis, also proclaimed by Clinton and Blair, according to which globalization is a phenomenon produced by the spontaneous evolution of economic life, which cannot be contrasted or controlled; ignoring that its characteristics, mechanisms and effects are to a large extent simply the result of specific policy choices (such as the decision to abolish all obstacles to the free international movement of goods and capital, or drastically reducing taxation and antitrust legal discipline); and that even to the extent that globalization is a consequence of uncontrollable factors (as innovations and technological developments largely are), the effects of these forces on the economy can be channelled in certain directions instead of others by the way markets are organized and the adoption of specific economic policy measures, as these two elements strongly influence the incentives of economic agents' action.

Considering all these limits of international economists, it is not surprising that, overall, they – like the main international economic institutions, the IMF in particular – not only did not anticipate many of the developments in international trade and globalization (which is a very difficult task; although they were equally unable to see the evident signs of a looming financial crisis before it exploded in 2008); but they also failed to identify them while they were taking place under their eyes, so that for some of these developments it was students of other disciplines who first realized the importance of the changes taking place.

Economists, with a few exceptions, did not understand, while it was under way (and at times even after), the historical and systemic significance of the Chinese economic advance, often reducing that experience to a simple problem of unfair competition by a mischievous new rival, and producing few analyses of the profound changes in the balance of world economic power that were taking place in favour of China and some other emerging countries at the expense of previously hegemonic economies. Economic debate concentrated on the negative effects that the exports from new industrial countries produced for the advanced countries' low-skilled workers (and even this effect was initially largely denied or played down). Only with a long delay did economists understand the importance of the GVC phenomenon, initially highlighted mainly by other scholars. They left it up to philosophers and other researchers to analyse the issue of where economic activity creates value and to debate on the exploitation in sweatshops and GVCs. Their theoretical limits – and/or their unwillingness to acknowledge unpleasant realities – led them to largely ignore the evident deficiencies, injustices and abuses of the globalization process. A typical example is the almost complete absence for decades until very recent years of any reaction by international economists to the shameful scandal of fiscal havens and, later on, to that of the ridiculous levels of taxation of the foreign activities of the New Economy's giants. Most of them also failed to underline the urgent need to reconsider the existing system of patents and IPR, whose deficiencies many of them recognized.

It was only when some outstanding economists (such as Samuelson, Stiglitz and partly Krugman), sometimes after a long period of silence on the issue, joined the few early critical voices, that a more realistic analysis of globalization was produced and reasonable proposals were formulated to manage its development, so as to make it more responsive to the common interest rather than mainly that of restricted business groups.

In all probability, had the unpleasant negative aspects of the globalization process been clearly pointed out by economists from the beginning, and measures to eliminate or minimize them advanced and adopted, the process would have proceeded with substantial advantages for most, if not all, participants without any need to have recourse to particularly drastic measures. As decades passed without any intervention, action to redress the situation would involve much higher costs (and sacrifices on the part of its former main beneficiaries), and much stronger efforts to bring different countries, with now consolidated divergent interests on most issues, to agree on a set of common rules.

* * *

This work has tried to show that many economic developments and innovative concepts and theories were anticipated by more far-sighted economists, whose ideas were not taken with the serious consideration they deserved, and who were at times relegated to a marginal position in what was considered respectable economics and basically ignored.

Throughout history scholars who identified new tendencies in economic life and proposed innovative measures to deal with them clashed with theories and interpretations of economic phenomena long since consolidated into powerful orthodoxies. This is also what happened during the period of predominance of the ultra-liberalist ideology, which, consigned to a marginal position from the 1929 crisis to the 1970s, enjoyed an unexpected revival in the UK and the USA, and then in other countries, reaching a position of intellectual supremacy that was maintained for a couple of decades. This result stemmed from the mistakes and excesses of previous Western policies inspired by Keynesian theory; but also from the intellectual predominance of the USA, thanks to its system of universities and economic research centres (whose scale, and financial support from private foundations, were enormously larger than those of other countries), and its overwhelming influence on the financial operations and research activity of the main international economic institutions – thus confirming the importance of economic power for the diffusion of ideas and influence on research and teaching. It took some extraordinary and dramatic events, such as the strengthening of Chinese export penetration in the US market and the 2008 global crisis, for a very different representation of the globalization process to spread among international economists, and for the evidence of China's successful economic catch-up to be fully recognized.

The development of trade in recent decades has taken place in a different way from what could be anticipated on the basis of the prescriptions derived from prevailing international trade theory. The same happened at the end of the 19th century, when Germany and the USA industrialized following policies opposed to the free trade then recommended by international economists; and it happened again in more recent times with the government policies of export stimulus adopted first by Japan and then by the 'Asian tigers'; although the fundamental positive role of the opening to trade and foreign investment – if properly managed on the basis of a well-structured development strategy – has been validated. It must be admitted that some recent unforeseeable crucial developments, both technological and political (the ICT revolution and the collapse of the communist system), have been so radical that unavoidably economists, like other scholars, found themselves unprepared to face the problems posed by the new reality. Yet a more open and less dogmatic theoretical attitude would have allowed them a better understanding of the changed economic environment.

It must also be pointed out that among economists challenging orthodox economic theory, those on the left were no less mistaken than their mainstream opponents in their view of the new developments. They continued to see in the capitalist system, the MNCs and the globalization process only negative forces, whose working inevitably put obstacles in the way of the industrialization and economic progress of developing countries; and they ostracized the very restricted group of economists who, on their political side, advanced less drastic and superficial negative judgements on the changes under way – so that they too were taken by surprise by the unforeseen success of the Chinese experience of transition to an open market economy.

* * *

The lack of foresight and the limited ability to understand, on the basis of the international trade theory predominant at each time, the changes taking place in the international economy, seem to have been the consequence of the general difficulty of conceiving explanations of reality different from traditional ones, and to the reluctance to recognize and analyse those aspects of economic life that create problems and complications for a firmly established theory as they prove unfit to be analysed with the current formal models or require the application of methodologies different from those approved by academic orthodoxy (as happened with technological progress, power relations and psychological phenomena). This applies not only to the trade theory that referred to the RHO model, but also to the 'New Trade Theory' of the 1980s. The latter, after demolishing some fundamental assumptions of the RHO model and consolidating to the point of becoming itself a new orthodoxy, has not satisfactorily analysed other realities of contemporary international economic life, such as persistent unemployment, trade balance disequilibria, the increasing role of absolute relative to comparative advantages and even oligopolies.

In this work, we have tried to underline the often very shaky foundations on which economic theories are based (for example, the current ambiguous conception of the factor capital, the critique of which by economists from Cambridge in the UK continues to be ignored by the majority of economists) and the difficulties that empirical research, particularly in the field of international economics, has to overcome in order to test the validity of different models and theories – largely owing to the fact, underlined by Krugman, that 'the changing nature of world trade has outpaced economists' ability to engage in secure quantitative analysis' (2008b, p.134). Trade theory – like most theories addressing social phenomena, but probably to a larger extent – shares this characteristic of running after a reality that is changing more and more rapidly and in unpredictable directions; so that, quite apart from the power relations and interests that consolidate around any theory, researchers have an inherent difficulty in formulating new ones, and tend to use as a guide – in reacting to, and interpreting, unexpected changes in economic life – ideas and concepts elaborated on the basis of past experience, which frequently prove obsolete in the new external environment.

Finally, we hope to have shown the uncertain and never definitive validity of apparently firmly established concepts and principles of international trade theory. However paradoxical that may appear, as indicated in Footnote 8 in Chapter 1 the very basic notions of absolute and comparative advantage of Smith and Ricardo, analysed in greater depth in recent years, have proved liable to interpretations very different from the ones previously considered as definitively consolidated.

Bibliography[*]

Acemoglu, Daron, Autor, David, Dorn, David, Hanson, Gordon H. and Price, Brendan (2016), 'Import Competition and the Great US Employment Sag of the 2000s', *Journal of Labour Labor Economics*, 34 (1): S141–S198.

Acemoglu, Daron and Linn, Joshua (2004), 'Market Size in Innovation: Theory and Evidence from the Pharmaceutical Industry', *Quarterly Journal of Economics*, 119 (3): 1049–1090.

Ádám, Gy (1971), 'New Trends in International Business: Worldwide Sourcing and Dedomiciling', *Acta Oeconomica*, 7 (3–4): 349–367.

Aerni, Philipp (2013), 'Do Private Standards Encourage or Hinder Trade and Innovation?', University of Bern, NCCR Trade Regulation Working Paper No. 2013/18.

Ahmad, Nadim (2019), 'Improving the Accounting Frameworks for Analyses of Global Value Chains', in World Bank Group et al. (2019), *Global Value Chain Development Report 2019: Technological Innovation, Supply Chain Trade, and Workers in a Globalized World*, Washington: World Bank Group.

Aichele, Rahel and Heiland, Inga (2019), 'Where Is the Value Added? Trade Liberalization and Production Networks', CESifo Working Paper No. 6026.

Aidt, Toke S. (2003), 'Economic Analysis of Corruption: a Survey', *Economic Journal*, 113 (491): 632–652.

Akamatsu, Kaname (1962), 'A Historical Pattern of Economic Growth in Developing Countries', *Journal of Developing Economies*, 1 (1): 3–25.

Alam, M. Shahid (2004), 'Colonialism and Industrialization: A Critique of Lewis', *Review of Radical Political Economics*, 36 (2): 217–240.

Aldrich, John (2004), 'The Discovery of Comparative Advantage', *Journal of the History of Economic Thought*, 26 (3): 379–399.

Amador, João and di Mauro, Filippo (eds.) (2015), *The Age of Global Value Chains: Maps and Policy Issues*, London: CEPR Press.

Amano, Akihiro (1966), 'Intermediate Goods and the Theory of Comparative Advantage: A Two-Country, Three-Commodity Case', *Weltwirtschaftliches Archiv*, 96 (2): 340–345.

Amnesty International (2004), *Clouds of Injustice: Bhopal Disaster 20 Years on*, London: Amnesty International Publications.

Andrias, Kate and Rogers, Brishen (2018), 'Building Worker Voice in Today's Economy', Roosevelt Institute, New York.

Anker, Richard and Anker, Martha (2017), *Living Wages Around the World: Manual for Measurement*, Cheltenham (UK): Edward Elgar.

[*] In the text of the book, quotations from works in foreign languages refer to the pages of the English translation, unless otherwise indicated.

Antràs, Pol (2005), 'Incomplete Contracts and the Product Cycle', *American Economic Review*, 95 (4): 1054–1073.
Antràs, Pol (2016), *Global Production: Firms, Contracts, and Trade Structure*, Princeton, NJ: Princeton University Press.
Antràs, Pol (2020), 'Conceptual Aspects of Global Value Chains' (Background Paper for the 2020 World Development Report), World Bank Group, Policy Research Working Paper No. 9114.
Antràs, Pol and Helpman, Elhanan (2004), 'Global Sourcing', *Journal of Political Economy*, 112 (3): 552–580.
Antràs, Pol and Rossi-Hansberg, Esteban (2009), 'Organizations and Trade', *Annual Review of Economics*, 1 (1): 43–64.
Antweiler, Werner and Trefler, Daniel (2002), 'Increasing Returns and All That: A View from Trade', *American Economic Review*, 92 (1): 93–119.
Arndt, Sven W. and Kierzkowski, Henryk (eds.) (2001), *Fragmentation: New Production Patterns in the World Economy*, Oxford: Oxford University Press.
Arrighi, Giovanni (2007), *Adam Smith in Beijing: Lineages of the Twenty-First Century*, London: Verso.
Arthur, W. Brian (1989), 'Competing Technologies, Increasing Returns, and Lock-In by Historical Events', *Economic Journal*, 99 (394): 116–131.
Arthur, W. Brian (1990), 'Positive Feedbacks in the Economy', *Scientific American*, 262 (2): 92–99.
Arthur, W. Brian (1994), *Increasing Returns and Path Dependence in the Economy*, Ann Arbor, MI: University of Michigan Press.
Ashford, Robert (2010), 'Binary Economics – An Overview', College of Law, Syracuse University. Available at: https://surface.syr.edu/lawpub/15 .
Atkinson, Anthony B. (2015), *Inequality: What Can Be Done?*, Cambridge, MA: Harvard University Press.
Ault, Hugh J. (2019), 'Tax Competition and Tax Cooperation: A Survey and Reassessment', in Jérôme Monsenego and Jan Bjuvberg (eds.), *International Taxation in a Changing Landscape: Liber Amicorum in Honour of Bertil Wiman*, Alphen aan den Rijn, Netherlands: Wolters Kluwer.
Austin, Kenneth (2011), 'Communist China's Capitalism: The Highest Stage of Capitalist Imperialism', *World Economics*, 12 (1): 79–94.
Autor, David H. (2018), 'Ricardan Models of Trade', 14.662 Spring 2018, Lecture Note 7. Available at: https//economics.mit.edu/files/15402.
Autor, David H., Dorn, David and Hanson, Gordon H. (2015), 'Untangling Trade and Technology: Evidence from Local Labour Markets', *Economic Journal*, 125 (584): 621–646.
Autor, David H., Dorn, David and Hanson, Gordon H. (2016), 'The China Shock: Learning from Labor Market Adjustment to Large Changes in Trade', NBER Working Paper No. 21906.
Avineri, Shlomo (ed.) (1968), *Karl Marx on Colonialism & Modernization*, Garden City, NY: Doubleday & Co.
Babbage, Charles (1832), *On the Economy of Machinery and Manufactures*, London: Charles Knight.
Bakan, Joel (2004), *The Corporation: The Pathological Pursuit of Profit and Power*, New York: Free Press.
Baker, Dean (2016), *Rigged: How Globalization and the Rules of the Modern Economy Were Structured to Make the Rich Richer*, Washington DC: Center for Economic and Policy Research.

Baily, Martin N., Burtless, Gary and Litan, Robert E. (1993), *Growth with Equity: Economic Policymaking for the Next Century*, Washington DC: Brookings Institution.

Bair, Jennifer (ed.) (2009), *Frontiers of Commodity Chain Research*, Stanford, CA: Stanford University Press.

Baldone, Salvatore, Sdogati, Fabio and Tajoli, Lucia (2007), 'On Some Effects of International Fragmentation of Production on Comparative Advantages, Trade Flows, and the Income of Countries', *World Economy*, 30 (11): 1726–1769.

Baldwin, Richard (2006), 'Globalisation: The Great Unboundling(s)', *The Economic Council of Finland*, 20 (3): 5–47.

Baldwin, Richard (2016), *The Great Convergence: Information Technology and the New Globalization*, Cambridge, MA: The Belknap Press of Harvard University Press.

Baldwin, Richard (2017), 'Ricardo's Comparative Advantage Has Been Denationalised', in Simon J. Evenett (ed.), *Cloth for Wine? The Relevance of Ricardo's Comparative Advantage in the 21st Century*, London: CEPR Press.

Baldwin, Richard and Krugman, Paul R. (2000), 'Agglomeration, Integration and Tax Harmonization', CEPR Discussion Paper No. 2630.

Baldwin, Richard and Robert-Nicoud, Frédéric (2007), 'Offshoring: General Equilibrium Effects on Wages, Production and Trade', NBER Working Paper No. 12991.

Baldwin, Richard and Robert-Nicoud Frédéric (2010), 'Trade-in-Goods and Trade-in-Tasks: An Integrating Framework', CEPR Discussion Paper No. 7775.

Banca d'Italia (2016), 'Global Value Chains: New Evidence and Implications', Workshops and Conferences, No. 21.

Banerjee, Abhijit V. and Duflo, Esther (2019), *Good Economics for Hard Times: Better Answers to Our Biggest Problems*, London: Allen Lane.

Banga, Rashmi (2014), 'Linking into Global Value Chains Is Not Sufficient: Do You Export Domestic Value Added Contents?', *Journal of Economic Integration*, 29 (2): 267–297.

Baran, Paul (1957), *The Political Economy of Growth*, New York: Monthly Review Press.

Baran, Paul A. and Sweezy, Paul M. (1966), *Monopoly Capital: An Essay on the American Economic and Social Order*, New York: Monthly Review Press.

Bardhan, Pranab (1991), 'The Concept of Power in Economics', *Economics and Politics*, 3 (3): 265–277.

Bardhan, Pranab (1997), 'Corruption and Development: A Review of Issues', *Journal of Economic Literature*, 35 (3): 1320–1346.

Bardhan, Pranab (2006), 'The Economist's Approach to the Problem of Corruption', *World Development*, 34 (2): 341–348.

Barratt Brown, Michael (1974), *The Economics of Imperialism*, Harmondsworth (UK): Penguin Books.

Barratt Brown, Michael (1999), 'Imperialism Revisited', in Ronald H. Chilcote (ed.), *The Political Economy of Imperialism: Critical Appraisals*, London: Kluwer Academic.

Barry, Christian and Reddy, Sanjay G. (2006), 'The False Dilemma of the Sweatshop', *Financial Times*, 24 July.

Barry, Christian and Reddy, Sanjay G. (2008), *International Trade and Labor Standards: A Proposal for Linkage*, New York: Columbia University Press.

Barry, Michael, Dundon, Tony and Wilkinson, Adrian (2018), 'Employee Voice: Conceptualisations, Meanings, Limitations and Possible Integration', in Adrian Wilkinson, Tony Dundon, Jimmy Donaghey and Alexander Colvin (eds.), *The Routledge Companion to Employment Relations*, London: Routledge.

Bartlett, Randall (1989), *Economics and Power: An Inquiry into Human Relations and Markets*, Cambridge: Cambridge University Press.

Baumol, William J. (2002), *The Free-Market Innovation Machine*, Princeton, NJ: Princeton University Press.

Bayard, Kimberly, Byrne, David and Smith, Dominic (2014), 'The Scope of U.S. Factoryless Manufacturing', in Susan Houseman and Michael Mandel (eds.), *Measuring the Effects of Globalization: Better Trade Statistics for Better Policy*, Kalamazoo, MI: W. E. Upjohn Institute.

Becattini, Giacomo (2004), *Industrial Districts: A New Approach to Industrial Change*, Cheltenham: Edward Elgar.

Bell, Daniel A. (2015), *The China Model: Political Meritocracy and the Limits of Democracy*, Princeton, NJ: Princeton University Press.

Belloc, Marianna (2006), 'Institutions and International Trade: A Reconsideration of Comparative Advantage', *Journal of Economic Surveys*, 20 (1): 3–26.

Bems, Rudolfs and Johnson, Robert C. (2015), 'Demand for Value Added and Value-Added Exchange Rates', NBER Working Paper No. 21070.

Bernanke, Ben S. (2005), 'The Global Saving Glut and the US Current Account Deficit', Board of Governors of the U.S. Federal Reserve System, Speech No. 77.

Bernard, Andrew B., Eaton, Jonathan, Jensen, J. Bradford and Kortum, Samuel (2003), 'Plants and Productivity in International Trade', *American Economic Review*, 93 (4): 1268–1290.

Bernard, Andrew B. and Fort, Teresa C. (2013), 'Factoryless Goods Producers in the US', NBER Working Paper No. 19396.

Bernard, Andrew and Fort, Teresa C. (2015), 'Factoryless Goods Producing Firms', *American Economic Review: Papers and Proceedings*, 105 (5): 518–523.

Bernard, Andrew and Fort, Teresa C. (2017), 'Factoryless Goods Producers in the U.S.', in Lionel Fontagné and Ann Harrison (eds.), *The Factory-Free Economy: Outsourcing, Servitization, and the Future of Industry*, Oxford: Oxford University Press.

Bernard, Andrew B. and Jensen, J. Bradford (1995), 'Exporters, Jobs, and Wages in U.S. Manufacturing, 1976–1987', *Brookings Papers on Economic Activity: Microeconomics*, 26: 67–112.

Bernard, Andrew B. and Jensen, J. Bradford (1999), 'Exceptional Exporter Performance: Cause, Effect, or Both?', *Journal of International Economics*, 47 (1): 1–25.

Bernard, Andrew B., Jensen, J. Bradford, Redding, Stephen J. and Schott, Peter K. (2007), 'Firms in International Trade', *Journal of Economic Perspectives*, 21 (3): 105–130.

Bernard, Andrew B., Jensen, J. Bradford, Redding, Stephen J. and Schott, Peter K. (2012), 'The Empirics of Firm Heterogeneity and International Trade', *Annual Review of Economics*, 4: 283–313.

Bernard, Andrew B., Jensen, J. Bradford, Redding, Stephen J. and Schott, Peter K. (2018), 'Global Firms', *Journal of Economic Literature*, 56 (2): 565–619.

Bernard, Andrew B. and Moxnes, Andreas (2018), 'Networks and Trade', *Annual Review of Economics*, 10: 65–85.

Bernhofen, Daniel M. and Brown, John C. (2018), 'On the Genius Behind David Ricardo's 1817 Formulation of Comparative Advantage', *Journal of Economic Perspectives*, 32 (4): 227–240.

Bhagwati, Jagdish (1958), 'Immiserizing Growth: A Geometrical Note', *Review of Economic Studies*, 25 (3): 201–205.

Bhagwati, Jagdish (1964), "The Pure Theory of International Trade: A Survey", *Economic Journal*, 74 (293): 1-84.

Bhagwati, Jagdish (1993a), 'Rough Trade', *The New Republic*, 31 May.

Bhagwati, Jagdish (1993b), 'The Case for Free Trade', *Scientific American*, 269 (5): 42–49.

Bhagwati, Jagdish (1994), 'Shock Treatments', *The New Republic*, 28 March, pp. 39–43.

Bhagwati, Jagdish (1998), *A Stream of Windows: Unsettling Reflections on Trade, Immigration, and Democracy*, Cambridge, MA: The MIT Press.

Bhagwati, Jagdish (2004), *In Defense of Globalization*, New York: Oxford University Press.

Bhagwati, Jagdish (2009), 'Don't Cry for Free Trade', in Jagdish Bhagwati, and Alan S. Blinder, *Offshoring of American Jobs: What Response from U.S. Economic Policy?*, Cambridge, MA: The MIT Press.

Bhagwati, Jagdish and Dehejia, Vivek H. (1994), 'Free Trade and Wages of the Unskilled: Is Marx Striking Again?', in Jagdish Bhagwati and Marvin H. Kosters (eds.), *Trade and Wages: Leveling Wages Down*, Washington DC: American Enterprise Institute.

Bhagwati, Jagdish, Panagariya, Arvind and Srinivasan, Thirukodikaval Nilacanta (2004), 'The Muddles over Outsourcing', *Journal of Economic Perspectives*, 18 (4): 93–114.

Bitzer, Jürgen, Görg, Holger and Schröder, Philipp J.H. (2012), 'Can Trade Really Hurt? An Empirical Follow-Up on Samuelson's Controversial Paper', *Economic Inquiry*, 50 (3): 724–738.

Black, Bernard, Kraakman, Reinier and Tarassova, Anna (2000), 'Russian Privatization and Corporate Governance: What Went Wrong?', *Stanford Law Review*, 52 (6): 1731–1808.

Blanchard, Olivier and Rodrik, Dani (2019), 'We Have the Tools to Reverse the Rise in Inequality', Peterson Institute for International Economics, Speeches and Papers, 20 November.

Blasi, Joseph R., Freeman, Richard B. and Kruse, Douglas L. (2017), 'Having a Stake: Evidence and Implications for Broad-based Employee Stock Ownership and Profit Sharing', Third Way/Economy (Internet), February.

Blattner, Niklaus (1973), 'Domestic Competition and Foreign Trade: The Case of the Excess Capacity Barrier', *Zeitschrift für Nationalökonomie/Journal of Economics*, 33 (3–4): 403–412.

Blaug, Mark (1985), *Economic Theory in Retrospect* (4th edition), Cambridge: Cambridge University Press.

Blecker, Robert A. (1997), 'The 'Unnatural and Retrograde Order': Adam Smith's Theories of Trade and Development Reconsidered', *Economica*, 64 (255): 527–537.

Blecker, Robert A. (2005a), 'International Economics after Robinson', in Bill Gibson (ed.), *Joan Robinson's Economics: A Centennial Celebration*, Cheltenham (UK): Edward Elgar.

Blecker, Robert A. (2005b), Statement Before the U.S.–China Economic and Security Review Commission. Hearing on China and the Future of Globalization. Panel III: China's Role in the Development of Globalization, Hearing of 19 May 2005.

Blecker, Robert A. (2009), 'Davidson on Keynes: The Open Economy Dimension', *Journal of Post Keynesian Economics*, 32 (1): 19–41.

Blecker, Robert A. and Razmi, Arslan (2010), 'Export-Led Growth, Real Exchange Rates and the Fallacy of Composition', in Mark Setterfield (ed.), *Handbook of Alternative Theories of Economic Growth*, Northampton, MA: Edward Elgar.

Blind, Knut (2013), *The Impact of Standardization and Standards on Innovation*, Manchester: Manchester Institute of Innovation Research, University of Manchester.

Blinder, Alan S. (2006), 'Offshoring: The Next Industrial Revolution?', *Foreign Affairs*, 85 (2): 113–128.

Blinder, Alan S. (2007), 'Offshoring: Big Deal, or Business as Usual?', CEPS Working Paper No. 149.

Blinder, Alan S. (2009), 'How Many US Jobs Might Be Offshorable?', *World Economics*, 10 (2): 41–78.

Bliss, Christopher (2007), *Trade, Growth, and Inequality*, Oxford: Oxford University Press.

Bloom, Nick, Draka, Mirko and Van Reenen, John (2011), 'Trade Induced Technical Change? The Impact of Chinese Imports on Innovation, IT and Productivity', London School of Economics, CEP Discussion Paper No. 1000.

Boldrin, Michele and Levine, David K. (2008), *Against Intellectual Monopoly*, Cambridge: Cambridge University Press.

Bolton, Patrick, Brodley, Joseph F. and Riordan, Michael H. (2015), 'Predatory Pricing: Strategic Theory and Legal Policy', US Department of Justice. Available at: https://www.justice.gov/atr/predatory-pricing-strategic-theory-and-legal-policy.

Bonvillian, William B. (2012), 'Reinventing American Manufacturing: The Role of Innovation', *Innovations*, 7 (3): 97–125.

Boyle, James (2003), 'The Second Enclosure Movement and the Construction of the Public Domain', *Law and Contemporary Problems*, 66 (1): 33–74.

Brahmbhatt, Milan, Canuto, Otaviano and Vostroknutova, Ekaterina (2010), 'Dealing with Dutch Disease', *Economic Premise*, No. 16, World Bank.

Brandis, Royall (1967), 'The Myth of Absolute Advantage', *American Economic Review*, 57 (1): 165–175.

Brandis, Royall (1968), 'The Myth of Absolute Advantage: Reply', *American Economic Review*, 58 (3): 520–522.

Brandly, Mark (2007), 'Review Essay' of Gomory and Baumol (2000), *Quarterly Journal of Austrian Economics*, 10 (2): 83–92.

Brandt, Loren, Ma, Debin and Rawski, Thomas G. (2014), 'From Divergence to Convergence: Reevaluating the History Behind China's Economic Boom', *Journal of Economic Literature*, 52 (1): 45–123.

Brennan, Jordan (2014), 'The Business of Power: Canadian Multinationals in the Postwar Era', Ph.D. Dissertation, York University, Toronto. Available at: https://core.ac.uk/download/pdf/77103363.pdf.

Brennan, Jordan (2016), 'Rising Corporate Concentration, Declining Trade Union Power, and the Growing Income Gap: American Prosperity in Historical Perspective', Levy Economic Institute of Bard College.

Brenner, Robert (1977), 'The Origins of Capitalist Development: a Critique of Neo-Smithian Marxism', *New Left Review*, No. 104: 25–92.

Brewer, Anthony (1980), *Marxist Theories of Imperialism: A Critical Survey*, London: Routledge & Kegan Paul.

Brewer, Anthony (1985), 'Trade with Fixed Real Wages and Mobile Capital', *Journal of International Economics*, 18 (1–2): 177–186.

Brewer, Anthony (1999), 'Imperialism in Retrospect', in Ronald H. Chilcote (ed.), *The Political Economy of Imperialism: Critical Appraisals*, London: Kluwer Academic.

Breznitz, Dan and Murphree, Michael (2013), 'The Rise of China in Technology Standards: New Norms in Old Institutions', Research Report Prepared on Behalf of the U.S.–China Economic and Security Review Commission, 16 January.

Brittan, Samuel (1984), 'The Politics and Economics of Privatization', *The Political Quarterly*, 55 (2): 109–128.

Brittan, Samuel (1993), 'The Two-way Switch in World Economy', *Financial Times*, 9 December.

Brittan, Samuel (2006), 'Globalisation Depresses Western Wages', *Financial Times*, 20 October.

Brolin, John (2006), *The Bias of the World: Theories of Unequal Exchange in History*, Lund Studies in Human Ecology 9, Lund, Sweden: Lund University.

Brown, Richard and Julius, Deanne (1993), 'Is Manufacturing Still Special in the New World Order?', in Richard O'Brien (ed.), *Finance and the International Economy, Vol. 7: The Amex Bank Review Prize Essays*, Oxford: Oxford University Press.

Bruins, Gijsbert W. J., Einaudi, Luigi, Seligman, Edwin R. A. and Stamp, Josiah (1923), *Report on Double Taxation Submitted to the Financial Committee Economic and Financial Commission*, Geneva: League of Nations.

Brunnermeier, Markus, Doshi, Rush and James, Harold (2018), 'Beijing's Bismarckian Ghosts: How Great Powers Compete Economically', *The Washington Quarterly*, 41 (3): 161–176.

Bruton, Henry J. (1980), Review of Lewis (1978a), *Economic Development and Cultural Change*, 28 (2): 409–412.

Bruton, Henry J. (1998), 'A Reconsideration of Import Substitution', *Journal of Economic Literature*, 36 (2): 903–936.

Brynjolfsson, Erik and McAfee, Andrew (2011), *Race Against the Machine*, Lexington, MA: Digital Frontier Press.

Brynjolfsson, Erik and McAfee, Andrew (2014), *The Second Machine Age: Work, Progress, and Prosperity in a Time of Brilliant Technologies*, NewYork: W.W. Norton & Company.

Buchanan, James M. and Yoon, Yong J. (2002), 'Globalization as Framed by the Two Logics of Trade', *Independent Review*, 6 (3): 399–405.

Buckley, Kenneth (1958), 'The Role of Staple Industries in Canada's Economic Development', *Journal of Economic History*, 18 (4): 439–450.

Busch, Lawrence (2011), *Standards: Recipes for Reality*, Cambridge, MA: The MIT Press.

Büthe, Tim and Mattli, Walter 2011), *The New Global Rulers: The Privatization of Regulation in the World Economy*, Princeton, NJ: Princeton University Press.

Caballero, Ricardo J., Farhi, Emmanuel and Gourinchas, Pierre-Olivier (2008), 'An Equilibrium Model of 'Global Imbalances' and Low Interest Rates', *American Economic Review*, 98 (1): 358–393.

Cadestin, Charles, De Backer, Koen, Desnoyers-James, Isabelle, Miroudot, Sébastien, Ye, Ming and Rigo, Davide (2018), 'Multinational Enterprises and Global Value Chains: New Insights on the Trade–Investment Nexus', OECD Science, Technology and Industry Working Papers 2019/05.

Cairncross, Frances (2001), *The Death of Distance: How the Communications Revolution Is Changing Our Lives* (2nd edition), Boston, MA: Harvard Business School Press.

Cambridge Econometrics (2020), 'Research on Trade in Value Added: Final Research Report', UK Department for International Trade.

Cammarosano, Joseph R. (2014), *John Maynard Keynes: Free Trader or Protectionist?*, Lexington, MD: Lexington Books.

Carabelli, Anna M. (2021), *Keynes on Uncertainty and Tragic Happiness: Complexity and Expectations*, London: Palgrave Macmillan.

Case, Anne and Deaton, Angus (2020), *Deaths of Despair and the Future of Capitalism*, Princeton, NJ: Princeton University Press.

Cattaneo, Olivier, Gereffi, Gary and Staritz, Cornelia (eds.) (2010), *Global Value Chains in a Postcrisis World: A Development Perspective*, Washington DC: World Bank.
Caves, Richard E. (1967) [1960], *Trade and Economic Structure*, Cambridge, MA: Harvard University Press.
Caves, Richard E. (1965), '"Vent for Surplus" Models of Trade and Growth', in Robert E. Baldwin et al., *Trade, Growth and the Balance of Payments: Essays in Honor of Gottfried Haberler*, Chicago: Rand McNally.
Caves, Richard E. (1982), *Multinational Enterprise and Economic Analysis*, Cambridge: Cambridge University Press.
Caves, Richard E. and Holton, Richard H. (1959), *The Canadian Economy, Prospect and Retrospect*, Cambridge, MA: Harvard University Press.
Cebr (2015), 'The Economic Contribution of Standards to the UK Economy', Report by the Centre for Economics and Business Research Ltd, London: British Standards Institution.
Chandra, Ramesh (2004), 'Adam Smith, Allyn Young and the Division of Labour', *Journal of Economic Issues*, 38 (3): 787–805.
Chang, Ha-Joon (2007) 'Understanding the Relationship between Institutions and Economic Development – Some Key Theoretical Issues', in Ha-Joon Chang (ed.), *Institutional Change and Economic Development*, London: Anthem Press.
Chang, Ha-Joon (2011), 'Institutions and Economic Development: Theory, Policy and History', *Journal of Institutional Economics*, 7 (4): 473–498.
Chang, Leslie T. (2008), *Factory Girls: From Village to City in a Changing China*, New York: Spiegel & Grau.
Chevalier, Michel (1851), *L'Exposition Universelle de Londres*, Paris: Librairie Scientifique-Industrielle L. Mathias.
Chor, Davin (2019), 'Modelling Global Value Chains: Approaches and Insights from Economics' in Stefano Ponte, Gary Gereffi and Gale Raj-Reichert (eds.), *Handbook of Global Value Chains*, Cheltenham (UK): Edward Elgar Publishing.
Christians, Allison (2018), 'Taxing According to Value Creation', *Tax Notes International*, 90: 1–8.
Christians, Allison and van Apeldoorn, Laurens (2018), 'Taxing Income Where Value is Created', *Florida Tax Review*, 22 (1): 1–39.
Cimoli, Mario, Dosi, Giovanni, Nelson, Richard and Stiglitz, Joseph (2006), 'Institutions and Policies Shaping Industrial Development: An Introductory Note', Sant'Anna School of Advanced Studies, Pisa, (Italy), LEM Working Paper Series, No. 2006/02.
Cipolla, Carlo M. (1965), *Guns and Sails*, London: Collins.
Coase, Ronald and Wang, Ning (2013), *How China Became Capitalist*, New York: Palgrave Macmillan.
Coe, Neil M. and Yeung, Henry Wai-Chung (2015), *Global Production Networks: Theorizing Economic Development in an Interconnected World*, Oxford: Oxford University Press.
Coe, Neil M. and Yeung, Henry Wai-Chung (2019), 'Global Production Networks: Mapping Recent Conceptual Developments', *Journal of Economic Geography*, 19 (4): 775–801.
Cohan, William D. (2011), *Money and Power: How Goldman Sachs Came to Rule the World*, New York: Doubleday.
Cohen, Avi J. and Harcourt, Geoffrey C. (2003), 'Whatever Happened to the Cambridge Capital Theory Controversies?', *Journal of Economic Perspectives*, 17 (1):199–214.
Cooper, Richard N. (2004), 'Is 'Economic Power' a Useful and Operational Concept?', Weatherhead Center for International Affairs, Working Paper Series, No. 04–02.

Corden, W. Max (1984), 'Booming Sector and Dutch Disease Economics: Survey and Consolidation', *Oxford Economic Papers*, 36 (3): 359–380.

Corden, W. Max (1994), *Economic Policy, Exchange Rates, and the International System*, Oxford: Oxford University Press.

Corden, W. Max and Findlay, Ronald E. (1977), 'Concluding Remarks', in Bertil Ohlin, Per-Ove Hesselborn and Per Magnus Wijkman (eds.), *The International Allocation of Economic Activity*, London: Macmillan.

Corden, W. Max and Neary, J. Peter (1982), 'Booming Sector and De-Industrialisation in a Small Open Economy', *Economic Journal*, 92 (368): 825–848.

Costinot, Arnaud and Donaldson, Dave (2017) 'Old Idea, New Insights: The Ricardian Revival in International Trade', *NBER Reporter*, 3: 11–15.

Costinot, Arnaud and Rodríguez-Clare, Andrés (2018), 'The US Gains from Trade: Valuation Using the Demand for Foreign Factor Services', *Journal of Economic Perspectives*, 32 (2): 3–24.

Costinot, Arnaud and Vogel, Jonathan (2015), 'Beyond Ricardo: Assignment Models in International Trade', *Annual Review of Economics*, 7: 31–62.

Crinò, Rosario and Epifani, Paolo (2014), 'Trade Imbalances, Export Structure and Wage Inequality', *Economic Journal*, 124 (576): 507–539.

Crouch, Colin (2011), *The Strange Non-Death of Neoliberalism*, Cambridge: Polity Press.

Crouch, Colin (2016), 'The Paradoxes of Privatization and Public Services Outsourcing', in Michael Jacobs and Mariana Mazzucato (eds.), *Rethinking Capitalism: Economics and Policy for Sustainable and Inclusive Growth*, Chichester (UK): Wiley-Blackwell.

Culberson, John M. (1984), *International Trade and the Future of the West*, Madison, WI: 21st Century Press.

Curott, Nicholas A. (2016), 'Adam Smith's Theory of Money and Banking', Johns Hopkins Institute for Applied Economics, Global Health and the Study of Business Enterprise, Baltimore, Studies in Applied Economics, No. 47.

Curzon Price, Victoria (2001), 'Some Causes and Consequences of Fragmentation', in Sven W. Arndt and Henryk Kierzkowski (eds), *Fragmentation: New Production Patterns in the World Economy*, Oxford: Oxford University Press.

Dallas, Mark, Ponte, Stefano and Sturgeon, Timothy J. (2019), 'A Typology of Power in Global Value Chains', *Review of International Political Economy*, 26 (4): 666–694.

Daly, Herman E. (1993), 'The Perils of Free Trade', *Scientific American*, 269 (5): 50–57.

Daly, Herman and Goodland, Robert (1994), 'An Ecological-Economic Assessment of Deregulation of International Commerce under GATT', *Ecological Economics*, 9 (1): 73–92.

D'Amico, Ronald and Schochet, Peter Z. (2012), *The Evaluation of the Trade Adjustment Assistance Program: A Synthesis of Major Findings*, Oakland, CA: Social Policy Research and Princeton, NJ: Mathematica Policy Research.

Daokui Li, David (2019), 'Lessons from the First 70 Years of the People's Republic of China', *Financial Times*, 1 October.

David, Paul A. (1985), 'Clio and the Economics of QWERTY', *American Economic Review*, 75 (2): 332–337.

Davidson, Paul (2007), *John Maynard Keynes*, London: Palgrave Macmillan.

Davis, Gerald F. (2016), *The Vanishing American Corporation: Navigating the Hazards of a New Economy*, Oakland, CA: Berrett-Koehler Publishers.

De Angelis, Massimo and Harvie, David (2008), 'Globalization? No Question! Foreign Direct Investment and Labour Commanded', *Review of Radical Political Economics*, 40 (4): 429–444.

Deardorff, Alan V. (2003), 'Time and Trade: The Role of Time in Determining the Structure and Effects of International Trade, with an Application to Japan', in Robert M. Stern (ed.), *Analytical Studies in U.S.–Japan International Economic Relations*, Cheltenham (UK): Edward Elgar.

Deardorff, Alan V. (2005), 'How Robust is Comparative Advantage?', *Review of International Economics*, 13 (5): 1004–1016.

Deardorff, Alan V. and Hakura, Dalia S. (1994), 'Trade and Wages – What Are the Questions?', in Jagdish Bhagwati and Marvin H. Kosters (eds.), *Trade and Wages: Leveling Wages Down*, Washington, DC: American Enterprise Institute.

Deaton, Angus (2013), *The Great Escape: Health, Wealth, and the Origins of Inequality*, Princeton, NJ: Princeton University Press.

De Cecco, Marcello (1971), *Economia e finanza internazionale dal 1890 al 1914*, Bari: Laterza (English translation: *Money and Empire: The International Gold Standard, 1890–1914*, Oxford: Basil Blackwell, 1974).

De Grauwe, Paul (2001), 'Competitiveness and Compassion', *Financial Times*, 11 August.

De Loecker, Jan and Eeckhout, Jan (2018), 'Global Market Power', NBER Working Paper No. 24768.

De Loecker, Jan, Eeckhout, Jan and Unger Gabriel (2020), 'The Rise of Market Power and the Macroeconomic Implications', *Quarterly Journal of Economics*, 135 (2): 561–644.

Denis, Henry (1961), 'Le rôle des 'débouchés préalables' dans la croissance économique de l'Europe occidentale et des Etats-Unis d'Amérique', *Cahiers de l'I.S.E.A.*, No.113, Série P: 3–90.

Depoortère, Christophe and Ravix, Joël Thomas (2015), 'The Classical Theory of International Trade after Sraffa', *Cahiers d'Économie Politique/Papers in Political Economy*, No. 69: 203–234.

Desai, Padma (2005), 'Russian Retrospectives on Reforms from Yeltsin to Putin', *Journal of Economic Perspectives*, 19 (1): 87–106.

Dickens, William T. and Rose, Stephen J. (2007), 'Blinder Baloney', *International Economy*, 21 (4): 18–23 and 83.

Díez, Federico J., Fan, Jiayue and Villegas-Sánchez, Carolina (2019), 'Global Declining Competition', IMF Working Paper WP/19/82.

Dixit, Avinash K. and Grossman, Gene (2005), 'The Limits of Free Trade' in 'Comments', *Journal of Economic Perspectives*, 19 (3): 241–245.

Dixit, Avinash K. and Stiglitz, Joseph E. (1977), 'Monopolistic Competition and Optimum Product Diversity', *American Economic Review*, 67 (3): 297–308.

Dosi, Giovanni, Pavitt, Keith and Soete, Luc (1990), *The Economics of Technical Change and International Trade*, Hemel Hempstead (UK): Harvester Wheatsheaf.

Dosi, Giovanni and Tranchero, Matteo (2018), 'The Role of Comparative Advantage, Endowments and Technology in Structural Transformation', Scuola Superiore Sant'Anna, Pisa,(Italy), LEM Working Paper Series, 2018/33.

Drèze, Jacques H. (1960), 'Quelques réflections sereines sur l'adaptation de l'industrie belge au Marché Commun', *Comptes rendus des travaux de la Société Royale d'Economie Politique de Belgique*, No. 275: 3-37.

Durst, Michael C. (2019), *Taxing Multinational Business in Lower-Income Countries: Economics, Politics and Social Responsibility*, Brighton: Institute of Development Studies.

Eaton, Jonathan and Kortum, Samuel (2012), 'Putting Ricardo to Work', *Journal of Economic Perspectives*, 26 (2): 65–90.

Edmonds, Eric V. and Pavcnik, Nina (2005), 'Child Labor in the Global Economy', *Journal of Economic Perspectives*, 19 (1): 199–220.

Egyedi, Tineke M. (2010), 'On the Implications of Competing Standards', in Konkurrensverket – Swedish Competition Authority (ed.), *The Pros and Cons of Standard Setting*, Vasteras, Sweden: Edita Vastra Aros AB.

Elliott, Kimberly Ann (2019), 'Developing a More Inclusive US Trade Policy at Home and Abroad', CGD Policy Paper 146, Center for Global Development, Washington DC.

Elliott, Kimberly Ann and Freeman, Richard B. (2001), 'White Hats or Don Quixotes? Human Rights Vigilantes in the Global Economy', NBER Working Paper No. 8102.

Elliott, Kimberly Ann and Freeman, Richard B. (2003), *Can Labor Standards Improve under Globalization?*, Washington DC: Institute for International Economics.

Elmslie, Bruce Truitt (1995), 'The Convergence Debate Between David Hume and Josiah Tucker', *Journal of Economic Perspectives*, 9 (4): 207–216. m

Elmslie, Bruce and James, Antoinette M. (1993), 'The Renaissance of Adam Smith in Modern Theories of International Trade', in Robert F. Hébert (ed.), *Perspectives on the History of Economic Thought*, Cheltenham (UK): Edward Elgar.

Elmslie, Bruce and Sedgley, Norman (2002), 'Vent for Surplus: a Case of Mistaken Identity', *Southern Economic Journal*, 68 (3):712–720.

Elmslie. Bruce and Vieira, Flavio (1999), 'A Primer on Technology Gap Theory and Empirics', in Johan Deprez and John T. Harvey (eds.), *Foundations of International Economics: Post Keynesian Perspectives*, London: Routledge.

Emmanuel, Arghiri (1969), *L'échange inégal: Essai sur les antagonismes dans les rapports économiques internationaux*, Paris: Maspero (English translation: *Unequal Exchange: A Study of the Imperialism of Trade*, London: New Left Books, 1972).

Emmanuel, Arghiri (1974), 'Myths of Development vs Myths of Underdevelopment', *New Left Review*, No. 85: 61–82.

Ernst, Dieter (2013), 'Standards, Innovation, and Latecomer Economic Development – A Conceptual Framework', East–West Center Working Papers, No. 134.

Ethier, Wilfred J. (1982), 'Decreasing Costs in International Trade and Frank Graham's Argument for Protection', *Econometrica*, 50 (5): 1243–1268.

Ethier, Wilfred J. (1984), 'Higher Dimensional Issues in Trade Theory', in Ronald W. Jones and Peter B. Kenen (eds.), *Handbook of International Economics*, vol. 1, Amsterdam: North Holland.

Faccarello, Gilbert (2015a), 'Comparative Advantage', in Heinz D. Kurz and Neri Salvadori (eds.), *The Elgar Companion to David Ricardo*, Cheltenham (UK): Edward Elgar.

Faccarello, Gilbert (2015b), 'A Calm Investigation into Mr Ricardo's Principles of International Trade', *European Journal of the History of Economic Thought*, 22 (5): 754–790.

Facchini, Giovanni and Willmann, Gerald (2001), 'Pareto Gains from Trade', *Economia Politica*, 18 (2): 207–216.

Fagerberg, Jan (1996), 'Technology and Competitiveness', *Oxford Review of Economic Policy*, 12 (3): 39–51.

Federico, Giovanni (1994), *Il filo d'oro; L'industria mondiale della seta dalla restaurazione alla grande crisi'*, Venice: Marsilio (English translation: *An Economic History of the Silk Industry, 1830–1930*, Cambridge: Cambridge University Press, 1997).

Feenstra, Robert C. (1998), 'Integration of Trade and Disintegration of Production in the Global Economy', *Journal of Economic Perspectives*, 12 (4): 31–50.

Felipe, Jesus (2003), 'Is Export-led Growth Passé? Implications for Developing Asia', Asian Development Bank, ERD Working Paper No. 48.

Ferguson, Benjamin (2018), 'Exploitation and Labour', in Eugene Heath, Byron Kaldis and Alexei Marcoux (eds.), *The Routledge Companion to Business Ethics*, London: Routledge.

Fibírová, Jana and Petera, Petr (2013), 'Profit-Sharing – A Tool for Improving Productivity, Profitability and Competitiveness of Firms?', *Journal of Competitiveness*, 5 (4): 3–25.

Findlay, Ronald E. (1970), *Trade and Specialization*, Harmondsworth (UK): Penguin Books.

Findlay, Ronald E. (1977), 'Comment' to Ohlin paper, in Bertil Ohlin, Per-Ove Hesselborn and Per Magnus Wijkman (eds.), *The International Allocation of Economic Activity*, London: Macmillan.

Findlay, Ronald E. (1981), 'The Fundamental Determinants of the Terms of Trade', in Sven Grassman and Erik Lundberg (eds.), *The World Economic Order: Past and Prospects*, London: Macmillan.

Findlay, Ronald E. and Lundahl, Mats (1994), 'Natural Resources, 'Vent-for-Surplus', and the Staples Theory', in Gerald M. Meier (ed.), *From Classical Economics to Development Economics*, New York: St Martin's Press.

Findlay, Ronald E. and O'Rourke, Kevin H. (2007), *Power and Plenty: Trade, War, and the World Economy in the Second Millennium*, Princeton, NJ: Princeton University Press.

Fitzgerald, Edmund V.K. and Perosino, Giorgio (1999), 'Trade Liberalization, Employment and Wages: a Critical Approach', in Giorgio Barba Navaretti, Riccardo Faini and Giovanni Zanalda (eds.), *Labour Markets, Poverty, and Development*, Oxford: Oxford University Press.

Fong, Mei (2016), *One Child: The Story of China's Most Radical Experiment*, London: Oneworld Publications.

Fontagné, Lionel and Harrison, Ann (eds.) (2017), *The Factory-Free Economy: Outsourcing, Servitization, and the Future of Industry*, Oxford: Oxford University Press.

Ford, Martin (2009), *The Lights in the Tunnel: Automation, Accelerating Technology and the Economy of the Future*, Lexington, KY: Acculant Publishing.

Fort, Teresa C. (2013), 'Breaking up Is Hard to Do: Why Firms Fragment Production Across Locations', US Census Bureau Center for Economic Studies Paper No. CES-WP-13-35.

Fort, Teresa C. (2017), 'Technology and Production Fragmentation: Domestic versus Foreign Sourcing', *Review of Economic Studies*, 84: 650–687.

Frank, Andre Gunder (1967), *Capitalism and Underdevelopment in Latin America*, New York: Monthly Review Press.

Frank, Charles (1973), 'Comment', in Helen Hughes (ed.), *Prospects for Partnership: Industrialization and Trade Policies in the 1970s*, Washington DC: International Bank for Reconstruction and Development.

Freeman, Richard B. (1995), 'Are Your Wages Set in Beijing?', *Journal of Economic Perspectives*, 9 (3): 15–32.

Freeman, Richard B. (2005), 'China, India and the Doubling of the Global Labor Force: Who Pays the Price of Globalization?', *The Globalist*, 3 June.

Freeman, Richard B. (2008a), 'The New Global Labor Market', *Focus*, 26 (1): 1–6.

Freeman, Richard B. (2008b), 'Labor Market Imbalances: Shortages, Surpluses, or What?', in Jane Sneddon Little (ed.), *Global Imbalances and the Evolving World Economy*, Boston, MA: Federal Reserve Bank of Boston.

Friedman, Thomas L. (2016), *Thank You for Being Late*, New York: Farrar, Strauss and Giroux.

Fröbel, Folker, Heinrichs, Jürgen and Kreye, Otto (1977), *Die neue internationale Arbeitsteilung: Strukturelle Arbeitslosigkeit in den Industrieländern und die Industrialisierung der Entwicklungsländer*, Reinbek bei Hamburg, Germany: Rewohlt Taschenbuch Verlag GmbH (English translation: *The New International Division of Labour: Structural Unemployment in Industrialised Countries and Industrialisation in Developing Countries*, Cambridge: Cambridge University Press, 1980).

Fuest, Clemens, Parenti, Mathieu and Toubal, Farid (2019), 'International Corporate Taxation: What Reforms? What Impact?', *Notes du Conseil d'analyse économique*, 6 (54): 1–12.

Galbraith, John Kenneth (1967), *The New Industrial State*, Boston, MA: Houghton Mifflin.

Galbraith, John Kenneth (1983), *The Anatomy of Power*, Boston, MA: Houghton Mifflin.

Garretsen, Harry and Peeters, Jolanda (2006), 'Capital Mobility, Agglomeration and Corporate Tax Rates: Is the Race to the Bottom for Real?', De Nederlandsche Bank Working Paper No. 113.

Gaulier, Guillaume, Sztulman, Aude and Ünal, Deniz (2019), 'Are Global Value Chains Receding? The Jury Is Still Out. Key Findings from the Analysis of Deflated World Trade in Parts and Components', Paris, CEPII Working Paper No. 2019-01.

Gehrke, Christian (2015), 'Ricardo's Discovery of Comparative Advantage Revisited: A Critique of Ruffin's Account', *European Journal of the History of Economic Thought*, 22 (5): 791–817.

Gehrke, Christian (2017), 'Foreign Trade, International Values, and Gains from Trade: Ricardo, Pennington, Whewell, and John Stuart Mill', in Shigeyoshi Senga, Masatomi Fujimoto and Taichi Tabuchi (eds.), *Ricardo and International Trade*, London: Routledge.

Gentilini, Ugo, Grosh, Margaret, Rigolini, Jamele and Yemtsov, Ruslan (eds.) (2020), *Exploring Universal Basic Income: A Guide to Navigating Concepts, Evidence, and Practices*, Washington DC: World Bank Group.

Gereffi, Gary (1994), 'The Organization of Buyer-Driven Global Commodity Chains: How U.S. Retailers Shape Overseas Production Networks', in Gary Gereffi and Miguel Korzeniewicz (eds.), *Commodity Chains and Global Capitalism*, Westport, CT: Praeger.

Gereffi, Gary, Humphrey, John and Sturgeon, Timothy (2005), 'The Governance of Global Value Chains', *Review of International Political Economy*, 12 (1): 78–104.

Gesell, Silvio (2012) [1916], *Die natürliche Wirtschaftsordnung durch Freiland und Freigelt*, Les Hauts Geneveys, Switzerland: Selbstverlag (English translation: *Establishing a Natural Economic Order Through Free-Land and Free-Money*, Lewiston, NY: Edwin Mellen Press, 2012).

Ghatak, Maitreesh and Maniquet, François, 'Universal Basic Income: Some Theoretical Aspects', *Annual Review of Economics*, 11: 895–928.

Gianni, Monica (2018), 'OECD BEPS (In)Action 1: Factor Presence as a Solution to Tax Issues of the Digital Economy', *Tax Lawyer*, 72 (1): 255–298.

Gibson, Christopher S. (2007), 'Globalization and the Technology Standards Game: Balancing Concerns of Protectionism and Intellectual Property in International Standards', *Berkeley Technology Law Journal*, 22 (4): 1403–1484.

Goldberg, Pinelopi K. (ed.) (2015), *Trade and Inequality*, Cheltenham: Edward Elgar.

Gollin, Douglas (2014), 'The Lewis Model: A 60-Year Retrospective', *Journal of Economic Perspectives*, 28 (3): 71–88.

Golub, Stephen S., Jones, Ronald W. and Kierzkowski, Henryk (2007), 'Globalization and Country-Specific Service Links', *Journal of Economic Policy Reform*, 10 (2): 63–88.

Gomes, Leonard (1987), *Foreign Trade and the National Economy: Mercantilist and Classical Perspectives*, New York: St. Martin's Press.

Gomory, Ralph E. (2009), 'Manufacturing and the Limits of Comparative Advantage', *The Huffington Post*, 8 July. Available at: huffpost.com/entry/manufacturing-and-the-lim_b_227870.

Gomory, Ralph E. and Baumol, William J. (2000), *Global Trade and Conflicting National Interest*, Cambridge, MA: The MIT Press.

Gomory, Ralph E. and Baumol, William J. (2009), 'Globalization: Country and Company Interests in Conflict', *Journal of Policy Modeling*, 31 (3): 540–555.

Gomory, Ralph E. and Baumol, William J. (2013), 'On Technical Progress and the Gains and Losses from Outsourcing', in Ashok Bardhan, Dwight Jaffee and Cynthia Kroll (eds.), *The Oxford Handbook of Offshoring and Global Employment*, Oxford: Oxford University Press.

Goodhart, Charles and Pradhan, Manoj (2017), 'Demographics Will Reverse Three Multi-Decade Global Trends', Bank for International Settlements Working Papers, No. 656.

Gordon, Robert J. (2018), Why Has Economic Growth Slowed When Innovation Appears to Be Accelerating?', NBER Working Paper No. 24554.

Gordon, Robert J. and Sayed, Hassan (2020), 'Transatlantic Technologies: The Role of ICT in the Evolution of U.S. and European Productivity Growth', NBER Working Paper No. 27425.

Graham, Frank D. (1923), 'Some Aspects of Protection Further Considered', *Quarterly Journal of Economics*, 37 (2): 199–227.

Griffin, Keith and Gurley, John (1985), 'Radical Analyses of Imperialism, the Third World, and the Transition to Socialism: A Survey Article', *Journal of Economic Literature*, 23 (3): 1089–1143.

Grinberg, Itai (2019), 'International Taxation in an Era of Digital Disruption: Analyzing the Current Debate', Georgetown University Law Center, *TAXES The Tax Magazine.* Available at: https://scholarship.law.georgetown.edu/facpub/2145.

Groenewegen, Peter D. (1977), 'Adam Smith and the Division of Labour: A Bicentenary Estimate', *Australian Economic Papers*, 16 (29): 161–174.

Grossman, Gene M. and Helpman, Elhanan (1995), 'Technology and Trade', in Gene M. Grossman and Kenneth Rogoff (eds.), *Handbook of International Economics*, Vol. 3, Amsterdam: North-Holland.

Grossman, Gene M. and Rossi-Hansberg, Esteban (2006), 'The Rise of Offshoring: It's Not Wine for Cloth Anymore', in *The New Economic Geography: Effects and Policy Implications*, Jackson Hole Symposium, Kansas City, MO: Federal Reserve Bank of Kansas City.

Grossman, Gene M. and Rossi-Hansberg, Esteban (2008), 'Trading Tasks: A Simple Theory of Offshoring', *American Economic Review*, 98 (5): 1978–1997.

Grullon, Gustavo, Larkin, Yelena and Michaely, Roni (2019), 'Are US Industries Becoming More Concentrated?', *Review of Finance*, 23 (4): 697–743.

Guillermo Peón, Sylvia B. (2004), 'The Terms of Trade Controversy', *Aportes*, 9 (27): 121–138.

Guriev, Sergei (2019), 'Gorbachev Versus Deng: A Review of Chris Miller's *The Struggle to Save the Soviet Economy*', *Journal of Economic Literature*, 57 (1): 120–146.

Gutiérrez, Germán and Philippon, Thomas (2017), 'Declining Competition and Investment in the U.S.', NBER Working Paper No. 23583.

Haberler, Gottfried (1930), 'Die Theorie der Komparativen Kosten und ihre Auswertung für die Begründung des Freihandels', *Weltwirtshaftliches Archiv*, 32: 349–370. (English translation: 'The Theory of Comparative Costs and Its Use in Defence of Free Trade', in Anthony Y. C. Koo (ed.), *Essays of Gottfried Haberler*, Cambridge, MA: The MIT Press, 1985).

Hachem, Hicham M. (2017), 'Innovation, Dynamics and the Myths about Knowledge, Technology and R&D-Driven Economic Growth: An Evolving Network Model', *Journal of Innovation Economics & Management*, 23: 13–32.

Hacker, Jacob S. (2011), 'The Institutional Foundations of Middle-Class Democracy', in *Priorities for a New Political Economy: Memos to the Left*, London: Policy Network.

Hadzhieva, Eli (2019), 'Impact of Digitalisation on International Tax Matters', Study requested by the TAX3 Committee, European Parliament.

Haldane, Andrew G. (2016), 'The Costs of Short-Termism', in Michael Jacobs and Mariana Mazzucato (eds.), *Rethinking Capitalism: Economics and Policy for Sustainable and Inclusive Growth*, Chichester (UK): Wiley-Blackwell.

Harrison, Ann, McLaren, John and McMillan, Margaret (2011), 'Recent Perspectives on Trade and Inequality', World Bank, Policy Research Working Paper 5754.

Harrod, Roy (1933), *International Economics*, Cambridge: Cambridge University Press.

Harvie, David (2005), 'All Labour Produces Value for Capital and We All Struggle Against Value', *The Commoner*, 10: 132–171.

Hauner, Thomas, Milanovic, Branko and Naidu, Suresh (2017), 'Inequality, Foreign Investment, and Imperialism', Munich Personal RePEc Archive Paper No. 83068.

Hausmann, Ricardo, Hwang, Jason and Rodrik, Dani (2007), 'What You Export Matters', *Journal of Economic Growth*, 12 (1): 1–25.

Havice, Elizabeth and Pickles, John (2019), 'On Value in Value Chains', in Stefano Ponte, Gary Gereffi and Gale Raj-Reichert (eds.), *Handbook of Global Value Chains*, Cheltenham (UK): Edward Elgar Publishing.

Hawtrey, Ralph G. (1930), *The Economic Aspects of Sovereignty*, London: Longmans.

Head, Keith and Spencer, Barbara J. (2017), 'Oligopoly in International Trade: Rise, Fall and Resurgence', NBER Working Paper No. 23720.

Headrick, Daniel R. (1981), *The Tools of Empire: Technology and European Imperialism in the Nineteenth Century*, New York: Oxford University Press.

Headrick, Daniel R. (2010), *Power over Peoples: Technology, Environments, and Western Imperialism, 1400 to the Present*, Princeton, NJ: Princeton University Press.

Heckscher, Eli (1919), 'The Effect of Foreign Trade on the Distribution of Income' (in Swedish), *Ekonomisk Tidskrift*, 21: 497–512 (English translation in Howard S. Ellis and Lloyd S. Metzler (eds.), *Readings in the Theory of International Trade*, Philadelphia, PA: Blakiston, 1949).

Helleiner, Gerald K. (1972), *International Trade and Economic Development*, Harmondsworth (UK): Penguin Books.

Helper, Susan, Krueger, Timothy and Wial, Howard (2012), 'Why Does Manufacturing Matter? Which Manufacturing Matters? A Policy Framework', Metropolitan Policy Program, Brookings Institution.

Helpman, Elhanan (1998), 'Explaining the Structure of Foreign Trade: Where Do We Stand?', *Weltwirtschaftliches Archiv*, 134 (4): 573–589.

Helpman, Elhanan (2006), 'Trade, FDI, and the Organization of Firms', *Journal of Economic Literature*, 44 (3): 589–630.

Helpman, Elhanan (2011), *Understanding Global Trade*, Cambridge, MA: Harvard University Press.

Helpman, Elhanan and Krugman, Paul R. (1985), *Market Structure and Foreign Trade*, Cambridge, MA: The MIT Press.

Hertz, Noreena (2001), *The Silent Takeover: Global Capitalism and the Death of Democracy*, London: Heinemann.

Hickland, Eugene, Cullinane, Niall, Dobbins, Tony, Dundon, Tony and Donaghey, Jimmy (2020), 'Employer Silencing in a Context of Voice Regulations: Case Studies of Non-Compliance', *Human Resource Management Journal*, 30 (4): 537–552.

Hicks, John R. (1953), 'An Inaugural Lecture', *Oxford Economic Papers*, 5 (2): 117–135.

Hira, Ron and Hira, Anil (2005), *Outsourcing America: What's Behind Our National Crisis and How We Can Reclaim American Jobs*, New York: AMACOM.

Hirsch, Seev (1965), 'The United States Electronics Industry in International Trade', *National Institute Economic Review*, 34: 92–107.

Hirschman, Albert O. (1969), *National Power and the Structure of Foreign Trade*, Berkeley, CA: University of California Press.

Hirschman, Albert O. (1976), 'On Hegel, Imperialism, and Structural Stagnation', *Journal of Development Economics*, 3 (1): 1–8.

Hirshleifer, Jack (1990), 'The Determinants of Power', UCLA Department of Economics Working Paper No. 582.

Hobson, John A. (1938) [1902], *Imperialism: A Study* (3rd edition), London: Allen & Unwin.

Hochschild, Adam (1998), *King Leopold's Ghost: A Story of Greed, Terror and Heroism in Colonial Africa*, Boston, MA: Houghton Mifflin.

Hoekman, Bernard and Javorcik, Beata Smarzynska (eds.) (2006), *Global Integration and Technology Transfer*, Washington DC: World Bank.

Hoynes, Hilary W. and Rothstein, Jesse (2019), 'Universal Basic Income in the US and Advanced Countries', NBER Working Paper No. 25538.

Hufbauer, Gary Clide (1966), *Synthetic Materials and the Theory of International Trade*, London: Gerald Duckworth.

Hufbauer, Gary Clide (1970), 'The Impact of National Characteristics & Technology on the Commodity Composition of Trade in Manufactured Goods', in Raymond Vernon (ed.), *The Technology Factor in International Trade*, New York: National Bureau of Economic Research.

Hughes, Kent H. and Sha, Lynn (eds.) (2009), *New Thinking in International Trade: Global Competition and Comparative Advantage*, Washington DC: Woodrow Wilson International Center for Scholars.

Hummels, David (2007), 'Transportation Costs and International Trade in the Second Era of Globalization', *Journal of Economic Perspectives*, 21 (3): 131–154.

Hunt, Diana (1989), *Economic Theories of Development: An Analysis of Competing Paradigms*, New York: Harvester Wheatsheaf.

Hyman, Jeff (2018), *Employee Voice and Participation: Contested Past, Troubled Present, Uncertain Future*, Abingdon (UK): Routledge.

Ingram, James C. (1968), 'The Myth of Absolute Advantage: Comment', *American Economic Review*, 58 (3): 516–520.

Irwin, Douglas A. (1996), *Against the Tide: An Intellectual History of Free Trade*, Princeton, NJ: Princeton University Press.

Irwin, Douglas A. (2017), 'Ricardo and Comparative Advantage at 200', in Simon J. Evenett (ed.), *Cloth for Wine? The Relevance of Ricardo's Comparative Advantage in the 21st Century*, London: CEPR Press.

Jacobs, Michael and Mazzucato, Mariana (eds.) (2016), *Rethinking Capitalism: Economics and Policy for Sustainable and Inclusive Growth*, Chichester: Wiley-Blackwell.

Jacques, Martin (2009), *When China Rules the World: The Rise of the Middle Kingdom and the End of the Western World*, London: Allen Lane.

Jaffe, Adam B. (2016), 'Patent Citation Data in Social Science Research: Overview and Best Practices', NBER Working Paper No. 21868.

Johnson, Harry G. (1954), 'Increasing Productivity, Income-Price Trends and Trade Balance', *Economic Journal*, 64 (255): 462–485.

Johnson, Harry G. (1955), 'Economic Expansion and International Trade', *Manchester School of Economic and Social Studies*, 23 (2): 95–112.

Johnson, Harry G. (1973), 'Trade, Investment and Labor, and the Changing International Division of Production', in Helen Hughes (ed.), *Prospects for Partnership: Industrialization and Trade Policies in the 1970s*, Washington DC: International Bank for Reconstruction and Development.

Johnson, Robert C. (2014), 'Five Facts about Value-Added Exports and Implications for Macroeconomics and Trade Research', *Journal of Economic Perspectives*, 28 (2): 119–142.

Johnson, Robert C. (2018), 'Measuring Global Value Chains', *Annual Review of Economics*, 10: 207–236.

Jones, Ronald W. (1980), 'Comparative and Absolute Advantage', *Schweizer Zeitschrift für Volkswirtschaft und Statistik*, 116 (3): 235–260.

Jones, Ronald W. (2000), *Globalization and the Theory of Input Trade*, Cambridge, MA: The MIT Press.

Jones, Ronald W. and Kierzkowski, Henryk (1990), 'The Role of Services in Production and International Trade: A Theoretical Framework', in Ronald W. Jones and Anne O. Kreuger (eds.), *The Political Economy of International Trade: Essays in Honour of Robert E. Baldwin*, Oxford: Basil Blackwell.

Jones, Ronald W. and Kierzkowski, Henryk (2001a), 'A Framework for Fragmentation', in Sven W. Arndt and Henryk Kierzkowski (eds.), *Fragmentation: New Production Patterns in the World Economy*, Oxford: Oxford University Press.

Jones, Ronald W. and Kierzkowski, Henryk (2001b), 'Horizontal Aspects of Vertical Fragmentation', in Leonard K. Cheng and Henryk Kierzkowski (eds.) (2001), *Global Production and Trade in East Asia*, Boston: Springer.

Jones, Ronald W. and Weder, Rolf (eds.) (2017), *200 Years of Ricardian Trade Theory: Challenges of Globalization*, Cham (Switzerland): Springer International Publishing.

Ju, Jiandong and Yu, Xinding (2018), 'China's Opening Up after 40 Years: Standing at a Historic Turning Point', *China & World Economy*, 26 (2): 23–49.

Kaldor, Nicholas (1980), 'The Foundations of Free Trade Theory and Their Implications for the Current World Recession', in Edmond Malinvaud and Jean-Paul Fitoussi (eds.), *Unemployment in Western Countries*, London: Macmillan.

Kano, Liena, Tsang, Eric W.K. and Yeung, Henry Wai-chung (2020), 'Global Value Chains: A Review of the Multi-Disciplinary Literature', *Journal of International Business Studies*, 51 (4): 577–622.

Kaplinsky, Raphael (2000), 'Spreading the Gains from Globalization: What Can Be Learned from Value Chains Analysis?', Institute of Development Studies, University of Sussex, IDS Working Paper 110.

Kaplinsky, Raphael (2010), 'The Role of Standards in Global Value Chains and Their Impact on Economic and Social Upgrading', World Bank Policy Research Working Paper No. 5396.

Kapstein, Ethan B. (1999), *Sharing the Wealth: Workers and the World Economy*, London: W.W. Norton & Company.

Karmakar, Krishanu and Martinez-Vazquez, Jorge (2014), 'Fiscal Competition versus Fiscal Harmonization: A Review of the Arguments', Georgia State University, International Center for Public Policy Working Paper 14–31.

Kay, John (2003), *The Truth About Markets: Why Some Nations Are Rich But Most Remain Poor*, London: Allen Lane.

Keen, Michael and Konrad, Kai A. (2013), 'The Theory of International Tax Competition and Coordination', in Emmanuel Saez, Martin Feldstein, Raj Chetty and Alan J. Auerbach (eds.), *Handbook of Public Economics*, Vol. 5, Amsterdam: North Holland.

Keesing, Donald B. (1965), 'Labor Skills and International Trade: Evaluating Many Trade

Flows with a Single Measuring Device', *Review of Economics and Statistics*, 47 (3): 287–294.

Keesing, Donald B. (1967), 'The Impact of Research and Development on United States Trade', *Journal of Political Economy*, 75 (1): 38–48.

Keller, Wolfgang (2004), 'International Technology Diffusion', *Journal of Economic Literature*, 42 (3): 752–782.

Kemp, Tom (1967), *Theories of Imperialism*, London: Dennis Dobson.

Kennedy, Scott (2006), 'The Political Economy of Standards Coalitions: Explaining China's Involvement in High-Tech Standards Wars', *Asia Policy*, 2: 41–62.

Keynes, John Maynard (1936), *The General Theory of Employment, Interest and Money*, London: Macmillan.

Keynes, John Maynard (1981), *The Collected Writings of John Maynard Keynes*, Vol. 20, Donald Moggridge (ed.), London: Macmillan.

Keynes, John Maynard (1982), *The Collected Writings of John Maynard Keynes*, Vol. 21, Donald Moggridge (ed.), London: Macmillan.

Kimura, Fukinari (2013), 'How Have Production Networks Changed Development Strategies in Asia?', in Deborah K. Elms and Patrick Low (eds.) (2013), *Global Value Chains in a Changing World*, Geneva: World Trade Organization.

Kindleberger, Charles P. (1983), 'Standards as Public, Collective and Private Goods', *Kyklos*, 36 (3): 377–396.

Klein, Matthew C. and Pettis, Michael (2020), *Trade Wars Are Class Wars: How Rising Inequality Distorts the Global Economy and Threatens International Peace*, London: Yale University Press.

Klein, Philip A. (1987), 'Power and Economic Performance: The Institutionalist View', *Journal of Economic Issues*, 21 (3): 1341–1377.

Kletzer, Lori G. (2003), `'Trade-related Job Loss and Wage Insurance: a Synthetic Review', UC Santa Cruz SCCIE Working Paper No. 02-28.

Kletzer, Lori G. and Litan, Robert E. (2001), 'A Prescription to Relieve Worker Anxiety', Brookings Institution, Policy Brief No. 73.

Kletzer, Lori G. and Rosen, Howard (2005), 'Easing the Adjustment Burden on Workers', in C. Fred Bergsten (ed.), *The United States and the World Economy: Foreign Economic Policy for the Next Decade*, Washington DC: Institute for International Economics.

Koebner, Richard (1959), 'Adam Smith and the Industrial Revolution', *Economic History Review*, 11 (3): 381–391.

Kravis, Irving B. (1956), '"Availability" and Other Influences on the Commodity Composition of Trade', *Journal of Political Economy*, 64: 143–155.

Kreuger, Alan B. (2018), 'Reflections on Dwindling Worker Bargaining Power and Monetary Policy', Luncheon Address at the Jackson Hole Economic Symposium, 24 August. Available at: pinguet.free.fr/krueger2018.pdf.

Kriesler, Peter, Halevi, Joseph and Setterfield, Mark (2020), 'Political Aspects of 'Buffer Stock' Employment: A Reconsideration', The New School for Social Research, New York, Working Paper No. 09/2020.

Krugman, Paul R. (1979), 'Increasing Returns, Monopolistic Competition, and International Trade', *Journal of International Economics*, 9 (4): 469–479.

Krugman, Paul R. (1989), 'Industrial Organization and International Trade', in Richard Schmalensee and Robert Willig (eds.), *Handbook of Industrial Organization*, Vol. 2, Amsterdam: North-Holland.

Krugman, Paul R. (1990), *Rethinking International Trade*, Cambridge, MA: The MIT Press.

Krugman, Paul R. (1991), 'Increasing Returns and Economic Geography', *Journal of Political Economy*, 99 (3): 483–499.

Krugman, Paul R. (1993) 'The Fall and Rise of Development Economics'. Available at http://www.wws.princeton.edu/pkrugman/dishpan.html. (Published in Paul R. Krugman, *Development, Geography and Economic Theory*, Cambridge, MA: The MIT Press, 1995).

Krugman, Paul R. (1995), 'Growing World Trade: Causes and Consequences', *Brookings Papers on Economic Activity*, 26 (1): 327–377.

Krugman, Paul R. (1996a), 'A Country is not a Company', *Harvard Business Review*, January–February: 40–44 and 48–51.

Krugman, Paul R. (1996b), *Pop Internationalism*, Cambridge, MA: The MIT Press.

Krugman, Paul R. (1997), 'In Praise of Cheap Labor', *Slate*, 21 March.

Krugman, Paul R. (2007a), 'Divided over Trade', *New York Times*, 14 May.

Krugman, Paul R. (2007b), 'Trade and Inequality, Revisited', *New York Times*, 15 June.

Krugman, Paul R. (2007c), 'Trouble with Trade', *New York Times*, 28 December.

Krugman, Paul R. (2007d), *The Conscience of a Liberal*, New York: Norton & Company.

Krugman, Paul R. (2008a), 'The Increasing Returns Revolution in Trade and Geography', in Karl Grandin (ed.), *Les Prix Nobel. The Nobel Prizes 2008*, Stockholm: Nobel Foundation.

Krugman, Paul R. (2008b), 'Trade and Wages, Reconsidered', *Brookings Papers on Economic Activity*, 39 (1): 103–137.

Krugman, Paul R., Obstfeld, Maurice and Melitz, Marc J. (2014), *International Economics* (10th edition), London: Pearson International.

Kruse, Douglas L., Freeman, Richard B. and Blasi, Joseph R. (eds.) (2010), *Shared Capitalism at Work: Employee Ownership, Profit and Gain Sharing, and Broad-Based Stock*, Chicago: University of Chicago Press.

Kurz, Heinz D. (1992), 'Adam Smith on Foreign Trade: A Note on the 'Vent-for-Surplus' Argument', *Economica*, 59 (236): 475–481.

Kuttner, Robert (1996), *Everything for Sale: The Virtues and Limits of Markets*, Chicago: University of Chicago Press.

Lal, Deepak (1983), *The Poverty of 'Development Economics'*, London: Institute of Economic Affairs.

Lall, Sanjaya (1975), 'Is 'Dependence' a Useful Concept in Analysing Underdevelopment?', *World Development*, 3 (11–12): 799–810.

Lancaster, Kelvin (1979), *Variety, Equity, and Efficiency*, New York: Columbia University Press.

Lassudrie-Duchêne, Bernard (1971), 'La demande de différence et l'échange international', Cahiers de l'ISEA, *Économies et Sociétés*, No. 6.

Lassudrie-Duchêne, Bernard (1972), 'La loi des proportions de facteurs et le régime de concurrence monopolistique', *Economie Appliquée*, No. 1.

Lavezzi, Andrea (2003), 'Smith, Marshall and Young on Division of Labour and Economic Growth', *European Journal of the History of Economic Thought*, 10 (1): 81–108.

Layne-Farrar, Anne (2010), 'Business Models and Standard Setting Process', in Konkurrensverket – Swedish Competition Authority (ed.), *The Pros and Cons of Standard Setting*, Vasteras (Sweden): Edita Vastra Aros AB.

Lazonick, William (2014), 'Profits Without Prosperity', *Harvard Business Review*, 92 (9): 46–55.

Leamer, Edward E. (1984), *Sources of International Comparative Advantage: Theory and Evidence*, Cambridge, MA: The MIT Press.

Leamer, Edward E. (2012), *The Craft of Economics: Lessons from the Heckscher–Ohlin Framework*, Cambridge, MA: The MIT Press.

L'Économie Politique (2006), 'What Economic Patriotism?', 31 (3).

Lennard, Michael (2018), 'Act of Creation: the OECD/G20 Test of 'Value Creation' as a Basis for Taxing Rights and Its Relevance to Developing Countries', *Transnational Corporations*, 25 (3): 55–84.

Lester, Richard K. and Piore, Michael J. (2004), *Innovation – The Missing Dimension*, Cambridge, MA: Harvard University Press.

Levinson, Marc (2006), *The Box: How the Shipping Container Made the World Smaller and the World Economy Bigger*, Princeton, NJ: Princeton University Press.

Levy, Frank and Murnane, Richard J. (2004), *The New Division of Labor: How Computers Are Creating the Next Job Market*, Princeton: Princeton University Press.

Lewis, W. Arthur (1954), 'Economic Development with Unlimited Supplies of Labour', *The Manchester School*, 22 (2): 139–192.

Lewis, W. Arthur (1955), *The Theory of Economic Growth*, London: Allen & Unwin.

Lewis, W. Arthur (1969), *Aspects of Tropical Trade 1883–1965*, Stockholm: Almquist.

Lewis, W. Arthur (1976), 'The Diffusion of Development', in Andrew S. Skinner and Thomas Wilson (eds.), *The Market and the State: Essays in Honour of Adam Smith*, Oxford: Clarendon Press.

Lewis, W. Arthur (1978a), *The Evolution of the International Economic Order*, Princeton, NJ: Princeton University Press.

Lewis, W. Arthur (1978b), *Growth and Fluctuations 1870–1913*, London: George Allen & Unwin.

Lewis, W. Arthur (1980), 'The Tropical Dilemma', *Challenge*, 23 (1): 26–30.

Li, Jinyan, Bao, Jin and Li, Huaning (Christina) (2019a), 'Value Creation: A Constant Principle in a Changing World of International Taxation', *Canadian Tax Journal*, 67 (4): 1107–1134.

Li, Jinyan, Bao, Jin and Li, Huaning (Christina) (2019b), 'BEPS and the Emerging Global Approach to Taxing Multinational Enterprises', Osgoode Hall Law School of York University, Conference Papers. Available at: https://digitalcommons.osgoode.yorku.ca/conference_papers.

Li, Yifan and Miao, Zhuang (2018), 'Globalization, Import Penetration and Markup', Munich Personal RePec Archive Paper No. 91757.

Lichtenstein, Peter M. (2016), *Theories of International* Economics, New York: Routledge.

Lin, Justin Yifu (2012), *The Quest for Prosperity: How Developing Economies Can Take Off*, Princeton, NJ: Princeton University Press.

Linder, Staffan Burenstam (1961), *An Essay on Trade and Transformation*, Uppsala, Sweden: Almqvist & Wiksells.

Little, Jane Sneddon (2008), 'Rebalancing Act: Global Imbalances in a Changing World', in Jane Sneddon Little (ed.), *Global Imbalances and the Evolving World Economy*, Boston: Federal Reserve Bank of Boston.

Litvin, Daniel (2003), *Empires of Profit: Commerce, Conquest and Corporate Responsibility*, New York: Texere.

Lutz, Mark A. (2008), 'Revisiting the Relevance of International Trade Theory', *Forum for Social Economics*, 37 (2): 147–164.

Lynn, Barry C. (2005), *End of the Line: The Rise and Coming Fall of the Global Corporation*, New York: Doubleday.

Lynn, Barry C. (2010), *Cornered: The New Monopoly Capitalism and the Economics of Destruction*, Hoboken, NJ: John Wiley & Sons.

Maalouf, Amin (2019), *Le naufrage des civilisations*, Paris: Éditions Grasset & Fasquelle (English translation: *Adrift: How Our World Lost Its Way*, London: World Editions, 2020).

MacDonald, Glenn M. and Markusen, James R. (1985), 'A Rehabilitation of Absolute Advantage', *Journal of Political Economy*, 93 (2): 277–297.

Machlup, Fritz (1943), *International Trade and the National Income Multiplier*, Philadelphia, PA: Blakiston Company.

Maneschi, Andrea (1992), 'Ricardo's International Trade Theory: Beyond the Comparative Cost Example', *Cambridge Journal of Economics*, 16 (4): 421–437.

Maneschi, Andrea (1998), *Comparative Advantage in International Trade: A Historical Perspective*, Cheltenham (UK): Edward Elgar.

Maneschi, Andrea (2002), 'How New is the 'New Trade Theory' of the Past Two Decades?', in Stephan Boehm, Christian Gehrke, Heinz D. Kurz and Richard Sturn (eds.), *Is There Progress in Economics?: Knowledge, Truth and the History of Economic Thought*, Cheltenham (UK): Edward Elgar.

Maneschi, Andrea (2004), 'The True Meaning of David Ricardo's Four Magic Numbers', *Journal of International Economics*, 62 (2): 433–442.

Maneschi, Andrea (2008), 'How Would Ricardo Have Taught the Principle of Comparative Advantage?', *Southern Economic Journal*, 74 (4): 1167–1176.

Maneschi, Andrea (2009), 'Comparative Advantage', in Kenneth A. Reinert and Ramkishen S. Rajan (eds.), *The Princeton Encyclopedia of the World Economy*, Vol. 1, Princeton, NJ: Princeton University Press.

Maneschi, Andrea (2015), 'Ricardo's Four Magic Numbers', in Heinz D. Kurz and Neri Salvadori (eds.), *The Elgar Companion to David Ricardo*, Cheltenham (UK): Edward Elgar.

Mankiw, N. Gregory and Swagel, Phillip (2006), 'The Politics and Economics of Offshore Outsourcing', Harvard Institute of Economic Research Working Papers 2120.

Marangos, John (2004), 'Social Dividend Versus Basic Income Guarantee in Market Socialism', *International Journal of Political Economy*, 34 (3): 20–40.

Marx, Karl (1867), Address for participation in the Lausanne 1867 Congress of the International Workingmen's Association, reproduced in 'On the Lausanne Congress'. Available at: https://www.marxists.org/archive/marx/iwma/documents/1867/lausanne-call.htm.

Mason, Paul (2015), *PostCapitalism: A Guide to Our Future*, London: Allen Lane.

Matthews, Robert C.O. (1949), 'Reciprocal Demand and Increasing Returns', *Review of Economic Studies*, 17 (2): 149–158.

Mattli, Walter and Büthe, Tim (2003), 'Setting International Standards: Technological Rationality or Primacy of Power?', *World Politics*, 56 (1): 1–42.

Mattoo, Aaditya, Wang, Zhi and Wei, Shang-Jin (eds.) (2013), *Trade in Value Added: Developing New Measures of Cross-Border Trade*, Washington DC: World Bank Group.

Maurin, Max (2013), 'Les fondements non néoclassiques du protectionisme', Doctoral Thesis, Université Montesquieu – Bordeaux IV. Available at: theses.fr/2013BOR40014.

Mayer, Jane (2016), *Dark Money: The Hidden History of the Billionaires Behind the Rise of the Radical Right*, New York: Doubleday.

Mayer, Jörg (2003), 'The Fallacy of Composition: A Review of the Literature', United Nations Conference on Trade and Development Discussion Papers No. 166.

Mazzucato, Mariana (2013), *The Entrepreneurial State: Debunking Public vs. Private Sector Myths*, London: Anthem Press.

Mazzucato, Mariana (2018), *The Value of Everything: Making and Taking in the Global Economy*, London: Allen Lane.

McCombie, John S.L. and Thirlwall, Anthony P. (eds.) (2004), *Essays on Balance of Payments Constrained Growth: Theory and Evidence*, London: Routledge.

McKinsey Global Institute (2019), 'Globalization in Transition: The Future of Trade and Value Chains', McKinsey & Company, January.

Mead, Walter Russell (1990), *The Low-Wage Challenge to Global Growth: The Labor Cost-Productivity Imbalance in Newly Industrialized Countries*, Washington DC: Economic Policy Institute.

Meade, James E. (1952), *A Geometry of International Trade*, London: George Allen & Unwin.

Meade, James E. (1964), *Efficiency, Equality, and the Ownership of Property*, London: Allen & Unwin.

Meier, Gerald M. (1963), *International Trade and Development*, New York: Harper & Row.

Melitz, Marc J. (2003), 'The Impact of Trade on Intra-Industry Reallocations and Aggregate Industry Productivity', *Econometrica*, 71 (6): 1695–1725.

Melitz, Marc J. and Redding, Stephen J. (2014), 'Heterogeneous Firms and Trade', in Gita Gopinath, Elhanan Helpman and Kenneth Rogoff (eds.), *Handbook of International Economics*, Vol. 4, Amsterdam: Elsevier North Holland.

Melitz, Mark J. and Trefler, Daniel (2012), 'Gains from Trade when Firms Matter', *Journal of Economic Perspectives*, 26 (2): 91–118.

Melvin, James R. (1969a), 'Increasing Returns to Scale as a Determinant of Trade', *Canadian Journal of Economics*, 2 (3): 389–402.

Melvin, James R. (1969b), 'Intermediate Goods, the Production Possibility Curve and Gains from Trade', *Quarterly Journal of Economics*, 83 (1): 121–131.

Melvin, James R. (1970), 'Commodity Taxation as a Determinant of Trade', *Canadian Journal of Economics*, 3 (1): 62–78.

Melvin, James R. (1990), 'Time and Space in Economic Analysis', *Canadian Journal of Economics*, 23 (4): 725–747.

Milanovic, Branko (2019), *Capitalism, Alone: The Future of the System That Rules the World*, Cambridge, MA: Harvard University Press.

Milberg, William (1994), 'Is Absolute Advantage *Passé*? Towards a Post-Keynesian/Marxian Theory of International Trade', in Mark A. Glick (ed.), *Competition, Technology and Money: Classical and Post-Keynesian Perspectives*, Aldershot (UK): Edward Elgar.

Milberg, William (2002), 'Say's Law in the Open Economy: Keynes's Rejection of the Theory of Comparative Advantage', in Sheila C. Dow and John Hillard (eds.), *Keynes, Uncertainty and the Global Economy*, Cheltenham (UK): Edward Elgar.

Milberg, William (2007), 'Export Processing Zones, Industrial Upgrading and Economic Development: A Survey', Schwartz Center for Economic Policy Analysis and Department of Economics, The New School for Social Research, New York, Working Paper 2007-10.

Milberg, William and Houston, Ellen (2005), 'The High Road and the Low Road to International Competitiveness: Extending the Neo-Schumpeterian Trade Model Beyond Technology', *International Review of Applied Economics*, 19 (2): 137–162.

Milberg, William and Winkler, Deborah (2010), 'Financialisation and the Dynamics of Offshoring in the USA', *Cambridge Journal of Economics*, 34 (2): 275–293.

Milberg, William and Winkler, Deborah (2013), *Outsourcing Economics: Global Value Chains in Capitalist Development*, Cambridge: Cambridge University Press.

Mill, John Stuart (1909) [1848], *Principles of Political Economy*, W. J. Ashley (ed.), London: Longmans (reproducing Mill's 7th edition, 1871).

Miller, John (2003), 'Why Economists Are Wrong about Sweatshops and the Antisweatshop Movement', *Challenge*, 46 (1): 93–122.
Mokyr, Joel (2018), 'The Past and the Future of Innovation: Some Lessons from Economic History', *Explorations in Economic History*, 69: 13–26.
Morales Meoqui, Jorge (2011), 'Comparative Advantage and the Labor Theory of Value', *History of Political Economy,* 43 (4): 743–763.
Morales Meoqui, Jorge (2012), 'Essence and Merits of David Ricardo's Proof of Comparative Advantage', Munich Personal RePEc Archive Paper No. 49114.
Morales Meoqui, Jorge (2020), 'Overcoming Absolute and Comparative Advantage: a Reappraisal of the Relative Cheapness of Foreign Commodities as the Basis of International Trade', Working Paper. Available at: https://ssrn.com/abstract=3095473.
Moretti, Enrico (2012), *The New Geography of Jobs*, New York: Houghton Mifflin Harcourt.
Morozov, Evgeny (2011), *The Net Delusion: The Dark Side of Internet Freedom*, New York: PublicAffair.
Morris, Charles R. (2012), 'We Were Pirates, Too: Why America Was the China of the 19th Century', *Foreign Policy*, 6 December.
Morse, Susan C. (2018), 'Value Creation: A Standard in Search of a Process', *Bulletin for International Taxation*, 72 (4–5): 196–202.
Mosca, Manuela (ed.) (2018), *Power in Economic Thought*, London: Palgrave Macmillan.
Moser, Petra (2013), 'Patents and Innovation: Evidence from Economic History', *Journal of Economic Perspectives*, 27 (1): 23–44.
Murrell, Peter (1995), 'The Transition According to Cambridge, Mass.', *Journal of Economic Literature*, 33 (1): 164–178.
Myint, Hla (1958), 'The 'Classical Theory' of International Trade and the Underdeveloped Countries', *Economic Journal*, 68 (270): 317–337.
Myint, Hla (1964), *The Economics of the Developing Countries*, London: Hutchinson & Co Ltd.
Myint, Hla (1976), 'Comment' on Lewis (1976), in Andrew S. Skinner and Thomas Wilson (eds.), *The Market and the State: Essays in Honour of Adam Smith*, Oxford: Clarendon Press.
Nayyar, Deepak (2007), 'Globalization and Free Trade: Theory, History, and Reality', in Anwar Shaikh (ed.), *Globalization and the Myth of Free Trade*, New York: Routledge.
Nayyar, Deepak (2013), *Catch Up: Developing Countries in the World Economy*, Oxford: Oxford University Press.
Neary, J. Peter (2001), 'Of Hype and Hyperbolas: Introducing the New Economic Geography', *Journal of Economic Literature*, 39 (2): 536–561.
Neary, J. Peter (2003a), 'Globalization and Market Structure', *Journal of the European Economic Association*, 1 (2–3): 245–271.
Neary, J. Peter (2003b), 'Competitive versus Comparative Advantage', *World Economy*, 26 (4): 457–470.
Neary, J. Peter (2009), 'Putting the 'New' into New Trade Theory: Paul Krugman's Nobel Memorial Prize in Economics', *Scandinavian Journal of Economics*, 111 (2): 217–250.
Neary, J. Peter (2010), 'Two and a Half Theories of Trade', *World Economy*, 33 (1): 1–19.
Neary, J. Peter (2016), 'International Trade in General Oligopolistic Equilibrium', *Review of International Economics*, 24 (4): 669–698.
Neill, Robin (1991), *A History of Canadian Economic Thought*, London: Routledge.
Nicholson, Joseph Shield (1897), *Principles of Political Economy*, Vol. 2, New York: Macmillan.

Nolan, Peter, Zhang, Jin and Liu, Chunhang (2008), 'The Global Business Revolution, the Cascade Effect, and the Challenge for Firms from Developing Countries', *Cambridge Journal of Economics*, 32 (1): 29–47.

North, Douglass C. (1990), *Institutions, Institutional Change and Economic Performance*, Cambridge: Cambridge University Press.

North, Douglass C. (1991), 'Institutions', *Journal of Economic Perspectives*, 5 (1): 97–112.

Nunn, Nathan and Trefler, Daniel (2014), 'Domestic Institutions as a Source of Comparative Advantage', in Gita Gopinath, Elhanan Helpman and Kenneth Rogoff (eds.), *Handbook of International Economics*, Vol. 4, Amsterdam: Elsevier.

O'Brien, Patrick K. (1984), 'The Third World in the International Economy, 1850–1950: Some Historiographical Perspective', *Rivista di storia economica*, 1, International Issue.

Ocampo, José Antonio and Parra-Lancourt, Mariángela (2010), 'The Terms of Trade for Commodities Since the Mid-19th Century', *Revista de Historia Económica, Journal of Iberian and Latin American Economic History*, 28 (1): 11–43.

OECD (1995), 'Profit-Sharing in OECD Countries', *Employment Outlook*, Paris: OECD.

OECD (2013), *Action Plan on Base Erosion and Profit Shifting*, Paris: OECD.

OECD (2016), *Multilateral Convention to Implement Tax Treaty Related Measures to Prevent Base Erosion and Profit Shifting*. Available at: oecd.org/tax/treaties/multilateral-convention-to-implement-tax-related-measures-to-prevent-BEPS.pdf.

OECD (2017), 'Basic Income as a Policy Option: Can it Add Up?', Policy Brief on the Future of Work, Paris: OECD.

OECD (2018), *Tax Challenges Arising from Digitalization: Interim Report 2018*, Paris: OECD.

OECD (2019), *Programme of Work to Develop a Consensus Solution to the Tax Challenges Arising from the Digitalisation of the Economy: Inclusive Framework on BEPS*, Paris: OECD.

Ohlin, Bertil (1967) [1933], *Interregional and International Trade*, Cambridge, MA: Harvard University Press (the 1967 edition includes a new Appendix on 'Reflections on Contemporary International Trade Theories').

Ohlin, Bertil (1977), 'Some Aspects of the Relations Between International Movements of Commodities, Factors of Production, and Technology', in Bertil Ohlin, Per-Ove Hesselborn and Per Magnus Wijkman (eds.), *The International Allocation of Economic Activity*, London: Macmillan.

Olson, Mancur (1965), *The Logic of Collective Action*, New Haven, CT: Yale University Press.

O'Neill, Martin (2020), 'Power, Predistribution, and Social Justice', *Philosophy*, 95 (1): 63–91.

Ortiz, Fernando (1940), *Contrapunteo cubano del tabaco y el azùcar*, La Habana: Jesùs Montero (English translation: *Cuban Counterpoint: Tobacco and Sugar*, New York: Alfred Knopf Inc., 1947).

Ottaviano, Gianmarco I. P. (2010), ''New' New Economic Geography: Firm Heterogeneity and Agglomeration Economies', *Journal of Economic Geography*, 11 (2): 231–240.

Owen, Roger and Sutcliffe, Bob (eds.) (1972), *Studies in the Theory of Imperialism*, London: Longman.

Owens, Jeffrey and Zhan, James X. (2018), 'Introduction to the Special Issue. Trade, Investment and Taxation: Policy Linkages', *Transnational Corporations*, 25 (2): 1–8.

Ozanne, Adam (2016), *Power and Neoclassical Economics: A Return to Political Economy in the Teaching of Economics*, London: Palgrave.

Ozawa, Terutomo (2019), 'A Note on Dani Rodrik, 'Populism and the Economics of Globalization'', *Journal of International Business Policy*, 2 (2): 182–193.

Pagrotsky, Leif (2000), 'Being Flexible about Flexibility', *Financial Times*, 5 October.

Pahl, Stefan and Timmer, Marcel P. (2020), 'Do Global Value Chains Enhance Economic Upgrading? A Long View', *Journal of Development Studies*, 56 (9): 1683–1705.

Palermo, Giulio (2000), 'Economic Power and the Firm in New Institutional Economics: Two Conflicting Problems', *Journal of Economic Issues*, 34 (3): 573–601.

Palermo, Giulio (2016), *Economics and Power: A Marxist Critique*, London: Routledge.

Palley, Thomas I. (1998), *Plenty of Nothing: The Downsizing of the American Dream and the Case for Structural Keynesianism*, Princeton, NJ: Princeton University Press.

Palley, Thomas I. (2006a), 'Is Globalization Destined to Fail?', *International Herald Tribune*, 2 April.

Palley, Thomas I. (2006b), 'Developing the Domestic Market', *Challenge*, 49 (6): 20–34.

Palley, Thomas I. (2008), 'Institutionalism and the New Trade Theory: Rethinking Comparative Advantage and Trade Policy', *Journal of Economic Issues*, 42 (1): 195–208.

Palley, Thomas I. (2011), 'The Rise and Fall of Export-led Growth', Levy Economics Institute of Bard College, Annandale-on-Hudson, New York, Working Paper No. 675.

Palley, Thomas I. (2018), 'Three Globalizations, Not Two: Rethinking the History and Economics of Trade and Globalization', *European Journal of Economics and Economic Policies*, 15 (2): 174–192.

Panagariya, Arvind (2004), 'Why the Recent Samuelson Article Is NOT about Offshore Outsourcing'. Available at: www.personal.umich.edu/-alandear/topics/documents/Panagiriya-OnSamuelson.htm.

Panagariya, Arvind (2005), 'Defending the Case for Free Trade', paper prepared for the U.S.–China Economic and Security Review Commission's hearing on the panel 'China and the Future of Globalization' to be held at the Council on Foreign Relations in New York, 19–20 May 2005. Available at: citeseerx.ist.psu.edu/viewdoc/summary?doi=10.1.1.413.3988.

Panagariya, Arvind (2007), 'Outsourcing: Is the Third Industrial Revolution Really Around the Corner?', paper presented at the Macro Research Foundation Conference 2007, Tokyo Club Foundation for Research Studies, 13–14 November. Available at: nomurafoundation.or.jp/en/wordpress/wp-content/uploads/2014/09/20071113-14_Arvind Panagiriya.pdf.

Pantaleoni, Maffeo (1898), 'An Attempt to Analyse the Concepts of "Strong and Weak" in Their Economic Connection', *Economic Journal*, 8 (30): 183–205.

Park, Albert, Nayyar, Gaurav and Low, Patrick (2013), *Supply Chain Perspectives and Issues: A Literature Review*, Geneva: World Trade Organization.

Parrinello, Sergio (2002), 'The 'Institutional Factor' in the Theory of International Trade: New vs. Old Trade Theories', in Stephan Boehm, Christian Gehrke, Heinz D. Kurz and Richard Sturn (eds.), *Is There Progress in Economics?: Knowledge, Truth and the History of Economic Thought*, Cheltenham (UK): Edward Elgar.

Parrinello, Sergio (2010), 'National Competitiveness and Absolute Advantage in a Global Economy', in John Vint, J. Stanley Metcalfe, Heinz D. Kurz, Neri Salvadori and Paul Samuelson (eds.), *Economic Theory and Economic Thought: Essays in Honour of Ian Steedman*, London: Routledge.

Pasinetti, Luigi L. (2007), *Keynes and the Cambridge Keynesians: A 'Revolution in Economics' to Be Accomplished*, Cambridge: Cambridge University Press.

Patel, Raj (2009), *The Value of Nothing: How to Reshape Market Society and Redefine Democracy*, London: Portobello Books.

Patnaik, Utsa (2005), 'Ricardo's Fallacy: Mutual Benefits from Trade Based on Comparative

Costs and Specialization?', in Jomo Kwame Sundaram (ed.), *The Pioneers of Development Economics: Great Economists on Development*, London: Zed Books.

Paus, Eva (ed.) (2007), *Global Capitalism Unbound: Winners and Losers from Offshore Outsourcing*, New York: Palgrave Macmillan.

Perelman, Michael (2012), 'The Power of Economics vs. the Economics of Power', *Challenge*, 55 (6): 53–66.

Perkins, John (2004), *Confessions of an Economic Hit Man*, San Francisco, CA: Berrett-Koehler Publishers.

Perroux, François (1948), 'Esquisse d'une théorie de l'économie dominante', *Économie Appliquée*, 1 (2–3): 243–300.

Perroux, François (1950), 'The Domination Effect and Modern Economic Theory', *Social Research*, 17 (2):188–206.

Phelps, Edmund S. (1997), *Rewarding Work: How to Restore Participation and Self-Support to Free Enterprise*, Cambridge, MA: Harvard University Press.

Phelps, Edmund S. (2015), 'What Is Wrong with the West's Economies?', *New York Review of Books*, 13 August.

Philippon, Thomas (2019), *The Great Reversal: How America Gave up on Free Markets*, Cambridge, MA: The Belknap Press of Harvard University Press.

Piketty, Thomas (2013), *Le capital au XXe siècle*, Paris: Éditions du Seuil (English translation: *Capital in the Twenty-First Century*, Cambridge, MA: The Belknap Press of Harvard University Press, 2014).

Ping, Wang (2011), 'A Brief History of Standards and Standardization Organizations: a Chinese Perspective', East–West Center Working Papers, Economics Series, No. 117.

Pogge, Thomas and Mechta, Krishen (eds.) (2016), *Global Tax Fairness*, Oxford: Oxford University Press.

Pomfret, Richard (1992), 'International Trade Policy with Imperfect Competition', Princeton University, Special Papers in International Economics, No. 17.

Ponte, Stefano, Gereffi, Gary and Raj-Reichert, Gale (eds.) (2019), *Handbook of Global Value Chains*, Cheltenham (UK): Edward Elgar Publishing.

Porter, Michael E. (1985), *Competitive Advantage: Creating and Sustaining Superior Performance*, New York: Free Press.

Porter, Michael E. (1998a), *On Competition*, Harvard, MA: Harvard Business School Press.

Porter, Michael E. (1998b), 'Clusters and the New Economics of Competition', *Harvard Business Review*, 76 (6): 77–90.

Porter, Michael E. (2000), 'Location, Competition, and Economic Development: Local Clusters in a Global Economy', *Economic Development Quarterly*, 14 (1): 23–32.

Posner, Michael V. (1961), 'International Trade and Technical Change', *Oxford Economic Papers*, 13 (3): 323–341.

Posner, Michael V. and Steer, Andrew (1979), 'Price Competitiveness and the Performance of Manufacturing Industry', in Frank Blackaby (ed.) *De-Industrialisation*, London: Heinemann Educational Books.

Powell, Benjamin (2014a), 'Sweatshop Blues: An Interview with Benjamin Powell', *The Freeman*, Jan. 22.

Powell, Benjamin (2014b), *Out of Poverty: Sweatshops in the Global Economy*, New York: Cambridge University Press.

Prasch, Robert E. (1996), 'Reassessing the Theory of Comparative Advantage', *Review of Political Economy*, 8 (1): 37–55.

Prebisch, Raúl (1950), *The Economic Development of Latin America and Its Principal Problems*, New York: United Nations.

Proost, Stef and Thisse, Jacques-François (2019), 'What Can Be Learned from Spatial Economics?', *Journal of Economic Literature*, 57 (3): 575–643.

Pullen, John (2006), 'Did Ricardo Really Have a Law of Comparative Advantage? A Comparison of Ricardo's Version and the Modern Version', *History of Economics Review*, 44 (1): 59–75.

Purvis, Douglas D. (1972), 'Technology, Trade and Factor Mobility', *Economic Journal*, 82 (327): 991–999.

Rae, John (1834), *Statement of Some New Principles on the Subject of Political Economy, Exposing the Fallacies of the System of Free Trade and of Some Other Doctrines Maintained in the 'Wealth of Nations'*, Boston: Hilliard, Gray, and Co..

Raffer, Kunibert (1987), *Unequal Exchange and the Evolution of the World System: Reconsidering the Impact of Trade on North–South Relations*, New York: St Martin's Press.

Raffer, Kunibert (1994), 'Disadvantaging Comparative Advantages: The Problem of Decreasing Returns', in Renée Prendergast and Frances Stewart (eds.), *Market Forces and World Development*, London: Macmillan.

Rajan, Raghuram G. and Zingales, Luigi (1998), 'Power in a Theory of the Firm', *Quarterly Journal of Economics*, 113 (2): 387–432.

Rand, Ayn (1967), *Capitalism: The Unknown Ideal*, New York: Signet.

Ranis, Gustav (1984), Review of Marc Gersovitzk (ed.), *Selected Economic Writings of W. Arthur Lewis*, New York University Press, 1983, *Journal of Economic Literature*, 22 (3): 1127–1129.

Rapp, Richard T. (1975), 'The Unmaking of the Mediterranean Trade Hegemony: International Trade Rivalry and the Commercial Revolution', *Journal of Economic History*, 35 (3): 499–525.

Reagan, Michael D. (1963), *The Managed Economy*, Oxford: Oxford University Press.

Redding, Stephen J. (2011), 'Theories of Heterogeneous Firms and Trade', *Annual Review of Economics*, 3: 77–105.

Reich, Robert B. (2007), *Supercapitalism: The Transformation of Business, Democracy, and Everyday Life*, New York: Alfred A. Knopf.

Reich, Robert B. (2015), *Saving Capitalism: For the Many, Not the Few*, New York: Alfred A. Knopf.

Reich, Robert B. (2020), *The System: Who Rigged It, How We Fix It*, New York: Vintage Books.

Reinert, Erik S. (1994), 'Catching-Up from Way Behind. A Third World Perspective on First World History', in Jan Fagerberg, Bart Verspagen and Nick von Tunzelmann (eds.), *The Dynamics of Technology, Trade and Growth*, Aldershot (UK): Edward Elgar.

Reinert, Erik S. (2007), *How Rich Countries Got Rich… and Why Poor Countries Stay Poor*, London: Constable.

Remond-Tiedrez, Isabelle and Rueda-Cantuche, José M. (eds.) (2019), *EU Inter-Country Supply, Use and Input–Output Tables – Full International and Global Accounts for Research in Input–Output Analysis (FIGARO)*, Luxembourg: Publications Office of the European Union.

Ricardo, David (1951) [1817], *On the Principles of Political Economy and Taxation*, Piero Sraffa and M.H. Dobb (eds.) *The Works and Correspondence of David Ricardo*, Vol. 1, Cambridge: Cambridge University Press.

Richardson, George B. (1972), 'The Organization of Industry', *Economic Journal*, 82 (327): 883–896.
Richardson, George B. (1975), 'Adam Smith on Competition and Increasing Returns', in Andrew S. Skinner and Thomas Wilson (eds.), *Essays on Adam Smith*, Oxford: Clarendon Press.
Richardson, J. David (2000), 'The WTO and Market-Supportive Regulation: a Way Forward on New Competition, Technological and Labour Issues', (Federal Reserve Bank of St. Louis) *Review*, 82 (2): 115–126.
Richardson, J. David (2001), 'Exports Matter … and so Does Trade Finance', in Gary C. Hufbauer and Rita M. Rodriguez (eds.), *The Ex-Im Bank in the 21st Century: A New Approach?*, Washington DC: Peterson Institute for International Economics.
Rifkin, Jeremy (2015), *The Zero Marginal Cost Society: The Internet of Things, the Collaborative Commons, and the Eclipse of Capitalism*, New York: Palgrave Macmillan.
Roach, Brian (2007), 'Corporate Power in a Global Economy', Global Development and Environment Institute, Tufts University, Medford, MA.
Roach, Stephen S. (2003), 'Outsourcing, Protectionism, and the Global Labor Arbitrage', Morgan Stanley, Special Economic Study.
Roach, Stephen S. (2009), Intervention in 'Panel I: Global Trade, Conflicting National Interests, and Comparative Advantage', in Lynn Sha and Kent H. Hughes (eds.), *New Thinking in International Trade: Global Competition and Comparative Advantage*, Washington DC: Woodrow Wilson International Center for Scholars.
Robertson, Dennis Holme (1938), 'The Future of International Trade', *Economic Journal*, 48 (189): 1–14.
Robinson, Joan (1946), 'The Pure Theory of International Trade', *Review of Economic Studies*, 14 (2): 98–112.
Robinson, Joan (1962), *Economic Philosophy*, London: Watts.
Robinson, Joan (1966a), *The New Mercantilism: An Inaugural Lecture*, Cambridge: Cambridge University Press.
Robinson, Joan (1966b), *An Essay on Marxian Economics* (2nd edition), London: Macmillan.
Robinson, Joan (1973), 'The Need for a Reconsideration of the Theory of International Trade', in Michael B. Connolly and Alexander K. Swoboda (eds.), *International Trade and Money*, London: George Allen & Unwin.
Robinson, Romney (1956a), 'Factor Proportions and Comparative Advantage: Part I', *Quarterly Journal of Economics*, 70 (2): 169–192.
Robinson, Romney (1956b), 'Factor Proportions and Comparative Advantage: Part II', *Quarterly Journal of Economics*, 70 (3): 346–363.
Roccas, Massimo (1975), *Nuove teorie del commercio internazionale*, Milan: Etas Libri.
Rodrik, Dani (1999), 'Globalization and Labour, or: If Globalization Is a Bowl of Cherries, Why Are There So Many Glum Faces around the Table?', in Richard Baldwin, Daniel Cohen, Andre Sapir and Anthony Venables (eds.), *Market Integration, Regionalism and the Global Economy*, Cambridge: Cambridge University Press.
Rodrik, Dani (2001), 'Development Strategies for the 21st Century', in Boris Pleskovic and Nicholas Stern (eds.), *Annual World Bank Conference on Development Economics 2000*, Washington DC: World Bank
Rodrik, Dani (2008), 'Is Export Led Growth Passé?', *Project Syndicate*, 11 September.
Rodrik, Dani (2011), *The Globalization Paradox: Democracy and the Future of the World Economy*, New York: W.W. Norton & Company.

Rodrik, Dani (2015), *Economics Rules: The Rights and Wrongs of the Dismal Science*, London: W.W. Norton & Company.

Rodrik, Dani (2016a), 'Put Globalization to Work for Democracies', *New York Times*, 17 September.

Rodrik, Dani (2016b), 'The Abdication of the Left', *Project Syndicate*, 11 July.

Rodrik, Dani (2018a), 'Populism and the Economics of Globalization', *Journal of International Business Policy*, 1 (1–2): 12–33.

Rodrik, Dani (2018b), 'Towards a More Inclusive Globalization: An Anti-Social Dumping Scheme', Econfip Research Brief, December.

Rodrik, Dani (2018c), 'What Do Trade Agreements Really Do?', *Journal of Economic Perspectives*, 32 (2): 73–90.

Rodrik, Dani (2019), 'Globalization's Wrong Turn and How It Hurt America', *Foreign Affairs*, 98 (4): 26–33.

Rodrik, Dani and van Ypersele, Tanguy (2001), 'Capital Mobility, Distributive Conflict and International Tax Coordination', *Journal of International Economics*, 54 (1): 57–73.

Rosenberg, Nathan (1982), *Inside the Black Box: Technology and Economics*, Cambridge: Cambridge University Press.

Rothkopf, David (2012), *Power, Inc.: The Epic Rivalry Between Big Business and Government – and the Reckoning That Lies Ahead*, New York: Farrar, Straus and Giroux.

Rothschild, Kurt W. (ed.) (1971), *Power in Economics*, Harmondsworth (UK): Penguin Books.

Rothschild, Kurt W. (2002), 'The Absence of Power in Contemporary Economic Theory', *Journal of Socio-Economics*, 31 (5): 433–442.

Rothschild, Kurt W. (2008), 'Economic Imperialism', *Analyse & Kritik*, 30 (2): 723–733.

Ruffin, Roy J. (2002), 'David Ricardo's Discovery of Comparative Advantage', *History of Political Economy*, 34 (4): 727–748.

Ruffin, Roy J. (2005), 'Debunking a Myth: Torrens on Comparative Advantage', *History of Political Economy*, 37 (4): 711–722.

Russell, Andrew L. (2005), 'Standardization in History: A Review Essay with an Eye to the Future', in Sherrie Bolin (ed.), *The Standards Edge: Future Generations*, Ann Arbor, MI: Sheridan Press.

Sako, Mari and Zylberberg, Ezequiel (2019), 'Supplier Strategy in Global Value Chains: Shaping Governance and Profiting from Upgrading', *Socio-Economic Review*, 17 (3): 687–707.

Salvati, Michele (1971), 'Lo scambio ineguale: una 'recensione polemica'', *Problemi del socialismo*, 13 (4): 475–495.

Samuels, Warren J. (ed.) (1979), *The Economy as a System of Power*, New Brunswick, N.J.: Transaction Books.

Samuelson, Paul A. (1948), 'International Trade and the Equalization of Factor Prices', *Economic Journal*, 58 (230): 163–184.

Samuelson, Paul A. (1972), 'Freud, Fear and Foreign Trade', *New York Times*, 30 July (the article is a synthesis of "International Trade for a Rich Country", Lectures before the Swedish-American Chamber of Commerce, New York City, May 10. Stockholm: Federation of Swedish Industries, 1972. Reproduced in *The Collected Scientific Papers of Paul A. Samuelson*, Vol. 4, Chapter 250, Cambridge, MA: The MIT Press, 1977).

Samuelson, Paul A. (2004), 'Where Ricardo and Mill Rebut and Confirm Arguments of Mainstream Economists Supporting Globalization', *Journal of Economic Perspectives*, 18 (3): 135–146.

Samuelson, Paul A. (2005), 'Response from Paul A. Samuelson', *Journal of Economic Perspectives*, 19 (3): 242–243.
Sandel, Michael J. (2012), *What Money Can't Buy: The Moral Limits of Markets*, London: Allen Lane.
Sandretto, René (2009), 'François Perroux, a Precursor of the Current Analyses of Power', *Journal of World Economic Review*, 5 (1): 57–68.
Sannassee, Raja Vinesh, Seetanah, Boopen and Jugessur, J. (2014), 'Export-Led Growth Hypothesis: A Meta-Analysis', *Journal of Developing Areas*, 48 (1): 361–385.
Sanyal, Kalyan K. and Jones, Ronald W. (1982), 'The Theory of Trade in Middle Products', *American Economic Review*, 72 (1): 16–31.
Scherer, Frederic M. (1992), *International High-Technology Competition*, Cambridge, MA: Harvard University Press.
Scherer, Frederic M. (2010), 'A Half Century of Research on Patent Economics', *WIPO Journal*, 2 (1): 20–27.
Scherer, Frederic M. (2015), 'First Mover Advantages and Optimal Patent Protection', *Journal of Technology Transfer*, 40 (4): 559–580.
Scheuerman, William E. (2001), 'Liberal Democracy and the Empire of Speed', *Polity*, 34 (1): 41–67.
Scheuerman, William E. (2004), *Liberal Democracy and the Social Acceleration of Time*, Baltimore, MD: Johns Hopkins University Press.
Schoechle, Timothy (2009), *Standardization and Digital Enclosure: The Privatization of Standards, Knowledge, and Policies in the Age of Global Information Technology*, London: Information Science Reference, IGI Global.
Schultze, Charles L. (1977), *The Public Use of Private Interest*, Washington DC: The Brookings Institution.
Schumacher, Reinhard (2012a), 'Free Trade and Absolute and Comparative Advantage', Universität Potsdam, WeltTrends Thesis 16.
Schumacher, Reinhard (2012b), 'Adam Smith's Theory of Absolute Advantage and the Use of Doxography in the History of Economics', *Erasmus Journal for Philosophy and Economics*, 5 (2): 54–80.
Schumacher, Reinhard (2015), 'Adam Smith's 'Two Distinct Benefits' from Trade: The Dead End of 'Vent-for-Surplus' Interpretations', *History of Political Economy*, 47 (4): 577–603.
Schumacher, Reinhard (2016a), 'Adam Smith, the Patterns of Foreign Trade and the Division of Labour: a Country as a Jack-of-All-Trades Rather Than a Specialist', Duke University, CHOPE Working Paper No. 2016-22.
Schumacher, Reinhard (2016b), 'Adam Smith and the 'Rich Country–Poor Country' Debate: Eighteenth-Century Views on Economic Progress and International Trade', *European Journal of the History of Economic Thought*, 23 (5): 764–793.
Schumacher, Reinhard (2020), 'Altering the Pattern of Trade in the *Wealth of Nations*: Adam Smith and the Historiography of International Trade Theory', *Journal of the History of Economic Thought*, 42 (1): 19–42.
Schumpeter, Joseph A. (1942), *Capitalism, Socialism and Democracy*, New York: Harper & Row.
Schumpeter, Joseph A. (1951), *Imperialism and Social Classes*, Oxford: Basil Blackwell.
Schumpeter, Joseph A. (1954), *History of Economic Analysis*, New York: Oxford University Press.
Schutz, Eric A. (2011), *Inequality and Power: The Economics of Class*, Abingdon (UK): Routledge.

Seragelding, Ismail (1998), 'Can We Feed Our World? An Interview with CGIAR Chairman', *CGIAR News*, December. Available at: cgspace.cgiar.org/bitstream/handle/10947/5652/dec98.pdf?sequence=1&isAllowed=y.

Serra, Antonio (1613), *Breve trattato delle cause che possono far abbondare l'oro e l'argento dove non sono miniere*, Naples: Lazzaro Scorriggio (English translation: Sophus A. Reinert (ed.), *A 'Short Treatise' on the Wealth and Poverty of Nations*, London: Anthem Press, 2011).

Sha, Lynn and Hughes, Kent H. (eds.) (2009), *New Thinking in International Trade: Global Competition and Comparative Advantage*, Washington DC: Woodrow Wilson International Center for Scholars.

Shaikh, Anwar (1980), 'The Laws of International Exchange', in Edward J. Nell (ed.), *Growth, Profits, and Property: Essays in the Revival of Political Economy*, Cambridge: Cambridge University Press.

Shaikh, Anwar (1991), 'Competition and Exchange Rates: Theory and Empirical Evidence', New School for Social Research, New York, Working Paper No. 25.

Shaikh, Anwar (1996), 'Free Trade, Unemployment, and Economic Policy', in John Eatwell (ed.), *Global Unemployment: Loss of Jobs in the '90s*, London: M.E. Sharpe.

Shapiro, Carl and Varian, Hal R. (1999), 'The Art of Standards Wars', *California Management Review*, 41 (2): 8–32.

Sharpston, Michael (1975), 'International Sub-contracting', *Oxford Economic Papers*, 27 (1): 94–135.

Sharpston, Michael (1976), 'International Subcontracting', *World Development*, 4 (4): 333–337.

Sideri, Sandro (1970), *Trade and Power*, Rotterdam: Rotterdam University Press.

Sideri, Sandro (1972), 'International Trade and Economic Power', in *Towards a New World Economy*, Papers and Proceedings, Fifth European Conference of the Society for International Development, Rotterdam: Rotterdam University Press.

Singer, Hans (1950), 'The Distribution of Gains between Investing and Borrowing Countries', *American Economic Review*, 40 (2): 473–485.

Sinn, Hans-Werner (2006), 'The Pathological Export Boom and the Bazaar Effect: How to Solve the German Puzzle', *World Economy*, 29 (9): 1157–1175.

Sinn, Hans-Werner (2007), 'The Welfare State and the Forces of Globalization', NBER Working Paper No. 12946.

Skidelsky, Robert and Craig, Nan (eds.) (2016), *Who Runs the Economy? The Role of Power in Economics*, London: Palgrave Macmillan.

Smith, Adam (1961) [1776], *An Inquiry into the Nature and Causes of the Wealth of Nations*, Edwin Cannan (ed.), London: Methuen.

Smith, John (2016), *Imperialism in the Twenty-First Century: Globalization, Super-Exploitation, and Capitalism's Final Crisis*, New York: Monthly Review Press.

Snyder, Jeremy (2010), 'Exploitation and Sweatshop Labor: Perspectives and Issues', *Business Ethics Quarterly*, 20 (2): 187–213.

Spence, Michael (2011), *The Next Convergence: The Future of Economic Growth in a Multispeed World*, New York: Picador-Farrar, Straus and Giroux.

Sraffa, Piero (1926), 'The Laws of Returns under Competitive Conditions', *Economic Journal*, 36 (144): 535–550.

Sraffa, Piero (1960), *Production of Commodities by Means of Commodities: Prelude to a Critique of Economic Theory*, Cambridge: Cambridge University Press.

Stansbury, Anna and Summers, Lawrence H. (2020), 'The Declining Worker Power Hypoth-

esis: An Explanation for the Recent Evolution of the American Economy', NBER Working Paper No. 27193.
Standing, Guy (2006), 'CI, COAG and COG: a Comment on a Debate', in Erik Olin Wright (ed.), *Redesigning Distribution: Basic Income and Stakeholder Grants as Alternative Cornerstones for a More Egalitarian Capitalism*, London: Verso.
Standing, Guy (2007), 'Offshoring and Labor Recommodification in the Global Transformation', in Eva Paus (ed.), *Global Capitalism Unbound: Winners and Losers from Offshore Outsourcing*, New York: Palgrave Macmillan.
Stango, Victor (2004), 'The Economics of Standards Wars', *Review of Network Economics*, 3 (1):1–19.
Stern, Robert M. (1998), 'Labor Standards and International Trade', University of Michigan, School of Public Policy, Research Seminar in International Economics, Discussion Paper No. 430.
Stiglitz, Joseph E. (2002), *Globalization and Its Discontents*, London: Allen Lane.
Stiglitz, Joseph E. (2006), *Making Globalization Work*, London: Allen Lane.
Stiglitz, Joseph E. (2012), *The Price of Inequality*, London: Allen Lane.
Stiglitz, Joseph E. (2015), *The Great Divide*, London: Allen Lane.
Stiglitz, Joseph E. (2019), *People, Power, and Profits: Progressive Capitalism for an Age of Discontent*, London: Allen Lane.
Stiglitz, Joseph E. and Charlton, Andrew (2005), *Fair Trade for All: How Trade Can Promote Development*, Oxford: Oxford University Press.
Stiglitz, Joseph E. and Hersh, Adam S. (2015), 'Opinion: The Trans-Pacific Partnership Charade: TPP Isn't about 'Free Trade' at All', *Project Syndicate*, MarketWatch, 5 October.
Sturgeon, Timothy J. (2013), 'Global Value Chains and Economic Globalization – Towards a New Measurement Framework', Report to Eurostat, Industrial Performance Center, Massachusetts Institute of Technology.
Sturgeon, Timothy J. and Gereffi, Gary (2008), 'The Challenge of Global Value Chains: Why Integrative Trade Requires New Thinking and New Data', prepared for Industry Canada. Available at: gvcc.duke.edu/wp.content/uploads/GVmetrics_Nov202008.pdf.
Sturgeon, Timothy J., Van Biesebroeck, Johannes and Gereffi, Gary (2008), 'Value Chains, Networks and Clusters: Reframing the Global Automotive Industry', *Journal of Economic Geography*, 8 (3): 297–321.
Sturgeon, Timothy J. and Van Biesebroeck, Johannes (2011), 'Global Value Chains in the Automotive Industry: An Enhanced Role for Developing Countries?', *International Journal of Technological Learning, Innovation and Development*, 4 (1–2–3): 181–205.
Suarez, Carmen (2010), 'The Invention of Capital in Comparative Advantage Theory', AHE 2010 Conference Papers, University of Bordeaux.
Summers, Lawrence (2008), 'A Strategy to Promote Healthy Globalization', *Financial Times*, 4 May.
Sutcliffe, Bob (1972), 'Imperialism and Industrialization in the Third World', in Roger Owen and Bob Sutcliffe (eds.), *Studies in the Theory of Imperialism*, London: Longman.
Suttmeier, Richard P., Yao, Xiangkui and Tan, Alex Zixiang (2006), *Standards of Power? Technology, Institutions, and Politics in the Development of China's National Standards Strategy*, Seattle, WA: National Bureau of Asian Research.
Swann, G. M. Peter (2010a), *The Economics of Standardization: An Update*, Manchester: Innovative Economics Limited.
Swann, G. M. Peter (2010b), 'International Standards and Trade: A Review of the Empirical Literature', OECD Trade Policy Working Papers No. 97.

Taylor, John B. (2006), 'Commentary: The Rise of Offshoring: It's Not Wine for Cloth Anymore', in *The New Economic Geography: Effects and Policy Implications*, Jackson Hole Symposium, Kansas City, MO: Federal Reserve Bank of Kansas City.

Tharoor, Shashi (2017), *Inglorious Empire: What the British Did to India*, London: C. Hurst & Co. Ltd.

Timmer, Marcel P., Erumban, Abdul Azeez, Los, Bart, Stehrer, Robert and de Vries, Gaaitzen J. (2014), 'Slicing up Global Value Chains', *Journal of Economic Perspectives*, 28 (2): 99–118.

Timmer, Marcel P., Miroudot, Sébastien and de Vries, Gaaitzen J. (2019), 'Functional Specialization in Trade', *Journal of Economic Geography*, 19 (1): 1–30.

Tokatli, Nebahat (2013), 'Towards a Better Understanding of the Apparel Industry: A Critique of the Upgrading Literature', *Journal of Economic Geography*, 13 (6): 993–1011.

Tolles, N. Arnold (1957), 'Labour Standards in Relation to Foreign Trade Policy', in *Foreign Trade Policy: Compendium of Papers on United States Foreign Trade Policy,* collected by the Staff for the Subcommittee on Foreign Trade Policy of the Committee on Ways and Means, Washington DC: Government Printing Office.

Tørsløv, Thomas R., Wier, Ludvig S. and Zucman, Gabriel (2018), 'The Missing Profits of Nations', NBER Working Paper No. 24701.

Travis, Hannibal (2000), 'Pirates of the Information Infrastructure: Blackstonian Copyright and the First Amendment', *Berkeley Technology Law Journal*, 15 (777): 777–864.

Tucker, Todd N. (2018), 'Seven Strategies to Rebuilt Worker Power for the 21st Century Global Economy: A Comparative and Historical Framework for Policy Action', Roosevelt Institute. Available at: https://ssrn.com/abstract=3456984.

Turnell, Sean (2001), 'The Right to Employment: Extending the Core Labour Standards and Trade Debate', Department of Economics, Macquarie University, Sidney, Macquarie Economic Research Papers, 1/2001.

Uchitelle, Louis (2006), *The Disposable American: Layoffs and their Consequences*, New York: Alfred Knopf.

UNCTAD (United Nations Conference on Trade and Development) (2016), *Trade and Development Report, 2016*, New York and Geneva: United Nations.

UNCTAD (2018), *Non-Tariff Measures: Economic Assessment and Policy Options for Development*, Geneva: United Nations.

van Apeldoorn, Laurens (2019), 'Exploitation, International Taxation, and Global Justice', *Review of Social Economy*, 77 (2): 163–183.

Vanek, Jaroslav (1963), 'Variable Factor Proportions and Interindustry Flows in the Theory of International Trade', *Quarterly Journal of Economics*, 77 (1): 129–142.

Van Parijs, Philippe and Vanderborght, Yannick (2017), *Basic Income: A Radical Proposal for a Free Society and a Sane Economy*, Cambridge, MA: Harvard University Press.

Van Reenen, John (2011), 'Wage Inequality, Technology and Trade: 21st Century Evidence', Centre for Economic Performance, London School of Economics and Political Science, Occasional Paper No. 28.

Van Trier, Walter E. (1989), 'Who Framed Social Dividend? A Tale of the Unexpected', Rapport 89/230, Universitaire Faculteiten St.-Ignatius, Antwerpen.

Van Trier, Walter (2018), 'From James Meade's "Social Dividend" to "State Bonus": An Intriguing Chapter in the History of a Concept', *Œconomia*, 8 (4): 439–474.

Veblen, Thorstein (1909), 'The Limitations of Marginal Utility', *Journal of Political Economy*, 17: 620–636.

Veblen, Thorstein (1920), *The Vested Interests and the Common Man*, New York: Heubsch.

Vernon, Raymond (1966), 'International Investment and International Trade in the Product Cycle', *Quarterly Journal of Economics*, 88 (2): 190–207.

Vernon, Raymond (1971), *Sovereignty at Bay*, Harmondsworth (UK): Penguin Books.

Viner, Jacob (1937), *Studies in the Theory of International Trade*, London: Allen & Unwin.

Walker, E. Ronald (1943), *From Economic Theory to Policy*, Chicago: University of Chicago Press.

Walker, Francis (1903), 'Increasing and Diminishing Costs in International Trade', *Yale Review*, 12: 32–57.

Wallerstein, Immanuel (1979), *The Capitalist World Economy*, Cambridge: Cambridge University Press.

Walzer, Michael (2018), *A Foreign Policy for the Left*, New Haven, CT: Yale University Press.

Warren, Bill (1973), 'Imperialism and Capitalist Industrialization', *New Left Review*, No. 81: 3–44.

Warren, Bill (1980), *Imperialism, Pioneer of Capitalism*, London: Verso.

Watkins, Melvin H. (1963), 'A Staple Theory of Economic Growth', *Canadian Journal of Economic and Political Science*, 29 (2): 141–158.

Wedel, Janine R. and Chandra, Siddharth (2004), 'Courtage international et institutions floues: des rôles multiples, ambigus et contradictoires dans les relations russo-américaines', *Actes de la Recherche en Sciences Sociales*, No. 151–152: 114–125.

Wei, Shang-Jin (2015), 'Freer Choice, Lower Growth, and Higher Welfare: Recent Changes in China's Population Control Policy and the Impact on Its Economy', in Reuven Glick and Mark M. Spiegel (eds.), *Policy Challenges in a Diverging Global Economy*, Federal Reserve Bank of San Francisco. Available at: http://www.frbsf.org/economic-research/events/2015/november/2015-asia-economic-policy-conference/.

Wei, Shang-Jin, Xie, Zhuan and Zhang, Xiaobo (2017), 'From "Made in China" to "Innovated in China": Necessity, Prospect, and Challenges', *Journal of Economic Perspectives*, 31 (1): 49–70.

Weil, David (2014), *The Fissured Workplace: Why Work Became So Bad for So Many and What Can Be Done to Improve It*, Cambridge, MA: Harvard University Press.

Weil, David (2019), 'Understanding the Present and Future of Work in the Fissured Workplace Context', *Russel Sage Foundation Journal of the Social Sciences*, 5 (5): 147–165.

Welz, Christian and Fernández-Macías, Enrique (2008), 'Financial Participation of Employees in the European Union: Much Ado about Nothing?', *European Journal of Industrial Relations*, 14 (4): 479–497.

Wertheimer, Alan (1996), *Exploitation*, Princeton, NJ: Princeton University Press.

Whalley, John (2009), 'Shifting Economic Power', First draft for an OECD Development Centre project on Shifting Global Wealth, September. Available at: oecd.org/dev/pgd/45337859.pdf.

Williams, John H. (1929), 'The Theory of International Trade Reconsidered', *Economic Journal*, 39 (154): 195–209.

Willmann, Gerald (2004), 'Pareto Gains from Trade: a Dynamic Counterexample', *Economics Letters*, 83 (2): 199–204.

Wolf, Martin (1990), 'Some Myths about Economic Power', *Financial Times*, 1 November.

Wolf, Martin (2004), *Why Globalization Works*, New Haven, CT: Yale University Press.

Wolszczak, Joanna and Parteka, Aleksandra (2015), 'Does Offshoring Affect Industry Employment? Evidence from a Wide European Panel of Countries', *Journal of International Studies*, 8 (1): 41–52.

Wood, Adrian (1994), *North–South Trade, Employment and Inequality*, Oxford: Clarendon Press.

Wood, Adrian (1995), 'How Trade Hurt Unskilled Workers', *Journal of Economic Perspectives*, 9 (3): 57–80.
Wood, Adrian (2008), 'Heckscher–Ohlin in Theory and Reality', in Philip Arestis and John Eatwell (eds.), *Issues in Economic Development and Globalization: Essays in Honour of Ajit Singh*, Basingstoke (UK): Palgrave Macmillan.
World Bank (2020), *World Development Report 2020: Trading for Development in the Age of Global Value Chains*, Washington DC: World Bank.
World Bank Group et al. (eds.) (2017), *Global Value Chain Development Report 2017: Measuring and Analyzing the Impact of GVCs on Economic Development*, Washington DC: World Bank Group.
World Bank Group et al. (eds.) (2019), *Global Value Chain Development Report 2019: Technological Innovation, Supply Chain Trade, and Workers in a Globalized World*, Washington DC: World Bank Group.
Wright, Greg C. (2014), 'Revisiting the Employment Impact of Offshoring', *European Economic Review*, 66 (C): 63–83.
WTO (2020a), *World Trade Report 2020: Government Policies to Promote Innovation in the Digital Age*, Geneva: WTO Publications.
WTO (2020b), *World Trade Statistical Review*, Geneva: WTO Publications.
Yamin, Mo and Sinkovics, Rudolf R. (2009), 'Infrastructure or Foreign Direct Investment? An Examination of the Implications of MNE Strategy for Economic Development', *Journal of World Business*, 44 (2): 144–157.
Yang, Xiaokai and Ng, Siang (1995), 'Specialization and Division of Labour: a Survey', Centre for International Economic Studies, University of Adelaide, Seminar Paper 95-06.
Yoshii, Satoshi, Fujimoto, Takahiro and Shiozawa, Yoshinori (2019), 'Was Adam Smith a Proponent of Absolute Advantage Theory? A Formative History of an Urban Legend and Lessons Learned', NUCB Business School, Nagoya,(Japan), Discussion Paper No. 19003.
Young, Allyn A. (1928), 'Increasing Returns and Economic Progress', *Economic Journal*, 38 (152): 527–542.
Zhang, Junsen (2017), 'The Evolution of China's One-Child Policy and its Effects on Family Outcomes', *Journal of Economic Perspectives*, 31 (1): 141–160.
Zhuravskaya, Ekaterina (2007), 'Whither Russia? A Review of Andrei Shleifer's *A Normal Country*', *Journal of Economic Literature*, 45 (1): 127–146.
Zingales, Luigi (2012), *A Capitalism for the People: Recapturing the Lost Genius of American Prosperity*, New York: Basic Books.
Zingales, Luigi (2017), 'Towards a Political Theory of the Firm', *Journal of Economic Perspectives*, 31 (3): 113–130.
Zucman, Gabriel (2013), *La richesse cachée des nations: enquête sur les paradis fiscaux*, Paris: Éditions du Seuil (English translation: *The Hidden Wealth of Nations: The Scourge of Tax Havens*, Chicago: University of Chicago Press, 2015).
Zwolinski, Matt (2007), 'Sweatshops, Choice, and Exploitation', *Business Ethics Quarterly*, 17 (4): 689–727.
Zwolinski, Matt and Wertheimer, Alan (2016), 'Exploitation' in Edward N. Zalta (ed.), *Stanford Encyclopedia of Philosophy*, Stanford, CA: Metaphysic Research Lab, Stanford University.

Index of Names